Contract Law Textbook

15th edition

Edited by E A Lichtenstein
BA, LLB, LLM

and P A Read
LLB, DPA, Barrister

HLT Publications

HLT PUBLICATIONS
200 Greyhound Road, London W14 9RY

First published 1979
15th edition 1993

© The HLT Group Ltd 1993

ISBN 0 7510 0322 0

British Library Cataloguing-in-Publication.
A CIP Catalogue record for this book is
available from the British Library.

Acknowledgement
The publishers and author would like to
thank the Incorporated Council of Law
Reporting for England and Wales for kind
permission to reproduce extracts from the
Weekly Law Reports.

Printed and bound in Great Britain

Contents

Preface

HLT Textbooks are written specifically for students. Whatever their course, they will find our books clear and precise, providing comprehensive and up-to-date coverage. Written by specialists in their field, our textbooks are reviewed and updated on an annual basis.

Since the last edition of *Contract Law Textbook* there has been no new legislation of any note, but a whole series of new cases have been incorporated into the text as appropriate.

Among these new cases are a number pertaining to construction and content of contracts, including the Privy Council case of *Graham* v *Pitkin* [1992] 1 WLR 403; a cluster of cases on intention to form legal relations (*Orion Insurance Co* v *Sphere Drake Insurance* [1992] 1 Lloyd's Rep 239; *G Percy Trentham Ltd* v *Archital Luxfer Ltd* [1993] 1 Lloyd's Rep 25); and an important Court of Appeal case on implied terms (*Chelsea Football & Athletic Co Ltd* v *S B Property Co Ltd* [1992] TLR 175). In addition, there are cases on mistake, duress and illegality, as well as an interesting Court of Appeal case on frustration (*McAlpine, Humberoak Ltd* v *McDermott International Inc* (1992) Financial Times 13 March).

The conflicting loyalties of estate agents is the main issue in the Privy Council case of *Kelly* v *Cooper* [1992] 3 WLR 936.

Unusually, since case law on this topic is rare, there are two recent cases on the Supply of Goods and Services Act 1982.

This textbook is now up to date as of 7 April 1993.

Table of Cases

Dunlop Pneumatic Tyre Co Ltd *v* Selfridge & Co Ltd [1915] AC 847   *41, 229*
Dunlop Pneumatic Tyre Co *v* New Garage [1915] AC 79   *320, 321*
Durham Fancy Goods Ltd *v* Michael Jackson (Fancy Goods) Ltd [1968] 2 QB 839
    56

East *v* Maurer [1991] 2 All ER 733   *127*
Eastham *v* Newcastle United Football Club [1964] Ch 413   *251*
Eastwood *v* Kenyon (1840) 11 Ad & El 438   *5, 44, 89*
Edgington *v* Fitzmaurice (1885) 29 Ch D 459   *120, 123*
Edler *v* Auerbach [1950] 1 KB 359   *255*
Edwards *v* Carter [1893] AC 360   *159*
Edwards *v* Skyways Ltd [1964] 1 WLR 349   *71*
Edwards *v* SOGAT [1971] Ch 354   *315*
Edwin Hill *v* First National Finance Corporation plc [1989] 1 WLR 225   *239*
Ellesmere *v* Wallace [1929] 2 Ch 1   *225*
Elliott *v* Freeman (1863) 7 LT 715   *198*
Elliott *v* Pierson [1948] 1 All ER 939   *313*
Ellis *v* Barker (1871) LR 7 Ch App 104   *217*
Elpis Maritime Co Ltd *v* Chartering Co Inc (The Maria D) [1991] 3 All ER 785
    91
Engell *v* Fitch (1868) LR 3 QB 314, at 330   *312*
England *v* Curling (1844) 8 Beav 129   *333*
England *v* Marsden (1886) LR 1 CP 529   *344*
English Hop Growers *v* Dering [1928] 2 KB 174   *253*
Entores *v* Miles Far East Corporation [1955] 2 QB 327   *34, 35, 39*
Erlanger *v* New Sombrero Phosphate Co (1878) 3 App Cas 1218   *130*
Errington *v* Errington and Woods [1952] 1 KB 290   *20, 24*
Ertel Bieber *v* Rio Tinto [1918] AC 260   *271, 272*
Esso Petroleum Co Ltd *v* Commissioners of Customs and Excise [1976] 1 WLR 1;
    [1976] 1 All ER 117   *71, 374*
Esso Petroleum Co *v* Harper's Garage (Stourport) Ltd [1968] AC 269   *249, 254*
Esso Petroleum *v* Mardon [1976] QB 801   *98, 127*
Evans *v* Merzario Ltd [1976] 1 WLR 1078   *72, 98*
Evenden *v* Guildford City AFC Ltd [1975] QB 917   *56, 57, 58, 65*
Evening Standard *v* Henderson (1986) The Times 15 November   *337*
Eves *v* Eves [1975] 1 WLR 1338   *70*
Exall *v* Partridge (1799) 8 TR 308   *344*
Exports Credit *v* Universal Oil Products [1983] 2 All ER 205   *322*
Eyre *v* Measday [1986] 1 All ER 488   *99, 109*

F Goldsmith (Sicklemere) Ltd *v* Baxter [1970] Ch 85   *84*
FA Tamplin SS Company Ltd *v* Anglo-Mexican Petroleum Products Company Ltd
    [1916] 2 AC 397   *268*

Table of Statutes

1

Introduction

1.1 The problems of studying the law of contract

1.2 Definitions

1.3 Historical development and the theories underlying contract

1.4 Overlap with other legal topics

1.5 Methods of studying law of contract

1.1 The problems of studying the law of contract

A number of problems arise in the study of any legal topic. In the case of contract law there are four basic problems in particular:

1. Concepts and terminology are specific. It is often not so much that terms used are strange or highly technical, but that there are ordinary everyday words or phrases which may have some specific definition in a contractual context.
2. There are large numbers of cases. The general principles of contract law are still, to a large extent, judge made. That is to say, the rules were formulated by the courts over a lengthy period of time. Even now, there are comparatively few statutes governing contractual law.
3. Contract law tends to overlap with other areas, in particular, with tort and property law.
4. The last century or so has seen the development of a number of 'specialist' areas, such as contracts of employment and shipping or insurance contracts. Often these subjects are really not much affected at all by ordinary contractual rules and, instead, are governed by legislation specially enacted for the purpose. Normally, a student will never really need to come into contact with these topics at all, but it can be quite confusing if he or she stumbles on, say, a contract of employment case which he reads about in the paper and tries to fit it into what he knows of ordinary common law rules of contract. While it is important to recognise that such specialised fields of contract exist, with one or two exceptions, they really have no great importance or relevance for a student embarking on a study of the law of contract.

(As to those exceptions, see, for example, Chapter 20.)
Items 1–3 will be examined more closely in the following paragraphs.

1.2 Definitions

It is notoriously difficult to define very generalised concepts like 'a contract'. It is perhaps an oversimplification to say that it is a 'legally enforceable agreement', but if we look at some standard definitions, we see that this is a common theme.
  Thus, in Treitel:

> 'A contract is an agreement giving rise to obligations which are enforced or recognised by the law. The factor which distinguishes contractual from other legal obligations is that they are based on the agreement of the contracting parties.'

And Anson:

> 'We may provisionally describe the law of contract as that branch of the law which determines the circumstances in which a promise shall be legally binding on the person making it.'

Pollock described a contract as 'a promise or set of promises which the law will enforce'.
  American Restatement (Second) of the Law of Contract, 1978:

> 'A contract is a promise or a set of promises for the breach of which the law gives a remedy or the performance of which the law in some way recognises as a duty.'

From these definitions it would appear that the law of contract is about promises and agreements; however, the scope and operation of the subject – and the meaning of 'agreement – cannot be adequately explained without a consideration of:

1. The historical development of the law of obligations and the emergence of contractual remedies.
2. The theories underlying the purpose of the law of contract which necessarily involve a consideration of prevailing economic and philosophical attitudes.

1.3 Historical development and the theories underlying contract

By the fourteenth century the common law courts had established jurisdiction over certain civil wrongs which were known as trespasses. Flexible forms of action came to be developed which allowed litigants to adapt these forms to the particular circumstances of the case. These actions included a form in which the plaintiff alleged that the defendant had undertaken (in Latin: assumpsit) a certain obligation and then by negligent misconduct had caused him damage. This was an important development because earlier the only form of obligation that could be enforced was a debt for a specific sum. Even more important was the fact that while the old debt actions were tried by jury, the new assumpsit action could be heard after the ritual of swearing an oath.

By 1602 (*Slade's Case* (1602) 4 Co Rep 92a) the writ of assumpsit had become the general remedy for informal contracts and it was the concept of assumpsit that became the basis for the modern law of contract and quasi contract.

This foundation of contract in assumpsit (and the earlier debt) is reflected, in broad terms, in two kinds of situations in which a contractual remedy might be sought:

1. When the plaintiff complains of an invasion of his rights by the defendant's breach of undertaking.
2. When the plaintiff seeks a contractual remedy to recover a sum of money owed to him by the defendant, often for goods sold or services supplied.

It could be said that the first situation reflects the assumpsit origin of contract and the second the origin in debt.

The other particularly important time, historically, for the law of contract was the nineteenth century. The philosophy of laissez faire which prevailed in the nineteenth century involved the belief that the law should interfere with people's activities as little as possible. In the area of the law of contract this belief found expression in the words of Sir George Jessel in *Printing and Numerical Registering Co v Sampson* (1875) LR 19 Eq 462:

'If there is one thing more than another which public policy requires, it is that men of full age and competent understanding, shall have the utmost liberty in contracting and that their contracts, when entered into freely and voluntarily, shall be held sacred and shall be enforced by the Courts of Justice.'

This robust view did not recognise that people are seldom free to choose whether or not to contract, or to choose the other contracting party, or to determine the terms of their contracts. In particular, when one party enjoys a monopoly or is otherwise economically dominant, the other party may be especially at a disadvantage.

However, not all nineteenth-century judges shared the vigorous opinions expressed above. In recognition of this, statutes – particularly towards the end of the nineteenth century and during this century – have sought to impose terms and limit the power of economically dominant parties. We shall be examining the scope and effect of this legislation in later sections.

Theories of contract

The main question here is: Why should promises be enforced? Several answers to this question can be isolated: each of which has gained prominence according to the prevalent economic/social/political theory of the period:

1. *Natural law: honour theory* When the church had considerable influence on the mores of society, it was thought that promises ought to be kept and the law should reflect this fact.
2. *Laissez faire: bargain theory* This idea, perhaps, represents the basis of 'classical' contract: the law should enforce bargains, supported by adequate quid pro quo moving from both sides, made by free men of full age and capacity. Such a theory was less acceptable when people realised that the market economy did not make all men free: accordingly, contract became the means of social control by the state, for example, Hire Purchase Act, food and drugs legislation etc.
3. *Welfare state: reliance theory* This theory is based on the notion that where one person has altered his position to his detriment on the basis of another's promise, the other should make good the detriment, or give compensation if he goes back on his promise.

1.4 Overlap with other legal topics

Contract and property

The main difference between the law of property and the law of contract is that the former is said to create rights 'in rem' while the latter creates rights 'in personam'.

Thus contracts and conveyances were always kept separate. In English law, however, a contract can act as a conveyance of property or rights and property (except for land), and this can lead to problems when a contract turns out to be defective for, say, mistake or illegality. Thus property problems can arise under the guise of contract, and some of the rules reflect historical attitudes to property, rather than principles that might be more appropriate to a consumer society.

This was recognised by Lord Denning, in particular, who was always concerned for the rights of the bona fide purchaser. See, for example, *Lewis* v *Averay* [1972] 1 QB 198.

Contract and tort

We have already seen that contract, quasi-contract and tort all have a common origin.

There is nowadays an increasing recognition by the judiciary that the traditional and long-accepted rigid division of the law of obligations into contract and tort is without historic foundation and unrealistic. See, for example, *Brooks Wharf and Bull Wharf* v *Goodman Bros* [1937] 1 KB 534; [1936] 3 All ER 695, *Hedley Byrne & Co Ltd* v *Heller and Partners Ltd* [1964] AC 465; [1963] 2 All ER 575, *The Albazero* [1977] AC 774; [1976] 3 All ER 129 and *Tennant Radiant Heat Ltd* v *Warrington Development Corp* [1988] 11 EG 71.

Contract and equity

Equity has contributed a wider view of the reasons for enforcing contracts than the narrow, consideration-based approach articulated at common law in cases such as: *Eastwood* v *Kenyon* (1840) 11 Ad & El 438, *Currie* v *Misa* (1875) LR 10 Exch 153.

In particular, courts of equity have shown greater concern to enforce promises than to uphold bargains; the focus of attention is the promisor and the need for him to keep substantive faith.

This approach is easily confused with the common law approach and the confusion was compounded once equity ceased to be administered by a separate court. The reason for the confusion is that equity is only applied at the court's discretion. And this discretion – to enforce promises – will only be exercised, inter alia, where not to do so would cause more harm to the plaintiff than to the defendant. In other words, the plaintiff must satisfy the court that, in the circumstances which exist *at the time of the hearing* (not, as in common law, those which existed at the time of the alleged breach), he will lose more if the court does not act than the defendant will if the court does act. See, for example: *Foster* v *Robinson* [1951] 1 KB 149 and *Binions* v *Evans* [1972] Ch 359. These cases are quite consistent with equity's general approach, but completely inconsistent and inexplicable, in terms of common law considerations.

The other major difference between law and equity relates to its remedies. Equity will enforce the promise directly through specific performance or injunction: when this is not appropriate, damages may be awarded but calculated not, as at common law, at the date of the breach of contract, but at the date when the court decides to act against the defendant for breaking his promise or undertaking.

1.5 Methods of studying law of contract

Contract is one of the few areas of law with which almost everyone comes into day-to-day contact. Whilst, superficially at least, that might be regarded as advantageous to the student embarking on a study of contract law, it is in reality often a hindrance rather than a help.

To the extent that everyone makes contracts in their daily lives – a week's supply of groceries, a newspaper, a car or even a house – everyone tends to regard themselves an expert in a rather 'do-it-yourself' area of law. Familiarity with the basic concept of a contract breeds, if not contempt, then perhaps a rather deceptive feeling of over-confidence.

The general body of contract law is immense, and this fact creates one of the student's greatest problems. The sheer volume of information facing a student may seem, at least initially, a daunting if not downright impossible task to grasp.

Nowhere is this more true than as to case law. The general principles of contract law are still, as noted earlier, of a judge-made origin. That is to say, most of the major principles are contained in judicial decisions rather than statute. Cases are still the most important source of contract law and it is important that the student becomes used, from a very early stage, to reading and researching his or her own case reports. While it *is* possible to go through an entire contract course without ever going near a law library, it is not a course of action to be recommended!

Students who depend on textbook resumés of cases and who never read a case report themselves are at a considerable disadvantage.

From reading as many cases as possible, right from the word go, it is possible to gain an insight into how the courts reach their decisions, how judges interpret facts and how they apply legal principles to those facts.

No casebook or textbook will give the student the sort of information to be found in a report. Although, in a textbook, the student may find some basic facts and the decision neatly documented, what he or she will *not* find, unless he or she reads the full report for him or herself, is whether the court was reluctant to reach its decision, or whether a dissenting judgment was of particular interest or importance, or what other cases the court considered or rejected.

Strictly speaking, it does not even matter what cases the student reads, though obviously the majority of students will seek out the 'classics' – the cases of major importance in a particular area. But *any* cases are useful reading; in working out what the courts took into account (or what they perhaps *should* have taken into account), will help to fix the topic in the memory and sharpen the student's own perceptions of the subject.

It does no good to learn a few (or even a lot) of cases off by heart – this will only give a static view of contract. Nor is it wise to think that each case establishes one rule or law.

Rather it is the relationship between whole groups of cases which may be of importance. It is only by careful study of a series of cases at a time that the student begins to pick out patterns of conduct and can begin to predict how the courts might react in future similar cases and how the law on the topic might progress.

The law of contract should never be studied in self-contained sections. Unfortunately it often is!

None of the rules relating to contract exists in a vacuum, and the student who is constantly revising and updating his or her notes, in the light of what he or she learns as the course progresses, will have a higher level of understanding of the topic as a whole.

It is also helpful to note that aspects of contract can be approached at differing levels of complexity. Offer and acceptance, for example, because it is dealt with at the beginning of the course, is often treated in a very simplistic way. Areas of contractual law which are traditionally dealt with towards the end of the course are often dealt with by lecturers in greater detail and, because of this, some areas seem deceptively simple and others gain a needless reputation for being complicated.

Unfortunately, most lecturers run to such a tight timetable that there is often no time for a retrospective look at the course. For this reason, it is worth paying particular attention to the final chapter in this book, which takes an overview of the law of contract. The student may find that, armed with a sound knowledge of the ground rules, to look at the area as a whole throws up some new ideas and perspectives.

In order for the student to have some idea of the rules of contract law before he or she starts to study the individual topics in details, it is strongly recommended that an elementary book should be read.

2

Offer and Acceptance

2.1 General principles

2.2 The offer

2.3 Duration and termination of offer

2.4 Acceptance

2.5 Communication of acceptance

2.1 General principles

There are three basic essentials to the creation of a contract which will be recognised and enforced by the courts. These are contractual intention, agreement and consideration. Contractual intention was dealt with in Chapter 1 and consideration will be examined in Chapter 3.

This chapter is concerned with the means by which the courts ascertain that the parties have, in fact, reached agreement. The method traditionally adopted is to analyse the dealings between the parties in terms of offer and acceptance. As we have already seen, this is an objective test, and the question asked is whether there has been a definite offer by one party and an unqualified acceptance by the other.

Note that often today, in a complex commercial transaction, it may be difficult to determine the precise stages of offer and acceptance. See *New Zealand Shipping Co Ltd* v *AM Satterthwaite & Co Ltd (The Eurymedon)* [1975] AC 154.

Note Lord Wilberforce's comment in this case that the traditional approach is 'often at the cost of forcing the facts to fit uneasily into the marked slots of offer, acceptance and consideration'.

It is worth contrasting the view expressed above with Lord Diplock's view that it is only exceptional cases 'which do not fit easily into the normal analysis of offer and acceptance'.

Clarke v *Earl of Dunraven* [1897] AC 59 is a good example of the sort of case Diplock probably had in mind. Here all the entrants to a race unambiguously agreed to be bound by the rules of the race. However, the large numbers of competitors and the different times at which they entered the race made it virtually impossible to identify individual offers and acceptances, and to attempt to categorise each entry into such divisions would be an artificial and pointless exercise.

In *Butler Machine Tool Co Ltd* v *Ex-Cell-O Corporation (England) Ltd* [1979] 1 WLR 401 and again in *Gibson* v *Manchester City Council* [1979] 1 WLR 294 (see also 'Invitation to treat' (below)) Lord Denning did, indeed, suggest a more flexible approach – assessing the presence (or absence) of agreement, not through the orthodox examination of offer and acceptance, but looking at all the circumstances to see if the parties have reached agreement.

However, in the first case (*Butler Machine Tool*), the Court of Appeal based their decision on the traditional offer and acceptance. In the second case (*Gibson*), the House of Lords reversed the Court of Appeal's decision that, looking at all the circumstances, there was overall evidence of agreement and, instead, held that there had been no matching offer or acceptance.

So far, therefore, although the courts have expressed from time to time a certain unease regarding the rigidity of the orthodox matching of offer and acceptance, there is no real sign of any concerted move towards a more flexible, free-ranging approach.

The courts still regard it as preferable, in examining a transaction, to break down the parties' actions into small, self-contained sections that they can classify as offers, counter offers or invitations to treat, or acceptances or revocations, or whatever. In thus examining every detail of the parties' conduct, it gives a (sometimes spurious) appearance of certainty and uniformity to the way in which the courts apply the objective test to look for evidence of agreement.

2.2 The offer

Definition

The offer is an expression of willingness to contract made with the intention (actual or apparent) that it shall become binding on the offeror as soon as it is accepted by the person to whom it is addressed.

An offer can be made to one person or a group of persons, or to the world at large. The offeror is bound to fulfil the terms of his offer once it is accepted.

The issue of whether there would be a valid offer to the world at large was considered in *Carlill* v *Carbolic Smoke Ball Co Ltd* [1893] 1 QB 256.

The offer was contained in a newspaper advertisement. Bowen LJ said:

> 'It was also said that the contract was made with all the world – that is with everybody, and you cannot contract with everybody. It is not a contract made with all the world. It is an offer made to all the world and why should an offer not be made to all the world which is to ripen into a contract with anybody who comes forward and performs the conditions?'

The offer may be made in writing, by words or conduct. All that is necessary is that the terms of the offer are clear and that the offer was made with the intention that it should be binding if accepted.

In ascertaining whether there has, in fact, been an offer capable of acceptance, the courts have applied the principles set out below.

Types of offer: unilateral

Some offers are purely one sided. They are made without the offeror's having any idea whether they will ever be taken up and accepted, and thereby be transformed into a contract.

Such an offer is said to be unilateral. An example has already been noted in *Carlill* v *Carbolic Smoke Ball Co Ltd* (the facts of which are set out below).

This offer, also classified as an offer to the world at large, was typical of the type in which manufacturers offer to pay compensation to users of their product, if the product does not live up to expectations. Often, such offers are part of a general publicity campaign popularising the product.

Similarly, other publicity offers, such as those occasionally mounted by newspapers, offering a reward for the first person to swim the Irish Sea, or find the Loch Ness monster, are unilateral offers.

On a more homely note, the 'lost and found' columns of any newspaper will carry offers of rewards for lost items or pets. A person making such an offer has no idea whether it will ever be accepted, hence it is unilateral.

Types of offer: bilateral

The majority of offers are bilateral. Most contracts are negotiated on a promise for a promise basis. While it is not always true, most people make an offer to one named offeree or, at most, a small group of potentially interested parties. Again it is not always the case, but many contracts are made with both parties present on a face-to-face basis.

Thus an offer to sell a house involves a promise by the offeror to sell, in return for the offeree's promise to pay. Similarly, an offer to build a house involves the builder's offer to construct the house in return for the customer's promise to pay for it. These are both examples of bilateral offers.

Invitation to treat

An invitation to treat made by one party to another is not an offer. An invitation to treat is made at a preliminary stage in the making of an agreement, where one party seeks to ascertain whether the other would be willing to enter into a contract and, if so, upon what terms. It is an invitation extended by one party to the other to enter into negotiations, or to make an offer. An invitation to treat cannot be accepted so as to form a binding contract, since it is nearly always the invitee who is being asked to make the offer.

To distinguish between an offer and an invitation to treat it is necessary to look at the intention of the person making it, as revealed by his words or actions, and at the surrounding circumstances. It is not an offer unless it was made with the intention that it should be binding as soon as the person to whom it was addressed communicates his assent.

The words used by the parties are not themselves conclusive. An 'offer' may, in fact, be 'an invitation to treat' or vice versa. The court looks at both the words used and the surrounding circumstances to determine the real intention of the parties.

See, for example, the forms of wording used in the following cases: *Spencer* v *Harding* (1870) LR 5 CP 561:

'We are instructed to offer ... for sale by tender'

which was held to be an invitation to treat (see below), and *Clifton* v *Palumbo* [1944] 2 All ER 497:

'I am prepared to offer you ... my ... estate for £600,000.'

The land in question was a large scattered estate. The Court of Appeal held that this was not a definite offer to sell, but a preliminary statement as to price, which was just one of the questions to be settled between the parties.

Lord Greene MR said:

'There is nothing in the world to prevent an owner of an estate of this kind contracting to sell it to a purchaser, who is prepared to spend so large a sum of money, on terms written out upon a half sheet of note paper of the most informal description and even, if he likes, on unfavourable conditions. But I think it is legitimate, in approaching the construction of a document of this kind, containing phrases and expressions of doubtful significance, to bear in mind that the probability of parties entering into so large a transaction and finally binding themselves to a contract of this description couched in such terms, is remote. If they have done it, they have done it, however unwise and however unbusinesslike it may be. The question is, Have they done it?'

A statement which expresses itself as an 'acceptance' may, in fact, be an offer: *Bigg* v *Boyd Gibbons Ltd* [1971] 1 WLR 913, [1971] 2 All ER 183. The relevant statement was 'for a quick sale I would accept £26,000'. This was held to be, in fact, an offer capable of acceptance so as to create a binding agreement. See also *Harvey* v *Facey* (below).

However, a statement is not an offer if the person making it states clearly that he is *not* to be bound by the acceptance of the other party, but only where he himself signifies his acceptance. See *Financings Ltd* v *Stimson* [1962] 1 WLR 1184. See also *Butler Machine Tool Co Ltd* v *Ex-Cell-O Corporation (England) Ltd*.

The following are examples of statements that have been held to be invitations to treat: *Harvey* v *Facey* [1893] AC 552. The plaintiffs telegraphed the defendants in relation to a piece of land.

'Will you sell us Bumper Hall Pen? Telegraph lowest cash price.'

The defendants replied:

'Lowest cash price for Bumper Hall Pen, £900.'

The plaintiffs then telegraphed:

'We agree to buy Bumper Hall Pen for £900 asked by you.'

The Judicial Committee of the Privy Council held that the defendants' telegram was not an offer, but an invitation to treat, telling the plaintiffs the lowest price that they would accept for the land. The plaintiffs' second telegram was an offer, but there was no contract because it had not been accepted. See *Gibson* v *Manchester City Council* [1978] 2 All ER 583 CA, [1979] 1 All ER 972 HL.

In 1970, Manchester City Council (Conservative) adopted a policy of selling council houses to their tenants. The respondent, a tenant of a council house, wrote to the Council asking for a form giving details of the purchase and mortgage terms available. On 10 February 1971, the City Treasurer wrote to the respondent that the Council 'may be prepared to sell the house to you at a purchase price of £2,725 less 20% = £2,180 freehold'. The letter also gave details of mortgages that might be available, and went on 'if you would like to make formal application to buy your council house please complete the enclosed application form and return it to me as soon as possible'. The application was headed, 'Application to buy a council house' and concluded: 'I ... now wish to buy my council house. The above answers are correct and I agree that they shall be the basis of the arrangements regarding the purchase'. The respondent completed the form except for the purchase price and returned it to the Council on 5 March 1971.

On 18 March he wrote again to the Council: 'I would be obliged if you will carry on with my purchase as per my application already in your possession.'

Before formal written contracts had been prepared and exchanged by the parties, Council policy changed and they decided only to sell houses where the contracts had already been exchanged.

The respondent brought an action seeking specific performance of the contract of sale, which he claimed to be constituted by the letter of 10 March from the City Treasurer and his application of 5 March.

The County Court judge and the Court of Appeal considered that there was an enforceable agreement. The House of Lords took a contrary view and adopted the dissenting judgment of Geoffrey Lane LJ in the Court of Appeal.

He said:

> 'It is said that the letter of 10th March 1971 constitutes a firm offer to sell.
>
> It is largely a matter of impression, but although to Lord Denning MR and Ormrod LJ it appears perfectly plain that that was a firm offer, to me it appears equally plain that it was not. First of all, the words used "may be" in the first paragraph and "may grant a mortgage" and finally the words "if you would like to make an application to buy your council house" are strange words to use if this was indeed a formal offer on behalf of the Council. It is in my judgment no more than one would expect of a letter coming from a City Treasurer. It is a letter setting out the financial terms on which it may be that the Council will be prepared to consider the sale and purchase in due course.'

Further grounds upon which Geoffrey Lane LJ held that there was no firm offer capable of acceptance were (1) that the letter was from the City Treasurer rather than the Town Clerk from whom a firm offer would have come; and (2) that the formal contract would have contained a number of provisions, such as restrictive covenants, to which the alleged agreement made no reference.

One interesting point arising from this case (*Gibson*) was originated by Lord Denning MR in the Court of Appeal [1978] 2 All ER at p586:

> 'To my mind it is a mistake to think that all contracts can be analysed into the form of offer and acceptance. I know in some of the textbooks it has been the custom to do so; but as I understand the law there is no need to look for strict offer and acceptance. You should look at the correspondence as a whole and at the conduct of the parties and see therefrom whether the parties have come to an agreement on everything that is material. If by their correspondence and their conduct you can see an agreement on all material terms, which was intended thenceforward to be binding, then there is a binding contract in law even though all the formalities have not been gone through. For that proposition I would refer to *Brogden* v *Metropolitan Railway Co* (1877) 2 App Cas 666.'

In the hearing in the Lords a year later, Lord Diplock seems to have accepted that Lord Denning MR's statement of the law in this matter could be valid, though not in the instant case:

> 'My Lords, there may be certain types of contract, though I think they are exceptional, which do not fit easily into the normal analysis of a contract as being constituted by offer and acceptance; but a contract alleged to have been made by exchange of correspondence between the parties in which successive communications other than the first are in reply to one another is not one of these ... I venture to think that it was by departing from ... (the) ... conventional approach that the majority of the Court of Appeal was led into error. ([1979] 1 All ER 972 at p974.)

(One such exceptional case is, perhaps, illustrated by *New Zealand Shipping* v *Satterthwaite & Co Ltd* [1974] 1 All ER 1015.)

The distinction between offers and invitations to treat is often hard to draw as it depends upon the intention of the person making the statement. However, in some cases the distinction is settled, presumptively, at least, by authority or by statute. These cases are dealt with below.

Display of goods in shops

The issue is whether the display of goods in shops, on shelves or in the window with a price tag attached is an offer or an invitation to treat. If it is an offer, then the customer can accept it by indicating his desire to buy the item and the shopkeeper must then sell it to him at the stated price. If, on the other hand, it is an invitation to treat, the offer is made by the customer in seeking to buy the item, and the shopkeeper can accept or refuse the offer as he wishes.

The leading case is *Pharmaceutical Society of Great Britain* v *Boots Cash Chemists (Southern) Ltd* [1952] 2 All ER 456; [1953] 1 All ER 482. The defendants adapted their shop, or one of them, to a self-service system. A customer, on entering, was given a basket and, having selected from the shelves the articles he required, put them in the basket and took them to the cash desk. Near the desk was a registered pharmacist who was authorised, if necessary, to stop a customer removing any drug from the shop. The court had to decide whether the defendants had broken the provisions of s18 Pharmacy and Poisons Act 1933, which made it unlawful to sell any listed poison 'unless the sale is effected under the supervision of a registered pharmacist'. The vital and obvious question is where the 'sale' in fact took place, and at what time, and this depended upon whether the display of goods was an offer or an invitation to treat. The plaintiffs contended that it was an offer which was accepted when the customer put an article into his basket, and if this article was a 'poison' it was therefore 'sold' before the pharmacist could intervene. According to the defendants, the display was only an invitation to treat. An offer to buy was made when the customer put an article in the basket, and this offer the defendants were free to accept or reject. If they accepted, they did so only when the transaction was approved by the pharmacist near the cash desk. Lord Goddard at first instance, had no hesitation in deciding that the display was only an invitation to treat so that the law had not been broken, and the Court of Appeal upheld his reasoning and adopted his decision. He said:

> 'The transaction is in no way different from the normal transaction in a shop in which there is no self-service scheme. I am quite satisfied it would be wrong to say that the shopkeeper is making an offer to sell every article in the shop to any person who might come in and that that person can insist on buying any article by saying "I accept your offer". I agree with the illustration put forward during the case of a person who might go into a shop where books are displayed. In most bookshops customers are invited to go in and pick up books and look at them even if they do not buy them. There is no contract by the shopkeeper to sell until the customer has taken the book to the shopkeeper or his assistant and said "I want to buy this book" and the shopkeeper says "yes". That would not prevent the shopkeeper, seeing the book picked up, saying, "I am sorry I cannot let you have that book; it is the only copy I have got and I have already promised it to another customer". Therefore, in my opinion, the mere fact that a customer picks up a bottle of medicine from the shelves in this case does not amount to an acceptance of an offer to sell. It is an offer by the customer to buy, and there is no sale effected until the buyer's offer to buy is accepted by the acceptance of the price.'

In *Fisher* v *Bell* [1961] 1 QB 394 a flick knife was displayed in a shop window with a price tag attached. The issue was whether the law prohibiting the display of such items for sale had been breached. Lord Parker stated:

> 'It is clear according to the ordinary law of contract that the display of an article with a price on it in a shop window is merely an invitation to treat. It is in no sense an offer for sale, the acceptance of which constitutes a contract.'

On the other hand, in *Chapleton* v *Barry Urban District Council* [1940] 1 KB 532, a display of deck chairs under a 'For Hire' sign was held to be an offer (see below).

Advertisements

Whether or not advertisements can amount to offers depends to a large extent on whether they are bilateral or unilateral, that is, capable of acceptance by one or a limited number of persons, or open to all the world to accept.

Advertisements of bilateral transactions

Such advertisements are usually held not to amount to offers. Two reasons are given. First, such advertisements may lead to further bargaining, as in the case of an advertisement of land for sale. Second, the vendor may wish to assure himself that the prospective purchaser will be able to pay for the goods before entering into a binding agreement.

The following have been held to be invitations to treat:

Advertisement in a newspaper of goods for sale – *Partridge* v *Crittenden* [1968] 2 All ER 421. Here the appellants inserted in a periodical entitled 'Cage and Aviary Birds' an advertisement, 'Bramblefinch cocks and hens, 25*s*.'. The words 'offer for sale' were not used, but the advertisement was placed under the heading, 'classified advertisements'. The appellants were charged with unlawfully offering for sale a wild live bird.

The Divisional Court quashed the conviction. Lord Parker said:

'I think that when one is dealing with advertisements and circulars, unless they come from manufacturers, there is business sense in their being construed as invitations to treat and not offers for sale.'

Circulation of a catalogue by a wine merchant – *Grainger & Son* v *Gough* [1896] AC 325. This was held to be an attempt to induce offers from recipients, not an offer itself.

Lord Herschell pointed out the inconvenience of a contrary interpretation:

'The transmission of such a price list does not amount to an offer to supply an unlimited quantity of the wine described at the price named, so that as soon as an order is received there is a binding contract to supply that quantity. If that were so the merchant might find himself involved in any number of contractual obligations to supply wine of a particular description which he would be quite unable to carry out, his stock of wine of that description being necessarily limited.'

Advertisement that a scholarship examination will be held. In *Rooke* v *Dawson* [1895] 1 Ch 480, this was held not to amount to an offer to a candidate that the examination would be held.

Advertisements of unilateral contracts

Such advertisements are commonly held to amount to offers. The leading case is *Carlill* v *Carbolic Smoke Ball Co Ltd* [1893] 1 QB 256.

The defendants issued an advertisement promising to pay £100 to any person who used carbolic smoke balls made by them as prescribed and then caught influenza. They stated that they had deposited £1,000 with their bankers 'shewing our sincerity in this matter'. The plaintiff used the smoke balls, caught influenza and claimed her £100. The defendants claimed, inter alia, that she was not entitled to payment because their advertisement had not amounted to an offer.

It was held that this advertisement did constitute an offer and the defendants had indicated their intention to be bound by the deposit with their bankers.

Bowen LJ said:

> 'It is not like cases in which you offer to negotiate or you issue advertisements that you have got a stock of books to sell, or houses to let, in which cases there is no offer to be bound by any contract. Such advertisements are offers to negotiate – offers to receive offers – offers to chaffer'.

Note that there is a strong presumption that advertisements in trade journals and the like are offers, not invitations to treat. For example, Lord Parker's comment in *Partridge* v *Crittenden* (above) clearly considers manufacturers' advertisements and circulars to be true offers. Advertisements promising rewards for the recovery of lost property or for information leading to the capture or conviction of a criminal are commonly regarded as offers. See *Gibbons* v *Proctor* (1891) 64 LT 594 and *Williams* v *Carwardine* (1833) 5 Car & P 566.

Ticket cases

An area which has caused difficulty, and is still far from clear, involves contracts where a ticket is given by one party to the other. The question usually arises in the context of whether the ticket is a contractual document, and hence whether the parties are bound by any conditions printed on that ticket, or referred to on the ticket, and further details may be sought in Chapter 8 on exclusion clauses.

Whether or not a ticket is a contractual document and its role in the formation of the contract depends upon: (1) whether that ticket was intended to be a contractual document; and (2) the mode and timing of its issue.

In *Chapleton* v *Barry Urban District Council* (above), deck chairs were offered for hire under a sign setting out the price per hour and which requested the public to obtain tickets from the attendant and retain them for inspection. The plaintiff took two chairs and obtained two tickets from the attendant, which he did not read. He sat on a chair which collapsed. He sued the Council who relied upon a clause printed upon the ticket excluding liability.

The Court of Appeal held the Council liable. The sign constituted the offer which the plaintiff accepted when he took two deck chairs. The tickets amounted to no more than receipts, and hence any terms on those tickets were not part of the contract, which had been concluded prior to their issue.

In some cases, it is clear that the ticket is a contractual document and that the request for a ticket is an offer and the issue of that ticket an acceptance. This would appear to be the case with cinema, raffle and cloakroom tickets.

In other cases, the proffering of the ticket has been held to be an offer and the taking of that ticket, an acceptance. See *Thompson* v *London Midland & Scottish*

Railway Co [1930] 1 KB 41 where a contract of carriage is booked by telephone the contract is not complete until the ticket has been received, whether or not paid for beforehand.

In *Cockerton* v *Naviera Aznar SA* [1960] 2 Lloyd's Rep 450, the question was discussed in relation to automatic ticket-issuing machines in *Thornton* v *Shoe Lane Parking Ltd* [1971] 2 QB 163

The plaintiff had parked his car in the defendant's automatic car park. At the entrance there was a sign setting out the charges and stating: 'All cars parked at customer's risk'. As the defendant drove in, a light changed from red to green and a ticket was pushed at him by a machine. The transaction was analysed in terms of offer and acceptance by Lord Denning:

> 'The customer pays his money and gets a ticket. He cannot refuse it. He cannot get his money back. He may protest to the machine, even swear at it; but it will remain unmoved. He is committed beyond recall. He was committed at the very moment when he put his money in the machine; the contract was concluded at that time. It can be translated into offer and acceptance in this way. The offer is made when the proprietor of the machine holds out as being ready to receive the money. The acceptance takes place when the customer puts money in the slot. The terms of the offer are contained in the notice placed on or near the machine, stating what is offered for the money. He (the customer) is not bound by the terms printed on the ticket because the ticket comes too late. The contract had already been made.'

A case that is hard to reconcile with the above, or indeed with common sense, is *Wilkie* v *London Passenger Transport Board* [1947] 1 All ER 258.

There the issue was the process of formation of a contract of carriage on a public transport bus. This part of the decision was obiter as the Court of Appeal found that the plaintiff was, in fact, a bare licensee, not a party to a contract at all. Lord Greene MR thought that a contract was made when an intending passenger 'puts himself either on the platform or inside the bus'. Hence the offer must be made by the transport authority in running the bus and that offer is accepted by a passenger when he gets on the bus. If this is the case, then there is a complete contract before any payment is made or a ticket issued, and that process results in the formation of a second contract.

The difficulty with Lord Greene's analysis is that the passenger gives no consideration when he gets on the bus, so that it could be argued that a passenger could not enforce the contract of carriage. A more realistic analysis of the formation of the contract is that the running of the bus or the advertisement of bus services is an invitation to treat. The offer is made by the passenger when he gets on the bus and it is accepted by the transport authority when they take his money. This leaves open the question of whether the ticket is a mere receipt or a contractual document.

Auction sales

The question of whether an auctioneer's call for bids was an offer or an invitation to treat was considered in *Payne* v *Cave* (1789) 3 Term Rep 148.

It was there decided that the call for bids is an invitation to treat, a request for offers. The bids made by persons at the auction are offers which the auctioneer can accept or reject as he chooses.

This principle now has statutory form in s57(2) Sale of Goods Act 1979, which provides that a sale by auction is completed by the fall of the hammer and, up until then, a lot can be withdrawn. Likewise, an auctioneer can generally withdraw lots before he accepts the bid.

Goods put in for sale by auction are sold either with a reserve price or without. If the former is the case, then there is no contract if the auctioneer mistakenly accepts a bid lower than the reserve price and the item can be withdrawn even after the hammer has fallen. See *McManus* v *Fortescue* [1907] 2 KB 1.

Where the auction is advertised as being held without reserve, there is no contract of sale between the owner of the property and the highest bidder if the auctioneer refuses to accept the highest bid. But in *Warlow* v *Harrison* (1859) 1 E & E 309, it was held (obiter) that the auctioneer is liable in such a case on a separate contract between himself and the highest bidder that the sale be without reserve. The request for bids at the auction is an offer by the auctioneer that he will, on the owner's behalf, accept the highest bid, and this offer is accepted by bidding. Hence if the auctioneer refuses to sell an item to the highest bidder, that bidder can sue the auctioneer for breach of contract.

An advertisement that an auction is to be held does not constitute an offer to hold it capable of acceptance. In *Harris* v *Nickerson* (1873) LR 8 QB 286, the plaintiff was held not to be entitled to recover the money expended on travelling to attend an auction that had been advertised and which was then cancelled.

Tenders

Where goods are advertised for sale by tender, the statement is not an offer, but an invitation to treat; that is, it is a request by the owner of the goods for offers to purchase them. It is not an offer to sell to the person making the highest tender. See *Spencer* v *Harding* (1870) LR 5 CP 561.

Likewise, where a building contract is put out for tender, this is a request for offers by contractors which can then be accepted or rejected.

In *Harvela* v *Royal Trust of Canada* [1985] 1 All ER 261, the Court of Appeal had to consider the proper construction of an invitation to submit tenders. The telex, inviting the tenders, contained the term that:

'We bind ourselves to accept (the highest offer) provided such offer complies with the terms of this telex.'

In his judgment Waller LJ said:

'If it were not for the words "We bind ourselves to accept", this would have been a mere invitation to treat; but those words in my opinion make it an offer which the bidder being highest accepted' (at p265).

(Note: the decision of the Court of Appeal in *Harvela* has now been reversed by the House of Lords, but not on these grounds [1985] 2 All ER 966.) See also acceptance of tenders (below).

Subject to contract

The words 'subject to contract' are used by parties who are negotiating as to the terms of a contract to indicate that documents passing from one to the other are not intended to be offers capable of acceptance so as to form a binding contract. This topic is dealt with more fully in Chapter 5.

2.3 Duration and termination of offer

An offer continues in existence, capable of acceptance until it is brought to an end. There are six ways in which this can occur:

Revocation

The offer may be revoked by the offeror at any time up until it is accepted. See *Payne* v *Cave* (above). This is the case even where the offeror has stated that the offer will remain open for a certain period, unless the offeree can establish the existence of a separate and distinct contract to keep the offer open. In *Routledge* v *Grant* (1828) 4 Bing 653 the offeror stated that the offer would remains open for six weeks. He was held entitled to revoke the offer prior to the end of six weeks. The offeree could only insist on the offer remaining in existence for that period if he could show that he had bought the option to purchase by a separate agreement.

Communication of revocation

The only requirement imposed on the offeror is that the revocation of the offer must be communicated to the offeree(s). Unless and until the revocation is so communicated, it is ineffective. There must be actual communication of the revocation. Deemed communication as in the case of the postal rule in acceptance (see 'Occurence of a terminating condition', below) is not enough. It must be shown that the offeree was actually aware of the revocation.

In *Byrne* v *Van Tienhoven* (1880) 5 CPD 344, the defendants posted a letter on 1 October offering to sell to the plaintiffs 1,000 boxes of tinplates. They posted a letter revoking that offer on 8 October, which reached the plaintiffs on 20 October. Meanwhile, the plaintiffs had posted a letter accepting the offer on 15 October. Under the postal rule of acceptance, the offer was accepted when the plaintiffs posted their letter of acceptance. The revocation was not effective until it actually reached the plaintiffs, on 20 October, by which time the contract had been formed.

There is no requirement that the revocation be directly communicated to the offeree. It is sufficient that it can be shown that he was aware of the revocation prior to his acceptance.

In *Dickinson* v *Dodds* (1876) 2 Ch D 463, on 10 June the defendant gave the plaintiff a written offer of sale of a house for £800, which stated that the offer would remain open until 9 am on 12 June. On 11 June the defendant sold the house to a third party, and the plaintiff was told of this sale by a fourth party on the evening of 11 June. Before 9 am on 12 June, the plaintiff handed the defendant a letter purporting to accept the offer. It was held that the plaintiff was fully aware of the revocation before he 'accepted' the offer and that the revocation was effective.

Revocation of unilateral offers

The cases set out above are all examples of bilateral offers, that is, the offer to be bound by a promise in exchange for a promise by the offeree. Where the offer is unilateral, the basic principle is the same, but a little more difficult to apply.

A unilateral offer is accepted by the offeree performing an act. Acceptance will not be complete until the act itself is complete. The question that then arises is whether the offer can be withdrawn at any time before complete acceptance, or whether it must be withdrawn before the offeree commences performance of the act that constitutes acceptance. The former position is in accordance with the general rules on the revocation of offers, but it could lead to injustice.

If, for instance, a man offers a reward of £1,000 to the first person to swim the English Channel, acceptance is not complete until a swimmer actually reaches the shore. An application of the conventional rules would allow the offeror to revoke his offer as the swimmer comes in sight of land.

The question of the revocability of unilateral offers once performance has commenced was considered in two Court of Appeal decisions.

In *Errington* v *Errington and Woods* [1952] 1 KB 290, a father bought a house for his son and daughter-in-law to live in. He paid one-third of the purchase price in cash and borrowed the remainder from a building society on mortgage. He told the son and daughter-in-law that if they paid the mortgage instalments, he would convey the house to them when the payments were complete. They duly paid the instalments. The father purported to revoke his offer to convey the house before the whole mortgage had been repaid. It was held that there must be a term implied into the offer that it would be irrevocable once performance had commenced.

In *Daulia* v *Four Millbank Nominees Ltd* [1978] 2 All ER 557, the defendants were the owners of land. They agreed in a telephone conversation with the plaintiffs that if the plaintiffs produced a banker's order for the amount of the deposit, and attended at the defendants' solicitors the next morning to sign and exchange contracts, then the defendants would enter into a binding contract to sell the land to the plaintiffs.

The plaintiffs duly fulfilled these conditions. The defendants, having had a higher offer, refused to enter into the contract of sale. The plaintiffs sued for damages for breach by the defendants of their unilateral contract.

Goff LJ said:

> 'The concept of a unilateral or "if" contract is somewhat anomalous, because it is clear that, at all events until the offeree starts to perform the conditions, there is no contract at all, but merely an offer which the offeror is free to revoke ... Whilst I think that the true view of the unilateral contract must in general be that the offeror is entitled to require full performance of the condition which he has imposed and short of that he is not bound, that must be subject to one important qualification, which stems from the fact that there must be an implied obligation on the part of the offeror not to prevent the condition becoming satisfied, which obligation it seems to me must arise as soon as the offeree starts to perform. Until then the offeror can revoke the whole thing, but once the offeree has embarked on performance it is too late for the offeror to revoke his offer.'

The effect of this decision is that unilateral contracts go through two stages. Once the offeree has commenced performance of the act that constitutes acceptance, the offer can no longer be revoked. But until that act has been completely performed, the offer has not been accepted so as to form a binding contract.

Hence, while the man who offered the £1,000 for swimming the English Channel cannot revoke his offer once someone has started the swim, the swimmer cannot claim the reward unless he completes the crossing.

Rejection by the offeree

An offer that is rejected by the offeree cannot be subsequently accepted by him, once the rejection has been communicated to the offeror. There must be a specific rejection of the offer, not merely an enquiry as to some of the details of the offer. This topic is dealt with in more detail below, in 'Acceptance' and 'Counter-offers'.

Lapse of time

Where an offer is stated to be open for a specific length of time, then the offer automatically terminates when that time limit expires. Where there is no express time limit, an offer is normally open only for a reasonable time.

What constitutes 'reasonable' will depend largely on the subject matter of the proposed contract. Thus an offer to sell perishable goods will remain open for far less long than an offer involving land or shares. In *Ramsgate Victoria Hotel Co* v *Montefiore* (1866) LR 1 Ex Ch 109, the defendant offered to buy the plaintiffs' shares in June. He heard nothing more until the end of November when he was told that his offer had been accepted and he was required to pay the purchase price. On his refusal, he was sued for that price. It was held that he was entitled to refuse as his offer had not been accepted within a reasonable time and had therefore lapsed.

Occurrence of a terminating condition

An offer may be made subject to a condition. If that condition is not satisfied, the offer is not capable of acceptance. Examples of such conditions are that the offer must be accepted within a stated time or, in an offer to sell goods, that the goods are in a saleable condition or that an applicant for life insurance is in the same state of health as he was when he made his application.

In *Financings Ltd* v *Stimson* [1962] 3 All ER 386, the Court of Appeal considered the case of a man who had offered to purchase a car. Between the making of the offer and its acceptance, the car was badly damaged when a stranger crashed into it outside the garage.

Donovan LJ said:

> 'The county court judge held that there must be implied a term that, until acceptance, the goods would remain in substantially the same state as at the date of the offer; and I think that this is both good sense and good law.'

Death

The effect of the death of the offeror depends upon the nature of the offer. If it involved the performance of a promise which was personal to the offeror, such as writing a book or singing at a concert, then the offer cannot be accepted once news of the death has been communicated to the offeree. There must be actual communication. Where the offer was not dependent upon the offeror personally, then his death has no effect, and the offer remains capable of acceptance, and if accepted, is binding upon the estate of the offeror.

In *Bradbury* v *Morgan* (1862) 1 H & C 249, there is no clear English authority on the effect of the death of the offeree. In *Reynolds* v *Atherton* (1921) 125 LT 690, the question was considered obiter by Warrington LJ, who considered that the death of the offeree operates as a revocation of an offer. This view was not endorsed by the House of Lords.

In *Re Irvine* [1928] 3 DLR 268, a Canadian decision, a letter of acceptance was handed by a man to his son for posting. The man died before the letter was posted and it was held that the acceptance was ineffective as the offer had lapsed on the offeree's death.

Insanity, incapacity, insolvency or impossibility

The power to make an offer may be inhibited by, or the power to accept an offer terminated by, the occurrence of any of the following events either before the making of the offer or before its acceptance: the insanity or drunkenness of either party; intervening incapacity in the case of a corporation; the intended contract becoming illegal; and the performance of the contract becoming impossible. These topics are dealt with in more detail in Chapters 9, 13 and 14.

2.4 Acceptance

Definition

An acceptance is a final and unqualified acceptance of the terms of an offer. Unless it can be shown that there was such an acceptance, then there is no contract. In some cases, it is obvious that there has been an unqualified acceptance of the exact terms of an offer. Where the offeror sets out his offer and requests an answer of 'yes or no' from the offeree, it is not difficult to determine whether or not there has been acceptance. Frequently, however, progress towards agreement involves long and arduous bargaining by the parties. In those circumstances, the courts must look carefully at the dealings between the parties to decide whether there has, in fact, been an agreement and upon which terms.

Where an offer is made in the alternative, the acceptance must stipulate which alternative has been accepted. In *Peter Lind & Co Ltd* v *Mersey Docks and Harbour Board* [1972] 2 Lloyd's Rep 234, an offer to build a terminal was made by a tender quoting two alternative prices, fixed and 'cost-plus'. The offeree purported to accept 'your tender', without stating which price. It was held that there was no acceptance and hence no contract.

In addition to being a firm and unqualified acceptance of all the terms of the offer, the fact of acceptance must normally be communicated to the offeror before there is a concluded contract. The rules as to communication are dealt with below (see 2.5).

Acceptance by conduct

Acceptance of a bilateral offer normally takes the form of words, either spoken or written. But in the case of unilateral offers, that is, the offer of a promise in return for the performance of some act by the offeree, the offeree's performance of that act is the acceptance of the offer.

In *Carlill* v *Carbolic Smoke Ball Co Ltd* (above), the offer was contained in the advertisement by the company. Mrs Carlill accepted the offer by inhaling the smoke balls in accordance with the instructions. Acceptance was complete without the need to communicate the fact of acceptance to the company, an exception to the usual rule which requires communication before acceptance is complete. In practical terms, there will normally be communication of the fact that the act has been performed in order to collect the reward that has been offered, but there is a complete contract in existence once the act of acceptance has been completely performed, whether or not the offeror is aware that this is the case.

Acceptance is not complete until the act of acceptance has been completely performed. Where the offer is of a reward for the return of a lost cat, the offer is accepted when someone looks for, finds and returns the cat. The offeree will not be entitled to enforce the contract and claim his reward until he returns the cat.

Starting to look for the cat is not enough.

The requirement that there be complete performance of the act of acceptance before there is a concluded contract was emphasised in the case of *Daulia* v *Four Millbank Nominees Ltd* (above), where Goff LJ said:

> ' ... the true view of the unilateral contract must in general be that the offeror is entitled to require full performance of the condition that he has imposed and short of that he is not bound'.

See also *Errington* v *Errington and Woods* (above) for a discussion of the acceptance by conduct of a unilateral offer.

In addition to the act of acceptance being completely performed, it must have been performed by the offeree with the intention of accepting the offer in order to amount to an acceptance.

In *Taylor* v *Allon* [1966] 1 QB 304, an insurance company offered to insure the plaintiff's car. He took the car on to the road. It was held that this act did not amount to acceptance of the offer to insure because there was evidence that the plaintiff had in fact intended to insure his car with another company.

Occasionally, both offer and acceptance are alleged to have been made by conduct. In such cases, it is difficult to ascertain the terms of the agreement or, indeed, if there was in fact agreement at all. In such cases, the courts may apply the standard of reasonableness, that is, imply a term that a reasonable price was to be paid for goods sent by A to B and used by B. Or the court might look at previous dealings between the parties.

In *Brogden* v *Metropolitan Railway Co* (1877) 2 App Cas 666, the existence and terms of an agreement between the parties were established by reference to a draft agreement which had not been formally agreed by either party. The railway company had submitted a draft agreement to the plaintiff (a coal merchant) for the supply of coal by the plaintiff to the railway company. The plaintiff had amended the draft, written 'approved' upon it and returned it to the railway company, who did not expressly approve the amendments, but put it away in a drawer. The coal merchant commenced deliveries of coal to the railway company, who accepted those deliveries for two years. The supply and payment were upon the terms of the draft agreement, as amended. When a dispute arose, the plaintiff refused to continue supplying coal, and when sued for non-delivery, claimed that there was not and never had been a binding agreement between the parties. The House of Lords held that a contract came into existence either when the railway company ordered the first load of coal from Brogden upon the new terms, or when the first delivery of coal was made by Brogden and accepted by the railway company.

The point to note from this decision is that if two parties act as though there is a contract between them, then the courts will try to spell out the terms of a contract by reference either to previous dealings between the parties, or to customary terms. Conduct of itself cannot, however, be construed as an acceptance of an order if the offer prescribes the form of acceptance, and the conduct alone does not fulfil the requirements.

In *Wettern Electric Ltd* v *Welsh Development Agency* [1983] 2 All ER 629, the defendants offered the plaintiffs a licence to occupy a factory in a letter which stated: 'If you accept this licence on the above terms, will you please complete the acknowledgement and acceptance at the foot of the enclosed copy and return it to us at your earliest convenience.' The plaintiff did not complete the acknowledgement, but went into occupation of the factory. It was held that the act of going into occupation of the factory by the plaintiffs was not an acceptance of the defendants' offer, since that offer had required acceptance in another manner.

Counter-offers

In order to create a binding agreement, the offer and acceptance must match. The offeree must accept all the terms of the offer. If in his reply to an offer, the offeree introduces a new term or terms, or varies the terms of the offer, then that reply cannot amount to an acceptance. Instead, the reply is treated as an offer itself, a counter-offer, which the original offeror is free to accept or reject.

In *Tinn* v *Hoffman & Co* (1873) 29 LT 271, the offeree responded to an offer to sell 1,200 tons of steel with a request to purchase 800 tons. He was told that there had been no acceptance of the offer of sale. Instead, there had been a counter-offer to purchase 800 tons, which the sellers were free to accept or reject.

A counter-offer not only fails as an acceptance, it also generally amounts to a rejection of the original offer, which cannot then be subsequently accepted. This is illustrated in *Hyde* v *Wrench* (1840) 3 Beav 334. The defendant offered to sell the plaintiff a farm for £1,000. The plaintiff offered £950, which the defendant refused. The plaintiff then purported to accept the offer of £1,000 and sought specific performance of a contract for the sale of land. It was held that no contract existed. The plaintiff had rejected the defendant's original offer with his counter-offer, and that original offer no longer existed so as to be capable of later acceptance.

In order to amount to a counter-offer, the offeree's reply must itself be capable of acceptance. That is, it must contain either expressly or impliedly all the necessity terms.

Request for information

It is necessary to distinguish between a reply that amounts to a new offer and a reply which is merely a request for further information as to the terms of the offer. If the offeree is merely seeking further information before deciding whether to accept an offer, or enquiring as to whether the offeror will modify his terms, then he is not necessarily making a counter-offer. Whether a reply does or does not amount to a counter-offer is a matter of construction for the court. If the reply does not amount to a counter-offer, then the original offer remains in existence and is still capable of acceptance.

In *Stevenson* v *McLean* (1880) 5 QBD 346, the defendant offered on Saturday to sell the plaintiffs 3,800 tons of iron 'at 40s. nett cash per ton, open until Monday'. On Monday, the plaintiffs telegraphed 'Please wire whether you would accept 40s. for delivery over two months, or if not, longest limit you would give.' No reply was received, so by a telegram sent at 1.34 pm the plaintiffs accepted the offer to sell at 40s. cash. Meanwhile, the defendants sold the iron to a third party and informed the plaintiffs of this by a telegram sent at 1.25 pm, which crossed with the plaintiffs' telegram. When the plaintiffs sued for non-delivery, it was held that there was a valid contract of sale between the plaintiffs and defendants. The plaintiff's first telegram was not a counter-offer which destroyed the defendants' offer, but 'a mere inquiry, which should have been answered and not treated as a rejection of the offer'.

Clarification of implied terms

Where the reply to an offer contains terms that are not expressly set out in the offer, the reply will not amount to a counter-offer if those terms would, in any case, be implied into the offer. This is because the offeree is not in fact introducing new terms into the offer.

An example of the above would occur if, in response to an offer to sell goods, the prospective purchaser stated in his reply that the goods must be suitable for the purpose for which he was purchasing them. In any case, such a term would be implied into the contract for sale by the Sale of Goods Act 1979. Hence no new terms have been included.

The test to determine whether a reply by an offeree amounts to a counter-offer or not is whether a reasonable person in the position of the offeror would regard the purported acceptance 'as introducing a new term into the bargain and not as a clear acceptance of the offer'. See *Global Tankers Inc* v *Amercoat Europa NV* [1975] 1 Lloyd's Rep 666.

The 'battle of forms'

The rule that offer and acceptance must correspond with each other gives rise to problems where each party wants to contract on the basis of standard terms and these terms differ. This would occur where neither of the contracting parties are private individuals. For instance, company A offers to sell goods to company B, stating that the sale will be subject to company A's standard terms, as printed on the back of the document containing the offer. Company B reply stating that they want to buy the goods, at the price offered, but that the sale should be subject to B's standard terms as printed on the back of B's order form, which differ materially from A's.

This problem, and the methods by which the courts should approach it, was considered by the Court of Appeal in *Butler Machine Tool Co Ltd* v *Ex-Cell-O Corporation (England) Ltd* (above).

FACTS:

23 May 1969: The sellers offered to sell a machine to the buyers for £75,535 to be delivered in 10 months. The offer included certain terms, including a clause for variation of the price to the price ruling at the date of delivery. The offer was subject to an overriding clause that the seller's terms and conditions, as stated in the offer, 'shall prevail over any terms and conditions in the Buyer's order'.

27 May 1969: The buyers placed an order subject to their own, materially different, terms and conditions including, in particular, a term for a fixed price. At the foot of the order was a tear-off acknowledgement slip stating 'We accept your order on the Terms and Conditions stated thereon.'

5 June 1969: The sellers completed and returned the buyers' acknowledgement slip with a letter stating that the order was accepted on the basis of their quotation of 23 May.

At the date of delivery, the sellers claimed an increase in price for the machine of about £3,000. The buyers refused liability to pay the extra price on the grounds that the contract was made under their terms and conditions at a fixed price. The sellers contended that it was their terms and conditions which prevailed and they were, therefore, entitled to the increased price.

HELD (at first instance): since in their opening offer the sellers had said that their terms should prevail over any sought to be imposed by the buyers, the subsequent dealings were subject to that condition and, therefore, all the other original conditions imposed by the seller.

The buyers appealed. The Court of Appeal upheld the appeal.

Lord Denning MR:

'No doubt a contract was ... (on receipt of the letter and form of the 5th June) ... concluded. But on what terms? The sellers rely on their general conditions and on their last letter which said "in accordance with our revised quotation of 23rd May" (which had on the back the price variation clause). The buyers rely on the acknowledgement signed by the sellers which accepted the buyers' order "on the terms and conditions stated thereon" (which did not include a price variation clause).

If these documents are analysed in our traditional method, the result would seem to me to be this:

The quotation of 23rd May 1969, was an offer by the sellers to the buyers containing conditions on the back. The order of 27th May 1969 purported to be an acceptance of that offer in that it was for the same machine at the same price, but it contained such additions as to cost of installation, date of delivery and so forth that it was in law a rejection of the offer and constituted a counter-offer. That is clear from *Hyde* v *Wrench* (1840) 3 Beav 334. As Megaw J said in *Trollope & Colls Ltd* v *Atomic Power Construction Ltd* [1962] 3 All ER 1035 at 1038 ... the counter-offer kills the original offer. The letter of the sellers of 5th June 1969 was an acceptance of that counter-offer, as is shown by the acknowledgement which the sellers signed and returned to the buyers. The reference to the quotation of the 23rd May 1969 referred only to the price and identity of the machine.

... In many of these cases our traditional analysis of offer, counter-offer, rejection, acceptance and so forth is out of date. This was observed by Lord Wilberforce in *New Zealand Shipping Co Ltd* v *A M Satterthwaite* [1974] 1 All ER 1015, pp 1019-1020. The better way is to look at all the documents passing between the parties and to glean from them, or from the conduct of the parties, whether they have reached agreement on all material points, even though there may be differences between the terms and conditions printed on the back of them. As Lord Cairns LC said in *Brogden* v *Metropolitan Railway Co* (1877) 2 App Cas 666 at 672 ... "there may be consensus between the parties far short of a complete mode of expressing it, and that consensus may be discovered from letters or from other documents of an imperfect and incomplete description."

Applying this guide it will be found that in most cases where there is a "battle of forms" there is a contract as soon as the last of the forms is sent and received without any objection being taken to it. The difficulty is to decide which form, or which part of which form, is a term or condition of the contract. In some cases the battle is won by the man who fires the last shot. He is the man who puts forward the latest terms and conditions and, if they are not objected to by the other party, he may be taken to have agreed to them. Such was the illustration given by Professor Guest in *Anson's Law of Contract* where he says that "the terms of the contract consist of the terms of the offer subject to the modifications contained in the acceptance". That may, however, go too far. In some cases the battle is won by the man who gets the blow in first. If he offers to sell at a named price on the terms and conditions stated on the back and the buyer orders the goods purporting to accept the offer on an order form with his own different terms and conditions on the back, then, if the difference is so material that it would affect the price, the buyer ought not to be allowed to take advantage of the difference unless he draws it specifically to the attention of the seller. There are yet other cases where the battle depends on the shots fired on both sides. There is a concluded contract but the forms vary. The terms and conditions of both parties are to be construed together. If they can be reconciled so as to give a harmonious result, all is well and good. If the differences are irreconcilable, so that they are mutually contradictory, then the conflicting terms may have to be scrapped and replaced by reasonable implication.

In the present case the judge thought that the sellers in their initial quotation got their blow in first ... But I think that the documents have to be considered as a whole. And as a matter of construction, I think the acknowledgement of 5th June 1969 is the decisive document. It makes clear that the contract was on the buyer's and not the seller's terms and the buyer's terms did not include a price variation clause. I would therefore allow the appeal and enter judgment for the buyers.'

The principles of law which emerge from this case are:

1. Where the contracting parties form a contract which purports to be on the terms and conditions of both parties and those terms and conditions are at variance then:

    a) if the variation is insignificant, the offeree can impose the variation without drawing the offeror's attention specifically to it. The offeree, despite imposition of minor amendments to the offeror's conditions, nonetheless accepts the original offer.

    b) Where there is a difference which is so significant as would affect the price, the offeree cannot take advantage of it unless he clearly draws it to the attention of the offeror. In this case, the original offeree is now offering to enter into a different contract. The offer is made by him and is a counter-offer, which may or may not be accepted by the original offeror, such counter-offer may act as non-acceptance or refusal of the original offer (or it may simply be an enquiry as to whether the offeror will accept the new terms, whilst leaving open the possibility of acceptance under the original terms).

2. Where a counter-offer is accepted on its terms, then the original offer becomes totally eradicated. This must be so for, in the instant case, the major factor in the letter of 23 May was the term that the conditions thereof would be paramount. If the reference by the sellers to this letter referred only to the price and identity of the machine, then the letter must be seen by the court as a nullity in that the price was, under the terms of that letter, subject to change and, therefore, the 'price' identified could only be the price from the buyer's point of view.

3. It is difficult to reconcile the concept of a 'battle of forms' with the fundamental idea that contracting parties should be ad idem. Both parties in this type obviously consider that their terms and conditions prevail, and are replying on those terms and conditions.

Note, however, that the case of *Hartog* v *Colin and Shields* [1939] 3 All ER 566 (see Chapter 10) would appear to suggest that the seller in such cases might rely on mistake.

Acceptance of tenders

A tender is an offer (see 'Tenders' above). Normally, the acceptance of a tender leads to the formation of a contract by which the person tendering is bound to perform that which he has offered, at the price stated in the tender. This would be the case, for instance, where tenders were invited by a town council for the building of a new town hall; various builders submit tenders and, mindful of their duty to the ratepayers, the council accept the lowest priced. That acceptance creates a single contract under which the builders are bound to erect the town hall and the council to pay for it.

Difficulties arise, however, where tenders are invited for the periodical supply of goods. In such circumstances, it is a matter of construction of the original invitation to tender as to whether or not 'acceptance' of that tender leads to the formation of a contract.

Such invitations to tender can be divided into two broad types. First, an advertisement by A Ltd for offers to supply a specified quantity of goods, to be supplied during a specified time. In response to this invitation, B Ltd offers to supply the required quantity at a stated price. Acceptance of B Ltd's tender creates a contract, under which B Ltd are bound to supply the goods and the buyers A Ltd, are bound to accept them and pay for them. The only matter which is not settled is the timing of the deliveries, but the fact that these are to be by instalments as and when demanded, does not prevent a concluded agreement coming into existence on the acceptance of the tender.

Secondly, an advertisement by A Ltd for offers to supply goods up to a stated maximum, during a certain period, the goods to be supplied as and when demanded. Acceptance by A Ltd of a tender received from B Ltd in response to this invitation does not create a contract under which A Ltd is bound to accept delivery of the goods up to the stated maximum. Instead, A's acceptance converts B's tender into a *standing offer* to supply the goods up to the stated maximum at the stated price as and when requested to do so by A. The standing offer is accepted each time A places an order, so that there are a series of separate contracts for the supply of goods. A will not be in breach of contract if no orders are placed at all. Likewise, B's standing offer may be revoked, providing that it is not revoked at a time when it has been accepted by the placing of a specific order by A Ltd.

This second type of tender is illustrated in *Great Northern Railway* v *Witham* (1873) LR 9 CP 16. The plaintiffs advertised for tenders for the supply of stores. The defendant replied: 'I undertake to supply the company for 12 months with such quantities of (specified items) as the company may order from time to time.' The company accepted the tender, and for some months gave various orders which were filled by the defendant. Later, the company ordered some of the specified items, within the 12 months, and the defendant refused to supply them. It was held that his non-delivery was a breach of contract, as the placing of the order for the goods by the company was an acceptance of the defendant's standing order, which created a contract binding on the defendant to supply the goods ordered. The defendant could revoke his offer, but not in respect of goods that had already been ordered.

The question of acceptance of tenders was also considered in *Blackpool & Fylde Aero Club Ltd* v *Blackpool BC* [1990] 1 WLR 1195.

The defendant local authority owned the local airport for which it granted concessions for the operation of scenic and pleasure flights. On the expiry date of the current concessions, it invited the plaintiffs and seven other companies to tender for the new concession. The plaintiffs currently held the existing pleasure flight concession. The invitation to submit tenders was accompanied by a condition that no tender received after a certain date/time would be considered. The plaintiff's tender was posted by hand in the town hall letterbox, before the expiry date but, unfortunately, the box was not cleared regularly and the town clerk received the tender, which was higher than any of the others submitted, after the deadline. The local authority announced that they were not considering it because it was too late.

HELD: by the Court of Appeal, that where invitations are issued to specified parties to submit tenders, and the submission procedure is clearly laid down, along with a fixed date for submission, then if an invitee complied with the submission procedure and submitted his tender within the deadline, he had not just a moral but a contractual right to be considered.

The Court of Appeal held that, though an invitation to tender was normally no more than an offer to consider bids, circumstances could exist whereby it gave rise to binding contractual obligations. Although the invitation did not specifically state this, a careful examination of what the parties said, and did, established a clear intention on the part of the defendants to be bound to examine, and give equal consideration to, all tenders submitted within the deadline. Since the plaintiffs had submitted on time, they were entitled to expect their tender to be considered in conjunction with all the other tenders.

Conditional acceptance

A conditional assent to an offer is not an acceptance of that offer. Conditional assents occur most often in the case of negotiation for the sale of land. The use of the phrase 'subject to contract' in a response to an offer is a conditional assent, which means that the offeree is stating that his assent to the terms of the offer is conditional upon a formal contract being drawn up. Until there is an acceptance which is not stated to be 'subject to contract', there is no contract.

Whether or not an assent is conditional is a matter of construction. The cases discussed above in relation to 'Subject to contract' dealt with the interrelationship between the use of the phrase and the requirements of s40(1) LPA 1925 (now repealed). It has never been suggested that an assent marked 'subject to contract' can amount to an effective acceptance of an offer, unless it has been agreed that the condition is to be waived. Where words other than 'conditional' or 'subject to contract' are used, the position is less clear.

In *Branca* v *Cobarro* [1947] 2 All ER 101, a vendor agreed to sell his mushroom farm for £5,000. He had stated in writing: 'this is a provisional agreement until a fully legalised agreement, drawn up by a solicitor, and embodying the conditions herewith stated is signed.' Branca paid a deposit of £500, which he subsequently sought to recover, arguing that there was no concluded contract.

At first instance, the plaintiff, Branca, obtained judgment. On appeal, Lord Greene MR said:

'A provisional agreement is going to have efficacy until a certain event happens, ie the efficacy of the agreement is not made conditional on the happening of that event.'

Asquith LJ said:

'The word "until" seems to me plainly to imply that the agreement is to be immediately fully binding unless and until superseded by a subsequent agreement.'

The appeal was allowed.

The test to be applied is whether the parties have made the operation of their agreement conditional upon the coming into existence, at some later date, of a further document. If that is the case, then there is no contract unless and until that further document is executed.

If, on the other hand, the parties have agreed that their existing agreement will subsequently be replaced by a more formal written agreement, they are bound by the existing informal agreement.

The abolition of s40(1) LPA 1925 (see Chapter 5) suggests that the use of the phrase 'subject to contract' will no longer have relevance in contracts for sale of land. However, in theory, it will still be possible for the parties to make an informal agreement until such times as a formal contract can be drawn up for all other types of contract.

Acceptance in ignorance of an offer

The question that arises is whether an offeree who performs the act that constitutes acceptance while ignorant of the existence of the offer thereby validly accepts that offer. There is little authority on this point, but it would seem illogical to consider such an acceptance to be valid, as it ignores the requirement of intention on the part of the offeree. In *Upton-on-Severn RDC v Powell* [1942] 1 All ER 220 the defendant, whose house was on fire, telephoned the police station and asked for the fire brigade. He was entitled to the services of the Pershore Fire Brigade free of charge as he lived in its district, but the police officer called the Upton Fire Bridage in the mistaken belief that the defendant lived in their district. At the time they put out the fire, the Upton Fire Bridage shared this view. Later the defendant was sued for payment by the Upton Fire Brigade. He was held contractually bound to pay for those services.

The decision is difficult to reconcile with principle as, at the time they performed the services, the fire brigade had no thought of reward of those services, so how could that amount to an acceptance?

Motive for the acceptance

An offeree may perform the act that constitutes acceptance of an offer, with knowledge of that offer, but for a motive other than accepting the offer. The question that then arises, is whether his act amounts to a valid acceptance.

In *Williams v Carwardine* (1833) 5 Car & P 566, the defendant offered a reward of £20 to anyone who gave information leading to the conviction of the murderers of Walter Carwardine. The plaintiff was aware of the offer, and thinking that she had not much longer to live, signed 'a voluntary statement to ease my conscience, and in the hopes of forgiveness hereafter'.

As a result of the statement, the murderer was convicted. The plaintiff was held entitled to enforce the agreement and obtain her reward. Patterson J said: 'We cannot go into the plaintiff's motives.'

A similar conclusion was reached in *Carlill v Carbolic Smoke Ball Co Ltd* (above), where the plaintiff's motive in doing the act of acceptance (taking the smoke balls) was to avoid catching influenza, not to accept the defendant's offer. The plaintiff was held entitled to recover.

In the Australian case of *R v Clarke* (1927) 40 CLR 227, a different conclusion was reached. The Government of Western Australia offered a reward of £1,000 'for such information as shall lead to the arrest and conviction of' the murderers of two police officers, and added that, 'if the information should be given by an accomplice, not being himself the murderer, he should receive a free pardon'. Clarke saw the offer, and he was an accomplice. Some time later he gave the necessary information. He claimed the reward from the Crown by Petition of Right. He admitted not only that he had acted solely to save his own skin, but that, at the time when he gave the information, the question of the reward had passed out of his mind.

The High Court of Australia held that his claim must fail. He was, in their opinion, in the same position as if he had never heard of the reward. Higgin J said:

> 'Clarke had seen the offer, indeed, but it was not present to his mind – he had forgotten it and gave no consideration to it in his intense excitement as to his own danger. There cannot be assent without knowledge of the offer; and ignorance of the offer is the same thing, whether it is due to never hearing of it or forgetting it after hearing.'

The position therefore seems to be that an acceptance which is wholly motivated by factors other than the existence of the offer has no effect. Where, however, the existence of the offer plays some part, however small, in inducing a person to do the required act, there is a valid acceptance of the offer.

Cross-offers

The third situation where ignorance might appear to be no bar to a completed contract is in the area of cross-offers. However, it seems that there is generally no contract if two persons make identical cross-offers, neither knowing of the other's offer when he made his own; for example, if X writes to Y offering to sell Y his car for £500 and Y simultaneously writes to X offering to buy his car for £500. The natural reaction would be for one or both parties to seek to confirm that they are in agreement, and that extra communication would be an acceptance. Without it there can be no contract implied. Certainty is thus guaranteed, and conventional practice promoted. Blackburn J, in *Tinn v Hoffman & Co* (1873) 29 LT 271, said:

> 'When a contract is made between two parties, there is a promise by one in consideration of the promise made by the other; there are two assenting minds, the parties agreeing in opinion and one having promised in consideration of the promise made by the other – there is an exchange of promises. But I do not think exchanging offers would, upon principle, be at all the same thing. The promise or offer being made on each side in ignorance of the promise or offer made on the other side, neither of them can be construed as an acceptance of the other.'

2.5 Communication of acceptance

The general rule

The general rule is that an acceptance must be communicated to the offeror. Until and unless the acceptance is so communicated, no contract comes into existence.

Hence where, as in *Brogden* v *Metropolitan Railway Co*, the offeree fails to inform the offeror whether or not the offer has been accepted, there is no acceptance. If the offeree decides to accept the offer and writes a letter of acceptance which he then forgets to post, again there is no effective acceptance of the offer. The same result would follow if the offeree communicated his acceptance only to his own agent.

In order for an acceptance to be accepted, it must be *brought to the attention of the offeror*. Hence, there is no contract if, as Lord Denning MR said in *Entores* v *Miles Far East Corporation* [1955] 2 QB 327 at p332:

> 'the words of acceptance are drowned by an aircraft flying overhead; or if they are spoken into a telephone after the line has gone dead or become so indistinct that the offeror does not hear them.'

Exceptions to the general rule

The general rule as to acceptance does not apply, or is modified in the following cases:

1. Where the offeror expressly or impliedly waives the requirement that acceptance be communicated. This is generally the case with unilateral contracts and may sometimes be the case with bilateral agreements. The topic is dealt with in more detail below (see 'Silence').
2. Where the offeror is estopped from denying that the acceptance was communicated. This will be the case if it was in fact sent or spoken by the offeree, but was not received or heard by the offeror as a result of his own fault or omission. This would be the case in the example given by Lord Denning MR in *Entores* v *Miles Far East Corporation* (above):

> 'if the listener on the telephone does not catch the words of acceptance but nevertheless does not ask for them to be repeated.'

A similar result would follow if the acceptance was sent by telex to the offeror's office during office hours, but is simply not read by anyone there after it has been transcribed on to the offeror's machine.

3. Where the acceptance is communicated to the offeror's agent and that agent has authority to receive that acceptance on behalf of his principal. See *Henthorn* v *Fraser* [1892] 2 Ch 27.
4. Where the postal rule applies, in which case the acceptance can be effective before it is in fact received by the offeror. This is dealt with in detail below, in 'The postal rule'.

There is no requirement that the acceptance must be communicated specifically by the offeree. All that is required is that the offeror knows of the acceptance and hence there can be a valid contract, even though the acceptance was not brought to his attention by the offeree. See *Bloxham's Case* (1864) 33 Beav 529.

But where the acceptance is communicated to the offeror by a person other than the offeree, there will be no contract if that third party had no authority to so act on behalf of the offeree, and the circumstances indicate that the offeree's decision to accept was not yet regarded by him as irrevocable. See *Powell* v *Lee* (1908) 99 LT 284.

What constitutes communication of acceptance?

An acceptance is communicated when and where it is brought to the attention of the offeror, unless the postal rule applies, in which case the acceptance is communicated when the letter of acceptance is posted by the offeree.

Methods of communication are divided into those where communication is more or less instantaneous: face-to-face conversation, telephone, telex and fax; and into those where there is a time lag between the dispatch and receipt: letters and telegrams. The postal rule applies only to letters and telegrams.

Where the method of communication is instantaneous, then the offer is accepted when the offeror actually hears the acceptance. If the offeree speaks his acceptance but it is not heard by the offeror, then it has not been effectively communicated.

In *Entores* v *Miles Far East Corporation* (above), the issue was where a contract had been made. The plaintiffs were a London company and the defendants an American corporation with agents in Amsterdam. Both the plaintiffs and the Amsterdam agents used telex machines. The plaintiffs made an offer to the Amsterdam agents by telex, to buy goods from them. This offer was accepted, also by telex. The defendants were alleged to have broken this contract and the plaintiffs wished to show that the agreement had been made in England, so that legal proceedings could be commenced in England for breach of contract. The defendants contended that the postal rule applied, so that the offer was accepted when the telex was dispatched, in Holland.

Parker LJ said:

> 'Where ... the parties are in each other's presence, or, though separated by space, communication between them is instantaneous, there is no need for such a rule of convenience (the postal rule). To hold otherwise would leave no room for the operation of the general rule that notification of the acceptance must be received. An acceptor could say: "I spoke the words in your presence, albeit softly, and it matters not that you did not hear me"; or "I telephoned you and accepted, and it matters not that the telephone went dead and you did not get my message" ... So far as telex messages are concerned, although the despatch and receipt of a message is not completely instantaneous, the parties are to all intents and purposes in each other's presence just as if they were in telephonic communication, and I can see no reason for departing from the general rule that there is no binding contract until notice of the acceptance is received by the offeror. That being so, and since the offer was made by the plaintiffs in London and notification of the acceptance was received by them in London, the contract resulting therefrom was made in London.'

The Court of Appeal decision was approved by the House of Lords in the recent case of *Brinkibon Ltd* v *Stahag Stahl* [1982] 1 All ER 293.

The plaintiffs were an English company and the defendants an Austrian company, based in Vienna. After negotiations, the defendants offered to sell steel bars to the plaintiffs. The plaintiffs accepted this offer by a telex sent to the defendants in Vienna. The contract was not performed and the plaintiffs commenced proceedings for breach of contract, in England. The defendants claimed that the contract was made in Austria, so that the English courts did not have jurisdiction.

The House of Lords held that where there was instantaneous communication between the offeror and the offeree, the formation of a contract was governed by the general rule that a contract was concluded where and when acceptance of the offer was received by the offeror. Since the telex communication from the buyers in London to the sellers in Austria was instantaneous, the contract was made in Austria. The House of Lords considered the possibility that there might be circumstances in which, although telex was used, communication was not in fact instantaneous. This could occur where a telex was sent at night or when the offeror's office was closed.

Lord Wilberforce said, in relation to such circumstances:

> 'No universal rule can cover all such cases; they must be resolved by references to the intentions of the parties, by sound business practice and in some cases by a judgment where the risk should lie.'

The postal rule

The postal rule applies where there is a lag between despatch of an acceptance and receipt of that acceptance by the offeror. That is, where acceptance is by letter or telegram. In such a case, acceptance is communicated when the offeree posts the letter or telegram. This is an exception to the general rule, under which acceptance is complete once it is brought to the attention of the offeror.

Attempts have been made to justify the rules of postal offer and acceptance. It is best explained as a (somewhat arbitrary) rule of convenience. Essentially, the main problem in negotiating a contract by post is that letters get delayed or lost. Probably the most telling argument is that if an offeror indicates he is willing to negotiate by post, he is indicating his willingness to bear the risks involved.

Where acceptance is by post, there are three possible moments when that acceptance could be complete:

1. when the letter is posted by the offeree;
2. when the letter is delivered to the offeror;
3. when the letter is actually brought to the attention of the offeror.

It is easier to keep accurate records of the date and time at which a letter was posted, than the moment when it was delivered or the time when the offeror actually became aware of its existence. Hence it can be argued that in the interests of certainty as to the time when the contract was formed, the time of acceptance should be the time of posting.

A second ground upon which this departure from the general rule can be supported is that of the allocation of risk. Where postal acceptance has been expressly or impliedly stipulated by the offeror (see below), then the offeree may reply by that method. Postal communication bears the risk of letters being lost or delayed in the post. If acceptance was only complete when a letter was received by the offeror, then the offeree would not know whether or not he was a party to a binding agreement until the letter was received, and if, in fact, the letter never does arrive, the offeree could find himself acting on the assumption that he was a party to a contract when this does not turn out to be the case.

The risk borne by the offeror where acceptance is complete upon the posting of the letter of acceptance is that he is then bound by the agreement before he actually is aware of the acceptance. If the letter of acceptance is delayed or lost, then the offeror may assume that his offer was not accepted and enter into a contract for the disposal of the same goods. This would be a breach of the original contract. However, it was the offeror who stipulated acceptance by post, and hence it can be argued that he should bear the risk.

Development of the postal rule
The present rule was first laid down in *Adams* v *Lindsell* (1818) B & Ald 681.

On 2 September the defendants wrote to the plaintiffs offering to sell them a quantity of wool and requiring acceptance in the course of post. On 5 September the letter arrived, having been misdirected in the post by the defendants. On receipt of the letter, the plaintiffs immediately posted an acceptance. On 9 September the letter arrived, but meanwhile the defendants had sold the fleeces elsewhere, not having received a reply as expected on 7 September. The court held that the contract was completed on 5 September.

Application of the postal rule
A letter is 'posted' when it is put into the control of the Post Office (for example, by placing it in a letter box) or one of its employees authorised to receive letters. Giving a letter to an unauthorised person will not amount to acceptance of an offer. See *Re London and Northern Bank* [1900] 1 Ch 220.

Jones wrote to a company applying for shares and the company's servant took a letter of acceptance to the post at 7 am. Outside the Post Office the servant handed the letter to a postman. On the same day, a letter withdrawing Jones' offer arrived at the company's office at 8.30 am and was opened at 9.30 am.

The question was whether there had been acceptance before communication of the withdrawal of the offer.

Cozens-Hardy J said:

'The postman was not an agent of the Post Office to receive letters. The Postal Guide at page 47 expressly stated that town postmen are not allowed to take charge of letters from the post ... The mere fact of handing the letter to the postman outside St Martin le Grand Post Office was not a posting of the letter.'

The rule is best explained as one for the convenience of an offeree, assuming that the offeror will take responsibility for loss or delay in the post since he chose to open negotiations by this method. This may be misguided if the offeror is in fact a counter-offeror.

Thesiger J, in *Household Fire Insurance* v *Grant* (1879) 4 Ex D 216, said:

> 'As soon as the letter of acceptance is delivered to the Post Office the contract is made as complete and final and absolutely binding as if the acceptor had put his letter in the hands of a messenger sent by the offeror himself as his agent.'

This was a case turning upon loss of the letter, but was decided by a majority, overruling a previous decision. It would seem, therefore, that the arguments of convenience for and against applying the postal rule to such a situation are finely balanced. On the one hand, it may be harsh to hold an offeror liable on an acceptance which through no fault of his own, was never received by him; on the other, it may be equally hard to deprive the offeree of the benefit of an acceptance if he had taken all reasonable steps to communicate it. English law favours the offeree on the grounds that it is the offeror who 'trusts to the post' and that the offeror can always safeguard himself by stipulating in the offer that the acceptance must be actually communicated to him, and that postal rules will not apply.

In *Holwell Securities* v *Hughes* [1974] 1 WLR 155, the defendants granted the plaintiffs a six-month option to purchase property; the option was to be exercised by notice in writing to the defendants. The plaintiffs' solicitors sent a written acceptance exercising the option, but the letter was never delivered. The plaintiffs sought specific performance of the contract. At first instance, Templeman J dismissed the action.

On appeal, the plaintiffs argued that the postal rule applied and the option was properly exercised when the letter was put in the post.

Lawton LJ said:

> 'The plaintiffs were unable to do what the agreement said they were to do, namely fix the defendant with knowledge that they had decided to buy his property. If this construction of the option clause is correct there is no room for the application of any rule of law relating to the acceptance of offers by posting letters ... It becomes clear that the parties cannot have intended that the posting of a letter should constitute the exercise of the option.'

In *Yates Building Co Ltd* v *R J Pulleyn & Sons (York) Ltd* [1975] 237 EG 183, the facts of this case were that an offer was made, stipulating that acceptance should be by recorded delivery or registered post. The acceptance was actually made by ordinary post. The offerors therefore returned the acceptance, which it was never disputed arrived within the stipulated time limit, saying that they were not bound by it since it did not accord with the prescribed mode. By that time it was too late for the offerees to accept by the prescribed means.

Lord Denning MR with Lord Scarman concurring said that one has to look at the overall purpose for stipulating a particular mode of acceptance. Though their terminology differed, both judges drew a distinguishing line between mandatory requirements, and those which were purely optional or permissive. In the instant case, the purpose for stipulating recorded delivery or registered mail was to protect the offeree. Since the acceptance had indubitably arrived, no one, least of all the offerors, had been prejudiced.

Telegrams and telexes

The 'postal rule' also applies to acceptance by telegram. See *Bruner* v *Moore* [1904] 1 Ch 305. It does not apply to acceptance by telex. The problem in relation to acceptance by telex is not *when* the offer has been accepted because communication is nearly instantaneous, but *where* it has been accepted. This is significant for determining whether English law governs the contract, or whether the English court has jurisdiction to hear a case or to order service of notice of a writ outside the jurisdiction. (Students interested in this aspect should refer to a textbook on conflict of laws.) It is axiomatic that the contract is complete on acceptance. If A in Belgium accepts an offer by telex made by B in England, the contract could be capable of being made in Belgium or England. It will, however, be very rare that the contract will be deemed to have been made in Belgium. This question was first discussed in *Entores Ltd* v *Miles Far East Corporation* (1955) (above), and has been upheld in the *Brinkibon* case. (See 'What constitutes communication of acceptance?', above).

Silence

An offeree who does nothing in respect to an offer is not bound by the terms of that offer. The offeror cannot, in other words, impose silence as acceptance by the offeree.

In *Felthouse* v *Bindley* (1862) 11 CBNS 869, the plaintiff and his nephew had been negotiating about the sale of the nephew's horse. Having apparently reached agreement, the plaintiff wrote to his nephew to clarify whether the amount was in pounds and shillings or guineas. He concluded his letter by saying: 'If I hear no more about him I consider the horse is mine at £3 15*s*.' The nephew did not reply, but had decided to accept the offer. He instructed the auctioneer who was selling his farming stock not to sell the horse as it had already been sold. The auctioneer mistakenly sold the horse and was sued by the plaintiff in conversion. The Common Pleas held that at the time of the auction, no contract had been concluded for the sale of the horse between the plaintiff and his nephew.

In view of the fact that the nephew had decided to accept the offer and had informed the auctioneer accordingly, this decision is perhaps difficult to understand. The Exchequer Chamber, in affirming the decision on appeal, appears to have emphasised the alternative ground for the decision that the then requirements of the Statute of Frauds had not been complied with because there had been no delivery, part payment or memorandum in writing to vest the property in the plaintiff.

Though the decision at first instance in *Felthouse* v *Bindley* has been criticised on the facts, the general principle laid down in that case, that an offeror cannot impose silence as acceptance, has not been challenged.

What has not been fully resolved in England is the extent to which an offeror may, expressly or impliedly, waive communication of acceptance by the offeree. If the principle in *Felthouse* v *Bindley* is for the protection of the offeree, it does not seem satisfactory for the offeror who has waived the necessity of communication to be able to deny the validity of the contract. This is recognised in unilateral contracts, but the extent of this recognition in bilateral contracts is uncertain.

Although silence cannot of itself amount to acceptance, inaction on the part of the offeree may justifiably entitle the offeror to infer that his offer has been accepted.

In *Rust* v *Abbey Life Insurance Co* [1979] 2 Lloyd's Rep 355, the plaintiff applied and paid for a 'property bond' which was allocated to her on the terms of the defendant's usual policy of insurance. After a period of some seven months, the plaintiff sought recovery of the payment she had made on the basis that there had been no concluded contract. Her claim was rejected on the grounds that her application had been an offer and the issue of the policy an acceptance. It was further held, however, that, even if the issue of the policy had been a counter-offer, that counter-offer had been accepted by the plaintiff by her conduct in taking no action for the period in question.

Note that the Unsolicited Goods and Services Act 1971 now gives further protection to offerees in respect of 'imposed silent acceptance'.

Revocation of posted acceptance

Can an offeree withdraw his acceptance, after it has been posted, by a later communication, which reaches the offeror before the acceptance? There is no clear authority in English law. A strict application of the postal rule would not permit such withdrawal. This view is supported by decisions in New Zealand in *Wenkheim* v *Arndt* (NZ) 1JR (1873) and South Africa in *A-Z Bazaars* v *Minister of Agriculture* [1974] (4) SA 392 (c). The contrary view is argued by Professor Hudson in (1966) 82 LQR 169. He holds that the postal rule is merely one of convenience and ought not to be inflexibly applied.

3

Consideration

3.1 Introduction

3.2 Definitions

3.3 Four principles

3.4 Promissory estoppel

3.1 Introduction

To speak of a doctrine of consideration is something of a misnomer. There is no one doctrine with a coherent rationale, but rather a body of rules evolved by the courts, the function of which is to put some limit on the enforceability of agreements in law.

It is a general principle of the English law of contract that an informal gratuitous promise is not enforceable as a contract. Either the promise must be formalised by being made under seal, or it must be supported by consideration. This does not mean that a promise for which there is no consideration is devoid of legal effect. (See 3.4 below.)

The problem discussed in this chapter is what, in law, constitutes consideration so as to make the promise it supports enforceable as a contract.

3.2 Definitions

The definition most often quoted is that of Lush J in *Currie v Misa* (1875) LR 10 Ex 153 at p162:

> 'a valuable consideration in the sense of the law may consist either in some right, interest, profit or benefit accruing to the one party, or some forbearance, detriment, loss or responsibility given suffered or undertaken by the other'.

However, this definition is fundamentally incomplete and, as such, subject to criticism by theorists.

Cheshire and Fifoot prefer the approach taken in *Dunlop Pneumatic Tyre Co Ltd v Selfridge & Co Ltd* [1915] AC 847 that 'consideration is the price for which the promise of the other is bought'.

This brings out the element of bargain, of exchange of the giving of consideration in return for a promise which is so essential to the notion of consideration.

The point is also made in the American Restatement of Contracts (1932), which was the original version, defining consideration as: 'something bargained for and given in return for the promise'. More recently in the Second Restatement (1981), an even more clearly explicit definition states:

1. To constitute consideration a performance or a return promise must be bargained for.
2. A performance or a return promise is bargained for if it is sought by the promisor in exchange for his promise and is given by the promisee in exchange for that promise.

But, though subjected to criticism, it is the traditional definition which the courts have consistently applied, and it is that traditional approach to which we shall largely confine ourselves.

The courts have always looked on consideration in terms of a dichotomy of benefit to the promisor (the person making the promise), or detriment to the promisee (the person to whom the promise is made). These requirements are alternative. For instance, where A guarantees B's bank overdraft, the promisee bank suffers detriment by advancing money to B but no benefit to A, the promisor, need be shown.

The benefit/detriment dichotomy can bear two separate meanings. First, it may be used in the sense of any act, forbearance or promise that has economic value ('factual' benefit/detriment). Secondly, it is used in the sense of an act, forbearance or promise the performance of which is not already legally due ('legal' benefit/detriment). The courts have never consistently drawn the above distinction but, as will be seen, there are a number of cases where there was undoubted actual benefit/detriment, but there has been held to be no legal consideration.

A further division of the types of consideration is that distinguishing executed consideration (an act or forbearance in return for a promise) and executory consideration (mutual promises).

3.3 Four principles

Generally, it can be said that there are four principles governing the sufficiency and nature of consideration. These principles are hedged about with exceptions. The principles are:

1. consideration must move from the promisee;
2. consideration need not move to the promisor;
3. past consideration is not good consideration;
4. consideration must be sufficient but need not be adequate.

The effect of the last principle is ameliorated by the operation of equity by what is now known as 'promissory estoppel'. The position at common law will be examined first. Each principle and the exceptions to it will be dealt with in turn.

Consideration must move from the promisee

As has been indicated above, a person may provide consideration either by conferring a benefit upon another, or by undertaking to suffer a detriment to himself. It is, however, a personal obligation. A cannot generally promise C that B will confer a benefit or suffer a detriment in consideration for a promise by C to A, unless, of course, A assumes liability to C for the non-performance of that activity by B. The justification for this is that the consideration has not moved from the promisee.

In *Thomas* v *Thomas* (1842) 11 LJ QB 104, a testator wanted to give a house to his widow. The executors of his will promised the house to the widow 'in consideration of such desire' provided that she promised to keep the house in repair and to pay ground rent of £1 per annum. It was alleged that no binding agreement had been reached because the consideration was expressed to be moving from the testator and not from the widow.

HELD: that the promise to repair and to pay £1 per annum ground rent constituted consideration provided by her. She was, therefore, entitled to remain in the house.

There was a similar search for consideration in *Bolton* v *Madden* (1873) LR 9 QB 55. The plaintiff and defendant were both subscribers to a charity and entitled to vote on the distribution of funds at two successive meetings. The plaintiff and defendant agreed that, at the first meeting, the plaintiff would vote for the defendant's chosen candidate, and that the defendant would vote for the plaintiff's chosen candidate. The defendant refused to vote for the plaintiff's candidate.

HELD: the defendant was bound by his promise because the plaintiff had provided consideration in the earlier week by voting for the defendant's preferred candidate.

De La Bere v *Pearson* [1908] 1 KB 280 is similarly an illustration of the need of the court to find consideration moving from the promisee. In this case, the defendants owned a newspaper. They invited readers to apply by letter for financial advice so that the letters could be published. The plaintiff's letter was published. He followed the advice and suffered a loss. He sued. The defendants said that the advice had been given gratuitously and that they were not, therefore, liable.

HELD: the plaintiff had given consideration by writing a letter which could be published, and there was a contract between the plaintiff and the defendants.

Where the only benefit is to the promisee, however, it seems that consideration cannot be found. This is illustrated in *Dickinson* v *Abel* [1969] 1 WLR 295. The occupier and beneficiary under a trust of a farm asked a prospective purchaser of the farm: 'What's in it for me?' The prospective purchaser said that he could have £10,000 if he (the purchaser) bought the farm for £100,000 or less.

HELD: no services were offered by the occupier or expressed by the purchaser. The occupier could not know what was in the mind of the purchaser so that there could not be any contractual consensus as to the consideration to be provided by the occupier. Unlike *The Moorcock* (see 6.8) no term could be implied which amounted to consideration.

Consideration need not move to the promisor

Where the consideration provided is the suffering of a detriment to the promisee, the consideration cannot move to the promisor.

So in *Carlill* v *Carbolic Smoke Ball Co Ltd* (above), the consideration for the promise by the Carbolic Smoke Ball Co was using the smoke ball which the plaintiff had bought. That conferred no direct benefit on the Carbolic Smoke Ball Co, and so did not move to the promisor. It was, however, a detriment to herself.

In *Tanner* v *Tanner* [1975] 1 WLR 1346, a mistress gave up her rent-controlled flat and moved into a house bought by her lover and brought up the children of their union.

HELD: that she had provided consideration by giving up her rent-controlled flat. She had a contractual licence to remain, which was irrevocable until the children were over school age.

The sustaining of the detriment must be part of the bargain struck between man and mistress. In *Horrocks* v *Foray* [1976] 1 WLR 230, the court thought that there would be no consideration in somewhat similar circumstances, because the mistress did not give up anything as part of the bargain.

Megaw LJ said:

'I say ... "(that there was no contractual licence)" ... without going on to consider what I think may well be an extremely difficult barrier in the way of the defendant (the mistress). Suppose that she had established something which otherwise could be regarded as being a contract, where is the consideration for that contract to be found? In *Tanner* v *Tanner*, the consideration was perfectly clear; the lady had given up her rent-controlled flat as part of the bargain that they would move into other accommodation. There is no such consideration here.'

Past consideration is not good consideration

The rule is well established. It can be seen in operation in *Roscorla* v *Thomas* (1842) 3 QB 234. The defendant promised the plaintiff that a horse which had been bought by him was sound and free from vice. In fact, it was not.

HELD: the express promise that the horse was sound and free from vice had been made after the sale and, therefore, no consideration for the promise was given.

Similarly, in *Eastwood* v *Kenyon* (1840) 11 Ad & El 438, the guardian of a young girl had raised a loan to pay for her education and maintenance. On her marriage, her husband agreed to repay the amount of the loan. He failed to do so. The guardian sued him.

HELD: there was no liability on the part of the husband because the consideration was past consideration. With reference to the argument that the husband had a moral obligation to repay the loan, the court said that no such argument could exist in English law. It would annihilate any need for consideration at all.

In *Re McArdle* [1951] Ch 669, a promise made 'in consideration of your carrying out certain alterations and improvements to the property' was held by the Court of Appeal to be unenforceable, as all the work had been done before the promise was made.

These cases contrast with that of *Lampleigh* v *Braithwait* (1615) Hob 105. Braithwait had murdered someone (M) and asked Lampleigh to do his best to obtain a pardon for him. Lampleigh journeyed to and from Newmarket for him. Braithwait afterwards promised to pay Lampleigh £100.

HELD: that the promise to pay £100, coupled with the prior request as part of the same activity, amounted to good consideration.

The principle extrapolated from this case crystallised into its modern form in *Re Casey's Patents* [1892] 1 Ch 104. A and B, who were joint owners of certain patent rights, wrote to C stating: 'In consideration of your services as the practical manager in working our patents we hereby agree to give you one third share of the patents.'

HELD: C could rely on this agreement. He was deemed to have given consideration for it. The court made the following observation:

> 'The fact of a past service raises an implication that at the time it was rendered it was to be paid for, and if it was a service which was to be paid for, when you get in the subsequent document a promise to pay, that promise may be treated as an admission which evidences, or as a positive bargain which fixes, the amount of that reasonable remuneration on the faith of which the service was originally rendered. So that here for past services there is ample justification for the promise to give the third share.'

Re Casey's Patents can, therefore, be said to be authority for the view that a subsequent promise to pay for an act done in the past will be good consideration where the plaintiff would be able to recover on a quantum meruit basis. (See Chapter 18). The subsequent agreement fixes the amount of the quantum meruit. Treitel, *The Law of Contract*, suggests that the promise could, alternatively, be regarded as being given in consideration of the promisee's releasing his quantum meruit claim. The decision in *Re Casey's Patents* was approved in 1979 in the case of *Pao On* v *Lau Yiu Long* [1979] 3 All ER 65 PC. The plaintiffs owned issued share capital in a company called 'Shing On'. The defendants were the majority shareholders in a company called 'Fu Chip' in Hong Kong. Two written agreements were entered:

1. The plaintiffs were to sell shares in 'Shing On' to 'Fu Chip' in exchange for certain shares in 'Fu Chip'.

2. The defendants agreed to buy back just over half of the shares at the same price at a later date.

The purpose of the second agreement was to protect the plaintiffs against a fall in the share prices of 'Fu Chip'. However, as the share prices were expected to rise, the plaintiffs realised that they had contracted a bad bargain. Accordingly, the plaintiffs refused to perform the contracts, unless a different agreement were reached. The defendants chose to avoid litigation by cancelling the second agreement and replacing it by an agreement by the defendants to indemnify the plaintiffs against a drop in the value of the shares. The document of indemnity referred to the first agreement, and incorporated into the guarantee the promise in the first agreement not to sell before a certain date.

In fact, the share prices fell. The defendant failed to idemnify the plaintiff.

HELD: the promise not to sell before a certain date provided consideration supporting the agreement to indemnify, even though it was made prior to that agreement. The promise had been made in anticipation of some sort of guarantee by the defendant which protected the plaintiff against loss. *Re Casey's Patents* was approved and applied.

The Privy Council, in *Pao On*, laid down the necessary preconditions for an act done before the giving of a promise to constitute consideration for the promise:

1. the act must be done at the promisor's request;
2. the parties must have understood that the act was to be remunerated either by a payment or the conferment of some other benefit; and
3. the payment, or the conferment of a benefit, must have been legally enforceable had it been promised in advance.

Consideration must be sufficient but need not be adequate

The word 'sufficient' in this context is incapable of precise definition. In reality, it is used as little more than shorthand for the body of rules which prevent certain acts or promises from constituting valid consideration even though the rules discussed above may have been satisfied.

Valuation

The court will look to see if the purported consideration contains any value. If it sees that there can be some value, then it will not concern itself with the accuracy of the valuation. That may be so even where the motive for undervaluation is a corrupt one. Equity may intervene but the position at law is unaffected.

In *Chappell* v *Nestlé* [1960] AC 87 the respondents sold gramophone records to consumers of their chocolate products for 1*s*. 6*d*. and three wrappers. The question whether the chocolate wrappers formed part of the consideration fell for determination. They were held to be part of the consideration, even though Nestlé only threw them away. It follows that the wrappers would have been good consideration even if no sums had been paid.

Similarly, in *Midland Bank* v *Green* [1981] AC 513, where a husband conveyed an estate to his wife at a very low price to avoid the operation of an option to purchase, the court would not look at the adequacy of the consideration, even though the transaction was in part a gift.

But the act or promise must have some economic value. In *White* v *Bluett* (1853) 23 LJ Ex 36, it was held that a son's promise not to bore his father with complaints (for the father's promise not to sue him on a promissory note) was not good consideration.

Knowledge

It may be the case that a person must know that he is giving value in order to find consideration, though this is still open to debate.

In *Arrale* v *Costain Civil Engineering* [1976] 1 Lloyd's Rep 98, a workman accepted compensation for injury under a Dubai ordinance and in satisfaction of his rights in Dubai and at common law.

HELD: the workman had not lost his right to sue at common law because, at the time he accepted the compensation and entered into the agreement, he did not know he had any rights. He therefore gave no consideration for giving them up.

Compromise of suit

The above case implies that the workman could have provided consideration by giving up rights of which he knew. Similarly, where a person gives up proceedings at law, the mere surrender of the right to continue or start the proceedings is good consideration. Provided that the compromise is reached in good faith, it does not render the consideration invalid if it subsequently transpires that the claim compromised was wholly unfounded.

In *Callisher* v *Bischoffsheim* (1870) LR 5 QB 449, the plaintiff claimed that money was owed to him by the Government of Honduras and others. The defendant offered to pay the plaintiff if he would drop his suit against the Government. The plaintiff did so. The defendant refused to pay. The plaintiff brought an action. The defendant said that the Government of Honduras did not owe any money to the plaintiff.

HELD: that was no defence to an action for breach of the agreement of compromise.

Duties owed to third parties

Where a duty is owed to a third party, its performance can also be consideration for a promise by another. The problem was considered in *Scotson* v *Pegg* (1861) 6 H & N 295. A agreed to deliver coal to B's order. B ordered A to deliver the coal to C, who promised A to unload it. A successfully sued to enforce C's promise, it being held that A's delivery of the coal was good consideration for C's promise notwithstanding that A was already bound to so deliver by his contract with B. However, it was also suggested there may have been a separate consideration for C's promise in that A may have had a lien on the coal, which he agreed to release in return for C's promise to unload the coal.

The same question also arose in *Shadwell* v *Shadwell* (1860) 9 CBNS 159, where an uncle promised to pay an annual sum to his nephew on hearing of his intended marriage (at the time a promise to marry was a binding contract that could be sued upon). Although the majority of the Court of Common Pleas held there was consideration for the uncle's promise, the suggested 'consideration' is unconvincing. They suggested that the nephew had made a material change in his position and incurred financial embarrassment, and that there had been a benefit to the uncle in that the welfare of his nephew was an object of interest to a near relative.

The principle that a promise to perform, or the performance of, a pre-existing contractual obligation to a third party can be valid consideration was affirmed by the Privy Council in *New Zealand Shipping* v *Satterthwaite (The Eurymedon)* [1974] 1 All ER 1015, where Lord Wilberforce said:

> 'An agreement to do an act which the promisor is under an existing obligation to a third party to do, may quite well amount to a valid consideration ... the promisee obtains the benefit of a direct obligation ... This proposition is illustrated and supported by *Scotson* v *Pegg* which their Lordships consider to be a good law.'

In *Pao On* v *Lau Yiu* (above), Lord Scarman stated that their Lordships did not doubt the principle.

Duties owed by law

If the duty relied upon to constitute consideration is already owed at law, it may not constitute good consideration. If, however, the promisor agrees to do more than is required at law, the consideration will be sufficient. This contrast can be illustrated by *Collins* v *Godefroy* (1831) 1 B & Ad 950 and *Glasbrook Brothers* v *Glamorgan CC* [1925] AC 270. In *Collins* v *Godefroy*, a plaintiff was subpoenaed to give evidence for the defendant. The plaintiff alleged that the defendant had promised to pay her expenses.

HELD: the defendant was obliged by law to answer to the subpoena, so that giving evidence could not be consideration for the promise to pay the witness's expenses.

The contrasting situation arose in *Glasbrook Bros* v *Glamorgan CC*. The police were under a duty to protect a coal mine during a strike. They were asked by the manager of a coal mine to provide a stronger guard than the police would otherwise have done. A rate was agreed for the provision of this service.

HELD: the extra protection was good consideration for the promise by the coal mine manager to pay for it. See also *Harris* v *Sheffield United Football Club* [1987] 2 All ER 838.

A case which is difficult to reconcile with the rationale expressed above is *Ward* v *Byham* [1956] 1 WLR 496. The father of an illegitimate child wrote to its mother from whom he was separated saying that she could have the child and an allowance of £1 per week if she proved that the child was well looked after and happy. The father refused to continue payments after the mother married another man.

HELD: the mother was entitled to enforce the father's promise. Denning LJ (as he then was) based his decision on the ground that the mother provided consideration by performing her legal duty to maintain the child. The alternative explanation is that the promise to make the child happy was further consideration. The latter explanation is problematical for two reasons:

1. it may be no more than a provision of natural love and affection; or
2. it may be too uncertain.

This latter view is also difficult to reconcile with *White* v *Bluett* (above).

Treitel, *The Law of Contract*, prefers the view of Lord Denning MR. He also suggests that, with the exception of the old and somewhat doubtful case of *Collins* v *Godefroy*, there is no conclusive authority to show that performance of a duty imposed by law cannot be consideration for a promise. In any event, it is hard to see why performance of a duty owed to a third party should be capable of amounting to consideration when performance of a duty owed at law cannot be so capable.

Duties imposed by prior contract with the promisor
The rule is that if A is bound to do something by virtue of a contract with B, performance of the duty or the promise to perform cannot be consideration for a further promise by B.

The same principle is said to be derived also from *Stilk* v *Myrick* (1809) 2 Camp 317. Some sailors had deserted a ship. The captain of the ship promised to divide their wages among the remaining sailors if they would work the ship home short-handed.

HELD: that there was no consideration because the sailors were already bound to work the ship home.

The reliability of this decision is suspect. One of the reports of *Stilk* v *Myrick* (1809) 6 Esp 129 does not mention consideration at all, but says that the court decided against the sailors on the basis of an earlier decision on the grounds of public policy that sailors might refuse to perform their contracts unless they were granted extra pay. The case is, however, arguably wrong for another reason. The promise to divide the wages of the deserters was made by the ship's master, who was the defendant in the action. The sailors' contracts to work the ship may have been with the ship owners. This question was not raised, at least according to the reports. However, the rule in *Stilk* v *Myrick* was recognised as still being good law in *North Ocean Shipping* v *Hyundai Construction (The Atlantic Baron)* [1978] 3 All ER 1170, though being held inapplicable on the facts.

A different conclusion was reached in *Hartley* v *Ponsonby* (1857) 7 E & B 872. Here the ship became so short-handed as a result of desertion that it was dangerous to sail the ship home with only the remaining crew. The crew were offered increased wages if they sailed the ship home.

HELD: the promise to pay extra money was supported by good consideration. The danger to the sailors discharged them from their original contract. Consequently, they were free to enter into the new contract.

Note that in the case of *Williams* v *Roffey Bros & Nicholls* [1989] NLJ 1713, it was held (by the Court of Appeal) that when a party to an existing contract later agrees to pay an extra 'bonus' in order to ensure that the other party performs his obligations under the original contract, that the agreement is binding if the party agreeing to pay the bonus has thereby obtained some new practical advantage or avoided a disadvantage.

In the course of his judgment, Glidewell LJ said that following the decision in *Pao On* v *Lau Yiu Long* [1979] AC 614 the state of the law on this subject may be expressed as follows:

1. if A enters into a contract with B to do work for or supply goods or services to B in return for payment from B; and
2. at some time before A has completely performed his obligations under the contract, B has reason to doubt whether A will, or will be able to, complete his side of the bargain; and
3. B therefore promises A an additional payment in return for A's promise to perform his contractual obligations on time; and
4. as a result of giving this promise, B obtains in practice a benefit or obviates a disbenefit; and
5. B's promise is not given as a result of fraud or economic duress on A's part;
6. the benefit to B is capable of being consideration so that B's promise will be legally binding.

This proposition refines and limits the application of the principle in *Stilk* v *Myrick* (1809) 2 Camp 317, but leaves the principle unscathed.

Russell LJ, concurring, noted that in the late twentieth century the rigid approach to *Stilk* v *Myrick* was neither necessary nor desirable.

It seems to follow from the proposition that performance of an existing duty cannot be consideration for a new promise that, a fortiori, partial performance of a duty cannot be consideration for a new promise. On the other hand, the introduction of a new element into the existing duty will support a new promise. The cases which are authority for this view are both cases which concern debts. In *Pinnel's Case* (1602) 5 Co Rep 117a, Pinnel sued Cole for £8 10s. due on a bond in November 1600. Cole's defence was that at Pinnel's request, he had paid him £5 2s. 6d. on 1 October, and that Pinnel had accepted this payment in full satisfaction of the original debt.

HELD: judgment was given for Pinnel on a point of pleading. The Court made it clear that, had it not been for a technical flaw, they would have found for Cole on the ground that payment in part had been made on an earlier day than that appointed.

The payment at the request of the plaintiff on an earlier date than is contractually required is a new element, and provides additional consideration to support the discharge of the debt. So payment of a smaller sum accompanied at the creditor's request by the delivery of a chattel is good consideration for a promise to forgo the balance. 'The gift of a horse, hawk or robe, etc in satisfaction is good. For it shall be intended that a horse, hawk or robe, etc might be more beneficial than money.' This observation does not apply to negotiable instruments (such as cheques), even though negotiable instruments are a form of chattel. See *D & C Builders Ltd* v *Rees* [1966] 2 QB 617.

Pinnel's Case is cited as the authority for the proposition that: 'Payment of a lesser sum on the day in satisfaction of a greater sum cannot be any satisfaction for the whole.' The rule was approved by the House of Lords – *Foakes* v *Beer* (1884) 9 App Cas 605 – although Lord Blackburn in the latter case, dissenting in all but name, said the true ratio of the former case was:

' ... that where a matter paid and accepted in satisfaction of a debt certain might by any possibility be more beneficial to the creditor than his debt, the court will not inquire into the adequacy of the consideration',

and that the further statement that a lesser sum on the day could never be satisfaction was unnecessary and erroneous.

The facts of *Foakes* v *Beer* were that B obtained judgment against F who subsequently asked for time to pay. B agreed to take no proceedings whatever on the judgment in consideration of an immediate payment with the balance paid by instalments. F complied with the terms of the agreement, and paid the whole of the judgment debt, but B thereafter sued for interest on the principal sum and the House of Lords held that she was entitled to succeed on that claim.

Part payment by third parties

Where a third party makes part payment which the creditor accepts as full satisfaction of the debtor's obligation, the creditor cannot then sue the debtor for the balance, for to do so would be a fraud upon the third party. That is not to say, however, that the breach of contract with the third party would be fraud at common law; it would not. For that reason, an alternative explanation for the rule that a third party can discharge a debtor's liability by part payment of the debt has been proffered. The court will not help the creditor to break his contract with the third party by allowing him to recover from the debtor. The third party can intervene so as to obtain a stay of the action. See *Snelling* v *Snelling* [1973] 1 QB 87. It is, of course, necessary that the creditor should have agreed with the third party not to sue the debtor. See *Gore* v *Van Der Lann* [1967] 2 QB 31.

Furthermore, where the part payment is made by a third party against a promissory note, a creditor cannot then sue the debtor on the note. In *Hirachand Punamchand* v *Temple* [1911] 2 KB 330, the court said that the promissory note was extinct as though it had been cancelled. The right of action on a promissory note is, however, distinct from a right of action in contract. The action on the note may be lost even though the contract remedy is not. The reverse is also true.

3.4 Promissory estoppel

Introduction

'Promissory estoppel' is the name that has been given to the equitable doctrine which has as its principal source the obiter dicta of Denning J (as he then was) in *Central London Property Trust Ltd* v *High Trees House Ltd* [1947] 1 KB 130.

Estoppel is a concept known both to law and to equity; estoppel at common law is commonly concerned to prevent a person from denying the existence of facts which he has himself previously asserted; as a rule of evidence, it debars him from leading evidence to rebut his own earlier assertion, where another, in consequence thereof, has acted to his detriment on the faith of the assertion.

Promissory estoppel is a type of equitable estoppel, but the two terms are not interchangeable, because the latter also embraces proprietary estoppel, a more certain and long-established concept. Proprietary estoppel provides that where a person expends money or effort on another's property in the mistaken belief that he has or will thereby acquire an interest in the property and the true owner encourages or acquiesces in the mistake, the latter is estopped, that is, prevented from asserting his full title against the former. Proprietary estoppel is permanent in effect, and may create a positive right of action (compare this with promissory estoppel as elaborated below).

Promissory estoppel is not concerned with facts but with promises and intentions:

> 'Where by his words or conduct one party to a transaction makes to the other an unambiguous promise or assurance which is intended to affect the legal relations between them (whether contractual or otherwise), and the other party acts upon it, altering his position to his detriment, the party making the promise or assurance will not be permitted to act inconsistently with it.' (Snell's 'Principles of Equity', 27th edn.)

The above definition might properly be called the conventional one; it is by no means universally accepted.

Evolution

The modern starting point is *High Trees*, but of necessity reference back must be made to nineteenth-century cases from which the doctrine purports to derive its authority and legitimacy.

The *High Trees* case

In 1937, the defendants leased a block of flats from the plaintiff for 99 years at a rent of £2,500 per annum. By 1940, because of the war, the defendants were unable fully to let the block, and the plaintiffs agreed to reduce the rent to £1,250. In 1945, when conditions had returned to normal and the block was fully let again, the plaintiffs sought to return to the full rent.

Denning J held that the plaintiffs could thereafter recover the full rent because their promise to accept half only was intended to apply during the war whilst the block was not fully let. Such is the ratio decidendi of the case. Promissory estoppel only raises its head in obiter dicta, because his Lordship said that had the plaintiffs sued for the balance in respect of the period 1940-5, they would not have recovered.

Circumnavigating the authorities

Denning J's obiter dicta caused eyebrows to be raised because of the way he characteristically dealt with apparently immovable obstacles in his path.

The problem his Lordship faced was that, under the lease, the plaintiffs were contractually entitled to £2,500. There was no variation of the contract, no consideration moving from the defendants to support the plaintiffs' bare promise, which according to conventional theory would thus be unenforceable. Up until *High Trees*, it was considered to be an entrenched rule of English law that part payment of a debt did not without more discharge the debtor's liability for the whole amount; *Pinnel's Case* (1602) 5 Co Rep 117a (Court of Common Pleas), affirmed by the House of Lords in *Foakes* v *Beer* (1884) 9 App Cas 605.

Between the contracting parties themselves, the problem was susceptible of a practical solution: if the part payment was made at a time earlier than that stipulated in the contract for payment of the whole sum, the debtor would be discharged – as held in *Pinnel's Case*. The earlier part payment was good consideration for the creditor's promise to accept half, because the debtor was doing something different to that which he was contractually bound to do. Likewise, payments in goods, even if considerably less valuable than the debt in money terms, discharged the debtor. In the immortal words of Jessel MR in *Couldery* v *Bartrum* (1881) 19 Ch D 394:

> 'According to English Common Law a creditor might accept anything in satisfaction of his debt except a less amount of money. He might take a horse, or a canary, or a tomtit if he chose, and that was accord and satisfaction; but by a most extraordinary peculiarity of the English Common Law, he could not take 19s. 6d. in the pound.'

Thus expressed the rule had little to commend it; it permitted creditors to renege on agreements and, in 1937, the Law Revision Committee recommended its abolition, but although some Commonwealth jurisdictions have adopted this recommendation, no legislative action has yet been taken in England.

How then did Denning J avoid the operation of the rule? He relied on *Hughes* v *Metropolitan Railway Co* (1877) 2 App Cas 439. The appellant landlord served on the respondent tenants a notice to repair within six months; the effect of the respondents' failure to comply being that the appellant could forfeit the lease. Following service of the notice, the parties commenced negotiations for the respondents to buy the lease, which proceeded for almost six months when the appellant terminated them, and sought to forfeit the lease for the respondents' failure to repair. The House of Lords held that, by the negotiations, the appellant impliedly promised that he would not bring proceedings upon the respondents' failure to repair within six months, and that he could not subsequently take advantage of the respondents relying on this.

In *High Trees*, Denning J cited what he regarded as the crucial speech of Lord Cairns in *Hughes*:

> 'It is the first principle upon which all Courts of Equity proceed, that if parties who have entered into definite and distinct terms involving certain legal results - certain penalties or legal forfeiture - afterwards by their own act or with their own consent enter upon a course of negotiations which has the effect of leading one of the parties to suppose that the strict rights arising under the contract will not be enforced, or will be kept in suspense, or held in abeyance, the person who otherwise might have enforced these rights will not be allowed to enforce them where it would be inequitable having regard to the dealings which have thus taken place between the parties.'

For the moment, two short points should be made. First, Lord Cairns cited no authority for his 'first principle' and, secondly, there is no mention anywhere of promissory or, indeed, any other type of estoppel.

It has been said that Denning J revived a moribund case and applied too widely a principle that, on one reading of *Hughes*, concerned only equity's power to mitigate against inequitable forfeiture at common law. This is a little unfair, because *Hughes* had been cited and applied beyond the landlord and tenant context in *Birmingham and District Land Co* v *L & N W Ry* (1888) 40 Ch D 268 where Bowen LJ said:

> 'If persons who have contractual rights against others induce by their conduct those against whom they have such rights to believe that such rights will either not be enforced or will be kept in suspense or abeyance for some particular time, those persons will not be allowed by a court of equity to enforce the rights until such time has elapsed, without at all events placing the parties in the same position as they were before.'

It must, however, be said that certain other authorities relied on by Denning J were somewhat less than convincing. In summary, his Lordship's conclusion was that the effect of Hughes was that a promise to accept a smaller sum in discharge of a larger sum, if acted upon, is binding notwithstanding the absence of consideration. This, he said, was a result of the fusion of law and equity; he summarily dealt with *Foakes* v *Beer* by saying that in that case the point had not been considered.

Foakes was not the only authority in Denning J's path. He was also faced with a further decision of the House of Lords in *Jorden* v *Money* (1854) 5 HL Cas 185, where the defendant told the plaintiff on a number of occasions that she did not intend to enforce a debt owed by him to her under a bond and warrant. The plaintiff sought to give effect to these assurances by bringing an action to have the bond released and the debt cancelled. Their Lordships held, insofar as it is possible to extract a ratio decidendi (and the accepted ratio), that only a representation of existing or past fact could give rise to an estoppel, not a mere representation as to intention.

Denning J dealt with this difficulty equally shortly: he said that in *Jorden*, 'the promisor made it clear she did not intend to be legally bound', whereas in *High Trees*, 'the proper inference was that the promisor did intend to be bound'. Nevertheless, his Lordship paid some respect to the decision by declining to call his equitable principle an estoppel, saying only that it was analogous to estoppel. In subsequent cases, his Lordship has not been so reticent.

Denning J's reasoning analysed

Hughes. Denning J undoubtedly rescued *Hughes* from the obscurity into which it had fallen after the *Birmingham Land* case. Since *High Trees*, it has commonly been cited and relied on (and not just by Lord Denning himself), so it is certainly now accepted as being authority for some principle of equitable relief. It is, however, unlikely that their Lordships appreciated that their speeches would have such profound repercussions, and in all probability considered they were dealing with a straightforward landlord and tenant matter; *Pinnel's Case* and *Jorden* v *Money* were never mentioned.

Foakes v *Beer*. In saying the *Hughes* point was never considered in *Foakes*, Denning J goes halfway to reconciling *High Trees* with *Foakes*. Estoppel was not pleaded in *Foakes* and was, therefore, never discussed (nor of course was it, in terms, in *Hughes*); arguably, if the defendant had taken the point he might have succeeded (and thereby rendered the present discussion superfluous). On the other hand, *Foakes* was only seven years after *Hughes*, and two members of the House of Lords sat in both cases. Perhaps they were in ignorance of the revolution they had initiated?

A possibly crucial factual distinction that is often overlooked is that in *High Trees*, the promise related to future payments (before the rent was due); in *Foakes*, the debt had already accrued. In the former case, the parties' future conduct would thereby be influenced, but can this reasoning apply to a presently outstanding debt? It may be that *High Trees* was correctly decided and that, at the same time, *Pinnel's Case* and *Foakes* remain good law.

Jorden v *Money*. *Jorden* was decided according to equitable principles and cannot be treated as laying down an inconsistent common law rule. Nor is it sufficient for Denning J simply to say that the promisor did not intend to be legally bound. With respect, his Lordship thereby put the cart before the horse. The reason the promisor was not legally bound was *because* the House of Lords held she could not be so bound by a mere representation of intention.

Jorden is a curious case. Lord Cranworth LC said:

> '... I think that the doctrine does not apply to a case where the representation is not a representation of fact but a statement of something which the party intends or does not intend to do. In the former case it is a contract, in the latter it is not'.

In effect his Lordship said that to enforce a representation of intention there must be a contract, and thereby failed properly to draw the distinction between an action upon a representation and an action upon a contract.

Two solutions have been suggested. First, that the criticism levelled at *High Trees* is aimed at the wrong target. *Jorden* may be the case incorrectly decided; the authorities relied on therein do not, it is said, support the limitation on estoppel imposed by that decision. Secondly, less drastically, *Jorden* might be said to lay down the general rule to which *Hughes* and *High Trees* are exceptions; namely, that where there is an existing contractual relationship between the parties, and one makes to the other a promise to vary, suspend or abandon his strict legal rights, he may be prevented from going back on that promise.

Post High Trees

High Trees, it appears, is here to stay, at least for the time being. It has been considered in a considerable number of recent cases, which are conveniently discussed under a number of headings defining and illustrating its principles and application.

The nature of the promise

The promise must be clear and unequivocal. See *Woodhouse Israel Cocoa Ltd* v *Nigerian Produce Marketing Co Ltd* [1972] AC 741 (HL) and *The Scaptrade* [1983] 2 All ER 763 (CA). Further, as Denning J emphasised in *High Trees*, the promise must be intended to affect legal relations and not be simply a gratuitous indulgence.

Contractual relationships and beyond

Can promissory estoppel arise where the parties are not bound by a contractual relationship? In *Hughes* and the *Birmingham Land* case, the parties were contractually bound, as they were in *High Trees*, although Denning J did not specify this as being a necessary precondition. In *Ajayi* v *Briscoe* [1964] 1 WLR 1326, Lord Hodson, giving the opinion of the Privy Council, said that: 'the principle applied when one party to a contract in the absence of fresh consideration agrees not to enforce his right'. In *Hughes*, Lord Cairns expressly referred to his remarks to 'contractual rights'. Further, all the cases relied on by Denning J in *High Trees* were cases of contract. In *Combe* v *Combe* [1951] 2 KB 215, Birkett LJ was prepared to consider that it might apply to a maintenance agreement between a divorced husband and wife, which fell short of being a contract proper but which clearly resembled one. Similarly, in *Durham Fancy Goods Ltd* v *Michael Jackson (Fancy Goods) Ltd* [1968] 2 QB 839, Donaldson J said that an existing contractual relationship was not necessary providing there was 'a pre-existing legal relationship which could, in certain circumstances, give rise to liabilities and penalties'.

Lord Denning endeavoured to go further still in *Evenden* v *Guildford City AFC Ltd* [1975] QB 917, and held that where an employee was promised by his new employer that he would be credited with his years of service for his old employer, which for the purposes of a redundancy payment would greatly increase the lump sum, and on the faith of the promise did not sue his old employer for a redundancy payment, the new employer was estopped from going back on his promise. His Lordship said:

> '(Promissory estoppel) applies whenever a representation is made, whether of fact or law, present or future, which is intended to be binding, intended to induce a person to act on it, and he does act on it.'

and he disclaimed any necessity for a contractual relationship, going considerably further than Birkett LJ and Donaldson J, who thought a legal relationship analogous to contract was required, to say that none at all was necessary.

Evenden has been overruled on its facts by the House of Lords in *Secretary of State for Employment* v *Globe Elastic Thread* [1979] 2 All ER 1077 where, on similar facts, their Lordships said promissory estoppel did not apply because, quite simply, there *was* a contract with the employee that he would retain the benefit of his previous years' service. Lord Denning's view was not commented on, but it is submitted that the assertion that there need be no existing legal relationship between the parties for promissory estoppel to apply is not supported by authority, and has serious and unexamined implications for the doctrine of consideration as a whole.

In a later case, *Crabb* v *Arun DC* [1976] Ch 179, Lord Denning was prepared to say that promissory estoppel could operate to prevent a person insisting on his strict legal rights 'whether arising under a contract, or on his title deeds, or by statute'. With respect to his Lordship, far from applying the judgment of Lord Cairns in *Hughes*, it extends it far beyond its original context – Lord Cairns was careful to confine his speech to instances where 'parties ... have entered into distinct terms involving certain legal results – certain penalties or legal forfeiture'. In *Brikom Investments Ltd* v *Carr* [1979] 2 All ER 753, Roskill and Cumming-Bruce LJJ expressed their dissent from Lord Denning's view in *Crabb* v *Arun DC*.

A shield not a sword

Here again the question seems to be, if promissory estoppel can create a cause of action on a bare promise, whither the doctrine of consideration? The answer is that the *doctrine operates as 'a shield not a sword'* (*Combe* v *Combe*), that it is defensive in nature, not offensive. As Denning J said in *High Trees*, the doctrine does not create an action for breach of promise, but it will prevent the promissor acting inconsistently with his promise.

In *Combe* v *Combe*, his Lordship expressed concern that the doctrine might be stretched too far and explicitly stated that it did *'not create new causes of action where none existed before'*. (His Lordship's judgment merits close reading in the light of his own remarks in later cases.) Asquith LJ agreed and said that the effect of the doctrine was that 'the promisor cannot bring an action against the promisee which involves the repudiation of his promise or which is inconsistent with it'.

This does not mean that a promisee can never be a plaintiff: if in a contract for the sale of goods a buyer promises not to insist on delivery by the date specified in the contract, and then subsequently refuses to accept the later delivery, it is surmised that the seller could sue for the price and that the buyer would, by his promise, be estopped from asserting that delivery was late.

In *Robertson* v *Minister of Pensions* [1949] 1 KB 227, the defendants refused to pay the plaintiff a disability pension, and the plaintiff sued. Denning J held that by reason of an earlier letter from the defendants to the plaintiff assuring him that his disability had been caused by war service, they were estopped from subsequently asserting the contrary.

As Asquith LJ said in *Combe* v *Combe*, the action was brought not on the promise, but on an independent statutory right which the defendants were estopped from denying.

The orthodox view that promissory estoppel is by definition a defensive doctrine only has recently been subject to attack. In *Re Wyvern Developments Ltd* [1974] 1 WLR 1097, Templeman J, without much explanation, appeared to think that this was no longer the case and that it could create rights; Lord Denning's judgment in *Evenden* also adopted this approach. The old view was, however, restated by Croom-Johnson J in *Argy Trading Development Co Ltd* v *Lapid Developments Ltd* [1977] 1 WLR 444.

It is true that proprietary estoppel (another form of equitable estoppel) *can* create rights, but this of itself does not seem sufficient to confer a similar quality on promissory estoppel. Its whole history and basis heretofore has been that it deals with promises in a pre-existing contractual framework. To extend it beyond this is to render actionable bare promises unsupported by consideration. What effect will this have on the doctrine of consideration which, according to Denning LJ in *Combe* v *Combe* 'is too firmly fixed to be overthrown by a sidewind'?

An equitable doctrine

Being an equitable doctrine, the promisee can only rely on promissory estoppel if he has himself acted equitably. In the words of the old maxim, 'He who comes to equity must come with clean hands.'

In *D & C Builders Ltd* v *Rees* [1966] 2 QB 617, the defendant owed the plaintiffs £482 for building work done. After failing to pay for several months, the defendant offered £300 or, in effect, nothing. The plaintiffs, as the defendant well knew, were in dire financial straits and were compelled to accept. They subsequently sued for the balance. Lord Denning held that the defendant had held the plaintiffs to ransom by taking advantage of their financial predicament, that there was no true accord between the parties and that accordingly the defendant could not rely on *High Trees* in his defence; it would not be inequitable for the plaintiffs to go back on their promise to accept £300 because it had been extracted by threats.

Acting on the promise

For the promisee to invoke the doctrine of promissory estoppel, he must in some way have acted on the promise, or altered his position in reliance on it. This much emerges with reasonable clarity from *High Trees, Ajayi* v *Briscoe* (Privy Council) and *Tool Metal Manufacturing Co Ltd* v *Tungsten Electric Co Ltd* [1955] 1 WLR 761 HL, although in the last two cases the doctrine was only considered en passant. The difficulty lies in the next step in the reasoning. The whole concept of estoppel is based on the principle that it would be inequitable to let the promisor resile on his promise, because the promisee will suffer prejudice or loss as a result, that is, on the faith of the promise he has altered his position to *his detriment*. Is detriment necessary for promissory estoppel?

Prima facie in *High Trees* there was none. Where is the detriment in paying half, when one is liable for the whole? It has been suggested that the defendants did act to their detriment by choosing to remain as tenants of the block on the faith of the plaintiffs' promise.

Whether or not this is so is unclear from the facts as reported and, in any event, appears unlikely in view of the (curious and often unnoticed) fact that the defendant company was a subsidiary of the plaintiffs. Such an exercise is reminiscent of the Court's occasional despairing efforts to find consideration where really none exists (for example, the majority in *Ward* v *Byham* [1956] 1 WLR 496). Lord Denning himself has admitted, extrajudicially, that there was no detriment in *High Trees* and in *W J Alan & Co* v *El Nasr Export and Import Co* [1972] 2 QB 189, has disclaimed detriment as a necessary condition for promissory estoppel.

The point is one of some difficulty. In *Tool Metal* and *Ajayi* v *Briscoe*, the House of Lords and Privy Council respectively simply referred to the promisee 'altering his position' with no mention of the necessity of detriment. It may be that they regarded the point as self-evident and sufficiently embraced within the idea of the promisee 'altering his position'; certainly, it would seem unusual that an equity could be raised by a man who had altered his position to his advantage. The resultant ambiguity of the decisions is that Lord Denning has been able to cite them as supporting his 'no detriment' approach in *Alan* v *El Nasr*.

It is instructive to refer back to the original source of promissory estoppel, *Hughes*. Clearly, the tenants did act to their detriment by failing to repair within the prescribed time, and thereby rendering themselves liable to forfeiture. To this extent, *High Trees* is not on all fours with *Hughes*. The point might be dealt with by saying that the general test is whether, in all the circumstances, it would be inequitable to permit the promisor to go back on his promise. Detriment would clearly be important in determining this, but that it is only a factor (albeit a weighty one) to be considered. To permit the promisor to resile might be, in all the circumstances, inequitable even in the absence of detriment; on the other hand, detriment would not necessarily of itself, without more, satisfy the inequitable test. ·

In *Société Italo-Belge* v *Palm Oils (The Post Chaser)* [1982] 1 All ER 19, Robert Goff J also expressed the view that it is not necessary to show detriment. His Lordship stated, further, that:

> '... indeed, the representee may have benefited from the representation, and yet it may be inequitable, at least without reasonable notice, for the representor to enforce his legal rights'.

However, in *Goldsworthy* v *Brickell* [1987] 1 All ER 853, Nourse LJ did regard detriment as a requirement of promissory estoppel. This point was not fully discussed by the Court of Appeal as it was found, on the facts, that a clear and unequivocal representation had not been established.

The issue is thus open for decision by the House of Lords should the opportunity arise. With respect to Lord Denning, it requires a deeper analysis than saying (as his Lordship has done extrajudicially) that promises ought to be kept and it is inequitable to permit a man to break a promise. The importance of the doctrine of consideration in the English law of contract means that, in the absence of consideration, as a general rule a man is allowed to do just that.

Suspensive or extinctive?

It has yet to be established beyond argument whether promissory estoppel operates only to suspend rights, that is, that the promisor can reassert his strict legal rights upon giving the promisee reasonable notice that he intends so to do, or whether it may operate totally to extinguish the promisor's rights, that is, is permanent in effect.

It will be remembered that in *High Trees* the defendants were under a continuing liability to pay rent annually under the lease. The doctrine operated suspensively only insofar as the landlords could insist on payment of full rent when wartime conditions had ceased and the block was fully let; at the end of the war, the landlord's rights revived. The contrary hardly seemed arguable because the nature of the landlord's promise was such that it was clear they only agreed to accept half rent during the continuance of the war; when it ceased, the promise no longer applied, nor could it have been understood by either party thereafter to apply. In one sense, however, the promise did extinguish certain of the landlord's rights, namely their rights to the full rent from 1940-5. Denning J held that they were forever estopped from claiming the balance. Suppose the promise, unlike that in *High Trees*, is not limited in nature, but is intended and understood to be permanent in effect? Lord Denning, in *D & C Builders* v *Rees* and *Alan* v *El Nasr*, expressed the view that, in these circumstances, the courts would not permit the promisor to revert to this strict legal right and that the estoppel would be final and permanent. It should be noted that *D & C Builders* did not concern periodical payments, but liability for a single lump sum. If promissory estoppel is to apply to such facts, then it can only be permanent in effect, otherwise *Foakes* v *Beer* will continue in full force and the promisor would be free at a future time to claim the balance; to say that the promisor is temporarily estopped from claiming the balance, but may do so upon giving reasonable notice, renders the estoppel virtually worthless from the promisee's point of view. In *Arrale* v *Costain Civil Engineering Ltd* [1976] 1 Lloyd's Rep 98, Lord Denning said that the rule in *Foakes* v *Beer* was no longer valid and had been replaced by equitable principles. The view preferred here is that *Foakes* remains good in law, but the strictness of the rule is mitigated in equity by promissory estoppel providing the necessary conditions are satisfied.

Other judges have been less certain than Lord Denning about this aspect of promissory estoppel. In *Tool Metal*, the House of Lords permitted the promisors to go back on a promise not to insist upon the payment of compensation for the exploitation of a patented manufacturing process (another case of periodical payments), because the promise was referrable to wartime conditions and could be terminated thereafter by giving reasonable notice.

In *Ajayi* v *Briscoe*, the Privy Council said that the promisor could resile from his promise on giving reasonable notice, which need not be formal notice, giving the promisee reasonable opportunity of resuming his position, but that the promise would become final and irrecovable if the promisee could not resume his former position, thus accepting extinctiveness in principle in certain circumstances.

Promissory estoppel was applied to extinguish all rights by a New Zealand judge in *P* v *P* [1957] NZLR 854. McGregor J held that where the Public Trustee, on behalf of a mentally ill wife, erroneously represented to a husband that the latter's liability to pay maintenance under a deed of separation was discharged by a subsequent divorce, the Public Trustee could not thereafter sue the husband under the deed.

Hughes itself is of little help in this respect. Admittedly, Lord Cairns did not limit his enunciated principle as being suspensive only, but on the facts the promisor's rights were only suspended, and as has already been pointed out, it would be wrong to read too much into the minutiae of his Lordship's speech because he was almost certainly unaware that he was in the act of laying down a principle that would be so closely scrutinised and widely applied.

Again, therefore, it must be said that the matter remains open for argument. The view of Lord Denning does command sympathy and respect. If the promise is such that the promisor unequivocally and permanently abandons his rights, how can a court be said to be preventing the promisor from acting inconsistently with his promise (the very basis of the estoppel) if it subsequently permits him to reassume those rights? It is submitted that the preferred approach is to look at the nature of the promise: if, as in *High Trees* and *Tool Metal*, it is intended to be temporary in application and to reserve to the promisor the right subsequently to reassert his legal rights, the effect will be suspensive only; if, on the other hand, it is intended to be permanent, then there is no reason why in principle or on authority the promise should not be given its full effect so as to extinguish the promisor's rights.

Promissory estoppel – fact or fantasy?

It might be thought to be lamentably late in the day to consider the reality or otherwise of promissory estoppel. The reason why only now the basic premise upon which all the above has been based falls for discussion is that it is only when one has fully understood what promissory estoppel purports to be, that one can stand back and judge the validity or otherwise of the thing itself.

It has been contended that promissory estoppel is not a true estoppel, properly so called. In support of this is cited the judgment of Denning J in *High Trees*, where his Lordship said that the cases from which he derived the *High Trees* principle were 'not really' cases of estoppel. In all probability, his Lordship's guarded language was at least partially motivated by the necessity to give due deference to the decision of the House of Lords in *Jorden* v *Money*, and, further, with all respect to his Lordship, at that stage he had probably not fully thought through the repercussions of his judgment. In later cases, his Lordship has unreservedly adopted the expression 'promissory estoppel'.

Those who argue against the estoppel view have sought to show the close connection between the doctrine and the common law doctrine of waiver or forebearance (see, for example, Treitel). Waiver was developed at common law to mitigate strictness of the rules as to variation, namely, that the terms of an existing contract could only be varied providing both parties furnished consideration and providing any necessary formalities were complied with. Where for the convenience of, and at the request of one party, the other forbears to insist on the precise mode or time of performance specified in the contract, the contract remains unchanged in the sense that there are no variations of its terms, but the party acceding to the request will be said to have waived his right to insist on strict compliance with one or more of them. The promissory estoppel cases, so it is said, are the counterpart in equity, and are better described as being cases of equitable forbearance.

There has so far been no attempt to explain the relationship between waiver and promissory estoppel, there is, indeed, an unfortunate tendency to speak of the two as if there is little or no difference: see *Combe* v *Combe* and, in particular, *Alan* v *El Nasr*. It may be that the answer lies in turning the microscope, not on the promissory estoppel cases, but on the waiver cases. These have always occupied a somewhat anomalous position in the law of contract, and no real attempt to explain them has ever been made (there can be no invocation of equity because the principles were developed by the common law courts before fusion in 1873). In *Charles Rickards Ltd* v *Oppenheim* [1950] 1 KB 616 (a waiver case), Denning LJ described waiver as being 'a kind of estoppel'. This may be the happiest explanation, and if waiver is, at common law, 'a kind of estoppel', then promissory estoppel may legitimately be said to be its specialised counterpart in equity, flowing from *Hughes* v *Metropolitan Rly Co*.

Although the relationship may be close, there are a number of important distinctions:

1. Promissory estoppel may extend beyond mere contractual relationships (see 'Contractual relationships and beyond' above).
2. In the opinion of certain judges, promissory estoppel may create new rights (see 'A shield not a sword' above); waiver can never do this.
3. Promissory estoppel is subject to special equitable principles (see 'An equitable doctrine' above).
4. Promissory estoppel requires the promisee to alter his position (arguably to his detriment) in reliance on the promise (see 'Acting on the promise' above); waiver makes no such demand.
5. Promissory estoppel may be permanent in nature (see 'Suspensive or extinctive?' above); waiver customarily permits the promisor to revert to his strict legal rights upon giving reasonable notice (*Rickards* v *Oppenheim*), though in *Alan* v *El Nasr* Megaw and Stephenson LJJ dealt with the case as being one of 'irrevocable waiver'.

Further complications

The sharp contrast between the views of Lord Denning MR and the more orthodox approach is manifest in the judgments of the Court of Appeal in *Brikom Investments Ltd* v *Carr* [1979] 2 All ER 753. The plaintiff landlords offered 99-year leases to their sitting tenants in four blocks of flats. At that time, the roofs of the blocks were in need of repair. The leases made the tenants liable to pay a contribution towards the repair costs, but the plaintiffs orally represented that they would carry out the repairs at their own expense. After the repairs were completed, the plaintiffs served contribution notices on (1) the first defendant, who was an original lessee and who admitted she would have taken the lease, even if the plaintiffs had not promised to pay for the repairs themselves; (2) the second defendant, who took the assignment of a lease with knowledge of the plaintiffs' representation; and (3) the third defendant, an assignee of an assignee without notice of the representation. The defendants relied in their defence, inter alia, on promissory estoppel.

Lord Denning held the *High Trees* principle in all three cases. As regards the first defendant, his Lordship was not impressed by the fact that she would have taken the lease irrespective of representations, dismissing this as hypothetical and held that she had acted on the promise.

As regards the second and third defendants, he held, simply, that the benefit and the burden ran with the lease to later assignees and assignors, apparently irrespective of whether or not they had notice.

Roskill and Cumming-Bruce LJJ, whilst arriving at the same result as Lord Denning, were careful to distance themselves from his Lordship's reasoning. Roskill LJ said:

> ' ... it would be wrong to extend the doctrine of promissory estoppel, whatever its precise limits at the present day, to the extent of abolishing in this back-handed way the doctrine of consideration'.

His Lordship disagreed with Lord Denning's idea of the estoppel running with the lease, and decided the case partly on the grounds of there being a collateral contract (the benefit of which had been assigned to the second and third defendants). Alternatively, his Lordship said: 'there was a plain waiver by the landlords of their right to claim the cost of these repairs from these tenants' and that this waiver subsisted notwithstanding subsequent assignments and sub-assignments, 'the relevant obligation ... had before the assignment been waived by the landlords'. His Lordship cited *Hughes* v *Metropolitan Rly Co* as supporting the ground of waiver, not promissory estoppel, and said of that case:

> 'For my own part, I would respectfully prefer to regard that as an illustration of contractual variation of strict contractual rights. But it could equally well be put as an illustration of equity relieving from the consequences of strict adherence to the letter of the lease.'

Cumming-Bruce LJ, in a brief judgment, agreed with Roskill LJ.

Regrettably the reasoning in all the judgments is profoundly unsatisfactory.

Lord Denning's judgment may be criticised on three grounds. First, his Lordship held that pre-contractual representations can give rise to an estoppel, whereas existing authority requires a contractual or analogous relationship (see 'Contractual relationships and beyond' above). Secondly, his Lordship appears to dismiss the requirement that the promisee must rely on the promise (see 'Acting on the promise' above), and seems to assert his old view that the unfairness of the promisor going back on his promise is sufficient, irrespective of any prejudice to the promisee. Thirdly, as a matter of property law, his idea of the estoppel running with the lease is unsound. His Lordship regards notice of the estoppel as irrelevant, yet it is a long established rule of property law that a bona fide purchaser for value of a legal estate takes free of equities.

Roskill LJ's judgment too leaves much to be desired. Whilst it is understandable that he refers to promissory estoppel as a 'somewhat uncertain doctrine', and wholly laudable that he is anxious to preserve the doctrine of consideration from underhand attacks, other parts of his judgment commend themselves far less. His Lordship fails to explain why he both rejects promissory estoppel and then applies *Hughes* v *Metropolitan Railway Co*. If, as appears to be the case, his Lordship adheres to the 'equitable waiver' rather than 'promissory estoppel' classification, then he fails to explain what the difference is between the two.

His Lordship regards *Hughes* as being an example of waiver 'as a matter of contract law or equity (call it what you will)', but for the reasons given in (1)–(5) above, it would be wholly wrong to regard the two as being the same; *Hughes* can be authority for one or the other, but not both. Nor can his Lordship be correct in referring to *Hughes* 'as an illustration of contractual variation of strict contractual rights'.

A contractual variation requires consideration and (in appropriate cases) due formality; neither are present in *Hughes*, which cannot, it is submitted, be regarded as a case of 'contractual variation' if his Lordship uses that term in its accepted sense. Unfortunately, therefore, *Brikom* v *Carr* served only to muddy even further already murky waters.

It remains to consider what has been termed 'estoppel by convention'. This may arise where the parties to a transaction act on an assumed state of facts. The effect of estoppel by convention is to preclude the parties from denying those facts. The difference between promissory estoppel and estoppel by convention is that the latter can arise without any representation having been made. If one party makes a mistaken assumption, which is not the result of a representation made by the other party, but is shared by that other party, this may be sufficient for an estoppel by convention to be created.

Thus in *Amalgamated Investment and Property Co* v *Texas Commerce International Bank* [1981] 3 All ER 577, the plaintiff requested the defendant to make advances of money to the plaintiff's subsidiary company, and gave a guarantee to the defendant in respect of those advances. The guarantee was for the repayment of any money advanced *by the defendant*. In order to circumvent the relevant currency restrictions, the defendant advanced money to one of its subsidiaries which, in turn, advanced money to the plaintiff's subsidiary. No money was directly paid by the defendant. On a literal reading, the guarantee did not, therefore, apply to the advances that were made. The plaintiff sought a declaration that it was under no liability to the bank under the guarantee. The Court of Appeal held, however, that the parties had acted on an assumed state of affairs that the guarantee would cover the loans that were actually made. That gave rise to an estoppel by convention, which estopped each party as against the other from questioning the truth of the facts which they assumed to be true.

In a subsequent case, *Keen* v *Holland* [1984] 1 All ER 75, the Court of Appeal was concerned to establish the limitations of estoppel by convention. In the *Amalgamated Investment* case, the parties had established a conventional basis on which they regulated their subsequent dealings. This was not authority for the proposition urged on the court in *Keen* v *Holland* that the mere fact that where the parties had a common view about the legal effect of contract, and that one of them would not to the other's knowledge have entered into it if he had appreciated its true legal effect, they are, without more, estopped from asserting its true legal effect. So broad a proposition could not be deduced from the actual decision in *Amalgamated Investment*, and could not be right.

Concluding thoughts

Promissory estoppel is ripe for examination in the House of Lords. The cases in the Lords in which the doctrine has been discussed have all, ultimately, turned on other issues, and their Lordships' remarks in that House had indicated that their Lordships feel that the time is ready for a pronouncement by the highest court in the land.

'I desire to add that the time may soon come when the whole sequence of cases based on promissory estoppel since the war, beginning with *Central London Property Trust Ltd* v *High Trees Houses Ltd* may need to be reviewed and reduced to a coherent body of doctrine by the courts. I do not mean to say that any are to be regarded with suspicion. But, as is common with an expanding doctrine, they do raise problems of coherent exposition which have never been systematically explored. However, this may be, we are not in a position to carry out this exploration here and in the present proceedings.'

Per Lord Hailsham LC in *Woodhouse* v *Nigerian Produce Marketing*:

'I am unable in any event to agree that any question of estoppel arises. There was a contract with the employee that he would retain the benefit of his previous employment. To convert this into an estoppel is to turn the doctrine of promissory estoppel (the validity or scope of which I do not now examine) upside down.'

Per Lord Wilberforce in *Secretary of State for Employment* v *Globe Elastic Thread Co Ltd*, overruling *Evenden* v *Guildford City AFC Ltd*:

'Pending such consideration, the validity, scope and necessary conditions for the application of promissory estoppel remain uncertain.'

4

Intention to Form Legal Relationships

4.1 Aims of the law of contract

4.2 Formation of the contract

4.3 Intention to create legal relations

4.1 Aims of the law of contract

As we have already noted in the Introduction, the common theme underlying all attempts to define the term 'contract' is that there must be agreement. To the extent that, having made such an agreement, the parties must be encouraged to honour their obligations, means that certain rules have been formulated which dictate the degree to which the courts will intervene to enforce an agreement. However, while it may seem to be stating the obvious, it must be remembered that initially (at least in theory) parties voluntarily enter into agreements, free of all pressures or outside forces.

The main aims of contract are usually stated as given below.

1. To realise expectations.
2. To guard against (or allocate) certain commercial risks.
3. To ensure smooth running of the commercial system – *Tsakiroglou and Co Ltd* v *Noblee Thorl GmbH* [1962] AC 93.
4. Not to rescue a party from a bad bargain (see *Tsakiroglou* case, above); however some relief may be afforded to a party in cases of duress or undue influence.
5. To be an instrument of social control (see, for example, employment, sale of goods and consumer credit law).

The remedial goals of a plaintiff in a contract action are traditionally said to be one of three possibilities.

1. Fulfillment of expectation interest. This is often said to be the primary goal: the plaintiff seeks to be put into the position he would have been in had the defendant carried out the contract.
2. Protection of the plaintiff's restitution interest. Here the plaintiff seeks just to be put in the position he was in before he entered into the contract, that is, return of any goods delivered or money paid.

3. Protection of the plaintiff's reliance interest. Here the plaintiff is seeking compensation for work carried out, or expenses incurred in reliance upon the contractual agreement. A good example is the case of *Anglia Television Ltd v Reed* [1972] 1 QB 60.

Note: Punishment of the defendant is not a contractual aim (see *Addis* v *Gramophone Co Ltd* [1909] AC 488).

Looking over these aims and goals it becomes clear that, while there must be agreement for a contract to be legally enforceable, enforcement of agreements using the law of contract may achieve certain other underlying purposes as well. (Look, for example, at (3) and (5) of the main aims of contract above.)

4.2 Formation of the contract

General

A plaintiff will not be able to succeed against a defendant, simply because he has suffered loss which has, in some fashion, been induced by the defendant.

He must be able to show that the defendant's conduct has given the plaintiff a course of action in law.

He must be able to show that a contract has been entered into, either with the defendant or his agent or, where a misrepresentation is alleged, with a third party.

If he cannot show that a contract has been entered into, he cannot succeed on an application of the law of contract. He may be able to succeed under the law of torts, or obtain relief in equity, but that does not fall to be discussed in this section.

Elements of contract

Accordingly, it is said that the plaintiff must show four things to exist in order to establish that a contract has been entered into, as listed below.

1. That the parties had an intention to enter into legal relations.
2. That one party made an offer to the other.
3. That the other accepted that offer.
4. That there was an exchange of consideration.

The terms of the agreement must be sufficiently certain, that is, capable of being ascertained, to enable the court to be sure that an agreement has been reached.

Broader questions

It may be argued that the search is less for static ingredients in a 'thing' called a contract than for positive evidence that the plaintiff was justified in relying upon the defendant, and should not, therefore, bear the loss of his disappointed expectation.

The following questions are relevant:

1. Was the plaintiff justified in assuming that there was agreement?
2. Is there any reason to suppose that the parties did not intend their arrangements to have legal results?
3. What is it in the nature of the plaintiff's reliance upon the defendant that would justify the court in interfering on his behalf?
4. If an arrangement was primarily between two or more others, is the plaintiff so closely connected to this arrangement that the court should intervene to give him a remedy?

It is necessary to ask such broad questions because if it is not understood that this seems to be the court's basic approach, the many recent changes that have taken place in this area will be bewildering. These broad issues should be borne in mind when the subject of contractual ingredients is studied through the traditional categories.

Note, in particular, that the courts, in assessing whether or not there has been agreement, apply an objective test. Thus, it is not the function of the courts to ask whether each of the parties believed he had reached agreement; but whether an objective outsider, armed with the same information as the parties possessed at the time of making the contract, would have concluded that they had reached agreement. This objective test is applied in order to achieve the certainty that commercial transactions require. It is a practical approach which has largely displaced the theory prevalent during the nineteenth century that there could be no contract unless there had been a consensus ad idem – a meeting of minds of the contracting parties.

Hence, it is not open to a party to a contract to assert that he did not intend to contract on certain terms, if the evidence shows he accepted an offer containing those terms. Unless, that is, one party can set up one of the four defences of misrepresentation, mistake, duress or undue influence, which may effectively negative apparent agreement.

4.3 Intention to create legal relations

Not every bargain gives rise to a contract. For example, if A says to B, his brother: 'If you drive to the pub, I'll buy the first pint', and B agrees, a reasonable person would not expect that B would be able to sue A when he refuses to buy the first pint. The reason is that the nature of the agreement and the relationship of the parties would lead a reasonable person to believe that there was no contractual intention.

So when will a contractual intention be found? A distinction has to be drawn between agreements which are merely social and/or domestic, and agreements which are commercial in nature.

Social and domestic agreements

The rule where agreements are social or domestic is that there is a *presumption* that the parties do not intend to create legal relations. The leading case is *Balfour* v *Balfour* [1919] 2 KB 571. The defendant, a civil servant based in Sri Lanka, came to England with his wife (the plaintiff) and later returned to Sri Lanka alone, the wife remaining in England for health reasons. The defendant promised to pay the plaintiff £30 per month as maintenance, but failed to keep up the payments. The wife sued.

HELD: the wife could not succeed because:

1. she had provided no consideration for the promise to pay £30; and
2. there was no intention to create legal relations. Where the parties were husband and wife, the onus was on the plaintiff to rebut the presumption that in social and domestic arrangements there was no intention to contract. This she had failed to do.

Note, however, that in *Pettit* v *Pettit* [1970] AC 777, it was observed that though many agreements between husband and wife were not intended to be legally binding, performance of such agreements might well give rise to legal consequences.

Lord Diplock said:

'It would, in my view, be erroneous to extend the presumption accepted in *Balfour* v *Balfour* that mutual promises between man and wife in relation to their domestic arrangements are prima facie not intended by either to be legally enforceable to a presumption that *no* legal consequences should flow from acts done by them in performance of mutual promises with respect to the acquisition, improvement or addition to real or personal property - for this would be to intend what is impossible in law.'

Similarly, in *Jones* v *Padavatton* [1969] 1 WLR 328, Mrs Jones offered a monthly allowance to her daughter if she would go to England and read for the Bar. Her daughter reluctantly gave up her job in America and came to take Bar Finals. She was not very successful. Mrs Jones bought a house in London. She stopped paying the monthly allowance, but she allowed the daughter to live in the house and receive rents from other tenants. Some three years later, Mrs Jones brought an action for possession. The daughter counterclaimed for breach of the agreement to pay the monthly allowance and/or to provide the daughter with accommodation.

HELD: the first agreement may have been made with the intention of creating legal relations, but was only to be deemed to be for a reasonable time; that is sufficient time to enable the daughter to pass her Bar Finals. It had lapsed after five years.

The second agreement was only a family arrangement and there was no intention to create legal relations.

Intention and consideration

In deciding whether there is a contractual intention, it is often difficult to distinguish the intention from the question of whether consideration has been given.

Natural love and affection is not consideration recognised at law. That is why no consideration was provided for the wife in *Balfour* v *Balfour*.

Interests in occupation
The presumption against contractual intention is sometimes rebutted where the occupation of real property is concerned. For example, in *Hardwick* v *Johnson* [1978] 1 WLR 683, a mother promised to buy for her son and daughter-in-law a suitable house in which to live. The arrangement was that she would buy it and they would pay her rent at £7 per week. After one year, the marriage broke down. The mother tried to get possession of the house. The daughter-in-law offered £7 per week.

HELD: It was a licence for occupation. Lord Denning said that it was equitable and Lords Justice Roskill and Browne said that it was contractual. They were clear that the court has to look at the intention of the parties by forming its own opinion as to what would have been the intention of reasonable men as to the effect of the exchange of promises if it had been present on their minds at the time. See also, *Eves* v *Eves* [1975] 1 WLR 1338 and *Tanner* v *Tanner* [1975] 1 WLR 1346. Distinguish *Jones* v *Padavatton*.

Separation agreements
Furthermore, the presumption may be rebutted where an agreement is reached between spouses who are unhappily married, or about to separate, or separated, but any agreement reached must be expressed in clear, unambiguous terms. In *Meritt* v *Meritt* [1970] 1 WLR 1211, the husband, separated from his wife, agreed in writing to transfer the matrimonial home out of their joint names into her name alone, provided she paid off the remaining mortgage debt.

HELD: the husband's promise was legally enforceable after his wife paid off the mortgage. Contrast *Gould* v *Gould* [1970] 1 QB 275.

Intention inferred from 'mutuality'
An illustrative case is *Simpkins* v *Pays* [1955] 1 WLR 975. The defendant, her granddaughter, and the plaintiff, a paying lodger, all entered weekly for a newspaper fashion competition in the defendant's name. There was no regular rule concerning the way in which payments were shared. One week a prize of £750 was won; on the defendant's refusal to share the prize, the plaintiff sued for a third.

HELD: that it was a joint enterprise to which cash was contributed in the expectation of sharing any prize. The court was unable to identify any offer, or acceptance, but said that there was a 'mutuality' about the arrangements.

Commercial agreements

Where the agreement is a commercial one, there is a presumption that the parties intended to enter into legal relations. This means that the plaintiff does not have to prove intention in order to succeed; the court will presume its existence. The presumption can, however, be rebutted if a contrary intention is expressed. In *Rose & Frank Co* v *J R Crompton Bros* [1925] AC 445, a commercial agreement stated:

> 'This agreement is not entered into ... as a formal or legal agreement, and shall not be subject to legal jurisdiction in the law courts.'

HELD: that no legally enforceable contract existed. The appellant company could not recover compensation for the respondent company's refusal to honour its obligation.

Similarly, in *Jones* v *Vernons Pools* [1938] 2 All ER 626, the plaintiff sued on a football coupon which was said to be binding in honour only.

HELD: the plaintiff could not recover.

Again in *Orion Insurance Co* v *Sphere Drake Insurance* [1992] 1 Lloyd's Rep 239 the plaintiffs claimed that the agreement between themselves and the defendants was a goodwill agreement only. The Court of Appeal conceded that from the overall impression (notes, memos, etc) there was no contractually binding agreement.

New England Reinsurance Corporation & First State Insurance Co v *Messoghios Insurance Co SA* [1992] 2 Lloyd's Rep 251, where the sole dealings between the parties consisted of a series of telexes, made it clear that even if the parties refer to a contract between them it may only be an informal agreement binding in honour only. The burden of proof that the agreement relied upon is contractually binding is on the plaintiff seeking to rely on it.

Most recently of all, the case of *G Percy Trentham Ltd* v *Archital Luxfer Ltd* [1993] 1 Lloyd's Rep 25, referred to the problem. Trentham were the main contractors on a scheme to build an industrial estate. They 'subcontracted' with the defendants to build doors, windows, shutters, etc. The dispute then arose as to defects in the completed work, and the defendants denied that a contract had even been formed. The Court of Appeal held that even though there were no written documents it was clear from the parties' conduct that contracts existed. The exchanges between them (memos, phone calls, meetings) made it clear that all supported the existence of a binding series of sub–contracts. The defendants could not disprove the contracts' existence.

Rebutting the burden of proof

The question of whether the burden of proof has been rebutted is, however, one of fact. In *Edwards* v *Skyways Ltd* [1964] 1 WLR 349, an airline pilot was offered a 'golden handshake', that is, a payment expressed to be ex gratia by his employers. They failed to pay. The pilot sued. The employers said that the offer of the ex gratia payment was not intended to be contractually binding.

HELD: that the burden of proof in a commercial agreement is on the person asserting that no legal effect was intended. The onus was said to be a heavy one and the employers had failed to discharge it.

A similar conclusion was reached in *Esso Petroleum* v *Commissioners for Customs and Excise* [1976] 1 WLR 1. Esso supplied garages with 'World Cup' coins. One coin was given away to motorists with every gallon of petrol. The issue, so far as the Customs and Excise were concerned, was whether there had been a contract of sale.

HELD (by 4:1): that there had been no *sale*. However, three members of the House of Lords thought that there was a contract with regard to the coins – a contract for *supply* – on the basis that Esso had not discharged the burden of proving an absence of contractual intent.

In *Evans* v *Merzario Ltd* [1976] 1 WLR 1078, a representative of a firm of forwarding agents, with whom the customer had dealt for a long time, said that goods would henceforth be packed into containers and carried below deck. At the time that the statement was made, no specific contract of carriage was designated.

HELD: that the promise was intended to be legally binding. The Court of Appeal relied on the importance of the place of carriage to the customer, and the fact that the customer would not have agreed to container carriage had that promise not been made.

In *Kleinwort Benson Ltd* v *Malaysia Mining Corp Bhd* [1989] 1 All ER 785, the plaintiff bank agreed with the defendants to make a loan facility to the defendant's wholly owned subsidiary. As part of the facility arrangement, the defendants furnished to the plaintiffs two 'letters of comfort', each of which stated that 'it is our policy to ensure that the business of (the subsidiary) is at all times in a position to meet its liabilities to you under the (loan facility) arrangements'.

The Court of Appeal held that, on the facts, the letters of comfort were statements of present fact, and not contractual promises as to future conduct. They were not intended to create legal relations, and gave rise to no more than a moral responsibility on the part of the defendants to meet the subsidiary's debt.

Walford v *Miles* [1992] 2 WLR 174, has in its progression through the courts, demonstrated that it is more closely concerned with the question of certainty (see Chapter 5). In this case the plaintiffs entered into negotiations with the defendants over the sale of the defendants' business, and reached the point of the plaintiffs agreeing to obtain a 'comfort letter' from the bank and not to withdraw from the negotiations. The defendants, in return, undertook to break off negotiations with a third party and deal only with the plaintiffs. In fact the defendants not only did not cease negotiations with the rival bidder, they eventually sold the business to that rival. The question arose as to whether this oral agreement was binding.

The House of Lords decided that although the law had, for more than 20 years, directed that an agreement to agree or an agreement to negotiate was not an enforceable contract, there was no reason why in English law, A should not perfectly validly negotiate an enforceable contract with B, that for consideration B would agree not to negotiate with anyone other than A for a fixed period of time.

Unfortunately, however, in *Walford* v *Miles* the agreement was deficient in one respect: it did not specify for how long this arrangement was to continue. This deficiency could not be cured by the court's implying, for example, a requirement that the arrangement should continue for a 'reasonable time' or some similar arrangement. For that reason the arrangement must fail for lack of certainty.

5

Certainty and Form of the Contract

5.1 Certainty

5.2 Form of the contract

5.3 Exceptions to the general rule

5.4 Contracts for the sale of land

5.5 Contracts of guarantee

5.6 Specific contracts required by statute to be in writing

5.1 Certainty

We have examined previously the mechanics of agreement, the process of analysing a transaction or negotiations in order to determine an offer and an acceptance. Even where an offer and acceptance have been established, it may not be clear precisely on what terms the parties have reached agreement. Whilst it is not the function of the courts to make an agreement for the parties, they will not defeat the intention of the parties to contract merely because the agreement has been loosely worded. Gaps in the contract may often be filled by reference to the custom of the trade, or the course of dealings between the parties. If, however, no such reference can be made, or it cannot be objectively determined what the parties intended, then the courts may be forced to conclude that the lack of certainty militates against contractual validity.

Statute

In the absence of express provision in an agreement, statute may be able to provide the missing terms.

Section 8 Sale of Goods Act 1979

(1) The price in a contract of sale may be fixed by the contract, or may be left to be fixed in a manner agreed by the contract, or may be determined by the course of dealing between the parties.
(2) Where the price is not determined as mentioned in subsection (1) above, the buyer must pay a reasonable price.

(3) What is a reasonable price is a question of fact dependent on the circumstances of each particular case.

Section 15(1) Supply of Goods and Services Act 1982

Where, under a contract for the supply of a service, the consideration for the service is not determined by the contract, left to be determined in a manner agreed by the contract, or determined by the course of dealing between the parties, there is an implied term that the party contracting with the supplier will pay a reasonable charge.

Vagueness

If an agreement is too vague to permit a meaning to be given to it, no enforceable contract can be construed. However, courts may be able to find a meaning to an apparently vague term by reference to custom, or to what is reasonable. Further, it may be possible to ignore certain meaningless words and still leave a valid contract. The approach of the courts is indicated by consideration of the following cases:

In *Scammel & Nephew v Ouston* [1941] AC 251, the order stated that it was given 'on the understanding that the balance of the purchase price can be had on hire-purchase terms ...' The House of Lords held that the phrase was so vague that it could not be given a definite meaning. There were no usual terms in such a contract to which reference could be made.

In *Hillas & Co v Arcos* (1932) 147 LT 503, a seemingly vague phrase was able to be interpreted. The agreement of sale was for timber 'of fair specification'. The parties were persons fully acquainted with the particular trade and, in the light of that, the House of Lords was able to affix a meaning to the phrase.

Nicolene v Simmonds [1953] 1 QB 543 illustrates that it may be possible to ignore certain words. A clause of the agreement stated that the sale was subject to 'the usual conditions of acceptance'. There were, in fact, no such usual conditions. The phrase was meaningless and the deletion of the phrase would not impair the validity of the contract.

The Scottish case, *Neilson v Stewart* 1991 SLT 523 HL, started as of general interest only, being concerned with Scots law. As now decided by the House of Lords, it would, no doubt, be similarly applicable to English cases. In the case, a sale of shares was agreed between seller and purchaser. The agreement included a loan repayment which was to be deferred for one year 'after which time repayment shall be negotiated to our mutual satisfaction'. The purchaser failed to complete the agreement and subsequently argued that the phrase in question rendered the whole agreement unenforceable by reason of uncertainty. The seller's argument was that there were two severable agreements, one for the sale of shares, which was enforceable, and one for the arrangements of the loan, which was not enforceable.

The House of Lords held that in fact both parts of the agreement were enforceable. The parties did not apparently intend the loan to be fixed as to time and manner of payment, all loans were repayable on demand and it was not essential that interest should be payable. Any apparent ambiguities could thus be resolved. The seller's action for damages for breach of contract by the buyer was successful.

The courts are concerned to ascertain whether or not the parties have actually reached agreement. In interpreting the language of the 'agreement', especially where there is a mixture of formal documents, verbal exchanges and later changes made to the basic document (as in the following case), problems may occur as to the construction of language used by the parties. See *Punjab National Bank* v *De Boinville* [1992] 1 WLR 1138 in which the plaintiff bank agreed to finance loans to a company (E Ltd) to purchase oil. One of the terms was that insurance cover be arranged to provide for any loss by the bank. Insurance was placed with various underwriters, most of the work being entrusted to two individual brokers. In all some five different policies were drawn up and assigned by customer to the bank by way of security. Once the first and second policies came into being, the remaining policies were based on simply deleting odd words and phrases and amending them. Thus references to 'assured' became 'a/c E Ltd' and 'net loss' became 'sum assured'. The question arose as to whether, in construing these later policies, regard could be had to the words which had been deleted, to give sense to the words substituted. It was held that since the later policies' construction was dependant on the earliest one, it was permissible to have regard to all aspects of the original policy, including deletions.

It should be noted also that a conditional acceptance is not true acceptance. This should, however, be distinguished from a contract which is conditional, which is quite different. In *Graham* v *Pitkin* (below) the question arose as to whether the condition in question was a condition precedent or not. Conditions of the sort found in this case are common in conveyancing cases, but not in other types of contract. *Graham* v *Pitkin* [1992] 1 WLR 403 concerned a sale of land in which the plaintiff purchasers stipulated a condition that a mortgage be arranged before the contract was considered binding. After considerable difficulty in arranging a mortgage the purchaser decided to pay cash. It was held that the contract was not uncertain or incomplete because of this condition. It was purely for the benefit of the purchaser who might waive the condition if she wished.

Incompleteness

If there is an essential term yet to be agreed, and there is no express or implied provision for its solution, there is no binding contract.

British Bank for Foreign Trade v *Novinex* [1949] 1 KB 623. Thus in *May and Butcher* v *R* [1934] 2 KB 17, the agreement provided that the price(s) to be paid and the date(s) of payment should 'be agreed upon from time to time' by the parties. The House of Lords held that there never was a concluded contract between the parties. As Treitel observed (6th edn p44), had the agreement been silent on these points, it may have been possible to resolve the matter by reference to the Sale of Goods Act (see 'Section 8' above).

There was an arbitration clause in the agreement, but this did not assist in resolution as this clause pre-supposed the existence of a binding contract.

A contrast with the above case is provided by *Foley* v *Classique Coaches* [1934] 2 KB 1, in which there were two related agreements put into separate documents. The one agreement concerned the sale of petrol; the latter agreement stated that the petrol was to be supplied 'at a price to be agreed by the parties in writing and from time to time'. The Court of Appeal was able to distinguish this case from that of *May and Butcher*. Here the agreement for the sale of petrol was acted on for three years; it formed part of a bargain involving the sale of land which had been conveyed; and it contained an arbitration clause, which was construed as applying to any failure to agree as to the price.

It would seem that a distinction must be drawn between an arrangement which is wholly executory on both sides, and one in which one party has performed all the obligations required of him by the agreement. An arrangement providing for 'a price to be agreed' may not constitute a binding contract whilst the matter is still executory, but if one party has completed the obligations required of him, it will be implied from the conduct of the parties that, in the absence of agreement, a reasonable price is to be paid. See *British Bank, etc* v *Novinex* (above).

An agreement will not be void for uncertainty if it provides a means for resolving the matters that are left open. In *Campbell* v *Edwards* [1976] 1 WLR 403 CA, the agreement provided that the price should be fixed by a valuer agreed on by the parties.

Lord Denning MR:

> 'If two parties agree that the price of property should be fixed by a valuer on whom they agree, and he gives that valuation honestly and in good faith they are bound by it. Even if he has made a mistake they are still bound by it.'

(It would of course, Lord Denning went on to say, be different if there were fraud or collusion).

In *Sudbrook Trading Estate* v *Eggleton* [1982] 3 All ER 1 HL, the agreement contained the provision for the purchase of the premises by the tenant 'at such price ... as may be agreed upon by two valuers', one to be nominated by each party. The landlord refused to appoint a valuer. The House of Lords interpreted this provision as an agreement to sell at a fair and reasonable price to be assessed by the two valuers. As the landlord had, in breach of his contractual obligation, made the agreed manner of assessment impossible, it was left open to the court to determine on expert evidence what was the fair and reasonable price.

5.2 Form of the contract

General rule

The general rule at common law is that contracts can be made informally. No writing or other document is necessary. A contract made orally is valid and enforceable, unless the contract falls into one of the exceptions set out below.

There may, however, be practical problems of proof when trying to enforce a verbal contract in the courts.

The exceptions to the general rule are all imposed by statute. The requirements as to form vary. Some contracts must be made by deed, some in writing, and some must be evidenced in writing.

A *deed* is a document containing all the terms of the agreement, which is signed (by both parties), sealed and delivered. Contracts made by deed are also referred to as specialties. The requirement of a seal dates from times when illiteracy was prevalent. A seal was used in place of a signature. The requirement of a signature to a deed was imposed in 1926 by s72 Law of Property Act 1925.

5.3 Exceptions to the general rule

Interests in land

The conveyance of existing legal interests in land, or the creation of new legal interests, must be by deed. *Section 52(1) Law of Property Act 1925.*

The grant of a lease for three years or less is excepted from this rule. Such leases may be validly created orally or in writing. *Section 54(2) Law of Property Act 1925.*

Contracts within the Statute of Frauds

The Statute, as originally enacted, required that six classes of contract must be supported by written evidence of the existence and terms of the contract before the contract could be enforced by the courts. The object of the Statute was to prevent fraud by witnesses giving false testimony as to the contents of an oral agreement. In practice, it worked badly as it enabled contracting parties to escape from performing their obligations under oral contracts and to avoid liability for breach of contract by relying on the technical defence afforded by the Statute. Hence the Statute was considerably narrowed in its scope by judicial interpretation prior to the repeal of most provisions by the Law Reform (Enforcement of Contracts) Act 1954.

Now only two classes of contract of those originally covered by the Statute of Frauds are required to be evidenced in writing:

1. Contracts of guarantee. The Statute of Frauds still applies to these contracts.
2. Contracts for the sale of land The provisions of the Statute of Frauds were

largely reproduced by s40(1) Law of Property Act 1925, so that such contracts were still required to be evidenced in writing. However, s40 has recently been abolished (see below).

Some contracts are required to be in writing by statute dealing with those specific contracts (see 5.6).

5.4 Contracts for the sale of land

In 1989, s40 Law of Property Act 1925 was repealed by the Law of Property (Miscellaneous Provisions) Act 1989.
Section 2 of the 1989 Act provides, inter alia, that:

1. a contract for sale or other disposition of an interest in land can only be made in writing, and only by incorporating all the terms which the parties have expressly agreed in one document, or when documents are exchanged, in each;
2. the terms may be incorporated in a document either by being set out in it, or by reference to some other document;
3. the document incorporating the terms, or when contracts are exchanged, one of the documents incorporating them (but not necessarily the same one) must be signed by or on behalf of each party to the contract.

The effect of this new legislation, which became effective on 27 September 1989, is that a contract for sale of land must be in writing, must be signed by each party, and the written document must contain all the terms agreed on. If an agreement does not comply with the statutory requirements, it will not be enforceable as a contract.

However, the statute does *not* apply to contracts made before the Act came into force, and there are also a number of exceptions, the most important of which are: short-term leases of less than three years duration; and contracts made in the course of a public auction.

Note that by virtue of s2(6) 'disposition' has the same meaning as in the old LPA 1925. 'Interest in land' means any estate, interest or charge in or over land or in or over the proceeds of sale of land.

Note that s1 Law of Property (Miscellaneous Provisions) Act 1989 came into force on 31 July 1990, abolishing previous rules as to the making of deeds. Section 1 abolishes the requirement of sealing for individuals, substituting instead a requirement for signature and attestation by a witness. Section 1 also introduces a new requirement that it should be clear on the face of it that the document is intended to be a deed, and abolishes the old rule that deeds must be made on paper or parchment.

Those contracts made before September 1989 and those exempt from the Act, will, therefore, presumably continue to operate under pre-existing law.

It is, therefore, necessary to examine s40 LPA in more detail, despite the fact that it has now been formally abolished.

Outline of the sequence of events involved in the sale of land

A complex and technical procedure for the sale of land or interests in land has evolved. Some understanding of this procedure is necessary to comprehend the significance of s40(1) LPA 1925.

The steps taken in the sale of land are as follows:

Negotiations

The vendor decides to sell the land and the purchaser to buy. Negotiations as to the price and other terms then commence. These usually take the form of letters between the parties or their solicitors or estate agents. The letters will usually include the words 'subject to contract', so as to avoid an enforceable contract coming into existence.

Exchange of contracts

Agreement as to all the terms of the sale having been reached, the vendor's solicitor draws up a contract setting out these terms. The vendor and purchaser sign a copy each and then exchange the copies, so that each holds a contract signed by the other. Normally at this point, the purchaser pays the vendor a deposit of 10% of the purchase price. One of the terms of the contract will be the date for completion of the sale.

At this point, the vendor is still the legal owner of the land as a deed is required to transfer the legal title to the purchaser (s52(1) LPA 1925). However, there is now an enforceable contract for the sale of land, enforceable, that is, under s40(1) LPA 1925.

The means of enforcement was by a decree of specific performance. This is an equitable remedy, previously available only in the courts of Chancery. After the Judicature Acts, the remedy is available in all courts, but the distinction between law and equity remains in the way in which the land is regarded after the exchange of contracts. Once there is an enforceable contract for the sale of land, equity regards the purchaser as the owner of that land, on the basis that equity regards as done that which ought to be done.

At law, however, until and unless there is a deed conveying the land to the purchaser, the vendor remains the owner of the land, and holds the legal interest on trust for the purchaser.

Completion

The sale of land is completed by the vendor's solicitor drawing up and executing a deed of *conveyance*, as is required by s52(1) LPA 1925 for the transfer of the legal title to the purchaser. On delivery of the conveyance to the purchaser, he pays the remaining 90% of the purchase price and becomes the full legal owner of the land.

Section 40 Law of Property Act 1925

This provided: Section 40(1):

> 'No action may be brought upon any contract for the sale or other disposition of land or any interest in land, unless the agreement upon which such action is brought, or some memorandum or note thereof, is in writing and signed by the person to be charged, or by some other person thereunto lawfully authorised.'

Contracts within s40(1)

The section applied to the 'sale or other disposition of land or any interest in land'.

Sale or other disposition

Disposition is defined by s205(1) LPA 1925 to include:

1. the grant of a lease;
2. the assignment of an existing lease;
3. the grant of a mortgage;
4. the disposition of land by will;
5. the release or gift of an interest in land.

In *Pritchard* v *Briggs* [1980] Ch 339, the grant of an option to purchase land and the grant of a right of pre-emption were held to be within s40(1).

In *Daulia Ltd* v *Four Millbank Nominees Ltd* [1978] Ch 231, an agreement to exchange contracts at a date in the future was held to be within the section.

Land or any interest in land

'Land' is defined by s205(1)(ix) LPA 1925 very widely. The following have been held to fall within s40(1):

1. *Equitable interest held by co-owners*. The leading case is *Steadman* v *Steadman* [1976] AC 536, where an oral agreement between husband and wife included an agreement by the wife to transfer her half share in the jointly owned matrimonial home to the husband for £1,500. The Court of Appeal held that the agreement as to the transfer of land fell within the section.
2. *Easements or profits a prendre*.
3. *Covenants*.
4. *Fixtures*. Moveable objects which are attached to land with the object of improving the land then themselves become part of that land. Hence bricks which are used to build a wall or a house become land, as do doors or windows. Objects such as these are fixtures. A contract for their sale separately from the land fell within s40(1).

In *Lee* v *Gaskell* (1876) 1 QBD 700, a contract for the sale of building materials comprised within a house due to be demolished was within the section.

5. *Licences.* A licence to occupy land does not confer any interest in land and hence a contract to grant a licence should be outside the section. There is some doubt where the licence granted is irrevocable, as such licences approach the status of interests in land, but there is as yet no decision on this point.

The note or memorandum

The nature of the document

The section did *not* require the contract itself to be in writing. All that was needed was some written evidence of the contract.

The writing which evidenced the oral contract may come into existence either before *or* after the contract is made. The more usual writing is a letter in which an offer to sell or purchase land is accepted and from which the words 'subject to contract' are missing. There is then a concluded contract.

However, a letter containing an offer which is accepted orally has been held to be a sufficient memorandum. See *Tiverton Estates Ltd* v *Wearwell Ltd* [1975] Ch 146. The offer must be sufficiently certain to be capable of acceptance, and not merely an invitation to treat. Note also *Grainger & Son* v *Gough* [1896] AC 325 and *Harvey* v *Facey* [1893] AC 552.

In *Bigg* v *Boyd Gibbons Ltd* [1971] 1 WLR 913, a letter of offer from the vendor stated the parties and the property, and also said 'for a quick sale I would accept £26,000'. This letter was held to constitute an offer capable of acceptance so as to create a binding contract of which specific performance was ordered.

A memorandum which has been lost or destroyed might still have satisfied s40(1) as oral or other secondary evidence of it was admissible. See *Barber* v *Rowe* [1948] 2 All ER 1050.

The form of the document

No special form of document was needed. The following have been held to constitute sufficient memoranda: a receipt for a deposit signed by the vendor, *Davies* v *Sweet* [1962] 2 QB 300; a telegram; a recital in a will; a letter written to a third party, *Godwin* v *Francis* (1870) LR 5 CP 295; a letter written by the defendant repudiating his liabilities under the contract, *Dewar* v *Mintoft* [1912] 2 KB 373; a letter merely denying the existence of a contract is not sufficient, *Thirkell* v *Cambi* [1919] 2 KB 590.

Subject to contract

The usual rule is that any document bearing the words 'subject to contract' could be relied upon for the purposes of s40(1). The reason for this was that the words indicate that no binding contract has been concluded.

Doubt as to this basic principle followed three Court of Appeal decisions.

In *Griffiths* v *Young* [1970] Ch 675, the written evidence of the contract consisted of a series of letters between the parties' solicitors all marked 'subject to contract', but oral evidence was allowed to show that the effect of the phrase had been waived by the parties. The letters were held to be sufficient evidence of a binding agreement.

In *Law* v *Jones* [1974] Ch 112, the decision was followed with the Court holding that it was the terms of the agreement rather than the fact of agreement which must be found recorded in the memorandum, and that the use of the phrase 'subject to contract' did not prevent the letters forming a sufficient memorandum.

Note *Tiverton Estates Ltd* v *Wearwell Ltd* (above). Shortly after the decision in *Law* v *Jones*, a differently constituted Court of Appeal reached a directly contrary decision: that the writing relied upon must acknowledge the existence of a concluded contract and the words 'subject to contract' are a denial of that.

There has been no resolution of this conflict, but the decision in Tiverton Estates is to be preferred as it allows the continued use of a formula hallowed by the years, and which solicitors and estate agents continue to use.

This use of the formula appears to have been accepted without argument in the later Court of Appeal decision in *Cohen* v *Nessdale* [1982] 2 All ER 97. See also *Alpenstow Ltd* v *Regalian Properties Ltd* [1985] 2 All ER 545.

It would seem, in any event, that the innovation of the Law of Property (Miscellaneous Provisions) Act 1989 will render the term 'subject to contract' totally irrelevant.

Joinder of documents

The words of the Statute of Frauds and then s40(1) clearly indicate that one document should contain all the contractual terms. The rigour of this requirement was progressively relaxed by judges, who generally viewed with disfavour a defendant who sought to rely on the technical defence afforded by s40(1).

By 1800, it was settled law that two or more documents could together constitute a sufficient memorandum, but it was necessary that one of those documents be signed, and that the signed document should refer expressly and directly to the other document(s). Oral evidence to link the documents was not admissible.

During the nineteenth century, the requirement that there be an express reference was relaxed, and implied references allowed with oral evidence being admissible to identify the document impliedly indicated.

This relaxation is illustrated by *Pearce* v *Gardner* [1897] 1 QB 688, where a letter and an envelope, shown by oral evidence to have contained the letter, were allowed to constitute the memorandum. The envelope was required to complete the terms of the contract as the plaintiff's name was not on the letter, along with the other terms, but was on the envelope which was addressed to him.

The modern state of the law was set out by Jenkins LJ in *Timmins* v *Moreland Street Property Co Ltd* [1958] Ch 110, and this remained true until 1989.

'It is still indispensably necessary, in order to justify the reading of documents together for this purpose, that there should be a document signed by the party to be charged, which, while not containing itself all the necessary ingredients of the required memorandum, does contain some reference, express or implied, to some other document or transaction. Where any such reference can be spelt out of a document so signed, then parol evidence may be given to identify the other document referred to, or, as the case may be, to explain the other transaction, and to identify any document relating to it. If by this process a document is brought to light which contains in writing all the terms of the bargain so far as not contained in the document signed by the party to be charged, then the two documents can be read together so as to constitute a sufficient memorandum for the purposes of section 40.'

Examples of the cross references that have been allowed are:

Stokes v Wicher [1920] 1 Ch 411. On a carbon copy of the plaintiff's agreement to purchase land (which did not contain the plaintiff's name, as required to satisfy the statute), the defendant's agent had signed both:

1. the agreement; and
2. a receipt for a deposit of £50.

The judge held that the signed carbon copy indicated the top copy and a cheque for £62(!), both signed by the plaintiff.

Law v Jones (above). A letter written explicitly in reply to another letter was held to incorporate that earlier letter by reference.

There are limits to cross reference. A document not in existence at the time the defendant signed cannot be relied upon.

Turnley v Hartley (1848) 3 New Pract Cas 96. This does not apply where the two documents came into existence at virtually the same time.

Timmins v Moreland Street Property Co Ltd (above).

Contents of the note or memorandum

The memorandum must contain all the material terms of the contract. These can be summarised as the four Ps: parties; property; price; plus any other provisions.

Parties

The parties and their respective positions, that is, which is vendor and which purchaser, must be indicated with certainty. However, it was not necessary that the parties be specifically named, merely that their identity was ascertainable.

In *Allen (AH) & Co Ltd* v *Whiteman* (1920) 89 LJ Ch 534, a reference to a party as 'mortgagees' was held sufficient as the identity of that party could be readily ascertained.

F Goldsmith (Sicklemere) Ltd v *Baxter* [1970] Ch 85. The name of the plaintiff vendor had been incorrectly set out in the memorandum as 'Goldsmith Coaches (Sicklemere) Ltd'. This was held sufficient.

On the other side of the line, a reference to 'vendor' was not sufficient. See *Potter* v *Duffield* (1874) LR 18 Eq 4.

Nor is a description of the purchasers in a solicitor's letter as 'my clients' adequate. See *Lovesy* v *Palmer* [1916] 2 Ch 233.

Property

The property which is the subject matter of the contract must be indicated. It need not be precisely named or described so long as it was identifiable.

The following descriptions have been held adequate: 'my house' *Cowley* v *Watts* (1853) 22 LJ Ch 591; '24 acres of land, freehold, at Totmonslow' *Plant* v *Bourne* [1897] 2 Ch 281; 'Land on which Evans Row houses previously stood' *Davies* v *Sweet* [1962] 2 QB 300; 'this chalet' *Smith* v *Mansi* [1963] 1 WLR 26.

There was no requirement that the memorandum specify the interest in the land that was to be transferred.

If no interest was specified, it was presumed that a freehold estate was to be conveyed.

Price

The price must be either stated or ascertainable. Where no price or method of determining the price has been stated, the courts would not imply a term that a reasonable price was to be paid.

However, a memorandum that explicitly states that the purchaser will buy land at 'a fair price' or at a 'reasonable valuation' will be valid and enforceable.

Other provisions

If the parties have agreed any other terms, then the memorandum would not be valid unless those terms are included.

If, under a contract for the sale of land, no date for completion was fixed, then the court would imply that completion take place within a reasonable time. If a date had been agreed, then the memorandum was insufficient unless the date was included.

Where the agreement is for the grant of a lease, the memorandum must include the date the lease is to commence and the length of the term. See *Harvey* v *Pratt* [1965] 1 WLR 1025.

An exception to the above rule arose where:

1. a provision had been omitted, but the contract was capable of being a complete agreement without that term; and
2. that term exclusively benefited the party seeking to enforce the contract; and
3. that party was willing to waive that provision.

The converse exception also applied where the provision was exclusively to the detriment of the party seeking to enforce the contract and he agreed to submit to it.

A final way around a missing provision is by means of a *collateral contract*.

If the party seeking to enforce the contract could show that the missing provision was the subject of a separate contract, then the main contract was enforceable despite the missing provision. The consideration for the collateral contract was usually found in the making of the principal contract. See *City and Westminster Properties* v *Mudd* [1959] Ch 129.

Signed

The statute required that the document be signed by the party to be charged (the defendant) or his agent. This has been very widely interpreted. All that was required was that the name or initials of the defendant should appear in *some form somewhere* on the document. The following, at any place on the document, have been held sufficient: handwriting, typewriting, printing, rubber stamp.

What was required was that the defendant had thereby indicated that he recognised the memorandum as being of the alleged agreement.

There was no requirement that the memorandum be signed by the plaintiff, although his name must be indicated or ascertainable from the memorandum.

Effect of non-compliance with s40(1)

Where there is no sufficient memorandum, then unless there has been part performance (see 'Part performance' below), the contract was unenforceable. The contract was not void or voidable. It was perfectly valid. It simply could not be enforced by legal proceedings seeking specific performance or damages.

As the contract was valid, the vendor of land under an oral contract might forfeit the purchaser's deposit, if the purchaser failed to complete, and keep that deposit. If the vendor defaulted, the purchaser might recover his deposit by a claim in quasi-contract based on total failure of consideration.

An unenforceable contract for the sale of land might serve as a defence where a purchaser who has taken possession of the land is sued in trespass by the vendor.

Part performance

Basis of doctrine
The doctrine of part performance was developed by Equity in response to the Statute of Frauds in accordance with the equitable maxim of not allowing a statute to be used as an instrument of fraud. The doctrine was preserved by s40(2) LPA 1925, which expressly exempted part performance from the effect of s40(1). It should be noted that part performance was *not* created by s40. Part performance is a distinct equitable doctrine, which continues independently of the statute.

Part performance, whilst not expressly abolished by the LP(MP)A 1989, will cease to have any relevance, as the 'note or memorandum' rule disappears. For the time being, it will still apply to contracts made before September 1989 and to exempted contracts.

The doctrine applied where the plaintiff, being a party to an oral contract for the sale of land, had partly or wholly performed his part of the contract in the expectation that the defendant would perform his part of the contract. In those circumstances, equity will not allow the defendant to escape from his obligations under the contract by reliance upon the lack of writing, but would order specific performance of the contract.

The principle underlying the doctrine is that the defendant might not set up s40(1) as a defence where the plaintiff had been induced, or allowed, by the defendant to alter his position on the faith of the contract, so that it would be fraud on the part of the defendant to rely on the statute.

Requirements of part performance

1. The act(s) of part performance relied upon must have been done by the person seeking to enforce the contract. Acts of part performance by the defendant cannot be relied upon.
2. The acts of part performance relied upon must point to the existence of some contract, and be consistent with the contract that is claimed to have been made.

These requirements, and the developments of the law relating to part performance, are illustrated by the cases set out below.

In *Maddison* v *Alderson* (1883) 8 App Cas 467, the plaintiff sought to enforce an oral agreement under which she had agreed to work as a man's housekeeper without wages in exchange for his promise to leave her a life estate in his land in his will. He died intestate. Specific performance of the oral agreement was refused on the grounds that the plaintiff's wage-free service up to the date of his death might have been for reasons other than the alleged contract.

In recent years, the requirements of part performance have been relaxed.

In *Wakeham* v *Mackenzie* [1968] 2 All ER 783, the plaintiff agreed orally with a widower that she would move into his house and look after him until his death, paying her share of coal and food in return for his promise to leave her the house and its contents in his will. In reliance upon this agreement, the plaintiff gave up the tenancy of her flat, and acted as his housekeeper until his death, paying her share of the expenses. She received nothing in the will. The court held that the giving up of her flat, the contribution to expenses and her work as housekeeper were sufficient acts of part performance in that they pointed to the existence of some contract and were consistent with the contract alleged.

In *Kingswood Estate Co* v *Anderson* [1963] 2 QB 169, the plaintiffs were the landlords of a house within the Rent Restriction Acts. The tenant defendant was a widow who lived there with her invalid son. In order to obtain possession of the house (under the Rent Restriction Acts), the plaintiffs offered the defendant alternative accommodation and agreed orally that the new tenancy would continue so long as she or her son lived. Four weeks after she had moved, the landlords served notice to quit and sought possession.

HELD: the giving up of possession of the protected tenancy of the house and taking possession of the flat were sufficient acts of part performance, and the oral contract was enforceable.

Until recently, it was settled law that the mere payment of money by the plaintiff to the defendant did not amount to part performance, as the payment could be pursuant to an agreement other than that alleged. This is no longer the case after the decision in *Steadman* v *Steadman* [1976] AC 536. The House of Lords held that an oral agreement between a husband and wife that included an agreement to transfer land was enforceable under the doctrine of part performance because the plaintiff had paid the defendant £100 in compliance with one of the terms of the agreement. Other acts amounting to a sufficient act of part performance include:

The plaintiff taking possession of land with the consent of the defendant, where the plaintiff had not previously occupied that land. See *Kingswood Estates Co* v *Anderson* (above).

Alterations to premises done by the plaintiff vendor at the request of and under the supervision of the defendant purchaser. See *Daniels* v *Trefusis* [1914] 1 Ch 788.

Note: it has been suggested that as the relevance of the doctrine of part performance fades, the doctrine of constructive trust may be developed to fill the gap.

While cases will continue to come before the courts for some time to come, concerning sales of land completed before September 1989, the foregoing rules are of less and less importance. Cases are already beginning to come before the courts concerning interpretation of the Law of Property (Miscellaneous Provisions) Act 1989. See, for example, *Record* v *Bell* [1991] 1 WLR 853 in which solicitors for the vendor and purchaser signed a contract for the sale of a house. On the day before exchange of contracts was due, the vendor's solicitor wrote to the purchaser's as to the question of Land Registry records recording the vendor's title. Further communications including another letter and a telephone call followed. The purchaser's solicitor wrote a letter which was to be attached to the contract of sale 'to be a part of the contract'. Later, the queries as to title were resolved.

By the date for completion of the contract, the purchaser had not paid, and so the vendor sought specific performance. The purchaser sought leave to defend on the basis that the contract of sale of the house did not comply with s2 LP(MP)A 1989.

The court held, in granting specific performance of the contract for the sale of the house, that although for that contract to comply with s2 LP(MP)A 1989 (which provides that either the expressly agreed terms for a contract for sale of land should be set out specifically or where the contract referred to some other document in which terms were to be found, that other document should be clearly identified in the contract as signed by the parties) the terms contained in the letters exchanged between the parties' solicitors should be clearly referred to in each of the parts of the contract which were exchanged between the parties. This was clearly not the case.

However, the court found that the vendor's solicitor's letter constituted an offer of a warranty that the vendor would be shown in the Land Registry files as the owner and this offer and its acceptance by the purchaser (as demonstrated by his agreeing to exchange contracts) formed a collateral contract between the parties. This collateral contract was independent of the sale of land and as such outside the provisions of s2 of the Act, and as such could be specifically enforced.

In *Spiro* v *Glencrown Properties* [1991] 2 WLR 931 the question of whether an option to purchase land is within s2 of the LP(MP)A 1989 arose. By a written agreement, the vendor of land granted an option to purchase land. The option could be exercised the same day and take-up of the option was to be signalled by notice in writing given by the purchaser to the vendor or his solicitor. The option agreement was executed in two exchanged parts, each containing the agreed terms and each signed by the party or his solicitor and exchanged. The purchaser took up the option by written notice in the agreed manner, but failed to complete. The question arose as to whether the agreement was within s2 LP(MP)A 1989.

The court held that an option to buy land could be defined as a sale of land within the meaning of the Act. The relevant contract was the agreement creating the option which consisted of two exchanged parts, containing all relevant terms and duly signed by or on behalf of both parties. This duly complied with the requirements of s2 and the contract could not be set aside as unenforceable merely because the taking up of the option required some unilateral action on the part of the purchaser.

5.5 Contracts of guarantee

Definition

A contract of guarantee is defined in the Statute of Frauds 1677 as 'a special promise to answer for the debt, default or miscarriage of another person'. Such contracts are not enforceable by legal proceedings unless evidenced in writing.

This definition of a contract of guarantee has been further refined by case law. A contract of guarantee now must fall into the form set out below.

1. There must be three parties:

   Creditor: A
   Debtor: B
   Guarantor: C

2. There must be a pre-existing liability between A and B. This liability may arise under a contract, or it may be tortious (*Kirkham* v *Marter* (1819) 2 B & Ald 613).

3. There must be a promise made by C to A that C will discharge B's liability to A if, and only if, B fails to do so himself.

In *Eastwood* v *Kenyon* (1840) 11 Ad & El 438, it was held that a promise made by C to B did not fall within the statute. The promise must be made by C to A.

Judicial limitations to the statute

The statute has been construed narrowly, in a continuing attempt to limit its application. There are four specific situations which have been held to fall outside its scope.

Substitution of third party for principal debtor

Where the effect of an agreement is to release the principal debtor (B) from his liability to the creditor (A) and put a third party in B's place, then there is no contract of guarantee.

In *Goodman* v *Chase* (1818) 1 B & Ald 297, a seller of goods was unwilling to fulfil further orders from a buyer unless he was paid, or given security, for goods already supplied. A third party orally promised the seller that he would assume sole responsibility for the payments due for goods already supplied. This was not a contract of guarantee because the third party assumed primary liability for the debt, rather than a liability conditional upon non-payment by the original debtor. The promise was, therefore, not within the statute and hence enforceable without writing.

No principal debtor

There must be a pre-existing liability between the debtor and the creditor. If the agreement is one under which A supplies goods to B in consideration of X's promise to pay for those goods, then B is never liable to pay for the goods. The primary liability is always that of X.

In *Mountstephen* v *Lakeman* (1871) LR 7 QB 196, the plaintiff was asked to do building works for the Brixham Local Board of Health. On asking how he was to be paid, the chairman of the Board told the plaintiff: 'Go on, *Mountstephen*, and do the work and I will see you paid.' The Board refused to pay on the grounds that there had never been any contract, express or implied, between it and the plaintiff. He then sued the chairman on his promise to pay. The defendant pleaded that the promise was a guarantee within the statute, and hence unenforceable for lack of writing. It was held that the defendant's promise was not a contract of guarantee as there had never been any liability to the plaintiff on the part of the Board. The primary liability for the payment had been assumed by the defendant from the start. The promise was hence enforceable without writing.

Promises falling within 'Substitution of third party for principal debtor' and 'No principal debtor' above are designated *contracts of indemnity* and are enforceable even though made orally.

Distinction between guarantee and indemnity

Indemnity:	C promises A that he, C, will satisfy an existing or future debt arising out of a benefit conferred on B by A. B is either released from liability to A or is never made liable to pay A.
Guarantee:	C promises A that he, C, will satisfy an existing or future liability owed by B to A if B fails to satisfy it himself. B is primarily liable. C is liable only if B defaults.

Guarantee part of larger contract

A guarantee which is merely an incidental part of a larger contract is not within the statute. This covers two types of contract:

Del credere agents is one who, for a commission, introduces buyers to sellers *and* guarantees any liability that may arise under the contract that results from his introduction.

In *Couturier* v *Hastie* (1856) 5 HL Cas 673, the plaintiffs employed the defendants under an oral agreement as del credere agents to sell a shipload of corn. The defendant sold it to X, in ignorance of the fact that at the time of the sale the corn was no longer in a saleable condition. X repudiated the contract when he discovered the condition of the goods, and the plaintiffs sued the defendant on his implied guarantee to pay for the corn if X failed to do so. The defendant pleaded the statute and the lack of writing. The court held that the guarantee was not within the statute, and hence enforceable despite the lack of writing.

The decision must be seen as a matter of public policy rather than one that can be explained by a strict interpretation of the statute.

Guarantees given by the owners of goods to safeguard their possession of those goods. This arises where C has a proprietary interest in goods arising under a contract of sale between himself and B, but there is a lien or charge on the goods in favour of A, arising out of an earlier contract of sale between A and B. In order to obtain undisputed possession of the goods, C guarantees payment to A should B fail to pay.

In *Harburg India Rubber Comb Co* v *Martin* [1902] 1 KB 778, the Court of Appeal held that a guarantee given as merely part of a contract for the sale of goods, or some other agreement, was not within the statute, provided the guarantor was the substantial owner of the goods, and had a proprietary interest in those goods.

Guarantee promise given to protect property

The requirement for contracts in writing does not apply when the guarantee promise is given in order to protect property. See *Fitzgerald* v *Dressler* (1858) 7 CBNS 374.

Summary

Before a contract under which a third party assumes liability for the debt of another falls within the statute, it is necessary to establish the following:

1. That the third party promised a creditor that he would pay the debtor of another.
2. That the agreement on its true construction was intended by the parties to be a guarantee and not an indemnity.
3. That the guarantee does not form part of a larger transaction.

Two recent cases concern aspects of contracts of guarantee. In the first, *Elpis Maritime Co Ltd* v *Marti Chartering Co Inc (The Maria D)* [1991] 3 All ER 785, the question of the 'note or memorandum' rule arose. This has already been dealt with in some detail, in the context of sales of land (see 5.4). In *Elpis* the owners chartered their vessel, *The Maria D*, to the charterers for a voyage from Izmir, Turkey, to Algeria for the carriage of a cargo of wheat. The contract was negotiated through brokers acting for both sides. Tramp Maritime acted for the owners and Marti Chartering for the charterers. During the course of the negotiations it was insisted that Marti should themselves provide a guarantee, initially only for demurrage, but later extended to include 5 per cent balance of freight. The written charterparty contract as finally drawn up consisted of several sheets. The first page was stamped and signed by Marti 'for and on behalf the charterers as brokers only'; other pages were signed or initialled, but with no indication that Marti were acting as brokers. The final page had stamp and signature for Marti below the heading 'Brokers'. The charterers signed separately.

The charterers failed to pay the $175,533 due for demurrage and freight. Arbitration proceedings awarded the owners this full amount plus interest, but no part of the sum outstanding was paid by the charterers. The owners then brought an action against Marti as guarantors.

The House of Lords found that s4 of the Statute of Frauds 1677 prescribed two separate ways in which a contract of guarantee might be made enforceable: by a written agreement signed by the guarantor; or secondly by a note or memorandum of the agreement. In this case, though the note or memorandum must be in writing and signed by the party to be charged, the basic agreement to guarantee might be verbal.

It was not disputed that there was a verbal undertaking by Marti to guarantee the liabilities of the charterers in respect of freight balance and demurrage. What was in question was whether clause 24 of the main charterparty contract constituted an 'adequate note or memorandum' for the purposes of s4. Clause 24 set out all the terms of the prior oral agreement of guarantee and was signed by Marti on the page containing the clause. The court considered that the question of whether Marti signed the page as brokers or on their own account to be irrelevant.

The charterparty, in whatever capacity Marti signed it, contained a sufficient note or memorandum to make the guarantee enforceable under the Statute of Frauds.

In the second case, *In re a Debtor (No 517 of 1991)* (1991) The Times 25 November, there was an oral agreement to vary a guarantee and the question arose as to whether such an oral variation was, under the requirements of the Statute of

Frauds, valid. The debtor had guaranteed performance of a monetary debt by an associated company IHL, but claimed that he had agreed with a representative of the creditor company that monies advanced by him through another company to IHL should go in reduction or extinction of his liability under the guarantee. That agreement was an oral one, not in writing as required by s4 of the Statute of Frauds.

The court found that an oral agreement varying the mode of performance of a guarantee could be relied upon by way of defence notwithstanding s4. That section merely had the effect of making any oral agreement unenforceable, thus it would be impossible to found a cause of action on it, but the agreement, whether verbal or written, could be relied on by way of defence.

5.6 Specific contracts required by statute to be in writing

1. Bills of exchange and promissory notes – ss3(1), 17(2) Bills of Exchange Act 1882.
2. Regulated consumer credit agreements (including hire-purchase agreements) under the Consumer Credit Act 1974.
3. Contracts of marine insurance are void unless made in writing in the form of a policy – Marine Insurance Act 1906.
4. A bill of sale is void unless it is in writing in the statutory form – Bills of Sale (1878) Amendment Act 1882.

6

Contents of Contracts

6.1 Introduction

Having established that a contract satisfies the requirements for validity, that is, that there has been an agreement supported by consideration and that it is in the necessary form (where that is required), the next stage is to determine the scope of the obligations incurred by the parties. The first step is to decide whether any statement (whether oral or in writing) forms part of the agreement or precedes the formation of the agreement. We have already seen that some such statements have been construed as invitations to treat, preceding the formation of the contract, and without legal effect.

Where a statement *induces* a contract, it may be construed as a representation, sometimes referred to as a 'mere' representation to distinguish it from terms which form part of the contract. Representations have legal effect, the examination of which we shall undertake later.

The task then is to define the nature and extent of the obligations. This involves determination of:

1. The terms of the contract.

2. The relative importance of those terms, that is, whether or not a breach of a term undermines a basic contractual obligation. This is of fundamental importance in determining the remedy available to the innocent party who has suffered a breach of contract.

3. The manner in which the terms formed part of the contract, that is, whether they were expressly provided for, and the rules applicable to, their construction, if not expressly provided for must they be implied by custom, by the courts or by statute.

We shall proceed by firstly examining the distinction between terms and representations and investigating the concept of the collateral contract.

6.2 Terms and representations

Statements made before or at the time of the conclusion of the contract

Problems can arise when statements are made before, or at the time, the contract is concluded. Such statements are usually oral, but may be in writing. The remedies available to a party who has suffered as a result of a false statement will depend on how the law construes the statement. Provided that the statement is not simply a eulogistic commendation of the subject matter of the contract, a common advertising usage, which is regarded as a 'mere puff' without legal significance, it can be one of the following:

1. a promise amounting to a term of the contract which, if unfulfilled, will allow a remedy for breach of contract; or
2. a mere representation, which, if false, will not give rise to an action for breach of contract, but may allow a remedy for misrepresentation; or
3. a collateral contract.

Terms or representations

The task of the court will be to ascertain the intention of the parties. In deciding whether a particular statement was intended to be a term of the contract, or merely amounted to a representation, the court may be guided by a consideration of the following factors:

The importance of the statement

A statement may well be a term of the contract if it is of such importance that if it had not been made the injured party would not have entered into the contract at all.

In *Bannerman* v *White* (1861) 10 CB NS 844, the buyer of hops asked whether sulphur had been used in their cultivation. He added that if it had he would not even bother to ask the price. The seller assured him that it had not. This assurance was held to be a condition of the contract. It was of such importance that, without it, the buyer would not have contracted.

Similarly, in *Couchman* v *Hill* [1947] KB 54, the buyer asked for the assurance that the heifer he was contemplating purchasing at an auction sale was unserved, as he required it for servicing by his own bull. He also stated that without this assurance, he would not bid. Both the seller and the auctioneer gave him this assurance. The Court of Appeal held that the assurance was a term of the contract, despite the fact that this was in conflict with the printed conditions to which the auction sale was subject, which provided that no warranty was given. In the alternative, the Court of Appeal found that the statement was a collateral contract (collateral contracts are discussed below).

In contrast is the case of *Oscar Chess* v *Williams* [1957] 1 WLR 370. A private seller of a car obtained the sum of £290 in part exchange on the basis that it was a 1948 model. It was, in fact, a 1939 model; the registration book had been fraudulently altered by a previous owner, but the seller was innocent of this. The price of a 1939 model was considerably lower. The plaintiff company, a motor dealer, would still have been prepared to buy the car, but at a 'lower price, had they known the true facts'. The Court of Appeal held, by a majority, that the statement was not a term of the contract. Morris LJ dissented, taking the view that the statement amounted to a condition in the contract; it related, he said, to a vitally important matter.

Did the party making the statement have special knowledge as against the other party?

An important factor may be the relative capability of the parties to know the truth.

Thus in *Harling* v *Eddy* [1951] 2 KB 739, the vendors of a heifer represented that there was nothing wrong with the animal but, in fact, it had tuberculosis from which it died within three months of the sale. A contributory factor in leading the Court of Appeal to decide that the statement was a term of the contract was that the vendors were in a special position to know of the heifer's condition. In his judgment, Lord Evershed MR distinguished the facts before him from what might appear to be similar facts in the earlier case of *Hopkins* v *Tanqueray* (1854) 15 CB 130. In that case, the conversation took place not at the sale, but the day before, and the contract was formed as a result of the sale at the auction and incorporated the conditions set out in the auction particulars.

In *Dick Bentley Productions Ltd* v *Harold Smith (Motors) Ltd* [1965] 1 WLR 623, the statement was made by a motor dealer to a private purchaser that the car had done only 20,000 miles since being fitted with a replacement engine and gearbox. This statement was untrue. A unanimous Court of Appeal held that the statement was a contractual term. Lord Denning MR referred to *Oscar Chess* v *Williams* and said 'in the present case it is very different ... Here we have a dealer, Mr Smith, who was in a position to know, or at least to find out, the history of the car'. See also *Schawel* v *Reade* [1913] 1 Ir Rep 81 and *Birch* v *Paramount Estates* (1956) 167 EG 196 (below).

Was the contract reduced to writing subsequent to the statement?
If the contract is subsequently reduced to writing and the written contract does not incorporate the statement, this would be suggestive of the view that the parties did not intend the statement to be a contractual term.

In *Routledge* v *McKay* [1954] 1 WLR 615, the defendant stated that a motor cycle, the subject matter of the proposed sale, was a 1942 model. In the written contract, signed a week later, no mention was made of the date of the model. It was held, on this point, that what the parties intended to agree on was recorded in the written agreement, and that it would be inconsistent with the written agreement to hold that there was an intention to make the prior statement a contractual term.

However, in *Birch* v *Paramount Estates* (1956) 167 EG 196, the defendants made a statement about the quality of a house. The contract, when reduced to writing, made no reference to the statement. The Court of Appeal regarded the statement as a contractual term. But here the defendants had special knowledge.

The lapse of time between the statement and the conclusion of the contract
This may be a relevant, but by no means a decisive, factor.

In *Bannerman* v *White*, the statement was made virtually at the same time as the conclusion of the contract. In *Routledge* v *McKay*, the lapse of a week between the two events weighed with the court as a factor militating against construing the statement as a contractual term.

On the other hand, in *Schawel* v *Reade* (above), the defendant told the plaintiff, who required a horse for stud purposes, that the animal was 'perfectly sound'. A few days later, the price was agreed and, three weeks later, the plaintiff bought the horse. The statement was held to be a term of the contract, but here again the defendant, who was the owner of the horse, would appear to have had special knowledge.

It must be emphasised that none of the above factors are conclusive. As Lord Moulton makes clear in *Heilbut, Symons & Co* v *Buckleton* [1913] AC 30, they may be criteria of value in deciding whether or not a contractual term is intended, but he said 'they cannot be said to furnish decisive tests ... The intention of the parties can only be deduced from the totality of the evidence ...' (Lord Moulton was commenting on the dicta of A L Smith MR in *De Lassalle* v *Guildford* (see below) in the course of which it was said that 'a decisive test is whether the vendor assumes to assert a fact of which the buyer is ignorant, or merely states an opinion or judgment upon a matter of which the vendor has no special knowledge ...' The use of the phrase 'decisive test' could not, Lord Moulton said, be defended).

A further observation must be made. Prior to the Misrepresentation Act 1967, the distinction between a representation and a contractual term was of more significance than it is today. The primary reason for this is that, before the 1967 Act, the only remedy for an innocent misrepresentation was rescission of the contract. Damages could not be obtained unless the misrepresentation was fraudulent. Moreover, there were (and still are) circumstances in which the right to claim rescission might be lost, leaving the injured party without any remedy.

The Misrepresentation Act introduced the right to obtain damages for certain non-fraudulent misrepresentations, though the measure of damages differs from that of contractual damages. However, damages for a wholly innocent misrepresentation still cannot be obtained while damages for breach of contract can be recovered as of right. The distinction between contractual terms and 'mere' representations remains of importance. This aspect will be dealt with more fully in Chapter 7.

6.3 Collateral contracts

If a promise is not a term of the principal contract, it is possible that it may be enforced as a collateral contract.

This was an important innovation used to circumvent the parol evidence rule, the formerly limited remedies for misrepresentation and privity of contract. The concept of a collateral contract is clearly illustrated by Lord Moulton in *Heilbut, Symons & Co* v *Buckleton* [1913] AC 30.

> 'It is evident, both on principle and on authority, that there may be a contract the consideration for which is the making of some other contract. "If you will make such and such a contract, I will give you one hundred pounds," is in every sense of the word a complete legal contract. It is collateral to the main contract, but each has an independent existence, and they do not differ in respect of their possessing to the full the character and status of a contract.'

Lord Moulton was also of the view, however, that such collateral contracts should be viewed suspiciously. He said:

> 'Such collateral contracts, the sole effect of which is to vary or add to the terms of the written contract, are therefore viewed with suspicion by the law ... Not only the terms of such contracts but the existence of an animus contrahendi on the part of all parties to them must be strictly shown.'

In an earlier case, the Court of Appeal in *De Lasalle* v *Guildford* [1901] 2 KB 215 had enforced an oral promise as a collateral contract.

The plaintiff and the defendant negotiated for the lease of a house. The terms of the lease were arranged, but the plaintiff (prospective tenant) refused to hand over the counterpart of the lease which he had signed unless the defendant assured him that the drains were in good order. The defendant gave this assurance, and the counterpart lease was thereafter handed to him. The drains were not in good order, and the plaintiff was held entitled to damages for breach of that undertaking.

This decision appears to be sound despite Lord Moulton's strictures on the dicta of A L Smith MR (see above).

A collateral contract was used for a similar purpose in *City and Westminster Properties* v *Mudd* [1959] Ch 129. The defendant, who had been a tenant of the premises for six years, was accustomed to sleep at the plaintiff's shop. The lease fell for renewal. The plaintiffs inserted a clause for use of the premises to be for 'showrooms, workrooms and offices only'. The defendant asked if he could sleep there. He was told that he could and he signed the lease.

It was held that the promise not to enforce the clause against him was a collateral contract which he could plead in answer to a claim for breach of contract.

The use of a collateral contract to avoid the stringency of written contracts, and where the remedy for misrepresentation is not available or unhelpful, used to be rare. It has, however, become increasingly popular. In *Evans* v *Merzario*, Lord Denning MR thought that the observations of Lord Moulton (above) were largely out of date.

In *Evans* v *Merzario* [1976] 1 WLR 1078, the plaintiffs, who had shipped goods for many years with the defendants who were forwarding agents, agreed to a changeover in the method of shipment to enable goods to be carried in containers. The defendants gave an oral assurance that the goods would be carried below deck on the ship. In fact, goods were carried above deck and the containers were washed overboard in a storm. The printed standard conditions of the forwarding trade enabled the defendants to carry containers above deck if they wished to do so.

HELD: that the plaintiffs could recover against the defendants. Lord Denning MR said that the promise to carry goods below deck was an enforceable collateral contract. Roskill and Geoffrey Lane LJJ also thought that the oral assurance was an express term of the contract of carriage, which was partly oral, partly in writing and partly by conduct.

Lord Denning explained the use for a collateral contract after the Misrepresentation Act 1967:

> 'We now have the Misrepresentation Act 1967 under which damages can be obtained for innocent misrepresentation of fact. This Act does not apply here because we are concerned with an assurance as to the future. But even in respect of promises as to the future, we have a different approach nowadays to collateral contracts. When a person gives a promise or an assurance to another, intending that he should act on it by entering into a contract, and he does act on it by entering into the contract, we hold that it is binding ...
>
> ... The cases are numerous in which oral promises have been held binding in spite of written exempting conditions.'

Esso Petroleum v *Mardon* [1976] QB 801 was a case which reached a similar conclusion. Esso induced Mardon to enter into a lease for a filling station by negligently misstating to him that the station would have a turnover of 200,000 gallons per year. In fact, it did not.

HELD: that Esso, although stating an opinion, also warranted that they had used reasonable care and skill in reaching that opinion. Damages were, therefore, recoverable for breach of that collateral warranty.

Accordingly, it seems that the collateral warranty can be implied as well as express. In *Esso* v *Mardon*, there was no express promise that the opinion had been achieved by the exercise of reasonable care and skill.

In *Eyre* v *Measday* [1986] 1 All ER 488 and *Thake* v *Maurice* [1984] 2 All ER 513, two differently constituted Courts of Appeal declined to find in sterilisation operations collateral warranties that the expected results would be achieved. Although permanent sterility was expected as a result of the operations, the Court of Appeal in both the above cases declined to find that there had been a collateral warranty that the operations would be completely successful.

The collateral contract may also be employed where the main contract is between the plaintiff and a third party. In *Shanklin Pier* v *Detel Products* [1951] 2 KB 854, the plaintiffs, wishing to paint the pier, consulted the defendants, paint manufacturers, who told them that their paint was suitable for the purpose. Acting on the faith of this statement, the plaintiffs caused to be inserted into the agreement with the contractors, who were to paint the pier, a term requiring the use of the defendants' paint. The paint proved unsuitable and the plaintiffs were entitled to damages for breach of the collateral promise. The plaintiffs, entering into the contract with the contractors, furnished consideration for the defendants' promise.

This principle has also been applied in hire-purchase cases where the dealer first sells the article to a finance company and the customer, on the faith of statements made to him by the dealer about the article, then enters into a contract with the finance company. The statements may amount to a collateral promise enforceable against the dealer. See *Andrews* v *Hopkinson* [1957] 1 QB 229. For a further application of the principle, see the Court of Appeal decision in *Wells* v *Buckland Sand & Silica* [1965] 2 QB 170.

6.4 Conditions

The ways in which the obligations under a contract are construed are various. The most important distinction is between those contractual obligations which entitle an innocent party to repudiate a contract in the event of a breach, and those which merely enable a person to claim damages. The classic division is between 'conditions', a breach of which gives the innocent party an option to repudiate, and 'warranties', a breach of which does not. The word 'warranty' is also used to mean a contractual promise, or term, so it is important to have in mind the use to which the word is being put. The word 'condition' also has another meaning. It may mean a stipulation that a contract should be brought to an end, or should not be enforceable, except on the happening of a given event. The condition is then properly called a 'condition subsequent', or a 'condition precedent' respectively.

In addition to the classic division between conditions and warranties, there is a third class of term called an intermediate term or innominate term (the names are interchangeable). This is usually thought to be different from a condition because it is not necessarily certain at the outset whether the term will enable a person to repudiate in the event of its breach. Conditions precedent and conditions subsequent will be examined first.

Condition precedent

Where the operation of an obligation or right is suspended until the happening of a certain event, there is said to be a 'condition precedent'. If the event never happens, the obligation or right never arises.

In *Pym* v *Campbell* (1856) 6 E & B 370, the defendants agreed in writing to buy from the plaintiff a share in an invention. The defendants gave oral evidence that it was not to operate until a third party had approved the invention, and that this had not happened.

HELD: that there was a condition precedent which had not been satisfied and the plaintiffs could not recover.

Erle J said that the evidence showed that there was never an agreement at all. It does not, however, necessarily follow that there is no agreement. The condition precedent may suspend, rather than negative, the agreement. The performance of the contract was only suspended in *Marten* v *Whale* [1917] 2 KB 480. P agreed with X to buy a plot of land subject to the approval by P's solicitors of 'title and restrictions'. At the same time, P agreed to sell his car to X in consideration of the first agreement and to be simultaneous. He gave possession of the car to X, who sold it to a bona fide purchaser (D) without notice. P's solicitor refused to approve the restrictions for the land. P sued to recover the car from D.

HELD: the solicitor's approval was only a condition precedent to the passing of property in the car, not to the creation of a contract of sale. Once an agreement to sell had been made, X became a buyer in possession and could pass good title under s25 SGA 1893 – now 1979.

It is always a matter of some difficulty to decide whether the failure of a condition precedent prevents the formation of the contract, or merely suspends the obligations created under it. In *Bentworth Finance* v *Lubert* [1968] 1 QB 680, P let a car to D who was to pay 24 monthly instalments. The car was delivered without a log book. D did not use the car and refused to pay the instalments. P recovered possession of the car and sued for the instalments.

HELD: the refusal to supply the log book was the failure of a condition precedent upon which liability for the instalments depended – that is, the contract did not come into existence until the log book was supplied.

Condition subsequent

The obligation of one or both parties may be subject to the condition that it is to be immediately binding, but in the event of a certain occurrence or the ascertaining of certain facts, the obligation will cease to be binding or the party will have the right to avoid the contract.

In *Head* v *Tattersall* (1871) LR 7 Ex 7, A bought a horse from B with a certain description. A was to have the right to return it by a certain day if it did not answer its description. It did not, and A returned the horse before the day. In the meantime, however, the horse had been injured without A's fault. It was held that the contract had been brought to an end by the fulfilment of the condition subsequent. A was entitled to recover the price, and the loss occasioned by the horse's injury fell on B.

When is a term a condition?

Frequently, the terms of a contract are not conveniently labelled by the parties as 'condition' and 'warranty'. Even if the parties do employ such labels, it does not follow that their use may be conclusive as to what may constitute a condition or warranty. For example, if the words 'it is warranted that ...' are used it will not follow that breach of the term will not be a breach of condition. If the parties have not expressed themselves on the issue of what is to be a condition enabling repudiation for breach and what is not, the courts have to decide. This may be a formidable task.

In *Poussard* v *Spiers & Pond* (1876) 1 QBD 410, an actress was employed to play the leading part in a French operetta as from the beginning of its run. She was unable to take up her role until a week after the season had started. The producers, who had had to engage a substitute, refused her services.

HELD: her promise to perform as from the first night amounted to a condition and that its breach entitled the producers to treat the contract as discharged.

On the other hand, in *Bettini* v *Gye* (1876) 1 QBD 183, a singer was engaged to sing for the whole of the season in theatres and at concerts. He undertook to appear six days in advance for rehearsals. He only arrived three days in advance. The defendant sought to terminate the contract.

HELD: that he could not. The rehearsal clause was subsidiary to the main part of the agreement. Accordingly, it was only a warranty that the singer would arrive six days in advance.

The courts, therefore, seek to distinguish a condition from a warranty by deciding upon the importance of the term to the contract as a whole, and from that decision inferring the intention of the parties.

In *Behn* v *Burness* (1863) 3 B & S 751, the court had to evaluate a statement in a charter party that a ship was now in the port of Amsterdam. The statement was inaccurate. The question was whether that promise was a condition or a warranty.

HELD: the term was a condition.

The intention of the parties is to be ascertained at the time of entry into the agreement. In *The Mihalis Angelos* [1971] 1 QB 164, the owners of a vessel let it to charterers for a voyage from Haiphong to Hamburg. The owners said that the vessel was 'expected ready to load about 1st July'. It was found as a fact that there was no reasonable ground for expecting that the vessel would be ready to load on 1 July.

HELD: the expected readiness clause was a condition.

6.5 Warranties

It is already suggested that the word 'warranty' is used in a multiplicity of senses. Chitty suggests that:

> 'the emergence of the new category of "intermediate" or "innominate" terms seems likely to have reduced the number of occasions when a term will be classified as a warranty in this sense (the breach of which by one party does not entitle the other to treat his obligations as discharged), almost to vanishing point, save in the very exceptional circumstances where a term has been specifically so classified by statute.'

He is referring principally to the Sale of Goods Act 1979.

6.6 Innominate terms

In *Hongkong Fir Shipping* v *Kawasaki Kisen Kaisha* [1962] 2 QB 26, the defendants chartered the vessel 'Hong Kong Fir' from the plaintiffs for 24 months; the charter party provided 'she being fitted in every way for ordinary cargo service'. It transpired that the engine-room staff were incompetent, and the vessel spent less than nine weeks of the first seven months of the charter at sea because of breakdowns and consequent repairs required to make her seaworthy. The defendants repudiated the charter party and claimed that the term as to seaworthiness was a condition of the contract, any breach of which entitled them to do so.

HELD: the term was neither a condition nor a warranty, and in determining whether the defendants could terminate the contract, it was necessary to look at the consequences of the breach to see if they deprived the innocent party of substantially the whole benefit he should have received under the contract. On the facts, this was not the case, because the charter party still had a substantial time to run.

Diplock LJ said:

> 'There are, however, many contractual undertakings of a more complex character which cannot be categorised as being "conditions" or "warranties" ... Of such undertakings all that can be said is that some breaches will and others will not give rise to an event which will deprive the party not in default of substantially the whole benefit which it was intended he should obtain from the contract; and the legal consequences of a breach of such undertaking, unless provided for expressly in the contract, depend upon the nature of the event to which the breach gives rise and do not follow automatically from a prior classification of the undertaking as a condition or warranty.'

Breach of an innominate term will enable the party not in default to treat the contract as repudiated only if the other party has renounced his obligations under the contract; or the other party has rendered his obligations impossible of performance; or the party not in default has been deprived of substantially the whole benefit which it was intended he should obtain from the contract.

A term is most likely to be an innominate term when it is capable of being broken in both a very trivial or a very serious manner, so that a duty to provide a seaworthy ship would fall within this category (*Hongkong Fir* (above)), as could a duty to proceed with 'all convenient speed' to a port of loading (*Freeman v Taylor* (1831) 8 Bing 124), and as would an obligation on a shipmaster to obey the charterer's orders (*Federal Commerce & Navigation v Molena Alpha* [1979] AC 757). Similarly, a term in a contract for the sale of goods that shipment be in good condition was an innominate term, the breach of which had to be serious as to go to the root of the contract in order for the buyer to reject. This was the case even though the Sale of Goods Act 1979 divides terms only into conditions and warranties. *Cehave v Bremer Handelsgesellschaft mbH* [1976] QB 44.

In *Reardon Smith v Hansen-Tangen* [1976] 1 WLR 989, two charter parties were in agreement for the charter of a ship to be built at a certain shipyard in Japan. In fact, the ship was built at another shipyard. The charterers sought to reject the vessel on the grounds that the description of the ship was a condition of the contract, any departure from which was a breach of condition of the contract which justified rejection.

HELD: the charterers were not entitled to repudiate. In order to reach the decision, the House of Lords looked at the background to the case. Lord Wilberforce expressed the view that 'the court ... must ... place itself in thought in the same factual matrix as that in which the parties were'. In order to place himself in that factual matrix, he asked what was the commercial purpose of the charter parties and what was the factual background against which they were made.

This description has been adopted in subsequent cases by other members of the House of Lords, for example, Lord Scarman in *Bunge v Tradax* (below). Notice, however, that he does not regard the expression 'the factual matrix' as describing anything other than the more common 'circumstances of the case'.

The question of whether time was of the essence (a condition) has arisen in a number of cases.

In *United Scientific Holdings v Burnley Borough Council* [1978] AC 904, the House of Lords held that the timetable set out in rent review clauses for the taking of pre-defined steps was not of the essence. In contrast, in *Bunge Corporation v Tradax Export SA* [1981] 1 WLR 711, the House of Lords thought that in mercantile contracts time would usually be of the essence and not an innominate term.

The distinction between clauses which would be likely to be regarded as innominate terms, and those which would be conditions were illuminated in *Bremer Handelsgesellschaft v Vanden Avenne-Izegem PVBA* [1978] 2 Lloyd's Rep 109.

The House of Lords had to consider two clauses:

1. A prohibition of export clause which required the sellers to advise the buyers 'without delay' of impossibility of shipment by reason of a prohibition.
2. A clause setting down a schedule for notifying, and acting upon, the notification of a force majeure occurrence.

HELD: the former was an innominate term because it would give rise to many varying breaches. The latter was a condition. The stipulation as to time required punctual compliance.

Lord Wilberforce said that the classification of a term as a condition or innominate term is dependent upon: the form of the clause; the relation of the clause to the contract as a whole; and the general considerations of law.

Notably, this categorisation also includes matters of policy, in particular, the question of unfairness to the seller or buyer of restricting the remedy to damages in any given instance. The House of Lords was anxious to convey the impression that they were not constrained to regard any clause as a condition unless there would be demonstrated good reason for doing so.

The last-mentioned case was referred to in *Bunge* v *Tradax* (above) where, similarly, a clause which specified a time was held to be a condition. The buyers in that case had an obligation to give the sellers notice that the vessel nominated for carriage of the goods was ready to load. Notice of readiness was to be given on 13 June. In fact, it was not given until 17 June.

HELD: that the failure to give notice on time was a breach of condition because the purpose of a clause designating a time for performance was to enable the other party to organise his affairs to meet his own obligations. The need for certainty in commercial contracts was great and to fail to provide certainty would be an unfairness. Time clauses in commercial contracts would generally be conditions, in particular because only one breach is possible; to be late.

Bunge v *Tradax* also disposed of a common fallacy, that is, that whether a clause was a condition or an innominate term was capable of decision only after the breach had occurred. The House of Lords and, in particular, Lord Wilberforce made it plain that the time for determining whether a clause was a condition or an innominate term was at the time of contracting. Lord Wilberforce said:

> 'The test suggested by the appellants was ... (to) ... consider ... the breach actually committed and then decide whether that default would deprive the party not in default of substantially the whole benefit of the contract. They even invoked certain passages in the judgment of Diplock LJ in *Hongkong Fir* to support it. One may observe in the first place that the introduction of a test of this kind would be commercially most undesirable ... I am clear that the submission is unacceptable in law ...'

The judicial approach in determining the intention of the parties as to the classification of a term of the contract is illustrated by the case of *Schuler AG* v *Wickman Machine Tool Sales Ltd* [1974] AC 235 HL. The respondents were the exclusive selling agents in the UK for the appellants' presses. The agency agreement provided:

> 'It shall be a condition of this agreement that (the respondent) shall send its representative to visit (the six largest UK motor manufacturers) at least once every week.'

The respondents committed some minor breaches of this term, and the appellants terminated the agreement, claiming that by reason of the term being a condition they were entitled so to do.

HELD: the parties could not have intended that the appellants should have the right to terminate the agreement if the respondents failed to make one of the obliged number of visits, which in total amounted to nearly 1,400. A provision elsewhere in the agreement gave the appellants the right to determine the agreement if the respondents committed a 'material breach' of the obligations, and failed to remedy it within 60 days of being required to do so in writing. The House of Lords had regard to the fact that the relevant clause was the only one referred to as a 'condition'. Lord Reid felt that it would have been unreasonable for the appellants to be entitled to terminate the agreement for the respondents' failure to make even one visit. But he would have been constrained so to hold were it not for the later provision. The word 'condition' made any breach of the clause a 'material breach', entitling the appellants to give notice requiring the breach to be remedied. But not, as the appellant sought, to terminate the contract forthwith without notice. In a persuasive speech Lord Wilberforce, dissenting, thought that the term was a condition. This view was shared by Stephenson LJ in his dissenting judgment in the Court of Appeal and by Mocatta J at first instance.

In *Lombard North Central plc* v *Butterworth* [1987] 1 All ER 267, the agreement was for the lease of a computer for a period of five years on payment of an initial sum of £584.05, and nineteen subsequent quarterly instalments of the same amount. The agreement provided that the plaintiffs had the right to terminate the agreement if the instalments were not paid punctually. The agreement also contained a clause providing that 'punctual payment of each instalment was of the essence of the agreement'. The Court of Appeal held that though the failure to pay promptly was not repudiatory, this clause had the effect of making failure to pay on time a breach of condition. A failure to pay on time did not normally go to the root of a contract, but the parties were at liberty to make any particular obligation of the essence of their contract and had done so on this occasion.

6.7 Express terms

All the terms which have been discussed above have been express terms of the contract, that is, the parties have communicated to one another that the form of words is to be a part of the contract between them. It frequently occurs, however, that the parties are at cross-purposes or become at cross-purposes about the meaning of the words used. This difficulty arises particularly in relation to written contracts where rules of law and evidence have been developed to enable one or other party to show what the words in the contract do in fact mean.

These rules can be shortly stated.

1. The aim is to discover the intention of the parties.
2. Their intention must be found in the document itself (although see the observations of Lord Wilberforce in *Reardon Smith* v *Hansen-Tangen* (above)). This is known as 'the parol evidence rule'.

3. The popular meaning of words is to be applied unless the context indicates that some other meaning is intended.
4. Technical words should be given their technical meaning.
5. The contract should be construed so as to avoid absurdity or inconsistency.
6. Mercantile contracts should be construed according to mercantile usage.
7. The courts may look at customs of particular places to interpret the contract.
8. The contract should be read as a whole.
9. Where clauses are inconsistent or repugnant to each other effect should be given to that part which is intended to carry the real intention of the parties on a consideration of the contract as a whole.
10. Where there are printed and written words, greater significance should be placed on the written words as more likely to exhibit a true intention.
11. Where a general word is preceded by several words illustrating a class of behaviour or meaning or intention, the general word shall be limited 'ejusdem generis', that is, it only applies to matters which are in a similar category to the preceding words. For example, the words, 'be destroyed by fire, flood, storm, tempest or other inevitable accident' could not cover losses caused by acts or default of the parties to the contract. See *Saner* v *Bilton* (1878) 7 Ch D 815.

There have recently appeared before the courts a whole string of contracts in which construction problems have arisen. For example, in *G A Estates* v *Caviapen Trustees Ltd* (1991) The Times 22 October the use of the contra proferentem rule was considered by the courts.

In this Scottish case, the plaintiffs, in a sale of land, warranted to the defendants that the land was fit for the purpose of constructing a particular development. The defendants, when they discovered that the land was not suitable for the purpose stated, refused to pay. The plaintiffs sought payment relying on the contra proferentem rule, contending the warranty had been drafted specifically in favour of the defendants and should, if ambiguous, be construed in the manner least favourable to them. The defendants, counterclaiming, argued that the clause was not conceived as a favour to them and was not intended to benefit one party more than another. The contra proferentem rule had no relevance. The court held that, in order for the contra proferentem rule to be justified, the argument that the warranty was a special feature and was never normally included in contracts for sale of land was to be rejected. No special rule of construction (such as contra proferentem) applied here.

In *Richco International* v *Bunge & Co Ltd* [1991] 2 Lloyd's Rep 93, on the other hand, the mercantile expression 'contracts in string' and the repercussions of such 'strings' were considered. Several contracts were negotiated in string. Among the clauses were conditions as to ports of shipment and loading arrangements. The charterers sought to interpret clauses differently in certain aspects of the contract.

Not surprisingly the court decided that, where contracts are in a string, exactly the same meaning must be given to clauses in contracts throughout the chain. The same weighting should also be given to the importance (or lack of it) of similar clauses.

Rules of evidence

The 'parol evidence rule' is frequently said to derive from the rule in *Goss* v *Lord Nugent* (1833) 5 B & Ad 58:

> '... verbal evidence is not allowed to be given ... so as to add to or subtract from, or in any manner to vary or qualify the written contract'.

There are, however, innumerable exceptions to the parol evidence rule.

To show that an implied term is inapplicable

Where the contract is silent on a subject where usually a term would be implied, parol (verbal evidence as to extrinsic matters) evidence is available to show that the usual term should not be implied. So if a person takes out a policy of marine insurance and evidence can show that the ship was unseaworthy, then the implied term of the contract as to seaworthiness can be excluded. See *Burgess* v *Wickham* (1863) 3 B & S 669.

To show when the contract is to commence

In *Pym* v *Campbell* (1856) 6 E & B 370, oral evidence was available to show that a contract for sale of a patent was not to commence until it had been approved by a third party.

To show the capacity of the party acting

In *Wake* v *Harrop* (1861) 6 H & N 768, oral evidence was available to show that an agent was acting as such when signing a charterparty and not as a principal acting on his own behalf – but note that the court indicated that the right to call such evidence existed only in equity where a person was a defendant.

Guidance on the position at law may be given by *Newell* v *Radford* (1867) LR 3 CP 52, where oral evidence could be called to say which party was a buyer and which party a seller in circumstances where that fact was not apparent from the face of the contract.

To defend an action for specific performance

Because an action for specific performance is an action for an equitable remedy, parol evidence may be given by a defendant. In *Martin* v *Pycroft* (1852) 2 De GM & G 785, parol evidence was also given to obtain specific performance of a written lease by giving evidence of an oral promise to pay.

To construe an ambiguous document

But the situation where oral evidence of prior negotiations is given to construe the document by reference to agreed meanings must be distinguished from evidence of prior negotiation alone. See *Robertson* v *Jackson* (1845) 2 CB 412, *Prenn* v *Simmonds* [1971] 1 WLR 1381 and *Arrale* v *Costains* [1976] 1 Lloyd's Rep 98.

Evidence of conduct after the contract is generally inadmissible to show the intention of the parties, unless it relates specifically to the terms of the original agreement. See *James Miller* v *Whitworth St Estates* [1970] AC 583 and *Ferguson* v *Dawson* [1976] 1 WLR 346.

To show a collateral promise

A perhaps classic example of where oral evidence was allowed to reverse the effect of a written agreement was in *City and Westminster Properties* v *Mudd* [1959] Ch 129 (see 6.3 above).

6.8 Terms implied by the courts

It is a moot point whether the implication of terms into a contract is a question of law, or whether it can, in some circumstances, be a question of fact. Treitel takes the view that the implication may be either of fact or law, whereas Chitty considers that the implication is one of law for the court. There are, in any event, generally said to be two circumstances in which terms are implied at common law:

1. Where the contract does not deal with a matter expressly, but a term is said to be intended by the parties. That intention is discovered by looking at the words of the agreement and their surrounding circumstances.
2. Where the contract does not expressly deal with the matter, but it creates a relationship in which such a term is usually implied.

Treitel treats the first type of implied term as one of fact and the latter as of law.

Intention of the parties

In *The Moorcock* (1889) 14 PD 64, a term was implied that a wharf was safe for the use of ships which contracted to lie at the wharf, so that the plaintiff was able to recover damages against the defendant when his ship was damaged because the water level fell and grounded her.

Bowen LJ gave the classic definition:

'Now, an implied warranty, or as it is called, a covenant in law, as distinguished from an express contract or express warranty, really is in all cases founded upon the presumed intention of the parties and upon reason. The implication which the law draws from what must obviously have been the intention of the parties, the law draws with object of giving efficiency to the transaction and preventing such a failure of consideration as cannot have been within the contemplation of either side; and I believe if one were to take all the cases, and there are many, of implied warranties or covenants in law, it will be found that in all of them the law is raising an implication from the presumed intention of the parties with the object of giving to the transaction such efficiency as both parties must have intended that at all events it shall have.'

Accordingly, the circumstances in which a term will be implied are where its inclusion can be inferred from the agreement. It is sometimes referred to as the 'officious bystander' test for an implied term, because of the test laid down in *Shirlaw* v *Southern Foundries* [1939] 2 KB 206; [1940] AC 701 HL.

'Prima facie that which in any contract is left to be implied and need not be expressed is something so obvious that it goes without saying; so that, if while one of the parties were making their bargain, an officious bystander were to suggest some express provision for it in the agreement, they would testily suppress him with a common, "oh, of course".'

In that case, a company managing director was appointed for ten years. He sought to say (when facing dismissal) that the term implied that the company would not remove him from his directorship in that time and that the Articles of Association would not be altered to enable him to be removed.
The court took the view that the former would be capable of being an implied term, but that the latter would not.
The dividing line between those cases where a term may be implied is narrow and difficult to draw. A few examples illustrate the problem.

In *Luxor* v *Cooper* [1941] AC 108, a term would not be implied that an estate agent was entitled to commission where he introduced a purchaser but no sale followed because the court was not satisfied that both parties, as reasonable men, would have agreed to it if it were suggested to both of them.

In *Reigate* v *Union Manufacturing* [1918] 1 KB 592, no term would be implied that a contract of sole agency was not to be terminated by the principal prematurely ceasing to carry on business. In order for a term to be implied, it must be *necessary* to give business efficacy and not just reasonable.

In *Trollope* v *NW Metropolitan Hospital Board* [1973] 1 WLR 601, no term as to overrunning on a building contract could be implied because the court could not say which of many types of term was to be implied.

In *Shell* v *Lostock Garages* [1976] 1 WLR 1187, no term could be implied forbidding abnormal discrimination between competing purchasers of Shell petrol because the parties would not have agreed to such a term. The court indicated that it would always be reluctant to find an implied term where the parties had agreed in the form of a carefully drafted written contract.

In *Courtaulds Northern Spinning* v *Sibson* [1988] ICR 451 CA, when deciding whether a term should be implied into a contract, the courts should consider what the parties would have agreed if acting reasonably at the time the contract was made.

In *Eyre* v *Measday* and *Thake* v *Maurice* (above), the Court of Appeal in both cases refused to imply a term that an undertaking was given that the operations would be successful.

Most recently see *Chelsea Football & Athletic Co Ltd* v *S B Property Co Ltd* [1992] TLR 175 in which the question of implied terms in a sale of land arose.

In August 1982 a lease for premises, including the Stamford Bridge stadium, was granted by the company to the club, for a period of seven years. At the same time

Chelsea Football Club sold the freehold of certain of this land to SB Property. The idea was to give the property company six years to find a developer, the club having an option to purchase the land back if a developer was not found. Exactly three days before the end of the six year period, the company granted a lease of all the land to a company called Crest Homes Ltd for 210 years. Notwithstanding this fact, a week later, the club gave notice that they proposed to exercise their option to purchase the freehold. The property company challenged the validity of this move. By 1991 the property market had collapsed and Crest Homes decided it was expedient to surrender their lease, and SB conceded, contrary to their earlier arguments, that the football club had indeed validly exercised its option.

In late 1991, Chelsea Football Club began a new action, alleging that the property company's delaying tactics amounted to a breach of an implied term and that the club had suffered substantial damages as a result of this delay, because the property market had now collapsed.

It was held by the Court of Appeal that there was no indication in the lease that time was to be of the essence, and it could find no justification at all for implying a term into the contract that the parties would do nothing to prevent or delay completion.

Implied from the relationship between the parties

The classic example of this is *Liverpool City Council* v *Irwin* [1977] AC 236 HL. It was held that it was an implied term of a lease of a maisonette in a Council block that the landlord should take reasonable care to keep the common parts of the block in a reasonable state of repair. The House of Lords did not consider *The Moorcock* test to be applicable, but held that the subject matter of the lease and the relationships created by the tenancy demanded, of its nature, the contractual obligation on the landlord.

It seems that courts are reluctant to extend implications from the relationships between the parties beyond the recognised categories of such relationships.

In *Shell* v *Lostock Garages* (above), Lord Denning MR, although tempted to do so, did not find that solus agreements, that is, agreements for the sole distribution of petrol, although increasingly common, yet fell into the category of recognised relationships.

This reluctance by the courts is manifested in *Harvela Investments Ltd* v *Royal Trust Company of Canada* [1984] 3 WLR 1280 CA; [1985] 1 All ER 261 HL.

The vendors of shares put them up for sale to two competing bidders, the plaintiffs and defendants. The notice of sale was made by telex, and expressed itself to be open for a specified period. The vendors bound themselves to sell to the higher of the two bidders, and reserved no right to choose between unequal bids. The defendants sent in an undisclosed bid, to be opened immediately before the period for making a bid expired. When opened, it proved to be made in terms that the defendants' bid fell into two parts: (1) a fixed bid of a specified sum, and (2) a bid to be calculated by reference to the bid made by the plaintiffs and expressed to be 101,000 Canadian dollars in excess of such bid. The defendants elected to make whichever bid should be higher of the two alternatives. Such a method of bidding is termed 'referential'. The plaintiffs, suing to prevent sale to the defendants, argued: (1) the telex was a mere invitation to treat, and (2) a term should be implied into this telex, if it was indeed an offer, to the effect that referential bidding was impermissible. The House of Lords found for the plaintiffs, but the greater consideration of implication of terms appears in the judgment of the Court of Appeal, which seems unaffected on this point.

In his judgment, Waller LJ distinguished the facts before him from those in *Liverpool City Council* v *Irwin* (above), which concerned a widespread group, namely landlords and tenants of high-rise flats. Here the case concerned a very small group, namely those vendors who have bound themselves to accept the highest bid and who have not in their offer excluded referential bids. Waller LJ said:

> 'If one considers the position of the reasonable man receiving this offer, would he immediately think that a referential bid would not be allowed? If not are there any other compelling reasons for implying such a term? In my judgment there are not.'

The House of Lords concluded that the parties had by their agreement forbidden referential bidding, thus the 'relationship' basis of implication was unnecessary.

In *Wettern Electric Ltd* v *Welsh Development Agency* [1983] 2 All ER 629, the main issue was whether the licence for the occupation of a factory which had been granted to the plaintiffs included an implied term that the factory was of sound construction and reasonably suitable for the purposes required by the plaintiffs. The court found that although there was no principle that the term was to be implied in licences of land, that is, the legal relationship did not demand it, the term could be implied under *The Moorcock* principle to give business efficacy to the contract.

Thompson v *ASDA-MFI Group plc* [1988] 1 WLR 1093 High Court. Share option scheme – sale of company. In 1981, the defendants established a savings-related share option scheme for the benefit of employees and their subsidiaries' employees. The plaintiff, employed by a subsidiary, accepted options to subscribe for shares. In 1985, the defendants sold the subsidiary and informed the plaintiff that his options had therefore lapsed. The scheme rules provided, inter alia, that options could only be exercised by employees (para (a)) and that an option would lapse if the holder ceased to be an employee (para (d)). However, the plaintiff contended that the defendants could not rely on their own acts to defeat his rights.

HELD: the rules took effect and the plaintiff's claim that his opinions had been wrongfully repudiated could not succeed.

Scott J:

> 'Whatever doubt there might previously have been ... the law is now, in my judgement, as stated by Lord Diplock in *Cheall* v *Association of Professional, Executive, Clerical and Computer Staff* [1983] 1 All ER 1130 at 1135. In order to attract the principle that a party is not entitled to rely on his own acts as fulfilling a condition subsequent and bringing a contract to an end, the act must be a breach of duty and (per Lord Diplock):

"...the duty must be one that is owed to the other party under that contract; breach of a duty whether contractual or non-contractual owed to a stranger to the contract does not suffice."

The principle expressed by Lord Watson in *Mackay* v *Dick* (1881) 6 App Cas 251 at 270 is not, in my view, a principle of English law. The fictional fulfilment of conditions precedent and the fictional non-fulfilment of conditions subsequent may be principles of the civil law; but they are not principles of English law. In this area of the law of contract English law proceeds, in my view, by means of implied terms. If a term can be implied that a party will not do an act that, if done, would prevent the fulfilment of a condition precedent, then the doing of that act will be a breach of contract; if a term can be implied that a party will not do an act that, if done, would cause a condition subsequent to be fulfilled, then the doing of that act will be a breach of contract. But if a suitable term cannot be implied into the contract then in my judgement, the contract will take effect according to its tenor. The condition precedent will fail and the condition subsequent will be fulfilled.

In the present case, ASDA was entitled to sell its shareholding in [the subsiduary]. The sale did not represent any breach of duty owed to the plaintiff. Nor, for that matter, was the sale wrongful in any other sense. A term to the effect that ASDA would not sell its [subsiduary] shares cannot be implied into the rules. So the rules take effect as they stand.

Paragraphs (a) and (b) ... represent conditions subsequent. The condition in each paragraph was fulfilled as a consequence of the sale of the [subsiduary] shares. Under para (a) the rights under the options ceased to be exercisable. Under para (d) the options lapsed. The conditions were fulfilled by acts of ASDA. That, in my judgement is immaterial because the acts did not represent any breach of the duty owed by ASDA to the plaintiff. In my judgement this action fails and must be dismissed.'

In *Alghussein Establishment* v *Eton College* [1988] 1 WLR 587, it was held that there is an implied term in every contract that neither party is entitled to take advantage of his own breach as against the other party unless there is an express agreement to the contrary.

In employment relationships, the implication of terms is less uncommon. In *Sterling* v *Patchett* [1955] AC 534, it was an implied term in a contract of employment that the employee, who had invented certain processes, was the trustee of his inventions for his employers.

In *Lister* v *Romford Ice and Cold Storage Co* [1957] AC 555, the implied duty of care and skill which an employee owed his employer meant that the employee who had negligently injured a fellow employee, for whom the employer was vicariously liable, was himself liable for the damages which the employer had been obliged to pay to the fellow employee. The employee, in turn, argued that the contract of employment implied a promise to indemnify him from such liability. The House of Lords held by a majority that no such term could be implied.

6.9 Terms implied by custom

Terms may be implied by custom or usage of a particular trade or business, market or locality. The custom must be invariable and certain. A contract may be construed as incorporating a relevant custom unless it is inconsistent with the terms of that contract.

Examples of terms implied by custom or usage are:

Hutton v *Warren* (1836) 1 M & W 466. A tenant established a right to a reasonable allowance for labour expended on the land, even though the lease did not contain a term to this effect.

Lord Eldon v *Hedley Brothers* [1935] 2 KB 1. The usage of a particular trade, the hay trade, was implied into a contract, to vary what would otherwise have been the time property in the goods passed. Section 18 Sale of Goods Act 1979 provides that when goods are subject to being weighed or measured to determine the price, property does not pass until that act is done. The usage in the trade, however, was that when hay was bought in the particular manner relevant in this case, property passed at the time the contract was made, and a term to this effect should be implied into the contract.

British Crane Hire v *Ipswich Plant Hire* [1975] QB 303. The owner of a crane hired it to a contractor who was engaged in the same business. It was held that the owner's terms, which were usual in the business, were binding on the hirer although they had not actually been communicated at the time of hiring. There was, in the view of the Court of Appeal, a 'common understanding' that these terms applied.

Terms of collective agreements between trade unions and employers may be incorporated into individual employees' contracts by implication. The most common basis for such implication will be that the terms of the collective agreement are uniformly observed for the group of workers of which the employee is a member.

Sagar v *Ridehalgh* [1931] 1 Ch 310 and *Donelan* v *Kerby Construction* [1983] IRLR 19. A custom or usage cannot be incorporated into a contract if it is expressly or impliedly excluded by the terms of the contract. Nor can it be incorporated if it is inconsistent with the tenor of the contract as a whole. See also *London Export Corp* v *Jubilee Coffee Roasting* [1958] 1 WLR 661.

6.10   Terms implied by statute

Sale of goods

Certain terms are implied in contracts for the sale of goods. These terms were originally implied by the common law, but they were codified in the Sale of Goods Act 1893, and are now re-enacted (with amendments) in ss12–15 Sale of Goods Act 1979.

Implied terms about title
Section 12 implies a *condition* on the part of the seller that he has the right to sell the goods and a warranty of freedom from encumbrance and quiet possession.

Sale by description

Section 12 implies a *condition* that, where goods are sold by description, the goods will correspond with the description.

Implied terms about quality

Section 14(2) provides that where the seller sells goods in the course of a business there is an implied *condition* that the goods are of merchantable quality, except where the defects were specifically drawn to the buyer's attention, or, where the buyer examined the goods before the contract was made, regarding defects which that examination ought to have revealed.

'Merchantable quality' is defined in s14(6) as being:

> ' ... as fit for the purpose or purposes for which goods of that kind are commonly bought as it is reasonable to expect having regard to any description applied to them, the price (if relevant) and all the other relevant circumstances'.

Implied terms about fitness

Section 14(3) provides that where the seller sells goods in the course of a business and the buyer makes known to the seller (expressly or by implication) any particular purpose for which the goods are being bought, there is an implied *condition* that the goods are reasonably fit for that purposes.

Subsections 14(2) and 14(3) overlap to some extent. Both the definition of 'merchantable quality' and s14(3) refer to 'fitness for purpose'. But if the buyer requires the goods for some particular purpose, he must make this known to the seller.

Sale by sample

Section 15 provides that in the case of a contract for sale by sample, there is an implied *condition* that the bulk will correspond with the sample in quality, that the buyer will have a reasonable opportunity of comparing the bulk with the sample, and that the goods will be free from any defect rendering them unmerchantable, not apparent on reasonable examination of the sample ('unmerchantable' is construed in accordance with s14(6) above).

Implied terms under the Sale of Goods Act 1979 are considered again, and in more detail, in Chapter 20. They are dealt with here, in outline, as some knowledge of these implied terms is required for an understanding of the Unfair Contract Terms Act 1977 which is dealt with in Chapter 8.

Contracts of hire purchase

Certain terms are implied into all contracts of hire purchase by ss8–11 Supply of Goods (Implied terms) Act 1973. They relate similarly to title, description, quality, fitness for purpose and sample and correspond very closely to the implied terms in contracts for the sale of goods.

Supply of goods and services

The Supply of Goods and Services Act 1982 implies certain terms into contracts for the supply of goods and services which, prior to this Act, were outside the realm of a statute, but were to some extent governed by the common law.

Part I of the Act deals with contracts for the transfer of property in goods, other than contracts for the sale of goods and hire purchase agreements, and contracts for the hire of goods. There are provisions corresponding to those in the Sale of Goods Act 1979. Thus in the 1982 Act for contracts for the transfer of property in goods, there are implied terms: about title, s2; where transfer is by description, s3; about quality or fitness, s4; where transfer is by sample, s5. And in contracts for the hire of goods, there are, similarly, implied terms: title, s7; description, s8; quality or fitness, s9; sample, s10.

Part II of the Act is concerned with the supply of services and represents an attempt to put into statutory form basic obligations owed by those who provide services. Because of the wide range of services provided to the public, no attempt is made to define a contract for the supply of a service except in the most general terms as 'a contract under which a person ('the supplier') agrees to carry out a service' (s12(1)). Contracts of employment and apprenticeship are specifically excluded.

The basic obligations are those relating to care and skill, time for performance and consideration. In respect of these obligations, certain terms are implied. The Act does not specify whether they are conditions or warranties.

Care and skill

Section 13 provides that in a contract for the supply of a service, where the supplier is acting in the course of a business, there is an implied term that the supplier will carry out the service with reasonable skill and care.

The obligation implied in this section merely restates the law as has been enunciated in many cases. See, for example, *Samuels* v *Davis* [1943] 1 KB 526 (repair of dentures) and *Greaves* v *Baynham Meikle* [1975] 1 WLR 1095 (design of a building).

Time for performance

Section 14 provides, where the supplier is acting in the course of a business, that where the time for the carrying out of the service is not fixed by the contract or by the course of dealing between the parties, there is an implied term that the supplier will carry out the service in a reasonable time. What is a reasonable time is a question of fact.

This section again merely codifies the common law. See *Rickards* v *Oppenheim* [1950] 1 KB 616.

Consideration

Section 15 provides that if the price for the service is not fixed by contract or determined by the course of dealing, the party contracting with the supplier will pay a reasonable charge. What is a reasonable charge is a question of fact.

This section does *not* enable an aggrieved party to re-open the contract if the price, though excessive, is one to which he has agreed.

7

Misrepresentation

7.1 Introduction

It is important to see this topic in its historical perspective, because it is still a developing area of contract law; most of the major changes took place in the 1960s. It is necessary to remember that two major events took place then; the decision in *Hedley Byrne* v *Heller* (see below) in 1963, and the enactment of the Misrepresentation Act 1967. The cases which predate these two events are not necessarily irrelevant or obsolete; but it is necessary to approach warily, asking all the time: 'would this case have been decided according to the same rules, if it were to be decided today?'

Prior to the enactment of the Misrepresentation Act 1967 (hereinafter MA 1967), the victim of misrepresentation had recourse solely to the courts for rescission of contract or, if fraud could be proven, damages in the tort of deceit. We shall see that the Act of 1967 substantially improved the situation with regard to the remedies available, in addition to widening the context of what constituted a misrepresentation.

We have already seen that contractual terms form the very cornerstone of bargains. Such contractual terms define the rights and obligations of the respective parties to a contract. If a particular term is broken then, dependent on the status of that term, the remedy will lie in breach of contract. The problem which presents itself is: what, if any, remedy lies in respect of incorrect statements inducing a contract, but which are not enshrined in the contract as contractual terms? Inevitably, certain oral statements are made prior to the conclusion of a contract which, although not terms of a contract, have some bearing on whether that contract is or is not concluded. If such a statement turns out to be incorrect, it follows that serious loss could be sustained by the innocent party.

We have already seen from our examination of cases such as *Oscar Chess* v *Williams* that the courts have, on occasion, shown a marked reluctance to construe certain undertakings made prior to the contract as terms of that contract.

Development of the concept of the 'mere' representation

The courts developed the concept of the 'mere representation' – being a statement of fact past or present which, though not intended to be a term of the contract, induces the other party to enter into the contract.

At common law, the remedy for misrepresentation was the award of damages for the tort of deceit, where the misrepresentation was fraudulent. Equity developed the remedy of rescission applicable to both fraudulent and innocent misrepresentation. Whilst rescission was a useful remedy, it was subject to the various 'bars' on the right to claim the remedy (see below) and, moreover, an innocent misrepresentation did not allow the award of damages, but only enabled the injured party to recover an indemnity.

However, there have been in recent times two major developments:

1. the decision by the House of Lords in *Hedley Byrne* v *Heller* in 1963 (see below), which provided a remedy in damages for negligent misstatements at common law;
2. the reforms provided by MA 1967.

As a consequence of these developments misrepresentations can now be categorised as given below.

1. Fraudulent misrepresentations.
2. Negligent misstatements at common law.
3. Misrepresentations under s2(1) MA 1967.
4. Innocent misrepresentations.

General requirements

A representation, then, is a statement which is made by one party to the contract to the other, which, although it is not a term of the contract, nevertheless is a reason that induced that other party to enter into the contract. Note that, in certain circumstances, misrepresentation can be by conduct. If the statement is untrue it is a misrepresentation.

For the untrue statement to constitute an actionable misrepresentation it must meet the following requirements:

1. it must be one of fact, not opinion or intention or law;
2. it must have induced the contract.

We shall proceed to examine each of these requirements in turn.

7.2 The misrepresentation must be of fact

Expression of opinion

An expression of opinion, the statement of a belief, incapable of actual proof, will not allow a claim based on misrepresentation.

In *Bisset* v *Wilkinson* [1927] AC 177, the vendor whilst in the process of selling his farm which had not previously been used as a sheep farm, was asked by the plaintiff as to the number of sheep the farm could sustain. An opinion, which turned out to be incorrect, was given.

It was held that this statement was merely the honest expression of an opinion, and not a statement of fact as to the actual capacity of the farm.

However, there can be circumstances in which an opinion is construed as a statement of fact. Where the person giving the opinion was in a position to know the true facts, and it can be proved that the person concerned could not reasonably have held such a view as a result, then in this situation the person's opinion will be treated as a statement of fact.

In *Smith* v *Land and House Property Corporation* (1884) 28 Ch D 7, the plaintiff put up his hotel for sale stating that it was let to a 'most desirable tenant'. The defendants agreed to buy the hotel. The tenant was bankrupt. As a result, the defendants refused to complete the contract and were sued by the plaintiff for specific performance.

The Court of Appeal held that the plaintiff's statement was not mere opinion, but was one of fact.

There is also the view that where a layman relies on an expert's statement and uses such a statement as a positive assertion to back up his own views 'as if they were true facts' liability in misrepresentation will ensue if it turns out to be incorrect. See *Reese River Silver Mining Co Ltd* v *Smith* (1869) LR 4 HL 64.

A more recent case is *Brown* v *Raphael* [1958] Ch 636 CA. The particulars of sale of the reversion on a trust fund stated that estate duty would be payable on the death of the annuitant 'who is believed to have no aggregable estate'. The vendor's solicitors believed this to be true, but had no reasonable grounds for the belief.

It was held that as the vendor was in a stronger position than the purchaser to be able to ascertain the facts, there must be implied a further representation that the vendor had reasonable grounds for his belief. A further example of the manner in which the court may be able to imply a representation appears from the decision in *Laurence* v *Lexcourt Holdings* [1978] 2 All ER 810, in which it was held that the description of premises as offices was a representation not merely as to the physical state of the premises, but contained, by implication, a representation as to the availability of planning permission for the premises to be used as offices.

Some expressions of opinion are mere puffs. The laudatory statements made about a product by sellers or advertisers cannot, for the most part, be regarded as representations. The description of land as 'fertile and improvable' was held not to constitute a representation in *Dimmock* v *Hallett* (1866) 2 Ch App 21.

There may well be liability, however, for more precise claims, ones that purport to be supported by facts and figures. The distinction is between mere laudatory remarks and specific promises or assertions of a factual nature.

Statements or promises as to the future

Representations as to the future will not attract liability in misrepresentation. A statement as to future intention will not be regarded as binding on a person unless the statement is incorporated into a contract. The situation is different if the stated intention is not in fact held. If a person knows that his promise which has induced another to enter into a contract will not, in fact, be carried out, then he will be liable.

In *Edgington* v *Fitzmaurice* (1885) 29 Ch D 459, the directors of a company issued a prospectus inviting subscriptions for debentures stating that the issue was for investment purposes. The plaintiff advanced the money in reliance on that statement and in the erroneous belief that the debenture holders would have a charge upon the property. It transpired that the real object of the loan was to enable the directors to pay off pressing debts.

The Court of Appeal held that the plaintiff was entitled to rescind the contract on the basis of misrepresentation.

Although the statement was a promise of intent, the court held that the defendants had no intention of keeping to such intent at the time they made the statement. The defendants knew that they would not be able to keep their promise.

In recent years, this view has become more prevalent. In *Esso Petroleum* v *Mardon* [1976] QB 801, a petrol company which offered an inaccurate forecast of the probable sales of a filling station was liable in damages to a tenant who contracted with the petrol company on the basis of the forecast.

In *McNally* v *Welltrade International Ltd* [1978] IRLR 497, an employment agency was liable for misrepresentation about a prospective employee's suitability for a job he had applied for.

It seems to follow that the rigidity of the rule that statements of opinion or as to the future are never actionable, is lessening and it may be necessary to analyse anew the traditional formula. One suggestion is that the essence of the rule is not the nature of the statement but the nature of the reliance. If it is reasonable to rely on the statement, then perhaps it should be regarded as actionable.

Misrepresentation cannot be one of law

The rule is simple, the distinction between fact and law is not. If A represents that 'The existing planning permissions cover use of this building as an office', and they do not, is that a misrepresentation of law or fact? It seems that it is a representation of fact: *Laurence* v *Lexcourt Holdings* (above). Where a landlord says that he accepts liability for repairs under a lease that is a representation of fact: *Brikom Investments* v *Seaford* [1981] 1 WLR 863. A statement of foreign law is always regarded as a statement of fact: *Andre et Cie SA* v *Ets Michel Blancs* [1977] 2 Lloyd's Rep 166. In *Cooper* v *Phibbs* (1867) LR 2 HL 149, a distinction was drawn between statements as to private rights and general statements as to the law. By and large, subsequent cases such as those mentioned above have followed that pattern. So if A makes two representations:

1. all contracts which are in writing are enforceable; and
2. this contract of employment between B and C is enforceable because it is in writing.

The former cannot give rise to an action because it is a statement of law (and opinion); the latter may be actionable as it is declaratory of private rights.

Silence

Prima facie silence is not a misrepresentation. Mere non-disclosure is generally not actionable. Remember the maxim is caveat emptor – let the buyer beware. The other party has no duty to disclose problems voluntarily. Thus if one party is labouring under a misapprehension, there is no duty on the other party to correct it. See *Smith* v *Hughes* (1871) LR 6 QB 597.

There are three fundamental exceptions to this rule:

1. The representor must not misleadingly tell only part of the truth. See *Dimmock* v *Hallett* (1866) 2 Ch App 21.
2. Later events falsifying a representation must be disclosed. This includes the situation where an individual makes a false statement believing it to be true. If he subsequently discovers that he was in error, he is under a positive duty to disclose the truth. Similarly, where later events falsify an initially correct assertion, for example, *With* v *O'Flanagan* [1936] Ch 575, where a medical practice became valueless between the time of making the statement and the date of sale. It was held that the vendor should have communicated this.
3. Contracts uberrimae fidei. Certain contracts impose a duty of disclosure. These are known as contracts uberrimae fidei (contracts of the utmost good faith). The main contracts that fall within this category are contracts of insurance, family settlements and contracts where there is a fiduciary relationship. Examples of a fiduciary relationship are: solicitor and client, trustee and beneficiary, bank manager and client, inter-family agreements (though this is not a closed list) but,

apparently, not master and servant. See *Bell* v *Lever Bros* [1932] AC 161 and contrast *Sybron Corporation* v *Rochem Ltd* [1983] 2 All ER 707.

7.3 The misrepresentation must have induced the contract

Reliance

There can be no liability in respect of a falsehood which does not induce the party to enter into the contract. The best illustration of this in operation is where A makes a false statement as an inducement for B to contract, but B contracts regardless, either knowing the statement to be false, or not even being aware of the statement in the sense that it did not influence his mind.

There will be no reliance, and hence no inducement, in the following circumstances:

1. The misrepresentation did not come to the plaintiff's notice. Thus where false reports of a company's financial affairs had been published but the plaintiff had not read them. See *ex p Biggs* (1850) 28 LJ Ch 50.
2. The plaintiff relied not on the misrepresentation but on his own judgment. In *Attwood* v *Small* (1838) 6 Cl & F 232, the plaintiffs negotiated with the defendant for the sale of certain mines. The plaintiffs asked questions as to the capabilities of the property. The defendant's answer was verified by persons appointed by the plaintiffs. Six months after the sale was complete, the plaintiffs found that the defendant's statement had been inaccurate, and they sought to rescind on the ground of misrepresentation.

   The court held that the plaintiffs could not rescind the contract since they had not been induced to contract by the defendant's statement, but rather by their own engineer's report.

   It must be stressed that this rule applies in cases of innocent (and probably negligent) misrepresentation, but not where the misrepresentation was fraudulent. See *Pearson* v *Dublin Corporation* [1907] AC 351.

   If, however, a plaintiff has been induced to enter into a contract by a misrepresentation, it is no answer to say that he had been afforded the means of verifying it. Thus in *Redgrave* v *Hurd* (1881) 20 Ch D 1, a party was induced to purchase a solicitor's house and practice by innocent misrepresentations as to the value of the practice. He was allowed rescission even though the books and papers which he had been invited to examine, and did not, would have revealed the falsity of the representations.

   In *Central Railway Co of Venezuela* v *Kirsch* (1867) LR 2 HL 99, the defendants issued a prospectus which contained representations which were untrue and deceptive. The plaintiffs were given the opportunity of inspecting certain reports and plans which supplied the correct data. It was held that it is not sufficient to mitigate a falsehood by giving the victim a chance to verify the statement from plans and documents. What would be the position if the plaintiffs checked the plans and documents (which contained the true position), and concluded that such inspection verified the statement made initially? Presumably the result would have been different.

It is not necessary for the plaintiff to show that the misrepresentation was the only inducement for him to enter into the contract. In *Edgington* v *Fitzmaurice* (above), there were two inducing factors. One was the statement of intent, where no such intention was held, the other was the plaintiff's own erroneous belief as to the security afforded by the debentures. The fact that the plaintiff could not rely on the latter did not disentitle him to relief.

The question of reliance was considered by the Court of Appeal in the context of a claim in tort based on negligence in *JEB Fasteners* v *Marks, Bloom & Co* [1983] 1 All ER 583. The plaintiffs wished to take over a company with the principal object of acquiring the services of the two directors. During the period of negotiations, the defendants produced some audited accounts. The figures in the accounts were inaccurate. The plaintiffs were aware that there was inaccuracy, but were not aware of the extent of the inaccuracy. The take-over was unsuccessful, and the plaintiffs sustained considerable loss as a result. The trial judge found that the plaintiffs did 'rely on' the accounts in the sense that they had studied the accounts before the take-over, and the picture presented by the accounts encouraged them to continue with the take-over. However, the judge found that because the motive for the take-over was to obtain the services of the company's two directors and the plaintiffs had formed their own view of the value of the company's stock, the plaintiffs would have proceeded in any event. There was an appeal on the ground that this approach was illogical.

The Court of Appeal upheld the judgment on the grounds that there was sufficient evidence to support the finding that there had been no 'true reliance'.

Stephenson LJ said that in the context of negligent misrepresentation, the false representation had to play a real and substantial, although not necessarily decisive, part in inducing the plaintiff to act.

Materiality

Treitel argues that a misrepresentation has no effect unless it is material. He says (the *Law of Contract*):

> 'That is, it must be one that would affect the judgment of a reasonable man in deciding whether, or on what terms, to enter into the contract; or one that would induce him to enter into the contract without making such enquiries as he otherwise would make.'

Chitty (25th edn para 407) states that there is no clear authority denying relief to a representee who has, in fact, been influenced by a representation which would not have influenced a reasonable man, and submits that where the representor knows or ought to know that the statement will be acted upon, the representee ought not to be denied relief. See also *Museprime Properties Ltd* v *Adhill Properties Ltd* [1990] 36 EG 114.

7.4 Fraudulent misrepresentation

Once misrepresentation has been established, it is necessary to direct the enquiry into the nature of the misrepresentation. A misrepresentation is fraudulent in the three instances set out by Lord Herschell in *Derry* v *Peek* (1889) 14 App Cas 337, where it is made with knowledge of its falsity, or without belief in its truth, or recklessly not caring whether it is true or false.

The victim of a fraudulent misrepresentation has the following courses of action open to him as listed below.

1. He may affirm the contract and claim damages for the tort of deceit.
2. He may rescind the contract and claim damages as aforesaid.
3. He may plead fraud as a defence to an action against him for breach of contract.

The remedies of rescission and for damages will be discussed further below.

Certain points should be noted in connection with fraudulent misrepresentation. The onus probandi is on the plaintiff – he who asserts fraud must prove it. Tactically, it may be difficult to prove fraud, in the light of Lord Herschell's requirements. Fraud carries with it moral obloquy. A defendant is, therefore, more likely to contest an allegation of fraud than of negligence. Protracted and expensive litigation may consequently ensue, making a compromise settlement unlikely.

7.5 Negligent misstatements at common law

An important development in the common law was initiated by the decision of the House of Lords in *Hedley Byrne* v *Heller* [1964] AC 465. The plaintiffs in this action had suffered loss by extending credit to a certain firm. They had been induced to do so by a reference, carelessly given by that firm's bank, which, in effect, vouched for the firm's creditworthiness. The bank escaped liability because of a disclaimer clause – the reference was stated to have been given 'without responsibility'. But the House of Lords made it clear that, without this clause, the bank would have owed a duty to the plaintiffs.

The importance of this case lies in its recognition that the duty arises not only in situations of fiduciary and contractual relationships, but also in situations where there is a 'special relationship' between the parties. This special relationship will arise where the representor has (or purports to have) some special skill or knowledge, and knows (or should know) that the representee will rely on the representation.

The main impact of the case for the law of contract was the clear emergence of the category of negligent misrepresentation for which a remedy lay in damages. But this has been somewhat overtaken by the enactment of MA 1967.

7.6 Representations under the Misrepresentation Act 1967

Section 2(1) of the Act provides:

> 'Where a person has entered into a contract after a misrepresentation has been made to him by another party thereto and as a result thereof he has suffered loss, then, if the person making the misrepresentation would be liable to damages in respect thereof had the misrepresentation been made fraudulently, that person shall be so liable notwithstanding that the misrepresentation was not made fraudulently unless he proves that he had reasonable ground to believe and did believe up to the time the contract was made that the facts represented were true.'

This section requires analysis.

It is clear that where the representation had induced the contract, there is no need to prove a 'special relationship'. See *Howard Marine* v *Ogden* [1978] QB 574.

It reverses the burden of proof. Once the representee has proved that there has been a misrepresentation which induced him to enter into the contract, the onus is on the representor to prove both his belief in the truth of the representation and reasonable ground for his belief.

Section 2(1) also applies where the representation is made by an agent on behalf of the contracting party (see *Gosling* v *Anderson* (1972) 223 EG 1743), but the agent is not personally liable (see *The Skopas* [1983] 2 All ER 1).

The effect of s2(1) was considered by the Court of Appeal in *Howard Marine* v *Ogden* (above). The defendants wished to hire two barges from the plaintiffs. The plaintiffs quoted a price for the hire in a letter which made no mention of the carrying capacity in weight of the barges. During subsequent negotiations, in response to a query, the plaintiffs' representative gave a figure for the carrying capacity, which though an honest answer was incorrect. The figure was given on the basis of the representative's recollection of the figure given in Lloyd's Register. The correct figure appeared in shipping documents which the representative had seen, but had forgotten. Because of their limited carrying capacity, the defendant's work was held up. They refused to pay the hire charges. The plaintiffs sued for the hire charges and the defendants counter-claimed damages. By a majority, the Court of Appeal found the plaintiffs liable under s2(1).

Lord Denning MR (dissenting) held that:

1. there was no collateral warranty;
2. there was nothing giving rise to a duty of care which would make the plaintiffs liable for negligent misstatement at common law;
3. the plaintiffs had discharged the burden of proof imposed by s2(1).

Bridge and Shaw LJJ held that there was no collateral warranty, but held the plaintiffs liable under s2(1) as the evidence adduced by the plaintiffs was not sufficient to show that their representative had an objectively reasonable ground for disregarding the carrying capacity figure given in the shipping document and preferring the figure in Lloyd's Register. Shaw LJ also held that the plaintiffs were liable for breach of their common law duty of care in making the representation. Bridge LJ expressed doubts on this point.

The recent case of *Gran Gelato Ltd* v *Richcliff Group Ltd* [1992] 1 All ER 865 makes it clear that as a general principle the defence of contributory negligence may be available in cases of negligent misrepresentation.

Section 2(2) of the Act provides that where the representee is entitled to rescission the court may, if it considers it equitable to do so, award damages in lieu of rescission. The court will consider the nature of the representation, the loss that would be caused if the contract were upheld, and the loss that would be caused to the representor if rescission were granted. Damages may be awarded under s2(2) whether or not the representor is liable under s2(1), but any award under s2(2) shall be taken into account in assessing the representor's liability under s2(1). This somewhat convoluted provision is contained in s2(3).

7.7 Innocent misrepresentation

The Act has only to a limited extent altered the position with regard to innocent misrepresentation, that is, where the representor has discharged the burden of proof imposed by s2(1).

Prior to the Act, the only remedy available for innocent misrepresentation was rescission, which as we shall see may be a doubtful remedy. Damages were not obtainable, but Equity devised a measure of compensation, known as indemnity compensation, for loss directly attributable to innocent misrepresentation. The difference between indemnities and damages is illustrated by the case of *Whittington* v *Seale-Hayne* (1900) 82 LT 49. The plaintiffs, poultry breeders, were induced to enter into a lease of property belonging to the defendants by an oral representation that the premises were in a sanitary condition. The lease that was later executed did not contain this representation, which was not, therefore, a term of the contract. The premises were, in fact, insanitary. The terms of the lease required the plaintiffs to pay rent to the defendants and rates to the local authority, and they were also obliged to effect certain repairs to the premises. The plaintiffs could recover these expenses as they were bound under the lease to make these payments. They could not recover removal expenses and consequential loss as these did not arise from obligations imposed by the lease.

MA 1967 allows by s2(2) damages in lieu of rescission, but this modification of the law is subject to certain limitations:

1. it is within the discretion of the court;
2. the award of damages is in lieu of rescission; a plaintiff cannot rescind and be awarded damages for innocent misrepresentation, whereas he can be entitled to both remedies for fraudulent or negligent misrepresentation;
3. it is not yet clear what the measure of damages is under s2(2).

7.8 Remedies

Damages

For fraudulent misrepresentation, the measure of damages is tortious; in tort the purpose of an award of damages is to put the injured party in the position he would have been in if the wrong had not been committed. The contractual measure is designed to put such party in the position he would have been in if the contract had been performed, that is, if the promise were true.

Normally, in tort actions, an award of damages is limited by the test of remoteness, that is, the defendant will be liable only for damages that were reasonably foreseeable.

In *Doyle* v *Olby (Ironmongers) Ltd* [1969] 2 QB 158, however, Lord Denning MR said that:

> 'The defendant is bound to make reparation for all the actual damage directly flowing from the fraudulent inducement ... It does not lie in the mouth of the fraudulent person to say that they could not have been reasonably foreseen.'

In the recent case of *East* v *Maurer* [1991] 2 All ER 733 the Court of Appeal stated that the 'reparation for all actual damage' as indicated by Denning in *Doyle* v *Olby* would include loss of profits. The assessment of loss of profits was, however, to be made on a tortious basis, that is, placing the plaintiff in the same position he would have been in, had the wrong not been committed. The result is that damages for loss of profits caused by a fraudulent misrepresentation must be based on the level of profits that might have been expected, had the false misrepresentation not been made, rather than on the basis of a contractual warranty that a particular state of affairs should continue. The overall effect of such an approach may well result in the amount of damages to be awarded for loss of profits being reduced. This case should also be considered in the light of *Royscot* v *Rogerson* (see page 126).

There is a conflict of views as to whether or not exemplary damages can be awarded for the tort of deceit. This question was raised, but not decided, in *Archer* v *Brown* [1984] 2 All ER 267 where the court held, however, that the plaintiff was entitled to aggravated damages for the distress he had suffered.

For negligent misrepresentation at common law the measure of damages is in tort, the normal rule applies that the loss must be reasonably foreseeable. See *Esso Petroleum* v *Mardon* [1976] QB 801.

The measure of damages under s2(1) MA 1967 is not made entirely clear by the wording of the subsection. The language employed suggests that a tortious measure was envisaged. However, in *Watts* v *Spence* [1976] Ch 165, the court gave damages for loss of bargain under s2(1), that is, the contractual measure. That decision was not followed in *Sharneyford Supplies* v *Edge* [1985] 1 All ER 976, where the matter was fully considered by Mervyn Davies J, who decided that the tortious measure was the correct one to apply. (The actual decision of Mervyn Davies J was reversed by the Court of Appeal – [1987] 1 All ER 588 – but not on this point.)

In *Royscott Trust Ltd* v *Rogerson* [1991] 3 WLR 57 it was held that the tortious measure of damages was the true one. In that case a car dealer agreed to sell a car on HP to a customer for a cash price of £7,600, of which the customer was to pay a deposit of £1,200. These amounts were mistakenly stated as £8,000 and £1,600 respectively to the finance company and all future transactions were based on these figures.

The customer paid part of the sum due to the finance company, but in 1987 he dishonestly sold the car; and later ceased to make any payments. The amount unpaid by that time was, the finance company claimed, £3,625. They based this figure on the difference between the amount repaid to them by the customer and the amount £6,400 which they had advanced to the car dealer. The figures supplied to the finance company, however, had been mistakenly set too high, and the finance company sued the car dealer for innocent misrepresentation and claimed damages under s2(1) Misrepresentation Act 1967.

The Court of Appeal held that the measure of damages recoverable under s2(1) MA 1967 was a tortious rather than contractual one. The finance company was entitled to recover damages in respect of all losses occurring as a natural consequence, including unforeseeable losses, subject to the normal rules on remoteness. It was in any event a foreseeable event that a customer buying a car on HP might dishonestly sell the car. The act by the customer was not a novus actus, the chain of causation was unbroken. The car dealers were liable for innocent misrepresentation and the finance company could claim the £3,625 plus interest.

There is considerable uncertainty as to the measure to be applied when damages are awarded in lieu of rescission under s2(2) MA 1967. Both Treitel (6th edn p277) and Chitty (25th edn para 436) are of the view that damages under s2(2) may be lower than the damages awarded under s2(1). Chitty suggests the possibility of a special measure to compensate the representee for the loss of his right to rescind. In Cheshire and Fifoot (11th edn pp286–7), the view is expressed that compensation should be limited to an indemnity.

Rescission

Rescission is available for any of the categories of misrepresentation. A contract can be rescinded by giving notice to the representor, but this is not always necessary. In *Car and Universal Finance* v *Caldwell* [1965] 1 QB 525, the owner of a car was induced by fraud to sell his car to a rogue, who disappeared and could not be traced. On discovering the fraud, the owner notified the police and the Automobile Association. These actions were held sufficient to rescind the contract, so that an innocent third party who had bought the car from the rogue acquired no title to it.

It has recently been established that it is not necessary to prove conclusively that reliance was placed on a misrepresentation, if it is conceded by all parties that misrepresentation has in fact taken place.

In *Museprime Properties Ltd* v *Adhill Properties Ltd* [1990] 36 EG 114, a sale by auction of three properties, the particulars wrongly represented the rents from the properties as being open to negotiation. The statements in the auction particulars and made later by the auctioneer himself misrepresented the position with regard to rent reviews. In fact, on two of the three properties, rent reviews had been triggered and new rents agreed.

The plaintiff company successfully bid for the three properties – commercial and residential premises in Finchley – and discovered the true situation. They commenced an action for rescission. The defendant company countered with the defence that the misrepresentations were not such as to induce any reasonable person to enter into a contract.

HELD: the plaintiffs had established and, indeed, the defendants conceded, that misrepresentation had occurred. Any material misrepresentation is a ground for rescission.

The judge referred, with approval, to the view of Goff and Jones: *Law of Restitution*, that the question whether representations would have induced a reasonable person to enter into a contract was relevant only to the onus of proof. Here the plaintiffs had established their claim to rescission of the contract on the ground of material misrepresentation. Reliance was, therefore, of no further relevance. The plaintiffs were awarded return of their deposit and damages in respect of lost conveyancing expenses.

Limits to rescission

There are several bars, or limits, to the right to rescind for misrepresentation.

If the representee has affirmed the contract
Long v *Lloyd* [1958] 1 WLR 753.

In *Peyman* v *Lanjani* [1985] Ch 457, the Court of Appeal held that the plaintiff had not lost his right to rescind because, knowing of the facts which afforded this right, he proceeded with the contract, unless he also knew of the right to rescind. The plaintiff here did not know he had such right. As he did not know he had such right, he could not be said to have elected to affirm the contract.

See also *Production Technology Consultants* v *Bartlett* [1988] 25 EG 121, in which the plaintiff bought a freehold house which had been divided into four flats from the defendant at an auction. The particulars supplied at the auction innocently failed to say that one of the flats was let on a 99 year lease. Before completion, the lease was sent to the plaintiff's solicitors, but without waiting, the plaintiff completed the transaction, then sued for damages under s2(1) of the MA 1967.

While, at first instance, the court held that by completing he had exhausted his remedies, on appeal the CA held that the plaintiff, while having lost his right to rescind, still retained the right to sue for damages.

Note that the point at which the existence of the 99 year lease became known to the solicitors became the point at which constructively knowledge was imputed to the plaintiff; his decision to complete was assumed to be affirmation and his right to rescind lost.

This case demonstrates, however, the courts' right to award damages in lieu, even when the right to rescind is lost for some reason.

If the representee has not acted within a reasonable time
See *Leaf* v *International Galleries* [1950] 2 KB 86. However, this may not be a bar in the case of fraudulent misrepresentation. See *Armstrong* v *Jackson* [1917] 2 KB 822.

If restitution is impossible
See *Clarke* v *Dickson* (1858) EB & B 148 and *Erlanger* v *New Sombrero Phosphate Co* (1878) 3 App Cas 1218.

If third parties have acquired rights in the subject matter of the contract
Phillips v *Brooks* [1919] 2 KB 243.

Two previous bars to rescission have been removed by MA 1967. Prior to the Act, it was doubtful whether the right to rescind for innocent misrepresentation survived if the misrepresentation had become a term of the contract. Section 1(a) now provides that a person shall be entitled to rescind notwithstanding that the misrepresentation has become a term of the contract if he would otherwise have been so entitled without alleging fraud.

Before the Act, there were decisions to the effect that certain contracts could not be rescinded for innocent misrepresentation after they had been 'executed', for example, contracts for the disposition of an interest in land and the sale of shares. This has now been reversed by s1(b).

7.9 Misrepresentation and exclusion clauses

Section 3 MA 1967 as amended by s8 Unfair Contract Terms Act 1977 provides that:

> 'If a contract contains a term which would exclude or restrict:
> a) any liability to which a party to a contract may be subject by reason of any misrepresentation made by him before the contract was made; or
> b) any remedy available to another party to the contract by reason of such a misrepresentation,
> that term shall be of no effect except insofar as it satisfies the requirement of reasonableness as stated in s11(1) of the Unfair Contract Terms Act 1977; and it is for those claiming that the term satisfies that requirement to show that it does.'

The requirement of reasonableness will be considered in the ensuing chapter on exclusion clauses.

There is one point to observe at this juncture. It may be difficult to draw a distinction between a clause excluding liability and one defining the authority of, for example, an agent. See *Overbrooke Estates* v *Glencombe Properties* [1974] 1 WLR 1335, in which it was held that a provision in the particulars of sale did not constitute an exclusion clause but a limitation on the apparent authority of the auctioneers.

8

Exclusion Clauses

8.1 Introduction

8.2 Notice by display

8.3 Notice in a document

8.4 Notice by a course of dealing

8.5 Signature

8.6 Avoiding or qualifying the clause

8.7 Interpreting the clause

8.8 The Unfair Contract Terms Act 1977

8.1 Introduction

An exclusion or exemption clause is one which purports to exclude wholly, or in part, liability for certain breaches of contract or for the happening of certain events. If the exclusion is only partial, then the clause may be called a 'limitation of liability clause'.

The whole area of exclusion and limitation clauses is a constantly developing one, and also one in which it is well to be aware of the historical background, in order to put the modern law in true perspective.

It should be recalled that the law in the nineteenth and early twentieth centuries was based on the dual concepts of 'laissez faire' and the doctrine of freedom of contract. With the Industrial Revolution and the growth of large, often monopolistic, businesses, came the standard form contract. No longer were parties on an equal footing, free to negotiate such terms as they wished. Often the new, large industries would not agree to do business except using these standardised contract forms. Worse, exclusion or limitation clauses were often inserted into such standard form contracts to exempt them from liabilities to which they would otherwise be bound. The unfortunate individual consumer, when faced with this 'take it or leave it' attitude, had no option but to accept the standard form contract, exclusion clause(s) and all, no matter how unsatisfactory that might be.

Initially, the courts' attachment to the doctrine of freedom of contract meant that they did not see it as a part of their function to interfere, even when an exclusion clause was patently unfair, and imposed oppressively on a party with unequal bargaining power. One can see this attitude as late as the 1930s, reflected in cases like *Thompson* v *LMS Railway* [1930] 1 KB 41 (see below).

When, eventually, the courts began to realise the undesirability of allowing exclusion clauses to be operated with no real controls at all, they initially tried to limit the effect by a series of interpretative rules. It is interesting to see how, manipulating such rules, judicial attitudes have hardened over the last century. Such rules included the 'contra proferentem' rule, and the basic requirement that an exclusion clause should be clear and unambiguous to be effective.

Also, the doctrine of 'fundamental breach' developed and was in its prime in the decade 1970–80. This concept (that once a contract had been brought to an end by a fundamental breach any exclusion clauses would no longer apply), was probably always an unsafe theory and, in 1980, in *Photo Production* v *Securicor Transport* (see below), the House of Lords overruled earlier cases and it was made clear that there was no real reason why, even when a fundamental breach occurred, it should not be covered by an exclusion clause, provided the clause was clear and specific.

The Unfair Contract Terms Act 1977 (UCTA) marks the beginning of the present statutory controls on exclusion clauses, although it was not by any means the first statute to bar exclusion clauses.

For example, the Misrepresentation Act 1967 gave powers to a court to bar certain types of exclusion clauses. The importance of UCTA is not only that it covers a wide range of potential clauses in different types of contract, but that it also has a real effect on the older common law rules. The provisions of common law and UCTA co-exist in many contracts. In some contracts, only parts of the Act will apply; to some contracts, UCTA does not apply at all, the contract being governed entirely by common law.

It is, therefore, necessary to be familiar with the common law as well as the statutory rules governing exclusion clauses.

At common law, in order for an exclusion clause to be binding, it must have been incorporated as a term of the contract. The courts have evolved stringent tests to check whether the relevant clause is incorporated. There are two main ways in which an exclusion clause may be incorporated: by advance notice to the other party that the exclusion is to be a term of the contract, and by the signature of the party agreeing to be bound by the exclusion clause.

When the incorporation is by virtue of notifying the other party, in advance, of its inclusion, then three situations should be noted: notice by display; notice in a document; and notice by a course of dealing.

8.2 Notice by display

Notices exhibited in premises which purport to exempt liability for loss or damage are common. For example: 'Car parked at owner's risk' in a car park, or 'The Management undertake no liability for loss or damage occasioned to customer's apparel' in a cloakroom, are instances of notices which are intended to have contractual force. Whether such clauses do have contractual force is dependent upon whether the notice is in a position where it can be seen before or at the time of entry into the contract. A leading case is *Olley* v *Marlborough Court* [1949] 1 KB 532. A husband and wife arrived at a hotel. They paid for their board and residence in advance. They went to the hotel room. A notice was displayed in the room exempting the hotel from liability for loss or damage to items left in the room. During their stay, the wife's fur coat was stolen.

HELD: the contract was made before the notice was seen, so that the contractual liability could not unilaterally be transferred back to the hotel guests. See also *Thornton* v *Shoe Lane Parking* [1971] 2 QB 163.

8.3 Notice in a document

There are five questions which should be asked:

1. Is the document contractual?
2. Has reasonably sufficient notice been given?
3. Is the clause unusual?
4. Could acceptance have been avoided?
5. When is the contractual dealing concluded?

A recent case heard in the Australian Court of Appeal provides a useful illustration of items (1)–(5) above. In *Dillon* v *Baltic Shipping Co* (*The Mikhail Lermontov*) [1991] 2 Lloyd's Rep 155 the plaintiff and her daughter booked a cruise on the 'Mikhail Lermontov' by paying a deposit. One week later they received a document headed 'Booking Form CTC Cruises'. This form contained, inter alia, the clause:

> 'Contract of Carriage for travel as set out ... will be made only at the time of issuing the tickets and will be subject to conditions and regulations printed on the tickets ...'

Having paid the balance, the plaintiff received tickets containing terms and conditions, limiting the shipping line's liability for personal injury and death. Just over a week into the cruise, the liner struck a rock and sank. The plaintiff suffered personal injury and nervous shock.

The plaintiff claimed damages for personal injuries, loss of property and loss of the enjoyment of the holiday. The defendants argued that limitation clauses, referred to on the ticket, formed part of the conditions of the contract and that they were entitled to rely on them. The court held that the statement in the initial brochure (supplied on receipt of the deposit) was insufficient to draw the attention of the customer to the fact that limitation clauses were contained in the ticket terms and conditions. The issue of a ticket with terms and conditions printed in full occurred after payment of the balance and a firm contract of carriage was already in existence. At the time the contract of carriage came into force, the plaintiff had not had a reasonable opportunity to see and agree to the conditions and terms referred to, and which the defendants sought to impose on all the passengers when tickets were delivered, which was about a month or more later.

Exclusion or limitation clauses thus referred to, on the ticket, could not be said to be incorporated into the contract and could not be relied upon.

Is the document contractual?

Where the clause is contained in a document, it is still essential that the clause is incorporated into the contract. A document proffered after the contract has been made cannot contain any terms of the contract, and so cannot be binding upon the recipient. For example, A makes an offer to B. B accepts. After he has done so, he gives A a sheet of 'Terms and conditions'. These are not part of the contract between A and B.

Even where the document which contains terms and conditions is proffered before the contract is concluded, the document must be one on which a person could reasonably expect to find 'terms and conditions'. The test is that of the expectation of 'the reasonable man'. The narrowness of the distinction between documents upon which the reasonable man would, and would not, expect to find contractual terms, can be illustrated by a comparison of the following four cases.

In *Parker v South Eastern Railway* (1877) 2 CPD 416, the plaintiff was given a ticket which read 'see back' in exchange for luggage left at a railway cloakroom. The reverse of the ticket contained exclusion clauses for loss or damage to the luggage.

HELD: the plaintiff was bound by the exclusion clause because notice of the clauses had been given, and the notice was sufficient 'in all the circumstances of the case'.

In *Chapelton v Barry UDC* [1940] 1 KB 532, deck chairs were stacked by a notice asking the public who wished to use the deck chairs to get tickets and retain them for inspection. The plaintiff paid for two tickets for chairs, but did not read them. The reverse of the ticket contained exclusion clauses from liability for personal injury. The plaintiff was injured when a deck chair collapsed.

HELD: the defendant could not rely on the exclusion clause because it was not contained in a contractual document. No one would have assumed that the ticket was anything but a receipt. Even if the ticket had been a contractual document, it was given to the plaintiff after he had accepted the offer to hire the chair.

In *McCutcheon v David MacBrayne* [1964] 1 WLR 125, exclusion clauses were contained in 27 paragraphs of small print contained inside and outside a ferry booking office and in a 'risk note' which passengers sometimes signed.

HELD: the exclusions clauses were not incorporated.

A different type of case is *Burnett* v *Westminster Bank* [1966] 1 QB 742. The plaintiff had accounts at branches A and B of the defendant bank. A new cheque book for branch A contained a notice that the cheques in the book would be applied to the account for which they had been prepared. No notice of contractual terms had been contained in previous cheque books. The plaintiff attempted to debit account B by writing on the cheque. The bank's computer failed to read the handwritten instruction, and the wrong account was debited.

HELD: the words in the cheque book were not contained in a contractual document and were therefore ineffective.

Has reasonably sufficient notice been given?

In *Parker,* the House of Lords held that the notice must be reasonably sufficient in all the circumstances of the case. This is a question of fact. The court must look at all the circumstances and the situation of the parties.

It has become almost axiomatic that where a document contains terms and conditions on its reverse, it must refer to them on the face of that document.

In *Sugar* v *London, Midland and Scottish Railway* [1941] 1 All ER 172, the words 'for conditions see back', which appeared on the face of the document, was obliterated by the date stamp.

HELD: that reasonably sufficient notice had not been given.

In *Richardson Spence & Co* v *Rowntree* [1894] AC 217, the plaintiff contracted with the defendant to be taken as a passenger on a steamer from Philadelphia to Liverpool. The fare was paid and the plaintiff received the ticket, which was folded up and in part obliterated by red ink. She knew that the ticket contained writing, but not that it contained terms.

HELD: no reasonably sufficient notice had been given.

The requirement is only that *reasonably* sufficient notice be given. It is an objective and not a subjective test. If the plaintiff has a peculiarity not common to the rest of the population, such that he does not know of the terms, he will not be protected by his ignorance if a reasonable man would have known of them.

In *Thompson* v *LMS Railway* [1930] 1 KB 41, the plaintiff was injured when she stepped off a train which had stopped before reaching the platform. Her ticket contained terms which referred to timetables which limited liability. She could not read the words on the ticket because she was illiterate.

HELD: that she was bound by the clauses limiting liability. A reasonable man would have been able to read the ticket and to know that exclusion clauses in the railway timetable could be referred to and were incorporated in the contract.

If the defendant knows of the peculiarity, the same result does not follow. In

Geier v *Kujawa* [1970] 1 Lloyd's Rep 364, a notice in English was displayed in a car to the effect that passengers travelled at their own risk. A German passenger who was known to speak no English travelled in the car.

HELD: the passenger was not bound by the term.

An interesting case which illustrates the application of the objective test occurred in *Smith* v *South Wales Switchgear* [1978] 1 All ER 18. A contractual document provided that the contract incorporated general conditions of business which were available on request. There were three editions of the general conditions, the last of which was March 1970. No copy had been requested, although the 1969 conditions had been supplied by mistake.

HELD: the 1970 version of the conditions was incorporated into the contract. It was common experience that trading conditions were revised from time to time. The meaning which could be reasonably attributed to the reference was that the conditions referred to were the current conditions.

Does it make any difference that the clause is unusual?

It seems that the more unusual or unreasonable the clause, the more difficult it may be to incorporate it into the contract at common law. This is principally an argument promoted by Lord Denning MR. He first made this observation in *Spurling* v *Bradshaw* [1956] 2 All ER 121, where he suggested that 'the more unreasonable the clause is the greater the notice which must be given of it'. He expressed like views in *Thornton* v *Shoe Lane Parking* [1971] 2 QB 163. In that case, a ticket was issued from an automatic machine in a car park. The car park premises contained a notice which was visible on approach that all cars were parked at owner's risk. The ticket, which was issued as the driver approached, emerged from the machine. He would take the ticket and drive on. The ticket contained printed wording that it was issued subject to conditions displayed inside the premises. The conditions inside the premises were in small print and very wide, and excluded liability for damage to cars and customers.

Lord Denning said that the clause was so wide and destructive of rights that, in order to be effective, it would have to have a red hand pointing to it and be printed in red ink.

Megaw LJ said that when a restriction was not usual, the defendant must show that he had fairly brought to the notice of the other party his intention to attach an unusual condition.

HELD: the plaintiff was not bound by the clauses inside the premises.

In *Interfoto Picture Library Ltd* v *Stiletto Visual Programmes Ltd* [1988] 1 All ER 348, the Court of Appeal re-affirmed the principle that where a condition in a contract was particularly onerous or unusual, and would not generally be known to the other party, the party seeking to enforce that condition had to show it had been fairly and reasonably brought to the other party's attention. Their Lordships stressed that this was a general principle of law and was not confined to exclusion clauses.

Could acceptance have been avoided?

The observances of the Court of Appeal in the *Shoe Lane* case support the proposition that if the plaintiff cannot resile from his prior intention to conclude the contract at the time when notice is given, the exclusion clause will not have been incorporated into the contract.

Have the contractual negotiations been concluded?

This is, of course, always a question of fact rather than law, but an interesting illustration of the difficulties which present themselves arose in *Levison* v *Patent Steam Carpet Cleaning Co* [1977] 3 All ER 498. The owner of a carpet requested that it be picked up and taken away for cleaning. When the cleaning company called for it, the owner was presented with a document containing exclusion clauses. He signed it. The cleaning company took away the carpet and a further rug.

HELD: that the exclusion clauses were incorporated into the contract, although they did not cover a fundamental breach. The reasoning is difficult to ascertain, although the Court of Appeal were unanimous. Lord Denning MR thought that the exclusion clauses were incorporated by a course of dealing and, in any event, the contract was not concluded until the signature of the form. Sir David Cairns and Orr LJ thought that the document would have been part of the contract even in the absence of a course of dealing. The most promising suggestion was on the basis of a novation (see below). During the telephone conversation, only a carpet had been mentioned, whereas the contract subsequently was for a rug plus a carpet. The alternative way of looking at this suggestion is to say that the telephone conversation was only an invitation to treat, but this seems artificial in the light of the detail of agreement which had been achieved. (Lord Denning's judgment on the fundamental breach question must be read in the light of *Photo Production* v *Securicor Transport Ltd* – see below.)

8.4 Notice by a course of dealing

If notice has not been given by display as in a contractual document, it may have been given by 'a course of dealing'. This situation will arise where the parties have dealt together in the past on a number of occasions such that one party can be presumed to know the terms and conditions upon which the other operates. It does not seem to matter that the party against whom the clause is used does not know in fact what those terms are, provided that he has had every opportunity to find out what they are.

In *Henry Kendall* v *William Lillico* [1968] 2 All ER 444, the parties had contracted on more than 100 occasions in the years preceding the contract which was broken. On each occasion, there was a verbal contract which was followed by a 'sold note'. The 'sold note' contained conditions. They would not have been incorporated into the first few contracts. On the other hand, the recipients knew that the notes contained conditions, but they had not read them.

HELD: their conduct in continuing to trade evinced an intention to be bound by the conditions.

In contrast with the above is *McCutcheon* v *David MacBrayne Ltd* (above). The plaintiffs' agent had dealt with the defendants on many occasions. Sometimes he had signed a 'risk note', and sometimes he had not. The risk note contained conditions. On this occasion no risk note was signed.

HELD: the plaintiffs were not bound by the conditions. There was no course of conduct because there was no consistency of dealing.

In *Hollier* v *Rambler Motors* [1972] 2 QB 71, Salmon LJ held that three or four transactions over a period of five years could not be described as 'a course of dealing'.

In *British Crane Hire* v *Ipswich Plant Hire* [1975] QB 303, the facts were that both parties were companies engaged in hiring out earth-moving equipment. The defendants needed a dragline crane urgently, and they contacted the plaintiffs by telephone. Subsequently, a printed form containing conditions arrived. In the previous year, there had been two occasions when the plaintiff contracted on those terms, with the defendant, although that was not known to the defendant's manager at the time of contracting.

HELD: the terms would be incorporated into the contract, not by a course of dealing, but because there was a common understanding between the parties, who were in the same line of business, that any contract would be on these standard terms.

If there had been some bizarre element in the terms and conditions relied upon by the plaintiff, the same result may not follow, because there could not then be a 'common understanding'. That observation would seem to follow from Sir Eric Sachs' judgment. It may not follow from that of Lord Denning MR. He thought that the mere fact that one party knew that the other would contract on conditions was sufficient regardless of what those conditions might be. He said that he:

> 'would not put it so much on the course of dealing but rather on the common understanding which is to be derived from the conduct of the parties, namely, that the hiring was to be on the terms of the plaintiff's usual conditions ... it is just as if the plaintiffs had said "We will supply it on our usual conditions" and the defendants had said "of course, this is quite understood".'

Sir Eric Sachs emphasised the distinction between the position then before him, and the position where the parties are in wholly different walks of life, as in *Hollier's* case (above) – where one, for instance, is an expert in a line of business and the other is not.

8.5 Signature

The effect of signing a written document was distinguished from the mere receipt of a notice in *Parker* v *South Eastern Railway* (above).

Mellish LJ said:

'Where an action is brought on a written agreement which is signed by the defendant the agreement is proved by proving his signature, and, in the absence of fraud it is wholly immaterial that he has not read the agreement and does not know its contents.'

This dictum was conclusively adopted in *L'Estrange* v *Graucob* [1934] 2 KB 394. The plaintiff was a café owner. She agreed to buy an automatic slot machine from the defendants. The agreement was to pay by instalments and it contained an exemption clause which the plaintiff signed. The machine was faulty and the plaintiff purported to terminate the agreement.

HELD: she could not do so because she was bound by the exclusion clause which she had signed.

Scrutton LJ observed:

'In cases in which the contract is contained in a railway ticket or other unsigned document, it is necessary to prove that an alleged party was aware, or ought to have been aware, of its terms and conditions. These cases have no application when the document has been signed. When a document containing contractual terms is signed, then, in the absence of fraud, or I will add, misrepresentation, the party signing it is bound, and it is wholly immaterial if he has read the document or not.'

8.6 Avoiding or qualifying the clause

The severity of the rule that signature will incorporate the clause can be mitigated in a number of ways.

If there has been a misrepresentation

In *Curtis* v *Chemical Cleaning and Dyeing Co* [1951] 1 KB 805, the plaintiff took a white satin wedding dress to the defendant's shop for cleaning. She was asked to sign a receipt containing an exemption clause. She asked for an explanation. She was told that it exempted liability from certain risks and, in the present instance, from the risk of damage to the beads and sequins in the dress. In fact, the clause purported to exempt liability for damage howsoever caused. The dress was stained.

HELD: because of the misrepresentation, the exemption clause could not be relied on. This has been subsequently endorsed in a number of cases, for example, *Jacques* v *Lloyd D George & Partners* [1968] 2 All ER 187.

If there is an independent oral undertaking

In *Couchman* v *Hill* [1947] KB 54 (see Chapter 6), a promise was given that a heifer was 'unserved'. This was untrue and an exemption clause excluded liability for warranties. The Court of Appeal found that the promise was nonetheless a term of the contract and, *alternatively*, that it was a collateral contract. (See 6.3.)

If the plea of 'Non est Factum' can be upheld.

(This plea 'it is not my deed' is dealt with in Chapter 10.)

If there has been fraud

Although see *Tullis* v *Jacson* [1892] 3 Ch 441. The parties to a building contract agreed that an arbitrator's decision was to be final, and was not to be set aside for any pretence, suggestion, charge or insinuation of fraud.

HELD: the award would be upheld and would not be set aside even if it had not been made in good faith.

Notably, this case dealt in terms with the question of fraud, so that the parties had clearly addressed their minds to the question of fraud. The fraud to which they had so addressed their minds was not their own fraud. This case, therefore, has no relevance to the proposition that the party cannot exclude liability for his *own* fraud. Furthermore, it is a case which has attracted some criticism, for example, that of Scrutton LJ in *Czarnikow* v *Roth, Schmidt & Co* [1922] 2 KB 478 at 488.

In *S Pearson & Son* v *Dublin Corporation* [1907] AC 351, the plaintiffs agreed to do work for the defendants. The plaintiffs had a duty to satisfy themselves that the plans were accurate.

HELD: this clause would not avail the defendants if the plans were fraudulent.

On the question of whether the parties could specifically exclude liability for their own fraud, the House of Lords made the following observations:

Lord Loreburn:

'No one can escape liability for his own fraudulent statements by inserting a clause in a contract that the other party shall not rely on them.' (He thought that a person could exclude liability for his agent's fraud, however.)

Lord Halsbury:

'No craft or machinery in the form of contract can estop a person who claims that he has been defrauded from having that question of fact submitted to a jury.'

Lord James:

'When the fraud succeeds, surely those who designed the fraudulent protection cannot take advantage of it ... As a general principle I incline to the view that an express term that fraud shall not vitiate a contract could be bad in law.'

8.7 Interpreting the clause

Where there has been a fundamental breach or a breach of a fundamental term

The first issue is the meaning of the expressions 'fundamental breach' and 'term'. A fundamental breach may be the breach of a fundamental term, but it could also be any other breach of contract which defeats the main purpose of the contract. A fundamental term (a phrase which has attracted great and, no doubt, well–deserved criticism as indistinguishable in principle from the description 'condition'), is one which is at the root of the contract so that it governs its main purpose.

Where there has been a breach of a fundamental term or a fundamental breach, it is a question of construction whether the exclusion clause is drafted sufficiently widely to apply to the breach. In *Suisse Atlantique Société d'Armament Maritime* v *Rotterdamsche Kolen Centrale* [1967] 1 AC 361, a charterparty contained a clause limiting damages to $1,000 per day for each lay-day beyond the permitted number (that is, days spent waiting in port). The number of excess days was 150. The owners claimed a greater loss.

HELD: the clause was an agreed damages clause and not an exclusion clause so that the question of fundamental breach did not arise and, even if it had, the clause would have been effective.

However, the House of Lords went on to say that as a rule of *construction* (not of law), an exemption clause should not, in the absence of clear words, be applied to breaches which tended to defeat the main purpose of the contract.

This was re-affirmed in *Photo Production* v *Securicor Transport Ltd* [1980] AC 827. The defendants agreed to provide a visiting patrol service to the plaintiffs' factory at £8 15s. per week. The contract contained an exemption clause to the effect that the defendants 'should not be responsible for any injurious act or default by any employee of the company unless such act or default could have been foreseen and avoided by the exercise of due diligence on the part of the company as his employer'. In fact, a patrolman deliberately lit a fire and the factory was substantially burnt down.

HELD: the defendants were protected by the exemption clause. The view expressed in *Harbutt's Plasticene Ltd* v *Wayne Tank and Pumps Co Ltd* [1970] 1 QB 447 that a breach of contract by one party, accepted by the other as discharging him from his further obligations under the contract, brought the contract to an end and, together with it, any exemption clause, was disapproved. The proper question was whether, as a matter of construction, the exemption clause relieved the defendants from liability. Here, there was an apportionment of the risk as between plaintiff and defendant, and the risk of arson was not accepted by the defendant.

The distinction between an exclusion clause and limitation of liability and agreed damages arose again for discussion in *Ailsa Craig Fishing* v *Malvern Fishing* [1983] 1 All ER 101. The appellants owned a boat which sank in Aberdeen Harbour. The vessel was a complete loss. The respondents were required by contract with inter alia the appellants to provide continuous security cover for the boat. The contract contained two contentious clauses and the issues were:

1. whether they were available to the respondents even though the respondents had completely failed to comply with the contract; and
2. how the clause was to be interpreted.

The court said that the clause was one which limited liability, and that the contract had to be construed as a whole to see whether the limitation of liability clause should apply to a fundamental breach. Although a limitation of liability clause had to be clearly and unambiguously expressed and construed contra proferentem, it should be given its ordinary and natural meaning. This should be construed less rigidly than an exemption clause because it would be more likely to accord with the true intention of the parties.

Note that the *Ailsa Craig Fishing* case was of particular importance with regard to limitation clauses.

While it is difficult to see just *why* limitation clauses should be construed less rigidly than an exclusion clause, the distinction has nevertheless been approved in *George Mitchell* v *Finney Lock Seeds* [1983] (see below).

See in particular Palmer (1982) 45 MLR 322, who points out that some limitation clauses are so close to zero (1.8% in *Ailsa Craig* and 0.33% in *George Mitchell* v *Finney Lock Seeds*) that they might almost be exclusion clauses anyway.

The contra proferentem rule

It has already been indicated that the clause should be construed contra proferentem, that is, against the interests of the person seeking to rely on it. Accordingly, where a clause fails to deal with a specific matter, it will not be deemed to cover that matter. A few examples will illustrate the point.

In *Lee & Son (Grantham) Ltd* v *Railway Executive* [1949] 2 All ER 581, the plaintiffs leased a warehouse from the defendants. In the lease was a clause which purported to exempt liability for loss and damage which would not have arisen but for the tenancy. The goods were damaged by a spark which gave rise to a fire.

HELD: on a construction contra proferentem, the loss did not arise from the relationship of landlord and tenant, and so the clause was not applicable to exempt liability for the loss.

In *Webster* v *Higgins* [1948] 2 All ER 127, a term in a hire-purchase contract said that no warranty, condition or description is given.

HELD: that the clause did not exempt liability for an undertaking which had already been given.

In *Wallis, Son & Wells* v *Pratt & Haynes* [1911] AC 394, a provision that a seller gave no 'warranty, express or implied' did not exclude him from liability for breach of a condition

In *Houghton* v *Trafalgar Insurance* [1954] 1 QB 247, the insurance policy excluded the insurer from liability 'whilst the car was carrying any *load* in excess of that for which it is construed'. It was held that the clause did not exclude liability where the car was carrying an excess number of passengers.

Similarly, in *Computer and Systems Engineering plc* v *John Lelliott Ltd* (1991) The Times 21 February, a standard form contract excluded liability for 'flooding or burst pipes'. Damage was caused to the plaintiff's property by a fractured sprinkler pipe.

The court interpreted the clause literally and strictly and held that the damage caused was not within the meaning of the exclusion clause. The plaintiff could claim compensation.

Exclusion clauses: enforcement by the party in breach

The recent case of *Micklefield* v *SAC Technology Ltd* [1990] IRLR 218 concerned an employment contract and was, as such, excluded from the operation of the Unfair Contract Terms Act 1977 by Schedule 1 paragraph 1 of that Act.

A company director was employed under a service agreement which, inter alia, allowed him to apply for share issues. An exclusion clause in the agreement provided that this privilege would lapse if, for any reason, he ceased to be employed by the company. He was dismissed without notice, wrongfully and in breach of contract. His employers held that since the exclusion clause said ceased to be employed 'for whatever reason', they could legitimately refuse to issue the shares applied for by the plaintiff some two weeks before he was wrongfully dismissed. The plaintiff argued that he should be permitted to recover damages for loss of the option to take up shares.

HELD: the principle that a party could not be permitted to take advantage of his own wrong was not a strict rule of law and could, in fact, be excluded. Provided the clause in question was decisive and explicit, it would be within either party's right to incorporate such a clause. The clause in question was sufficiently clear and specific, and would apply. The plaintiff was refused damages.

Negligence

The Unfair Contract Terms Act now renders clauses purporting to exclude liability for negligence largely ineffective (see below), but even where the statute does not apply, the courts have required clear words to satisfy the exclusion of liability for negligence.

Where a party can be made liable on some ground other than negligence, the clause will be construed as applying to that other ground, and not to negligence. The principle was stated by Lord Greene MR in *Alderslade* v *Hendon Laundry* [1945] KB 189 as follows:

> '... where the head of damage in respect of which limitation of liability is sought to be imposed by such a clause is one which rests on negligence and nothing else, the clause must be construed as extending to that head of damage, because if it were not so construed it would lack subject-matter. Where, on the other hand, the head of damage may be based on some ground other than that of negligence, the general principle is that the clause must be confined to loss occurring through that other cause to the exclusion of loss arising through negligence. The reason for that is that if a contracting party wishes in such a case to limit his liability in respect of negligence, he must do so in clear terms, and in the absence of such clear terms the clause is to be construed as relating to a different kind of liability and not to liability based on negligence.'

The reasoning behind this approach was made clear in *Gillespie Brothers* v *Roy Bowles Transport* [1973] QB 400, where Buckley LJ said:

'... it is inherently improbable that one party to the contract should intend to absolve the other party from the consequences of the latter's own negligence. The intention to do so must therefore be made perfectly clear for otherwise the court will conclude that the exempted party was only to be free from liability in respect of damage occasioned by causes other than negligence for which he is answerable.'

In *Smith* v *South Wales Switchgear* [1978] 1 All ER 18, the House of Lord held that a clause did not contain an *express* provision excluding liability for negligence unless it contained the word 'negligence', or some synonym for 'negligence'.

The courts have distinguished between cases where the defendant could be held liable only if he were negligent, and cases where liability could arise from some other cause. Thus in *Hollier* v *Rambler Motors* (above), the clause purported to exclude liability 'for damage caused by fire to customers' cars on the premises'. The Court of Appeal held that the clause did not apply to negligence. Fire could occur from a large variety of causes, only one of which is negligence on the part of the occupier of the premises.

This case should be compared with that of *Rutter* v *Palmer* [1922] 2 KB 87, where the clause provided that 'customers' cars are driven by our staff at customers' sole risk'. It was held that the clause excluded liability for negligence, as the garage was *only* liable where such loss was due to negligence.

8.8 The Unfair Contract Terms Act 1977

Ambit of the Act

The Act applies to contract terms and to notices which are non-contractual, and which purport to exclude or restrict liability in tort. It seeks to limit the circumstances in which terms and notices restricting or limiting liability may apply, but it does not affect the basis of liability, nor does it apply to any other 'unfair' terms. The Act, furthermore, does not affect the issues of incorporation and interpretation which must be left to the common law.

Generally, the Act can be said to cover three areas:

1. The exclusion or restriction of liability for negligence (defined in s1(1)) to apply to a contractual duty of care, a tortious duty of care and a common duty of care under the Occupiers Liability Act 1984.
2. The exclusion or restriction of liability for certain terms implied by statute into sale of goods contracts, hire purchase agreements and some other supply contracts.
3. Some contract terms which exclude or limit liability for breaches of contract, or which purport to entitle the other party to render a contractual performance substantially different from that which was reasonably expected of him.

The general effect of the Act

Where the act or omission complained of is covered by an exemption clause or limitation of liability clause, the Act may:

1. render it wholly ineffective;
2. render it effective only in so far as it may satisfy the requirement of reasonableness.

Although the Act only applies to clauses which 'exclude or restrict' liability, those words have an extended meaning. Section 13 provides:

> '(1) To the extent that this Part of this Act prevents the exclusion or restriction of any liability it also prevents:
> a) making the liability or its enforcement subject to restrictive or onerous conditions;
> b) excluding or restricting any right or remedy in respect of the liability, or subjecting a person to any prejudice in consequence of his pursuing any such right or remedy;
> c) excluding or restricting rules of evidence or procedure;
> and (to that extent) ss2 and 5 to 7 also prevent excluding or restricting liability by reference to terms and notices which exclude or restrict the relevant obligation or duty.
> (2) But an agreement in writing to submit present or future differences to arbitration is not to be treated under this Part of this Act as excluding or restricting any liability.'

Thus the Act will apply to terms: imposing a time limit for making claims, s13(1)(a); limiting a buyer's right to reject defective goods, s13(1)(b); stating that acceptance of goods shall be regarded as proof of their conformity with the contract, s13(1)(c).

Business liability and dealing as a consumer

Apart from s6 (implied terms in sales of goods and hire purchase agreements), the Act is concerned with terms which purport to exclude business liability. The person intended principally to benefit from the Act is the person who is dealing as a consumer. A distinction is drawn between a person who is dealing as a consumer, and a person who is not. Section 12 provides:

> '(1) A party to a contract "deals as consumer" in relation to another party if:
> a) he neither makes the contract in the course of a business nor holds himself out as doing so; and
> b) the other party does make the contract in the course of a business; and
> c) in the case of a contract governed by the law of sale of goods or hire purchase, or by s7 of this Act, the goods passing under or in pursuance of the contract are of a type ordinarily supplied for private use or consumption.
> (2) But on a sale by auction or by competitive tender the buyer is not in any circumstances to be regarded as dealing as consumer.
> (3) Subject to this, it is for those claiming that a party does not deal as consumer to show that he does not.'

('Business' includes a profession and government, local government, local authority or public authority activities, s14.)

The Court of Appeal has recently given consideration to the question of 'dealing as a consumer' in *R & B Customs Brokers Co Ltd* v *United Dominions Trust Ltd* [1988] 1 All

ER 847. The plaintiff company had purchased a car from the defendant company for the use of one of its directors. It was held that where a transaction was only incidental to a business activity, a degree of regularity was required before a transaction could be said to be an integral part of the business carried on and so entered into in the course of that business. Since here the car was only the second or third vehicle acquired by the plaintiffs, there was not a sufficient degree of regularity capable of establishing that the contract was anything more than part of a consumer transaction.

Negligence liability

This is set out in s2 of the Act:

> '(1) A person cannot by reference to any contract term or to a notice given to persons generally or to particular persons exclude or restrict his liability for death or personal injury resulting from negligence.
> (2) In the case of other loss or damage, a person cannot so exclude or restrict his liability for negligence except in so far as the term or notice satisfies the requirement of reasonableness.
> (3) Where a contract term or notice purports to exclude or restrict liability for negligence a person's agreement to or awareness of it is not of itself to be taken as indicating his voluntary acceptance of any risk.'

This is a section which only applies to business liability which, so far as death or personal injury resulting from negligence is concerned, can no longer be excluded or restricted. Liability for other types of negligence can be excluded or restricted, but only in so far as the contract term or notice satisfies the requirement of reasonableness within s11(1) (below).

Subsection (3) seems to be an attempt to distinguish between the exclusion or restriction of liability and the defence of volenti non fit injuria.

Note that s2(1) does not preclude the wrongdoer from making arrangements with a third party as to sharing or bearing the burden of compensating the victim. See *Thompson* v *T Lohan (Plant Hire) Ltd* [1987] 2 All ER 631.

If, however, a clause purports merely to transfer liability to a third party, but has the effect of excluding all liability on the part of the wrongdoer, such clause *will* fall within the Act. See *Phillips Products* v *Hyland* [1987] 2 All ER 620.

Liability arising in contract

Section 3 provides:

> '(1) This section applies as between contracting parties where one of them deals as consumer or on the other's written standard terms of business.
> (2) As against that party, the other cannot by reference to any contract term:
> a) when himself in breach of contract, exclude or restrict any liability of his in respect of the breach; or
> b) claim to be entitled:
> i) to render a contractual performance substantially different from that which was reasonably expected of him, or

ii) in respect of the whole or any part of his contractual obligation, to render no performance at all,
except in so far as (in any of the cases mentioned above in this subsection) the contract term satisfies the requirement of reasonableness.'

It would seem that the expression 'deals on the other's written standard terms of business' applies even where these standard terms are the terms of a third party – so that the National Conditions of Sale drawn up by the Law Society for the benefit of vendors and purchasers of land would be within the scope of s3 of the Act.

Section 3(2)(b)(i) would appear to apply to contracts with tour operators, which contain provisions entitling the tour operators to arrange accommodation or transport other than that specified. A contract for concert tickets providing that the management reserves the right to cancel the concert at any time might be subject to s3(2)(b)(ii).

Unreasonable indemnity clauses

An indemnity clause is one where a party agrees to reimburse losses sustained by another whether on the happening of a specified event or not. Section 4 of the Act applies to such a clause. The liability against which an indemnity is sought must be a business liability, and the person who is benefited by the clause is the consumer. He is not bound by the clause unless it satisfies the requirement of reasonableness. An example of the situation in which such a clause may be used is to indemnify a car hire company against third party claims arising out of the hirer's use of the car.

Section 4 provides:

'(1) A person dealing as consumer cannot by reference to any contract term be made to indemnify another person (whether a party to the contract or not) in respect of liability that may be incurred by the other for negligence or breach of contract, except in so far as the contract term satisfies the requirement of reasonableness.
(2) This section applies whether the liability in question:
a) is directly that of the person to be indemnified or is incurred by him vicariously;
b) is to the person dealing as consumer or to someone else.'

Guarantee of consumer goods

Section 5 prevents the implementation of terms or notices in manufacturer's guarantees which exclude or restrict liability for the negligence of the manufacturer or distributor for loss or damage from defects in the goods.

'(1) In the case of goods of a type ordinarily supplied for private use or consumption, where loss or damage;
a) arises from the goods proving defective while in consumer use, and
b) results from the negligence of a person concerned in the manufacture or distribution of the goods
liability for the loss or damage cannot be excluded or restricted by reference to any contract term or notice contained in or operating by reference to a guarantee of the goods.
(2) For these purposes:
a) goods are to be regarded as "in consumer use" when a person is using them, or has

them in his possession for use, otherwise than exclusively for the purposes of a business; and

b) anything in writing is a guarantee if it contains or purports to contain some promise or assurance (however worded or presented) that defects will be made good by complete or partial replacement, or by repair, monetary compensation or otherwise.

(3) This section does not apply as between the parties to a contract under or in pursuance of which possession or ownership of the goods passed.'

Sales and hire-purchase

Section 6 deals with both business and non-business liability, and makes some clauses totally ineffective and others subject to the test of reasonableness. It provides:

'(1) Liability for breach of the obligations arising from
a) s12 of the Sale of Goods Act 1979 (seller's implied undertakings as to title, etc);
b) s8 of the Supply of Goods (Implied Terms) Act 1973 (the corresponding thing in relation to hire-purchase)
cannot be excluded or restricted by reference to any contract term.
(2) As against a person dealing as consumer, liability for breach of the obligations arising from:
a) ss13, 14 or 15 of the 1979 Act (seller's implied undertakings as to conformity of goods with description or sample, or as to their quality or fitness for a particular purpose);
b) ss9, 10 or 11 of the 1973 Act (the corresponding things in relation to hire-purchase),
cannot be excluded or restricted by reference to any contract term.
(3) As against a person dealing otherwise than as consumer, the liability specified in subsection (2) above can be excluded or restricted by reference to a contract term, but only in so far as the term satisfies the requirement of reasonableness.
(4) The liabilities referred to in this section are not only the business liabilities defined by s1(3), but include those arising under any contract of sale of goods or hire-purchase agreement.'

Notice that the requirement of reasonableness referred to is that under s11(2) of the Act, which refers the reader to the guidelines set out in Schedule 2. See below.

Miscellaneous contracts under which goods pass

Section 7 applies to contracts (other than sale or hire-purchase) for the supply of goods now governed by the Supply of Goods and Services Act 1982.

'(1) Where the possession or ownership of goods passes under or in pursuance of a contract not governed by the law of sale of goods or hire-purchase, subsections (2) to (4) below apply as regards the effect (if any) to be given to contract terms excluding or restricting liability for breach of obligation arising by implication of law from the nature of the contract.
(2) As against a person dealing as consumer, liability in respect of the goods' correspondence with description or sample, or their quality or fitness for any particular purpose, cannot be excluded or restricted by reference to any such term.
(3) As against a person dealing otherwise than as consumer, that liability can be excluded

or restricted by reference to such a term, but only in so far as the term satisfied the requirement of reasonableness.

(3A) Liability for breach of the obligations arising under s2 of the Supply of Goods and Services Act 1982 (implied terms about title etc in certain contracts for the transfer of the property in goods) cannot be excluded or restricted by reference to any such term.

(4) Liability in respect of:

a) the right to transfer ownership of the goods, or give possession; or

b) the assurance of quiet possession to a person taking goods in pursuance of the contract

cannot (in a case to which subsection (3A) above does not apply) be excluded or restricted by reference to any such term except in so far as the term satisfies the requirement of reasonableness.

(5) This section does not apply in the case of goods passing on a redemption of trading stamps within the Trading Stamps Act 1964 or the Trading Stamps Act (Northern Ireland) 1965.'

The requirement of reasonableness

Section 11 has already been referred to. It provides:

'(1) In relation to a contract term, the requirement of reasonableness for the purposes of this Part of this Act, s3 of the Misrepresentation Act 1967 and s3 of the Misrepresentation Act (Northern Ireland) 1967 is that the term shall have been a fair and reasonable one to be included having regard to the circumstances which were, or ought reasonably to have been, known to or in the contemplation of the parties when the contract was made.

(2) In determining for the purposes of ss6 or 7 above whether a contract term satisfies the requirement of reasonableness, regard shall be had in particular to the matters specified in Schedule 2 to this Act; but this subsection does not prevent the court or arbitrator from holding, in accordance with any rule of law, that a term which purports to exclude or restrict any relevant liability is not a term of the contract.

(3) In relation to a notice (not being a notice having contractual effect), the requirement of reasonableness under this Act is that it should be fair and reasonable to allow reliance on it, having regard to all the circumstances obtaining when the liability arose or (but for the notice) would have arisen.

(4) Where by reference to a contract term or notice a person seeks to restrict liability to a specified sum of money, and the question arises (under this or any other Act) whether the term or notice satisfies the requirement of reasonableness, regard shall be had in particular (but without prejudice to subsection (2) above in the case of contract terms) to:

a) the resources which he could expect to be available to him for the purpose of meeting the liability should it arise; and

b) how far it was open to him to cover himself by insurance.

(5) It is for those claiming that a contract term or notice satisfies the requirement of reasonableness to show that it does.'

These guidelines specified in clause 11(2) appear in Schedule 2.

' "Guidelines" for application of reasonableness test

The matters to which regard is to be had in particular for the purposes of ss6(3), 7(3) and (4), 20 and 21 are any of the following which appear to be relevant:

a) the strength of the bargaining positions of the parties relative to each other, taking into account (among other things) alternative means by which the customer's requirements could have been met.

b) whether the customer received an inducement to agree to the term, or in accepting it had an opportunity of entering into a similar contract with other persons, but without having to accept a similar term;

c) whether the customer knew or ought reasonably to have known of the existence and extent of the term (having regard, among other things, to any custom of the trade and any previous course of dealing between the parties);

d) where the term excludes or restricts any relevant liability if some condition is not complied with, whether it was reasonable at the time of the contract to expect that compliance with that condition would be practicable;

e) whether the goods were manufactured, processed or adapted to the special order of the customer.'

The requirement of reasonableness was considered by the House of Lords in *George Mitchell* v *Finney Lock Seeds* [1983] 2 All ER 737. The purchasers of cabbage seeds were supplied with commercially useless seed of the wrong description so that their crops were lost. The contract contained an exclusion clause which purported to limit the liability of the seller to the cost of the seeds, some £200. The purchasers' claim was for damages of £61,513 for breach of contract.

The House of Lords held: although a limitation clause was to be construed contra proferentem, it was not subject to the very strict principles of construction applicable to clauses of complete exclusion of liability; the limitations clause was enforceable at common law. Lord Bridge observed that the *Photo Production* case (above) 'gave the final quietus to the doctrine that a "fundamental breach" of contract deprived the party in breach of the benefit of clauses in the contract excluding or limiting his liability'. However, the test of reasonableness (imposed by an enactment now superseded by s6(3) UCTA) was not satisfied. The reasons for this were: that it appeared that the normal practice of the seller was not to rely on the limitation clause, but to negotiate settlements of reasonable claims; the breach was due to the seller's negligence; and the seller could have insured against the loss without materially raising his charges.

A contrasting case is *R W Green* v *Cade Bros Farm* [1978] 1 Lloyd's Rep 602. Here the contract was for the sale of seed potatoes by potato merchants. The contract limited the liability of the sellers to returning the price. The potatoes proved to be infected with a virus. As the potatoes were uncertified, and hence cheaper, Griffiths J upheld the limitation clause as reasonable. However, he struck down as unreasonable a clause requiring the buyers to give notice of a claim within three days of delivery.

In *Stag Line Ltd* v *Tyne Shiprepair Group Ltd* [1984] 2 Lloyd's Rep 211, it was held, in respect of a shiprepairing contract, that a term excluding liability for economic loss was reasonable, but a term that the shipowner should have no remedy unless he returned the vessel to the shiprepairer's yard for repair, was unreasonable.

The House of Lords has recently considered the question of the exclusion of liability for negligence and whether such exclusion meets the requirement of reasonableness in hearing appeals in the two cases of *Smith* v *Eric S Bush* and *Harris* v *Wyre Forest District Council* [1989] 2 All ER 514. (The appeals were heard together.)

In the first case, the plaintiff applied to a building society for a mortgage and signed an application form which stated that a copy of the survey report and valuation would be given to the plaintiff. The form contained a disclaimer to the effect that neither the society nor its surveyor warranted that the report and valuation would be accurate, and that the report and valuation would be supplied without any acceptance of responsibility. The plaintiff subsequently received a copy of the report which contained a disclaimer in terms similar to those on the application form. The report stated that no essential repairs were required. On the strength of that report, and without obtaining an independent survey, the plaintiff purchased the house. In their inspection of the house, the surveyor had observed that certain chimney breasts had been removed, but had not checked to see whether the chimneys above were adequately supported. Eighteen months after the plaintiff purchased the house, bricks from the chimney collapsed and fell through the roof, causing considerable damage.

In the second case, the plaintiffs applied to a local authority for a mortgage to enable them to purchase a house. The local authority instructed their valuation surveyor to carry out a valuation. The plaintiffs signed an application form which stated that the valuation was confidential and was intended solely for the information of the local authority, and that no responsibility was accepted for the value or condition of the property by reason of the inspection and report. The surveyor valued the house at the asking price of £9,450, and the local authority offered to advance the plaintiffs 90% of that sum subject to certain minor repairs being done to the house. The plaintiffs, assuming that the house was worth at least the amount of the valuation and that the surveyor had found no serious defects, purchased the property for £9,000 without obtaining an independent survey. Three years later, they discovered that the house was subject to settlement, was virtually unsaleable and could only be repaired, if at all, at a cost of more than the purchase price.

In affirming the decision of the Court of Appeal in *Smith*, and reversing the Court of Appeal's decision in *Harris*, the House of Lords held that a valuer who valued a house for a building society or a local authority owed a duty of care to the purchaser of the house. However, the valuer could disclaim liability to exercise reasonable skill and care by an express exclusion clause, but such a disclaimer had to satisfy the requirement of reasonableness in s2(2) of the Act. In both these cases, it would not be fair and reasonable to impose on the purchasers the risk of loss arising from the incompetence or carelessness on the part of the valuers. The disclaimers were, therefore, not effective to exclude liability for the negligence of the valuers.

In his speech, Lord Griffiths said that it was impossible to draw up an exhaustive list of factors to be taken into account in deciding whether an exclusion clause met the requirement of reasonableness, but certain matters should always be considered. These were:

1 Were the parties of equal bargaining power?
2. In the case of advice, would it have been reasonably practicable to obtain the advice from an alternative source, taking into account considerations of costs and time?

3. How difficult is the task of being undertaken for which liability is being excluded?
4. What are the practical consequences of the decision on the question of reasonableness? This involves the sums of money at stake and the ability of the parties to bear the loss, which raises the question of insurance.

The case of *Davies* v *Parry* [1988] BTLC 236, for example, concerned the question of whether a disclaimer, seeking to absolve a surveyor from liability for negligence in the preparation of a valuation report, was reasonable. It was held that whether or not such a clause was reasonable depended on the facts of each case and, in particular, whether it was reasonable to assume that such a report would be relied on by non-experts, that is, potential buyers.

The test of reasonableness and the ambit of s11(1) was further considered in *Flamar Interocean Ltd* v *Denmac Ltd (The Flamar Pride and Flamar Progress)* [1990] 1 Lloyd's Rep 434.

The owners of the two vessels claimed damages for breach of contract against the defendants, the technical managers of the vessels. The contract(s) in question was a ship's management contract for each vessel, pertaining to pre-delivery inspection of the vessels, maintenance inspections, insurance and so on. The question arose as to whether the technical managers (the defendants) could rely on an exclusion clause in the contract.

HELD: under s2(2) UCTA 1977, a person could not exclude or restrict his liability for negligence, save insofar as the clause might satisfy the test of reasonableness. It was incontestable that there had been negligence, in (inter alia): (1) failure to require adequate and thorough pre-delivery tests to be carried out; (2) failure to engage someone with experience of refrigerated vessels; and (3) failure to provide liability insurance cover.

Potter J remarked:

'The clauses in question did not satisfy the test of reasonableness as laid out in s11(1) of the UCTA, providing that the term shall be fair and reasonable having regard to the circumstances "which were, or ought to have been, known to, or in the contemplation of the parties, at the time when the contract was made". The exclusion clause could not be relied on by the defendants.'

The Act prevents evasion of its provisions by means of a secondary contract

Section 10 provides:

'A person is not bound by any contract term prejudicing or taking away rights of his which arise under or in connection with, the performance of another contract, so far as those rights extend to the enforcement of another's liability which this part of the Act prevents that other from excluding or restricting.'

A possible application of this section is to an attempt to exclude liability under an agreement for the sale of an article by means of a secondary maintenance agreement. The case of *Tudor Grange Holdings Ltd* v *Citibank NA and Another* [1991] 4 All

ER 1 helps to cast further light on s10 of the UCTA 1977. The section was aimed at controlling future exemptions and exclusions rather than retrospectively limiting or adjusting liability.

At a hearing in chambers the defendant bank and others applied to have an action by the plaintiff company struck out. Judgment was given in open court. By a deed of release, dated March 1989, the plaintiffs purported to release Citibank and its associates from 'all claims, demands and causes of action prior to the date hereof'. The question arose as to whether this release was, under s10 UCTA 1977, reasonable. The argument lay that it was not, and since it failed to satisfy the test of reasonableness it could not be binding.

The court repudiated this argument and held that s10 was held not to be intended to cover the present situation; it did not cover settlements and compromises on events that had already occurred. In the view of the court the Act was aimed soley at exemption clauses, clauses modifying future liability – it was not concerned with retrospective claims or settlements. Since s10 did not apply to the deed of release which bound the plaintiffs, it (the deed) formed a complete defence to the claims against the banks.

Exceptions

The Act does not apply to the following:

1. The liability of people not acting within the course of business (except s6).
2. Insurance contracts.
3. Certain parts of contracts relating to land.
4. Apart from s2(1), which does apply, contracts of marine salvage, such as towage, charterparties of ships or hovercraft, contracts for the carriage of goods by ship or hovercraft.
5. The s2(1) and (2) do not apply to contracts of employment except in favour of the employee.
6. Contracts for the international supply of goods.

Save as set out above, a contract properly governed by English law may not include provisions excluding the Act. A person cannot exclude liability by choosing a foreign law wholly or mainly to avoid the Act.

9

Incapacity

9.1 Introduction

Prima facie the law presumes that everyone has capacity to contract. A few classes of person are under a disability: minors, mentally disordered persons, drunken persons, and corporations.

9.2 Minors

General

Who is a minor?
Anybody who is under 18 years is a minor: s1 Family Law Reform Act 1969. A person becomes legally 18 years at the commencement of the day which is his birthday: s9 Family Law Reform Act 1969.

The issues involved

These are that the minor must have some contractual capacity so that he can survive; and unfairness to the other party to a transaction with him ought to be avoided, where possible; but, exploitation of a person who may lack insight into the nature of legal transactions by reason of his age, ought to be avoided. The parents of a minor are not liable for his contracts unless they acted as his agent in law.

There are two kinds of contract:

1. Contracts for necessaries (which are valid).
2. Voidable contracts.
    At common law these are of two types:
    a) those binding on the minor, unless he repudiated them during minority or within a reasonable time thereafter; and
    b) those which were not binding upon him, unless and until he ratified them after attaining his majority.

9.3 Necessaries

Necessary goods

What are necessary goods?

There are goods 'suitable to the condition of life of the ... (minor) and to his actual requirements at the time of the sale and delivery': s3(3) Sale of Goods Act 1979. It must be shown, first, that the class into which the goods fall is capable of being described as necessary, and, secondly, that the goods supplied, even if within such a class, were actually necessary at the time of the contract. See *Chapple* v *Cooper* (1844) 13 M & W 252.

Thus, given the style of dressing at the time, a waistcoat would fall into a class of objects capable of being called 'necessary', but the eleven fancy waistcoats supplied to an undergraduate in *Nash* v *Inman* [1908] 2 KB 1 were not deemed to be necessary to him. Clothes, food, drink, medicine, etc will fall within the definition of necessaries. The onus of showing that the goods are necessaries lies on the supplier. See *Nash* v *Inman* (above).

Executory contracts for necessary goods

It is not entirely certain whether a minor is bound by an executory contract for necessary goods. Section 3(2) Sale of Goods Act provides that a minor must pay a reasonable price for 'necessaries sold and delivered' and, as we have seen, 'necessaries' are defined in s3(3) in relation to 'the time of the sale and delivery'. What if the goods are sold but not yet delivered? Can the minor repudiate the contract before delivery?

The answer depends on whether the minor is liable in re: that is, because he has received the item in question, or by virtue of of consensus: that is, because he made the contract in the first place. The wording of s3 suggests that the goods must be 'necessary' both when the infant buys them and when they are delivered (if these two happenings are at different times). This implies that the basis of the minor's liability is that he has been supplied with the goods. Moreover, the requirement of s3 is for the minor to pay 'a reasonable price' which may not be the contract price. This does not support a contractual liability. In *Nash* v *Inman*, Fletcher Moulton LJ said that the minor was liable because he had been supplied, and not because he had contracted. Buckley LJ, however, said that the minor had a limited capacity to contract, and a contract for necessaries was one that the minor could make.

The position remains in doubt, but in *Roberts* v *Gray* [1913] 1 KB 520, it was held that an infant is bound by an executory contract for necessary services and education. Treitel (6th edn p413) considers that no distinction should be drawn between goods and services on this point.

Necessary services

These would include contracts by an infant for legal and medical assistance. In *Chapple* v *Cooper* (above), a contract by a widow for her husband's funeral was a contract for a necessary. A trading contract, is not, however, a necessary.

Contracts for necessaries must be for the benefit of the minor taken as a whole

If it contains terms which are harsh and onerous, the contract will not be enforceable against the infant. See *Fawcett* v *Smethurst* (1914) 84 LJ KB 473. Similarly, in *Flower* v *London and North Western Railway* [1894] 2 QB 65, a contract of carriage, which contained a clause exempting the defendants from liability for injury to the minor even if caused by negligence. It was void as against the minor.

Loans for necessaries

At common law it has been held that a minor cannot be made liable on a loan to him to purchase necessaries. See *Darby* v *Boucher* (1694) 1 Salk 279. But the common law position is not beyond doubt. See Treitel (1957) 73 LQR 194. By statute the former position was that contracts of loan were declared to be 'absolutely void'. This provision was contained in the Infants Relief Act 1874, but this Act has now been repealed by the Minors' Contracts Act 1987.

If the loan is actually spent on necessaries, it can be recovered (or such part of it as may have been so spent) in equity. See *Marlow* v *Pitfield* (1719) 1 P Wms 558.

A person who purchases necessaries at the request of a minor may be able to recover against the minor under an agency.

Contracts for service, apprenticeship and education

Contracts of service are valid if the service is, taken as a whole, beneficial to the minor, for example, an apprenticeship, or articles of clerkship, which may on occasions appear exploitive, but which have beneficial consequences long term. See *Clements* v *L & NW Railway* [1894] 2 QB 482. However, an apprenticeship was said to be oppressive, and not beneficial, in *De Francesco* v *Barnum* (1890) 45 Ch D 430, where the dancing master stipulated in the contract that his pupil should not accept remunerative engagements without his consent during the apprenticeship, nor marry until it was over.

On the other hand, there was an interesting clash of values in *Chaplin* v *Leslie Frewin (Publishers) Ltd* [1966] Ch 71. A minor made a contract to sell the story of his disreputable life; Lord Denning MR concluded that:

> '... it is not for his good that he should exploit his discreditable conduct for money, no matter how much he is paid',

but Dankwerts and Winn LLJ considered the contract beneficial in so far as Chaplin was well paid at a time when he would otherwise have had to rely on National Assistance. The scandal, the majority felt, would not be harmful, for there was 'clear proof that he had no taste nor decency' and 'no right to claim to any reputation'.

If he is grossly underpaid for his services, the contract would, unless there were off-setting, long-term benefits, be held invalid.

Other beneficial contracts

Some other beneficial contracts, but not all contracts, for example, trading contracts (see *Cowern* v *Nield* [1912] 2 KB 419), will be binding on a minor. In *Doyle* v *White City Stadium* [1935] 1 KB 110, a minor who was a professional boxer contracted with the British Boxing Board of Control and agreed to adhere to the rules of the Board.

HELD: the contract was binding on him because he could not have earned his living otherwise.

See also *Denmark Productions* v *Boscobel Productions* [1969] 1 QB 699.

9.4 Voidable contracts

Valid until repudiated

Voidable contracts generally are contracts which subsist unless and until avoided as contrasted with void contracts, which are a complete nullity ab initio. In the case of minors' voidable contracts, only one party, the minor, may avoid them. The rules as to liability are that once the minor has avoided the contract, he avoids liabilities which accrue after that date, but remains bound to meet obligations which have already arisen. See *Blake* v *Concannon* (1870) Ir R 4 CL 323. He cannot receive back money that was paid prior to the date of his avoiding the contract. See *Steinberg* v *Scala (Leeds) Ltd* [1923] 2 Ch 452. A minor applied for and was allotted shares in a company. She paid the amounts due on allotment and on the first call.

HELD: that although she could repudiate while under age, she could not recover moneys paid. She had received the very consideration she bargained for even though she had not been paid any dividend.

What kinds of contract are voidable?

1. Real property contracts.
2. Contracts involving shares.
3. Partnership agreements.
4. Marriage settlements.

Why?

In none of the above categories could the contracts be considered as for 'necessaries', except a contract for a lease of tenancy which would, in that event, be valid. Thus, if they were not voidable, they would have to be void. If so, the minor would have no obligation to make any payments, and could retain the benefit he had obtained. This may prove unjust to the other party in any transaction, but particularly so in these types of contract for they envisage reciprocal liability extending over a period of time.

There are, of course, other types of contract which involve such long-term reciprocal liability, notably contracts of hire-purchase, and these are void, except in so far as they are for necessaries. The reason is that the categories of voidable contracts became frozen in the late nineteenth century, and have not been added to. Perhaps they should be – this whole area of law is ripe for reform by legislation.

How are minors' voidable contracts avoided?

This is usually accomplished by notice, which the minor may revoke before he attains his majority. Notice that he wishes to avoid a voidable contract must be given before the minor becomes 18 years old, or within a reasonable time thereafter. What is reasonable time varies with the circumstances, but in a marriage settlement case Lord Watson said that a 'period of four years and eight months ... cannot possibly be regarded as a reasonable time'. See *Edwards* v *Carter* [1893] AC 360.

Contracts valid when ratified

At common law, all contracts which are not enforceable against the minor during his minority may be ratified by him when he attains his majority. Upon ratification, they become enforceable. The common law position has been restored by s1(a) Minors' Contracts Act 1987, which repeals the former provisions of the 1874 Act prohibiting ratification.

9.5 The Minors' Contracts Act 1987

As previously noted, the Infants Relief Act 1874 (which invalidated certain contracts and prohibited actions to enforce contracts ratified after majority) no longer applies – s1(a) of the 1987 Act. The new Act provides protection to creditors of minors in respect of guarantees. Section 2 provides that:

> 'Where:
>   a) a guarantee is given in respect of an obligation of a party to a contract made after the commencement of this Act, and
>   b) the obligation is unenforceable against him (or he repudiates the contract) because he was a minor when the contract was made,
> the guarantee shall not for that reason alone be unenforceable against the guarantor.'

9.6 Liability of a party contracting with a minor

So far in this discussion it is the minor's liability which has been considered. Generally, the rule is that lack of capacity is a personal advantage, so that the person contracting with the minor cannot rely upon it to invalidate the contract. To permit that to happen would transform the advantage to the minor into a disadvantage. Accordingly, a minor can recover damages from a person who refuses to peform his part of the contract. He would not, however, be able to obtain an order for specific performance: not, at least, unless he had himself performed the contract, because there would not be mutuality. See *Flight* v *Bolland* (1824) 4 Russ 298.

9.7 Liability of a minor in tort

A minor cannot be sued for an act which was within the contemplation of a void contract. In *Fawcett* v *Smethurst* (1914) 84 LJ KB 473, a minor hired a car to fetch a bag from the station. On the way he met a friend. He drove on further than the station. During the extra journey, the car accidently caught fire and was damaged.

HELD: he was not liable in tort as the extra journey did not take his actions out of the scope of the contract.

A similar finding was made in *Jennings* v *Rundall* (1799) 8 Term R 335, where a minor hired a horse and injured it by riding it too hard. On the other hand, in *Burnard* v *Haggis* (1863) 14 CB (NS) 45, a minor who hired a mare 'merely for a ride' and was warned that she was unfit for jumping was held liable for her death when jumped by his friend.

In *Ballett* v *Mingay* [1943] KB 281, a minor was liable when he improperly parted with a microphone that he had hired.

The rule that a minor is not liable in tort applies, not only where he commits a tort in breaking the invalid contract, but also where he commits a tort in procuring it.

In *R Leslie Ltd* v *Sheill* [1914] 3 KB 607, it was held that a minor could not be sued in deceit for inducing an adult to lend him money by fraudulently misrepresenting his age.

9.8 Restitution

Equity had the power to order the restoration of gains obtained by a minor under a contract unenforceable against him. This equitable power is now enshrined in statute. Section 3 Minors' Contracts Act 1987 provides that:

'(1) Where –
a) a person ("the plaintiff") has after the commencement of this Act entered into a contract with another ("the defendant"), and
b) the contract is unenforceable against the defendant (or he repudiates it) because he was a minor when the contract was made,
the court may, if it is just and equitable to do so, require the defendant to transfer to the plaintiff any property acquired by the defendant under the contract, or any property representing it.
(2) Nothing in this section shall be taken to prejudice any other remedy available to the plaintiff.'

9.9 Mentally disordered persons

There are two categories:

1. If a person is certified by two medical practitioners as being incapable of dealing with his property, then the court will have control over his property, and will delegate the day-to-day management of it, often to a relative, who will then be accountable to the court: Part VII Mental Health Act 1983. The person certified cannot then dispose of any of his property.
2. If there has been no certification, the contract may be set aside:
   a) if the other party knew of the disorder;
   b) if the disordered person did not understand the transaction by reason of his disorder.

The contract may be ratified by the disordered person once the disorder has ceased temporarily or permanently.

A person who supplies necessaries (see 9.2) may recover a reasonable price, therefore, even if he knew of the disorder: s3 Sale of Goods Act 1979.

9.10   Persons who are drunk

The contract may be set aside if: one party was very drunk and this prevented his understanding the transaction, and the other party knew of this.

Note *Gore* v *Gibson* (1843) 13 M & W 623. The drunken person is liable to pay a reasonable price for necessaries, and may in any event ratify the contract when he is sober.

9.11   Corporations

What is a corporation?

Where two or more persons associate in order to enter transactions, their association may be incorporated or unincorporated. If it is unincorporated – by a partnership – then it cannot incur liability apart from its members. No one can sue the partnership as such, but only its members, who are personally liable for any debts, to the full extent of their assets.

An incorporated association can incur liability apart from that of its members. It can hold assets in its own name, and is liable for its own debts. The liability of members and controllers is limited in some pre-arranged way, for example, as in a company limited by guarantee, or, the most common form of corporation, the 'limited liability' company. An incorporated association has contractual capacity.

What limitations are placed on a corporation's contractual capacity?

This depends upon whether the corporation is chartered or statutory.

A chartered corporation is created by Royal Charter. It has full contractual capacity so far as the other contracting party is concerned, but if it exceeds what it is authorised to do by its charter, the Attorney-General may bring proceedings to revoke the charter, or a member may seek a declaration that the contract is invalid. See *Pharmaceutical Society* v *Dickson* [1968] 2 All ER 686.

A statutory corporation is one which has been set up in the manner prescribed by statute. For example, after the Local Government Act 1972, virtually all local authorities in England and Wales are statutory corporations. Probably the most common type is the limited company, which can be created by individuals following the procedure laid down in the Companies Act 1985.

A limited company must register a Memorandum of Association with the Registrar of Companies in order to be validly incorporated. This will contain an 'objects clause' specifying the purpose(s) for which the company has been formed. While a company can, subsequently, change its objectives, for example, diversifying and expanding, any such change must be notified to the Registrar and the 'objects clause' amended. A company entering into a contract outside the scope of its stated objectives is said to be acting ultra vires and the contract is void. See *Ashbury Railway Carriage and Iron* v *Riche* (1875) LR 7 HL 653.

To verify whether or not the company was acting in a way which was ultra vires is not, however, always a simple matter of comparing the proposed contract with the objects clause. Any contract may come within the ambit of the objects clause if it can be considered 'reasonably incidental' to the overall purpose for which the company was set up.

To further facilitate the making of contracts with no restrictions imposed by the ultra vires doctrine, certain companies have, additionally, drafted the objects clause in very wide terms. See *Cotman* v *Brougham* [1918] AC 514. In order to curtail such broadly drafted memorandums, some courts have interpreted stated 'objectives' to be no more than powers ancillary to the main objects. See *Re Introductions Ltd* [1970] Ch 199. The effect of such a distinction is to make the exercise of such a power ultra vires, unless done in pursuit of a main objective as defined by the court.

A new approach by the courts may be seen in *Rolled Steel Products* v *BSC* [1984] BCLC 466, in which the exercise of a power for a purpose inconsistent with the stated main objectives was treated not as an ultra vires act, but as a breach of the directors' duties. Note that a change in the directors' duties may be ratified by shareholders, while an ultra vires act may not be. Thus the potential importance of this case is considerable.

Reason for disability?

It is felt that shareholders and other persons doing business with the corporation on the faith of its publicly declared enterprise should not suffer as a result of its going beyond those bounds.

Reservations

Objects clauses were drafted very widely, in the case of companies, so as to render them useless as a guide to what the company intended to do. Moreover, a company may not raise ultra vires against a party who contracts with it in good faith, though such a person may use ultra vires as a defence to an action under the contract by the company against him. This provision was introduced into English legislation as a result of an EEC Directive in 1972, and now appears in s35 Companies Act 1985. While the protection to be afforded to s35 is potentially wide, the importance of this section may be largely illusory. The conditions to be met with in complying with s35 are severely limiting.

10

Mistake

10.1 Introduction

It has been said that there is no single coherent doctrine of mistake in English law. Certainly, the single word 'mistake' can have so many different meanings it really indicates little more than a distant connection between assorted instances in which for various reasons the parties may, in everyday language, be said to have been 'mistaken'. The rules relating to mistake, when more closely examined, may be found to have more to do with other areas of contractual law, such as offer and acceptance and the formation of contracts generally.

The effect of a mistake at common law is that when the mistake is operative, it usually operates to make the contract void ab initio. No property will pass under it and no obligations can arise under it. The effect is literally that the law assumes there never has been a contract. Because of the fundamental importance of this doctrine insofar as sale of goods is concerned (no title may pass under a void contract), the courts have always been reluctant to extend the doctrine of operative mistake.

As often happens, equity has stepped into the breach (see 10.6). In equity, the contract may be voidable. Property will pass and obligations will arise unless or until the contract is avoided. However, the right to rescission may be lost in a number of cases and avoidance of the contract will be impossible.

10.2   Types of mistake

This is an area which abounds with confusing terminology. No two authorities seem agreed as to the forms mistake may take and, often, the same terminology is used to cover different forms of mistake.

Cheshire and Fifoot adopt the threefold classification of unilateral, common and mutal mistake. Unilateral is where A makes a mistake and B knows that A is mistaken. In mutual mistake, each party mistakenly makes a wrong assumption as in *Raffles* v *Wichelhaus* (see below). In common mistake, both parties make exactly the same mistake as in *Solle* v *Butcher* (see below), when both parties mistakenly believed that a rented property was not subject to the Rents Acts. Other authorities (such as Anson) combine all forms of mistake into either unilateral or mutual.

There are also other, really unrelated, doctrines concerned with documents. In the first type of case, there may be a simple transcription error in drawing up the contract, so that in its written form it does not accurately reflect what the parties agreed earlier. Secondly, a party may assert that the document containing his signature is not the document he thought he was signing. These will be dealt with below (see 10.5).

For the purposes of this book, the terms 'mutual' and 'unilateral' mistake only will be used. Thus a *mutual mistake* is one when the parties have arrived at a genuine agreement in the erroneous belief that some fact lying at the heart of the contract is true, when it is not.

A *unilateral mistake* is one where though superficially the parties appear to be in agreement, in fact, there is no genuine agreement and no binding contract has been concluded.

In the first case, mutual mistake, if both parties, on becoming aware of the true state of affairs, regret making the agreement, they may usually extricate themselves from the contract without recourse to the courts. Problems arise where one party, though originally mistaken, is unwilling to surrender an advantage gained under the contract that has resulted.

In the second case, unilateral mistake, here again if the parties themselves recognise that despite appearances they have not truly come to any agreement, there is no great problem, and they can usually extricate themselves without resorting to the courts. However, where one party continues to assert that an agreement exists, on terms he mistakenly understood to form the basis of the contract, then litigation may become necessary.

10.3   Mutual mistake

Bell v Lever Brothers Ltd

The concept of mutual mistake was extensively examined by the House of Lords in the leading case of *Bell* v *Lever Bros* [1932] AC 161.

The appellants were employed by a subsidiary company of the respondents and, during their term of office as chairman and vice-chairman respectively, they committed breaches of duty by certain speculative dealings. This conduct would have entitled the respondents to terminate their contracts without notice.

The appellants became redundant after company reorganisation, and large payments were made to them by the respondents, at that time unaware of their misconduct. When the appellants' misconduct came to light, the respondents sought rescission of the redundancy agreements and return of the sums paid.

At first instance, it was found that the appellants had never sought to actively conceal their past misconduct, and they simply did not appreciate its likely effect. In other words, the agreements were entered into under a mutual mistake.

By a 3–2 majority, the Lords held the agreements to be valid and binding.

It is generally agreed that the effect of *Bell* v *Lever Bros* is to confine the doctrine very narrowly. Specific types of mistake will be considered shortly, but it is convenient first to consider what their Lordships said concerning the general nature of common law mistake. Both Lords Atkin and Thankerton agreed that the mistake must be a false and fundamental assumption going to the root of the contract, and which both parties must be taken to have had in their minds at the time the contract was made as being the basis of their agreement. What is required is more than simply one party being able to demonstrate that had he known the true facts, he would never have made the contract. Lord Thankerton said:

'The phrase "underlying assumption by the parties", as applied to the subject matter of a contract, may be too widely interpreted so as to include something which one of the parties had not necessarily in his mind at the time of the contract; in my opinion it can only properly relate to something which both must have necessarily accepted in their minds as an essential and integral element of the subject matter.'

Applying this test to *Bell* v *Lever Bros*, it clearly was not satisfied. As Lord Atkin said, the respondents got exactly what they bargained for, release of the contracts, and it was immaterial that the same objective would have been achieved by other means, or that had they known the true facts, they would not have made the bargain. The discovered facts could not be said to destroy the identity of the contract.

In *Sheikh Brothers Ltd* v *Ochsner* [1957] AC 136, the appellants, who were lessees of an estate in Kenya, granted the respondent a licence to cut and manufacture sisal on the estate. The terms of the licence provided that the respondents should deliver to the appellants 50 tons of manufactured sisal fibre per month. It transpired that the net yield of the estate was insufficient to comply with this condition. *Bell* v *Lever Bros* was cited to the Judicial Committee, and the contract was held to be void.

Examples of contracts void under English law because of a sufficiently false and fundamental assumption, all preceding *Bell* v *Lever Bros* and which must, therefore, be read subject to it, are:

Scott v *Coulson* [1903] 2 Ch 249. The parties entered into a contract for the assignment of a life insurance policy wrongly believing that the object of the policy was still alive. The contract was held to be void and the vendor recovered the policy and the moneys payable under it on the assured's death.

Galloway v *Galloway* (1914) 30 TLR 531. The parties entered into a separation deed, believing themselves to be husband and wife. In fact, they had not contracted a valid marriage, the deed was held to be void and the man not liable to make the payments promised under it.

Griffiths v *Brymer* (1903) 19 TLR 434. The plaintiff contracted to hire a room from the defendant to watch the King's coronation procession. Shortly before the contract was made, the procession was cancelled. The plaintiff recovered moneys paid to the defendant on the grounds that the agreement was made on a missupposition of facts which went to the whole root of the contract.

An example of a case subsequent to *Bell* v *Lever Bros* is *Norwich Union Fire Insurance Society* v *Price* [1934] AC 455. The respondents shipped a cargo of lemons, insured under a policy of marine insurance, with the appellants. In the belief that the lemons had been damaged by an insured-against peril, and sold in consequence, the appellants paid over the insurance moneys. In fact, the lemons had not been damaged and had been sold because they were ripening. The Judicial Committee of Privy Council held that the appellants could recover the moneys as having been paid under a mistake of fact. The mistake was 'vital' and the contract was therefore void. The Judicial Committee said there was nothing in *Bell* v *Lever Bros* to suggest otherwise.

See also *Rover International* v *Cannon Film Sales* [1989] 1 WLR 912. Here a mutual mistake as to an essential question of fact meant that the contract was held to be void ab initio. Both parties were under the mistaken impression that a contract entered into earlier was valid. In fact, it was not. All their subsequent dealings were grounded on this mistaken belief. On appeal it was held since all agreements between the parties, and monies paid pursuant to such agreements, were based on a mutual mistake of fact, then any such agreements must be void ab initio and any monies paid be returned.

Having considered the general approach of the law to the problem of mutual mistake, three specific areas of contract, which have generated much case law, will now be considered. They are mistake as to quality; mistake as to the existence of the subject matter; and mistake as to title. In *Bell* v *Lever Bros*, Lord Atkin gave examples of all three.

Mistake as to quality

In the ordinary course of events, a mistake as to quality will not avail a party seeking to avoid a contract. He will usually be taken to have received the article or goods that constituted the subject matter of the contract and which the vendor contracted to supply. The buyer's only remedy may be to sue for breach of condition or warranty, providing there is some term in the contract relating to quality. The situations in which the contract may be void for mistake as to quality were said by

Lord Atkin to be where:

> '... it is the mistake of both parties, and is as to the existence of some quality which makes the thing without the quality essentially different from the thing as it was believed to be.'

He came to this conclusion on consideration of *Kennedy* v *Panama Royal Mail Co* and *Smith* v *Hughes*.

In *Kennedy* v *Panama Royal Mail Co* (1867) LR 2 QB 580, the plaintiff applied for shares in the defendant company in reliance on a prospectus which stated wrongly, but in good faith, that the company had concluded a contract with the Government of New Zealand to carry mails.

The shares were allotted to him and subsequently fell in value. On discovering the true facts, the plaintiff brought an action to recover the money he had paid for the shares. Dismissing the action, the Court of Queen's Bench held that the plaintiff had received that which he had contracted for, namely shares in the defendant company, and that the invalidity of the contract with the New Zealand Government did not make them different in substance. Blackburn J said that the difference must be:

> '... such as to show that there is a complete difference in substance between what was supposed to be and what was taken, so as to constitute a failure of consideration.'

Smith v *Hughes* (1871) LR 6 QB 597 involved a contract for the sale of oats by sample. The defendant wished to purchase old oats, but the oats sold to him by the plaintiff were new oats and useless for the defendant's purpose. The Court of Queen's Bench held that even if both parties believed the oats to be old oats, there would nevertheless be a binding contract.

In the light of these cases, the problem seems to be exactly when a mistake as to quality will avoid a contract. As has been said with some justification, if a mistake as to £50,000 (the sum at issue in *Bell* v *Lever Bros*) is not fundamental, then what is? The speeches in the House of Lords offer some assistance. Lord Atkin gave the following examples of contracts that would not be avoided:

1. Where a buyer purchases a horse believing it to be sound, pays accordingly, and would not have bought the horse had he known that it was, in fact, unsound. In the *absence of any contractual term as to soundness,* the buyer is bound.
2. Both buyer and seller believe a painting to be an old master; in reality it is a copy. If there is no representation or warranty the buyer has no remedy (contrast *Peco Arts* v *Hazlitt Gallery* [1983] 3 All ER 193, where the decision was, however, on the question of limitation of action).
3. A buyer purchases a house which, unbeknown to him, is uninhabitable, the contract is valid.
4. In the sale of a roadside garage, the buyer is unaware that shortly a by-pass route will be constructed to divert a substantial amount of traffic and thus business elsewhere; he has no remedy.

As with much of the law of mistake, mistake as to quality is defined by exclusion, and examples of where the plea might have or has succeeded are rare. In the Court of Appeal in *Bell* v *Lever Bros*, Greer LJ said that the contract would be void where the intention was to buy and sell a racehorse whereas, in fact, the animal was a carthorse. This example may be usefully contrasted with Lord Atkin's unsound horse. Three more cases in which the plea failed should also be mentioned:

In *Harrison & Jones Ltd* v *Bunten and Lancaster Ltd* [1953] 1 QB 646, the buyers agreed in writing to purchase from the sellers '100 bales of Calcutta kapok, sree brand', equal to an exhibited sample. Both parties believed it to be pure kapok consisting of sree cotton, but the commodity turned out to be a mixture containing bush cotton and commercially inferior. Pilcher J said that although the mistake may be fundamental from the point of view of the purchaser, the fact that the parties were unaware that the goods commercially thus described lacked a particular quality did not affect the validity of the contract.

In *Leaf* v *International Galleries* [1950] 2 KB 86, the plaintiff purchased from the defendants a painting which both mistakenly believed to be by Constable. The plaintiff sought rescission for misrepresentation, but the Court of Appeal said, obiter, that although the mistake may have been in one sense essential or fundamental, it did not avoid the contract.

The facts in *Peco Arts* (above) were substantially similar, but there was no decision on this point. It is clear, therefore, that although a particular quality may be of great importance to the contracting parties themselves, the courts look at the matter in a slightly different way by considering the essential nature of the subject matter, and not necessarily giving any weight at all to the hopes, desires and disappointments of the parties.

In *Solle* v *Butcher* [1950] 1 KB 671, the defendant let a flat to the plaintiff at a rent of £250 pa. Both parties assumed that in view of the considerable alterations that had been carried out on the property, it was in law a 'new' flat and no longer subject to rent control. The assumption was incorrect, and the maximum permitted rent was £140, and the plaintiff sought the return of the rent overpaid. The defendant in his counterclaim alleged that the lease was void for mistake. The Court of Appeal held that although there was a mutual mistake as to fact, the contract was not void. Denning LJ took a robustly critical view of the doctrine of mistake at common law (to be dealt with later), but the case is important because Bucknill LJ agreed that the mistake was not sufficient to avoid the contract. It has been argued that if ever a mistake as to quality were to operate, then it should be here, because the difference between a rent-controlled and a de-controlled flat is such as to make the one essentially different from the other. The opposite view is that the difference is simply as to commercial value, which will rarely, if ever, afford grounds for avoiding a contract. If the latter view is correct, and on balance it may be preferred, the case still illustrates the extent to which the mistake must be 'an essential and integral element' of the subject matter of the contract. It is suggested that the case does not hold that a mistake as to substance, as opposed to quality, can never operate.

There is a comparative dearth of authority in which contracts have been held to be void for mistake as to quality/substance – the following cases may be considered:

Gompertz v *Bartlett* (1853) 2 E & B 849. In a contract for the sale of a bill of exchange, the parties assumed it to be a valid unstamped foreign bill; in fact, it was an inland bill and therefore invalid. The purchaser was able to recover the purchase price on the grounds that the contract was void.

In *Nicholson and Venn* v *Smith-Marriott* (1947) 177 LT 189, table linen was advertised at a sale by auction as being 'with the crest of Charles I and the authentic property of that monarch'. The linen was Georgian and, in consequence, the buyer recovered damages though the judge was of the opinion that the buyer could have treated the contract as void. In *Solle* v *Butcher*, Denning LJ disagreed with this conclusion.

In attempting to produce a coherent exposition of the above law, it has been suggested that the test to apply in a given situation is whether the parties can be said to use the quality in question to identify the thing that is the subject matter of the contract, such that if it lacks this quality, the contract is void, per *Bell* v *Lever Bros*. Thus in *Bell*, the parties, if asked, would have replied that they were contracting for a service agreement, not an 'unbroken' service agreement; in *Nicholson and Venn*, the parties would have said that the contract was for the sale of Carolean table linen, and in Lord Atkin's examples of an unsound horse and an uninhabitable house, the answer would be that the contracts concerned a horse and a house respectively. His example of an old master would not necessarily fit into this text, and presumably the parties' answer in *Leaf* v *International Galleries* would have been that they were dealing with a Constable painting, which, in fact, it was not.

Apart from its obvious uncertainties, the principal weakness of this test is that it is really only a useful rule of thumb and no more. It fails to answer the essential point of why certain articles may be identified by their quality, and why others may not be. The significance of a fundamental mistake as to quality, for the mistake to operate, lies in the importance that the Court attach to the quality taking into account the pre-contractual negotiations of the parties (if any), and the express and implied terms of their final agreement. Such an approach has led to a further attempt to restate the law relating to mistake as to quality, by rejecting the quality/substance distinction as being both arbitrary and imprecise.

Glanville Williams (1945) 23 Can Bar Rev has argued that there is no 'metaphysical' substance independent of qualities, and that qualities considered compositely produce the essence of the substance of an article. Arguably preferable, instead, is to look at the matter from the point of view of exactly what the parties intended and undertook when entering into the contract. Ignoring the possibility of any term implied by statute (for example, Sale of Goods Act 1979), a mistake as to quality would normally have one of two possible results – applying the rule caveat emptor, the risk, that the goods were not of the quality that the parties believed them to be, will fall on the buyer, and he will have no remedy; or the seller may be held to have expressly or impliedly warranted that the goods were of the assumed quality and the buyer will have an action for damages.

Generally, it is argued, a mutual mistake as to quality will fall into either category, but there may be special circumstances in which, on the true construction of the contract, neither party could be held to have accepted the risk that the subject matter of the contract might be what in fact it proves to be, and to enforce the contract would cause either or both to have imposed upon them contractual obligations that the parties never intended to create. In such a situation, the contract would be void. This solution accords with the general object of the doctrine of common law mistake, that in exceptional cases contractual liabilities should be discharged because of matters unknown to the parties that render the contract utterly different to the contract that they intended to make.

In *Associated Japanese Bank International Ltd* v *Credit du Nord SA* [1988] 3 All ER 902, the effect of mistake as to quality was subject to detailed examination by Steyn J. His Lordship observed that the decision in *Bell* v *Lever Brothers* had been interpreted as virtually excluding mistake as to quality being operative at common law. He referred, in particular, to the judgments of Lord Denning in *Solle* v *Butcher* and *Magee* v *Pennine Insurance Co*, and the arguments advanced in Cheshire, Fifoot and Furmston's *Law of Contract* (11th edn pp225–6). In his view, this interpretation did not do justice to the speeches of the majority in that case. Lord Atkin had recognised that mistake as to quality might well operate to nullify consent, although in limited circumstances, when he held that:

'... a mistake will not affect assent unless it is the mistake of both parties, and is as to the existence of some quality which makes the thing without the quality essentially different from the thing as it was believed to be'.

Lord Thankerton had enunciated almost precisely the same test. Steyn J adopted the test formulated by Lord Atkin and held further that a party who seeks to rely on such a mistake to avoid the contract must have had reasonable grounds for the belief which gave rise to the mistake.

After a careful examination of the speeches in *Bell*, he concluded that the majority view was that there did exist a narrow, but perceptible, doctrine of common mistake where the mistake renders the subject matter of the contract essentially and radically different from the subject matter the parties believed to exist.

Mistake as to the existence of the subject matter

In *Bell* v *Lever Bros*, Lord Atkin clearly contemplated that where there was an agreement to purchase a specific article, and the article had perished prior to the making of the contract, then the contract was void and the parties' consent was nullified, with the qualification that the seller would be liable in damages if he knew this when the contract was concluded.

In addition, s6 Sale of Goods Act 1979 provides that:

'Where there is a contract for the sale of specific goods, and the goods without the knowledge of the seller have perished at the time when the contract was made, the contract is void.'

However, the cases suggest that the matter is not as plain as it might appear. Section 6 was widely believed to embody in statute form the principle of law to be found in *Couturier* v *Hastie* (1856) 5 HL Cas 673. The plaintiffs agreed to sell and the defendant to buy a cargo of Indian corn, which, unknown to both of them, had deteriorated to such an extent in transit that it had been sold en route to England in order to minimise losses, as it would not have survived the remainder of the voyage. The contract included a policy of insurance, and the plaintiffs alleged that the defendant had bought a chance, that is, he had taken a commercial risk as to whether or not the corn existed and, in any event, he had the insurance policy, and was therefore liable to pay the agreed price. The defendant argued that the contract was for the sale of specific goods, and that as the plaintiffs were unable to sell them, he was not bound to pay. It should firstly be noted that the case was not decided on the grounds of mistake, nor was the contract held to be void, though the inference to be drawn from the judgments is that it was. The Court of Exchequer Chamber and the House of Lords decided that it was a contract for specific goods, and that because the plaintiffs could not deliver them, they were unable to sustain an action for the price. This is equally well a finding that there has been a total failure of consideration.

If the case is correctly cited as dealing with non-existent subject matter, then it follows a number of earlier decisions in the nineteenth century to the same effect.

In *Strickland* v *Turner* (1852) 7 Exch 208, the plaintiff purchased an annuity and, unknown to the parties, the annuitant was already dead. He was able to recover the price paid, the consideration having totally failed.

In *Hitchcock* v *Giddings* (1817) 4 Price 135, the plaintiff bought a remainder in fee expectant upon an estate tail which had in fact been barred. The plaintiff recovered his purchase money.

It can be seen from these two cases, and also from *Couturier* v *Hastie*, that a buyer is not liable for the price where the seller has completely failed to deliver that which he promised, and as such they merely illustrate a total failure of consideration. If a contract is void for mistake, it is void ab initio and the buyer need not pay the price, and if he has done so then he may recover it. The two concepts thus have this much in common, and because they may often have the same effect, some confusion has arisen in distinguishing between them.

In *Barrow, Lane and Ballard Ltd* v *Phillips & Co* [1929] 1 KB 574, the plaintiffs contracted to sell the defendants 700 bags of nuts, believed by both parties to be lying in a warehouse. In fact, at the time the contract was made, 109 had disappeared, apparently stolen, and before the defendants tried to take delivery of them, a further 450 went missing. The contract was held to be void under s6.

Wright J said that where a contract relates to specific goods which do not exist, the case is not to be treated as one in which the seller warrants the existence of those specific goods, but one in which there has been a failure of consideration and mistake. As a matter of law, a failure of consideration is a breach of contract for which the injured party may recover damages, to be assessed in accordance with the principles of *Hadley* v *Baxendale* (1854) 9 Exch 341. He may content himself with merely recovering the price paid; this is, however, his only remedy in a case of mistake, and may be substantially less than the sum he would recover as damages. In this respect, therefore, the statement of Wright J is misleading, and the problems that may be caused by treating the matter in this way arose in a particularly acute form in *McRae* v *Commonwealth Disposals Commission* (1950) 84 CLR 377.

The defendants accepted the plaintiff's tender of £285 for the purchase of a wrecked oil tanker, described as laying on Jourmaund Reef, off Papua New Guinea. There was no such reef, nor any wrecked tanker in the indicated area, and in consequence of this, and of having incurred considerable expense in preparing the salvage operation, the plaintiff sued for damages for breach of contract. At first instance, the judge held himself bound by *Couturier* v *Hastie* to hold that the contract was void, but on appeal in the High Court of Australia, it was held that the defendants had warranted that the tanker existed and were liable accordingly. *Couturier* had been concerned with the construction of the terms of the contract, and was not to be regarded as an authority on mutual mistake; it was decided on the grounds of a failure of consideration and not with reference to the validity or otherwise of the contract. Had this been at issue, it would have been necessary to decide whether there was an implied condition precedent that the corn existed at the time the contract was made, and that if it did not, the parties were to be excused. The court held in the present case that no such term could be implied; the buyer relied on and acted on the assertion of the seller that the tanker existed, and there was no common assumption of fact to lead to the conclusion that the creation of contractual obligations depended on the correctness of the assumption.

As an Australian case, *McRae* is of only persuasive authority in the English courts. The decision has, in fact, led to a wide reappraisal of the law relating to non-existing goods (res extincta).

Slade, at (1954) 70 LQR 385, argues that, since *McRae*, the doctrine of mutal mistake had become redundant and that there will in every case be a binding contract unless the implied term precedent referred to in the judgment is present in the contract.

Atiyah, at (1957) 73 LQR 340, adopts a similar approach to *Couturier* v *Hastie*. He says that the case is open to four possible interpretations:

1. The contract was void for mistake. Such an explanation is dismissed as being discredited because the case had nothing to do with mistake. Strictly this is true; the case was not decided in mistake, nevertheless, their Lordships probably did have the concept of mistake in their minds when they formed their judgments. Atiyah is therefore correct in as much as the case is not a binding authority on mistake, as the court held in *McRae*.

2. The contract was void for attempting the impossible; that there can never be a contract for the sale of a res extincta because a contract must have subject matter. Atiyah replies that whether or not this is so depends on the intention of the

parties. The seller may contract that the goods exist, and although he may in reality have nothing to sell, that does not mean that the contract also does not exist. The obligation on the seller may be an absolute one, just as it may be to prevent the doctrine of frustration operating.

3. The contract is void on the grounds of a condition precedent; and

4. that it illustrates that a party cannot enforce a contract where there is a failure of consideration. He considers these possibilities together, and says that there are three alternatives: (1) that if there are no goods there is no binding contract, or (2) the buyer is not absolutely bound to pay, or (3) the seller is liable for non-delivery. *Couturier* only decided (2), and it is sufficient for the buyer to establish either (1) or (3) as in neither case is he liable to pay the price.

Couturier, Hitchcock and *Strickland* are, therefore, distinguished leaving *McRae* as good law concerning the validity of a contract for non-existent goods.

In a previous edition, Cheshire and Fifoot had suggested that *McRae* would not be followed, for a number of reasons, which in the light of modern developments now seem incorrect.

In fact, as has been noted, though only of persuasive authority, *McRae* has led to considerable rethinking of the law on res extincta. Certainly, *McRae* suggests that the operation of this area of mistake is extremely limited and subject to stringent restrictions.

Mistake as to title

In *Bell* v *Lever Bros*, Lord Atkin said that where unknown to both parties the buyer already possesses legal title to that which the seller purports to transfer to him, then the transaction is inoperative in law because the transfer is impossible. He cited *Cooper* v *Phibbs* (1867) LR 2 HL 149. A agreed to take the lease of a fishery from B, though contrary to the belief of the parties at the time, A was tenant for life of the fishery and B had no title. The House of Lords granted rescission in equity, though Lord Atkin was of the opinion that the contract was void at common law and regarded the case as analogous to a situation where a contract is void for mistake owing to non-existent subject matter (above).

The principle is a restricted one, however, and it must not be thought that when a seller 'sells' to the buyer what is already the buyer's in law, the contract is thereby avoided. Although the seller may have no title, as a rule this will not mean there is no contract; the effect will be that the seller is in breach of contract as being unable to perform his obligations and correspondingly unable to enforce the contract himself. It will still be open to the buyer to sue. Thus in the case of the sale of goods, s12(1) of the 1979 Act provides that there is:

'... an implied condition on the part of the seller that in the case of a sale, he has a right to sell the goods, and in the case of an agreement to sell, he will have such a right at the time when the property is to pass'.

Generally, the contract will only be avoided when there is no implied condition or warranty as to title, where it would be correct to say that the parties have regarded ownership of the subject matter as being, in the words of Lord Thankerton, 'an essential and integral element' of it.

Negligence

There is no English authority as to the position where the mutual mistake entertained by the parties is caused by the failure of one party to take reasonable care. Section 6 only precludes from its scope a case where the seller knew the goods had perished, that is, effectively fraud, and the normal rule would apparently apply to cases of negligence.

The suggestion to the contrary is to be found in *McRae*, where the defendants were held to be guilty of the 'grossest negligence' in that they knew that the buyer would rely on their assertion that the tanker existed, and they took no steps to verify what they were asserting. In such circumstances, the guilty party cannot rely on mutual mistake:

> 'In these circumstances it seems out of the question that they should be able to assert that no contract was concluded. It is not unfair or inaccurate to say that the only "mistake" the plaintiffs made was that they believed what the Commission told them.'

The common sense of this view appears unimpeachable, subject only to the caveat that normally in contract questions of fault are not relevant because liability in contract is strict. *McRae* is noted in (1952) 68 LQR 30, where it is suggested that the law would be in an extraordinary state if a defendant, however unequivocally he has represented a state of affairs as existing, is entitled to plead mistake and avoid liability to a plaintiff who has relied on his representation of fact. The law relating to mutual mistake is, therefore, to be qualified by a rule that in such a case, an estoppel will arise against the representor. Having regard to the present trend of decisions against holding contracts void for mistake, it is safe to say that a court would regard negligence as important where a defendant sought to escape liability, as in *McRae*. Note also that new cases are coming before the courts in which fault is for the first time becoming relevant in contract cases. (See Chapter 16.)

Mutual mistake and frustration

The distinguishing feature between a contract which is void for mistake and a contract which is frustrated, is the time of the occurrence of the event. If the vitiating factor occurs *before* the contract is made and the parties are in ignorance of it, the contract may be void for mutual mistake. If, on the other hand, the event occurs after the contract is made, the contract will be frustrated. It may not always be easy to ascertain the time of the relevant event.

In *Amalgamated Investment and Property Co* v *John Walker & Sons* [1976] 3 All ER 509, the plaintiffs contracted to buy a valuable property from the defendants.

Shortly afterwards, the local authority 'listed' the building so that it could not be pulled down or altered. The value of the property was greatly reduced. The plaintiffs argued that the contract was void for mistake. They said that the relevant event was not the listing of the building, but the administrative decision to list the building. This occurred before the contract was made.

HELD: the relevant act was the official act of listing the building which occurred only after the contract was made. Mistake did not apply since the building was not listed when the contract was signed. Nor was the contract frustrated. The parties were aware of the risk that the building might be listed, and it was a risk the plaintiffs had to bear.

10.4   Unilateral mistake

In the cases discussed above, the parties have been under a mutual misapprehension, that is, they have both made the same mistake. In this section, the matters to be considered concern instances where the mistake is made by one party only or, more exceptionally, though both are mistaken each is as it were differently mistaken. The difference between mutual and unilateral mistake may be illustrated by contrast; in the former the parties are agreed on the terms of the contract and have apparently concluded a binding agreement, it is the existence or non-existence of facts unknown to the parties that operates to negative or nullify their agreement. In unilateral mistake, the mistake occurs at the time the 'contract' is concluded (a void contract is, of course, no contract at all), and the effect of the unilateral mistake is such that these parties are, unknowingly, not, in fact, in agreement at all. In this respect, the cases concern as much offer and acceptance as mistake, and turn on the principle that no contract can be formed if there is no correspondence between the offer and the acceptance. In considering whether there is a concluded agreement, the intention of the parties is usually to be construed objectively, and whatever one party's real intention is, if the language used may be reasonably construed to mean what the other party reasonably believed it to mean, then a contract will exist.

It will be necessary for the party seeking to avoid the agreement to show either that there is such ambiguity that it is impossible reasonably to impute any agreement to the parties' dealings; or that the other party has knowingly accepted an offer in terms different to those in which it was intended to be by the offeror.

These matters will be considered under the following headings:

1. Where the parties are at cross purposes.
2. Where there is a mistake as to the terms of the contract.
3. Where there is a mistake as to identity: parties not inter praesentes.

Where the parties are at cross purposes

In order to succeed under this heading the party seeking to avoid the contract must show that it would be impossible, by applying the objective test, to decide that the parties intended the contract to take one form rather than another. If the 'reasonable man' test leads to the conclusion that, in the objective approach, the contract could be understood in one sense only, both parties will be bound by the contract in this sense. The following cases illustrate the circumstances under which the court will hold that there is no concluded contract:

Raffles v *Wichelhaus* (1864) H & C 906. In a contract for the sale of cotton, the goods were specified as being those 'to arrive ex *Peerless* from Bombay'. Two ships called the *Peerless* had recently sailed from Bombay, the one to which vendors believed the contract referred had left in December, whereas the buyers believed the cotton to be on board a ship that had sailed in October. There was no evidence to ascertain to which of the two ships the contract related, and the ambiguity was held to prevent a binding contract coming into existence.

In *Falck* v *Williams* [1900] AC 176, the parties used a code for business purposes, and the plaintiff sent to the defendant an offer in code by telegraph. The message was unpunctuated and could be understood in one of two senses, the plaintiff intending it in one sense and the defendant accepting it in the other. The Privy Council held that in the absence of any evidence to resolve in which sense the offer might reasonably be said to have been intended, no contract had been concluded.

In *Scriven Bros & Co* v *Hindley & Co* [1913] 3 KB 564 the defendants wished to purchase a quantity of hemp being offered for sale by the plaintiffs by auction. Prior to the sale, the defendants inspected a sample of the hemp, but unknown to them there was also some tow for sale, in similar bales and bearing identical markings. Tow is a commercially inferior commodity; but there was nothing in the auction catalogue to distinguish between the different goods, and the defendants bid for and had knocked down to them a quantity of tow at a price extravagant for the defendants' purposes. The plaintiffs sued for the price. Lawrence J held that the defendants' conduct did not suggest, according to the objective test, that they intended to buy tow; the offer and acceptance did not coincide, the parties were never ad idem as to the subject matter of the sale, and no contract existed.

The effect of the objective test is that negligence or blameworthiness is relevant in deciding whether, despite a party's private intentions, he may objectively be held to have entered into a contract. The concept, therefore, has something in common with the approach of the High Court of Australia in *McRae* (above). In each case, carelessness will prevent a party from asserting that the contract is void. In *McRae*, he is estopped, here he is bound by the impression he induced the other party reasonably to hold.

Where there is a mistake as to the terms of the contract

Here the objective test gives way to a subjective one, because the law is concerned not with reasonable inferences, but with circumstances in which one party is actually aware of the other party's mistake.

The grounds on which one party may avoid a contract because the other knew of his mistake are, at common law, narrowly and finely drawn. Generally, in English law, parties are assumed to possess equal bargaining power, and are treated accordingly. The rule is caveat emptor, let the buyer beware, and it is upon the contracting parties to ensure, in concluding an agreement, that it properly represents their intentions and desires. Certain contracts, for example, contracts of insurance, do impose duties on the parties to make a full and frank disclosure regarding contractual matters, but at common law in the absence of, for example, a misrepresentation, there is no such duty. Of course, this position has been eroded by statute which now affords much consumer protection. The position being considered here is one of classic common law contract, and the rule is this: that it is only where one party is mistaken as to the nature of the promise made by the other party, and the other is aware of the mistake, that the contract is void.

Thus, for example, in a contract for the sale of a painting, it is insufficient that the buyer thinks he is purchasing a Rembrandt, even if the buyer is aware of this delusion. It must be the case that the seller knows that the buyer thinks that he, the seller, is contracting to sell the painting as being by Rembrandt, but, in fact, the seller is simply selling it as a painting with no undertaking as to its origin. The mistake must be more than merely being in relation to the subject matter, it must be as to the nature of the offer the seller is making regarding the subject matter.

This can be illustrated by *Smith* v *Hughes* (1871) LR 6 QB 597. In a contract for the sale of oats by sample, the defendant buyer wished to purchase, and alleged the plaintiff had described the goods as being, 'old oats'. The plaintiff denied he had thus described them; the oats were new oats and of no use to the defendant. The trial judge left the following questions to the jury:

1. If the plaintiff had described the oats as 'old oats', then should the defendant succeed?
2. If the word 'old' was not used, did the plaintiff believe the defendant believed or was under the impression that he was agreeing to buy 'old oats' and, if so, should the defendant succeed?

The Court of Queen's Bench held that the second question had not been phrased with sufficient clarity to draw the jury's attention to the difference between the plaintiff knowing or believing that the defendant thought the oats were 'old', and his knowing or believing that the defendant thought that he was contracting to sell him oats as 'old oats'. Only in the latter case is there any operative mistake as to the nature of the offer which renders the contract void.

Thus, in *Hartog* v *Colin and Shields* [1939] 3 All ER 566, the plaintiff accepted the defendants' offer to sell 30,000 hare skins at a given price per pound. The previous negotiations had been conducted on the basis of a price per piece, as was the custom of the trade, and the evidence showed that at the rate per pound, the overall price would be absurdly low. The plaintiff sought to enforce these terms. Singleton J held the plaintiff could not reasonably have supposed that the offer contained the defendants' true intention; he must have known that the defendants were mistaken as to the offer made by them regarding the price, and the contract was void as a result.

Where there is a mistake as to identity: parties not inter praesentes

The most difficult area in unilateral mistake is where a contract is void because one contracting party was unaware of the true identity of the other party. Normally, it is said, the identity of the person with whom one contracts is immaterial; this will be particularly so in, for example, a shop sale or a public auction, for example, *Dennant* v *Skinner & Colborn* [1948] 2 KB 164.

At a car auction sale, several cars were knocked down to a bidder who, for the purposes of the memorandum of sale, gave his name as King of King's of Oxford, which was false. On the strength of this, he was allowed to take the cars away in return for a worthless cheque. It was held the property passed to him when the hammer fell; being an auction, his identity was immaterial. To avoid the contract for mistake as to identity, the matter must be material to the contract. It should firstly be borne in mind that a person may not accept an offer which he knows, or ought to know, is addressed to a third person.

In *Boulton* v *Jones* (1857) 2 H & N 564, the defendant had, over a period of time, established a course of dealing with one Brocklehurst. The two had a running account against which the defendant set-off sums owed to him by Brocklehurst. Unknown to the defendant, the plaintiff took over Brocklehurst's business, and when the defendant ordered goods from Brocklehurst, the plaintiff executed the order without informing him of the changed circumstances. The defendant refused to pay for the goods, and the plaintiff sued for the price. The Court held that the defendant was not liable, and Pollock CB said:

> 'Now the rule of law is clear, that if you propose to make a contract with A, then B cannot substitute himself for A without your consent, and to your disadvantage, securing to himself all the benefit of the contract.'

It may be that the crucial factor in this case was the existence of the defendant's right to set-off Brocklehurst's debts against his account, and conceivably had this not been the case, then he might never have sent the order in the first place. As a statement of law, the ratio decidendi is undoubtedly correct, but it may be that the rule only applied to small businesses or to contracts involving some personal element, and that in the present day when large, impersonal commercial concerns predominate, it will be less readily applied. Further, it may be that what is important is the company's standing, and (in law) its independent legal personality, and not the persons who either manage or own it.

A further qualification is that a party may not avoid a contract by merely asserting that the offer was, in fact, addressed to some third person. As is the case where the parties are at cross purposes as to offer and acceptance, the test is objective; one must ask how the reasonable man in the offeree's position would have interpreted the offer. If the irresistible conclusion is that he would have reasonably believed that the offer was addressed to him, then his acceptance will be effective.

Upton-on-Severn RDC v Powell [1942] 1 All ER 220. In consequence of a fire on his property, the defendant telephoned the Upton police and asked them to send for the fire brigade. The police called the Upton fire brigade, who duly put out the fire. It subsequently transpired that although the defendant was in the Upton police area, his property fell within the province of the neighbouring Pershore fire brigade, and the plaintiff sought to recover payment for the services of the Upton fire brigade. It was held that the Upton fire brigade had acted reasonably in effect, in accepting the defendant's offer, and could recover reasonable remuneration for their services.

The converse of this situation is the proposition that no valid contract is concluded when a person accepts an offer reasonably believing that the offer is from someone other than the actual offeror, and the offeror is aware of this. This is a logical corollary, because just as a party cannot accept an offer not made to him, there is no intention to contract with the person with whom the agreement is apparently concluded.

In *Cundy v Lindsay* (1878) 3 App Cas 459, one Blenkarn, a rogue, ordered a quantity of handkerchiefs from the respondents giving his address as 37 Wood Street, Cheapside, and signing the signature to make it appear as if the order came from Blenkiron & Co, a reputable firm of 123 Wood Street, and already known to the respondents. The respondents wrote to and sent goods to Benkiron & Co of 37 Wood Street, and the rogue sold the goods to the appellants who purchased them bona fide. In the Queen's Bench Division, Blackburn J held that although the rogue had obtained the goods by false pretences, the respondent had intended to contract with the addressee of 37 Wood Street, and that the contract, though voidable for fraud, was at first valid, and the appellants therefore acquired good title. The Court of Appeal and the House of Lords thought differently. Lord Cairns said:

> 'I ask the question, how is it possible to imagine that in that state of things any contract could have arisen between the respondents and Blenkarn, the dishonest man? Of him they knew nothing and of him they never thought. With him, they never intended to deal. Their minds never even for an instant of time rested upon him, and as between him and them there was no consensus of mind which could lead to any agreement or any contract whatever. As between him and them there was merely the one side to a contract where, in order to produce a contract, two sides would be required.'

Had Blenkarn been an honest man, and if nothing had put him on inquiry that the respondents did not intend to deal with him, then a valid contract would have been concluded, following *Upton v Powell*.

The crucial fact in *Cundy* was the question of identity. Lindsay's never intended to contract with Blenkarn, but with Blenkiron & Co. Suppose, however, that they intended so to do, having being induced by Blenkarn to believe that he was a reputable firm not a rogue?

This problem arose in *King's Norton Metal Co Ltd* v *Edridge Merrett & Co Ltd* (1897) 14 TLR 98. The plaintiffs were metal manufacturers, and received a letter requesting a quotation for a quantity of rivet wire purporting to come from 'Hallam & Co' on headed notepaper containing a drawing of a large factory and details of its overseas depots and agencies. The plaintiffs delivered the quotation and, in reply to orders, despatched the wire to Hallam & Co. The scheme was a fraud by a rogue, one Wallis, who never paid for the wire and resold it to the defendants. The plaintiffs claimed its return on the grounds that the contract was void. The Court of Appeal held that it was voidable only, because the plaintiffs had always intended to deal with the person who wrote the letter, and as there was no such entity as Hallam & Co, this clearly was Wallis. The property had, therefore, passed to him, and he could in turn pass good title to the defendants. The distinction drawn from *Cundy* v *Lindsay* was that here there was no mistake as to the identity of the offeror, but simply to his attributes. They thought he was a solvent international company; in reality he was a rogue.

Two conclusions are commonly drawn from these two cases: (1) that to succeed in the case of a mistake as to identity, there must be an indentifiable third party with whom one intended to contract (considered shortly); (2) the mistake must be as to identity and not attributes. This approach has been the subject of much academic and judicial criticism, and as a practical test has been compared in its value (or lack of it) with the quality/substance distinction enunciated in *Bell* v *Lever Bros*, that has proved so difficult to apply (above).

In *Lewis* v *Averay* (below), Lord Denning MR said:

' ... this is a distinction without a difference. A man's very name is one of his attributes. It is also a key to his identity. If then he gives a false name, is it a mistake as to his identity or a mistake as to his attributes? These fine distinctions do not make good law'.

It should also be noted that his Lordship, current to his reformulation of the law of mistake, is of the opinion that the contract in *Cundy* v *Lindsay* was voidable only.

Glanville Williams, at (1945) 23 Can Bar Rev 278, has argued that the distinction between identity and attributes is based on a fundamental misconception, namely, that they are treated as being two inherently different things which is, in reality, not the case. What the courts have chosen to call a mistake as to identity is, in fact, a mistake as to attributes. Despite this compelling reasoning, the distinction persists, and was relied on by Megaw LJ, sitting alongside Lord Denning in *Lewis* v *Averay*.

Treitel suggests a compromise, that where the attribute is used to identify a person, either as an individual or as being a member of a particular class of persons, then a mistake in this respect nullifies the contract. He adds two qualifications; first that an attribute as to credit-worthiness can never render a contract void, this is something which the parties must risk in the course of their dealings. Secondly, that the law makes certain presumptions as to identity, for example, that in a contract concluded by letter, the presumption is that it is the intention to contract with the writer of the letter. A further such presumption is considered under the next heading.

Mistake inter praesentes

Mistake as to identity is further complicated by the difficulty of fitting into the analysis a succession of cases concerning contracts inter praesentes (when the parties are face to face). Prima facie the offeror will be presumed to have intended to contract with the person in front of him. Thus, in *Phillips v Brooks* [1919] 2 KB 243, a man called North entered the plaintiff's shop and asked to see some jewellery, and selected some pearls and a ring, of total value £3,000. He wrote a cheque, saying as he did so, 'You see who I am. I am Sir George Bullough', a person known by reputation to the plaintiff, and gave an address which the plaintiff checked in a directory. The plaintiff allowed North to take the ring away, valued £450, and North pledged it with the defendants for £350, who took it bona fide and without notice of the fraud. When North's cheque was dishonoured, the plaintiff sought the return of the ring, claiming the contract was void. The issue was whether the plaintiff intended to sell the ring to the person present in the shop, or whether the offer was directed at Sir George Bullough only. It was held that the plaintiff's intention was the former; he may have thought his customer was Bullough, but the evidence did not bear out the argument that the offer was made to him alone.

The inference that the judge drew was that the parties intended to thus contract. Two cases have gone the other way.

In *Hardman v Booth* (1863) 1 H & C 803, the plaintiff went to the office of Thomas Gandell & Co, where a clerk by the name of Edward Gandell was employed, though Thomas Gandell was the sole owner of the firm. The clerk dishonestly persuaded the plaintiff that he was, in fact, a partner in the firm, and induced the plaintiff to send goods to Gandell & Co, being addressed to 'Edward Gandell & Co'. The clerk pledged the goods with the defendant as security for advances, and the plaintiff sued for their return. It has held that the plaintiff's offer related to the firm 'Thomas Gandell & Co' only, and the clerk, knowing this, could not purport to accept the offer for himself, and the contract was void.

In *Lake v Simmonds* [1927] AC 487, the appellant was a jeweller, and he had in the past made a number of small sales to a woman, Esme Ellison, who described herself as the wife of a wealthy customer, Van der Borgh. He permitted her to take away two extremely valuable necklaces 'on approval' to show to her 'husband'. She was, in fact, Van der Borgh's mistress, and she absconded with the jewelry. The appellant sought to claim for the loss on his insurance policy which excluded liability for jewelry 'entrusted to a customer', but covered theft. The question turned on whether there was a contract between the jeweller and Ellison, and the House of

Lords held there was no contract; the jeweller intended to deal with the wife of Van der Borgh, and that was the reason he parted with the goods. This was held to be a mistake as to identity and not merely attributes. *Phillips* v *Brooks Ltd* was distinguished on the ground that the sale had been concluded before North made his claim to be Bullough, the effect of which had been to affect the mode of payment the jeweller was prepared to accept and to induce him to let North take the ring away. It should be stated that although this is an arguable interpretation of the facts, it was in no way at the heart of the decision of the case, and Horridge J did not rely on it. Further, in *Lake* v *Simmonds,* this line of reasoning was adopted by Viscount Haldane alone, and is not supported by the other speeches. The logical conclusion of the chain of thought is that if North had at the outset announced himself as Sir George Bullough, the contract would have been void because the jeweller intended to contract with Bullough only, as the jeweller in *Lake* was held to have intended to contract with the wife of Van der Borgh only.

Another case in which the apparent intention to contract with the person immediately present was rebutted is *Ingram* v *Little* [1961] 1 QB 31. The plaintiffs were three elderly ladies who advertised their car for sale. A rogue calling himself Hutchinson visited their home and agreed to purchase the car for £717. When he tried to make payment by cheque, they refused to accept it, and to persuade them otherwise he told them what he claimed to be his full name and address and of his local business interests. One of the plaintiffs checked his details in a telephone directory at the local post office, and found them apparently correct. As a result he was permitted to take the car away in return for his cheque, which was dishonoured. The defendant bought the car from him in a good faith. The majority of the Court of Appeal held the contract was void. Pearce LJ said that after the initial refusal to take a cheque, the parties became involved in a credit sale in which the identity of the purchaser was of the utmost importance, and that the plaintiffs were only prepared to sell after checking his name and address; they were said to attach importance to the individuality of Hutchinson of the given address, and his Lordship would not disagree with the trial judge's finding that the plaintiff's offer was capable of acceptance only by the true Hutchinson.

Devlin LJ dissenting said that the evidence merely showed that if the plaintiffs had known the truth about the rogue, they would not have contracted with him, something that is at the bottom of every contract voidable for fraud. Their mistake as to his identity did not matter; even if he had been Hutchinson, this was no guarantee that his cheque would have been met. It was as to his creditworthiness that they were mistaken, and this was not a fact at the basis of the contract, but only a belief that each contracting party has that the other will honour his promise.

The most recent case disagrees with *Ingram* v *Little*: *Lewis* v *Averay* [1972] 1 QB 198. The plaintiff advertised his car for sale and a rogue called round to see it and offered to buy it, claiming to be the actor 'Richard Greene'. He signed a cheque for £450 'R A Green' and asked to take the car away with him. The plaintiff asked for proof of his identity, and the rogue showed him an admission pass to Pinewood

Studios in the name of 'Richard A Green'. The plaintiff, in consequence, allowed him to take the car. The cheque was dishonoured and the defendant purchased it bona fide for £200. The Court of Appeal held that the contract with the rogue was voidable only, that the plaintiff had failed to show that he did not intend to contract with the person actually present.

Lord Denning MR endorsed the judgments in *King's Norton Metal* and *Phillips* v *Brooks* and said:

'When two parties have come to a contract – or rather what appears, on the face of it, to be a contract – the fact that one party is mistaken as to the identity of the other does not mean that there is no contract, or that the contract is a nullity and void from the beginning. It only means that the contract is voidable, that is, liable to be set aside at the instance of the mistaken person, so long as he does so before third parties have in good faith acquired rights under it.'

The other two members of the court were less sweeping in their judgments, though nonetheless critical of the decision in *Ingram* v *Little*. Phillimore LJ thought it turned on its 'very special and unusual facts', and Megaw LJ held that, in both cases, the mistake was simply as to attributes, namely the rogue's creditworthiness, and that identity was not a matter of vital importance.

In the light of this decision, it is probably correct to say the presumption against holding a contract void where it is concluded inter praesentes, is very strong indeed, and the facts would have to be very special (more so than in *Ingram* v *Little*) to rebut it. A possible formulation is suggested in a note in (1972) 88 LQR 161; that the test ought to depend on an analysis of the terms of the agreement between the parties, and that where they meet face to face it is not usual to regard their identity as a vital term of the contract, but that a different conclusion will be reached if the seller has made it clear that the purchaser's identity is an essential point. It is suggested that this is a fair resolution of the authorities as they stand at present.

Lord Denning's view in *Lewis* v *Averay* finds support in the Twelfth Report of the Law Reform Committee (1966) Cmnd 2958, which recommended that where goods are sold under a mistake as to the buyer's identity, the contract should, so far as third parties are concerned, be voidable not void. This also suggests that the members of the Committee think that this can only be established by legislative enactment and is not as yet, despite his Lordships' judgment, part of the English law of contract.

The Committee also considered the suggestion of Devlin LJ in *Ingram* v *Little* that the courts should be given a power to apportion in such cases. The importance of such a concept will be readily appreciated. The authorities concern, almost universally, the problem as to who should suffer the loss caused by a rogue's fraudulent activities, the original vendor seeking to re-establish title to the goods by proving the contract was void, or the third party who has acquired the goods from the rogue, bona fide for value without notice of the fraud? Devlin LJ suggests that the:

'... loss should be divided between them in such proportion as is just in all the circumstances. If it be pure misfortune, the loss should be borne equally; if the fault or imprudence of either party has caused or contributed to the loss, it should be borne by that party in the whole or in the greater part.'

The Committee considered that such a power would be undesirable, because it would create uncertainty in an area of the law where certainty and clarity are particularly important, that it would be likely to increase litigation; and it would make it difficult for businessmen to obtain reliable legal advice or assess the likely financial outcome of their dealings and insure against the risks involved. In particular, the Committee highlighted the practical and procedural difficulties where there were more than two persons involved, that is, where there was a string of innocent purchasers.

An innocent third party might face the gravest problems in showing that the vendor was negligent; after all, that was a transaction to which he was not a party and about which he knows nothing. Also, the Committee disagreed with Devlin LJ regarding the position when the original vendor is not at fault, and was unable to see why, if he has a right in law to retain title to his chattel, he should be penalised, although his behaviour has fallen below the required standard.

It is not clear if the Committee is correct in fearing an increase in litigation and complications in apportionment. It may be that in the majority of cases it would simply be a matter of apportioning between seller and third party, and that usually there is no entangling chain of purchasers. Additionally, the view that it would make life difficult for businessmen is also arguable; Devlin LJ was probably contemplating private sales, which are where real injustices do arise. It seems unlikely that the power of apportionment would be an intolerable extra burden on businessmen. It might finally be said that although such a discretionary power would create a degree of uncertainty, it cannot be stated with confidence that the law is as clear and as certain as the Committee seems to think it is.

In the cases considered above, in all but *King's Norton Metal Co*, the offeror has contemplated making a contract with a clearly identifiable third party, be he Brocklehurst, Sir George Bullough, or Richard Greene. It is suggested that it need not be the case that the third person need be alive, or even have ever existed. This was impliedly the view of Lord Haldane in *Lake* v *Simmonds* and, whatever the correctness of the decision, it seems that in principle providing A can show that he made an offer to B in the erroneous belief that he was making an offer to C (whether or not C existed), then if B knew or reasonably ought to have known this, the contract would be void. *King's Norton* would be distinguished on the grounds that the contract was made with the author of the letter and as such was not an identifiable third party; it was the party with whom the seller had been corresponding, albeit fraudulently masquerading under another name.

It must be conceded, however, that the judge was of the opinion that an independent third party, that is, Hallam & Co would have had to exist in order to avoid the contract, and it would follow that a belief in a non-existent third party would not avail the seller. Bearing in mind the Court's increasing reluctance to permit the plea of mistake at common law, although the proposition that the third party need not, in fact, exist may be based on sound legal reasoning, it might not meet with approval when argued.

A further refinement to this hypothesis is where A makes an offer to B in the belief that B is not B (but otherwise does not entertain any belief as to his identity). Goodhart (1941) 57 LQR 228 has illustrated that such a case is fundamentally different to the one where A believes that B is C. Generally in the postulated case, the offer has been made to B, and whether or not he is aware that A would not have made the offer had he known B's identity, he may accept it, although it may be voidable at the suit of A. The contract will only be void ab initio if A proves an express or implied term in the contract, either that B is not B, or else that the offer is not one capable of acceptance by B. In such a case, there would be a mistake as to the terms of the contract known to B which would avoid the contract. See *Smith* v *Hughes*, *Hartog* v *Colin & Shields* (above). Thus in *Said* v *Butt* [1920] 3 KB 497, the plaintiff, a theatre critic knowing that the manager of a theatre would refuse to sell a ticket to him, employed a third party to buy on his behalf.

HELD: he knew the theatre would not contract with him, and he could not, by using an agent, cause the theatre to so contract against their knowledge and contrary to their express refusal. It is rare that such a term is ever expressly incorporated into a contract, and the job of the courts is, therefore, to consider where such a term may properly be implied into the contract.

In *Sowler* v *Potter* [1940] 1 KB 271, in May 1938, the defendant was convicted under the name of Ann Robinson of permitting disorderly conduct in a café. In July she began calling herself Ann Potter, and obtained from the plaintiff the lease of certain property in that name. The agent who conducted the negotiations over the lease with the defendant for the plaintiff said in evidence that he knew of the record of Ann Robinson, and had he known that the two were one and the same, he would not have completed the contract. Accordingly, the plaintiff alleged that the lease was void. The judge concluded that the agent thought he was entering into a contract with someone other than Ann Robinson, and said that in the grant of a lease, as between landlord and tenant, the consideration of identity was a vital element in the contract, and that the plaintiff's mistake rendered it void ab initio.

This case has been criticised – Goodhart (1941) 57 LQR 228 and judicially by Lord Denning MR in *Solle* v *Butcher* and *Lewis* v *Averay* – and is probably no longer to be regarded as good law. *King's Norton Metal Co* was apparently not cited to Tucker J in *Sowler* v *Potter*, and that case is authority that it is not enough that had the seller known the true facts about the buyer, he would not have entered into the contract, his motive for contracting is in this respect not relevant. It cannot be reasonably argued that at the time the lease was granted, it was uppermost in the agent's mind that the lessee should not be Ann Robinson and, therefore, no term could be implied into the offer that Ann Robinson was excluded from it and the contract would be voidable only. The case is really on all fours with *King's Norton Metal Co*, which has subsequently been affirmed, and must be the preferred authority.

The rule that a contract will only be void where A contracts with B thinking B is some identifiable third party, C, was criticised by Wilson in (1954) 17 MLR 515, who argues that the third party approach is only a useful guide for proving mistake, and that in any given situation what is important is that A should show an absence of an intention to contract with B. The example is given that if A refuses to deal with B, and B therefore disguises himself as C, the contract is void because A will be held to have intended to deal with C, whereas if B merely conceals his own identity, the contract is not void, there being no identifiable third party. This is said to be artificial, and is a conclusion only reached because of self-imposed limitations on the doctrine of mistake. Wilson suggests the question to be posed is: Did A intend to contract with B, with whom he has apparently entered into legal relations? and not 'With whom did A intend to contract?' Thus the case where A intends to contract with C is merely illustrative of an intention not to contract with B, and ought not to be the central point around which the law revolves. He relies on the writings of the French jurist Pothier, who said that where the consideration of the person with whom a party is willing to contract enters as an element into the contract, an error in this respect destroys consent and annuls the contract.

The contrary view, first cogently set out by Goodhart at (1941) 57 LQR 228 (above), is put in reply by Unger in (1955) 18 MLR 259. He argues, first, that Wilson's approach would have the effect of extending the doctrine of mistake at common law, and that it should be the policy of the law to uphold contracts rather than destroy them. Secondly, he says that Wilson's thesis, laying emphasis as it does on the alleged logical inconsistency of the third party approach, completely ignores the fact that even where there is no third party, the contract is still voidable and the full range of equitable remedies is available, at the court's discretion, to do justice between the parties, and that any inconsistency there may be is of little consequence. Thirdly, and perhaps least convincingly, he says that the third party approach goes hand in hand with the identity/attributes distinction considered above. In view of the criticism this distinction has attracted, this point must be taken with care.

The importance of third party purchasers for value in the mistake cases previously discussed has already been considered. The final point for inquiry in this section is whether it is possible for a third party to intervene and allege that a contract is void for mistake where the contracting parties themselves choose not to do so. The issue has not yet been considered by the English courts, but was raised in the New Zealand case: *Fawcett* v *Saint Merat* [1959] NZLR 952.

The plaintiff advertised her car for sale and the defendant, accompanied by a Mrs D, made an offer to purchase it, which was accepted. The plaintiff gave the defendant possession of the car and of the certificate of registration in return for a post-dated cheque, which was subsequently dishonoured. Judgment in default was obtained against the defendant but never satisfied. In the meantime, Mrs D, representing that she was the plaintiff, sold the car to the claimant company, and the plaintiff sought to satisfy the judgment by issuing a writ of sale under which the car was seized from the company by the sheriff. As the plaintiff had obtained judgment, it was not open to her to argue that the original contract between her and the defendant was voidable, because by suing on it she had affirmed it. To succeed she therefore had to show that the sale between Mrs D and the claimant company was void and that no title passed. Hardie Boys J held, following *Phillips* v *Brooks* and distinguishing *Hardman* v *Booth*, that the company had intended to contract with the person present, identified by sound and hearing, that is, Mrs D; the offer was not made to the plaintiff only. Secondly, he held that the plaintiff was not allowed to raise 'in the name of one of the contracting parties' the question of mistake as to identity so as to have the contract avoided, relying on an absence of any authority that such an action 'would lie'. Guest (1960) 76 LQR 207 argues that where a contract is void at common law, it is void ab initio, and that therefore the plaintiff is not raising the invalidity 'in the name of one of the contracting parties', but is asserting it on his own behalf. Further, *Lake* v *Simmonds* allowed an insurer to argue that the appellant jeweller had made a valid contract with a third party. His conclusion is that a third party has locus standi to intervene, but that here the plaintiff should be estopped from so doing because by her conduct in parting with the car registration certificate and accepting a post-dated cheque in return, she had armed the defendant with the appearance of being the owner of the car.

Some such restriction would be necessary, or the doctrine would appear to have some very odd results, for example, if the defendant in *Boulton* v *Jones* had accepted the goods from the plaintiff, would it be open to a third party to allege that the contract was void and that the property never passed? It may be that the courts would look to see if the third party had some legitimate interest for intervening, and only permit it in such circumstances.

Some cases concerning mistaken identity are more complex. Because the fraud involved in the case below took some considerable ingenuity to set up, the parties might be said to be inter praesentes, or not, depending on the exact stage at which one considers the mistake as to identity to have occurred.

In *Citibank NA* v *Brown Shipley & Co Ltd; Midland Bank* v *Brown Shipley & Co* [1991] 2 All ER 690, in several separate transactions involving different banks a person claiming to be a signatory of a company's account at one bank (the issuing bank) telephoned another bank (the receiving bank) with a request to buy substantial amounts of foreign currency, payment to be made by a bankers' draft issued by the issuing bank. The caller then telephoned the issuing bank, instructing them to prepare this bankers' draft to be drawn on the company's account. This the issuing company did: they handed the draft over to a messenger who purported to be from the company, in exchange for a letter that purported to confirm the telephone instructions, with forged signatures. The draft was then paid to the receiving bank, who after checking that the draft was genuinely issued by the issuing bank and had been issued in the ordinary course of business, paid the cash to the fraudster. In due course the receiving bank presented the draft to, and were paid by, the issuing bank. When the fraud was finally discovered the issuing bank brought an action against the receiving bank to recover the value of the draft on the basis that title in the draft had never passed to the receiving bank, as it could not derive good title from the fraudster, and the banks did not have a contract between them. The court decided that it was irrelevant that the delivery of the bankers' draft from the issuing bank to the receiving bank with the authority of the issuing bank established a voidable contract between the two banks.

The fact that the issuing bank had mistakenly dealt with a fraudster instead of the company with whom they thought they were dealing did not affect the formation of the contract between the two banks; admittedly the fraudster, because of mistaken identity had no title, but he was merely a 'conduit'. Title did not have to pass from the fraudster to the receiving bank. Of the two innocent parties, the issuing bank must bear the loss.

Mistake at common law – an appraisal of the different views

It will be appreciated from what has already gone before that explaining mistake at common law poses many problems. Some writers have concluded that these problems are not simply concerned with the interpretation of cases, but with the more fundamental point that, in fact, on consideration it is the case that authorities treated as being concerned with mistake are, in fact, not authority for this at all, and as Slade says at (1954) 70 LQR 405 the whole thing is a 'myth'. Some of these arguments will now be considered.

Cheshire and Fifoot (1944) 60 LQR 175, and *Law of Contract* 9th edition, argue that, since *Bell* v *Lever Bros*, mutual mistake will now only operate where the mistaken assumption is that the very subject matter of the contract is in existence, and that the wide language of the speeches suggesting that any false and fundamental assumption will suffice is not borne out by the decision in the case. The argument is that if, in Lord Atkin's words, 'the new state of facts makes the contract something different in kind from the contract in the original state of facts' renders the contract void, then if this test was not satisfied in *Bell* v *Lever Bros*, it will hardly ever be. The conclusion is that if the subject matter has ceased to exist, then there is nothing on which a binding contract can operate, and the parties have thus attempted the impossible. The reply is that, first, their Lordships in their speeches explained why the contract in *Bell* was not different in kind under the newly discovered facts, namely, that it was still possible of performance entirely in the way the parties had envisaged it at the outset. Regarding non-existent subject matter, it is suggested that the learned editors fail to appreciate both the correctness and the importance of the decision in *McRae*.

A forceful attack on the traditional doctrine of mistake at common law is to be found in the judgments of Lord Denning, and in the writings of Atiyah and Slade. Thus in *Solle* v *Butcher*, Denning LJ (as he then was) said:

> 'All previous decisions on this subject must now be read in the light of *Bell* v *Lever Bros*. The correct interpretation of that case, to my mind, is that once a contract has been made, that is to say, once the parties, whatever their inmost states of mind, have to all outward

appearances agreed with sufficient certainty in the same terms on the same subject matter, then the contract is good unless and until it is set aside for failure of some condition on which the existence of the contract depends, or for fraud, or on some equitable ground. Neither party can rely on his own mistake to say it was a nullity from the beginning, no matter that it was a mistake which to his mind was fundamental, and no matter that the other party knew that he was under a mistake. A fortiori if the other party did not know of the mistake, but shared it.'

And he reiterated this view in *Magee v Pennine Insurance Co Ltd* [1969] 2 QB 507.

Atiyah (1975) 73 LQR 340, and Atiyah and Bennion (1961) 24 MLR 421, argue for the implied term theory considered under 'Mistake as to the existence of the subject matter' above, that is that the risk of the facts on the basis of which the buyer and seller concluded their agreement not being correct will normally lie on either one or the other, and that only if there is an implied condition precedent that the contract will be inoperative if the facts are not as they are believed to be, are the parties discharged from their obligations.

Slade (1954) 70 LQR 405 adopts a similar stance, and starts from the proposition that a mistake as such may be a ground for affording a party some relief in equity, but in itself is irrelevant at law. A contract is void at law only if there is an implied term as referred to above, or if offer and acceptance are found on a true interpretation to be divergent. He divides the cases into three categories.

1. Where one party is unaware of the other's true intention.
2. Where one party is aware of the other's true intention.
3. Where the parties contract under the same mistaken assumption.

Where one party is unaware of the other's true intention
This is simply a question of whether one party has accepted the other's offer on the terms in which one party could enforce in court; if so, there is a contract. Because of the objective approach to offer and acceptance, a party is, in effect, estopped from denying the existence of a contract where his mistake is self-induced. The corollary of this is that the parties are not bound where the offer and acceptance are ambiguous. The general rule, therefore, is that if offer and acceptance are in identical terms, judging objectively, there is a contract.

Where one party is aware of the other's true intention
Here the approach is subjective; the promisor is not bound to fulfil a promise in a sense in which the promisee knew at the time of the promise he did not intend it. Thus in *Hartog v Colin & Shields*, there was no consensus as to terms.

Where the parties contract under the same mistaken assumption
Under this heading, Slade argues the implied term theory, and cites *Pope & Pearson v Buenos Aires New Gas Co* (1892) 8 TLR 758 per Lindley LJ: 'the defendants might have succeeded if they could have proved that it was an implied condition of the contract that it was not to be binding unless the information ... was correct', and

Lord Atkin in *Bell* v *Lever Bros*: 'the proposition does not amount to more than this, that if the contract expressly or impliedly contains a term that a particular assumption is a condition of the contract, the contract is avoided if the assumption is not true.'

He further argues that because it must be the presumed intention of both the parties, it is almost impossible to imply such a term regarding the quality of the subject matter, and that is why the contract in *Leaf* v *International Galleries* was not void. The conclusion is, therefore, that it is the Court's task to discover what are the terms, express or implied, of the offer and acceptance.

As statements of the law, (1) and (2) are almost unarguable, and it is really a matter of classification whether such matters should be treated as ones of 'mistake' or of offer and acceptance. It is sufficient for present purposes that examiners treat them as separate topics falling within mistake.

The real difficulty arises under (3). There is a danger of relying too much on extracts from *Bell*, the judgments of which are not obviously clear as is desirable. The proposition Lord Atkin refers to is immediately qualified by the statement that it does not take the Court very far in its inquiry in ascertaining whether a contract contains such a term, and his Lordship warns against constructing for the parties contracts which they have not in terms made, by importing implications which would appear to make the contract more businesslike and more fast. It is suggested that the general approach of the majority in *Bell* is that there is scope for an independent doctrine of mistake. Grunfield (1952) 15 MLR 297 argues that in the judgments of neither Lord Atkin nor Lord Thankerton is there to be found the severe curtailment of the function of the common law of contractual mistake, which is the primary feature of Lord Denning's restatement of the law in *Solle* v *Butcher* and subsequent cases. This, it is submitted, is correct; what the court was trying to do in *Bell* was to define the circumstances in which the doctrine operated, not to deny its very existence, and the judgments proceeded on the basis that certain types of mistake will avoid a contract. The conclusion that may tentatively be drawn is that the doctrine operates, where on the true construction of the contract, it is apparent that it was never the intention of the parties that the contract should apply to the newly discovered situation. Some support may be derived from an article by Wade 7 CLJ 341, one of the few writers to support the decision in *Bell* v *Lever Bros*. He argues that the correct approach following that case is as follows: that the subject matter of the contract consists of all the points that are contained within the contract as agreed by the parties, and those points which are outside it go at most to motive and are irrelevant in mistake. If the parties intend their agreement to depend for its validity on any one fact, they must state this in the contract, that is, the distinction is between what they ask for and the test, which is, did each party get what he bargained for? If either did not, as the result of a common error between the parties, then there must have been a mistake within the terms of the contract. This was not the case in *Bell*, where respondents did get what they bargained for; it was simply a bad bargain. Therefore, if it is possible for the agreement to be executed exactly according to its terms, there is a valid contract and no mistake. This is, in a sense the reverse of the implied term theory, in which the parties must have made provision for the contract to be inoperative for mistake, whereas in the suggested approach, the contract does not operate because the parties have not made provision for these unexpected facts. The jurisprudential difference is fundamental; the end result may be much the same, because in either case the court is considering the application of the terms of the contract. Depending on which view is adopted, the matter is initially considered from opposite ends but, by a course of construction, the two may well strike common ground in the middle.

10.5   Non est factum

Where a person, by signing a document, enters into contractual relations with another party, it may be possible for him to avoid liability under the contract if he signed the document under a mistaken belief as to the essential nature of the document, by raising the plea 'non est factum', namely, that 'it is not my deed'. This is an exception to the general rule that a person who signs a document is bound by it, whether or not he reads it or understands it, and was originally applicable where the mistaken party was unable to read the document owing to illiteracy or blindness; further, it could also only be pleaded where the document was, in fact, a deed. The plea has evolved through judicial decision such that now it applies to any written contract, and though some special circumstance must now attach to the mistaken party, it no longer needs to be inability to read.

The nature of the mistake

To define and delineate the nature of the mistake to which the plea may successfully be raised has proved difficult. The former approach was that the mistake must be as to the character of the document as opposed to its contents, and this was exemplified in *Howatson* v *Webb* [1907] 1 Ch 537 affirmed; [1908] 1 Ch 1.

The defendant was the trustee and nominee of land held for a solicitor, who induced the defendant to sign deeds which he believed were deeds of transfer. In fact, one of them was a mortgage to a third party as security for a loan, and the third party subsequently transferred the mortgage to the plaintiff. Warrington J held that the plea of non est factum failed because the defendant had been told that the documents were deeds relating to the property, and they did so relate, and his mind was therefore applied to dealing with the property, he was simply mistaken as to contents.

As a workable distinction, to differentiate between character and contents left much to be desired. It attracted criticism similar to that levelled against the substance/quality distinction in *Bell* v *Lever Bros*, and against the contrast between attributes and identity, *King's Norton Metal Co* v *Edridge Merrett & Co* and *Cundy* v *Lindsay* (above). In the case of non est factum, the unworkable rule was eventually rejected in the leading case in the House of Lords *Gallie* v *Lee* [1971] AC 1004 (*sub nom Saunders* v *Anglia Building Society*).

The plaintiff gave the deeds of her leasehold interest in the house in which she resided to her nephew, P, for him to raise money on its security providing that she could continue to reside there rent free until her death. She knew that a friend of P's, L, was helping him to arrange the loan, and L requested her to sign a document to this end. She had broken her spectacles and signed the document unread, though in reply to her inquiry she was told that it related to the gift by deed to her nephew. The document thus signed conveyed the house by sale to L, who did not pay the price, and subsequently mortgaged the house to a building society. The House of Lords, affirming the Court of Appeal, held that the object of the exercise was to raise money for the nephew, and that this would have been equally achieved by the alternative means envisaged by P and L, and would have been so achieved had L been honest, as by the plaintiff's original plan. Their Lordships rejected the test used in *Howatson* v *Webb*, and preferred to say, in the words of Lord Pearson, that it must be the case that the document was 'fundamentally different' or 'radically different' or 'totally different' to what the mistaken party believed it to be. Other terms employed by their Lordships were that the difference must be 'serious', 'essential' or 'very substantial'.

Undoubtedly, the new test is considerably more satisfactory than the character/contents approach. It now means, for example, that a mistake as to the size of a financial transaction – where an undertaking or guarantee is, in fact, for £10,000 rather than the £1,000 it is believed to be – could give rise to the plea. Formerly, it would have been excluded as being a mistake relating to contents only. Equally, if the difference between £10,000 and £1,000 is fundamental, the borderline case of £1,000 to £5,000 or £2,000 cannot be answered with confidence. Nor is it clear whether the nature of the mistake should be considered in an objective or subjective sense – the difference between £10,000 and £1,000 might be fundamental to an improverished law lecturer, but not necessarily to a multi-millionaire. In the test's flexibility, is also its uncertainty, and it may be that the end result is not very different – where a mistake is fundamental or radical, it would not strain judicial reasoning too much to classify the difference as being one of character as opposed to contents. Nevertheless, *Gallie* v *Lee* is probably logically and academically a happier solution to the difficulty, so long as the degree of discretion that lies in the Court's hands is appreciated.

As examples of cases in which the plea succeeded, reference may be made to two cases which, although decided before *Gallie* v *Lee*, are correct on their facts, even if the reasoning thereto could not stand with the new propositions formulated by their Lordships.

In *Foster* v *Mackinnon* (1869) LR 4 CP 704, the defendant, an elderly gentleman, was induced to indorse a bill of exchange, having been told that it was merely a guarantee and not having seen the face of the bill. The bill was later indorsed to the plaintiff who sued on it. Byles J held it invalid:

'... not merely on the ground of fraud ... but on the ground that the mind of the signer did not accompany the signature; in other words, that he never intended to sign and therefore in contemplation of law never did sign the contract to which his name is appended'.

Likewise, in *Lewis* v *Clay* (1898) 67 LJQB 224, at the request of a third party, one N, the defendant signed in a number of cut-open spaces on otherwise concealed documents, believing he was witnessing N's signature. In reality, he had signed promissory notes in favour of the plaintiff worth approximately £11,000. The plea succeeded on the grounds that promissory notes were altogether different to merely attesting a formal signature. See *Lloyds Bank* v *Waterhouse* (1990) The Independent 27 February.

Who may plead non est factum?

From originating as a plea to protect the illiterate, it appeared at one time as if the doctrine had been sufficiently extended such as to make it available to all persons. In *Gallie* v *Lee*, the House of Lords sought to disabuse lawyers of this idea. Lord Pearson said that the plea was open to persons who, for some permanent or temporary reason (not limited to blindness or illiteracy), are incapable of both reading and sufficiently understanding the deed or other document to be signed, that is, that such persons must be unable to understand to the extent that they are unable to detect a fundamental difference between the actual document, and the document as the signer had believed it to be. Lord Reid spoke of persons unable to understand the purport of a particular document, whether due to defective education, illness, or innate incapacity, and Lord Wilberforce included senile persons. It is apparent that normally a literate person of full understanding and capacity will be unable to plead non est factum.

Note that non est factum may not be used by a party who, having granted a power of attorney to another, finds that the power of attorney has been abused; or, the power having not been properly allocated, is used by a person who is incompetent. In *Norwich & Peterborough Building Society* v *Steed* [1992] 3 WLR 669, a power of attorney was granted to his mother by the defendant. She never properly understood the concept of power of attorney and was tricked into signing the necessary documents for the sale of the defendant's house at a very low price. The plea of non est factum could not be used by the defendant.

Negligence

Surprisingly, the effect of the signer's negligence was in considerable doubt until *Gallie* v *Lee*. One might have presumed that in view of the special nature of the plea, it was essential for the signer to show that he had not contributed to his mistake by failing to take reasonable care. However, prior to *Gallie* v *Lee*, the authoritative decision was that of the Court of Appeal in *Carlisle & Cumberland Banking Co* v *Bragg* [1911] 1 KB 489, in which it was held that negligence did not prevent a party from raising the plea, except in the special case of negotiable instruments where an indorser or an acceptor owes a duty to every subsequent bona fide holder for value. The Court clearly had tortious principles in mind in coming to the decision, and held that the plaintiff's loss was not caused by the signer's negligence, but by the fraud of a third party who had induced the defendant to sign a document without reading it. In *Gallie* v *Lee*, the House of Lords said that the tortious concept of a duty of care to one's neighbour had no relevance here, and it was simply a question of whether the signer had acted reasonably or carelessly in signing the document. Lord Wilberforce said that the signer has the responsibility of the normal man of prudence, and that the onus of proof lies on him to prove that he acted carefully. In considering this, the Court may pay particular attention to the nature of document signed and, in general, will consider all the circumstances of the case.

Mistake as to identity

The plea is not applicable where A signs a document believing it to be in favour of B whereas, in fact, it is in favour of C, thus it was that the plea failed in *Howatson* v *Webb* and *Gallie* v *Lee*. The rationale has been suggested as being that even if a party cannot understand a document, normally by reading it he would be able to discern to whom it is made out.

Ignorance

The essence of the plea is that there must be a mistake as to the essential nature of the document, thus to sign in complete ignorance of what is contained within does not permit the plea.

In *Gillman* v *Gillman* (1946) 174 LT 272, a wife signed a document in ignorance of its contents. In fact, it was a separation deed, and shortly afterwards her husband left her.

HELD: she was bound by the deed.

Nor is the plea applicable to documents signed in blank; it pertains only to documents that as and when signed impose some liability on the signer.

For a detailed analysis of *Gallie* v *Lee* see Stone (1972) 88 LQR 190.

Non est factum and undue influence

It may be useful to remember that although non est factum may not lie as a defence – at least against a third party – other defences may be available, for example, duress or undue influence (although the extent to which the latter can be of assistance may be limited). Undue influence was a defence, nevertheless, in *Avon Finance Co Ltd* v

Bridger [1985] 2 All ER 281 CA: a son induced his elderly parents to sign a mortgage in favour of a moneylender as security for a loan to him. The parents were in the course, as they believed, of selling their house and not executing a mortgage.

HELD: the parents were negligent in executing the mortgage deed and, therefore, could not rely upon non est factum as against the plaintiff. They could, however, rely on a defence of undue influence. The plaintiffs had sufficient notice of the circumstances to be bound by the equity.

10.6   Mistake in equity

In view of the uncertainties discussed above concerning the operation of mistake at common law, the courts are making increasing use of the special remedies available in equity that enable the court to do justice between the parties, whilst refraining from making the all or nothing decision on the validity of the contract which it must do at common law. In equity, the contract is not void ab initio, and the old rule was that equity will follow the law such that if the contract is valid at law, in general, the Court will not intervene. The scope of the new equitable jurisdiction that the courts have been claiming for themselves will be considered in the light of the three equitable remedies available, which are: specific performance; rectification of a written agreement; and rescission.

Specific performance

Where one party to a contract refuses to perform his part of the bargain, the other party may request the court to make an order for specific performance, which directs the party in breach to carry out the contract in accordance with its terms. The remedy is discretionary and the court will usually not order specific performance where damages would adequately compensate the injured party. In mistake in contract, although damages might fail to do this, the remedy will be refused, at the Court's discretion, where it would be inequitable to permit the plaintiff to enforce the contract on the terms in which it stands. Thus in *Webster* v *Cecil* (1861) 30 Beav 62, the defendant, having previously refused the plaintiff's offer of £2,000 for certain land which he had put up for sale, wrote to the plaintiff offering to sell the land for £1,250, which the plaintiff accepted. The defendant had intended to offer the land for £2,250 and, in the light of the previous dealings, the plaintiff must have known that the defendant had made a mistake. The contract was probably void at law, *Hartog* v *Colin and Shields* (above), but the plaintiff brought an action for specific performance. This was refused, and the plaintiff was left 'to bring such action at law as he might be advised'.

Specific performance may also be refused in the case of mutual mistake: *Grist* v *Bailey* [1967] Ch 532. The plaintiff agreed to buy a house, freehold, from the defendant, 'subject to the existing tenancy thereof'. Although the market value of the house with vacant possession was £2,250, the contract price was only £850 because both parties believed that the sitting tenant was protected by the Rent Acts. This was wrong and the tenant left the house shortly afterwards. Goff J, following *Solle* v *Butcher*, held the mistake did not make the contract a nullity at law, but that it was a mutual fundamental misapprehension which enabled the defendant to resist the action for specific performance. In addition, the defendant was granted rescission of the contract.

In the case of unilateral mistake, specific performance will be refused if the plaintiff had contributed, albeit innocently and unintentionally, to the defendant's mistake.

In *Denny* v *Hancock* (1870) LR 6 Ch App 1, intending to bid for a property being sold by auction, the defendant inspected a plan which showed the western side bounded by shrubs or trees. He located what he thought were the marked trees, bounded by an iron fence. In fact, these were not marked on the plan, and the real boundary was denoted by stumps, which were so covered by shrubs that they could not easily be seen. The Court of Appeal held that he had been misled by both the plan and the actual state of the grounds, and that his mistake was 'occasioned by at least crassa negligentia on the part of the vendor' and specific performance was refused.

The position is more difficult where the defendant's mistake is in no way attributable to the plaintiff's conduct, but is, nevertheless, a reasonable mistake to make in the circumstances. The following cases may be contrasted:

In *Malins* v *Freeman* (1837) 2 Keen 25, at a sale of land by auction, the defendant mistakenly thought that because lot 2, the property of the plaintiff, had been sold, lot 3 was the lot he wished to buy, that is, the land to be offered for sale after the plaintiff's land. In fact, lots 1–5 belonged to the plaintiff, and lot 3 was knocked down to the defendant. It was held that although the defendant was 'hurried and inconsiderate', he had never intended to enter into this contract, and it would be inequitable to compel him to perform it.

In *Tamplin* v *James* (1880) 15 Ch D 215, an inn and adjoining premises were being offered for sale by auction, and exhibited plans clearly showed that two plots of land at the rear were not included in the sale. The defendant purchased this property in the belief that the lot did include the additional two plots, and sought to resist an action for specific performance. Baggallay LJ said:

> 'But where there has been no misrepresentation and where there is no ambiguity in the terms of the contract, the defendant cannot be allowed to evade the performance of it by the simple statement that he has made a mistake'.

The cases are not easily reconciled because, in each, unlike *Denny* v *Hancock*, the fault lay with the purchaser, and it would be a futile exercise to attempt to define the degree of fault in each case, except that the standard of care must be that approved in *Tamplin* v *James* that if there was no reasonable ground for the defendant's mistake, specific performance should be ordered. One explanation of the cases is that even if the mistake is unreasonable, then the contract should not be enforced where it would cause hardship to the defendant, and that in *Malins* v

Freeman the defendant would have been forced to complete the purchase of an entirely different piece of land to the one he intended to buy, whereas in *Tamplin* v *James* the difference was arguably peripheral. The solution is a neat one, though it leaves a degree of uncertainty in predicting which way a court will decide. As the relief sought is discretionary, this is to a certain extent inevitable, and one must confine oneself to saying that particular cases will turn on their particular facts. This conclusion is reinforced by the judgment at first instance in *Van Praagh* v *Everidge* [1903] 1 Ch 434.

At a sale of land by auction, the order of sale was clearly displayed on a notice affixed to the auctioneer's rostrum and was also given on a number of distributed handbills. The defendant bid for and had knocked down to him a property other than the one he wished to purchase. It was held that the mistake was entirely due to his own fault, and the plaintiff could succeed in an action for specific performance.

Rectification

The remedy of rectification is available where by a mistake a written document does not accord with the true agreement between the parties. In these circumstances, the court has the equitable power to rectify the agreement so as to bring it into line with the true agreement. The mistake is not in the agreement, but in the way it has been written down: *Mackenzie* v *Coulson* (1869) LR 8 Eq 368 'Courts of Equity do not rectify contracts; they may and do rectify instruments purporting to have been made in pursuance of the terms of the contracts' per James VC.

As with specific performance, the remedy is discretionary, and to obtain rectification, three conditions must be satisfied:

1. There must be no other suitable alternative remedy. That which is omitted from the instrument may be enforceable as a collateral contract; a voluntary rectification will suffice, although unlike a decree it is not retrospective and may be less advantageous; or the matter may be solved by construction of the agreement, and in reported cases omitted words have been read into an agreement; words incorrectly included have been ignored; and '£1,000' has been read as '£100', *Elliott* v *Freeman* (1863) 7 LT 715. In these instances, rectification is unnecessary.
2. There must be very weighty evidence to establish the mistake. The burden of proof is on the party seeking rectification, though the standard is not that of the criminal trial (beyond reasonable doubt), *Joscelyne* v *Nissen* [1970] 2 QB 86 (see below). It must, therefore, be possible to adduce evidence of what the parties intended prior to the execution of the document; if their dealings were on an uncertain basis, the document will be treated as the best evidence of their intentions, and an action for rectification will be unlikely to succeed.
3. There must be a mistake common to all parties. This is the most important condition and may be sub-divided into three heads:

First, the parties must have come to an agreement, though this need not be in itself an enforceable contract; it is sufficient that the parties have agreed certain common terms that will be included in their agreement, and to this end the court will usually look for some outward expression of accord.

Secondly, it must be shown that it was the parties' continuing and unchanged intention that the common term be included in the written agreement up to the time of its execution.

In *Joscelyne v Nissen* [1970] 2 QB 86, the plaintiff shared a house with the defendant, his daughter, and it was orally agreed that she should take over his car-hire business and, in return, he would continue to reside in the house, but she would pay all the household expenses, including the cost of gas, coal and electricity. The subsequent written agreement failed to incorporate this term, and after paying these bills for some time, she then refused to do so on the grounds that she was not bound so to do under the written contract. The father sought to have the contract rectified. The court held that the agreement that she should make such payments had continued up until the time of the execution of the document, and it should be rectified accordingly.

Thirdly, the written document must clearly fail to represent the agreement.

In *Frederick Rose (London) Ltd v William Pim & Co Ltd* [1953] 2 QB 450, the plaintiff company received from their Egyptian house an order for 'Moroccan horsebeans described here as feveroles'. Not being familiar with 'feveroles', they consulted the defendants who explained that it was merely another term for horsebeans. The parties concluded an oral contract for the sale of horsebeans in Egypt. It was discovered that horsebeans were not 'feveroles' as the Egyptian house had requested, and the plaintiffs sought to rectify the contract to include the word feveroles in order that they could then claim for damages for breach of contract. The Court of Appeal refused the application because there was no disparity between the oral and the written agreements. Both had referred to horsebeans which had duly been delivered. The mistake of the parties lay in failing to apprehend that horsebeans and feveroles were different commodities.

In *Craddock Brothers Ltd v Hunt* [1923] 2 Ch 136, the plaintiffs orally agreed to sell to the defendants a house, excluding an adjacent yard. In the subsequent written agreement, the yard was included, and in the deed of conveyance the whole of the property was transferred to the defendants. The plaintiff was held entitled to rectification of both the written agreement and the conveyance.

An interesting example of the court's exercise of its discretion to permit rectification was in *Re Slocock's Will Trusts* [1979] 1 All ER 358. The plaintiffs were beneficiaries under a will, and in order to administer the proceeds of sale of land held on trust for them, a management company was formed and nominal shareholdings taken out. The first plaintiff wished to surrender her share of the money to the second and third plaintiffs in order to reduce or avoid tax. By a solicitor's mistake, the executed deed transferred only her shares in the management company and not her beneficial interest in the proceeds of sale. The plaintiff sought rectification to give effect to their common intention. Graham J granted the application and held that the parties were entitled to legitimately arrange their affairs in order to avoid paying tax, and it was not a ground to refuse to exercise the discretion to rectify because the Crown would be deprived of revenue.

Rectification is granted in only exceptional cases where the mistake is unilateral, because such a mistake normally fails to reflect the intentions of only one of the parties to the agreement, and the issue is likely to be whether or not the parties ever agreed that the alleged term should be incorporated in the contract. Rectification may be granted in cases involving fraud and misrepresentation, and estopped where one party knows of the mistake in the document, but fails to correct it. He will be estopped from resisting rectification on the grounds that the mistake is unilateral.

In *Agip SpA* v *Navigazione Alta Italia SpA* [1984] 1 Lloyd's Rep 353, the Court of Appeal insisted that rectification can only be ordered in a case of unilateral mistake where the other party has actual knowledge of the mistake.

Rescission

Of the three equitable remedies, rescission is the most controversial in operation for two reasons. First, it is said that the Courts are rescinding contracts which are valid at common law, and that in the absence of, for example, misrepresentation or fraud, the parties should be bound by their bargains and left to pursue their remedies at common law, if any. Secondly, rescission is often granted on certain terms, and this is said to be exercise of a power not justified by authority. To consider these views, rescission as it has evolved through the cases must be considered. It should also be borne in mind that rescission operates to set a transaction aside, and to put the parties in the position they were in prior to the contract.

Unilateral mistake

Similar considerations apply here to those discussed above concerning the refusal of specific performance for unilateral mistake, that there must be some vitiating element in the transaction that would make it inequitable to refuse to permit a party to rescind, because the other is in some way guilty of misrepresentation, negligence or unfair dealing.

In *Torrance* v *Bolton* (1872) LR 8 Ch App 118, property was being offered for sale by auction, and in the advertisement for the sale was described as an 'absolute freehold reversion'. It was only revealed by the auctioneer at the time of sale that it was, in fact, subject to three mortgages. The plaintiff was deaf and did not hear the announcement, and he bid for the property on the faith of the advertisement and it was sold to him. The sale was rescinded because the buyer was clearly under a misapprehension induced by the seller, and Lord Denning has said that the court held that it 'had power to set aside the contract whenever it was of opinion that it was unconscionable for the other party to avail himself of the legal advantage which he had obtained'.

The case could, perhaps, have been decided in misrepresentation, but the wide language of the judgments indicated that this 'advantage' need not affect the validity of the contract.

Mutual mistake

Cooper v *Phibbs* (above). It will be recalled that the appellant agreed to take the lease of a fishery from the respondents to which, in fact, he was already entitled. The contract was set aside in equity. In *Bell*, Lord Atkin thought it was void at law, but in *Solle* v *Butcher* Denning LJ agreed with the decision and said the mistake as to title did not render the lease a nullity, it was liable to be set aside on such terms as the Court thought just. The terms were that the respondents should have a lien on the fishery to the amount which they had spent in improving it. The equitable doctrine was expressed as follows: 'If the parties contract under a mutual mistake and misapprehension as to their relative and respective rights, the result is, that the agreement is liable to be set aside as having proceeded upon a common mistake.'

The case is regarded as the starting point of two related ideas: first, that where a contract is not void for mistake at common law, it may be set aside in equity if the mistake is, nevertheless, fundamental; secondly, that in thus setting aside, the Court may impose such terms as seem to it to be just.

The first principle was adopted in *Huddersfield Banking Co Ltd* v *Henry Lister & Son Ltd* [1895] 2 Ch 273. The defendant company went into liquidation and the plaintiffs, as mortgagees of the company's mills and fixtures therein, claimed to be entitled to the looms in the mills. If the looms were not fixtures, they would have had no claim on them, and the looms would pass to the liquidator. Upon inspection of the premises by both parties, it was agreed that the looms were not attached to the mills and were, therefore, not fixtures, and the plaintiffs agreed to a consent order for their sale. It later became known that the looms had been attached to the mills when the mortgage was executed, and they had been wrongfully loosened by a third party. The bank sought to have the consent order set aside for common and mutual mistake, and the court held, following *Cooper* v *Phibbs*, that the agreement was concluded on the basis of a common mistake as to a material fact, and it had the jurisdiction to set the order aside.

The importance of the court's power of rescission, if these two cases are correct, is considerable: it allows valid contracts to be set aside in equity. How would this apply to the facts of *Bell* v *Lever Bros*? The matter was raised in a case turning on remarkably similar facts: *Magee* v *Pennine Insurance Co Ltd* [1969] 2 QB 507.

The plaintiff purchased a motor car for his son to drive, and on his insurance proposal form, mistakenly, but innocently, stated that he, the plaintiff, held a licence. The defendants accepted the proposal and later the car was seriously damaged in an accident. The two sides came to an agreed settlement regarding the damage, but the defendants subsequently discovered the plaintiff's incorrect statement on the proposal form, which would enable them to repudiate liability. On the authority of *Bell* v *Lever Bros* and *Solle* v *Butcher*, the majority of the Court of

Appeal held the contract was not void at law, but that there was a common mistake which was fundamental to the whole agreement. Lord Denning side-stepped the factual similarities, simply saying that *Bell* had given 'enough trouble ... already'. Winn LJ, dissenting, said that although there was a misapprehension as to rights there was no misapprehension as to the subject matter of the contract, and the case fell within the ratio decidendi of *Bell* v *Lever Bros*.

In a note at (1969) 85 LQR 454, it is argued that *Magee* on its facts cannot be properly distinguished from *Bell* – in both there was an assumption that the contract comprised was valid and enforceable. The appropriate test advocated in such cases is: is there an express or implied term in the compromise that the contract is valid and enforceable and, if there is not, the agreement will be effective whatever the mistake as in *Bell*. What is important is to concentrate on the interpretation of the terms of the promisor's promise.

This argument is similar to the implied term theory regarding non-existent goods, that is, that it approaches the problem from the point of view of the allocation of risk; which of the parties undertook to bear the possibility that the common assumption was false?

The difficulty is that frequently they have not addressed their minds to the issue at all, and an order to find such an implied term would usually involve a degree of judicial creativity normally eschewed in the field of contract.

It may also be noted that an important factual distinction is that in *Bell*, the money had actually been paid over, in *Magee*, the plaintiff was suing the insurance company for the agreed sum. No reference is made to this in *Magee*, but it may be common sense to treat payment over of the money in such cases as discharging all obligations and liabilities once and for all.

Putting the defendant to his election

This has been described as equitable election, and has arisen where a plaintiff has been seeking rectification on the ground of unilateral mistake. As was noted above, rectification is usually only avalable in a case of mutual mistake; there is, however, a line of cases holding that in certain circumstances where a plaintiff seeks rectification and the mistake is not mutual, the defendant is given the choice to either submit or to have the contract rescinded.

In *Garrard* v *Frankel* (1862) 30 Beav 445, the parties were negotiating over the lease of some property, based on a rent of about £230 pa. When the lease was executed, the figure was incorrectly written in by the plaintiff as £130. It was held that the defendant must have been aware of the mistake, and should not be permitted to take advantage of it, and he was put to his election of rectification or rescission.

In *Paget* v *Marshall* (1884) 28 Ch D 255, the plaintiff offered to let a block of houses to the defendant, and mistakenly failed to exclude from his offer the first floor of one of the houses, which he had intended to keep for his own use. On the plaintiff's action for rectification 'the defendant was put to his election'. The court made no finding of fraud on the part of the defendant, but was of the opinion that he was aware of the mistake.

The problem with these decisions is that they appear to offer two illogical and irreconcilable alternatives: on the one hand if the parties were never ad idem, the contract ought to be rescinded, and might even be void at law; and if they did agree, then either the document records that agreement or it must be rectified. The cases were approved in *Solle* v *Butcher* by Denning LJ, and have been said to exemplify the flexible use of equitable remedies to achieve justice between the parties, and the effect is to put the parties back in their original position prior to the conclusion of the contract.

Their standing is now in grave doubt following *Riverlate Properties Ltd* v *Paul* [1975] Ch 133. The defendant leased a maisonette from the plaintiff, who intended that the former should be liable for half of the cost of exterior and structural repairs. In the lease liability rested entirely on the plaintiff, who, as a result, sued for rectification or, alternatively, rescission. The action was dismissed by the Court of Appeal, which held that there was no power to grant such relief in the case of unilateral mistake where it has neither been caused by the other party, nor was the other party aware of it.

Russell LJ said that to do so would be to venture into the field of moral philosophy, if it considered setting aside a good bargain because one party had made a miscalculation or other mistake, or because one party had obtained the goods at a bargain price. *Garrard* and *Paget* were said to turn on the fact that in both the defendant was aware of the plaintiff's mistake and was trying to take advantage of it. As such, the court still has the power to intervene, though apparently now only with a view to rectification, and it has no jurisdiction to offer rescission as an alternative. To this extent, *Garrard* and *Paget* must be taken to be disapproved and overruled. The decision in *Riverlate Properties* has effectively stopped optimistic plaintiffs from trying to withdraw from unfavourable transactions in the absence of any other mitigating factors. (For a note on this case see (1974) 90 LQR 439.)

Whether *Riverlate* represents the start of a reversal or at least a halting of the line of authority conferring on the courts a wide power to intervene in equity on the ground of mistake remains to be seen. Before this case, it could be stated with confidence that the courts were developing new equitable tools. The first recent authority was *Solle* v *Butcher* (above).

It will be recalled that the parties erroneously believed a house was no longer rent controlled, and let it at a higher than permitted rent, and when the plaintiff sought to recover the rent overpaid, the defendant counterclaimed that the lease was void and should be rescinded. The court held that the parties were under a common mistake of fact in believing that the flat was no longer rent controlled, and that the plaintiff should, on rescission of the lease, be permitted either to accept it or to take a new lease at the rent originally agreed which it was not permissible for the landlord to recover.

Denning LJ relied heavily on *Cooper* v *Phibbs* and *Huddersfield Banking Co Ltd*, and said those cases were in no way impaired by *Bell* v *Lever Bros* which, if it had been considered on equitable grounds, might have been decided differently. His Lordship was clearly thinking of rescission for mutual mistake as to a fundamental fact. The judgment depends on accepting that *Bell* either as a matter of law, or anyway in reality, has laid down that a contract will not be void at law for mistake (see discussion of this above), and that mistake is now only relevant in equity. Mistakes said to make a contract voidable were described as follows:

1. unilateral mistake: where there has been a material misrepresentation, whether or not it is fraudulent or fundamental; or where one party knowing the other is mistaken about the terms of an offer or the identity of the person by whom it is made, lets him remain under his delusion and concludes the contract on that basis;
2. mutual mistake: where the parties are under a common misapprehension, either as to facts or as to their relative and respective rights, provided that the misapprehension was fundamental and that the party seeking to set it aside was not himself at fault.

One might also add a caveat that it should be inequitable to allow the party contending there is a valid contract to insist on his strict contractual rights.

Regarding the question of fault under (2), Goff J in *Grist* v *Bailey* said that the point was not entirely clear, and that it must denote some degree of blameworthiness beyond the mere fault of having made a mistake: 'question is, how much, or in what way?'. The matter was considered in *Laurence* v *Lexcourt Holdings Ltd* [1978] 2 All ER 810.

In 1971, the plaintiff obtained permission to use the ground and part of the first floors of a property it owned for offices. In 1974, they offered to let the first and second floors of the property as offices to the defendants for 15 years, completely forgetting that the planning permission did not cover the whole building. The defendants assumed permission did exist, accepted the offer and took possession immediately without making any of the usual searches or enquiries. When the defendants learned of the true facts, they immediately vacated the building. The plaintiffs sued for specific performance, and the defendants counterclaimed for rescission on the grounds of, inter alia, common mistake. Deputy Judge Dillon QC held, following *Solle* v *Butcher* and *Grist* v *Bailey*, the mistake was fundamental, and that although the defendants were imprudent in proceeding without checking on the planning permission, they did not owe a duty of care to the plaintiff's forgetfulness or mistake, they were therefore not disentitled from relying on the mistake.

This new doctrine of equity thus appears well established, and it seems that in practice where there is an element of fundamental mistake in a contract, that a party is now more likely to obtain a remedy in equity than at common law. The criticisms that have been levelled against the doctrine have been principally that it has developed on the basis of tenuous authority, and that as a matter of strict law (or rather equity) it is unsupportable. Slade, at (1954) 70 LQR 385, has argued that equity may intervene in the following circumstances only:

1. If one party is unaware of the other's true intention, for example, on the seller's version of the events in *Smith* v *Hughes*, then rescission may only be granted if

there is misrepresentation or fraud, though it may at its discretion refuse to order specific performance.

2. If one party is aware of the other's true intentions, then if the contract is not void and there is not misrepresentation, the court grants rescission. Denning LJ in *Solle* v *Butcher* thought that where one party knew the other was mistaken as to the terms of the offer, an action for rescission would lie but, as Slade points out, such a contract is void at law, *Smith* v *Hughes*, and although Denning LJ considered nowadays that the contract would be set aside in equity, the line of authority is too firmly established to regard it without more as overruled. Slade also argues in the case of error in persona, that where the other party knows of the mistake, the contract would be voidable for misrepresentation, but if there was no representation, for exampe, the rogue never claimed to be anyone in particular, there would be no jurisdiction to grant rescission.

3. His strongest criticism is of Denning LJ's views on the position where the parties are under a common misapprehension. He argues that in *Cooper* v *Phibbs*, there was an active, albeit innocent misrepresentation that the would-be lessor had good title to the fishery, and that the rest of the judgment was therefore obiter dicta and, on a true reading of the case, Lord Westbury could not be said to have intended to lay down the wide rule that he is commonly held to have done. He also makes the point, considered in a note at (1950) 66 LQR 169, that the power the court exercised in relation to the parties' relative and respective rights was derived from the fact that the vendor had a valid lien for the amount he had spent on improving the fishery prior to the 'contract', and the court was, therefore, able to place terms on which it permitted the appellant to rescind. The conclusion is that *Cooper* can hardly be said to support the view that the court has the equitable power to set aside a valid lease because it considers that it would be unconscionable for the lessee to enforce it, or that it may impose terms on the parties when doing so. *Solle* v *Butcher*, Slade suggests, is wrongly decided on four counts.

1. There is no suggestion in *Cooper* that contracts not void at law may be set aside in equity.
2. That case is authority for setting aside void contracts.
3. The terms imposed in *Cooper* related to existing rights which would have been enforced independently.
4. *Bell* v *Lever Bros* was concerned with equity as well as the common law.

This last point is interesting in view of Denning LJ's suggestion in *Solle* that *Bell* might have been decided differently in equity. The action in *Bell* was, in fact, for the equitable remedy of rescission, and it is argued that the correct interpretation of the case is that as the contract was valid at common law, their lordships considered that no equitable relief could be sought in the absence of fraud, misrepresentation or the like.

Supporters of *Solle* v *Butcher* – and academically these are few and far between – argue that as the doctrine of mistake at common law is so narrow in operation (witness the almost total lack of recent authority), it is important that the courts should have a residuary discretion in order to impose a just solution where the exceptional case warrants it. It is conceded that this represents a radical extension of present (or in the light of recent cases) past principles, but this is justified principally on grounds of policy rather than authority. Bearing in mind *Riverlate Properties*, it may be that no precise limits can be drawn with respect to this new doctrine pending a possible pronouncement on it by the House of Lords.

Loss of the right to rescission
A party may lose the right to rescind in one of three ways:

By acquiescence. When a person has full knowledge of the facts giving him the right to rescind, and he elects to waive his right and affirm the contract, the right is lost forever. Mere possession of the knowledge is not itself acquiescence, but failure to act after acquiring it may be treated as evidence of an intention to waive the right.

Impossibility of restitutio in integrum. The contract is valid until set aside, and may be incapable of rescision where the parties cannot be restored to their original position. However, the rule is not strictly applied, and it is not necessary to restore the parties to their previous state in every detail.

Intervention of third parties. When the third party is a bona fide purchaser for value, the right is lost; it is not lost when he is a volunteer.

10.7   Common law and equity considered

Given that there is still such a thing as operative mistake at common law, one of the hardest things to define is precisely how this, and the doctrine of mistake in equity, operate side by side. Historically, common law and equity developed as separate jurisdictions, each having its own particular remedies, and neither relying on the other in coming to a decision. The two systems were fused by the Supreme Court of Judicature Act 1873, and with the remedies of both systems now available in one court, the decision in any given case has depended upon the nature of the action brought by the plaintiff. Thus in *Cundy* v *Lindsay*, *King's Norton Metal* and *Phillips* v *Brooks* the plaintiffs alleged the contract was void at common law, and the cases decided accordingly. The trend is now to plead mistake in equity; in *Laurence* v *Lexcourt Holdings* the common law was not mentioned and *Bell* v *Lever Bros* never cited. (It should be remembered that a party may not raise at trial matters that have not been pleaded.)

The present difficulty has arisen in the light of the robust view asserted by Denning LJ in *Solle* v *Butcher* and repeated in *Magee* v *Pennine Insurance* that contracts are no longer void for mistake at common law, except where the mistake has prevented the formation of any contract at all, and that mistake cases now fall to be decided in equity. However desirable such a solution may be, Grunfeld, at (1952) 15 MLR 297, had shown that Lord Denning's reasoning is based on an incorrect interpretation of the systems of law and equity before the 1873 Act. On the one hand, Lord Denning suggests that the Courts of Equity would take it for granted that a contract was valid at law, that there was a presupposition that this was the case. Grunfeld says there is virtually not a scintilla of authority to support this view; they approached the matter straightforwardly in equity, indifferent to the common law. Alternatively, his lordship suggests that the courts would first look to see if the contract was valid at law before applying equity, which Grunfeld says is based on a misreading of *Cooper* v *Phibbs*, and Grunfeld then argues for a complete substitution of equity for the common law. Subsequent cases have shown that this is what Lord Denning is doing in practice, even if his judgment in *Solle* allows some scope for common law mistake.

The contrary argument is that although since the Act of Fusion, where equity and common law conflict, the former prevails; mistake in contract is not an example of conflict, but of the complementary operation of law and equity, and that equitable remedies only become relevant once it is known the contract is valid at law. Thus in *Grist* v *Bailey*, where a house was sold at undervalue because the parties believed the sitting tenant was protected by statute, Goff J said:

'... the first question which arises is one of law, namely, what is the effect of common mistake? The leading case on this subject is *Bell* v *Lever Bros*. This is, of course, binding upon me and if exhaustive is really fatal to the defendant since it lays down very narrow limits within which mistake operates to avoid a contract.'

His Lordship held the contract valid at common law, and then applied the rules of equity derived from *Solle* v *Butcher*:

'Then I have to decide first, was there a common mistake in this case? Secondly, was it fundamental? And perhaps thirdly was the defendant at fault?'

The learned judge granted rescission in equity as a result of a fundamental common mistake.

It should be borne in mind, as Goff J said, that operative mistake at common law is now very restricted, and a mistaken party's best chance of success will be in equity. Common law will still be important in cases involving third party bona fide purchasers; the vendor's only hope of keeping title to his goods after being cheated out of them by a rogue, will be to show the contract was void at law, and that title never passed.

11

Duress and Undue Influence

11.1 Introduction

11.2 The common law doctrine of duress

11.3 The equitable rules of undue influence

11.4 The limited, and now suspect, principle of inequality of bargaining power

11.5 The protection afforded by certain statutory provisions

11.1   Introduction

We have examined, in earlier chapters, the situations in which a party may be afforded relief where he has been induced to enter into a contract by a misrepresentation, and the circumstances in which a contract may be void or voidable because a party has contracted on the basis of mistake.

We now turn to examine the situations in which the law gives relief to a person where the contract into which he has entered has been obtained by some form of improper pressure. It is important to emphasise at the outset that, for the law to intervene, the pressure must be 'improper'. People may be compelled to enter into unfavourable transactions by a number of factors: the demands of their own personal circumstances; the lack of an alternative source for the benefit they seek; or, more generally, the bargaining strength of the other party to the transaction. It would be contrary to all legal principle to permit a party to escape from the consequences of a transaction into which he has freely and voluntarily entered merely because of the restraints imposed upon him in the exercise of his freedom. However, there are situations in which the pressure is such that the victim of such pressure cannot be said to have acted freely and voluntarily. For certain forms of improper pressure, the law does afford the victim relief. The kinds of improper pressure that are recognised fall within the following categories.

1. The common law doctrine of duress.
2. The equitable rules of undue influence.
3. The limited, and now suspect, principle of inequality of bargaining power.
4. The protection afforded by certain statutory provisions.

We shall proceed to a consideration of each of these in turn.

11.2   The common law doctrine of duress

The origin of duress

The original common law of duress confined the doctrine within very narrow limits. Only duress to the person was recognised during the nineteenth century, and this required actual or threatened violence to the victim. Instances of duress to the person, in these terms, are rare in the present day. A modern example of such duress is *Barton* v *Armstrong* [1976] AC 104. A decision of the Privy Council, in which A threatened B with death if B's company did not pay a substantial sum of money to A. This is an important decision on the question of whether or not the victim would have entered into the contract but for the threat. This question provoked a difference of opinion both in the Court of Appeal of New South Wales and in the Privy Council. It will be considered further, below.

The nineteenth century limitation on duress meant that it could not be applied to 'duress of goods'. If a person, unlawfully detained, or threatened to detain, another's goods, this was not considered to be sufficient duress to enable a contract to be avoided. Note *Skeate* v *Beale* (1840) 11 Ad & El 983. There is a line of decisions to this effect in the nineteenth century.

However, while *Skeate* v *Beale* lays down the rule that a contract entered into in pursuance of a threat to retain goods cannot be thereby set aside, there is a wider restitutionary rule to the effect that money paid to obtain the release of goods wrongfully retained, or to avoid their seizure, may be recovered in an action for money had and received.

In *Maskell* v *Horner* [1915] 3 KB 106, tolls were levied on the plaintiff under a threat to seize goods and close down his business in a market. These tolls were, in fact, demanded with no right in law, and the Court of Appeal held the plaintiff entitled to recover the tolls paid, even though the payments had been made over a considerable period of time. Lord Reading CJ said:

> 'If a person pays money, which he is not bound to pay, under the compulsion of urgent and pressing necessity or of seizure ... he can recover it as money had and received.'

The distinction between the *Skeate* v *Beale* line of cases and the decision in *Maskell* v *Horner* is hard to follow, and it has been pointed out that the peculiar result would follow that although an agreement to pay money under duress of goods is enforceable, sums paid in pursuance of such an agreement by the coerced can be recovered in an action for money had and received.

A line of decisions prior to *Maskell* v *Horner* had upheld this wider restitutionary rule. It was said by Lord Denman CJ in *Skeate* v *Beale* that the distinction between that case, and the ones involving the application of the restitutionary rule, was that in the former the agreement had been entered into not compulsorily, but voluntarily. This was strongly criticised (though obiter) by Kerr J in *Occidental Worldwide Investment Corp* v *Skibs A/S Avanti (The Siboen and The Sibotre)* [1976] 1 Lloyd's Rep 293.

Kerr J said that *Skeate* v *Beale* would not justify a decision that:

'If I should be compelled to sign a lease or some other contract for a nominal but legally sufficient consideration under an imminent threat of having my house burnt down or a valuable picture slashed through without any threat of physical violence to anyone, I do not think that the law would uphold the agreement.'

This view was endorsed by Mocatta J in *North Ocean Shipping* v *Hyundai Construction (The Atlantic Baron)* [1979] QB 705. In the light of the modern developments of duress, it would seem that *Skeate* v *Beale* is no longer good law.

The effect of duress

Before discussion of the modern developments, it is necessary to examine the effect of duress. It is clear that if duress is established, it makes the contract voidable at the instance of the victim, not void.

This is emphasised because in some of the cases we shall be considering language is used in the judgments which might give the contrary impression. The use of the term 'to vitiate consent' (employed in *Pao On* – see below – and *The Siboen and The Sibotre*) suggests that duress destroys or negatives consent. If there were no consent, the contract would be void. However, it is clear from the tenor of the judgments being considered and, as Lord Scarman made explicit in *Universe Tankships* v *ITF* (below), the effect of operative duress is to make the contract voidable.

Duress in the modern law

A forerunner to the modern developments in contract was the decision in the law of torts by the House of Lords in *Rookes* v *Barnard* [1964] AC 1129, where the hitherto neglected tort of intimidation was revived and expanded in its application to trade union activities. Prior to this decision, it had been thought that the 'unlawful means', which is an essential ingredient of the tort, involved some form of physical violence. The concept of unlawful means was extended to include a threat of a breach of contract.

In *Morgan* v *Fry* [1968] 2 QB 710, Lord Denning MR defined the tort of intimidation as follows:

'The essential ingredients are these: there must be a threat by one person to use unlawful means (such as violence or a tort or a breach of contract) so as to compel another to obey his wishes and the person so threatened must comply with the demand rather than risk the threat being carried into execution. In such circumstances the person damnified by the compliance can sue for intimidation.'

In *D & C Builders* v *Rees* [1966] 2 QB 617 (which has been previously considered in connection with promissory estoppel), Lord Denning equated the undue pressure brought to bear on the plaintiffs with the tort of intimidation.

The relationship between duress and the tort of intimidation finds expression in the words of Lord Scarman in *Universe Tankships* v *ITF* [1982] 2 All ER 67, where his Lordship said that: 'duress, if proved, not only renders voidable a transaction into which a person has entered under its compulsion but is actionable as a tort, if it causes damage or loss'.

In recent times, the courts have extended the concept of duress from its earlier confines so as to recognise that certain forms of commercial pressure could amount to economic duress. The first modern case to make this clear was *The Siboen and The Sibotre*. At a time of recession in the shipping trade and a sharp fall in the market rates of hire of vessels, the charterers of two ships renegotiated the rates of hire, after a threat by them that they would go bankrupt and cease to trade if instalments under contracts of hire were not lowered. Since they also represented that they had no substantial assets, this would have left the owners with no effective legal remedy. It was especially coercive for the owners, who would have had to lay up the vessels and would then have been unable to meet mortgages and charges – a fact known by the charterers. The threats themselves were false in that there was no question of the charterers being bankrupted by high rates of hire.

Kerr J rejected the earlier confines of duress. But, he said, commercial pressure was not, in itself, enough to constitute duress. 'The court must', he said, 'be satisfied that the consent of the other party was overborne by compulsion so as to deprive him of any animus contrahendi.'

This would depend on the facts in each case. Kerr J considered that the owners would have been entitled to set aside the renegotiated rates on the ground of economic duress, but that on the present facts their will and consent had not been 'overborne' by what was ordinary commercial pressures.

In the subsequent case of *The Atlantic Baron* (above), Mocatta J confirmed that duress could take the form of economic duress. The facts were: under a ship construction contract, the building company demanded a 10% increase in instalments from the owners largely because of a devaluation of the US dollar. The owners did pay the increased rate demanded from them, although they protested that there was no legal basis on which the demand could be made. The owners were commercially compelled to pay since, at the time of the threat, they were negotiating a very lucrative contract for the charter of the ship to be built. Mocatta J decided that this constituted economic duress. The illegitimate pressure exerted by the building company was their threat to break the construction contract. Where, accordingly, a threat to break a contract had led to a further contract, that contract, even though it was made for good consideration, was voidable by reason of economic duress. However, the right to have the contract set aside could be lost by affirmation. By their delay in taking any action, once they were free of the duress, the owners had affirmed the contract. Furthermore, the judge held the fact that it was not the owner's intention to affirm did not entitle them to avoid the contract if that intention had not been indicated to the building company.

The Privy Council had occasion to consider economic duress in *Pao On* v *Lau Yiu* [1980] AC 614, Lord Scarman read the judgment of the board. Their Lordships agreed with the observations of Kerr J in *The Siboen and The Sibotre* that in a contractual situation, commercial pressure is not enough. There must be present some factor 'which could be regarded as a coercion of his will so as to vitiate his consent'. The material factors to consider were, Lord Scarman said:

1. whether the person alleged to have been coerced did or did not protest;
2. whether at the time of the alleged coercion he did or did not have an adequate legal remedy;
3. whether he was independently legally advised; and
4. whether after entering into the contract he took steps to avoid it.

His Lordship drew attention to the decisions of American judges which stressed the *effectiveness* of the alternative legal remedy. Thus, it would appear, it is no answer to an allegation of duress that the victim had a legal remedy which, in due course, he could have pursued.

A further important development was in *Universe Tankships* v *ITF* (above). In this case, the ITF, a trade union, had 'blacked' one of the plaintiffs' (a Liberian company's) ships, *The Universe Sentinel*, in port for sailing under a flag of convenience, only releasing the ship on payment of a large sum of money, part paid to the union welfare fund. The shipowners succumbed, made the payment and then sought to recover it as having been made under economic duress. Most of the judgments of the House of Lords were concerned with the union's statutory defence under the Trades Union and Labour Relations Act 1974, but they did find that the payments could be recovered – the House of Lords not challenging the Court of Appeal's finding of economic duress.

Lord Diplock stated that the rationale of economic duress is:

'... that his apparent consent was induced by pressure exercised on him by that other party which the law does not regard as legitimate, with the consequence that the consent is treated in law as revocable unless approbated either expressly or by implication after the illegitimate pressure has ceased to operate on his mind'.

Lord Scarman dealt with the two elements in the wrong of duress: that is, pressure amounting to compulsion of the will of the victim; and the illegitimacy of the pressure exerted.

In his discussion of 'compulsion', Lord Scarman modified the approach previously adopted by Kerr J in *The Siboen* and by the Privy Council in *Pao On*. His Lordship said:

'Compulsion is variously described in the authorities as coercion or the vitiation of consent. The classic case of duress is, however, not the lack of will to submit but the victim's intentional submission arising from the realisation that there is no other practical choice open to him ... The absence of choice can be proved in various ways, eg by protest, by the absence of independent advice, or by a declaration of intention to go to law to recover the money paid or the property transferred ... But none of these evidential matters goes to the essence of duress. The victim's silence will not assist the bully, if the lack of any practicable choice but to submit is proved.'

In the present case, Lord Scarman observed:

'There was no protest at the time, but only a determination to do whatever was needed as rapidly as possible to release the ship.'

A significant feature of this judgment is its departure from the previously stringent requirement of *The Siboen* and *Pao On* that the victim's will and consent should have been 'overborne' by the pressure. This approach of Lord Scarman was cited and approved by the Court of Appeal in *B & S Contractors* v *Green* [1984] ICR 419

The decision in *Universe Tankships* also involves the clear rejection by the House of Lords of the contention on behalf of the defendants that a plea of duress requires the party guilty of the duress to realise that his victim is acting under it.

The concept of economic duress received further recognition in the recent case of *Atlas Express Ltd* v *Kafco (Importers and Distributors) Ltd* [1989] 1 All ER 641. Also, see *Vantage Navigation Corp* v *Suhail* [1989] 1 Lloyd's Rep 138.

While it adds little that is new to the doctrine of economic duress, the recent decision in *Dimskal Shipping Co SA* v *International Transport Workers' Federation (The Evia Luck)* [1991] 4 All ER 871 is a useful reminder of the fact that the pressure applied must be improper in the legal sense.

The '*Evia Luck*' was a ship owned by the plaintiffs, a Panamanian registered company whose vessels sailed under the Panamanian flag of convenience. The International Transport Workers Federation (ITF) had been conducting a long campaign against flags of convenience. While the ship was in harbour in Sweden, it was boarded by agents of ITF, who informed the master, and the owners, that the ship would be blacked and loading would not be continued until the company entered into certain agreements with ITF. These included payment of back pay to the Greek and Filipino crew, new contracts of employment at higher wages and guarantees for future payments. At first the owners would not agree and the ship was in fact blacked. Yielding to pressure, the company agreed to sign the various agreements, which were expressly declared to be governed by English law. The company incurred loses of some £100,000 or more, due to delays in loading and sailing, and having to pay backpay to the crew.

They sought a declaration that the agreements were void on the grounds of duress and claimed restitution of all sums paid under such void agreements.

The House of Lords in discussing what constituted economic duress, said the fact that ITF's conduct was quite legal in Sweden was irrelevant. In stipulating that the agreements were to be governed by English law, the defendants had to accept English law as the proper law of conduct. Under English law a contract obtained by duress was voidable, and improper economic pressure (blacking the ship) constituted one form of duress. The owners were thus entitled to avoid the agreements they entered into because of pressure from ITF.

In some other countries, notably the USA, a clear distinction is made between substantive unfairness (when the terms are unfair or the consideration blatantly inadequate); and procedural unfairness (where there is some impropriety in making the contract such as undue influence).

This may now be gaining some recognition in this country. In a Privy Council decision, *Hart* v *O'Connor* [1985] 3 WLR 214, Lord Brightman recognised the distinction between two types of unfairness as contractual imbalance (substantive unfairness); and procedural unfairness.

The Privy Council disapproved of an earlier case, *Archer* v *Cutler* [1980] 1 NZLR 386, in which a New Zealand court refused to enforce a contract for the sale of land on the grounds of contractual imbalance alone. Some sort of procedural unfairness would also be required before the courts would intervene, according to the decision in *Hart*.

It would appear that English courts are starting to recognise the procedural versus substantive unfairness distinction, but so far there seems to be no concerted move to adopt the US doctrine of 'unconscionability'.

Pressure

The initial point to be observed is that it is not necessary to show that the duress was the sole cause of the victim's entry into the transaction.

In *Barton* v *Armstrong* (above) a case, it will be recalled, concerning duress to the person, the Privy Council held that if A's threats were a contributory reason for B entering into the transaction, B was entitled to relief. Once the duress had been established, the onus was on A to show that it had no bearing on the making of the contract. The Court of Appeal of New South Wales, by a majority, had taken the contrary view, holding that the onus was on B to show that, but for the duress, he would not have entered into the contract. The Privy Council allowed the appeal against that decision.

The presence or absence of duress is illustrated by consideration of the facts in *Atlantic Baron, The Siboen* and *Pao On*. Duress having been established in the former case, but not in the latter two. In *Pao On*, there had been unanimity amongst the judges in the courts below that the party alleging duress had not been subject to coercion. They had formed the opinion that he had considered the matter, chosen to avoid litigation, and formed the opinion that the risk in entering into the transaction was more apparent than real. There was, in short, no coercion. The Privy Council was not disposed to take a different view, but even if it had been it would not have substituted its opinion for that of the judges below on a question of fact.

The illegitimacy of the pressure

Threats to commit unlawful acts

Prima facie the threat to commit an unlawful act would constitute illegitimate pressure. It is not certain, however, that all threats to commit a breach of contract would, of necessity, be so regarded. Changes in circumstances, short of frustration of the contract, may make it commercially impossible for a party to continue the performance of a contract on the terms originally concluded. Pressure brought to bear on the other party to renegotiate the terms might not be regarded as illegitimate. There is a US authority to this effect: *Goebel* v *Linn* (1882) 47 Mich 489. In *Pao On*, the pressure for a variation might be regarded as legitimate as it was necessary to remedy the inadequacy of the original transaction.

Threats to commit a lawful act

For such threats to constitute duress can only be rare. It cannot, as a rule, be illegitimate for a person to threaten to do what he is lawfully entitled to do. If, however, it is coupled with a demand which is itself illegitimate, the pressure will assume the nature of the illegitimacy. Lord Scarman in *Universe Tankships* cites blackmail as an example.

In *Scolio Property* v *Cote* (1992) Supreme Court of Western Australia (unreported), after the auditors had been in, it was apparent that the defendant, an employee of the plaintiff company, had misappropriated large sums of money. Allegedly both parties signed a deed, in which the defendant promised to pay back the money missing. He defaulted and the plaintiff brought proceedings for that sum. Although the threat was undoubtedly made, it was quite legitimate to threaten to call the police in such cases and so it did not amount to duress.

Threats not to contract

As in 'Threats to commit a lawful act', a threat not to contract is usually no more than the exercise of a lawful right. There are, however, salvage cases where contracts for extortionate payments have been refused enforcement or set aside. See *The Rialto* [1891] P 175 and *The Crusader* [1907] P 196.

Threats to institute civil proceedings

Such threats can, again, rarely amount to illegitimate pressure. Apart from certain limited categories, there is no general tort of maliciously instituting civil proceedings. See *Metall und Rohstoff AG* v *Donaldson Lutkin & Jenrette Inc* [1989] 3 All ER 14 at p51.

Warnings

At common law it was once thought necessary to distinguish a threat from a warning. See *Biffin* v *Bignall* (1862) 7 H & N 877 and *Cumming* v *Ince* (1847) 11 QB 112. Chitty (25th edn para 495) suggests that this distinction is untenable in modern law.

Remedies for duress

As has been previously submitted, it is now clear that the effect of duress is to make the contract voidable, not void. The injured party will, therefore, be entitled to have the contract set aside for operative duress, unless he has expressly or impliedly affirmed it (see above).

As duress has been equated with the tort of intimidation (see the judgments of Lord Denning MR in *D & C Builders* and Lord Scarman in *Universe Tankships*), it would follow that a remedy for damages would lie in tort. (For the measure of damages for the tort of intimidation, see *Rookes* v *Barnard*, above.) There is, as yet, no authority on the question of whether or not an injured party who has affirmed the contract may nevertheless recover damages in tort. Chitty (para 501) has the view that damages should be recoverable, since otherwise a party who has lost the right to avoid the contract is left without a remedy for a clearly unlawful act.

11.3   The equitable rules of undue influence

Undue influence is an equitable doctrine. It must be kept distinct from the common law concept of duress. The equitable rules developed in consequence of the originally narrow confines of the common law.

The basis of the equitable doctrine was explained in *Allcard* v *Skinner* (1887) 36 Ch D 145 where Cotton LJ said:

> 'First, where the Court has been satisfied that the gift was the result of influence expressly used by the donee for the purpose; second, where the relations between the donor and donee have at or shortly before the execution of the gift been such as to raise a presumption that the donee had influence over the donor. In such a case the Court sets aside the voluntary gift, unless it is proved that in fact the gift was a spontaneous act of the donor acting under circumstances which enabled him to exercise an independent will and which justified the Court in holding that the gift was the result of a free exercise of the donor's will. The first class of cases may be considered as depending on the principle that no one shall be allowed to retain any benefit arising from his own fraud or wrongful act. In the second class of cases the Court interferes, not on the ground that any wrongful act has in fact been committed by the donee, but on the ground of public policy, and to prevent the relations which existed between the parties and the influence arising therefrom being abused.'

This passage requires elucidation in the light of Lord Scarman's speech in *National Westminster Bank* v *Morgan* (below). First, although the transactions in question were gifts in *Allcard* v *Skinner*, Cotton LJ did not exclude the applicability of his observations to other transactions. Secondly, the presumption of undue influence only arises where the transaction is one of manifest disadvantage to the party conferring the benefit. Thirdly, the principle involved is not one of vague public policy, but the prevention of victimisation of one party by another.

It is necessary to examine, therefore, (1) express influence; and (2) influence presumed from the special relationship between the parties.

Express influence

In this category, the onus of proving that the gift or contract was the result of improper pressure is on the party seeking to avoid the transaction. An example is *Williams* v *Bayley* (1866) LR 1 HL 200, where a promise to pay money was set aside because it was obtained by a threat to prosecute the promisor's son.

Influence presumed from a special relationship

A transaction can be set aside in equity where undue influence is presumed from the relationship between the parties. The presumption can be rebutted (see below), the onus is on the party receiving the benefit to show that it was not obtained by undue influence. See *Powell* v *Powell* [1900] 1 Ch 243.

The relationships where undue influence is presumed have been held to be:

1. Parent and child – *Wright* v *Vanderplank* (1855) 2 K & J 1.
2. Solicitor and client – *Wright* v *Carter* [1903] 1 Ch 27.
3. Doctor and patient – *Mitchell* v *Homfray* (1881) 8 QBD 587.
4. Trustee and beneficiary – *Ellis* v *Barker* (1871) LR 7 Ch App 104.
5. Religious adviser and disciple – *Roche* v *Sherrington* [1982] 1 WLR 599.

The presumption does not apply between husband and wife. See *Bank of Montreal* v *Stuart* [1911] AC 120, *Kings North Trust* v *Bell* [1986] 1 WLR 119 CA and *Midland Bank* v *Shephard* [1988] 3 All ER 17.

A presumption of undue influence might arise, even though the parties were husband and wife, in particular circumstances of dependency coupled with mutual trust. See *Simpson* v *Simpson* (1988) The Times 11 June.

In the case of master and servant, a recent decision, *Mathew* v *Bobbins* (1980) 256 EG 603, has held that servants are not today dominated by their masters, and as a result of modern employment legislation, there is no longer any presumption of undue influence.

There have been a number of reported cases in this area of the law in recent years. We shall consider, first, the decisions of the Court of Appeal and the House of Lords respectively in *Lloyds Bank* v *Bundy* [1975] QB 326 CA and *National Westminster Bank* v *Morgan* [1985] 1 All ER 821 HL.

What is critical in the application of the equitable doctrine is the nature of the transaction. This principle is not a new one, but has been re-emphasised by Lord Scarman in *Morgan*. His Lordship referred to the judgment of Lindley LJ in *Allcard* v *Skinner*, where Lindley LJ had said:

> 'Where a gift is made to a person standing in a confidential relation to the donor the Court will not set aside the gift of a small amount simply on the ground that the donor has no independent advice. In such a case, some proof of the exercise of the influence of the donee must be given. The mere existence of such influence is not enough in such a case; ... But if the gift is so large as not to be reasonably accounted for on the ground of friendship, relationship, charity or other ordinary motives on which ordinary men act, the burden is upon the donee to support the gift.'

Lord Scarman also referred to a passage in the judgment of Lord Shaw in *Poosathurai* v *Kannappa Chettiar* (1919) 47 Ind App 1, which is apparently not elsewhere reported and which he (Lord Scarman) regarded as of critical importance:

> 'It must be established that the person in a position of domination has used that position to obtain unfair advantage for himself, and so as to cause injury to the person relying upon

his authority or aid. Where the relation of influence, as above set forth, has been established, and the second thing is also made clear, namely that the bargain is with the "influencer" and in itself unconscionable, then the person in a position to use his dominating power has the burden thrown upon him, and it is a heavy burden, of establishing affirmatively that no domination was practised so as to bring about the transaction, but that the grantor of the deed was scrupulously kept separately advised in the independence of a free agent.'

As Lord Scarman observes, the doctrine applies not only to transactions of gift. A commercial relationship can become one in which one party assumes a role of dominating influence over the other.

Sir Eric Sachs in *Bundy* held that there were no finite categories of the special relationship. Such relationship, he said, tended to arise where someone relied on the guidance or advice of another, where the other was aware of that reliance and where the person on whom reliance is placed obtains a benefit from the transaction. This must be read subject to the requirement that the transaction was wrongful in itself as set out in the quotations given above.

It is necessary at this juncture to examine the facts in the two cases under discussion. In *Lloyds Bank* v *Bundy*, a guarantee was given to the bank by an elderly farmer, a customer of the bank, for his son's indebtedness. The guarantee was secured by a mortgage of Bundy's house in favour of the bank. It was held that as Bundy was liable to be influenced by the bank, which was obtaining a benefit, there was a duty on the bank to ensure that Bundy formed an independent judgment on the transaction. This duty the bank had failed to discharge. The obligation undertaken by Bundy was an onerous one; he had mortgaged his house to the hilt and it did not appear that his son's financial circumstances were likely to improve.

Sir Eric Sachs made it clear that, in ordinary circumstances, a bank does not incur the duty consequent upon a special relationship where it obtains a guarantee from a customer. But he said that:

'... once ... it is possible for a bank to be under that duty, it is, as in the present case, simply a question for "meticulous examination" of the particular facts to see whether that duty has arisen. On the special facts here it did arise and it has been broken.'

In *National Westminster Bank* v *Morgan*, the husband and wife owned a home jointly. The husband was unable to meet his mortgage commitments and made refinancing arrangements with the bank secured by a mortgage in favour of the bank over the matrimonial home. The bank manager called at the home to get the wife to execute the charge. She did not wish the charge to cover her husband's business liabilities. The bank manager assured her, in good faith but incorrectly, that it did not. It was, in fact, unlimited in extent and could, therefore, extend to all the husband's liabilities to the bank, though it was the bank's intention to confine it to the amount needed to refinance the mortgage. The wife had not received independent legal advice before executing the mortgage. The husband and wife fell into arrears with their payments, and the bank obtained an order for possession of the home. Shortly afterwards, the husband died without owing the bank any indebtedness for business advances. The wife contended that she had executed the mortgage because of undue influence and that it should be set aside. Lord Scarman made the only speech and his findings may be summarised as follows:

1. A transaction would not be set aside on the grounds of undue influence unless it could be shown that it was manifestly disadvantageous to the party alleged to be influenced.
2. The basic principle was not a vague public policy, but the prevention of victimisation of one party by another. On this point, Lord Scarman, with whose speech all their Lordships concurred, referred to the 'public policy' principle formulated by Cotton LJ in *Allcard* v *Skinner* (above). He stressed that it would be an error in applying the principle to ignore the requirement that the transaction was itself wrongful.
3. The transaction in the instant case was not unfair to the wife.
4. Although the doctrine of undue influence could extend to commercial transactions, including those between banker and customer, it could not be maintained on the present facts that the relationship was one in which the banker had a dominating influence.
5. The bank, therefore, was not under a duty to ensure that the wife had independent advice.

Note that in *Bank of Credit and Commerce International SA* v *Aboody and Another* [1989] 2 WLR 759, the Court of Appeal in disallowing an appeal by a wife alleging undue influence, held that there was no manifest disadvantage to the wife; and there was a strong probability the wife would have entered the transaction anyway.

Lord Scarman's use of the expression 'dominating influence' was the subject of much scrutiny by the Court of Appeal in the recent case of *Goldsworthy* v *Brickell* [1987] 1 All ER 853.

The Court held that in order for the presumption to arise that a transaction had been procured by the undue influence of one person over another, there had to be a relationship wherein the latter had ceded such a degree of trust or confidence to the former that the former was in a position to influence the latter into effecting the transaction. But it was not necessary to show that the person in whom the trust and confidence had been placed had assumed a dominating influence over the other. The Court thought that the decision of the Privy Council in *Poosathurai* v *Kannappa Chettiar* (above), which was much relied on by Lord Scarman, was not an accurate statement of English law on undue influence.

Nourse LJ referred to a number of leading cases, in particular, *Tufton* v *Sperni* [1952] 2 TLR 516, from which it clearly appeared that the presumption arose from a relation of trust and confidence, well short of domination. Nourse LJ doubted that the House of Lords in *Morgan* intended to the contrary, but if they did his Lordship respectfully disagreed with them, and observed that such holding was not necessary to the decision in that case. His Lordship added that it was to his mind inconceivable that the House of Lords intended, sub silentio, to overrule *Tufton* v *Sperni* and many other leading cases.

Parker LJ held the view that Lord Scarman had used the expression 'dominating influence' merely as a convenient means of describing a relationship in which one party was in a position to exercise influence over the other.

For Sir John Megaw it was beyond belief that the House of Lords could have intended to change the law by defining undue influence by reference to the words 'domination' or 'dominating'.

The Court of Appeal reiterated that the presumption of undue influence did not arise unless the transaction in question was manifestly and unfairly disadvantageous to the person alleged to be influenced. This requirement of manifest disadvantage has been insisted upon in a number of recent Court of Appeal decisions. See *Cornish* v *Midland Bank* [1985] 3 All ER 513 and *Woodstead Finance* v *Petrou* (1986) 136 NLJ 188.

Where a creditor entrusts the task of obtaining the signature of a debtor to an agreement to a person whom the creditor knows is in a position to influence the debtor, the transaction is liable to be set aside. See *Avon Finance* v *Bridger* [1985] 2 All ER 281 and *Kings North Trust* v *Bell* (above). In the absence of such knowledge, the creditor will not be tainted by the undue influence. See *Coldunell* v *Gallon* [1986] QB 1184, *Midland Bank* v *Perry* (1987) The Times 28 May and *Bank of Baroda* v *Shah* [1988] 3 All ER 24.

Rebutting the presumption

As has been indicated, where the presumption of undue influence arises it can be rebutted. The usual way of doing this is by showing that the other party had independent advice before entering into the transaction.

In *Inche Noriah* v *Shaik Allie bin Omar* [1929] AC 127, the Privy Council was also of the view that independent advice might be effective even though it was not taken. It must be given, however, in that case 'with a knowledge of all the relevant circumstances and must be such as a competent and honest adviser would give if acting solely in the interests of the donor.'

Where the influence is particularly strong, it may be necessary to show that the adviser approved the transactions and that his advice was followed. See *Powell* v *Powell* [1900] 1 Ch 243.

Loss of the right

The right to have the contract set aside for undue influence is barred by affirmation after the influence has ceased; delay; and third party rights.

Unconscionable bargains

Equity may also give relief where advantage is taken of a 'poor and ignorant man'. See *Fry* v *Lane* (1880) 40 Ch D 312. There are two more recent decisions: *Cresswell* v *Potter* [1978] 1 WLR 255n (decided in 1968), and *Backhouse* v *Backhouse* [1978] 1 WLR 243.

11.4 The limited, and now suspect, principle of inequality of bargaining power

In *Lloyds Bank* v *Bundy*, Lord Denning MR, after examining duress, the various forms of improper pressure and unconscionable bargains, sought to derive a general principle from these categories. They all rested on inequality of bargaining power. He said:

> 'By virtue of it, English law gives relief to one, who, without independent advice, enters into a contract on terms which are very unfair or transfers property for a consideration which is grossly inadequate, when his bargaining power is grievously impaired by reason of his own needs or desires, or by his own ignorance or infirmity, coupled with undue influences or pressures brought to bear on him by or for the benefit of the other.'

The principle did not, Lord Denning said, depend on proof of any wrongdoing. This principle was an alternative ground for his decision in *Bundy*. The other members of the Court of Appeal based their decision on undue influence, and did not find it necessary to express an opinion on Lord Denning's principle.

In subsequent cases, Lord Denning reiterated his view that English Law recognises this principle: *Clifford Davis* v *WEA Records* [1975] 1 WLR 61 and *Levison* v *Patent Steam Carpet Cleaning Co* [1978] QB 69. Some support for the principle is derived from the speech of Lord Diplock in *Schroeder Music Publishing* v *Macaulay* [1974] 1 WLR 1308, but Lord Diplock was dealing with the particular problem of standard form contracts in the context of restraint of trade. There has been little other judicial support for inequality of bargaining power as a general principle.

In *Pao On* v *Lau Yiu* (above), Lord Scarman stated that, where duress was not established, to treat the unfair use of a dominant bargaining position as a ground for invalidating a contract was unnecessary for the achievement of justice and unhelpful in the development of the law. In *Burmah Oil* v *Bank of England* (1981) The Times 4 July, the court rejected the argument that inequality of bargaining power is of itself a ground of invalidity. In *Alec Lobb (Garages)* v *Total Oil* [1985] 1 All ER 303, the plaintiff sought to have the transaction set aside on the grounds, inter alia, that the bargain was harsh and unconscionable. It was argued that because of Total's superior economic position and the financial pressures faced by the plaintiff, the parties were in a position of unequal bargaining power, and that, in this situation, the test should be whether the terms of the contract were fair and reasonable.

The Court of Appeal rejected this as a proposition of law. Dillon LJ observed that it was seldom in any negotiation that the bargaining position of the parties was absolutely equal. 'The Courts', said Dillon LJ, 'would only interfere in exceptional cases where as a matter of common fairness it was not right that the strong should be allowed to push the weak to the wall.' Concepts of unconscionable conduct and the exercise by the dominant party of coercive power would then be brought in.

The plaintiffs' shortage of money, the fact that they were already tied to Total by mortgages and had no alternative sources of finance, all of which was known to Total, did not render the transaction unconscionable. It was also clear, in the present case, that no pressure had been placed on the plaintiffs, who had taken independent advice from their accountants and solicitors. Total had been reluctant to enter into the transaction.

Most recently in *National Westminster Bank* v *Morgan* (above), Lord Scarman said:

'I question whether there is any need in the modern law to erect a general principle of relief against inequality of bargaining power. Parliament has undertaken the task – and it is essentially a legislative task – of enacting such restrictions upon freedom of contract as are in its judgment necessary to relieve against the mischief: for example, the hire-purchase and consumer protection legislation, of which the Supply of Goods (Implied Terms) Act 1973, Consumer Credit Act 1974, Consumer Safety Act 1978, Supply of Goods and Services Act 1982 and Insurance Companies Act 1982 are examples. I doubt whether the courts should assume the burden of formulating further restrictions.'

The two most recent cases confirm Treitel's view (6th edn p318) that it is unlikely that the principle will find literal acceptance in English law. The recent widening of the scope of duress has, Treitel observes, greatly reduced the need for such a principle.

11.5   The protection afforded by certain statutory provisions

Brief mention must be made of the Consumer Credit Act 1974, which empowers the court to 'reopen' any 'extortionate credit bargain'; and the Fair Trading Act 1973, which controls practices which 'subject customers to undue pressure' and which cause the terms of certain transactions to be so adverse to consumers as to be inequitable.

12

Privity of Contract

12.1 Introduction

The traditional approach to the rights and liabilities which are subject to a contract is to assert that they can vest only in a party to the contract. This is because the law only seeks to enforce bargains supported by consideration. Such a bald assertion does, however, in some cases, cause hardship and, in recent years, a departure may be witnessed from the strict application of that rule. See, for example, *Jackson* v *Horizon Holidays* (below). Where the rule has not been departed from it has been distinguished, and complex analyses of factual situations have resulted in the discovery of consideration where, at first glance, there was none to be found. See, for example, *New Zealand Shipping* v *Satterthwaite (The Eurymedon)*.

12.2 Privity and consideration

A party can either be privy to the agreement or to the consideration. It is disputed whether the rule that consideration must move from the promisee is the same as, or different from, the rule that only a party to the agreement can sue. See Furmston

223

(1960) 23 MLR at pp383–4. English judges have acted ambivalently and referred to both rules interchangeably. The two rules are capable, however, of being distinguished. Chitty on contracts furnishes an example:

> 'A man might ... promise his daughter to pay £1,000 to any man who married her. A person who married the daughter with knowledge of and in reliance on such a promise might provide consideration for it, but could not sue on it as it was not addressed to him.'

That is to say, he was not party to the agreement. A person can be party to an agreement, but not provide consideration. If, at the request of A, B promises C that he (B) will pay A £50 pa if C will dig his garden, A can be said in one sense to be 'party' to the agreement, but he does not provide consideration. A will not be able to enforce the contract.

Kepong Prospecting v *Schmidt* [1968] AC 810 is a decision of the Privy Council which supports the view that the doctrine of privity is distinct from the rule that consideration must move from the promisee.

12.3   Circumstances falling outside the rule

There are some circumstances in which the rule that only a party to the contract can enforce it, does not apply. These situations are not properly regarded as 'exceptions' to the rule because the question of privity is not in issue if the situation exists.

Collateral contracts

In *Shanklin Pier* v *Detel Products* [1951] 2 KB 854, the plaintiffs had employed contractors to paint a pier. They told them to buy paint made by the defendants. The defendants had told them that the paint would last for seven years. It only lasted for three months.

HELD: the plaintiffs could sue the defendants on a collateral contract. They had provided consideration for the defendants' promise by entering into an agreement with the contractors, which entailed the purchase of the defendants' paint. See also *Andrews* v *Hopkinson* [1957] 1 QB 229 and *Wells* v *Buckland* [1965] 2 QB 170 referred to in Chapter 6.

The court was able to find consideration moving from the plaintiffs – *Shanklin Pier* – without substantial difficulty. The case of *Charnock* v *Liverpool Corporation* [1968] 1 WLR 1498 gives rise to some doubts about the presence of consideration. The plaintiff's car was damaged. A contract existed between his insurance company and a garage (the defendant) for repairing the plaintiff's car. It was held that there was also a collateral contract between the plaintiff and the defendant to do the repairs within a reasonable time. The court found that the consideration was the leaving of the car at the garage. This was not, of course, a detriment to the plaintiff, but it was a benefit to the garage.

There must, however, be an intention to create a collateral contract before that contract can be formed. In *Alicia Hosiery Ltd* v *Brown Shipley Ltd* [1970] 1 QB 195, the owner of goods in a warehouse pledged them to a bank. The owner then sold to a buyer. The bank gave the buyer a delivery order addressed to the warehouseman (to instruct the warehouseman to give delivery of the goods). The warehouseman refused. The buyer sued the bank on a collateral contract. It was held that there was none.

A well-established example of a collateral contract is that which arises between the seller of goods and a bank when a buyer opens an irrevocable letter of credit in favour of the seller. When the buyer 'opens' the letter of credit, it means that a contract has been formed between the buyer of goods and the bank wherein the bank undertakes to pay the seller. Once the bank informs the seller, it seems that there is a collateral contract. But where is the consideration? There are two possible solutions: first, that the bank was making a unilateral offer to the seller which was accepted by performance of the contract between the buyer and seller; and, secondly, that the seller provided consideration by forbearing to sue the buyer for the price.

Under the Consumer Credit Act 1974, a dealer who conducts preceding negotiations for a 'regulated agreement' is, in certain circumstances, deemed to do so as agent of the creditor as well as in his actual capacity. The representation can, therefore, make the company liable under the main contract, while the dealer may still be liable on the representation as a collateral contract.

Multi-partite agreements

Clubs or unincorporated associations

Where a person joins a club or other unincorporated association, he may contract with all the other members, even though he may not know any of them. For example, in *Clarke* v *Dunraven* [1897] AC 59 HL, the owners of two yachts entered them in a regatta. Each owner undertook in a letter to the secretary to obey all the rules of the club. These included a rule that members were to pay 'all damages' caused by fouling. 'The Satanita' fouled 'The Valkyrie'. The owner sued the owner of 'The Satanita'. The owner of 'The Satanita' relied on a statutory limitation of liability to £8 per ton on the registered tonnage of the ship. The owner of 'The Valkyrie' said that the promise to pay 'all damages' excluded the statutory provision.

HELD: that the owner of 'The Valkyrie' could rely on the promise to pay 'all damages' because a contract between them on the terms specified with the club was formed, either when they entered the race, or at the latest at the time of sailing.

In contrast, in *Ellesmere* v *Wallace* [1929] 2 Ch 1, people entering horses for races were held to be contracting with the Jockey Club and not among themselves.

Companies

The position is not dissimilar where a person becomes a member of an incorporated body. The Companies Act 1985 provides that the Memorandum and Articles of a company (which contain its rules) bind the company and its members as though signed and sealed by each member, and amount to a covenant between each member and every other member.

Agency

A person may contract as agent for a third party (his principal). The principal is then bound and the agent is not privy to the contract and cannot (generally) sue or be sued upon it. Sometimes problems arise regarding sub-agencies. An agent can create privity of contract between himself and a sub-agent. See Chapter 19.

12.4   Attempts to impose liabilities on third parties

The general rule is that a contract only binds the parties to it. The reason that this is so, is that C is a stranger to the contract effected between A and B. In *Taddy* v *Sterious* [1904] 1 Ch 354, the plaintiffs were manufacturers of tobacco and they stipulated that this tobacco should not be sold under a fixed minimum price. Some tobacco was sold by the plaintiffs to a wholesaler, and a term of this contract was 'that acceptance of the goods will be deemed a contract between the purchaser and Taddy & Co, that he will observe these stipulations'. The contract also provided that:

> 'In the case of purchase by a retailer through a wholesaler the latter shall be deemed to be an agent for Taddy & Co.'

The wholesalers resold the tobacco to the defendants who had notice of this condition but, nevertheless, sold the tobacco at below the prescribed price. Taddy & Co brought an action against the defendants on three grounds:

1. The printed notice amounted to a contract between themselves and the defendants – the court held that this was not so, there was no contract between the plaintiff and the defendant.
2. The wholesaler was only an agent of the plaintiff – the court rejected this view as their 'agent' did not agree to any of the terms of agency.
3. The doctrine of restrictive covenants should be extended to manufactured goods – the court rejected this argument as it went against common sense.

There are various ways in which the strict harshness of this rule may be circumvented, for example, by:

1. The creation of a lien (where goods are entrusted to a person who has a right to retain them pending payment. So, if A contracts with B – a common carrier – that goods belonging to C should be carried from London to Newcastle to be paid for by C, C is not bound by the obligation under the contract between A and B, but he may not be able to get his goods from B because B has a right to retain them pending payment. This right is called a lien).
2. The creation of an equitable interest or irrevocable lience. In *Binions* v *Evans* [1972] Ch 359, a purchaser of land was bound by a promise made by the vendor

of the land to an occupant of a cottage that the occupant could remain in the cottage for the rest of her life. The purchaser took with notice of this promise. He would not have been bound by the promise if he had no notice.

3. The law of tort. In *Lumley* v *Gye* (1853) 2 E & B 216, the plaintiff had employed Johanna Wagner as an opera singer. The defendant induced her to refuse to perform because he wanted her to sing in his opera house. He was liable for his wrongful interference with contractual rights. The same rule may apply where a stranger to a contract uses a chattel in a manner which is inconsistent with a party's contractual rights. He may be liable in conversion as in the tort of wrongful interference. See *British Motor Trade Association* v *Salvadori* [1949] Ch 556, where A bought a car, convenanting with B that he would not resell it for one year without offering it to B. C bought the car with notice of the covenant within one year of the contract. He was held to be liable in tort for wrongful interference with the contractual rights of B.

Equity may impose liability although the common law does not

The principal application of the imposition of liability in equity is in relation to negative covenants which may, if certain conditions are satisfied, run with the land and bind purchasers of it to observe the covenants for the benefit of adjoining owners. The leading case is *Tulk* v *Moxhay* (1848) 2 Ph 774. The plaintiff who owned several houses in Leicester Square sold the garden in the centre of the Square to one Elms, who covenanted that he would keep the gardens and railings around them in their present condition and continue to allow individuals the use and enjoyment of the gardens.

The land in question was sold to the defendant although the conveyance to him did not contain the convenant in similar terms. The defendant did know of the restriction contained in the contract between the plaintiff and Elms. The defendant announced that he was going to build on the land, and the plaintiff, who was still owner of several adjacent houses, sought an injunction to restrain him from doing so.

HELD: that the covenant would be enforced in equity against all subsequent purchasers with notice. The reason for this decision was partly due to the defendant acting as he did whilst knowing of the plaintiff/Elms covenant and the plaintiff, it was said, must also have some interest in the land in question. The injunction was granted.

Attempts have been made to extend the operation of a restrictive covenant to cover contracts for the hire of ships as well as contracts restraining certain uses of land. The leading case is *Lord Strathcona Steamship Co* v *Dominion Coal Co* [1926] AC 108. The plaintiffs, Dominion Coal Co, had a charter right of the Lord Strathcona, and during the period of the charter, the ship was sold to the defendants who refused to let the plaintiffs use the ship in accordance with the terms of the charter. The plaintiffs sought an injunction to stop the defendants retaking the ship, but the defendants argued that as they were not privy to the contract (original charter contract) they could not be bound. Strictly speaking, the plaintiffs would have lost if they had sued in contract but, instead, they asked the court to extend the doctrine of *Tulk* v *Moxhay* from land to sea. The Judicial Committee of the Privy Council agreed to this and so the plaintiffs succeeded.

CRITICISM: under the doctrine of *Tulk* v *Moxhay*, an essential condition was that the plaintiff kept an interest in the *land*. There cannot be an analogy with ships in which case. The judgment was couched in such wide terms that it could have been applied to all chattels.

There is some doubt today as to whether the decision has much legal status due to Diplock J's judgment in *Port Line Ltd* v *Ben Line Steamers Ltd* [1958] 2 QB 146. A ship chartered to the plaintiffs by its owners for 30 months was sold to the defendant within this period. The defendant agreed to honour the charter. However, the ship was soon requisitioned by the government and compensation was paid to the defendant. The plaintiffs sued the defendant for compensation. Diplock J (as he then was) held that even if the *Strathcona* case was rightly decided it could not be applied to this case as (1) the defendant was not in breach of any duty by his act – it was the government who had acted, and (2) the plaintiff had not sought an injunction but *financial compensation*, which was thus outside the ambit of *Tulk* v *Moxhay* – also the defendants did not know of the plaintiff's actual charter rights.

The point about *Tulk* v *Moxhay* is that it opened a possible line of argument extending the ambit of the exception to the doctrine of privity. The argument raised in *Tulk* v *Moxhay* was naturally attractive to the lawyers of the time in that it presented a way round the doctrine. Thus, it came as no surprise to see the *Tulk* v *Moxhay* argument being raised in subsequent cases. You will recollect that the courts rejected the view that an agreement between A and B with regard to goods could run with the goods so as to bind C (*Taddy* v *Sterious*). In the *Strathcona* case (above), it was held by the Privy Council that a third party could effectively be bound by an agreement made between two parties and to which he was thus not a party.

Diplock J (as he then was) said in *Port Line*:

'The *Strathcona* case, although decided over thirty years ago, has never been followed in the English courts and has never come up for direct consideration.'

In *Bendall* v *McWhirter* [1952] 2 QB 466, Denning LJ said:

'It seems, therefore, that in this case for the first time after more than 30 years that an English court has to grapple with the problem of what principle was really laid down in the *Strathcona case*, and whether that case was rightly decided. The difficulty I have found in ascertaining its ratio decidendi, the impossibility which I find of reconciling the actual decision with well-established principles of law, the unsolved and, to me, insoluble problems which that decision raises combine to satisfy me that it was wrongly decided. I do not propose to follow it. I naturally express this opinion with great diffidence, but having reached a clear conclusion it is my duty to express it.

If I am wrong in my view that the case was wrongly decided, I am certainly averse from extending it one iota beyond that which, as I understand it, it purported to decide.

In particular, I do not think that it purported to decide (1) that anything short of actual knowledge by the subsequent purchaser at the time of the purchase of the charterer's rights, the violation of which it is sought to restrain, is sufficient to give rise to the equity; (2) that the charterer has any remedy against the subsequent purchaser with notice except a right to restrain the use of the vessel by such purchaser in a manner inconsistent with the terms of the charter; (3) that the charterer has any positive right against the subsequent purchaser to have the vessel used in accordance with the terms of his charter.'

12.5   Attempts to impose benefits on third parties

If A and B cannot impose liabilities on C, the corollary of this rule would logically seem to be that neither can they confer benefits on him or, more importantly, C cannot enforce such benefit by contractual action in the courts. The reason is simple: C is not a party to the bargain between A and B. The leading case on this aspect is *Tweddle* v *Atkinson* (1861) 1 B & S 393. The plaintiff married Mr Guy's daughter. The plaintiff's father and Mr Guy effected an agreement whereby each would pay a sum of money to the plaintiff. Both the fathers reneged on this agreement and subsequently died. The executor faced a problem due to the fact that the plaintiff sued the executor of Mr Guy for the sum promised. Crompton J:

'It is admitted that the plaintiff cannot succeed unless this case is an exception to the modern and well-established doctrine of the action of assumpsit. At the time when the cases which have been cited were decided the action of assumpsit was treated as an action of trespass upon the case, and therefore in the nature of a tort; and the law was not settled, as it now is, that natural love and affection is not a sufficient consideration for a promise upon which an action may be maintained; nor was it settled that the promisee cannot bring an action unless the consideration for the promise moved from him. The modern cases have, in effect, overruled the old decisions; they shew that the consideration must move from the party entitled to sue upon the contract. It would be a monstrous proposition to say that a person was a party to the contract for the purpose of suing upon it for his own advantage and not a party to it for the purpose of being sued. It is said that the father in the present case was agent for the son in making the contract but the argument ought also to make the son liable upon it. I am prepared to overrule the old decisions, and to hold that, by reason of the principles which now govern the action of assumpsit, the present action is not maintainable.'

Wrightman J:

'Some of the old decisions appear to support the proposition that a stranger to the consideration of a contract may maintain an action upon it, if he stand in such a near relationship to the party from whom the consideration proceeds, that he may be considered a party to the consideration. But there is no modern case in which the proposition has been supported. On the contrary, it is now established that no stranger to the consideration can take advantage of a contract, although made for his benefit.'

The rule in effect laid down by *Tweddle* v *Atkinson* has become accepted as one of the tenets of the common law.

Lord Haldane LC remarked in *Dunlop* v *Selfridge* [1915] AC 847:

'My Lords, in the law of England certain principles are fundamental. One is that only a person who is a party to a contract can sue upon it. Our law knows nothing of a jus quaesitum tertio arising by way of contract.'

The facts in this case were that Dunlop sold tyres to a wholesaler who sold them to Selfridges. Part of the contract of sale between the wholesaler and Selfridges was that Selfridges should pay compensation to Dunlop if they sold the tyres at below the fixed minimum price. Selfridges later sold below the minimum price and refused to pay compensation. They were sued by Dunlop for breach of contract.

The House of Lords held that Dunlop were not entitled to succeed. They were seeking to enforce a right in a contract to which they were not a party. The argument that the wholesalers were the agents of Dunlop was also rejected.

In *Scruttons* v *Midland Silicones Ltd* [1962] AC 446, a contract was made between a shipping company and a chemical manufacturer concerning the transportation of drums of chemicals. It was agreed that in case of damage by the shipping company, their liability would not exceed £500. A stevedore company damaged the drums and damage was above the £500 limit. They pleaded that they could rely on the provisions of the contract and only pay £500.

HELD: that as they were strangers to the contract they could not rely on its rights – and so they were liable to pay compensation by way of damages.

Scruttons v *Midland Silicones* (above) should be read in the light of *New Zealand Shipping* v *Satterthwaite (The Eurymedon)* [1975] AC 154, in which, on similar facts, the stevedore was able to rely on the provisions of the contract between the cargo owner and carrier. It was said that the bill of lading (which evidences the contract between the cargo owner and the carrier) brought into existence a bargain, initially unilateral, but capable of becoming mutual, between the shipper and the stevedore, made through the carrier as agent, which became a full contract when the stevedore performed services by unloading the goods. The performance of the services was for the benefit of the shipper, and the consideration was that the stevedore should have the benefit of the exemptions in the bill of lading.

This has been affirmed in *Port Jackson Stevedoring* v *Salmond and Spraggon (The New York Star)* [1981] 1 WLR 138. However, in the more recent case of *Southern Water Authority* v *Carey* [1985] 2 All ER 1077, subcontractors sought to rely on a limitation of liability clause in a main contract. They were held not to be entitled to the benefit of the clause in the absence of evidence that the main contractor had authority from the subcontractors at the time of making the contract.

12.6   Creation of a benefit by equity

Trusts

Although contractual rights cannot be established for a stranger, a trust can occur, conferring benefits on such a person, giving rights that can be legally enforced. Any form of property can form a trust. If A and B contract, B promising to pay C £100, then C cannot sue for the £100, because he is a stranger to the contract. But, if it can be proved that A and B had not created a contract but a *trust*, then A, the trustee, or C, the beneficiary, under the trust can sue for the £100 – in equity.

In *Re Flavell* (1883) 25 Ch D 89 a contract between two parties provided that in the event of one of the parties' death, the widow would be entitled to certain payments. The action was brought by one such widow. Her claim in contract failed, but she succeeded in equity as she managed to show to the court that she was the beneficiary under a trust made by the above parties in her favour.

Compare this decision, however, with *Re Schebsman* [1944] Ch 83. Schebsman was employed by a Swiss company, who agreed that his appointment should be ended by means of a golden handshake to the value of £5,500 to be paid in instalments and in the event of death to his widow. The widow sued for the failed payment, but it was held that she would fail as she could show no evidence of a trust. (In contract she failed because she was not privy to the contract.)

It appears from these two cases that two conditions must be fulfilled in order for the court to be convinced of the existence of a trust.

1. There must be a clear intention to create a trust; the words 'trust' and 'beneficiary' need not be used, although it would clarify matters if they were.
2. It must be clear that the parties did not intend to *alter* in any way whatever, the rights they had created, for example, if A and B make a contract to pay C £100, they have created a non-enforceable benefit to C (non enforceable by C) and C cannot sue. But if A and B create a trust, their freedom to modify the trust is curtailed.

That is, a £100 trust cannot be altered/reduced. In *Re Schebsman*, the court thought that this condition was lacking because it appeared that the employee and the employer still had the freedom to negotiate the golden handshake.

Commentary

One can derive an analysis of the discussion above on the equitable concept of trust in the following terms:

If A and B make an agreement for the benefit of C, C cannot enforce that contract since he is not a party to it. However, if they make a trust – or a trust is implied – then one of two analyses is relevant:

1. In the first instance of A and B making a trust for the benefit of C, C is a beneficiary of the trust created between A and B. The Law of Trusts indicates that provided all the parameters of trusts are satisfied then, C, as a beneficiary, can enforce the trust in his own right.
2. But in the instance of a trust being implied from a contractual situation, the analysis seems to be different.

For example, A agrees with B that B will do something for C. If a trust can be implied per *Flavell* above, then, it seems that A is the trustee for B of his own contractual rights. Thus A is, in effect, holding his own contractual rights for the benefit of C in trust. If that is the case, then C as a beneficiary of A's contractual rights can enforce the trust by virtue of those 'trust rights'.

The possibility stated in (2) above has been accepted by the courts. In *Les Affreteurs Reunis Société Anonyme v Leopold Walford* [1919] AC 801, it is suggested that although it is theoretically possible for a trust still to be found in these situations, it must be clear beyond a peradventure that a trust was intended. In *Knight v Knight* (1840) 3 Beav 148 at 173, Lord Langdale referred to the required three certainties:

1. certainty of words,
2. certainty of subject matter; and
3. certainty of objects.

Vandepitte v Preferred Accident Insurance Corporation of New York [1933] AC 70 held that:

> 'It is not legitimate to import into the contract the idea of a trust when the parties have given no indication that such was their intention. To interpret this contract as creating a trust would, in my judgment, be to disregard the dividing line between the case of a trust and the simple use of a contract made between two parties for the benefit of a third.'

Since the Privy Council decision in the above case, there has been very little mention of the trust concept in English courts in the context of privity.

Restrictive covenants

The benefit of a restrictive covenant can also run with land from vendor to purchaser. See *Tulk v Moxhay* (above).

12.7   Section 56 Law of Property Act 1925

Lord Denning MR believed that privity of contract never really existed as true law, and that the only reason it was recognised was due to constant erroneous interpretations over the years. He claims that the LPA 1925 puts this belief into statute form.

Section 56 LPA 1925:

> 'A person may take an interest in land or other property or the benefits concerning land or other property although he may not be named a party to the conveyance or other instrument.'

In both *Smith and Snipes Hall Farm Ltd v River Douglas Catchment Board* [1949] 2 KB 500 and *Drive Yourself Hire Co Ltd v Strutt* [1954] 1 QB 250, Lord Denning launched his campaign against privity – he argued that s56 LPA 1925 was intended to destroy the whole doctrine altogether. Certainly, the words are wide enough to support Denning's view. But it was questionable whether it was wise to take one section out of the context of an entire Act and use it to displace an established doctrine. Lord Denning's view was rejected by other judges in succeeding cases, but it was not until *Beswick* v *Beswick* [1968] AC 58 that the matter came before the House of Lords.

By a written agreement, PB assigned his business as a coal merchant to his nephew JB; in consideration, JB agreed to employ PB as a consultant at £6.50 pw for the rest of his life and, further, to pay PB's wife an annuity of £5 pw for her life after PB's death. PB's wife was not privy to the contract. After PB's death, JB only paid one sum of £5 to the widow and then refused to pay any more. The widow sought an order for specific performance of the agreement in her capacity as *executrix/administratrix* of the estate of her husband and in her *personal capacity*.

At first instance, the judge decided against the widow because he saw no evidence of a trust, and he rejected Lord Denning's interpretation of s56 LPA 1925 (above).

The Court of Appeal, with Lord Denning sitting, decided in favour of the widow however, basing their judgment on s56 LPA 1925 and on the fact that she was the administratrix of her husband's estate.

The House of Lords decided in favour of the widow on the *sole* ground that she was the administratrix of her husband's estate.

Lord Denning's view was rejected outright, the House of Lords holding that s56 should not be taken outside its context despite the wideness of the wording.

12.8   Remedies of the contracting party

Consideration must be given of (1) specific performance, and (2) damages.

Specific performance

This remedy was allowed in *Beswick*. It is, however, a discretionary remedy which will be examined in more detail in Chapter 15.

Damages

The majority view in *Beswick* v *Beswick* was that the widow qua administratrix would have been able to recover only nominal damages. This is presumably based on the general principle that, in an action for damages, the plaintiff cannot recover more than he has lost as a result of the breach. The estate would not have suffered any direct loss. Lord Upjohn was of the view that the basis for the conclusion that only nominal damages would be available is that the promisee had no other assets. Presumably he meant that had the promisee had other assets, they would have had to be diverted from the estate to keep the widow, and the estate would have sustained damage.

The question of the extent to which a contracting party may recover for loss sustained by a stranger who is intended to benefit from the contract was raised in *Jackson* v *Horizon Holidays* [1975] 1 WLR 1468. The plaintiff entered into a contract for himself and his family. The holiday provided failed to comply with the description given by the defendants in a number of important respects.

At first instance, the plaintiff recovered damages including a sum for mental distress. The defendants appealed against the amount of the damages.

In the Court of Appeal, James LJ, in dismissing the appeal, regarded the damages as compensation for the plaintiff's own distress. The plaintiff had, however, brought the action on behalf of himself and his family. Lord Denning MR thought the amount awarded was excessive compensation for the plaintiff himself, but he upheld the award on the ground that the plaintiff had made a contract for the benefit of himself and his family, and that he could recover for their loss as well as for his own. Lord Denning accepted as an established rule of law that if A makes a contract for the benefit of B, A can sue on the contract for the loss sustained by B as a result of the breach.

In *Woodar Investment Development* v *Wimpey Construction* [1980] 1 WLR 277, the House of Lords rejected the basis on which Lord Denning had arrived at his decision, and reaffirmed the view that a contracting party cannot recover damages for the loss sustained by the third party.

Their Lordships did not dissent from the actual decision in *Jackson*, which they felt could be supported either because the damages were awarded for the plaintiff's own loss; or because booking family holidays or ordering meals in restaurants calls for special treatment.

The facts of the *Woodar* case were: a contract for the sale of land provided that on completion the purchaser should pay £850,000 to the vendor and also £150,000 to a third party. The vendor claimed damages for wrongful repudiation. In fact, there was found to be no wrongful repudiation, but the House of Lords expressed the above views. At the same time, they suggested that the position at law might be unsatisfactory.

In *Forster* v *Silvermere Golf and Equestrian Centre* (1981) 125 Sol Jo 397, Dillon J refered to the results produced by the application of the rule that parties to the contract can only recover their personal loss as 'a blot on our law and most unjust'. The plaintiff had transferred land to the defendant who undertook to build a house on it and to allow the plaintiff and her children to live in it rent free for life.

HELD: that she could recover damages for her own loss, but not for the loss of the rights of occupation which her children might have enjoyed after her death.

Promises not to sue

If A promises B for consideration not to sue C, can B prevent this?

In *Gore* v *Van Der Lann* [1967] 2 QB 31, the Court of Appeal held that B could only obtain a stay of proceedings if there was a definite promise by A not to sue C; and B must have a sufficient interest in the enforcement of a promise, for example, where B would be exposed to a legal liability to C if A sues.

It is not clear that a 'sufficient interest' was required in *Snelling* v *Snelling Ltd* [1973] 1 QB 87. Three brothers lent money to a family company of which they were directors. They agreed that if one of them resigned he should forfeit any money due to him by the company. One resigned and sued the company. The company relied on the agreement. Because a company has an independent legal personality, it was not a party to the agreement. The brothers applied to be joined as defendants, adopted the defence and counter-claimed for a declaration that the loan was forfeit.

Ormrod J held that they were entitled to the declaration and that it was a proper case for the stay of proceedings.

12.9   Statutory exceptions

Certain exceptions to the doctrine of privity have been created by statute, including price maintenance agreements; and certain contracts of insurance enforceable in favour of third parties.

For example, under s148(4) Road Traffic Act 1972, an injured party may recover compensation from an insurance company once he has obtained judgment against the insured person.

12.10   Proposals for reform

In 1937, the Law Revision Committee recommended in its 6th Interim Report that:

> 'Where a contract by its express terms purports to confer a benefit on a third party it shall be enforceable by the third party in his own name subject to any defences that would have been valid between the contracting parties.'

The subsequent failure of the legislature to act on this recommendation prompted the remark by the House of Lords in *Woodar* v *Wimpey* (above) that if Parliament did not soon act, the courts would be forced to.

Note that the Law Commission has recently published 'Privity of Contract: Contracts for the Benefit of Third Parties' (Consultation Paper No 121, 1992). The Commission has provisionally recommended that legislation should be enacted to enable third parties, as well as promisees to enforce contractual provisions which have been made in their favour and which the parties intended to be enforced in favour of and by third parties. The rights should, however, only be enforceable within the contract. The promisor would have the same defences to any action, and the same rights of set-off and counter-claim as he would have against the promisee and performance of the contract, or release by the third party would discharge the promisor's contractual obligations.

The Commission recommends that parties to a contract should not be able thereby to impose duties on third parties, but should be able to impose conditions on the enjoyment by them of any benefits under the contract.

13

Illegality

13.1 Introduction

Different methods of classification of illegal contracts have been adopted by writers, some of whom prefer to classify illegal contracts according to the effects of the illegality. The effects, however, vary, depending on the nature of the contract and the behaviour of the parties. For example, one or both parties may be prevented from suing on the contract at all, or one or both parties may be prevented from suing on a particular undertaking, or, if the doctrine of severance applies (see below), one or both parties may be prevented from suing on part of a particular undertaking. The classification that is adopted here is into: contracts contrary to some principle of law; and contracts contrary to public policy.

Contracts in restraint of trade fall into the second category but are dealt with separately because of their importance. We shall examine, first, the types of illegal contracts and then the effect of the illegality.

13.2 Contracts which break the law

It is traditional to distinguish the situation where the object of a contract is the deliberate infringement of the provisions of a statute or a statutory instrument or the common law, then the court will not enforce that contract regardless of whether the

236

infringement is a civil or a criminal one; or where the law has been broken through carrying into effect the terms of a contract, then that contract may be upheld as valid at the instance of a party who was ignorant of such breach of the law or who innocently caused the breach.

Contracts which break the criminal law

Contracts to commit a crime

If a contract has as its object the deliberate commission of a crime, then it is illegal and the courts will not enforce it.

In *Bigos* v *Bousted* [1951] 1 All ER 92, D wished to send his daughter to Italy for health reasons, but because of Exchange Control Regulations could not get sufficient funds out of the country to make her an adequate allowance while abroad. He contracted with P that if she made £150 of Italian money available to his daughter in Italy, he would give her £150 in England and gave P some share certificates as security. The whole transaction failed and D sought recovery of his share certificates.

HELD: the court would not aid D to recover his share certificates as the whole transaction was illegal.

Property under the contract to be used for unlawful purposes

The contract itself may be legal, but the purpose to which its subject matter is to be put may not. If P enters into a contract with D knowing that D is going to use the subject matter for an illegal purpose, then it will not be enforceable.

In *Langton* v *Hughes* (1813) 1 M & S 593, P sold D Spanish juice, isinglass and ginger. P knew D was a brewer and that he intended to use these ingredients in flavouring his beer. In fact, the use of anything other than hops or malt in flavouring beer was illegal. P sued D for the price of the goods.

HELD: P was not entitled to recover anything, he knew D was going to use them for a purpose contrary to statute.

The contract performed in an unlawful manner

The manner in which the contract is performed may be sufficient to turn it into a contract which is prohibited by statute.

In *Anderson* v *Daniel* [1924] 1 KB 138, P sold D some agricultural fertilizer, but failed to give him an invoice showing the composition of it as statute required.

HELD: he could not recover the price since he had not performed the contract in the only manner which was permitted by statute.

The question may arise whether the purpose of the statute is merely to penalise conduct or, in addition, to prohibit performance of the contract.

In *St John's Shipping* v *Joseph Rank Ltd* [1957] 1 QB 267, D's defence to a claim by P for freight was that P had so overloaded his ship with the cargo in respect of which the freight was claimed, that the ship had been submerged below the load line, which was a statutory offence.

HELD: although P's conduct was an offence, it did not affect the contract between P and D.

> 'A court should not hold that any contract or class of contract is prohibited by statute unless there is a clear implication, or "necessary inference" as Parke B put it that the statute so intended. If a contract has as its whole object the doing of the very act which the statute prohibits it can be argued that you can hardly make sense of a statute which forbids an act and yet permits to be made a contract to do it; that is a clear implication' per Devlin J.

The problem of illegality is expressly dealt with in some statutes, for example, the Trades Description Act 1968 states that a contract for the supply of goods is not void merely because it contravenes that Act. This raises the question whether, if P sells D a television set, can he recover the price if he fails to give notice of the transaction to the Post Office as required by statute?

Contracts to idemnify against criminal liability

A contract to idemnify a person against liability resulting from the deliberate commission of a crime cannot be enforced at law.

In *Askey* v *Golden Wine Co* [1948] 2 All ER 35, P, a wholesaler, was fined as a result of breaches of the Food and Drugs Act and had to refund money to retailers. The breaches were due to his own gross negligence and failure to prevent them when he could have done so. He sought to recover the loss from the suppliers of the goods.

HELD: it would be against public policy to allow him to recover this loss, which was incurred through his own fault.

It is clearly established that a contract to indemnify a person against a crime which requires mens rea is illegal. See *Colburn* v *Patmore* (1834) 1 C M & R 73. However, where the offence is one of strict liability, it appears that a person can recover an indemnity for the innocent commission of such an offence.

In *Gregory* v *Ford* [1951] 1 All ER 121, X was employed to drive D's lorry which had third party insurance as required under s35 Road Traffic Act 1930. However, there were conditions attached to the insurance. X had an accident while on an errand for D and it transpired that the insurance policy was inoperative. P sued D for damages and D in turn claimed to be indemnified by X. X argued D had a duty to insure him against third party risks.

HELD: there was no duty on D to insure X against third party risks merely because he was their servant. However, X was entitled to assume that it was an implied term of his contract of employment that he should not be asked to do anything unlawful. He was entitled to assume the lorry was lawfully insured and was, therefore, not liable to indemnify D.

Contracts which break the civil law

Contract to commit a civil wrong

If the contract is to deliberately commit a civil wrong, such as to assault a third party (*Allen* v *Rescous* (1677) 2 Lev 174), or give fraudulent preference to a creditor (*Cockshott* v *Bennet* (1788) 2 TR 763), it is illegal and unenforceable.

If the parties are ignorant of the fact that by the contract they are committing a civil wrong, then it is not illegal. Therefore, if X agrees to sell Y goods which, in fact, belong to a third party, both are liable in conversion. However, no case seems to have held such contracts illegal and s12 Sale of Goods Act 1979 would appear to lend support to the theory that they are not.

If one of the parties to the contract knows that the contract is illegal, for example, where the seller of goods knows they belong to a third party, then it appears that only the innocent party is entitled to rely on the contract.

In *Clay* v *Yates* (1856) 1 H & N 73, P agreed to print a book for D which had a libellous dedication. P discovered afterwards that the dedication was libellous and printed the book without it. He then claimed the cost of printing the book. D argued it was an entire contract and that P could not recover anything as he had only given part performance.

HELD: there was an implied undertaking to pay for so much of the book as was lawful.

Whether a contract to break a contract is illegal is not, as yet, clearly decided. In some instances it is clear that the courts will declare such contracts bad on grounds of public policy. Lauterpacht in his article in 52 LQR 494 (1936) suggests that the proper approach is to accept that a contract to break a contract is illegal and unenforceable, and then to inquire what exceptions are engrafted onto that rule.

In *Edwin Hill* v *First National Finance Corporation plc* [1989] 1 WLR 225, the defendant bankers held a charge on land scheduled for redevelopment. The defendants agreed to pay the developer the necessary funds, provided the plaintiffs were replaced by other architects. The plaintiffs sued claiming damages against the defendants for procuring breach of the contract that they had with the developer. The Court of Appeal held that the defendants' interference with the plaintiffs' contract was justified as being in defence and protection of an equal and superior right of the defendants to be repaid under the legal charge.

This suggests that certain types of contract while prima facie illegal may be defensible on the grounds of public policy.

Contract to indemnify against civil liability

If the civil wrong is deliberately committed, then it appears that the general rule is that any contract of indemnity in respect of that wrong is illegal, for example, if X publishes a libel at the instigation of Y he cannot recover an indemnity from Y. See *W H Smith* v *Clinton* (1909) 99 LT 840. Where, however, the tendency of such a contract would be to restrict the circulation of the libel as published in a communication which the parties have agreed is to remain confidential, it would appear that an indemnity is recoverable if any liability is incurred through its disclosure. See *Weld-Blundell* v *Stephens* [1920] AC 956.

Where a civil wrong is innocently committed, then the general rule is that P can sue on a contract of indemnity. Therefore, an employer can insure himself against civil liability for the tort of his employee, whether or not it is a crime, and he can obtain an indemnity for torts committed by one employee on another from the wrongdoer under the contract of employment. See *Lister* v *Romford Ice and Cold Storage Co* [1957] AC 555.

Where a civil liability arises out of the commission of a crime, the rule is that any contracts to indemnify are not effective.

In *Gray* v *Barr* [1971] 2 QB 554, P shot and killed his wife's lover. He had an insurance policy which indemnified him against liability through causing death, and consequently sought to be indemnified under it for damages he had paid to the lover's estate.

HELD: P's actions in shooting D amounted to manslaughter and, as a matter of policy, he should not recover as armed violence should be deterred.

For further application of this principle, see *Re K (deceased)* [1985] 1 All ER 403.

In two exceptional cases, P may recover where he is liable in civil law for a crime, where the crime is one of strict liability (see *Gregory* v *Ford* (above)); and under a motor insurance policy where the crime is committed negligently, but not if it is committed deliberately.

In *Tinline* v *White Cross Insurance* [1921] 3 KB 327, P, a motorist, insured against 'accidental personal injury' to third parties, killed a third party through negligent driving. He was convicted of manslaughter and later was successfully sued by the estate of the third party. P sought to recover from the insurers the damages he paid.

HELD: he could recover from the insurers.

Contracts to waive rights conferred by statute
Whether a statutory right can be waived depends upon its overall purpose, and upon whether the intention of the statute would be frustrated by 'contracting out'. This is, therefore, the application of the provisions of public policy to the decision, because the courts will not allow the intentions of Parliament to be frustrated.

In *Johnson* v *Moreton* [1980] AC 37, the House of Lords held that a tenant could not contract out of the protection provided by s24 Agricultural Holdings Act 1948, because to do so would undermine the purpose of the Act.

Contract is illegal per se

The making of the contract itself may amount to an illegality and, in such circumstances, it may not only remain unenforced by the court but, in addition, it may be punishable with a fine or imprisonment. This is true, for example, of a conspiracy to defraud.

Therefore, if the purpose of a contract is to perpetrate a fraud on the prospective shareholders of a company (see *Begbie* v *Phosphate Sewage Co Ltd* (1875) LR 10 QB 491), the contract is illegal and criminal.

Contracts declared illegal by statute

Although the statute itself may not be repealed, the impact of certain sections of it may be diminished by changing circumstances. Consider *City Index* v *Leslie* [1990] NLJR 9 November.

The plaintiff company carried on a business which included wagers on the stock market index movements. The defendant opened a credit account with the plaintiff company, and after a number of unsuccessful bets owed the company nearly £35,000. He stated he was unable to pay. The plaintiff company sued for the amount outstanding on the basis that, although betting and wagering contracts had for many years been unenforceable under the Gaming Act 1845, the recent Financial Services Act 1986 meant that such wagers were now exempt from the Act.

HELD: section 63 Financial Services Act 1986 covers wagers entered into by way of business with a party entitled to trade under the Act. (The plaintiff company was a member of the Association of Futures, Brokers and Dealers and recognised by the Secretary of State.) Such wagers on differences in the market are 'investments' for the purposes of the Act, and the buying and selling of such forecasts are excluded from the unenforceability provisions of the Gaming Act 1845. The full sum owed was, therefore, not considered to be an 'illegal' contract and, as such, was recoverable.

The increasing number of City 'deals' means that transactions made by way of trade or business regarding futures and forecasts of commodity shares and prices, although highly speculative, cannot be regarded as gambles or wagering contracts. Although before the 1986 Act became law, actions could not have been entertained regarding them, by reason of s18 Gaming Act, they will now be fully enforceable at law.

13.3 Contracts contrary to public policy

Contracts to pervert the course of justice

Concealing and compounding crimes

Any agreement to conceal a crime is illegal and against public policy. See *Gardside* v *Outram* (1857) 26 LJ Ch 113.

Though the question as to whether if, in order to obtain information relating to crimes a promise to proceed no further by, say, the police, would be contractually binding, has never been tested in the courts.

The compounding of an offence other than treason is not an offence, except where it falls within s5 Criminal Law Act 1967, which provides that anyone:

'... who knows or believes that an arrestable offence has been committed and that he has information which might be of material assistance in securing the prosecution or conviction of any offender for it is guilty of an indictable offence if he accepts, for not disclosing that information, any consideration other than (a) the making good of loss or injury occasioned by the offence or (b) the making of reasonable compensation for that loss or injury'.

Where an agreement is an offence under s5 it is not enforceable in law.

If the agreement is not to initiate a prosecution or report an offence to the police, then it may be considered as stifling a prosecution and contrary to public policy.

Again, the question as to whether it would be contrary to public policy if P has a civil claim arising out of an offence and he compromises this with D has not been tested in a court of law, nor whether it would make any difference if he offered not to report the matter to the police.

But note *Fulham Football Club Ltd* v *Cabra Estates plc* (1992) The Times 11 September in which a development company and a local authority applied separately for planning consent to redevelop land. The plaintiffs covenanted with the development company that, for a substantial fee, they would not in any way support the council's application, including the provision of witnesses or evidence at any resultant public inquiry. Later, however, despite the covenant, the plaintiffs refused to support the development company, arguing that any agreement was void by reason of illegality. At first instance they were successful. The development company appealed. The Court of Appeal held that no agreement which required the giving of false evidence, or purported to prevent a witness responding to subpoena could be legal; it would always be contrary to public policy. But in commercial transactions such as this, involving disposition of land, an agreement to refrain from objecting, or to support, such a scheme would be considered valid. The plaintiffs could not rely on the rule concerning public policy to ignore the covenant they had agreed to as illegal. It would be an enforceable agreement and the defendants' appeal succeeded.

Interfering with proceedings
It is illegal to conduct criminal proceedings so that a person's name shall not be mentioned, or shall only be mentioned in a manner that does not damage or implicate him. An agreement not to appear and give evidence is illegal. A contract with a person who has 'stood bail' as a surety to indemnify the amount that the surety has stood is illegal and unenforceable. It is also an indictable offence.

Fraudulent preferences
Agreements to prefer creditors (who are unsecured) in winding up and bankruptcy proceedings are illegal and unenforceable. They may be set aside by statute, which declares them void rather than unenforceable.

Contracts which oust the jurisdiction of the courts

Such contracts are contrary to public policy as they would have the effect of evading many peremptory rules of law.

In *Anctil* v *Manufacturers Life Insurance* [1899] AC 604, a clause in an insurance policy provided that it should be 'incontestable' in certain events. P attempted to sue on it and it was held that this clause did not stop the court from deciding if he had an insurable interest.

Maintenance agreements

The House of Lords decided in *Hyman* v *Hyman* [1929] AC 601 that a wife could not validly contract with her husband not to apply for maintenance on a divorce, and that a contract of that kind did not prevent her from applying. For a recent application of this, see *Sutton* v *Sutton* [1984] 1 All ER 168.

Arbitration

It is perfectly legal to have a clause in an agreement to refer a matter to a private tribunal for a decision before going to court. But, if such a clause deprives the parties of their right to go to court, it is contrary to public policy and void.

In *Czarnikow* v *Roth, Schmidt & Co* [1922] 2 KB 478, a contract for the sale of sugar contained a clause that all disputes should be referred to arbitration, but that the arbitrator should not be required by any party to state a special case for the court to decide a point of law.

HELD: the clause was an attempt to deprive the court of its jurisdiction to decide points of law and was, therefore, contrary to public policy.

The parties to a contract are, however, at liberty to make it a condition precedent of going to court that arbitration should have taken place.

In *Scott* v *Avery* (1856) 5 HLC 811, an insurance policy contained a clause providing that the assured should not be 'entitled to maintain any action on his policy until the matters in dispute shall have been referred to and decided by arbitrators ... and the obtaining of the decision of such arbitrators is hereby declared to be condition precedent to the right of (the assured) to maintain any action'.

HELD: the clause was valid – it did not oust the jurisdiction of the court, but only laid a timetable for when that jurisdiction arose.

Maintenance and champerty

Maintenance is the unjustified meddling in, support of, or instigation of litigation by a person who has no concern or interest in it. A contract, for example, in which X agrees to help Y finance litigation to have Z's will set aside when X has no interest in the will may be within this category.

Champerty is where a person who is maintaining another extracts an agreement for a share in the winnings of the action. For example, X, a solicitor, agrees to help Y who is poor, to bring an action in defamation against Z, provided Y gives X 50% of the damages recovered.

Both maintenance and champerty were formerly a crime and a tort, but by ss13 and 14 Criminal Law Act 1967 both were abolished as such. However, the Act went on to provide that such abolition would 'not affect any rule of law as to the cases in which a contract is to be treated as contrary to public policy or otherwise illegal'. Therefore, a contract concerning maintenance or champerty is still illegal.

The leading case is *Martell* v *Consett Iron Co Ltd* [1955] Ch 363. An association for the protection of rivers from pollution supported an action by one of its members in connection with a river that ran through his land. The defendant said that the action was unlawfully maintained.

Danckwerts J, whose decision was upheld by the Court of Appeal, held that 'support of legal proceedings based on a bona fide community of pecuniary interest or religion or principle or problems', did not constitute maintenance.

The area of maintenance and champerty was re-examined by the Court of Appeal and House of Lords in *Trendtex Trading Corporation* v *Credit Suisse* [1982] AC 679. The issue arose out of a purported assignment of the right to litigate. The plaintiff sold cement. Payment was to be by confirmed letter of credit. The bank failed to honour the letter of credit. The plaintiff sued. After the Court of Appeal hearing, the plaintiff assigned the right to sue to Credit Suisse to whom the plaintiff was very substantially indebted. Credit Suisse then assigned the right to a third party. Subsequently, the plaintiff thought that the transfer of the right to sue was undervalued. As part of the indebtedness to Credit Suisse arose out of the cement contract and the financing of litigation, the plaintiff then claimed that the agreement was champertous.

HELD: by the House of Lords, that the assignment was void.

The Court of Appeal held it valid and Oliver LJ said that as the defendants had a close commercial relationship with the plaintiff, which would have justified them maintaining the action and participating in the profits, he could see no reason why they should not have the right to litigate as well.

Lord Denning MR saw no reason why the benefit of the right to sue should not be assignable, given that the benefit of the contract before breach is assignable. But note: that this would not extend to purely personal actions, nor where the assignment was to a solicitor. Such assignments would be champertous.

The House of Lords held that it was void here because the assignment was the first step in a transaction which involved further assignment to the third party. Lord Roskill thought that Oliver LJ should have distinguished between the interest necessary to support an assignment of a cause of action, and an interest necessary to justify maintaining the cause of action. It does not follow that the interest is the same. It was necessary to show that there was a commercial interest in the enforcement of the claim before the assignment would be valid. The burden of proof is on the assignee.

In *Picton Jones & Co* v *Arcadia Developments* [1989] 3 EG 85, the plaintiffs, who were a firm of surveyors, agreed to act for the defendants in relation to the aquisition of some amusement arcades. Their fees were only to be payable 'in the event of ultimate success'.

Though the plaintiffs were successful in carrying out their assignments, the defendants refused to pay, stating that the contract was one of champerty and, as such, illegal and unenforceable. Further, they alleged that entering such contracts was contrary to rules established by the plaintiffs' professional institute and, as such, contrary to public policy and illegal.

HELD: judgment was given to the plaintiffs since, first, the doctrine of champerty was confined to agreements regarding the outcome of litigation. Also, secondly, the fact that a professional institution forbids a particular type of contract does not necessarily mean that it is contrary to public policy and thus illegal.

It is worth considering, in view of the 'Code of Practice' issued by the Bar Council in which 'contingency fees' have been introduced for the first time, whether maintenance and champerty, in particular, may not now be obsolete.

Contracts promoting sexual immorality

Contracts which fall within this category are those which promote extramarital sexual intercourse. Pictures, books and films which are illegal by virtue of the Obscene Publications Act 1959 fall within the category of contracts which break the law.

A promise by a man to pay a woman money, either to become his mistress or to secure the continuance of cohabitation, used to be thought illegal. See *Franco* v *Bolton* (1797) 3 Ves 368. Any bond given after cohabitation to secure payment on such promises was, likewise, illegal. It does not follow that the same remains true. Values change and stable domestic relations between unmarried couples are no longer regarded as a departure from the norm. In recent cases, the illegality of these domestic relations has not been raised and, probably, would not be welcomed. An example of a case where a contract (a contractual licence) was found is *Tanner* v *Tanner* [1975] 1 WLR 1346. A married man who had twins by his mistress, provided her with a house. When the man subsequently attempted to evict her, it was held that there was an implied contract that she could remain there. The consideration provided by her was the relinquishment of a rent-controlled flat.

If the payment does not promote immorality by promoting cohabitation, then it is not illegal. Thus, a promise to pay money to a woman with whom a man has in the past cohabited is not illegal, it is a contract which lacks consideration in any case. See *Beaumont* v *Reeve* (1846) 8 QB 483. A gift by a man to a woman either during or after cohabitation is also, without more, valid. See *Ayerst* v *Jenkins* (1873) LR 16 Eq 275.

Contracts which have the effect of promoting prostitution are illegal. Thus, a contract to hire out a brougham to a prostitute for her profession is illegal. See *Pearce* v *Brooks* (1866) LR 1 Ex 213. But, apparently, it is not illegal to contract to wash a prostitute's linen which included a quantity of gentlemen's nightcaps. See *Lloyd* v *Johnson* (1798) 1 B & P 340.

Contracts to lease premises to prostitutes for their profession are illegal, but a contract to let a room to a prostitute who practises her profession at another place is valid 'because persons of that description must have a place to lay their heads'. See *Appleton* v *Campbell* (1826) 2 C & P 347.

Contracts concerning family matters

Contracts relating to divorce or separation

A contract by the parties to divorce proceedings is invalid if made with a corrupt intention, for example, where one party bribes the other to institute the proceedings or to deceive the court on certain matters relevant in the proceedings like family finances. But, bona fide attempts to come to arrangements which overcome the difficulties resulting from a broken marriage are valid.

In *Brodie* v *Brodie* [1917] P 271, an agreement was made between a man and a woman, who felt obliged to marry after the woman gave birth to a child, that they would not live together after the marriage. This was held to be invalid.

Spouses who are already married may agree to separate and, if they are already separated, they may make further agreements concerning their position. Where spouses attempt reconciliation, then any agreements relating to future separation are valid as it may aid the reconciliation. See *Harrison* v *Harrison* [1910] 1 KB 35.

Contracts to marry

By s1 Law Reform (Miscellaneous Provisions) Act 1970, actions for breach of promise to marry were abolished. Prior to this, only a promise by a married man to marry was unenforceable as against public policy on the ground that it tended to promote sexual immorality. However, a promise of marriage between the decree nisi and decree absolute was, then, permissible.

Marriage brokage contracts

An undertaking for reward to procure a marriage between two parties is against public policy and void. The same rule applies if the contract is merely to find a marriage partner for a client. See *Hermann* v *Charlesworth* [1905] 2 KB 123. This rule, if still applicable nowadays, raises an interesting question as to the status of contracts between marriage bureaux and their clients.

Contracts in restraint of marriage

A contract which attempts to restrain or prevent a party from marrying is void and against public policy. See *Lowe* v *Peers* (1768) 4 Burr 2225. But a contract which deters a person from marrying by providing some inducement which will end when he or she marries is not void, for example, a promise to let a house to a person until marriage is valid. See *Gibson* v *Dickie* (1815) 3 M & S 463.

Contracts to assign parental rights

A contract to transfer parental rights and liabilities is against public policy and void. Therefore, if X agrees to sell his child to Y, it is illegal. But a separation agreement between husband and wife for one or the other to relinquish such rights is valid – s1(1) Guardianship Act 1973.

Contracts interfering with government or foreign relations

Procurement of public offices and honours

Contracts for the sale of public appointments, such as a directorship in a public company, are contrary to public policy and void. Likewise, any agreement to pay money to procure an honour for the payer is also contrary to public policy, as it may result in improper methods being employed. It is also an offence under the Honours (Prevention of Abuses) Act 1925. See *Parkinson* v *Royal College of Ambulance* [1925] 2 KB 1.

Contracts by employees and members of public authorities

By s117 Local Government Act 1972, any officer with a direct or indirect pecuniary interest in a contract entered into by a local authority must declare his interest and can take no fees or rewards beyond his ordinary remuneration. Formerly, at common law, it was an offence for a public officer to accept a bribe or show favour. See *Re Wallace* [1920] 2 Ch 274.

Contracts to deceive public authorities

If a contract is made either to conceal or misrepresent facts to a public authority or body, for example, tax returns to the Inland Revenue, then it is illegal and void.

In *Alexander* v *Rayson* [1936] 1 KB 169, P let a service flat to D for £1,200 by a contract which was drawn up in two separate documents. In the first document, D agreed to pay £450 for the flat and services and, in the second, D agreed to pay £750 for the flat and services and the use of a refrigerator. The purpose was to deceive the local authority in respect of rates.

HELD: the contract was illegal and unenforceable.

If a contract is an attempt to evade the provisions of a statute, the purpose of which is to protect one of the contracting parties, then it is illegal.

In *Farrell* v *Alexander* [1976] 2 All ER 721, D wished to assign the unexpired term of four years of her tenancy to P. The assignment was to be done by means of a surrender by D to her landlord, who would grant P a new lease and, as a term of the agreement, P was to pay D £4,000 for fixtures and fittings, although they were worth much less. P claimed that the balance of the £4,000 was an illegal premium under the Rent Acts.

HELD: P was entitled to recover so much as exceeded the value of the fixtures and fittings. This was because the Rent Act only made the excess recoverable and not the whole sum.

Contracts which interfere with foreign relations

Where a contract has as its object the doing of an act illegal by the law of a friendly foreign country, it is illegal and void.

In *Regazzoni* v *KC Sethia* [1958] AC 301, a contract was made to export Indian jute to Italy with the ultimate purpose of re-exporting it from Italy to South Africa. Indian law prohibited the export of goods to South Africa and the contract could only be performed by making false declarations as to the destination of the jute.

HELD: the court would not help P to enforce the contract as it was an attempt to contravene Indian law.

If a contract has as its purpose the breach of the customs regulations of a foreign country or aiding terrorists to attack that country, it is illegal. See *De Wutz* v *Hendricks* (1824) 2 Bing 314.

The public policy of a friendly foreign state could not of itself prevent the enforcement of a contract in England. But if the contract was contrary to English public policy, and the same public policy applied in the friendly foreign country, the combination of the two factors would prevent enforcement. See *Lemenda Trading Co Ltd* v *African Middle East Petroleum Co Ltd* [1988] 1 All ER 513.

See also *Howard* v *Shirlstar Container Transport Ltd* [1990] 1 WLR 1292, where the defendant company agreed to pay the plaintiff £25,000 to 'remove' from Nigeria an aircraft belonging to them. He flew the aircraft out of Lagos without obtaining the necessary clearance and in breach of air traffic controls. After pursuit by a Nigerian Air Force plane, he made a forced landing in the Ivory Coast; the plane was impounded and later returned to Nigeria.

The defendant company said that because the contract required the plaintiff to 'successfully' remove the aircraft from Nigerian airspace, he had not performed the contract as agreed and they were, therefore, justified in withholding the agreed fee.

HELD: on a strictly technical interpretation the aircraft had (for a short time) left Nigeria and, therefore, the full sum was payable. A court would not allow a person to benefit from an illegal act, whether or not arising under foreign law, if to do so would be an affront to public conscience. Whether an illegal act might be considered against public policy was a question of fact in each case. In this case, the plaintiff's illegal act had been to save his own and his crew's lives and, on hearing that this would have been an acceptable defence under Nigerian law, the court permitted the plaintiff to recover the full amount.

Contracts to trade with the enemy

Under the Trading with the Enemy Act 1939, it is an offence to trade or attempt to trade with the enemy. Contracts to trade with the enemy are therefore illegal.

An enemy is anyone voluntarily resident or carrying on business in an enemy territory (*Porter* v *Freudenberg* [1915] 1 KB 857), and if the contract tends to aid the economy of the enemy that is sufficient.

Covenants in restraint of trade 249

Contracts interfering with personal liberty

If a contract imposes conditions on an individual which restrict his liability unduly without cause it is illegal.

In *Horwood* v *Millar's Timber and Trading Co* [1917] 1 KB 305, P borrowed money from D on terms that P would not, without D's written consent, leave his job, dispose of his house, borrow more money or move home.

HELD: the contract imposed unreasonable restrictions on P's liberty and was, therefore, void.

Restrictions imposed by a father on his son would not appear to fall within this category provided there are reasons for them.

In *Denny* v *Denny* [1919] 1 KB 583, a son who associated with gamblers, swindlers and other disreputable characters went bankrupt. His father promised to pay his debts and an allowance provided he did not become bankrupt again and reformed his character, gave up these friends, did not go within 80 miles of Piccadilly Circus without his father's consent, and did not have any contract with moneylenders, bookmakers or their servants.

HELD: the contract was valid; it was an attempt by a father to act for his son's moral benefit and not intended to restrict his liberty merely for commercial reasons.

13.4 Covenants in restraint of trade

Where a contract contains a covenant in restraint of trade, it will generally only be the covenant which is unenforceable (or part of it) and not the whole contract. The whole contract will be unenforceable, of course, if the promise to restrict trading activities is the only consideration moving from the promisee, for example, if the contract is: 'I will give you £100 if you will agree not to sell fish in the United Kingdom.' If the promise not to sell in the UK is unenforceable, the whole contract may fail.

All covenants in restraint of trade are prima facie unenforceable at common law. They become enforceable only if they are reasonable.

Definition of restraint of trade

The leading case is *Esso Petroleum Co* v *Harper's Garage (Stourport) Ltd* [1968] AC 269 (see below). Various definitions were attempted, or not, as the case may be.

Lord Reid would not attempt to define the dividing line between contracts which are, and contracts which are not, in restraint of trade.

Lord Wilberforce: 'no exhaustive test can be stated – probably no non-exhaustive test'. The common law has often (if sometimes unconsciously) thrived on ambiguity and it would be mistaken, even if it were possible, to try to crystallise the rules of this, or any aspect of public policy, into neat propositions. The doctrine of restraint of trade is one to be applied to factual situations with a broad and flexible rule of reason.

Lord Hodson adopted a test attempted by Diplock LJ in *Petrofina (Great Britain) Ltd* v *Martin* [1966] Ch 146:

'A contract in restraint of trade is one in which a party (the covenantor) agrees with any other party (the covenantee) to restrict his liberty in the future to carry on trade with other persons not parties to the contract in such manner as he chooses.'

Lord Morris thought that the above was a helpful exposition, but not to be taken too literally. He also referred to dicta of Lord Denning MR in the *Petrofina case*:

'Every member of the community is entitled to carry on any trade or business he chooses and in such manner as he thinks most desirable in his own interests, so long as he does nothing unlawful; with the consequence that any contract which interferes with the free exercise of his trade or business, by restricting him in the work he may do for others, is a contract in restraint of trade. It is invalid unless it is reasonable as between the parties.'

Lord Pearce:

'Somewhere there must be a line between those contracts which are in restraint of trade ... and those contracts which merely regulate the normal commercial relations between the parties.'

Note, for example, the case of *Watson* v *Prager* [1991] 1 WLR 726 in which the relationship between a professional boxer and his manager was held to come within the ambit of restraint of trade. The court held that the contract was not a normal commercial contract freely entered into by both parties, but was, by virtue of the British Boxing Board of Control's monopoly, to be subject to more stringent than usual judicial supervision. The contract would only be enforced if it was reasonable. Reasonableness would be tested by the nature of the terms, not how fairly or otherwise the defendant had adhered to conditions laid down by the BBBC. The fact that the manager had negotiated higher than average 'purses' did not alter the fact he was unilaterally able to agree the 'purse' for fights; the plaintiff was unable to negotiate on his own behalf. This was unreasonable, even if the actual sums negotiated were good.

The court decided that the contract contained restrictions on the plaintiff which were restrictive and unreasonable and was therefore unreasonable as a whole.

The origin of modern law is in the speech of Lord Macnaghten in *Nordenfelt* v *Maxim Nordenfelt Guns & Ammunition Co* [1894] AC 535 from which the proposition emerged that: although a covenant in restraint of trade is prima facie unenforceable, it will become enforceable if it is reasonable. Note that the recent case of *Allied Dunbar* v *Frank Weisinger* [1987] IRLR 60 has confirmed that the proper test is to consider whether the restraint is reasonably necessary for the protection of the interests of the covenantor. The concept of 'proportionality' in testing a covenant in restraint of trade is *not* a valid test. The matters which are pertinent in assessing reasonableness are the legitimate interests of the parties; and the public interest.

The criteria for determining reasonableness will depend on the nature of the transaction in which the restraint is imposed.

Although the categories of covenants in restraint of trade are not closed, the bulk of case law falls into the following categories: sale of a business and employment; restrictive trading; solus agreements; and others.

Sale of a business and employment

Covenants which restrain an employee's activities after the termination of the employment have always been construed more zealously than covenants which restrict the trading activities of the vendor of a business. The reason is that there is a greater parity of bargaining power between the vendor and purchaser of a business than between an employee and employer. That does not mean, however, that the court will go to extravagant lengths to find a covenant restricting the employee's activities void. In *Home Counties Dairies* v *Skilton* [1970] 1 WLR 526, the defendant (a milkman) covenanted that he would not serve or sell 'milk or dairy produce' to any customer or former customer of his employer for a period of one year. It was argued that this was too wide, because it would prevent him from working in a grocer's shop.

HELD: from the obvious intentions of the parties, the clause was intended to apply only to occupation as a roundsman, which was a business similar to that of his employer. The clause was reasonable.

The legitimate interests which can be protected by an employer are less than those which can be protected by the purchaser of a business. Whereas the purchaser of a business can be deemed to be entitled to the goodwill of the business free of competition, the same is not true of an employer. He cannot protect himself against competition, but only against the use of something in which he has a proprietary interest, such as a list of customers. See *Fitch* v *Dewes* [1921] 2 AC 158.

Although an employer's principal concern is likely to be about soliciting customers, it does not follow that this is the only interest which he can protect. In *Eastham* v *Newcastle United Football Club* [1964] Ch 413, Wilberforce J thought that other covenants in restraint might protect legitimate interests and be enforceable. In that case, he was considering the 'retain and transfer' system (where an employee could not transfer sides without the consent of both the sides from which, and to which, he wished to change). In fact, he did not find that this was an interest to be protected.

Reasonableness

Nature of the relationship with the covenantee's customers
The nature of the relationship which the vendor or employee would have had with customers of a business is relevant. For instance, a covenant imposed on the bookkeeper of a small business not to deal with customers or former customers of the business is unlikely to be reasonable because the employee would not have come into contact with the customers and would not be in a position to solicit them.

Area of restraint

The area to which an employee or vendor can be limited in plying his trade is a matter which goes to the reasonableness of the clause. Again, it may follow that a purchaser of a business has a greater interest to protect than an employer and can impose wider restraints.

In *Nordenfelt* v *Maxim Nordenfelt Guns and Ammunition* [1894] AC 535, a worldwide restraint was held valid. N entered into a contract for the the sale of his worldwide business. He undertook not to compete with it (inter alia) in the trade or business of guns, gun making, explosives, etc, for 25 years or anywhere in the world. The clause was held valid in so far as set out above. Certain words were deleted.

On the other hand, in *Mason* v *Provident Clothing* [1913] AC 724, a covenant by a canvasser, employed to sell clothes in Islington, not to enter into a similar business within 25 miles of London was held void. The area was too large.

In *Spencer* v *Marchington* [1988] IRLR 392, a restrictive covenant to prevent a former employee being engaged in a similar business within a radius of 25 miles of the ex-employer's business was too wide and contrary to public policy.

The recent case of *Briggs* v *Oates* [1991] 1 All ER 407 concerned a restraint of trade clause as agreed between solicitors. The solicitor's contract of employment with the firm contained a restriction that he would not set up in practice on his own, nor go to any rival firm, within a five mile radius of his present employers. The restriction was to last for five years. The court found that the restrictions were reasonable and binding.

Scope of restraint

Only those activities which pose a threat to an employer's legitimate interests may be covered. So in *Attwood* v *Lamont* [1920] 3 KB 571, the plaintiff carried on business as a draper, tailor and outfitter in Kidderminster. The defendant, who was head cutter and manager of the tailoring department, agreed that he would not at any time carry on the trades of tailor, dressmaker, general draper, milliner, hatter, haberdasher, or outfitter within 10 miles of Kidderminster.

HELD: only the restraint of him as a tailor was reasonable. Note that the Court of Appeal refused to apply the 'blue pencil test' below.

In *Clarke* v *Newland* [1991] 1 All ER 397, a restraint of trade clause covering members of a medical partnership contained a clause agreeing 'not to practise in the area of the practice'. The Court of Appeal had to consider not only what the exact 'practice area' was, but also whether the phrase meant that the defendant could not practise as a medical practitioner of any sort, or whether the bar was simply applicable to general medicine.

Duration of the restraint

In *Fitch* v *Dewes* (above), a life-long restraint was upheld. The circumstances in which this may be upheld, however, were said in *Fellowes* v *Fisher* [1976] QB 122 to be rare.

Public interest

It is frequently said that a covenant will be void if it is contrary to the public interest. There is little direct authority. In *Wyatt* v *Kreglinger & Fernau* [1933] 1 KB 793, the employers of a wool broker promised him a pension on his retirement provided that he did not re-enter the wool trade and did nothing to their detriment. He claimed for arrears of his pension.

HELD: he could not recover. One of the reasons given in the judgments was that the stipulation against competition was contrary to the public interest.

In *Deacons* v *Bridge* [1984] 2 All ER 19, the Privy Council upheld a restraint on a former partner in a firm of solicitors the effect of which was that he would not act as a solicitor in Hong Kong for a period of five years for any client of the firm or any person who had been a client during the three years preceding his departure from the firm. Their Lordships did not consider that a five-year restriction was unreasonable, and also thought that such a restriction was reasonable in the public interest.

In *Kerr* v *Morris* [1986] 3 All ER 217, the Court of Appeal held that a restraint on a doctor, a member of a partnership practising within the National Health Service, which precluded him from practising within a certain area, or treating patients of the partnership, was not contrary to the public interest.

Restrictive trading

Where suppliers and acquirers contract not with each other but suppliers contract inter se, and acquirers contract inter se, the rules about restraint of trade do not cease to apply. It is, however, more difficult to discover the interest that deserves to be protected.

In *English Hop Growers* v *Dering* [1928] 2 KB 174, hop growers undertook to deliver their crops to a central selling agency to avoid 'cut-throat' competition during a period of surplus.

HELD: the agreement was valid.

Compare *McEllstrim* v *Ballymacelligot Cooperative Society* [1919] AC 548. An association of farmers in Ireland promised to buy all the milk produced by its members in the area. The members promised not to sell milk to anyone except the association.

HELD: the agreement was invalid, because no farmer could withdraw from the association without the consent of the association, and that consent could be unreasonably withheld.

An agreement was held invalid in a more recent case because it would be prejudicial to a group of people, even though it would not prejudice the general public.

In *Kores Manufacturing* v *Kolok Manufacturing* [1959] Ch 108, both organisations produced carbon paper and typewriter ribbons. They agreed not to employ each other's former employees for five years after leaving that employment.

HELD: the area of restraint was too wide. It covered all employees no matter what they knew, and was of excessive duration.

Solus agreements

Many of these agreements have arisen between oil companies and garage proprietors, and some in respect of tied public houses. The leading case is *Esso Petroleum* v *Harper's Garage* [1968] AC 269. The defendants had undertaken to purchase from the plaintiffs petrol for two filling stations operated by them. In one case, the promise was of four years and five months duration. In respect of the other filling station, the agreement was for 21 years.

HELD: that the agreement for four years and five months was valid; that the agreement for 21 years was not valid. Further, as the purchase of the filling station was secured by a mortgage in favour of the plaintiffs containing the covenant, the covenant would be regarded as a clog on the equity of redemption of the mortgage.

In *Alec Lobb (Garages)* v *Total Oil* [1985] 1 All ER 303 CA, in 1969 the plaintiffs' garage business was in financial straits. In return for financial support from the defendants, they granted to the defendants a 51-year lease of their premises at a full market rent, then took for themselves an underlease (a 'leaseback') at a low rent for 21 years, which contained a tie to buy all their petrol from the defendants for a period of at least seven, and possibly as much as 21 years. In 1979, the plaintiffs sued to have the lease set aside and the exclusive purchase agreement declared void as being in unreasonable restraint of trade. The Court of Appeal held the exclusive sale agreement valid, and refused to set aside the lease.

The court had regard to the overall transaction, in particular (1) it was a rescue operation, benefiting the plaintiffs; (2) there was ample consideration for the grant of the lease to the defendants; (3) there were break clauses in the underlease; and (4) there was a public interest in encouraging a transaction which enabled a plaintiff to continue trading. See also *Amoco* v *Rocca Bros* [1975] AC 561 and *Cleveland Petroleum* v *Dartstone* [1969] 1 WLR 116.

Other agreements

The categories of restraint of trade are not closed, although the approach of the courts is that it is a rule which should be extended only cautiously.

In *Pharmaceutical Society of Great Britain* v *Dickson* [1970] AC 403, a rule of the Society which restricted the trading of chemists was invalid. A majority view was that this was because it was in restraint of trade.

Also, in *Greig* v *Insole* [1978] 1 WLR 302, a restriction on cricketers was held to be in restraint of trade.

13.5   Enforcement of illegal contracts

Where the contract itself is prohibited

If the contract itself is prohibited by law, then it is unenforceable and neither party to it can plead ignorance or innocence as an excuse.

The party which instigated the illegality will not be able to enforce the contract itself in any circumstances; thus, in *Pearce* v *Brooks* (above), the owner of a brougham who let it to a prostitute, knowing it was for the purposes of her profession, could not sue for the hire fee.

Any attempts by either party to enforce a contract prohibited by law by indirect means will be nullified by the court. Therefore, if the contract provides for arbitration, the court will set aside any awards made by the arbitrator, *David Taylor* v *Barnett Trading Co* [1953] 1 WLR 562.

If either party to an illegal contract commits wrongs which are independent of the contract, then the court will recognise and enforce remedies for such wrongs.

In *Edler* v *Auerbach* [1950] 1 KB 359, P let premises to D under an illegal lease which was unenforceable by either party. D removed a bath from the premises and promised P he would replace it at the end of the tenancy. He failed to do so and P sued for damages.

HELD: that D's promise was independent of the illegal lease and, therefore, P could recover damages for the failure to replace the bath.

Where the contract is lawful but performance is not

If the contract is lawful but the method of performance is one which *both parties knew is illegal*, then both parties are without remedies in enforcing it.

In *Ashmore, Benson & Pease* v *A V Dawson Ltd* [1973] 1 WLR 828, P contracted with D that D should carry two 25 ton loads of goods for him by using lorries which could not lawfully carry more than 20 tons apiece. Both P and D knew this and, in consequence, the goods were damaged.

HELD: P's claim for damages for the goods must be rejected as he not only knew of the illegality, but also permitted D to perform in such illegal manner in the hope of saving the expense of having the goods carried on three vehicles or two 25 ton vehicles.

As already mentioned above, Lord Devlin, in the *St John Shipping case,* drew a distinction between cases where the law penalises conduct and cases where the law penalises conduct and, in addition, makes that conduct an illegal mode of performing a contract.

A contract may be lawful in its formation, but one party intends to use it for illegal purposes while the other party is innocent of these purposes. The general rule is that the innocent party will not be affected by the illegal intentions of the guilty party.

If the innocent party, or indeed both parties, make a *mistake of law* , either in making the contract or concerning the consequences, then the general rule does not apply and the contract is unenforceable.

In *J M Allan* v *Cloke* [1963] 2 QB 340, a roulette wheel was let for the purpose of playing roulette royale at a country club. The parties honestly believed that this game was lawful when, in fact, it was not. The hirer sued for his hiring fee.

HELD: the parties had a 'common design to use the subject matter for an unlawful purpose' and, therefore, the contract was illegal and neither party could enforce it.

Could the party who hired the roulette wheel have enforced the contract if he intended to use the wheel for a purpose other than roulette royale?

Where the innocent party makes a *mistake of fact* as to the circumstances which will give rise to illegality, then he may be able to enforce the contract. The test for deciding whether he can enforce the contract is unclear, and the best solution to the problem seems to be that proposed by Devlin LJ in *Archbolds v S Spanglett Ltd* [1961] 1 QB 374 that one should consider whether declaring the contract illegal and denying a remedy to an innocent party will further the principles on which the contract has been declared illegal. In particular, he referred to contracts which are illegal by statute:

> 'I think that the purpose of this statute is sufficiently served by the penalties prescribed for the offender; the avoidance of the contract would cause grave inconvenience and injury to innocent members of the public without furthering the object of the statute.'

In *Archbolds v S Spanglett Ltd*, D contracted to carry P's whisky in a van which was not licensed to carry goods belonging to a third party. P did not know that the van was not so licensed to carry his whisky and that D was committing an offence thereby.

HELD: since P did not know that as a fact the van was improperly licensed, he could recover damages for D's breach of the contract.

Would the result have been different if the law had imposed a duty on P to ensure that his goods were carried in a licensed van?

In *Re Mahmoud and Ispahani* [1921] 2 KB 716, P was licensed to sell linseed oil to licensed dealers. D fraudulently misrepresented to P that he was a licensed dealer, and was thereby able to purchase some linseed oil from P. It was an offence to buy or sell linseed oil without a licence. P sued to enforce the contract.

HELD: that even if P lacked the mens rea of the offence, he still could not enforce the contract because both parties were prohibited from entering into the contract. It was illegal from its inception and, even though P was an innocent party, he was without remedy.

It is possible to conclude that *Re Mahmoud* could be distinguish from the *Archbolds* case on the basis that the former contract was illegal as formed, while the latter was illegal as performed. However, this is not a suitable test to distinguish between cases where the innocent party can enforce his rights, and where he cannot because, in several cases, the contract has been enforced where its formation was illegal, for example, *Bloxsome v Williams* (1824) 3 B & C 232.

P bought a horse from D on Sunday. D was a licensed horsedealer and, under the Sunday Observance Act 1677, he was prohibited from selling horses on Sunday and committed an offence if he did so. P did not know D was a dealer. D breached the contract and P sued for damages.

HELD: P could recover damages for breach of contract.

In *Phoenix Insurance* v *Adas* [1987] 2 All ER 155, Kerr LJ summarised the position with regard to the statutory prohibition on contracts as follows:

'i) Where a statute prohibits both parties from concluding or performing a contract when both or either of them have no authority to do so, the contract is impliedly prohibited: see *Mahmoud and Ispahani*'s case [1921] 2 KB 716, [1921] All ER Rep 217 and its analysis by Pearce LJ in the *Archbolds* case [1961] 1 All ER 417, [1961] 1 QB 374 with which Devlin LJ agreed.

ii) But where a statute merely prohibits one party from entering into a contract without authority and/or imposes a penalty on him if he does so (ie a unilateral prohibition) it does not follow that the contract itself is impliedly prohibited so as to render it illegal and void. Whether or not the statute has this effect depends on considerations of public policy in the light of the mischief which the statute is designed to prevent, its language, scope and purpose, the consequences for the innocent party, and any other relevant considerations.'

The Court of Appeal was considering the effect of the carrying on of insurance business without proper authorisation in breach of statute, where the statute only provided for criminal sanctions. It was held that the statute prohibited the business of effecting and performing contracts of insurance in the absence of proper authorisation and, therefore, such contracts were unenforceable and void. The Court of Appeal applied the decision of Parker J in *Bedford Insurance* v *Instituto de Reseguros de Brasil* [1985] QB 966. The contrary decision of Leggat J in *Stewart* v *Oriental Fire and Marine Insurance* [1985] QB 988 was overruled.

If the innocent party is unable to enforce the contract he may have alternative remedies

1. Where such contract has been induced by misrepresentation. See *Shelley* v *Paddock* [1980] QB 348.
2. Where it is possible to rely on a collateral contract.

In *Strongman* v *Sincock* [1955] 3 All ER 90, P, a firm of builders, agreed to modernise houses belonging to D, an architect. It was illegal to do this work without licences, and D promised to get these. P did the work and D only got some licences, and refused to pay for the work for which he did not get licences on the ground that the contract was illegal.

HELD: the building contract was illegal and the plaintiff could not sue on it. The plaintiff could, however, support an action for damages based on the defendant's breach of his collateral promise to obtain the licences.

13.6 Severance

If the contract is only partly illegal, then it may not be totally unenforceable. In *Wallis* v *Day* (1837) 2 M & W 273, Lord Abinger said:

'The defendant demurred on the ground that the covenant being in restraint of trade was illegal, and that therefore the whole contract was void. I cannot, however, accede to that conclusion. If a party enters into several covenants, one of which cannot be enforced against him, he is not therefore released from performing the others.'

There can be no severance if one of the promises is to do an act which is itself a criminal offence or contra bonos mores; in such cases, the whole transaction is regarded as void.

In the majority of cases where severance is allowed, the contracts have been concerned with restraint of trade. It has been used in the cases in two ways, either to cut out the offending promise altogether, or to nullify so much of it as is repugnant.

Excluding consideration

If the whole of the consideration for a promise is illegal, then the promise is unenforceable and void.

In *Lound* v *Grimwade* (1888) 39 Ch D 605, P was promised £3,000 by D in return for an undertaking not to take legal proceedings in respect of a fraud which D had committed.

HELD: P could not enforce payment of the £3,000 as the main consideration was to do an illegal act, that is, stifle a prosecution, and was as such inseverable.

If the main consideration for a promise is lawful, then the court will enforce the contract, even if the contract is supported by subsidiary illegal consideration.

In *Goodinson* v *Goodinson* [1954] 2 QB 118, a contract was made between a husband and wife who were separated to the effect that the husband would pay the wife a weekly sum of maintenance and, in consideration, the wife would indemnify him against all debts incurred by her, would not pledge his credit and would not take any proceedings for maintenance.

HELD: the promise by the wife not to sue for maintenance was void as it ousted the jurisdiction of the courts, but it was not the main consideration provided by the wife. Therefore, her promise on maintenance would be excluded and the contract upheld.

In *Alec Lobb* v *Total Oil* (above), the question of severance did not arise for decision in the Court of Appeal as the court had held that the restraint of trade clause was reasonable. Dunn LJ, in an exhaustive review of the authorities, nevertheless conducted an investigation into the law on this point. He formulated the principle of law on severance as follows:

'... if the valid promises are supported by sufficient consideration, then the invalid promise can be severed from the valid even though the consideration also supports the valid promise. On the other hand if the invalid promise is substantially the whole or main consideration for the agreement then there will be no severance.'

On the present facts, Dunn LJ had the view that the main consideration was that given for the lease, and the transaction was not dependent on the tie clause (the restraint of trade) in the underlease. Waller LJ agreed.

In *Carney* v *Herbert* [1985] 1 All ER 438 Privy Council, the respondents owned shares in a company. They entered into contracts to sell their shareholding to a company controlled by the appellant. The proceeds of sale were to be cash, payment secured by certain guarantees from the purchaser and (the term which rendered the sale potentially illegal) secured also by mortgages on land owned by the very company which issued the shares subject matter of the sale. Without doubt, the purported mortgages were illegal, but the question arose whether such illegality was so much a part of the sale agreement and guarantees as to render them also illegal and unenforceable. The Privy Council severed the mortgages from the sale agreement, and enforced the latter. In the words of the judgment of the entire Board:

> 'Subject to a caveat that it is undesirable, their Lordships venture to suggest that, as a general rule, where parties enter into a lawful contract of, for example, sale and purchase, and there is an ancillary provision which is illegal but exists for the exclusive benefit of the plaintiff, the court may and probably will ... permit the plaintiff, if he so wishes, to enforce the contract without the illegal provision.'

Excluding promises

This is concerned with reducing the scope of a promise so as to exclude a part which is illegal and, thereby, making the contract enforceable. In order that this can be done, three conditions must be satisfied:

The promise itself must be capable of severance

Promises which are illegal in themselves are incapable of severance, for example, a criminal or immoral promise. There may, however, be some grounds for believing that a promise made without mens rea, as required by the relevant crime, may be severable.

The 'blue pencil' test must be applied

The illegal promise must be amenable to severance by merely drawing a blue pencil through the offending words. The court will not redraft the covenant so that it makes sense, or add or substitute words for the same purpose.

In *Mason* v *Provident Clothing & Supply Co Ltd* [1913] AC 724, a contract in restraint of trade provided that a canvasser should not enter into a similar business, (that is, selling clothes), 'within 25 miles of London'. An application was made to substitute 'in Islington'.

HELD: this amounted to redrafting the covenant and not severance and could not be done.

Mason's case would appear to imply that severance is only possible under the blue pencil test with regard to the actual words of the contract. It is not possible to sever the covenant by limiting definitions in the covenant itself.

The nature of the contract must remain unaltered by severance
If the result of severance is that the contract becomes entirely different to that as envisaged by the parties, then the court will not order severance.

At one time, a distinction existed between contracts between employer and employee, and contracts between purchaser and vendor. In the former, severance would only be permitted where the restraint or restriction on an employee was trivial. However, it is now clear that this view is no longer held by the courts and, if it is possible, as a matter of construction, to interpret the contract as containing two separate covenants, one of which can be deleted without altering the nature of the contract, then the court will do this.

In *Attwood* v *Lamont* [1920] 3 KB 571, P owned a general outfitters business in Kidderminster which had several departments, each with a supervisor who signed a contract that he would not after leaving P's service: 'be concerned in any of the following trades ... a tailor, dressmaker, general draper, milliner, hatter, haberdasher, gentlemen's, ladies' or children's outfitter within 10 miles of Kidderminster'. D, the supervisor in the tailoring department, started up a tailor's shop and P, attempting to enforce the covenant, admitted that it was too wide and should be limited to tailoring only.

HELD: severance as proposed by P would alter the nature of the covenant, which was intended to protect the whole business and not merely part of it and, therefore, could not be effected. Further, the clause could not be regarded as a series of covenants for the protection of each department.

A contrasting case is *Goldsoll* v *Goldman* [1915] 1 Ch 292. The seller of imitation jewellery undertook that he would not deal in real or imitation jewellery in the United Kingdom, or certain named places abroad, for two years. The covenant was too wide in area as the seller had not traded abroad, and in the subject matter as he had scarcely dealt in real jewellery. It was held, however, that the reference to the places abroad and to real jewellery could be severed.

If the 'blue pencil' test is satisfied, the court still will not order severance if the result is to change the nature of the contract.

In *British Reinforced Concrete Engineering* v *Schelff* [1921] 2 Ch 563, P, who made and sold road reinforcement in the UK, bought D's business, which was solely concerned in selling road reinforcements. D covenanted not to 'directly or indirectly carry on or be concerned or interested in or act as a servant of any person concerned or interested in the business of the manufacture or sale of road reinforcements in any part of the United Kingdom'.

HELD: the covenant was too wide, and it could not be severed as it was one entire covenant. Further, the blue pencil test could not be applied to it in any case as it made the covenant worse instead of better, particularly in relation to the wide and offending phrase: 'in any part of the United Kingdom'.

13.7 Recovery of money or property paid or transferred under an illegal contract

The courts will not help the parties to enforce an illegal contract, and the general rule is that the court will not assist either party to an illegal contract to recover money paid or property transferred under the contract. Since the parties have embarked on an illegal transaction, they can expect no assistance from the court in respect of it and if money is paid or property passes, this will not be interfered with even if it appears unjust.

The courts' attitude may be summed up in the phrase, 'the loss lies where it falls'. Several exceptions exist where the court will aid a party to recover property or money.

Recovery authorised by statute

A statute may provide for the protection of a class of persons by making payments of money or property transferred to them under the illegal contract recoverable.

Under s125 Rent Act 1977, the payment of a premium in consideration of being granted a tenancy is illegal and an offence, and is expressly stated to be recoverable by the paying party, that is, the tenant. However, the Act also allows for the fact that payments may be made for fittings and fixtures in a lease, and provides that any excess payment for these is also a premium and recoverable. See *Farrell* v *Alexander* (above) as an example.

In some older statutes, certain conduct is made an offence, but nothing is said as to the recovery of property where such conduct is the basis of a contract. In such cases, it appears one must look to see for what purpose the statute was passed before allowing recovery of money or property.

In *Green* v *Portsmouth Stadium* [1973] 2 QB 190, P, a bookmaker, was charged an entrance fee in excess of that permitted by statute at a racecourse.

HELD: he could not recover it as the relevant Act only made such conduct an offence, and was silent as to whether the excess was recoverable and, in any case, it was passed to regulate racecourses and not to protect bookmakers.

Repudiation of illegal purpose

If a party who has entered an illegal contract repudiates that contract or the illegal purpose in the contract in time, then the law will assist him to recover money or property under the contract. Some authorities refer to this as repentance, but this does not always reflect the repudiating party's state of mind!

Two conditions must be satisfied:

The repudiation must be in time
There can be no recovery of money or property if the party who is attempting to

recover has already begun to perform the illegal purpose or has accepted illegal performance.

In *Kearley* v *Thomson* (1890) 24 QBD 742, P paid D £40 not to appear at his friend's public examination in bankruptcy. D stayed away from the examination, but before the friend was discharged from bankruptcy, P claimed the £40 back.

HELD: there had been a partial carrying into effect of the illegal purpose in a substantial manner since P had intended to interfere with the course of justice and achieved his object to some extent.

In *Taylor* v *Bowers* (1876) 1 QBD 291, P, who was being pressed by his creditors, fraudulently assigned some machinery to X to prevent it falling into their hands. He then called several creditors' meetings, but failed to reach a settlement with the creditors. P then claimed the machinery from D who had obtained it from X knowing of the fraudulent scheme.

HELD: the illegal purpose of defrauding the creditors had not been carried out, and P could, therefore, recover the machinery.

Repudiation must be voluntary

If the party is forced to repudiate by either a third party or a repudiation of the illegal contract by the other party, he cannot recover his property. Further, if the illegal transaction proves abortive, but only after a party has participated in it, then there can be no voluntary repudiation.

Oppression

Where a party is forced to enter into an illegal contract, then he can recover his money or property back at any stage, either before or after performance. Oppression is, for these purposes, given a wide meaning, and may include the circumstances in which the contract was made. The use of the word 'forced' in the first sentence of this paragraph may sometimes give a misleading impression. Certainly, if the parties are not 'in pari delicto', that is, not on an equal footing, with one party at a marked disadvantage, oppression is more likely to apply.

In *Kiriri Cotton Co* v *Dewani* [1960] AC 192, P paid his landlord, who was committing an offence by accepting it, a premium for a flat. However, the relevant statute, then the Rent Restriction Ordinance, did not expressly provide that such premiums were recoverable.

HELD: P was not to blame for attempting to evade the Ordinance, but his landlord was. He was using his property rights to exploit those in need of a roof over their head. P therefore had but little choice if he wanted a home.

Fraud

Where a party enters into the contract in reliance on a fraudulent misrepresentation, then he can recover his money or property given under the contract even if it was illegal. For these purposes, an innocent misrepresentation is insufficient.

In *Hughes* v *Liverpool Victoria Legal Friendly Society* [1916] 2 KB 482, P took out a life insurance policy on the advice of D's agent on the life of a person in which he had no insurable interest. The contract was therefore illegal.

HELD: P could recover the money he had paid as he had entered into the contract as a result of a fraudulent representation.

Mistake

Where there has been a mistake of fact, then it may be possible to recover money or property under the illegal contract. In *Oom* v *Bruce* (1810) 12 East 225, the parties to an insurance policy, one of whom was a Russian, were unaware of the fact that war had broken out between Britain and Russia at the time they effected the policy, and it was held that the premium was recoverable.

Where there has been a mistake of law, then there can be no recovery of money or property. See *Harse* v *Pearl Assurance Co* [1904] 1 KB 558.

Recovery other than under illegal contract

In several cases, a party may recover money paid or property given under the contract by means which do not require reliance on the contract.

Goods transferred under illegal contract

It is settled law that property in goods can pass under an illegal contract. See *Singh* v *Ali* [1960] AC 167. Therefore, if the property has passed from the seller to the buyer and the goods have been delivered either to the buyer or his agent, the seller will not be able to get them back.

Where goods are pledged, hired or lent under an illegal contract, then a right to possession passes when the goods are transferred. This right to possession will endure until it is brought to an end either by effluxion of time, or the occurrence of certain events, and until then the transferor cannot recover the goods. However, if the hirer, for example, commits a fundamental breach of contract, then his right to possession may come to an end otherwise than under the illegal contract, and the transferor can recover the goods.

In *Bowmakers* v *Barnet Instruments* [1945] KB 65, D possessed machine tools under several illegal hire-purchase agreements. They failed to pay the instalments due, and sold some of the goods, but kept the rest. P claimed damages for conversion of all the goods.

HELD: P did not have to found their claim on the illegal contract or plead illegality to support their claim, they could rely on their title. The hirer's right to possession had come to an end by fundamental breach of contract by selling the thing hired to him, and P could, therefore, recover their property.

Note: it is unclear in the *Bowmaker* case whether the contract provided for the hirer's right of possession to determine on any breach. But it is assumed that this must have been the case as P recovered the whole goods back, including those D had not sold and with respect to these, it is established law that failure to pay instalments is not a fundamental breach of contract.

Goods obtained under an illegal contract

Since property can pass in goods from the seller to the buyer under an illegal contract, the buyer has all the usual remedies to protect his property even if he pays nothing for them in return. Thus, if the seller attempts to recover them, the buyer can sue for them or their value. See *Singh* v *Ali* (above).

This rule operates irrespective of whether the goods have actually been delivered to the buyer.

In *Belvoir Finance Co* v *Stapleton* [1971] 1 QB 210, P agreed to finance the purchase of cars by one Belgravia from one Francis. Each purchase was effected by two contracts: the sale of the car by Francis to P, and the letting on hire-purchase by P to Belgravia. In fact, these contracts were illegal. Although P had never acquired possession of the cars, as Francis delivered them directly to Belgravia, it was held that P could recover the cars from Belgravia in an action for conversion.

Note: although this case is concerned with rights between the buyer and a third party, it is clear authority for the proposition that property can pass under an illegal sale, even if there has been no delivery to the buyer. But it should not be taken as authority that a buyer can recover goods which have passed under an illegal contract in, for example, an action for conversion where there has been no delivery by the seller.

Money paid under an illegal contract

Where money is paid under an illegal contract, the general rule is that it is irrecoverable.

Where money is paid as a deposit to a stakeholder under an illegal contract, it can be recovered so long as the stakeholder has not paid it over as instructed. See *O'Sullivan* v *Thomas* [1895] 1 QB 698.

13.8   Collateral agreements

Any agreement which is made to help with the performance of an illegal contract is itself illegal and unenforceable. Thus, an insurance policy on an illegal agreement is illegal (see *Toulmin* v *Anderson* (1808) 1 Taunt 227) and any loans or payments of money to aid the performance of an illegal contract are also illegal (see *M'Kinnell* v *Robinson* (1838) 3 M & W 434).

If an agreement is in itself legal, it will not, however, be rendered illegal merely because a collateral transaction to aid or further its performance happens to be illegal. Therefore, if a charterparty is itself legal, it will not be invalidated merely because a policy of insurance relating to it is illegally drawn up. See *South Western Mineral Co* v *Ashmore* [1967] 1 WLR 1110.

14

Frustration

14.1 Introduction

The doctrine of frustration operates in situations where it is established that due to subsequent change in circumstances, the contract is rendered impossible to perform, or it has become deprived of its commercial purpose by an event not due to the act or default of either party.

This is not to be confused with initial impossibility, which may render the contract void ab initio. See Chapter 10 and s6 Sale of Goods Act 1979, *Couturier* v *Hastie* (1856) 5 HL Cas 673 and *Barrow Lane & Ballard* v *Phillips* [1929] 1 KB 574.

Originally, the law declared that if a man bound himself by contract, then that man was absolutely bound notwithstanding anything which may subsequently have transpired making it difficult or impossible to perform the contract.

> 'It amounts to this: when the law casts a duty upon a man which, through no fault of his, he is unable to perform he is excused from non-performance; but if he binds himself by contract to do a thing, he cannot escape liability for damage by proof that as events turned out performance is futile or even impossible.'

In *Paradine* v *Jane* (1647) Aleyn 26, the classic statement of the concept appears in the above, a Civil War case involving dispossession of tenants by one Prince Rupert of the Rhine. The tenant pleaded that he should be relieved under the contract with the landlord for he had been evicted and thus had obtained no material benefit from the lease.

HELD: he was liable under the lease – broadly, for the reasons given in the extract above.

The 'absolute' approach to the determination of a legal problem is harsh without doubt, and the subsequent evolution of the doctrine of frustration bears witness to this.

14.2   Initial development of the doctrine

The turning point away from absolutist construction of contractual obligation came with the decision in *Taylor v Caldwell* (1863) 3 B & S 826.

Caldwell agreed to let a music hall to Taylor so that four concerts could be held there. Before the date of the first concert, the hall was destroyed by fire. Taylor claimed damages for Caldwell's failure to make the premises available.

HELD: that the claim for breach of contract must fail since it had become impossible to fulfil. The contractual obligation was dependent upon the continued existence of a particular object.

The interesting point to note was that until this time, the law refused to acknowledge that a party could be relieved from a contract unless there was some express condition entitling him to be so relieved in the event of subsequent impossibility.

Blackburn J gave the judgment of the Court of Queen's Bench, holding that the defendants were not liable under the contract.

The rationale of this decision was (broadly):

1. The doctrine of 'sanctity of contracts' does not apply where the contract is subject to conditions express or *implied*.
2. The doctrine of 'sanctity' only applies, therefore, to contracts based on positive or absolute promises.

Blackburn J stated the principle in the following terms:

'The principle seems to us to be that, in contracts in which the performance depends on the continued existence of a given person or thing, a condition is implied that the impossibility of performance arising from the perishing of the person or thing shall excuse the performance.

In none of the cases is the promise other than positive, nor is there any express stipulation that the destruction of the person or thing shall excuse the performance; but that excuse is by law implied, because from the nature of the contract it is apparent that the parties contracted on the basis of the continued existence of the particular person or chattel.'

From this he was able to derive in the particular case that the contract was subject to the implied condition that the music hall would continue to exist and that, if it did not, the parties were to be relieved of their obligations.

14.3 Tests for frustration

There are principally two tests which compete for recognition as the test for frustration:

1. The 'radical change in the obligation' test. This was adopted by the majority of the House of Lords in *Davis Contractors Ltd* v *Fareham UDC* [1956] AC 696. It is also sometimes referred to as 'the construction test'.
2. The implied term theory, as in *Taylor* v *Caldwell* (above). Contrast *Blackburn Bobbin & Co* v *Allen* [1918] 2 KB 467.

Notably, in *National Carriers* v *Panalpina (Northern) Ltd* [1981] AC 675, Lord Wilberforce was reluctant to choose between the theories. He took the view that they merged one into the other and that the choice depends upon 'what is most appropriate to the particular contract under consideration'.

This observation is criticised by Chitty (25th edn at para 1530). He gives four reasons why it does matter which test is chosen. (He favours the 'radical change in the obligation' test.)

1. Although it is possible that the two tests arrive at the same conclusion in the majority of cases, there may be borderline cases which could produce a different result if one test rather than the other were applied. It is reasonable that parties should be able to know in advance the view that a court may take and avoid litigation rather than seeking the intervention of the court to see which one the court may think 'most appropriate'.
2. The application of the implied term test (which Chitty denigrates as artificial) may prevent a proper understanding of the court's function.
3. The implied term test might be treated as a matter of fact, whereas the question of whether a contract has been frustrated is really one of law.
4. Lord Reid suggested in the *Davis* case that if the 'radical change' test were applied, the ordinary rules about the admissibility of extrinsic evidence could apply. (Note, however, that the ordinary rules of evidence could also apply to the implied term test.)

Atiyah (*An Introduction to the Law of Contract*. Oxford Clarendon Law Series, 1989, 4th edn) suggests that these two theories are not mutually inconsistent, but signify attempts to answer different questions. Atiyah distinguishes the following questions:

1. Is frustration based on the will of the parties or not?
2. How do the courts actually reason about cases concerning frustration?
3. In what situations are contracts actually found to be frustrated?
4. What is it that justifies the practice of holding contracts frustrated?

Even when one splits up questions as to the basis of frustration in this way, there are not always immediate easy answers. Some authorities choose to single out one question as being more important than any of the others. One can find support for all the various theories in decided cases and, ultimately, most attempts to define the 'basis' of the doctrine of frustration in unsatisfactory.

The 'radical change in the obligation' test

This has been upheld in two recent cases: in *Pioneer Shipping Ltd* v *BTP Tioxide Ltd* [1982] AC 724 and *National Carriers* v *Panalpina* (above).

Lord Simon restated the test in the latter case at p63:

> 'Frustration of a contract takes place when there supervenes an event (without default of either party and for which the contract makes no provision) which so significantly changes the nature (not merely the expense or onerousness) of the outstanding contractual rights and/or obligations from what the parties could reasonably have contemplated at the time of its execution that it would be unjust to hold them to the literal sense of its stipulations in the new circumstances; in such case the law declares both parties to be discharged from further performance.'

Lords Reid and Radcliffe in the *Davis* case found that the application of this test was a three-tiered process. It necessitated the following:

1. To construe the contractual terms in the light of the contract and surrounding circumstances at the time of its creation.
2. To examine the new circumstances and decide what would happen if the existing terms are applied to it.
3. To compare the two contractual obligations and see if there is a radical or fundamental change.

Accordingly, it is the nature of the *obligation* that must have changed, and not just the circumstances.

The implied term theory

Following the *Pioneer* and *Panalpina* cases, this test can be regarded as abandoned, although it is significant in the development of the doctrine of frustration. The traditional exposition is found in the speech of Lord Loreburn in *FA Tamplin SS Company Ltd* v *Anglo-Mexican Petroleum Products Company Ltd* [1916] 2 AC 397:

> 'A court can and ought to examine the contract and the circumstances in which it was made, not of course to vary but only to explain it, in order to see whether or not from the nature of it the parties must have made their bargain on the footing that a particular thing or state of things would continue to exist.
>
> And if they must have done so, then a term to that effect will be implied, though it be not expressed in the contract ... In most of the cases it is said that there was an implied

condition in the contract which operated to release the parties from performing it, and in all of them I think that was at bottom the principle upon which the Court proceeded.

It is, in my opinion, the true principle, for no court has an absolving power, but it can infer from the nature of the contract and the surrounding circumstances that a condition which was not expressed was a foundation on which the parties contracted ... Were the altered conditions such that, had they thought of them, the parties would have taken their chance of them, or such that as sensible men they would have said "if that happens, of course, it is all over between us".'

The traditional criticism of this test directed itself at the artificial implication of a term to deal with a situation which the parties would not have contemplated.

14.4   Examples of frustration

Destruction of the specific object essential for performance of the contract

See *Taylor* v *Caldwell* (above). Note s7 Sale of Goods Act 1979.

Personal incapacity where the personality of one of the parties is significant

In *Condor* v *The Barron Knights* [1966] 1 WLR 87, a drummer engaged to play in a pop group was contractually bound to work on seven nights a week when work was available. After an illness, Condor's doctor advised that it was only safe to employ him on four nights a week, although Condor himself was willing to work every night. It was necessary to engage another drummer who could safely work on seven nights each week.

HELD: that Condor's contract of employment had been frustrated in a commercial sense. It was impracticable to engage a stand-in for the three nights a week when Condor could not work, since this involved double rehearsals of the group's music and comedy routines.

Compare this with *Phillips* v *Alhambra Palace Co* [1901] 1 QB 59. One partner in a firm of music hall proprietors died after a troupe of performers had been engaged.

HELD: the contract with the performers was not frustrated because the contract was not of a personal nature, and could be enforced against the surviving partners.

In *Graves* v *Cohen* (1929) 46 TLR 121, the court held that the death of a racehorse owner frustrated the contract with his employee, a jockey, because the contract created a relationship of mutual confidence.

In *FC Shepherd & Co* v *Jerrom* [1986] 3 All ER 589 CA, it was held that a sentence of imprisonment imposed on an employee was capable of frustrating the employee's contract of employment if the sentence was such that it rendered the performance of the contract radically different from that which the parties contemplated when they entered into the contract.

The non-occurrence of a specified event

See *Krell* v *Henry* [1903] 2 KB 740. Henry hired a room from Krell for two days, to be used as a position from which to view the coronation procession of Edward VII, but the contract itself made no reference to that intended use. The King's illness caused a postponement of the procession.

HELD: that Henry was excused from paying the rent for the room. Holding of the procession on the dates planned was regarded by both parties as basic to enforcement of the contract.

Compare this with *Herne Bay Steamboat Company* v *Hutton* [1903] 2 KB 683. Herne Bay Steam Boat Company agreed to hire a steamboat to Hutton for a fee of £250 for a period of two days for the purpose of taking passengers to Spithead to cruise round the fleet and see the naval review on the occasion of Edward VII's coronation. The review was cancelled, but the boat could have been used to cruise round the assembled fleet.

HELD: that the contract was not frustrated. The holding of the naval review was not the only event upon which the intended use of the boat was dependent. The other object of the contract was to cruise round the fleet, and this remained capable of fulfilment.

Also see *Amalgamated Investment and Property Co* v *John Walker* [1977] 1 WLR 164.

Interference by the government

In *Metropolitan Water Board* v *Dick Kerr & Co* [1918] AC 119, Kerr & Co agreed to build a reservoir for the Water Board within six years. After two years, Kerr & Co were required by a wartime statute to cease work on the contract and to sell their plant.

HELD: the contract was frustrated because the interruption was of such a nature as to make the contract, if resumed, a different contract.

Supervening illegality

In *Denny, Mott & Dickson* v *James Fraser* [1944] AC 265, a contract for the sale and purchase of timber contained an option to purchase a timber yard. By a wartime control order, trading under the agreement became illegal. The appellants wanted to exercise the option.

HELD: the order had frustrated the contract so the option could not be exercised.

In a similar case, *Re Shipton Anderson and Harrison Brothers* [1915] 3 KB 676, a contract was concluded for the sale of a quantity of wheat lying in a warehouse. The Government requisitioned the wheat, in pursuance of wartime emergency regulations, for the control of food supplies, before it had been delivered, and also before ownership in the goods had passed to the buyer under the terms of contract of sale.

HELD: that the seller was excused from further performance of the contract as it was now impossible to deliver the goods due to the Government's lawful requisition.

Notice that where there is a supervening illegality, the parties cannot rely on the contractual terms to prevent the contract being frustrated. See *Ertel Bieber* v *Rio Tinto* [1918] AC 260. Apart from this exception, the parties can contract with the frustrating event in mind. This will prevent frustration.

Delay

Inordinate and unexpected delay may frustrate a contract. The problem is to know how long a party must wait before the delay can be said to be frustrating. In *Pioneer Shipping Ltd* v *BTP Tioxide Ltd* [1982] AC 724, Lord Roskill said:

> '... it is often necessary to wait upon events in order to see whether the delay already suffered and the prospects of further delay from that cause, will make any ultimate performance of the relevant contractual obligations "radically different" from that which was undertaken by the contract. But, as has often been said, businessmen must not be required to await events too long. They are entitled to know where they stand. Whether or not the delay is such as to bring about frustration must be a question to be determined by an informed judgment based on all the evidence of what has occurred and what is likely thereafter to occur. Often it will be a question of degree whether the effect of delay suffered and likely to be suffered, will be such as to bring about frustration of the particular event in question.'

Also see *Jackson* v *Union Marine Insurance* (1873) LR 10 CP 125. A ship was chartered in November 1871 to proceed with all possible despatch, danger and accidents of navigation excepted, from Liverpool to Newport where it was to load a cargo of iron rails for carriage to San Francisco. She sailed on 2 January, but the next day ran aground in Caernarvon Bay. She was refloated by 18 February and taken to Liverpool, where she underwent extensive repairs, which lasted till August. On 15 February, the charterers repudiated the contract.

HELD: such time was so long as to put an end in a commercial sense to the commercial speculation entered upon by the shipowner and the charterers. The express exceptions were not intended to cover an accident causing such extensive damage.

Leases

In *Cricklewood Property and Investment Trust* v *Leightons Investment Trust* [1945] AC 221, the House of Lords held unanimously that there was no frustration of a long-term building lease by the imposition of building restrictions following the outbreak of war. On the question of whether a lease could ever be frustrated, Lords Russell and Goddard thought that it could not because it created an estate in land which could not be defeated, even though some purpose for which the parties wished to use the land might become prohibited. Viscount Simon and Lord Wright, on the other hand, thought that a lease could be frustrated in rare circumstances, such as an earthquake or flood.

The question arose again in the *Panalpina* case. This concerned a ten-year lease of a warehouse. By a temporary order, the street, which gave the only access to the warehouse, was closed. On the question of whether the lease was frustrated:

HELD: since the closure was expected to last only a year or more, which would leave three or more years of the lease left to run, the lease was not frustrated. The House of Lords were anxious to say that, in principle, a lease could be frustrated. They cited with approval a passage from Corbin '*Contracts*' (1962) Vol 6 s1356:

> 'If there was one principal use contemplated by the lessee, known to the lessor, and one that played a large part in fixing rental value, a government prohibition or prevention of that use has been held to discharge the lessee from his duty to pay the rent. It is otherwise if other substantial uses permitted by the lease and in the contemplation of the parties, remain possible to the lessee.'

Frustration of contract by constant revision

McAlpine, Humberoak Ltd v *McDermott International Inc* (1992) Financial Times 13 March raised the question of whether continual alteration of the contractual terms could be said to give rise to frustration.

Both parties signed a contract for construction of an oil rig: the defendants were one among a large number of sub-contracting firms. Delays occurred in the plaintiffs' work, largely caused, the plaintiffs argued, by the late submission of large numbers of revised drawings which hindered production. The defendants' counterclaim suggested among other arguments, that the contract was in fact frustrated by the constant revision of plans.

The Court of Appeal stated that the numerous revisions of plan did not transform the contract so as to frustrate it. Indeed, the contract provided for changes of instruction in the form of new construction drawings. Also, since the contract was signed retrospectively, some months after work had begun, the parties were both fully aware of changes necessary at the time of signing the contract.

14.5   Scope of the doctrine

'The doctrine of frustration must be applied within very narrow limits', per Viscount Simonds in *Tsakiroglou and Company* v *Noblee Thorl GmbH* [1961] 2 All ER 179.

More recently, Lord Roskill said that the doctrine of frustration was 'not lightly to be invoked to relieve contracting parties of the normal consequences of imprudent commercial bargains'. See *Pioneer Shipping* v *BTP Tioxide* [1982] AC 724.

The doctrine is subject to the following limitations.

The doctrine cannot override express contractual provision for the frustrating event.

However, this does not apply if the supervening event is illegality. See *Ertel Bieber* v *Rio Tinto* (above).

The mere increase in expense or loss of profit is not a ground for frustration.

See *Davis Contractors* v *Fareham UDC* [1956] AC 696. The plaintiff agreed to build 78 houses in eight months at a fixed price. Due to bad weather, and labour shortages, the work took 22 months and cost £17,000 more than anticipated. The builders said that the weather and labour shortages, which were unforeseen, had frustrated the contract, and that they were entitled to recover £17,000 by way of quantum meruit.

HELD: the fact that unforeseen events made a contract more onerous than was anticipated did not frustrate it.

Also see *Tsakiroglou* v *Noblee Thorl* (above). Tsakiroglou agreed to sell Sudanese groundnuts to Noblee, the nuts to be shipped from Port Sudan to Hamburg, November/December 1956. As a result of the 'Suez crisis', the Suez Canal was closed from 2 November 1956 until April 1957. Tsakiroglou failed to deliver, arguing that shipment round the Cape was commercially and fundamentally different.

HELD: the contract was not frustrated. Tsakiroglou were, therefore, liable for breach – the change in circumstances was not fundamental. (Note that there was no implied term that the shipment should be via Suez; also, the nuts would not have deteriorated on the longer journey.)

Frustration must not be self-induced

In *Maritime National Fish* v *Ocean Trawlers* [1935] AC 524, Maritime chartered from Ocean a vessel which could only operate with an otter trawl. Both parties realised that it was an offence to use such a trawl without a government licence. Maritime was granted three such licences, but chose to use them in respect of three other vessels, with the result that Ocean's vessel could not be used.

HELD: that the charterparty had not been frustrated, consequently Maritime was liable to pay the charter fee. Maritime freely elected not to license Ocean's vessel, consequently their inability to use it was a direct result of their own deliberate act.

The burden of proving events which prima facie frustrate the contract lies on the party relying on frustration. If there is an allegation that the frustration is self-induced, the burden then shifts to the person alleging self-inducement. See also *Joseph Constantine* v *Imperial Smelting* [1942] AC 154.

The question of self-induced frustration arose before the House of Lords in *Paal Wilson* v *Blumenthal* [1983] AC 854. Where there had been a delay in proceeding with an arbitration which had been caused by breaches by both parties of their mutual obligations to one another to avoid delay, the House of Lords held that the fact that the parties were under a mutual obligation to keep the arbitration moving meant that neither party could claim that delay by the other party had frustrated the agreement to arbitrate.

Dealing with the requirements for frustration Lord Brandon said:

'There are two essential factors which must be present in order to frustrate a contract. The first essential factor is that there must be some outside event or extraneous change of situation, not foreseen or provided for by the parties at the time of contracting, which either makes it impossible for the contract to be performed at all, or at least renders its performance something radically different from what the parties contemplated when they entered into it. The second essential factor is that the outside event or extraneous change of situation concerned, and the consequences of either in relation to the performance of the contract, must have occurred without either the fault or the default of either party to the contract.'

Neither requirement had been met in the present case. The contract had not been subject to an extraneous event, but simply to the delay of the parties, and that delay was a breach by each party of its obligation.

In *FC Shepherd & Co* v *Jerrom* (above), although the employee was to blame for the offence for which he was sentenced, this was not a case of self-induced frustration. The employee could not plead his own default in order to establish a claim for unfair dismissal. Lawton LJ also held that the frustrating event was not the offence, but the outside event of the sentence imposed by the court.

In *Lauritzen AS* v *Wijsmuller BV* [1990] 1 Lloyd's Rep 1, the defendant agreed to transport the plaintiff's drilling rig by one of two transportation units. One unit was sunk and the defendant refused to use the other transportation unit. Two questions arose:

1. Did the extra time and cost involved entitled the plaintiff to treat the contract as frustrated?
2. If it was frustrated, could the contract be considered as terminated by self-induced frustration?

14.6   Effects of frustration

Frustration discharges the contract automatically: no question of election of one of the parties (compare with breach). However, this discharge does not relate back to the making of the contract, therefore, on principle, rights and liabilities already acquired up to the termination of the contract remain intact; only subsequent obligations are discharged. Accordingly, in the case of *Chandler* v *Webster* [1904] 1 KB 493, the Court of Appeal held that the loss would lie where it fell. However, this case was subsequently considered unjust and was overruled in *Fibrosa* v *Fairbairn* [1943] AC 32, where the House of Lords held that money paid over on a total failure of consideration was recoverable. This case, however, was equally inflexible: recovery was dependent upon a total failure of consideration, and there was no provision for restitution of prefrustration expenditure by one of the parties. As a result, Parliament intervened with the Law Reform (Frustrated Contracts) Act 1943.

The Law Reform (Frustrated Contracts) Act 1943

This statute remedies the defects of the common law. It is very flexible, and this is probably why there are no reported English decisions in the Act. The main provisions of the Act are as follows:

> 'Section 1(2) All sums paid or payable to any party in pursuance of the contract before the time when the parties were so discharged (in this Act referred to as "the time of discharge") shall, in the case of sums so paid, be recoverable from him as money received by him for the use of the party by whom the sums were paid, and, in the case of sums so payable, cease to be payable:
>
> Provided that, if the party to whom the sums were so paid or payable incurred expenses before the time of discharge in, or for the purpose of, the performance of the contract, the court may, if it considers it just to do so having regard to all the circumstances of the case, allow him to retain or, as the case may be, recover the whole or any part of the sums so paid or payable, not being an amount in excess of the expenses so incurred.
>
> Section 1(3) Where any party to the contract has, by reason of anything done by any other party thereto in, or for the purpose of, the performance of the contract, obtained a valuable benefit (other than a payment of money to which the last foregoing section applies) before the time of discharge, there shall be recoverable from him by the said other party such sum (if any) not exceeding the value of the said benefit to the party obtaining it, as the court considers just, having regard to all the circumstances of the case.'

Section 1(6) allows an action given by subs1(3) to be brought against one party even though the benefit was bestowed on a third party.

Section 2(3) permits contracting out.

Section 2(4) enables severance of a part of a contract which has been performed from a part which has been frustrated, but only where a part of a contract 'can properly be severed from the remainder of the contract'.

The effect of s1(2)

Section 1(2) provides three rules:

1. All sums actually paid at the time of discharge are recoverable.
2. All sums payable at the time of discharge cease to be payable.
3. The party to whom the sums were paid or payable at the time of the discharge may be allowed, if the court considers it just and equitable, to retain or recover the whole or part of the sums paid or payable if he has incurred expenses in, or for the purposes of, performing the contract. Recovery will not be allowed of any amount in excess of the expenses incurred.

It must be noted that recovery for expenses is only allowed from sums 'paid or payable' at the time of discharge. If, therefore, the party incurring the expenses had not stipulated for prepayment, he will not be able to obtain recovery.

The effect of s1(3)

There is academic controversy over the meaning of 'valuable benefit': one school of thought holds the view that it should be construed widely, for example, if a painter begins work on X's house, and the house is burnt down before completion of the job, X is nevertheless deemed to have received a benefit. A Canadian case on this problem, *Parsons Brothers* v *Shea* (1965) 53 DLR (2d) 86, favours this view.

A case has occurred which has discussed, inter alia, the meaning of the words 'valuable benefit'. In *BP Exploration* v *Hunt* [1982] 1 All ER 925, the defendant had a licence to explore the Libyan desert for oil. The defendant agreed to assign to the plaintiff a half share in the oil concession, and the plaintiff undertook to explore from its own resources and make payments to the defendants. There was a revolution in Libya. The plaintiff's half share was expropriated in 1971. In 1973, the defendants' share was expropriated. The plaintiffs said that the contract was frustrated in 1971, and that payments to the defendant could be recovered under s1(3) of the Act.

HELD: (at first instance and in the Court of Appeal) that the plaintiff could recover those sums under the Act that had been paid to the defendant together with interest. In the House of Lords, the only points taken by the defendant were whether the agreement was entered into with a view to the events that occurred and whether interest was payable.

Robert Goff J examined the relationship between the subsections at length. The following principles can be extracted from his judgment:

1. The Act was designed to prevent unjust enrichment.
2. Under subs1(3), the court is not concerned with restitution of value for net benefits, but with achieving justice between the parties. Subsection 1(2) may be concerned with the net benefit being the benefit to one party less an appropriate deduction for expenses incurred by him.
3. The court should, however, try to achieve consistency between these two sections, because they flow from the same principle (preventing unjust enrichment).
4. The Act was *not* designed to do certain things: for example, to apportion the loss between plaintiff and defendant; or to put the parties in the position they would have been in if the contract had been performed; or to restore the parties to the position they were in before the contract was made.
5. The valuable benefit should be the end product of services rendered and not just the service itself. He takes the example set out above.

'Suppose that a contract for work on a building is frustrated by a fire which destroys the building and which, therefore, also destroys a substantial amount of work already done by the plaintiff. Although it might be thought just to award the plaintiff a sum assessed on a quantum meruit basis, probably a rateable part of the contract price, in respect of the work he has done, the effect of s1(3)(b) will be to reduce the award to nil, because of the effect, in relation to the defendant's benefit, of the circumstances giving rise to the frustration of the contract.

... This will not be so in every case, since in some cases the services will have no end product; for example, where the services consist of doing such work as surveying, or transporting goods.

In each case it is necessary to ask the question: what benefit has the defendant obtained by reason of the plaintiff's contractual performance?'

6. The date of valuing the benefit is the date of frustration.
7. A just sum is restitutionary. If money has been paid, then it is recoverable. If the benefit does not consist of money, it is the reasonable value of the plaintiff's performance. In the case of services, it is reasonable remuneration. In the case of goods, it is a reasonable price.

The Court of Appeal, although suggesting that unjust enrichment was an inappropriate expression to use in connection with frustrated contracts, did not overturn this approach. It was not a live issue in the House of Lords.

Exclusion from the Act

Four types of contract are excluded:

1. Certain charterparties (voyage charterparties).
2. Contracts for carriage of goods by sea.
3. Insurance contracts.
4. Contracts for the sale of specific goods which perish.

15

Discharge of the Contract – Performance, Agreement and Breach

15.1 Introduction

15.2 Performance: the general rule

15.3 Modification of the general rule

15.4 Stipulations as to time of performance

15.5 Agreements

15.6 Bilateral discharge

15.7 Unilateral discharge

15.8 Breach

15.1 Introduction

In the previous chapter, we examined the circumstances in which the parties to a contract could be discharged of their obligations by the frustration of the contract. We turn now to an examination of discharge of contractual obligations by performance, by agreement and by breach.

The performance of his obligations by a contracting party discharges that party from his obligations under the contract. It should be noted that unless a term of the contract is expressly stated to have effect after the existence of the contract has ceased, all restrictions, liabilities and duties end with the discharge or breach of the contract.

In *Harrods Ltd* v *Schwartz-Sackin & Co Ltd* [1991] FSR 209 the plaintiffs terminated their contract with the defendants, who had operated the fine arts department at Harrods. One of the clauses in the contract was a no-advertising clause – that the defendants would not indicate their connection with Harrods, or use Harrods' name in any way. Once the contract had been ended, the defendants began to advertise their previous association with Harrods, who sought an interlocutory injunction to stop this.

The Court of Appeal held that unless a clause is specifically and expressly worded so as to make it clear that its effect is to continue beyond the existence of the contract, no such effect will be implied. All restrictive clauses terminate along with the contract.

What constitutes performance is the subject matter of our initial discussion. The parties may elect to discharge their obligations under the original contract by a subsequent agreement so to do.

A party who fails to perform his obligations under the contract is in breach of contract. It is perhaps unnecessary to state that what constitutes a breach depends on the terms of the contract. We have seen in Chapter 6 that certain breaches entitle the injured party to treat the contract as repudiated. If he elects to do so, he is himself discharged of his obligations under the contract, and is able to seek a remedy against the party in breach.

15.2   Performance: the general rule

Generally, parties must perform *precisely* all the terms of the contract in order to discharge their obligations.

Note that the question of whether a contract must be *personally* performed came before the courts in *Southway Group Ltd* v *Wolff* (1991) The Independent 30 August. The question as to whether a contract must be performed in person arose in this contract for services. Before the sale of a warehouse and adjoining land was completed with the plaintiffs, B agreed to carry out certain improvements in accordance with outline specifications. The question asked was whether B could then subcontract the work to an independent contractor. B had entered into a resale agreement with the defendants and then on purchase of the land had delegated all obligations.

The Court of Appeal decided that where, as in this case the essence of the contract lay in the provision of a special skill or expertise, the party who had agreed to provide the skill or expertise did not have the right to unilaterally delegate the responsibility to another person.

In contracts for the sale of goods, the Sale of Goods Act 1979 contains strict rules. Section 30 affords the buyer the right to reject goods if the seller delivers less or even more goods than he contracted to sell. Section 13 imposes the condition that the goods must correspond with the description. An illustration of the precise requirement of this section appears from *Re Moore and Landauer & Co* [1921] 2 KB 519. Tins of fruit delivered in cases of 24 and not the stipulated cases of 30 constituted a breach of s13.

The decision in this case is now, perhaps, doubtful. It was criticised as being excessively technical by Lord Wilberforce in *Reardon Smith Line* v *Hansen-Tangen* [1976] 3 All ER 570 at p576.

A classic example of hardship caused by this rule is *Cutter* v *Powell* (1795) 6 Term Rep 320. A seaman who was to be paid his wages after the end of a voyage died just a few days away from port. His widow was able to recover none of his wages because he had not completed performance of his contractual obligation.

The strict rule as to performance is mitigated in a number of instances.

15.3   Modification of the general rule

Divisible contracts

It is a question of construction whether a contract is entire or divisible. An *entire* contract is one where the agreement provides that complete performance by one party is a condition precedent to contractual liability on the part of the other party. With a *divisible* contract, part of the consideration of one party is set off against part of the performance of the other. Divisible contracts are frequently to be found in the building trade, for example, where a builder agrees to build a house for £2,500, with £1,000 to be paid on completion of the foundations, £1,000 on erection of the superstructure, and £500 six months after completion of the house in accordance with the specifications. Then, if after the foundations are laid the builder fails to do any further work, he can, nevertheless, recover £1,000.

However, in *Sumpter* v *Hedges* [1898] 1 QB 673, the plaintiff had agreed to erect upon the defendant's land two houses and stables for £565. He did part of the work to the value of about £333 and then abandoned the contract. The defendant completed the buildings.

HELD: the plaintiff could not recover the value of the work done, as he had abandoned the contract; and see below.

Acceptance of partial performance

Where the plaintiff to whom the promise of performance was made receives the benefit of partial performance of the promise under such circumstances that he is able to accept or reject the work and he accepts the work, then the promisee is obliged to pay a reasonable price for the benefit received. But it must be possible to infer from the circumstances a fresh agreement by the parties that payment shall be made for the goods or services in fact supplied.

In *Christy* v *Row* (1808) 1 Taunt 300, a ship freighted to Hamburg was prevented 'by restraint of princes' from arriving. Consignees accepted the cargo at another port *to which they had directed it to be delivered.*

HELD: the consignees were liable upon an implied contract to pay freight pro rata itineris (contract implied from their directions re alternative port of delivery).

In *Sumpter* v *Hedges* (above), Collins LJ said:

'Where, as in the case of work done on land, the circumstances are such as to give the defendant no option whether he will take the benefit of the work or not, then one must look to other facts than the mere taking of the benefit in order to ground the inference of a new contract. In this case I see no other facts on which such an inference can be founded. The mere fact that a defendant is in possession of what he cannot help keeping, or even has done work upon it, affords no ground for such an inference. He is not bound to keep unfinished a building which in an incomplete state would be a nuisance on his land.'

Completion of performance prevented by the promisee

Where a party to an entire contract *is prevented by the promisee* from performing all his obligations, then he can recover a reasonable price for what he has in fact done on a quantum meruit basis in an action in quasi-contract.

In *Planché* v *Colburn* (1831) 8 Bing 14, the plaintiff was to write a book on 'Costume and Ancient Armour' for a series, and was to receive £100 on completion of the book. After he had done the necessary research but before the book had been written, the publishers abandoned the series. He claimed alternatively on the original contract and on a quantum meruit. The claim on the original contract seems to have disappeared in the course of the argument but, on the alternative submission:

HELD:

1. that the original contract had been discharged by the defendants' breach (or, more properly, that the plaintiff had accepted the defendants' breach as discharging the contract?);
2. that no new contract had been substituted;
3. that the plaintiff could obtain 50 guineas as reasonable remuneration on a quantum meruit. This claim was independent of the original contract and was based on quasi-contract.

Substantial performance

When a man fully performs his contract in the hope that he has done all that he agreed to do, or has supplied all he agreed to supply, but subject to defects of so minor a character that he can be said to have *substantially* performed his promise, it is regarded as far more just to allow him to recover the contract price diminished by the extent to which his breach of contract lessened the value of what was done, than to leave him with no right of recovery at all.

The doctrine of substantial performance dates back to the judgment of Lord Mansfield in *Boone* v *Eyre* (1779) 1 Hy Bl 273n. In *Dakin & Co* v *Lee* [1916] 1 KB 566, builders promised to build a house according to specification and failed to carry out exactly all the specifications, for example, concrete not 4 feet deep as specified, wrong joining of certain rolled steel joists and concrete not properly mixed.

HELD (by the Court of Appeal): the builders were entitled to recover the contract price, less so much as ought to be allowed in respect of the items found to be defective.

Note that in requiring a standard of substantial performance, the court must not apply an excessively strict standard. In *Ateni Maritime Corporation* v *Great Marine*

(1991) Financial Times 13 February the buyers agreed to buy a ship under a contract based on a Norwegian Standard Sale form. The contract provided, inter alia, that if on arrival the ship was in any way so defective as to affect its certification, the defects would be made good at the seller's expense. The work should be to the satisfaction of a named third party, the classification society. The propeller was found to be severely damaged. A damages award against the sellers was appealed by them, on the grounds that in assessing damages the judge had applied too high a standard.

The Court of Appeal held that the buyers could not complain if the sellers did no more than was necessary to obtain a clean certificate. They were not able to demand the sellers did work that would restore it to its pre-contractual condition. The buyers were only entitled to such damages as would cover the cost of reasonable repair work.

Tender of performance

Tender of performance is equivalent to performance in the situation where one party cannot complete performance without the assistance of the other and the one party makes an offer to perform which the other refuses.

In *Startup* v *M'Donald* (1843) 6 M & G 593, the plaintiffs agreed to sell 10 tons of oil to the defendant and to deliver it to him 'within the last 14 days of March', payment to be in cash at the end of that period. Delivery was tendered at 8.30 pm on 31 March. The defendant refused to accept or pay for the goods because of the late hour.

HELD: the tender was equivalent to performance and the plaintiffs were entitled to recover damages for non-acceptance.

Rolfe B said:

'In every contract by which a party binds himself to deliver goods or pay money to another, he in fact engages to do an act which he cannot completely perform without the concurrence of the party to whom the delivery or the payment is to be made. Without acceptance on the part of him who is to receive, the act of him who is to deliver or to pay can amount only to a tender. But the law considers (the latter) as having substantially performed it if he has tendered the goods or the money ... provided only that the tender has been made under such circumstances that the party to whom it has been made has had a reasonable opportunity of examining the goods or the money tendered, in order to ascertain that the thing tendered really was what it purported to be. Indeed, without such an opportunity an offer to deliver or pay does not amount to a tender.'

Where goods are tendered they must be correct in quantity and quality.

Where *money* is tendered as payment, it must be in the form of 'legal tender' or such other form as is agreed, for example, a cheque.

To amount to a valid tender of money, the party seeking to perform must produce the correct sum of money (change cannot be required) in the form of 'legal tender', that is, Bank of England notes for any amount; gold coins for any amount;

coins of cupro-nickel or silver exceeding 10p in value for any amount up to £10; coins of cupro-nickel or silver of not more than 10p in value up to £5; coins of bronze for any amount up to 20p. See s2 Coinage Act 1971.

If the party making the tender of payment is sued for breach of contract, he must make payment of the sum tendered into court, whereupon the costs of the action will be borne by the plaintiff. See *Griffith* v *School Board of Ystradyfodwg* (1890) 24 QBD 307.

It is the duty of the party obliged to pay to seek out his creditor and, if he sends the money in any way and it is lost in the course of transit, the risk is on the debtor, and he will have to pay again, unless the creditor requests a particular manner of delivery, for example, by post, in which case the debtor will be discharged as long *as he exercises reasonable care* even where the money is lost in transit, viz the risk is on the creditor.

Where there is a valid tender of *goods*, the party tendering is discharged, but where there is a tender of *money*, although the debtor is absolved from further obligation to tender, the obligation to pay the debt, when called upon, remains.

15.4 Stipulations as to time of performance

At common law

The principle used to be that, in the absence of evidence of a contrary intention, time was essential, even though it has not been expressly made so by the parties. Thus, at common law, a party who did not perform on time could not perform his part of the contract late and enforce the contract against the other party. This rule was modified in part by s41 Law of Property Act 1925 which provides:

'Stipulations in a contract, as to time or otherwise, which according to the rules of equity are not deemed to be or to have become of the essence of the contract, are also construed and have effect at law in accordance with the same rules.'

The effect of this section in that, if time is not of the essence, late performance does not give rise to a right to terminate, but does give rise to a right to damages. See *Raineri* v *Miles* [1981] AC 1050.

In equity

Equity does not regard time as of the essence of a contract as long as the stipulations as to time can be disregarded without injustice to the parties, and, generally, in contracts for the sale of land, they can be disregarded because the delay of one party does not usually deprive the other of the substance of his bargain. However, even in equity time may, in certain circumstances, be regarded as of the essence of a contract:

1. Where the contract expressly provides that time 'is of the essence', or uses other clear words to the same effect. Then equity will give effect to the manifest intention of the parties.
2. Time can be made of the essence by the giving of notice (during the currency of the contract) to perform within a reasonable time. What amounts to a reasonable time is a question of fact depending on the circumstances of each case.

   In *Rickards (Charles)* v *Oppenheim* [1950] 1 KB 616, the defendant ordered a Rolls Royce chassis early in 1947, and in July the plaintiffs agreed that a body should be built for it within six or seven months. The body was not completed seven months later, but the defendant agreed to wait another three months. At the end of this period, the body was still not built. The defendant gave a final notice that if the work was not finished within a further four weeks, he would cancel the order. The body was not finished. The defendant cancelled the order.

   HELD: by giving the final indulgence and indicating that time was of the essence, and giving reasonable notice of that condition, he was not to be regarded in breach of the agreement. It was the plaintiff who was in breach.

   In *British & Commonwealth Holdings plc* v *Quadrex Holdings Inc* [1989] 3 WLR 723, the two companies entered into a written agreement to divide between them different divisions of a third company in which they were both interested. Initially, no time limit was set, but following delays, the plaintiffs served on the defendant company a notice making time 'of the essence' and setting a date for completion.

   The Court of Appeal held that while normally the plaintiffs would undoubtedly be within their rights to issue such a notice, their own conduct was not blameless. Because the plaintiffs' status was not that of an innocent party, their ability to issue a notice, making time 'of the essence', was in doubt.
3. Where from the nature of the surrounding circumstances or from the subject matter of the contract it is clearly essential that the stipulation as to time should be observed, for example, where ripe bananas or a short lease are the subject matter of the contract.

Stipulations as to time in conditional contracts

Note that contractual stipulations as to time may occur, not only as to the time by which performance must be completed but also, in certain types of conditional contracts, the dates by which certain contingent events must take place.

In *Millers Wharf Partnership Ltd* v *Corinthian Column Ltd* (1990) 61 P & CR 461 the plaintiffs agreed to grant the lease of a flat to the defendants, on condition that the plaintiffs should obtain planning permission for redevelopment by a certain date. Either party should have a right of rescission if planning permission was not obtained by the relevant time. The plaintiffs obtained planning consent, some months after the due date. The defendants eventually exercised their power of rescission. The plaintiffs argued that since the due date had passed and the condition had not been fulfilled yet the defendants had not rescinded, then they had lost the right to rescind. The obtaining of planning consent, the condition on which the contract depended, had been fulfilled by a later date; the defendants had waived their right to rescind by not acting immediately once it became apparent planning permission would not be obtained in the time specified.

The court held, however, that the right to rescind still existed. Planning permission had not been obtained by the due date and the plaintiffs' delay in seeking rescission was not to be taken as evidence of waiver.

15.5   Agreements

Eodem modo quo oritur, eodem modo dissoluitur – what has been created by agreement may be extinguished by agreement.

An agreement by the parties to an existing contract to extinguish the rights and obligations that have been created is itself a binding contract, provided that it is either made under seal or supported by consideration. Accordingly, a distinction needs to be drawn between agreements which are executed on one side, where the party seeking to be released must show that he has been giving consideration for the release, or that the release is under seal, and agreements which are wholly executory, where consideration may be found in the mutual release by each party of his rights under the contract.

Discharge by deed is equally effective as regards unilateral or bilateral discharge but where the agreement for discharge is not under seal, the legal position varies according to whether the discharge is bilateral or unilateral.

15.6   Bilateral discharge

This occurs whenever *both* parties to the contract have some right to surrender, as where the contract is in no way performed by either party, or is partly performed by one or both sides to the contract. Where neither party has performed his obligations, the contract is said to be executory.

The agreement by the parties to discharge their contract may be designed to have one of several effects:

1. the parties may intend to rescind their present agreement and nothing more, for example, R has agreed to make weekly deliveries of new materials to J as from 1 July. In June, both parties agree to the termination of the contract (*accord and satisfaction*); or
2. the parties may intend rescission plus agreement on the terms of a new contract as where A has agreed to supply B with a Ford Escort and, by agreement, his contract is rescinded and A agrees to supply B with a Renault 5; or

3. the parties may agree on the variation of an existing contract, for example, where delivery dates are changed for the convenience of both parties. Here, the parties intend to deal on the varied terms of basically the same contract.

The main area of discussion as regards the above surrounds the situation where the original contract is one for which the law requires either that it be in writing, or that there be written evidence of it.

Accord and satisfaction

'Accord and satisfaction is the purchase of a release from an obligation whether arising under a contract or tort by means of any valuable consideration, not being the actual performance of the obligation itself. The accord is the agreement by which the obligation is discharged. The satisfaction is the consideration which makes the agreement operative.' *British Russian Gazette* v *Associated Newspapers* [1933] 2 KB 616.

Thus, where there is an agreement mutually to release the other from the obligations under the first agreement, there is an accord and satisfaction.

See, most recently, the case of *Stour Valley Builders* v *Stuart* (1993) The Times 9 February, in which the Court of Appeal stressed the importance of the fact that there must be agreement between the parties for accord and satisfaction to apply.

Rescission

Although the law requires writing or written evidence for the formation or forceability of certain types of contract, *no* writing is required for their discharge. Thus, where an oral agreement seeks to provide for the rescission of such a contract and the creation of another in its place, the oral words will effectively discharge the existing contract, but if the new contract is of a type required to be evidenced in writing, then it will fail, for lack of writing, to be legally effective.

For example, where A enters into a written contract for the sale of Blackacre to B and later the parties orally agree that instead of selling Blackacre to B, A shall sell Whiteacre, the effect of the oral agreement is to discharge A from his obligation to convey Blackacre to B, but the agreement fails to give B any enforceable rights in respect of Whiteacre.

A rescission and substitution of a new contract is different from a variation, which merely changes or qualifies one or more of the existing contractual provisions. An example of rescission and substitution arose in *Morris* v *Baron* [1918] AC 1. Because there was a substituted agreement, the court drew the necessary inference that the original contract was discharged by rescission. A written contract was entered into for the sale and purchase of dates. A dispute arose and legal proceedings commenced. The parties agreed that the action and counter-claim should be withdrawn, and that an extension should be given to the buyer for payment of a sum owed by him under the contract, and that he should have an option to purchase the goods remaining due, instead of being bound to take delivery.

HELD (by the House of Lords): that the original contract of sale was discharged by the executory agreement.

A contract under seal has always been capable of oral dissolution in equity. Since the Judicature Act 1873, the equitable rule has prevailed. This formula is now embodied in s49 Supreme Court Act 1981.

Novation

This is the name given to a particular type of discharge by agreement. It occurs where there are two contracts each with a creditor and debtor, and the same person is the debtor under the second contract and the creditor under the first. The creditor under the second contract agrees for the release of his own debtor and to accept the debtor under the first contract, and the debtor under the first contract agrees to pay the creditor under the second contract in return for his creditor's promise to release him.

For example, A owes B £100. C owes A £100. C agrees to pay £100 to B in return for A's promise to release him. B agrees to release A in return for C's promise of £100. A agrees to release C in return for C's promise to pay off A's debt to B.

Old contracts: C – £100 – A   A – £100 – B

New contract: C – £100 – B

All are parties to the agreement and all three give consideration. The first contracts are discharged and a new one is created.

Variation

The parties may effect a variation by modifying or altering the terms of the original agreement. In *Berry* v *Berry* [1929] 2 KB 316, husband and wife entered into a separation deed whereby the husband promised to pay to the wife a certain sum each year for her support. Subsequently, they agreed in writing to vary the agreement.

HELD: the variation was valid and enforceable, and could be set up as a defence to an action on the deed.

So it seems that an oral or written agreement may be sufficient to vary a deed (compare the situation under the parol evidence rule, which relates to the *formation* of the contract and not the variation of it). An oral or written agreement may not be sufficient, however, to vary a contract which is required by law to be in writing or evidence in writing. See *Gross* v *Nugent* (1833) 5 B & Ald 58.

The vendor of certain land contracted to make a good title, and this he was unable to do. The purchaser by oral agreement agreed to accept the defective title, but later failed to complete. The vendor brought an action to enforce the contract, that is, the written contract as orally varied.

The court held against the vendor on the ground that there was no written evidence of the contract he wished to enforce.

Note: probably the purchaser could have enforced the original contract (subject to the possible effect of waiver – see later) because the variation of the original contract was ineffective. But if the oral agreement were construed as a rescission of the original contract and its replacement by a new contract, then there would be nothing for the purchaser to enforce.

So the distinction whether the oral agreement was intended by the parties to extinguish the original contract altogether and create a new one, or merely vary the original contract, can be crucial. It is a question of fact to be determined in the light of all the circumstances of each particular case.

See *British and Benington Ltd* v *NW Cachar Tea Co* [1923] AC 48, *Morris* v *Baron* (above) and *United Dominions Corporation (Jamaica) Ltd* v *Shoucair* [1969] 1 AC 340.

A variation should also be distinguished from:

1. A collateral agreement. This is concluded before the contract is entered into or under which one party agrees not to enforce a term of the main agreement. See *City & Westminster Properties* v *Mudd* [1959] Ch 129.
2. The mere elucidation of the contract by correcting mistakes or filling in details.

Waiver

Where one party voluntarily accedes to a request by another party to forbear his right to strict performance of the contract, or where he represents to another that he will not insist upon his right to strict performance of the contract, the court may hold that he has *waived* his right to performance as initially contemplated by the parties. Under the ordinary pressures of commerce and industry, such as postal delays and labour troubles, it frequently arises that it is not possible for one of the parties to keep strictly to the terms of his contract.

For example, the seller of goods may ask the buyer to let him deliver less than the agreed number of items one month, and make up the number on later monthly deliveries. If the buyer agrees, he is said to *waive* his strict rights under the contracts.

The waiver may be oral, written or inferred from conduct, even where the contract itself is one which is required by law to be in, or evidenced in, writing. In *Besseler Waechter Glover & Co* v *Derwent Coal* [1938] 1 KB 408, Goddard J said at p416:

> 'If the parties agree to rescind their original contract and to substitute it for a new one, the latter must be evidenced in writing; so, too, if as a matter of contract the parties agree that the terms of the original agreement shall be varied, the variation must be in writing. But if what happens is a mere voluntary forbearance to insist on delivery or acceptance according to the strict terms of the written contract, the original contract remains unaffected and the obligation to deliver and accept the full contract quantity still continues ... It does not appear to me to matter whether the request comes from one side or the other, or whether it is a matter which is convenient to one party or to both. What is of importance is whether it is a mere forbearance or a matter of contract.'

The effect of the waiver is that, in the absence of reasonable notice requiring contractual performance (if that is possible – it would not be possible where compliance with a time period has been waived), the party extending the forbearance will not be permitted to sue, and the party in whose favour the waiver has been granted will not be able to rely on the contractual obligations of the parties to allege that the other is in breach. For example, in *Levy* v *Goldberg* [1922] 1 KB 688, the defendants agreed in writing to buy cloth from the plaintiffs during a specified period. The defendants asked the plaintiffs not to deliver within that period. When the plaintiffs effected delivery subsequently, the defendants refused to accept delivery. The plaintiffs sued. The defendants said that the plaintiffs were in breach as the oral terms were insufficient to vary the contract (which was then required by the Statute of Frauds to be evidenced in writing).

HELD: that the plaintiffs had waived their contractual rights to insist on delivery during the contractual period, and so they were entitled to maintain their action against the defendants.

In *Hartley* v *Hymans* [1920] 3 KB 475, a buyer of cotton agreed to allow the seller to make late delivery.

HELD: he was liable in damages for refusing to take delivery after the contract period had expired.

In *Leather Cloth Co* v *Hieronimus* (1875) LR 10 QB 140, a buyer of goods to be shipped via Ostend agreed that they could be shipped via Rotterdam. The goods were lost.

HELD: the buyer was still liable for the price because he had assented to the altered mode of performance.

Proctor & Gamble Philippine Manufacturing Corpn v *Peter Cremer GmbH* [1988] 3 All ER 843 is an interesting recent case on waiver. In two contracts for copra cake being shipped from the Philippines, the buyers sought to repudiate on the grounds that the bills of lading were incorrectly dated. In fact, the cargo had not in any event been completely loaded on time, but was 11 days late.

HELD: if a party has a right to reject, which he is not aware of, he cannot be held to have waived his rights of rejection, since he is ignorant that such rights exist.

An example of the revocable nature of waiver is provided in *Rickards* v *Oppenheim*, the facts of which are set out above. The defendant (the buyer) had waived his original rights as to time of delivery, but could give reasonable notice that a new final date was to be complied with and treat the contract as at an end if that date was not complied with.

Of course, there must be circumstances in which the waiver cannot be revoked, for example, where the goods have been lost in the *Hieronimus* case and, possibly, where transportation via Rotterdam had already occurred.

The position relating to waiver at common law is also open to objection on the ground that, in effect, it often makes enforceable a promise which is unsupported by consideration, being given for the benefit of one party only.

The cases on waiver have much in common with the doctrine of promissory estoppel, which has been discussed in Chapter 3. See obiter dicta of Denning LJ in *Rickards* v *Oppenheim*:

'If the defendant, as he did, led the plaintiffs to believe that he would not insist on the stipulation as to time, and that, if they carried out the work, he would accept it, and they did, he could not afterwards set up the stipulation to regard to time against them. Whether it be called waiver or forbearance on his part, or an agreed variation or substituted performance, does not matter. It is kind of estoppel. By his conduct he evinced an intention to affect their legal relations. He made, in effect, a promise not to insist on his strict legal rights. That promise was to be acted on, and was in fact, acted on. He cannot afterwards go back on it.'

Although in many instances waiver and promissory estoppel produce the same results, there is authority for the view that the doctrines must be kept distinct. See *Brikom Investments* v *Carr* [1979] QB 467.

Provision for discharge in the contract itself

The contract can provide for discharge in its terms, for example, upon certain breaches of contract, or upon the occurrence of certain events, such as the bankruptcy of a party or conviction of a criminal offence, or on an event unconnected with the parties, or upon the giving of notice by one party. A common illustration of these provisions is found in partnership agreements. See also *Head* v *Tattersall* (above, 6.4).

15.7   Unilateral discharge

This takes place where only one party has rights to surrender. Where one party has entirely performed his part of the agreement, he is no longer under obligations but has rights to compel the performance of the agreement by the other party.

For example, A agrees to sell 1 cwt of coal to B for £X and A delivers the coal only to find out that B has suddenly incurred a tremendous expense. A, out of sympathy, agrees that B shall not pay for the coal. But where is the consideration moving from B in support of A's promise to forgo his right to the £X? There is none. There is merely a bare promise from A.

For unilateral discharge, unless the agreement is under seal, consideration must be furnished in order to make the agreement enforceable.

In this context, the agreement is termed the *accord,* and the consideration which makes it binding is known as the *satisfaction.* See above under 'Bilateral discharge'.

The Bills of Exchange Act 1882 provides an exception to the general rule that a unilateral discharge requires consideration: where the holder of a bill of exchange or promissory note unconditionally renounces his rights against the acceptor, the bill is discharged. The renunciation must be in writing, or the bill must be delivered up to the acceptor.

15.8   Breach

The nature of a breach

A failure to perform the terms of a contract constitutes a breach. As we have seen in Chapter 6, not all breaches entitle the innocent party to treat the contract as repudiated.

A breach does not automatically discharge a contract. Indeed, note the recent case of *Thornton* v *Abbey National plc* (1993) The Times 4 March, in which the Court of Appeal ruled that where a breach of contract occurs which in no way disadvantages the plaintiff, the defendants may, effectively, take advantage of their own breach of contract. It is simply that a sufficiently serious breach (breach of a condition or a breach with serious consequences) will give the innocent party the option of treating the contract as repudiated (viz treating the contract as 'at an end'). It is not rescinded ab initio, and the word rescission is, accordingly, a misleading term to use. The word 'repudiation' is more satisfactory. When a contract is said to be 'at an end', it means that the innocent party or, in some cases, both parties are discharged from further performance of their primary obligations under the contract, but in place of the primary obligation a secondary obligation may arise. This secondary obligation is (usually) to pay a monetary compensation for the non-performance. See *Photo Production Ltd* v *Securicor Transport Ltd* [1980] AC 827.

Note: the innocent party may choose to continue with the contract and simply sue for damages.

A breach which is sufficiently serious to give the innocent party this option of treating the contract can occur in one of two ways: either one party may show by express words or by implications from his conduct at some time before performance is due that he does not intend to observe his obligations under the contract – called anticipatory breach; or he may 'in fact' break a condition or otherwise break the contract in such a way that it amounts to a substantial failure of consideration.

Anticipatory breach

Where the breach occurs before the time fixed for performance, this is known as anticipatory breach. The innocent party is not under any obligation to wait until the date fixed for performance before commencing his action, but may immediately treat the contract as at an end and sue for damages. Alternatively, he may affirm the contract by treating it as still in force. The innocent party has this right of election, and is bound by his choice. If within a reasonable time he does not indicate that he accepts the other party's repudiation so that the contract is discharged, then the contract remains open for the benefit of, and the risk of, both parties.

The breach was accepted in *Hochster* v *De La Tour* (1853) 2 E & B 678. An employer told his employee (a travelling courier) before the time for performance arrived that he would not require his services. The courier sued for damages at once.

HELD: he was entitled to do so. See also *Frost* v *Knight* (1872) LR 7 Ex 111.

The breach was not accepted in *Avery* v *Bowden* (1855) 5 E & B 714. A charterparty provided that a ship should proceed to Odessa and there take a cargo from the charter's agent. The ship arrived at Odessa and the master demanded a cargo, but the agent could not provide one. The ship's master continued to ask for one. A war broke out. The charterer sued.

HELD (inter alia): that if the agent's conduct amounted to an anticipatory repudiation of the contract, the master had elected to keep the contract alive until it was discharged by frustration on the outbreak of war.

It appears that the right to keep the contract alive subsists even where the innocent party is increasing the amount, and not mitigating, the damages which he may receive from the party in breach. In *White & Carter* v *McGregor* [1962] AC 413, the appellants (advertising contractors) agreed with the respondent (a garage proprietor) to display advertisements for his garage for three years. The respondent repudiated the agreement and cancelled on the same day. The appellants refused to cancel and performed their obligations. They sued for the contract price.

HELD (by a majority of 3:2): that they were entitled to the full contract price.

Where a party elects to treat the contract as continuing, that is, he 'affirms' the contract, the affirmation can be regarded as a species of waiver. The innocent party waives his right to treat the contract as repudiated (see, for example, s11 Sale of Goods Act 1979) and may be 'estopped' from changing his election.

In *Panchaud Freres SA* v *Etablissements General Grain Co* [1970] 1 Lloyd's Rep 53, buyers of maize rejected it on a ground which was subsequently found to be inadequate. Three years later, they discovered that the grain had not been shipped within the period stipulated for in the contract. They, therefore, sought to justify their rejection on this ground.

HELD: they were not entitled to do so. Lord Denning MR stated that the buyers were estopped by their conduct from setting up late delivery as a ground for rejection because they had led the sellers to believe they would not do so.

If a party elects to affirm a contract after an anticipatory breach by the other party, he is not absolved from tendering further performance of his own obligations under the contract. Accordingly, if a repudiation by anticipatory breach was followed by affirmation of the contract, the repudiating party could escape liability if the affirming party was subsequently in breach of the contract. See *Fercometal Sarl* v *Mediterranean Shipping Co SA* [1988] 2 All ER 742.

Whether the anticipatory breach amounts to a repudiation depends on the actual circumstances of the case:

> '... you must examine what (the) conduct is to see whether it amounts to a renunciation, to an absolute refusal to perform the contract ... and whether the other party may accept it as a reason for not performing his part.'

per Lord Selborne in *Mersey Steel and Iron Co* v *Naylor Benzon & Co* (1884) 9 App Cas 434 at 438–9.

The difficulty that can arise in determining whether the conduct amounts to a repudiation is illustrated by a comparison of two decisions in the House of Lords.

In *Federal Commerce and Navigation* v *Molena Alpha* [1979] AC 757, the owners of the ship gave instructions not to issue bills of lading without which the charterers would not be able to operate the ship. The owners believed that they were entitled to take these measures. This belief did not weigh with the House of Lords, their Lordships holding that their conduct constituted a wrongful repudiation of the contract.

In *Woodar Investment* v *Wimpey Construction* [1980] 1 WLR 277, in a contract for the sale of land, the purchasers sought a right to rescind the contract. The right to rescind was afforded by the contract, but was only exercisable on grounds which did not, in fact, exist. The purchasers' motive was to escape from an unprofitable transaction, but they honestly believed that they were entitled to the right they brought.

The House of Lords held, by a majority, that the purchasers' conduct did not amount to a repudiatory breach. Lord Wilberforce distinguished this case from *Molena Alpha* by drawing a distinction between the erroneous assertion of a view, as here, and threatening a breach with serious consequences, as in *Molena Alpha*.

Lords Salmon and Russell, dissenting, held the view that the two cases were identical.

Cheshire and Fifoot (10th edn p486) suggests three possible grounds of distinction between these two cases:

1. In *Woodar*, there was no call for the sellers to take immediate action, they could have tested their rights by legal process.
2. In *Woodar*, the time for completion was some way off, if the purchasers had actually refused to complete this would then have amounted to a repudiation.
3. In *Molena Alpha*, the gap between repudiation and performance was fairly short, and the pressure on the charterers accordingly greater.

Questions of whether or not repudiation can be established often arise in contracts for the sale of goods where delivery or payment is to be made by instalments.

In *Mersey Steel and Iron* (above), the buyers were acting under the genuine, but mistaken, belief that they could not continue making payments without leave of the court, because of the initiation of insolvency proceedings. It was held that this conduct could not be construed as a repudiation.

Some guidance is given by the Court of Appeal in *Maple Flock Co Ltd* v *Universal Furniture Products (Wembley) Ltd* [1934] 1 KB 148 where it was stated that whether, in an instalment contract, a certain breach could be treated as repudiation is to be determined by considering, first, the ratio quantatively which the breach bears to the contract as a whole and, secondly, the degree of probability or improbability that the breach will be repeated.

In *Decro-Wall International* v *Practitioners in Marketing* [1971] 1 WLR 361, a company was persistently – though only slightly – late in making payments under the contract. This was not held to constitute a repudiation because the other party had not been prejudiced by the late payments, except in having to pay a small amount of interest on the outstanding sums, which could have been recovered from the party in default; moreover, there was no reason to doubt that payment would be made as soon as the goods in question had been disposed of. See also *Afovos Shipping* v *Pagnan* [1983] 1 All ER 449 where the House of Lords affirmed the principle that the doctrine of anticipatory breach related only to repudiation arising out of fundamental breach. The delay, in this instance in paying one instalment of hire, did not amount to a fundamental breach.

16

Remedies for Breach of Contract – Damages

16.1 Introduction

As we have seen from the discussion in earlier chapters, a breach of contract may be of such a nature that the injured party is justified in treating the contract as discharged. In such a case, the normal remedy of the injured party is to obtain damages for the breach to compensate him for the promise to him not being fulfilled, as well as to repudiate the contract. Alternatively, he may limit his remedy to damages. Not every breach of contract will entitle a person to treat himself as discharged, of course. Where a breach has only been a breach of warranty, the only remedy at common law is damages. The right to repudiate does not arise.

Equity may assist

By declaration
Damages for breach of contract may not always be satisfactory as a remedy. If the injured party feels that he made a bad bargain in the first place in entering into the contract, he may choose to obtain a declaration that the contract is terminated.

Specific performance

It may be the case that damages are an inadequate remedy to the injured party, for example, there may be no satisfactory substitute for that which the injured party had bargained for, as in a contract for the sale of a specific piece of land. In such cases, the appropriate remedy will be specific performance of the contract itself.

Injunction

Damages may be a useless remedy to the injured party who may seek specific performance of the contract in such cases. However, the breach may take the form of doing something contrary to the terms of the contract, for example, where an employee agrees not to go into competition against his employer or to work for his employer's competitors. The appropriate remedy there will be an injunction to restrain the defaulting party from acting in breach of contract.

Quasi-contractual remedies

Restitution for total failure of consideration

If the injured party had performed his side of the contract but has not received counter-performance in full, then the appropriate remedy may be restitution in respect of his own performance, for example, where the injured party has paid the price for the goods which he has not received.

Quantum meruit

In cases where the injured party has performed, under the contract, work the value of which exceeds what would have been due to him if the contract had been fully performed, then he may claim on a quantum meruit the value of that work already done. Such a claim will be quasi-contractual in nature.

16.2   Damages

General

Damages are meant to compensate the injured party for any consequences of the breach of contract which the law recognises. The underlying principle is to put the injured party financially as near as possible, into the position he would have been in had the promise been fulfilled.

Damages are assessed on the actual loss to the plaintiff, and not on the gain to the defendant. They are compensation, not punishment.

In *Teacher* v *Calder* [1889] 1 F (HL) 39, a financier broke a contract by which he agreed to invest £15,000 in the business of a timber merchant; instead, he invested the same sum in a distillery.

HELD: that the timber merchant's damages were to be based on the loss to his business – not on the much larger profits the financier had derived from investing in the brewery.

An exception exists to this rule in cases concerning a contract for the sale of land; here, the defendant must hand over the profits. In *Lake* v *Bayliss* [1974] 1 WLR 1073, the position was explained: the vendor is considered to be a trustee of the land for the purchaser after the contract is made. Therefore, if the vendor wrongfully resells the land to a third party, the purchaser is entitled to the proceeds of sale, even though they may exceed his loss.

If there has been no actual loss inflicted on the plaintiff as a result of the breach, he may still, in rare circumstances, recover damages.

In *Penarth Dock Engineering* v *Pound* [1963] 1 Lloyd's Rep 359, the defendant bought a floating dock from the plaintiff but failed to remove it from its berth within the stipulated time. The plaintiff claimed damages on the basis that he was deprived of the use of the berth during the time it was there in breach of the agreement. The defendant argued that the plaintiff should get only nominal damages, as he would not have made any use of the berth anyway.

HELD: the defendant should pay a fair rental value for the berth.

The general principle to be observed is that: *there must be a loss to the plaintiff in consequence of the breach.* Loss is widely defined and includes any harm to a person or his property and any other injury to his economic position. The plaintiff will be awarded *substantial damages* for such losses, and they will be based on the compensatory principle. If no such loss has been sustained, he will only be able to recover *nominal damages*.

See, for example, *Surrey CC* v *Bredero Homes Ltd* [1992] 3 All ER 302 in which nominal damages only were awarded to a local authority who had waited so long to make a claim that they had lost any rights to enforce the covenant they had claimed was breached. The loss of the value of the right to enforce the covenant (for instance by injunction) meant that the plaintiffs' failure to act no longer had any contractual rights to enforce.

Substantial damages are only recoverable if the plaintiff's position has been adversely affected. In *Staniforth* v *Lyall* (1830) 7 Bing 169, a shipowner who claimed damages for a charterer's breach to load his ship could not recover as he had found an alternative and more profitable means of employing the ship in the meantime.

Exemplary damages are not normally awarded in breach of contract. Such damages are awards of sums far greater than the pecuniary loss suffered by the plaintiff (see below).

C & P Haulage v *Middleton* [1983] 1 WLR 1461 illustrates the general proposition that the victim of a breach should not make a profit out of it, and that to recover substantial damages, the plaintiff must show actual loss suffered.

Compensation for the plaintiff's loss

There are several ways in which the plaintiff can be compensated for his loss; the plaintiff is entitled to choose whichever form of compensation he feels is most appropriate to his case.

Loss of bargain

Damages for loss of bargain are assessable to put the plaintiff 'so far as money can do it ... in the same situation as if the contract had been performed'.

In a contract for the sale of goods which are defective, the plaintiff will, under this heading, be entitled to damages reflecting the differences between the price paid under the contract and the actual value of the defective goods.

Reliance loss

Damages to put the plaintiff in the position he would have been, if the contract had never been made, by compensating him for expenses he has incurred in his abortive performance. Under this heading, expenses which the plaintiff was never obliged to incur may be recovered.

In *McRae* v *Commonwealth Disposals* (1950) 84 CLR 377, the plaintiff recovered £3,000 spent on sending out a salvage expedition to salvage a wrecked tanker, in a specified position, which they had purchased from the defendant. The tanker had never, in fact, existed. Reliance loss incurred before the contract was entered into may be recovered in certain instances.

In *Anglia Television* v *Reed* [1972] 1 QB 60, the plaintiffs incurred expenses in preparation for filming a television play. They subsequently entered into a contract with the defendant to play the leading role. The defendant repudiated the contract. The plaintiffs tried hard to find a substitute but failed, and had to abandon the play. The plaintiffs sued the defendant for expenses of production amounting to £2,750 incurred by the plaintiffs on production before the contract.

HELD: they were entitled to recover the whole of the wasted expenditure.

> 'Mr Reed must have known perfectly well that much expenditure had already been incurred on director's fees and the like. He must have contemplated – or at any rate, it is reasonably to be imputed to him – that if he broke his contract, all the expenditure would be wasted, whether or not it was incurred before or after the contract.' (per Lord Denning MR.)

Compare *C & P Haulage* v *Middleton* (above) where the expenditure was wasted, not because of the defendant's breach, but because the contract was unwise.

Restitution

Where a bargain is made, and the price paid, but the defendant fails to deliver the goods, then the plaintiff is entitled to recover the price paid plus interest thereon.

Choosing the claim

The plaintiff's choice in the above claims is limited to an extent. In loss of bargain, he must give some evidence of the value of his expectations and, if he is unable to do so, or his expectations are so speculative that no value can be put on them, then he is limited to claims in reliance loss and restitution. Further, if he wishes to pursue his remedy on a claim for restitution, then he must show a total failure of consideration.

The plaintiff's choice of claim may be aided by the fact that more than one of the claims is available to him; for example, both loss of bargain and reliance loss may be available. In such cases, the plaintiff can combine the claims.

In *Millar's Machinery Co* v *David Way* (1935) 40 Com Cas 240, the plaintiff bought some machinery which was installed in his factory and paid for. However, the machinery was not in accordance with the specifications laid down by the contract and the plaintiff rejected it.

HELD: that the plaintiff could recover the price (restitution), installation expenses (reliance loss) and the net loss resulting from the breach (loss of bargain).

The plaintiff is limited in combining his claims to the extent that he cannot recover the same loss more than once.

In *Cullinane* v *British 'Rema' Manufacturing Co* [1954] 1 QB 292, the plaintiff contracted to buy a clay pulverising plant from the defendant which should have pulverised clay at 6 tons per hour.

The plant never, in fact, pulverised clay at more than 2 tons per hour, and the plaintiff claimed damages under five headings:

1. Cost of buildings to house plant, less break up value.
2. Cost of plant less residual value.
3. Cost of ancillary plant less its residual value.
4. Interest on capital sums under the three headings above.
5. Loss of profit which would have been made on 6 tons per hour from date of installation of plant to date of trial.

HELD: the first three headings could not be awarded as damages as the plaintiff was attempting to recover both the whole of his original capital loss, and the whole of the profit he could have made. It was really a self-evident proposition as a claim for loss of profits could only be founded on the footing of capital expenditure.

For example, if a buyer pays for goods in advance which are not delivered, he cannot have both his payment (restitution) and the full value of the goods at the time of delivery (loss of bargain).

In *CCC Films* v *Impact Quadrant Films* [1984] 3 WLR 245, this case illustrates the choice of claim available – wasted expenditure or loss of profits. It makes the logical point that if the victim of the breach is claiming wasted expenditure because he cannot begin to estimate the expectation loss, then it would be impossible to make him have to prove at least sufficient expectation loss to cover the wasted expenditure. The onus falls on the defendant to prove that the expenditure would not have been recovered had the contract been performed.

The *CCC Films* decision will operate happily when the object of the contract is to make a profit. It produces difficulties for cases similar to *Anglia TV* v *Reed*, where the object of the contract is not to make a profit. The TV company expected to make their profits from increased advertising revenue if the programme was a success. Hutchinson J fails to deal with those problems.

Students will only understand all the cases in this area if they keep in the back of their minds the distinction the Court of Appeal failed to make clear in *Cullinane* v *British 'Rema'*. 'Loss of profits' is used in two senses – loss of *gross* profit and loss of *net* profit, that is, after deduction of the necessary spending to earn that pure profit.

Claims can be made combining reliance loss + restitution + net profit, but *not* combining reliance loss + restitution + gross profit.

For example, A contracts to buy a washing machine from B to install in his laundry to increase the capacity of his business. A spends £10 altering his premises in preparation and £100 in consideration for the new machine. The machine is installed but, in breach of contract, breaks down the next day losing A the chance of doing C's washing. A would have charged C £8 for this comprising £5 for electricity, soap powder, wear and tear on the machine and £3 pure profit.

A can sue B for   £10   +   £100   +   £3
                (Reliance)   (Restitution)   (Expectation *net* profit)

Incidental and consequential losses

Incidental losses are those which the plaintiff incurs after the breach has come to his notice. They include the administrative costs of buying a substitute, or sending back defective goods, or hiring a replacement in the meantime.

Consequential losses may be loss of profits, for example, reliance loss, or further harm such as personal injury or damage to property. Thus, if the defendant sells the plaintiff a cow which is diseased and infects the plaintiff's other cows, then the plaintiff can claim for not only damages in selling a defective cow, but the losses caused to the other cows.

Contributory negligence

Until comparatively recently, contributory negligence was not considered relevant in assessing damages for breach of contract.

There have, however, been a number of interesting cases, mainly at first instance, concerning this issue. See *AB Marintrans* v *Comet Shipping Co Ltd* [1985] 3 All ER 442 and *Basildon DC* v *J E Lesser (Properties)* [1985] 1 All ER 20.

The recent Court of Appeal decision in *Forsikringsaktieselskapet Vesta* v *Butcher* [1988] 2 All ER 43 looks carefully at these earlier cases. In *Forsikringsaktieselskapet*, the plaintiffs, a Norwegian insurance firm, insured a Norwegian fish farm and re-insured 90 per cent of the risk with London underwriters. It was a condition of the insurance that a 24-hour watch be kept on the farm; the owners said this could not be arranged. The plaintiffs telephoned the brokers and awaited confirmation that a non-continuous security arrangement was acceptable. Because of a breakdown in communications, the brokers never followed this up, and the reinsurers were never aware that a 24-hour watch was not being kept.

A severe storm resulted in heavy losses of fish. Although even if there had been a 24 hour-watch, losses would have been the same, the reinsurers repudiated liability on the ground inter alia of the breach of the 24-hour watch condition. The main issue was whether, on the facts of the case, the court had power to apportion under the Law Reform (Contributory Negligence) Act 1945, and thus reduce the damages recoverable by the plaintiffs.

The Court of Appeal held that the 1945 Act might apply in a number of categories of case:

'Three categories in particular can be conveniently identified:

1. Where the defendant's liability arises from some contractual provision which does not depend on negligence on the part of the defendant.
2. When the defendant's liability arises from a contractual obligation which is expressed in terms of taking care (or something similar) but does not correspond to a common law duty of care which would exist in the given case independently of contract.
3. Where the defendant's liability in contract is the same as his liability in the tort of negligence independently of the existence of any contract ...'

The Court of Appeal agreed that the present case was an example of category (3), and that in category (3) the defendant must be allowed to raise the defence of contributory negligence, so that the result of the case would be much the same whether the plaintiff chose to sue in contract or in tort.

16.3 Remoteness of damage

Hadley v Baxendale

Not every type of damage caused to the plaintiff as a result of the breach of contract will be recoverable. If the loss flowing from the breach of contract is too remote then it cannot be recovered. Losses, to be recoverable, must have been within the reasonable contemplation of the parties.

In *Hadley* v *Baxendale* (1854) 9 Exch 341, a shaft in the plaintiff's mill broke and had to be sent to the makers at Greenwich to serve as a pattern for the production of a new one. The defendant agreed to carry the shaft to the makers but, in breach of contract, delayed it so that a stoppage of several days occurred at the plaintiff's mill. The plaintiff claimed damages for £300 for loss of profits during this period, and was awarded £50. The defendant appealed.

HELD: that there were two principles upon which the jury should have been directed.

'Where the parties have made a contract which one of them has broken, the damages which the other party ought to receive in respect of such breach of contract should be such as may fairly and reasonably be considered as either arising naturally, ie according to the usual course of things, from such breach of contract itself, or such as may be reasonably supposed to have been in the contemplation of both parties at the time they made the contract as the probable result of the breach' (per Alderson B).

Damages are recoverable under two limbs under *Hadley* v *Baxendale*:

1. Damages which may fairly and reasonably be considered as arising naturally.
2. Damages which may reasonably be supposed to have been in the contemplation of the parties at the time of the contract.

If the loss resulting from the damage falls within either category under *Hadley* v *Baxendale*, then it is recoverable. Therefore, in *Hadley* v *Baxendale*, as the stoppage was not the natural consequence of the delay, the defendant was not liable under the first limb. He was not liable under the second limb either, as this required that the damage, that is, the stoppage would be contemplated by both parties at the time of the contract, as a probable result of the breach. The plaintiff had only told the defendant that the shaft was the broken shaft from a mill; if he had told the defendant that the mill would be idle if there was any delay, then the defendant might have tried to limit his liability as he would then, in the circumstances, have been clearly in breach.

The first limb covers loss which would usually be expected to result from the breach. The second limb will only operate where special circumstances under which the contract was actually made are communicated to the defendant by the plaintiff.

Developments after Hadley v Baxendale

Both rules can be put together to say what ought the reasonable man in the defendant's position to know and expect.

In *Victoria Laundry* v *Newman Industries* [1949] 2 KB 528, Victoria Laundry wished to expand business and needed a new boiler. Newman Industries wished to supply one, but delivered six months late after a road accident. During this time, Victoria Laundry were losing profits the new boiler would have earned, and this included certain lucrative contracts for the Ministry of Supply. Victoria Laundry claimed these profits as damages.

HELD: Newman Industries knew nothing of these orders and could not be held responsible for this loss. But Newman Industries, as an experienced firm, must have known that the new boiler was needed to cut losses or increase profits, thus they were liable for a reasonable sum representing some loss along those lines.

The Court of Appeal took the opportunity to review and restate the principles governing the measure of damages in the *Victoria Laundry* case, and Asquith LJ found six propositions which emerged from the authorities:

'i) It is well settled that the governing purpose of damages is to put the party whose rights have been violated in the same position, so far as money can do so, as if his rights have been observed. This purpose, if relentlessly pursued, would provide him with a complete indemnity for all loss de facto resulting from a particular breach however improbable, however unpredictable. This in contract at least is recognised as too harsh a rule. Hence:

ii) In cases of breach of contract the aggrieved party is only entitled to recover such part of the loss actually resulting as was, at the time of the contract, reasonably foreseeable as liable to result from the breach.

iii) What was at the time reasonably foreseeable, depends on the knowledge then possessed by the parties or, at all events, by the party who later commits the breach.

iv) For this purpose knowledge "possessed" is of two kinds – one imputed, the other actual. Everyone, as a reasonable person, is taken to know "the ordinary course of things" and consequently what loss is liable to result from a breach of that ordinary course. This is the subject matter of the "first rule" in *Hadley* v *Baxendale*, but to this knowledge, which the contract-breaker is assumed to possess, whether he actually possesses it or not, there may have to be added in a particular case knowledge which he actually possesses of special circumstances outside the "ordinary course of things", of such a kind that a breach in those special circumstances would be liable to cause more loss. Such a case attracts the operation of the "second rule" so to make the additional loss also recoverable.

v) In order to make the contract-breaker liable under either rule it is not necessary that he should actually have asked himself, "What loss is liable to result from a breach?" As has often been pointed out, parties at the time of contracting contemplate, not the breach of the contract, but its performance. It suffices that, if he had considered the question, he would as a reasonable man, have concluded that the loss in question was liable to result.

vi) Nor, finally, to make a particular loss recoverable, need it be proved that on a given state of knowledge the defendant could, as a reasonable man, forsee that a breach must necessarily result in that loss. It is enough if he could foresee it was likely to so result.'

The principles relating to remoteness of damage were further considered in the House of Lords in 1967 and given greater refinement.

In *The Heron II* [1969] 1 AC 350, the owner of 'Heron II' agreed to carry a cargo of sugar from Constanza (Rumania) to Basrah (Iraq). The voyage normally took 20 days but, in breach of contract, this voyage took 29 days. In those nine days, the Basrah sugar market fell and the plaintiff suffered loss of profit.

HELD: the plaintiff was entitled to damages for loss of profit since the defendant knew there was a sugar market in Basrah. The whole matter was a question of the likelihood of what the defendant knew; it was quite likely that the plaintiff was intending to sell on the sugar market.

'The present case is one in which no special information was given to the carrier as to what the charterers intended to do with the goods after they arrived at Basrah. In those circumstances in deciding what damages would fairly and reasonably be regarded as arising, if the delivery of the goods was delayed, I think that such a shipowner must reasonably have contemplated that, if he delivered the sugar at Basrah some nine or ten days later than he could and should have delivered it, then a loss by reason of a fall in the market price for sugar at Basrah was one that was liable to result or at least was not unlikely to result' (per Lord Morris).

In *The Heron II*, the House of Lords did not agree upon a general formulation. Lords Morris, Hodson and Pearce generally approved these propositions. Lords Reid and Upjohn modified the propositions in part.

Neither was happy with the words 'foreseeable' or 'reasonably foreseeable' in the *Victoria Laundry* formation. Lord Upjohn said:

'It is clear that on the one hand the test of foreseeability as laid down in the case of tort is not the test for breach of contract; nor on the other hand must the loser establish that the loss was a near certainty or odds-on probability. I am content to adopt as the test a "real danger" or a "serious possibility". There may be a shade of difference between these two phrases, but the assessment of damages is not an exact science and what to one judge or jury will appear a real danger may appear to another judge or jury as a serious possibility.'

All the members of the House of Lords used phrases to denote the degree of probability of loss resulting from the breach which would be recoverable.

Lord Reid: 'not unlikely', which meant, he thought, a degree of probability considerably less than an even chance but, nevertheless, not very unusual and easily foreseeable.

So away from balance of probabilities [handwritten marginal note]

Lord Morris: 'not unlikely to occur', or 'liable to result'.
Lord Hodson: 'liable to result'.
Lords Pearce
and Upjohn: 'a real danger', or 'a serious possibility'.

Four of them thought that the colloquialism 'on the cards' should not be used – the phrase employed by Asquith LJ in *Victoria Laundry*.

Effects of 'The two limbs'

Losses which occur 'in the ordinary course of things' only are recoverable under the first limb

In *Pilkington v Wood* [1953] Ch 770, the plaintiff bought a house in Hampshire and his solicitor, in breach of contract, negligently failed to notice that the house had a defective title, and was held liable for the amount by which the house's value had been lessened by the title not being good. The plaintiff shortly afterwards took up work in Lancashire and suffered added loss as the house was hard to resell.

HELD: that the solicitor was not liable for the latter loss as he could not anticipate that the plaintiff would shortly move.

If the parties are not ad idem in their contemplation of the use for which the subject matter of the contract is needed, then no loss is recoverable beyond that which would have resulted if the intended use had been that reasonably within the contemplation of the defendant.

In *Cory v Thames Ironworks Co* (1868) LR 3 QB 181, the defendant agreed to supply the plaintiff with the hull of a floating boom derrick, but delivered it six months late. The defendant reasonably believed the plaintiff intended to use the hull as a coal store. If this belief was well founded, then the plaintiff's loss would have been £420. But, unknown to the defendant, the plaintiff intended to use the hull for a new method of transferring coal from colliers to barges, and lost profits of £4,000. The plaintiff claimed £420 damages. The defendant argued that this represented a loss not actually suffered.

HELD: there would be 'no hardship or injustice' in awarding the plaintiff £420 when he had lost a larger amount.

However, it is doubtful if damages could be recovered for a loss suffered which is quite different in kind from that which would have occurred in the ordinary course of things. For example, if A sells B poisonous dog food and B eats the dog food himself and dies, could B's executor sue A for the loss of a dog?

Knowledge of special circumstances

The defendant's knowledge of special circumstances under the second limb is not in itself sufficient to make him liable. There must be knowledge and acceptance by the defendant of the purpose and intention of the plaintiff.

In *Horne* v *Midland Railway* (1873) LR 8 CP 131, the defendant contracted to carry a consignment of shoes to London by 3 February, but delivered a day late. As a result of the delay, the plaintiff lost an opportunity of selling the shoes at an exceptionally high price.

HELD: that the defendant was not liable for this loss, although he knew the plaintiff would have to take the shoes back if they were not delivered by 3 February, he did not know the plaintiff would lose an exceptionally high profit.

In *Simpson* v *L & N Railway* (1876) 1 QBD 274, the defendant contracted to carry the plaintiff's samples of cattle food from an agricultural show at Bedford to another at Newcastle. He delivered certain goods to an agent of the defendant at Bedford showground. The goods were marked 'must be at Newcastle by Monday certain'. No express reference was made in the contract of carriage to the Newcastle show. The samples arrived at Newcastle after the show was over.

HELD: the defendant was liable for loss of profits which the plaintiff would have made had the samples reached Newcastle on time. The plaintiff's purpose and intention could readily be inferred from the circumstances, which clearly indicated that the contract was one to carry samples to the Newcastle show and not simply to Newcastle.

Therefore, if the defendant could anticipate circumstances leading to an extra loss to the plaintiff on the facts known to him if the contract was breached, he will be liable. For example, a seller will be liable to a buyer for loss of profit on a sub-sale of which he knew.

Type or kind of loss

The test of remoteness determines whether the plaintiff is entitled to damages, and not the quantum.

In *Wroth* v *Tyler* [1974] Ch 30, the defendant contracted to sell his house to the plaintiff, but later refused to complete the transaction in breach of contract. In the meantime, house prices rose sharply and the plaintiff claimed the difference between the contract price and the market value at the date of the trial. The defendant argued that he should not be liable for the full difference between the contract price and the market price, because he could not have contemplated the exceptionally large rise in house prices between 1971 and 1973. However, he admitted he could have contemplated some rise in house prices.

HELD: the defendant might escape liability for a type or kind of loss which he could not have contemplated, but there was no authority to show that the quantum should be contemplated.

However, the test does not mean that the defendant is liable for all losses once liability has been founded. In the *Victoria Laundry* case, the defendant was only held liable for a reasonable amount of the profits, not for the actual amount of profits the plaintiff lost on not having the contracts for the Ministry of Supply.

Accordingly, whether or not a plaintiff may recover damages depends substantially upon the type of loss that the court is prepared to identify. So, in *Parsons* v *Uttley Ingham* [1978] QB 791, the court thought that it was within the contemplation of the parties that a hopper which was unfit for its purpose of storing food in a suitable condition for feeding pigs might lead to 'illness' of, or 'physical injury' to, the pigs, even though the pigs had died of a rare intestinal disease, which could not have been foreseen. See the judgment of Scarman LJ, in particular, on remoteness of damage in contract and in tort.

16.4   Causation

Where remoteness of damage is in issue between the parties, there will be no dispute about whether the breach caused the state of affairs leading to the damage. The issue will be whether that state of affairs was one which the law should recognise as permitting the plaintiff to recover damages for the breach.

Where causation is in issue between the parties, the dispute between the plaintiff and the defendant will be whether the state of affairs which the plaintiff alleges caused him damage, was one which resulted from a breach at all.

One event in the sequence of events leading to a loss might not be held to be the cause of the loss, for example, a shipowner is not liable to a charterer if, as a result of delay, the ship ran into a typhoon, as such a catastrophe may occur anywhere. See *The Monarch SS Co case* [1949] AC 196.

If there are two causes of the state of affairs resulting in damage, and both causes co-operate and have equal efficacy, one will be sufficient to carry a judgment for damages.

In *Smith, Hogg & Co* v *Black Sea Insurance* [1940] AC 997, a shipowner was held liable to a charterer in damages for loss of a cargo which had been caused by a combination of perils of the sea and the unseaworthiness of the ship. The latter was sufficient to carry a claim for damages.

An intervening act of a third party which itself causes the loss, or aggravates the loss, caused by the defendant's breach, will not absolve the defendant from liability if the intervening act was reasonably foreseeable – *Victoria Laundry* and *The Heron II* principles.

In *Weld-Blundell* v *Stephens* [1920] AC 956, the plaintiff employed an accountant, the defendant, to investigate the affairs of a company he had invested in. The defendant's partner negligently dropped a letter from the plaintiff in the office of the company's manager, which the manager picked up and showed to his directors, who sued the plaintiff in libel and won. The plaintiff sued the defendant for breach of contract to recover the damages he paid out in the libel action.

HELD: the claim must be dismissed since (1) the plaintiff's liability for libel existed apart from contract, and (2) the loss was not caused by breach of contract, but by the act of the company's manager showing the letter to the directors. This was an act the defendant could not have foreseen.

In *De La Bere* v *Pearson* [1908] 1 KB 280, the defendant was held liable for loss where he recommended a dishonest stockbroker to the plaintiff who wished to make investments, even though it was the dishonest stockbroker who caused the losses.

In *Stansbie* v *Troman* [1948] 2 KB 48, a painter in breach of contract after he had completed decorations, left unlocked a house, which was later burgled by thieves.

HELD: the defendant was liable for the value of goods taken as this was exactly the sort of loss he should have guarded against and foreseen.

Where loss is suffered on two or more separate occasions, the question will arise as to causation, limitation of actions and, possibly, the Latent Damage Act 1986 (see below). In *Iron Trade Mutual Insurance Co* v *Buckenham* [1989] 2 Lloyd's Rep 85, the plaintiffs were underwriters and brokers agents. The defendant firm were insurance and re-insurance brokers. From 1981, the defendants began refusing to pay out on certain contracts and, in 1984, they repudiated the contracts altogether, alleging that the contracts were voidable for non-disclosure of material facts. The plaintiffs sued the brokers for losses occasioned by this, framing their action in contract and tort. The defendants' main defence was limitation – the contracts were mainly from 1976 to 1981.

Three questions arose:

1. When did the plaintiffs' cause of action accrue?
2. Could the plaintiffs rely on the Latent Damage Act as a means of delaying the limitation period?
3. If the LDA, applied, what was the relevant starting date for the purposes of the Act?

HELD: the decision of the court, based as it was on the three questions listed above, found that the Act had no application to claims founded on contract, even when the duty concerned is simply a contractual duty to take reasonable care. Therefore, the questions as listed need not be considered further.

This is a difficult point of law, illustrating the present uncertainty of the law over the notion of concurrent liability in contract and tort. It has always been accepted that the Latent Damage Act 1986 applied to tort; whether or not the provisions of the Act can be extended to cover contractual liability is now open to doubt. Despite the negative decision in this particular case, this issue is not fully resolved.

Note that the Law Commission has, in Working Paper 114, August 1990, entitled 'Contributory Negligence as a Defence in Contract' provisionally recommended that when loss results partly from the plaintiff's own conduct and partly from the defendant's breach of contract, damages should be apportioned as appropriate. It suggests that apportionment is particularly appropriate for breaches of contractual duty to take care, but should also be applicable for breaches of strict contractual duty. In considering apportionment of damages, a court should have regard to the nature and extent of the duty and, possibly, how far it is possible to exclude apportionment in the relevant contract.

16.5   Measure of damages

Damages will be quantified on one of three bases as stated above:

1. Reliance loss, that is, cost to the plaintiff of reliance on the contract.
2. Restitution, that is, benefits obtained by the defendant under the contract.
3. Loss of bargain, that is, the plaintiff claims to be put in the same position as if the contract had been performed.

The last named requires further investigation.

Loss of bargain

Where the plaintiff claims for loss of bargain and that he be put in the position as if the contract had been performed, two bases of assessment are available: cost of cure; and difference in value.

In *Peevyhouse* v *Garland Coal Co* (1962) 382 P 2d 109, a coal company took a mining lease of farmland, covenanting to restore the land to its original state at the end of the lease. The work at the end of the lease would have cost $29,000, while the result of not doing it would reduce the value of the land by only $300.

HELD: damages for the company's failure to do the work should be assessed at the latter sum.

In the majority of cases where there is a discretion, the court will exercise this to use the most appropriate basis of assessment in the case. Certain prima facie rules exist for working out the appropriate mode of assessment.

1. In sale of goods contracts if a defect can be cured at a reasonable cost, the cost of cure will be awarded, otherwise the difference in value is awarded.
2. In building contracts, cost of cure basis is usual, and the builder must put the defects right. However, if the cost of cure is greater than the whole value of the

building, then only the difference in value will be awarded. See *Morris* v *Redland Bricks* [1970] AC 652.

3. Certain statutes prescribe which method of assessment is to be used, for example, s18 Landlord and Tenant Act 1927, the difference in value is to be used.

Actual and market values

Where damages are based on the difference in value principle, then market values may be taken into account to assess the plaintiff's loss.

If there is a market value against which the plaintiff's loss can be assessed, then the loss will be, prima facie, quantified by reference to it, but other factors may be taken into account.

Where the defendants fail to deliver goods or render services, then the plaintiff can go into the market and obtain these goods or services at the prevailing price. Therefore, the plaintiff's damages will be the difference between the market price and the price of the goods or services in the contract. See *Watts, Watt & Co* v *Mitsui* [1917] AC 227.

HELD: that if a carrier completely fails to deliver goods which he has contracted to carry, then the owner of the goods is entitled to their market value at the place and time fixed for delivery.

Under s51 Sale of Goods Act 1979, where a seller wrongfully neglects or refuses to deliver the goods to the buyer, the buyer may maintain an action against the seller for damages for non-delivery. But such an action will not allow the seller to recover for anything more than the difference between the market value and the actual value. Therefore, the plaintiff will not be able to recover any losses incurred by reason of not being able to make sub-sales.

In *Williams* v *Agius* [1914] AC 510, coal was sold at 16s. 3d. per ton. The buyer resold an equivalent amount at 19s. per ton. When the seller failed to deliver, the market price was 23s. 6d. The buyer went into the market to buy coal at 23s. 6d. and claimed damages.

HELD: The buyer could recover the difference between 16s. 3d. and 23s. 6d. The fact he had made a sub-sale at 19s was irrelevant, and the seller could not take advantage of this.

The sub-sale is irrelevant in assessing damages whether it was above or below market price.

In *Williams* v *Reynolds* (1865) 6 B & S 495, cotton was sold to the plaintiff at 16s. 3/4d., and the plaintiff resold it at 19s. 3/4d.. The defendant failed to deliver when the market price was 18s. 1/4d. The plaintiff failed to go into the market at that time to purchase to satisfy his sub-sale and market prices subsequently rose.

HELD: the plaintiff could only recover 1s. 1/2d. per ton damages as he should have gone into the market and mitigated. He was not entitled to the difference between the purchase price (16s. 3/4d.) and the sub-sale price (19s. 3/4d.).

Therefore, the defendant may not be allowed to take advantage of a sub-sale, as *Williams* v *Agius* illustrates. However, the plaintiff is at the same time permitted to have any mitigation which he undertakes taken into account, and the fact he goes into the market to do so is considered. If he fails to mitigate, then this is held against him.

Sub-sales are taken into consideration on one exceptional occasion, where the contract is one for specific or particular goods.

In *Re Hall and Pim's Arbitration* (1928) 139 LT 50, a cargo of wheat was sold for 51s. 9d. per quarter and resold by the buyer for 56s. 9d. per quarter. The seller refused delivery when the market price was 53s. 9d.

HELD: that the seller were liable for the difference between 51s. 9d. and 56s. 9d. The market price was to be disregarded because the buyers could not buy this particular cargo, which they had resold, on the market.

Late delivery as opposed to non-delivery has entitled the court to take into account a sub-sale.

In *Wertheim* v *Chicoutimi Pulp* [1911] AC 301, the defendant sold the plaintiff 3,000 tons of wood pulp for delivery in November at 25s. a ton. The pulp was not delivered until the following June. In November, the market value was 70s. per ton but in June it was only 42s. per ton. The plaintiff had in fact resold at 65s. per ton.

HELD: the plaintiff was entitled to damages of 5s. per ton, that is, the difference between the actual price and the market price at the agreed date of delivery, 65s. and 70s. He was not entitled to the difference between 42s. 6d., the market price in June, and 70s., the market price at the agreed date for delivery.

The latter, that is, damages of 27s. 6d. would allow the plaintiff to make a profit out of the breach.

It is submitted that the above is incorrect since the plaintiff would not have been making a profit out of the breach but, instead, his sub-sale would appear to have given the defendant the advantage of the plaintiff's business acumen.

Where there has been a delivery of goods which are defective, then the loss will, prima facie, be the difference between the market value and the value of the goods actually delivered. The sub-sale above or below the market price is ignored unless the sub-sale concerns some sort of unique goods. If the buyer chooses, he may reject the defective goods and then demand restitution of the price paid.

If the buyer refuses to accept and pay for goods, then the seller can go into the market and sell the goods at the prevailing price. The seller is not entitled to any damages if he sells in the market above the contract price, but he can claim for loss of bargain if he sells below the contract price.

Where there is no market

In the case of non-delivery of such goods, the court will assess the loss as best it can on the evidence before it. Relevant facts may include loss of the goods, their carriage and a reasonable profit.

In *The Arpad* [1934] P 189, sale of a cargo of wheat which was not marketable. The plaintiff made a sub-sale at 36s. per quarter, but the wheat was never delivered. The court did not assess the plaintiff's damages at the difference between the purchase price and, in this case, the sub-sale price since the court decided the price of other wheat in the market ought to be considered in any case.

Failure to accept and pay for goods which do not have a market will result in damages being quantified by reference to the actual proceeds of a sub-sale, so long as such sub-sales are reasonable.

Loss of profit

If the plaintiff has lost profit on the resale of the subject matter of the contract because of the defendant's breach, then the defendant will only be liable for this, subject to the rules above, if he should have reasonably seen or contemplated that the plaintiff was going to make a resale.

If the defendant wrongfully refuses to accept and pay for the goods, then the plaintiff can sue for the loss of profit on that transaction in certain circumstances.

In *Thompson v Robinson (Gunmakers) Ltd* [1955] Ch 177, the defendant bought a Vanguard car from the plaintiff, and later refused to accept and pay for it. The plaintiff's profit would have been £61.

HELD: where, as here, the supply of Vanguard cars exceeded the demand, had the plaintiff found another customer and sold to him as well as the defendant, then there would have been two sales and two profits. Therefore the defendant was liable for £61.

If there is a limited number of sales which the plaintiff could make because of, for example, shortages of the goods or services he is supplying, then there will be no damage for loss of profits if the defendant defaults.

In *Charter v Sullivan* [1957] 2 QB 117, the defendant bought a Hillman Minx car from the plaintiff but refused to accept it. The plaintiff's profit would have been £97, but he failed to recover this from the defendant as he could only sell as many cars as he could get from the makers.

Damages for distress and (see below) inconvenience

These are always assessed fairly stringently. The case of *Watts v Morrow* [1991] 1 WLR 1421 concerned inter alia the measure of damages for 'distress and inconvenience' caused by a negligent surveyor's report. The Court of Appeal felt that subject to certain restricted categories of exceptions damages for distress and inconvenience had little part to play in contractual compensation and an award of £4,000 was drastically reduced to £1,500.

16.6   Type of damage recoverable

In *Addis* v *Gramophone Co Ltd* [1909] AC 488, Lord Atkinson said:

> 'I have always understood that damages for breach of contract were in the nature of compensation, not punishment.'

The general rule of law applicable to such cases was in effect stated by Cockburn CJ, in *Engell* v *Fitch* (1868) LR 3 QB 314, at 330:

> 'By the law of England as a general rule, a vendor, who from whatever cause fails to perform his contract, is bound, as was said by Lord Wensleydale in the case referred to, to place the purchaser, so far as money will do it, in the position he would have been had the contract been performed.'

To the above principle there are exceptions. In some cases, as a matter of policy, or because of inherent difficulties in assessing whether any actual damage has occurred, damages are irrecoverable. In other cases, exemplary damages are recoverable because the type of breach is looked upon by law as socially reprehensible and, therefore, is discouraged in this way. Finally, damages are recoverable in circumstances which do not readily fall within the compensatory principle.

Damages which are irrecoverable

Injury to reputation
If the plaintiff's reputation in injured as a result of a breach of contract, then he cannot recover damages for this in addition to damages for the breach itself. The plaintiff's remedy in these circumstances is in tort, for example, defamation, and he should pursue the appropriate remedy in tort.

In *Hurst* v *Picture Theatres Ltd* [1915] 1 KB 1, the plaintiff was forcibly ejected from a cinema seat for which he had paid 6*d*. He brought an action in tort for assault and false imprisonment and not in contract, and recovered £150 damages. Much of this £150 was compensation for the injury the plaintiff had suffered to his reputation; such damage would clearly have been irrecoverable in contract. Indeed, the damages recoverable in contract would appear to have been minimal – probably only the 6*d*. price of the seat.

Injury to feelings
The plaintiff may be able to recover damages for such injuries in tort, but in contract such damages are irrecoverable.

In *Addis* v *Gramophone Company* [1909] AC 488, the plaintiff could be dismissed by his employers on six months' notice, which he was given but, at the same time, a new manager was appointed to take his place and the plaintiff was prevented from acting as manager. The plaintiff claimed damages for the harsh and humiliating manner in which he was dismissed, as well as for loss of salary and commission after his dismissal.

HELD: the plaintiff was only entitled to the commission and salary he had lost, and not to damages because his dismissal was harsh and humiliating.

'I can conceive nothing more objectionable and embarrassing in litigation than trying in effect an action of libel or slander as a matter of aggravation in an action for illegal dismissal' (per Lord Atkinson).

The principle established in *Addis* was reaffirmed by the Court of Appeal in *Bliss v South East Thames Regional Health Authority* [1985] IRLR 308.

Failure to make title to land

No damages are recoverable in this situation in the absence of fraud because of 'the peculiar difficulty in making a title to land in England'.

Elliott v *Pierson* [1948] 1 All ER 939 per Harman J applying the rule laid down by the House of Lords in *Bain* v *Fothergill* (1874) LR 7 HL 158.

In *Sharneyford Supplies Ltd* v *Edge* [1987] 1 All ER 588, the Court of Appeal expressed the view that now that registered title to land is general the rationale for the rule in *Bain* v *Fothergill* is no longer valid and the rule should be abolished.

Note that s3 Law of Property (Miscellaneous Provisions) Act 1989 did, finally, abolish the rule in *Bain* v *Fothergill* as from September 1989.

Now that the rule of *Bain* v *Fothergill* has been formally abolished, the following case is of interest.

In *Grangeville Marketing Inc* v *Seven Seas Properties Ltd* [1990] EGCS 23, in a contract for the sale of land there occurred, because of delay, a breach of contract; the vendor's delay was due to an inability to show good title. The plaintiff claimed damages for loss of profit on a prompt resale of the property in question, and loss of profit from renovating the property and selling individual flats. The defendant conceded that the delay amounted to breach of contract, but argued that the delay was caused by defect in title, and the plaintiff was precluded by the rule in *Bain* v *Fothergill* from recovering for loss or profit of the failure of the bargain.

HELD: a certificate was granted for leave to appeal direct to the House of Lords. It was for the Appellate Committee of the House of Lords to consider whether the rule in *Bain* v *Fothergill* (which had been criticised and subsequently abolished by s3 Law of Property (Miscellaneous Provisions) Act 1989, as from September 1989) should be applied in the present case.

At the time of writing, the House of Lords' decision is not known. On the face of it, it seems unlikely that the rule will, after so much criticism, be resurrected in any form whatsoever.

Exemplary damages

Dishonoured cheque

Where a cheque is wrongfully dishonoured, a trader on whose account it is drawn is entitled to substantial damages without pleading and proving actual damages.

In *Gibbons* v *Westminster Bank Ltd* [1939] 2 KB 882, this exception would appear from the cases to apply to traders only, and seems to be based on the principle that commercial reputation must be protected. If this is so, then not only is there an exception to the rule that damages are irrecoverable for injury to reputation, but that the exception operates merely on the proof of the cheque being dishonoured.

A non-trader would appear to be capable of recovering damages for dishonour of his cheque only if he pleads and proves them and then only as compensation.

Wrongful eviction

Under the Rent Act 1977 and Protection from Eviction Act 1977, a landlord who fails to give the appropriate notice to quit to his tenant will be liable for exemplary damages if he then attempts to wrongfully evict him. See *Drane* v *Evangelou* [1978] 1 WLR 455 as an example.

Other types of damage

Damage to commercial reputation

If the plaintiff's cheques are dishonoured and he is a trader, then he will have alternative remedies. But, if a plaintiff's commercial reputation is damaged in other ways, then he may recover.

In *Anglo-Continental Holidays* v *Typaldos Lines* [1967] 2 Lloyd's Rep 61, a travel agent recovered damages for loss of 'goodwill' from a shipowner who broke a contract to supply passengers with accommodation on a pleasure cruise.

The plaintiff may even be able to recover damages for loss of an opportunity to enhance his commercial reputation.

In *Herbert Clayton* v *Oliver* [1930] AC 209, an actor or author it was held, could recover damages for 'loss of publicity', but not for injury to existing reputation.

If the plaintiff's commercial reputation is damaged because he has been supplied with defective goods by a manufacturer or wholesaler, then he may recover damages. See *Cointat* v *Myham* [1913] 2 KB 220.

Discomfort, vexation and disappointment

In *Jarvis* v *Swan Tours* [1973] 2 QB 233, the plaintiff, a solicitor, went on a Swan Tour and, as a result, he sued for damages because the hotels fell short of the standards promised, and the buses were not of the standard promised.

HELD: that the plaintiff could recover damages for the disappointment and discomfort he had been caused as a result.

And see again *Jackson* v *Horizon Holidays* – discussed in Chapter 12 – where the plaintiff was allowed damages for distress and disappointment when his holiday fell far short of the defendant's promises.

There is, however, a limit to damages for distress for breach of contract. In *Bliss* v *South East Thames Regional Health Authority* [1987] ICR 700, Dillon LJ stated that such damages should be confined to cases 'where the contract which has been broken was itself a contract to provide peace of mind or freedom from distress'. In *Hayes* v *James and Charles Dodd* (1988) The Times 14 July, Staughton LJ said that:

'... it might be that the class was somewhat wider than that. But it should not include any case where the object of the contract was not comfort or pleasure or the relief of discomfort, but simply carrying on a commercial activity with a view to profit.'

Currency of damages

In the normal way of things, the currency in which damages are actually estimated and awarded has little significance. The amount will be the same, whatever foreign currency is nominated. In a very few cases, however, the choice of currency may make a considerable difference to the fairness, or otherwise, of the award.

In *The Texaco Melbourne* (1991) Financial Times 7 August following a breach of contract, it fell to be decided whether damages should be paid in US dollars or Ghanaian cedis.

The court held that in deciding such a matter regard should be had to the currency in which the loss was felt, but also to what was fair and equitable. Although the ship owners had felt the loss in cedis, because the value of the cedi had fallen drastically since the time of the contract, and because of stringent Ghanaian currency controls, it would be more reasonable to quantify the award in dollars.

Inconvenience

In *Bailey* v *Bullock* [1950] 2 All ER 1167, a solicitor failed to take proceedings to recover his client's house for him and was held liable in damages for the inconvenience caused by reason of the client having to live with his wife's parents for two years.

In *Cook* v *Spanish Holidays* (1960) The Times 6 February, a honeymoon couple recovered damages for the disappointment and inconvenience caused to them by a travel agent who failed to provide them with holiday accommodation.

Diminution of future prospects

In *Dunk* v *George Waller* [1970] 2 QB 163, an apprentice was wrongfully dismissed, but had he been allowed to complete his apprenticeship he would have got a certificate entitling him to certain jobs at certain wages. Without this certificate, his chances were lessened and he claimed damages for diminution of future prospects.

HELD: he was entitled to damages on this basis as the object of his apprenticeship was to enable him to get better employment.

In *Edwards* v *SOGAT* [1971] Ch 354, the plaintiff was wrongfully expelled from a trade union which resulted in his loss of employment. It was held that he could recover damages for the loss of employment opportunities which would follow from this.

Speculative damages

If the plaintiff's loss is the chance of doing something or benefiting from doing something, and this contingency is outside the control of the parties, then he is entitled to damages if the defendant's breach of contract denies him this chance.

In *Chaplin* v *Hicks* [1911] 2 KB 786, the plaintiff recovered damages for loss of the chance to take part in a beauty contest.

Speculative damages are usually a last resort since if the plaintiff could prove the value of his loss, then he could claim for loss of bargain. In *Simpson* v *L & N Railway* and *Victoria Laundry* v *Newman Industries*, the loss of profits on contracts which might have been made were speculative in character.

There can be no damages for the loss of a chance which depends entirely on the discretion of the defendant and he exercises this discretion against the plaintiff.

In *Lavarack* v *Woods of Colchester Ltd* [1967] 1 QB 278, the defendant contracted to employ the plaintiff at £4,000 pa plus such bonus, if any, as the defendant should from time to time determine. The defendant wrongfully dismissed the plaintiff and, afterwards, discontinued their bonus scheme, but increased salaries in lieu of the bonus.

The question arose as to whether the plaintiff's damages be increased to include increase in salary in lieu of bonus.

HELD: the plaintiff was not entitled to the increase in salary in lieu of bonus. His contract provided only for £4,000 pa plus bonus. The defendant was under no contractual obligation to the plaintiff to continue the bonus, and the fact that it was discontinued meant the plaintiff was only entitled to £4,000.

Quantification of speculative damages requires a valuation of the expected benefit and an assessment of the plaintiff's chances of getting it. Therefore, if the lost chance was that of entering a beauty contest, the plaintiff can only recover for this lost chance and not the full prize which she might have won.

16.7   Mitigation of damages

It is the duty of every plaintiff to mitigate his loss, that is, to do his best not to increase the amount of damage done.

There are three rules:

1. The plaintiff cannot recover for loss which is consequent upon the defendant's breach of contract where the plaintiff could have avoided the loss by taking reasonable steps.
2. The plaintiff cannot recover for any loss he has actually avoided, even though he took more steps than were necessary in compliance with the rule above.
3. The plaintiff may recover loss incurred in taking reasonable steps to mitigate his loss, even though he did not succeed.

Avoidable loss

The plaintiff must minimise the loss resulting from the breach by taking all reasonable steps available to him. If he fails to do so, then he cannot recover anything in respect of that extra loss.

In *Payzu* v *Saunders* [1919] 2 KB 581, the plaintiff agreed to buy certain goods from the defendant over a period of nine months with payment within one month of delivery, and deliveries monthly. The plaintiff failed to make prompt payment for the first instalment, and the defendant, in breach of contract, refused to deliver any more instalments under the contract, but offered to deliver the goods at the contract price if the plaintiff paid cash on delivery of the order. The plaintiff refused this and claimed damages, these being the difference between the contract price and the market price.

HELD: the plaintiff had permitted himself to sustain a large measure of the loss which, as prudent and reasonable people, they ought to have avoided. He had the cash available to meet the defendant's demands and could have mitigated by purchasing off the defendant at the contract price as the defendant offered, instead of going into the market to purchase at a higher price. He was, therefore, not entitled to damages.

However, not every new offer by the defendant will be regarded as one which the plaintiff must accept in order to mitigate the effects of the breach. In a contract of employment situation, if the plaintiff is wrongfully dismissed for alleged dishonesty made before others, he need not return if his employer offers to take him back. Similarly, if the plaintiff is wrongfully dismissed, he need not take a labouring job where he previously had a professional job. If, however, the plaintiff is offered alternative employment by an employer who has wrongfully dismissed him without cause, then the plaintiff must accept this in mitigation if it is a reasonable alternative.

In *Brace* v *Calder* [1895] 2 QB 253, the common law in the area of dismissals from employment has now been largely superseded by the statutory provisions of the Employment Protection (Consolidation) Act 1978.

The plaintiff is not expected to take risks in order to mitigate losses caused by the defendant's breach.

In *Pilkington* v *Wood* [1953] Ch 770, a solicitor in breach of contract obtained for the plaintiff a house which had a defective title. The plaintiff tried to sue the solicitor, who argued that the plaintiff should have mitigated by suing the vendor under the covenants for title under s76 LPA 1925.

HELD:

'The so-called duty to mitigate does not go so far as to oblige the injured party, even under an indemnity, to embark on a complicated and difficult piece of litigation against a third party ... it is no part of the plaintiff's duty to embark on the proposed litigation in order to protect his solicitor from the consequences of his own carelessness' (per Harman J).

The plaintiff must not take unreasonable steps which would actually increase the loss; if he does, he will not recover such losses. Therefore, if the plaintiff is aware of the defendant's breach, he must not continue to incur expense in order to prepare for performance when it is clear the defendant will not accept it.

In *Gebruder Metalmann* v *NBR* [1984] 1 Lloyd's Rep 614, Gebruder Metalmann sold goods to NBR, both being dealers in sugar. NBR repudiated the contract before the date for delivery of the goods, and Gebruder Metalmann accepted the repudiation. On the question whether the proper date for assessment of damages was the date the repudiation was accepted, or the date performance should have been made by delivery, the Court of Appeal held that the correct date was the date for delivery, subject to the seller doing everything reasonable, between the date of repudiation and the date for delivery, to sell the goods or otherwise mitigate its loss.

This case illustrates the need for the mitigating step taken to be *reasonable*, and where there are two reasonable courses of action open to the plaintiff, either will be sufficient to mitigate the damage.

No recovery for avoided loss

If the plaintiff obtains any benefits as a result of his mitigation, these must be brought into account; for example, if the plaintiff is wrongfully dismissed and then finds a comparable job elsewhere, the earnings of this job will be taken into account in assessing damages for wrongful dismissal. Other benefits which accrue to the plaintiff, but which he was not bound to do in mitigation, may be taken into account.

A benefit in order to be considered as received in mitigation, must be a direct benefit resulting from the breach and not a collateral benefit.

In *British Westinghouse* v *Underground Electric Rly of London* [1912] AC 673, A agreed to supply B with turbines of stated efficiency, but supplied less efficient ones, which used more coal. B accepted them and used them for some years before replacing them with turbines which were even more efficient than those specified in the contract with A. After replacement B, claimed damages from A.

HELD: B was under no duty to mitigate by buying new turbines, but since he had done so, the financial advantages he had gained from new turbines had to be taken into account. Thus, as B's saving in coal exceeded the cost of the new turbines, he was not entitled to damages. If B had claimed damages before buying the new turbines, A would have had no defence.

If P insures against a loss which may occur in the event of a breach, then this cannot be relied on by the defendant as mitigation, since it is a collateral benefit.

Note *Bradburn* v *GW Rly* (1874) LR 10 Ex 1. The defendant cannot rely on a profitable sub-sale by the plaintiff as mitigation either. See also *Williams Bros* v *Agius* (above).

Mitigation and anticipatory breach

The duty to mitigate does not apply to compel an innocent party to accept an anticipatory breach of contract, even though by failing to do so the plaintiff can increase the defendant's liability. See *White & Carter* v *McGregor*.

Compare with *Clea* v *Bulk Oil* [1984] 1 All ER 129. C chartered a ship to B. After a year (the charter was for two years), the ship broke down and was put in for repairs. B informed C that it no longer wanted the ship, but C carried out the repairs and, on their completion, offered the ship as ready once again; again B said it was not wanted. C took no steps to find an alternative charterer, and kept the ship fully crewed. On the question whether C was entitled to continue performance of the contract, or should have repudiated it and sued for damages, Lloyd J refused to interfere with the arbitrator's finding that C should have accepted the repudiation made on completion of the repairs, and could not recover the cost of hire under the charterparty; instead C had to sue for breach of contract.

In this case, Lloyd J confirmed the general principle that the victim of a repudiation of contract has a right to choose whether to accept the repudiation and bring the contract to an end, or to waive the repudiation and contined his performance of it. Where the contract is a continuing one, and the parties have future obligations under it, this right must be subject to the court finding that a victim has no 'substantial interest' in continuing to perform, and must repudiate: in *White & Carter* there was such an interest.

16.8 Liquidated damages clauses

General

The parties to the contract may make a genuine assessment of the losses which are likely to result in the event of a breach, and stipulate that such sum shall be payable in the event of a breach of contract.

Such clauses enable a party to know his liability in advance. If, however, the clause is not an assessment of losses, but intended as punishment on the contract-breaker, then the clause is a penalty clause and is void.

Note in this context the recent Privy Council case of *Golden Bay Realty Ltd* v *Orchard Twelve Investments Ltd* [1991] 1 WLR 981 in which it is made clear that contracts drawn up in statutory form cannot be said to incorporate penalty clauses.

A contract made in Singapore for the sale of commercial property was made in accordance with the relevant statutes as applicable locally. This included the Sale of Commercial Properties Act 1979, which provided inter alia that if the vendor failed to complete by the prescribed date he should pay liquidated damages, calculated as according to the SCP Act. The vendors failed to complete on the appointed day and were thus liable to pay the purchaser liquidated damages until he did finally complete, some two years later. The vendor appealed against this payment on the basis that it amounted to a penalty clause.

The Privy Council, supporting the Singapore Court of Appeal, refused relief from the provisions of the Act; holding that where the terms and conditions of a contract are prescribed by legislation, the usual rules as to penalty clauses do not apply. The vendor was not entitled to question the validity of the provision relating to liquidated damages by claiming it was penal in nature. Regardless of the purpose of the Act, damages were entitled to be recovered, calculated in accordance with the statutory formula.

A liquidated damages clause will be effective in the event of a breach, and the plaintiff will not recover more than that sum. No action for unliquidated damages will be allowed. Where the clause is a penalty clause, then in an action for breach of contract it is disregarded.

Penalty or liquidated damages?

The parties may often be in dispute over whether the clause was a penalty or a liquidated damages clause. Various rules have been formulated to deal with such contingencies.

The mere fact that a payment is described in a contract as a 'penalty' is not, of itself, decisive. The court will look at the construction of the clause itself and the surrounding circumstances and may, on these, conclude that what is described as a penalty clause is, in fact, a liquidated damages clause. See *Kemble* v *Farren* (1829) 6 Bing 141.

In *Dunlop Pneumatic Tyre Co* v *New Garage* [1915] AC 79, Lord Dunedin laid down three rules concerning penalty clauses:

1. The use of the words 'penalty' or 'liquidated damages' may prima facie be supposed to mean what they say, yet the expression used is not conclusive.
2. The essence of a penalty is a payment of money as in terrorem of the offending party; the essence of liquidated damages is a genuine convenanted pre-estimate of damage. See *Clydebank Engineering* v *Don Jose Ramos* [1905] AC 6.
3. Whether a sum stipulated is penalty or liquidated damages is a question of construction to be decided upon the terms and inherent circumstances of each particular contract, judged as of the time of making the contract, not as at the time of breach.

In *Public Works Commissioners* v *Hills* [1906] AC 368, Lord Dunedin then mentioned four tests which would prove helpful, or even conclusive, in deciding if the clause was a 'penalty' or 'liquidated damages'.

First, it will be held to be a penalty if the sum stipulated for is extravagant and unconscionable in amount in comparison to the greatest loss that could conceivably be proved to have followed from the breach. For example, if a builder contracts to do work worth £50 with a clause stipulating that he pay £1m if he fails to do the work, it is clearly a penalty.

Secondly, it will be held to be a penalty if the breach consists only in not paying a sum of money, and the sum stipulated is a sum greater than the sum which ought to have been paid. For example, a clause to make a debtor pay £1,000 if he failed to pay £50 on the due day.

In cases under this category, the rule will apply even if the contract is in every respect a fair one. Thus, in *Betts* v *Birch* (1859) 4 H & N 506, a contract for the sale of the furniture and stock in trade of a public house which contained a clause for the payment of £50 if either party should default, was held to be a contract with a penalty clause even though the bargain was fair.

In subsequent cases, the courts have attempted to overcome the effects of this rule by narrow construction. The cases on this point were decided before the *Dunlop* case and whether they are still good law is undecided. If they are, equity would, in many cases, be able to strike down the bargains as unconscionable.

In *Proctor Loan Co* v *Grice* (1880) 5 QBD 592, a debtor owing a debt payable in instalments, promised that on default on any instalment he would pay the whole balance.

HELD: this clause was not penal as it only accelerated, rather than increased, the liability of the debtor.

In *Wallis* v *Smith* (1892) 21 Ch D 243, a contract to develop a building estate stipulated that the defendant was to pay £500 on signing and £5,000 on the occurrence of 'any substantial breach'. The defendant failed to pay the £500 on signing and repudiated the whole contract.

HELD: that the failure to pay the £500 was not a substantial breach, but the plaintiff could recover the £5,000 from the defendant in any case because the defendant had repudiated the whole contract.

Thirdly, there is a presumption (but no more) that it is a penalty when

'a single lump sum is made payable by way of compensation on the occurrence of one or more or all of several events, some of which may occasion serious and others but trifling damage' (Lord Watson in *Lord Elphinstone* v *Monkland* (1886) 11 App Cas 332).

Finally, it is no obstacle to the sum stipulated being a genuine pre-estimate of damage, that the consequences of the breach are such as to make precise pre-estimation almost an impossibility.

In *Dunlop Pneumatic Tyre Co* v *New Garage* [1915] AC 79, the defendant bought tyres from the plaintiff and agreed not to: tamper with manufacturer's marks; sell below the list price; sell to any person blacklisted by the plaintiff; exhibit or export tyres without the plaintiff's consent. The defendant agreed to pay £5 for every tyre he sold or offered in breach of the agreement. In breach, the defendant sold to the public below the list price.

HELD: the provision for payment of £5 was not penal. Looking at the language of the contract itself, the character of the transaction and the circumstances, it was clear that the provision was to prevent a price war and so protect the plaintiff's sales. The clause was, therefore, an attempt to estimate damage at a certain figure and as the figure was not extravagant, it could only be concluded that it was a bargain to truly assess damages and not a penalty clause.

In *Jobson* v *Johnson* [1989] 1 WLR 1026, in a transaction for the transfer of shares in a football club, provision was made for default. The Court of Appeal held that whether a particular clause was penal or not was entirely a question of construction, to be decided in the light of circumstances at the time of making the contract.

Careful drafting of a contract may, however, enable a party to circumvent the rules relating to penalty clauses as appears from the case of *Lombard North Central plc* v *Butterworth* [1987] 1 All ER 267. A contract of hire provided that should the defendant default in the payment of any one instalment, he would be required to pay all past arrears of the hire charges, plus all future charges for the entire remaining period of hire. The Court of Appeal held that the term was a penalty. The plaintiffs, however, recovered the same sum as damages, as under the agreement punctual payment was a condition, the breach of which entitled the plaintiffs to repudiate the contract and recover damages for the loss of the whole transaction.

Clauses which underestimate damages

Where the contract has underestimated damages in the event of a breach, either because of inflation, or through bad bargaining, then damages will be limited to the amount stipulated by the contract.

A distinction may be drawn in such cases between a pure limitation clause, which specifies that damages shall be limited to a maximum figure of, for example, £10,000, and that the plaintiff can have such loss as he can prove up to this limit, and liquidated damages clauses. In the former, the plaintiff, as stated, can only receive what he proves. Thus, if he can only prove £100 damages, he will receive only £100. In the latter, the plaintiff will, on proving the breach, receive the stipulated sum regardless of whether these damages were above or below that amount, subject to the rule about penalty clauses.

In *Cellulose Acetate* v *Widnes Foundries* [1933] AC 20, the defendant agreed to build a chemical plant for the plaintiff in 18 weeks. If it took longer than this, they agreed to pay 'by way of penalty £20 per working week'. The defendant completed 30 weeks late, and the plaintiff lost £5,850 as a result of the delay. The defendant argued they were only liable for £600 damages.

HELD: the plaintiff could only receive £600. The clause was not a penalty clause although it was described as such, because its object was not to act in terrorem. The parties must have known that the actual loss would be more than £20 per week, and the clause would, therefore, appear to have been an attempt to limit liability. However, the clause was not a pure limitation clause, because it also fixed the minimum payable for delay. The defendant would, therefore, still have had to pay £20 per week had the plaintiff lost less.

If the clause is, in fact, a penalty clause, then as it is void, the plaintiff can ignore it and sue for his actual loss.

In *Wall* v *Rederiaktiebolaget Luggude* [1915] 3 KB 66, it was held that a shipowner could disregard a penalty clause and sue for the actual loss he suffered where it exceeded the amount of the penalty. If the clause provides for a payment in excess of the loss and is a penalty clause, it is unclear whether the plaintiff can rely on it. However, it would appear wrong to allow the plaintiff to take the benefit of such clauses when he can ignore them when they are to his detriment.

If the clause has been affected by inflation, then it would appear that the only remedy for the parties is to revise it themselves. However, it may be possible as a matter of construction to have it revised by the court, if it is clear that the clause is no longer effective for the purposes envisaged by the parties. See *Staffs Area Health Authority* v *Staffs Waterworks* [1978] 3 All ER 769 at p777 per Lord Denning MR.

Payments which are not liquidated damages

Some contracts stipulate for payment of a particular sum on the happening of certain events other than breach of the contract itself. These payments are not liquidated damages, and the distinction between liquidated damages and penalties is inapplicable.

In *Alder* v *Moore* [1961] 2 QB 57, the defendant, a professional footballer, received £500 from an insurance company for an injury which was supposed to have disabled him. He signed a declaration that he would not play professional football again and that 'in the event of infringement of this condition, he will be subject to a penalty of the amount paid him in settlement of his claim'. The defendant began playing football four months after signing the declaration and the plaintiff sought recovery of the £500. The defendant argued the clause was a penalty and that the underwriters had suffered no loss by his playing football again.

HELD: that this was a contract for the payment of a certain sum in a certain event which was not a breach of contract, and that the event having happened, the sum was payable. See also *Exports Credit* v *Universal Oil Products* [1983] 2 All ER 205.

Problems arise where a clause contains provision for payments on the occurrence of several different events and some of these are penal and some are not. The problem is usually associated with hire purchase agreements. The rules are as follows:

1. If the clause stipulates for payment on the hirer's breach, then the clause is penal and void. See *Cooden Engineering* v *Stanford* [1953] 1 QB 86.
2. If the agreement is determined on some ground other than the hirer's breach, then the law as to penalties does not apply. For example, where the hirer exercises his right to return the goods. See *Associated Distributors* v *Hall* [1938] 2 KB 83.
3. Where the agreement contains a minimum payment clause, then it will be regarded as penal unless the minimum payment is very small. See *Lamdon Trust*

v *Murrell* [1955] 1 WLR 391. A minimum payment clause which provided for the payment of three-quarters of the hire-purchase price on determination, was held to be penal, because it was payable regardless of whether the hirer defaulted on the first or last instalment.

Any attempts to apportion the minimum payment clause according to the seriousness of the breach is disapproved of. In *Bridge* v *Campbell Discount* [1962] AC 600, the plaintiff bought a car on hire-purchase and paid a deposit plus one monthly instalment. He could not keep up the payments and returned the car to the finance company. Clause 9 of the agreement required the plaintiff to pay, by way of depreciation, such sum as would make his total payments up to two-thirds of the purchase price (£206 in this case). Although this clause was to compensate for depreciation, it in fact decreased the amount payable, the longer the plaintiff kept the goods and continued the payments.

HELD: that the clause was penal because if the plaintiff was liable to pay the

'penal sum of £206 without relief of any kind ... It means that equity has committed itself to this absurd paradox: it will grant relief to a man who breaks his contract but will penalize the man who keeps it' (per Lord Denning).

Withholding payments

This can often be a penalty unless the contract stipulates that there will be no payment until performance is completed.

In *Gilbert-Ash* v *Modern Engineering* [1974] AC 689, a subcontractor was entitled to payments on the issue of architects' certificates, but the main contractor had, in the same contract, the right to withhold or suspend payments if the subcontractor 'failed to comply with any provisions' of the contract.

HELD: this provision was invalid as a penalty clause.

16.9   Deposit and part payment

Where a contract provides that the purchaser makes a part payment in advance, then this is recoverable by the plaintiff unless the contract provides to the contrary.

A deposit is a guarantee that the contract will be performed, and it is irrecoverable unless the contract specifies to the contrary. In most cases, the deposit, will also be regarded as part satisfaction of payment, for example, in contracts for the purchase of land, a deposit of 10 per cent is normal by the purchaser. This will be retained by the vendor if the purchaser fails to complete the contract but, in any event, if the purchaser completes it is regarded as part of the purchase price unless the contract provides to the contrary.

A deposit differs from a penalty in that it is payable before, not after, the breach. However, there is in substance no real difference between a deposit and a penalty.

In *Pye* v *British Automobile Commercial Syndicate* [1906] 1 KB 425, a car dealer agreed to buy ten cars, and paid a 'deposit' of £300 to be forfeited if he refused to accept any of the cars. He broke the contract and claimed back the £300.

HELD: the forfeiture clause was not penal because a breach was likely to have serious consequences for the seller's whole selling organisation and, therefore, their precise loss could not be assessed accurately in advance.

Whether or not the dealer could have got his 'deposit' back if the clause had been a penalty clause seems open to doubt.

Where a deposit is made on the purchase of land, then under s49(2) LPA 1925 the court can order repayment of the deposit even though it was not penal.

Where payment is to be by instalments and there is a forfeiture clause for default, the purchaser may obtain relief in two situations:

1. If the purchaser was willing and able to perform, then equity may extend the time for payment and/or order repayment of the forfeited payments. See *Starside Properties* v *Mustafa* [1974] 1 WLR 816.
2. If the purchaser was not willing and able to perform, he will not get his instalments back unless it is unconscionable for the vendor to keep them.

Mussen v *Van Diemen's Land Co* [1938] Ch 253 concerns sale of land for £321,000 with the price payable in instalments. The defendant could rescind if the plaintiff defaulted in payment. The plaintiff, in fact, defaulted after payment of £42,000 and claimed the return of this.

HELD: the plaintiff's claim must be rejected as he had freely entered the contract on agreed terms, which included terms that instalments paid were forfeited on default. If, however, the plaintiff had paid 90 per cent of the price, then it may well be regarded as unconscionable to allow the defendant to keep this.

16.10 Action for an agreed sum

General

This is an action for an agreed sum and neither more nor less. For example, the price of goods delivered or agreed remuneration for work done. Such actions differ from damages in that there are no questions of remoteness or quantification. The question is whether the plaintiff is entitled to the agreed sum, and the defendant will usually raise defences that either the goods were defective, or the work done unsatisfactorily.

Requirements for the action

The duty to pay the price must have arisen. Whether this has actually occurred will depend on the terms of the contract itself.

In *Mount* v *Oldham Corporation* [1973] 1 QB 309, a private school taking state scholars had an agreement with the Corporation for payment of fees which stipulated that fees were payable in advance. On the introduction of the comprehensive system, the Corporation withdrew pupils from the school without giving the customary one term's notice.

HELD: the headmaster could sue for fees payable in advance.

Section 49(2) Sale of Goods Act 1979 provides that if payment is to be made on a certain day irrespective of delivery, then the seller can sue for the price any time after that day.

In *Workman* v *Lloyds Brasileno* [1908] 1 KB 968, the plaintiff was constructing a ship for the defendant which was to be paid for by instalments.

HELD: the seller was entitled to sue for instalments as they became due.

The conduct of the injured party

The plaintiff can elect to terminate the contract and sue for damages which will take account of any sums payable under the contract but, in such cases, sums due after the contract terminated, under the terms of the contract, cannot be claimed.

The plaintiff can elect to treat the contract as still subsisting, and claim for what is due to him under it. In such cases, the plaintiff has done all that is required of him. For example, a seller who has delivered goods can sue for the price. But if the plaintiff has not done all that is required of him under the contract, he cannot bring an action for an agreed sum.

In *Denmark Productions* v *Boscobel Productions* [1969] 1 QB 699, a singer wrongfully repudiated a contract with his agent and the latter could not continue performance without the co-operation of the singer.

HELD: despite the fact that the agent could not perform without the co-operation of the guilty party, he could not be permitted to bring an action for an agreed sum, and could only claim for damages.

If the plaintiff continues performance after repudiation of the contract by the other party, he may be regarded as having an option which he, the plaintiff, has exercised to continue the contract and he can claim for agreed sums under the contract.

In *White and Carter Councils* v *MacGregor* [1962] AC 413 (and see above), the plaintiffs agreed to advertise the defendant's garage business on their litterbins for three years. The payment was to be 2s. per week for plates on litterbins and 5s. per annum towards the cost of a plate. The defendant repudiated on the day the contract was made, but the plaintiff nevertheless made the plates and displayed them. Then he sued for the full amount due on the contract.

HELD: the defendant's repudiation did not bring the contract to an end, but only gave the injured party an option as to whether to go on with the contract, but since the plaintiff had affirmed the contract it remained in full effect.

'It is settled as a fundamental rule of the law of contract that repudiation by one of the parties to a contract does not itself discharge it ... It follows that, if, as here, there was no acceptance (of the breach), the contract remains alive for the benefit of both parties and the party who has repudiated can change his mind, but it does not follow that the party at the receiving end of the proffered repudiation is bound to accept it before the time for performance and is left to his remedy in damages for breach' (per Lord Hodson).

If the plaintiff cannot perform without the co-operation of the defendant, then the contract will be at an end, and the plaintiff can only get damages. If the plaintiff could only have carried on with the defendant's co-operation, in the *MacGregor* case he would have only got damages in the circumstances. In *Sanders* v *Neale* [1974] 3 All ER 327, the plaintiff was wrongfully dismissed from his employment, and it was held he could only obtain damages and not an agreed sum.

In the *MacGregor* case, much depends on commercial considerations. If there is a small demand for the plaintiff's goods, then it may be reasonable for him to carry on with the contract. However, if demand is strong, the plaintiff would be acting unreasonably in not accepting repudiation, and may be penalised for not mitigating his loss. However, it is arguable that mitigation only applies to damages and not to an action for an agreed sum. Similarly, the plaintiff is entitled to continue performance where he would injure his repudiation if he discontinued, or when he has already entered contracts with third parties, to honour his contract with the defendant. In short, the rule in the *MacGregor* case will not be applied if the injured party has no 'substantial or legitimate interest' in completing performance. See *Clea* v *Bulk Oil* (above).

17

Remedies for Breach of Contract – Equitable Remedies

17.1 Specific performance: introduction

17.2 When damages are an inadequate remedy

17.3 Factors considered in awarding specific performance

17.4 Particular contracts

17.5 Specific performance and third parties

17.6 Injunction: introduction

17.7 Types of injunction

17.8 Damages in lieu of specific performance or injunction

17.1 Specific performance: introduction

There are cases where damages, although obtainable for the breach, are an inadequate remedy because they will not give the plaintiff adequate compensation for his loss. For example, the plaintiff may have contracted to purchase a particular plot of land from the defendant for which compensation can provide no satisfactory equivalent in the event of the defendant's breach.

Specific performance is an equitable remedy for breach of contract. The court has a discretion to order specific performance where it is just and equitable to do so. The plaintiff is not entitled to it as of right.

Note, however, that while specific performance (and other equitable remedies) may not be available as of right, any attempt in a contract to exclude such remedies will be void. In *Quadrant Visual Communications Ltd* v *Hutchinson Telephone (UK) Ltd* (1991) The Times 4 December in a contract made between the two parties one particular clause apparently purported to exclude equitable remedies. The Court of Appeal held that once there was a request for an equitable remedy (in this case specific performance) its discretion could not be fettered. Whatever the construction of the clause it was the decision of the court alone as to whether to grant or refuse any equitable remedy.

17.2   When damages are an inadequate remedy

If the plaintiff can show that damages are inadequate, then the court may entertain his claim for specific performance. Damages will be inadequate in the following cases:

Where the plaintiff cannot get a satisfactory substitute

Where land or other premises are involved, their specific performance is readily granted as the law takes the view that a buyer is not readily compensated by damages.

Antiques, valuable paintings and other irreplaceable items may be the subject of an action for specific performance. See *Nutbrown* v *Thornton* (1804) 10 Ves 159. Specific performance was ordered of a contract to supply machinery or plant which could not be readily obtained elsewhere.

In cases where the plaintiff has contracted to obtain services of a personal quality from the defendant, for example, to sing or take part in a film, then he will *not* get specific performance, but may obtain an injunction.

Where damages are difficult to assess

For example, specific performance will be ordered of a contract to sell or pay annuities.

Where the amount allowable as damages is not a secure financial equivalent

In *Beswick* v *Beswick* [1968] AC 58, A promised B to pay an annuity to C in consideration of B's transferring the goodwill of the business to A.

HELD: although the promise did not give C any right of action, because she was not a party to the contract (see Chapter 12), it could be specifically enforced by B's personal representative against A. This was because damages would have been purely nominal as the promisee or his estate had suffered no loss. A would have been unjustly enriched by being allowed to retain the entire benefit of the other contracting party's performance without performing his own promise.

Section 52 Sale of Goods Act 1979. The court has a discretion to order specific performance in the case of 'specific or ascertained goods'. This discretion is heavily influenced by pre-1893 equity cases and is used very sparingly.

Note *Behnke* v *Bede Shipping* [1927] 1 KB 649, a decree of specific performance was granted in the case of a ship.

However, in *Cohen* v *Roche* [1927] 1 KB 169, the court refused specific performance to a buyer of a set of Hepplewhite chairs saying that they were 'ordinary articles of commerce and of no special value or interest'. It was crucial in this case that the buyer was contracting with a view to resale and not to use. If the latter had been the case the result, it is submitted, would have been different.

In *Re Wait* [1927] 1 Ch 606, a case which failed under s52 because the goods were not 'specific or ascertained', Atkin LJ said the 'only remedy by way of specific performance was a statutory one'. This dictum appears to have been departed from in one recent case.

In *Sky Petroleum* v *VIP Petroleum* [1974] 1 All ER 954, the plaintiff agreed to buy all its petrol from the defendant for ten years, that is, unascertained goods. In November 1973, the defendant purported to terminate the contract for alleged breach of contract by the plaintiff. The plaintiff sought an interlocutory injunction in the circumstances, restraining the defendant from withholding petrol supplies because petrol shortages meant the plaintiff had either to get petrol from the defendant or close down since no alternative sources were available.

HELD: the plaintiff could get an injunction.

It would appear that the court grants specific performance according to the appropriateness of that remedy in the circumstances of each case. In this case, an injunction was granted for unascertained goods despite s52 and *Re Wait*. Damages would not have been an adequate remedy since the plaintiff could not have gone to the market to buy petrol.

17.3   Factors considered in awarding specific performance

Mutuality

There must be mutuality before specific performance is available. Therefore, the plaintiff can only have this remedy if the contract can also be enforced by the defendant.

There will be no mutuality if there exist some unperformed obligations of the plaintiff which cannot by their nature be enforced, for example, personal service contracts or contracts requiring constant supervision.

'The court does not grant specific performance unless it can give full relief to both parties' per Lord Cranworth LC in *Blackett* v *Bates* (1865) LR 1 Ch App 117 at 124.

The date of the hearing and not the date of the contract is the relevant time for dealing with mutuality. See *Price* v *Strange* [1977] 3 All ER 371.

'The time at which the mutual availability of specific performance and its importance must be considered is, in my opinion, the time of judgment, and the principle to be applied can, I think, be stated simply as follows: the court will not compel a defendant to perform his obligations specifically if it cannot at the same time ensure that any unperformed obligations of the plaintiff will be specifically performed' (per Buckley LJ).

In *Sutton* v *Sutton* [1984] 1 All ER 168, the court held that lack of mutuality might have been a good argument while the contract was executory but, by the time the case came before the court, the plaintiff had performed her side of the agreement, and it was too late for the defendant to rely on that defence.

Hardship

This is a ground for not ordering specific performance where it would cause the defendant hardship. In *Denne* v *Light* (1857) 8 De GM & G 774, the court refused to order specific performance against the buyer of farmland, which was wholly surrounded by land belonging to others, and over which there was no right of way.

A rare modern case where specific performance was refused on this ground is *Patel* v *Ali* [1984] 1 All ER 978. Specific performance may be refused against the defendant on grounds of hardship where the cost to the defendant is wholly out of proportion to the benefit which performance will confer on the plaintiff.

Unfairness

The court will refuse the remedy to the plaintiff if he has acted unfairly or dishonestly. The equitable principle is that the plaintiff must come to equity with clean hands. See *Coatsworth* v *Johnson* (1886) 54 LT 520 and *Walters* v *Morgan* (1861) 3 De GF & J 718, where the defendant agreed to grant the plaintiff a mining lease over land he had just bought. Specific performance was refused as the plaintiff had produced a draft lease and induced the defendant to sign the agreement in ignorance of the value of the property. The plaintiff had hurried the defendant into signing the lease before he knew the value of the property.

Mere inadequacy of consideration is not a ground for refusing specific performance, *Collier* v *Brown* (1788) 1 Cox CC 428, unless it is coupled with factors such as mistake or fraud.

Conduct of the plaintiff

Specific performance will be refused if the plaintiff fails to perform a promise which induced the defendant to contract.

In *Lamare* v *Dixon* (1873) LR 6 HL 414, the plaintiff induced the defendant to agree to take a lease of cellars by orally promising they would be made dry. The promise had no effect as a misrepresentation as it related to the future. The court refused the plaintiff specific performance since he had made no attempt to perform his promise. See also *Shell* v *Lostock Garages* [1976] 1 WLR 1187.

Impossibility

Equity will do nothing in vain, thus specific performance will not be ordered, for example, against the defendant who has contracted to sell land which he either does not own, or has already conveyed elsewhere. See *Castle* v *Wilkinson* (1870) LR 5 Ch App 534.

Supervision

The court is reluctant to grant specific performance where this would require constant supervision.

In *Ryan* v *Mutual Tontine Assoc* [1893] 1 Ch 116, a lease of a service flat provided that the lessors should provide a porter who was to be 'constantly in attendance'.

HELD: that this undertaking could not be specifically enforced. It would require 'that constant superintendence by the court which the court has always in such cases declined to give'.

In *Posner* v *Scott-Lewis* (1987) The Times 12 December, however, the court granted an application for specific performance of a lessor's covenant to employ a resident porter for certain duties. Mervyn Davies J distinguished the facts before him from those in *Ryan*, where supervision of the execution of the undertaking had been required. Here neither personal services, nor a continuous series of acts, were required, but merely the execution of an agreement containing provision for such services.

Contracts to cultivate a farm in a particular manner, keep an airfield in operation, deliver goods in instalments, etc, have not been enforced for this reason.

It has been argued that supervision is only a factor to be taken into account and is not a bar to specific performance.

In *Luganda* v *Service Hotels* [1969] 2 Ch 206, a mandatory injunction ordering the defendant to allow the plaintiff, who had been wrongfully locked out of a room in a hotel, to resume his residence was granted. This shows that the court attaches more importance to the plaintiff's interest than the difficulty of supervision.

Uncertainty

The agreement must be definite enough to be enforced both legally and specifically, that is, the court must be able to formulate its decree.

In *Joseph* v *National Magazine Co* [1959] Ch 14, the defendant undertook to publish an article to be written by the plaintiff, but could not agree with him as to the precise wording.

HELD: that specific performance must be refused as there was no definite manuscript, publication of which could be ordered.

Delay

There is no limitation period for obtaining specific performance, however, the plaintiff should pursue his remedy within a reasonable time, otherwise the equitable doctrine of laches may operate to bar his claim, that is, 'equity assists the vigilant, not the indolent'.

If both sides regard the contract as a leisurely transaction, then the plaintiff may obtain specific performance after two years. See *Lazard Bros* v *Fairfield Properties* (1977) 121 SJ 793.

If the plaintiff takes possession of land relying on his equitable title, then he may obtain a decree for specific performance of the contract regardless of the delay. See *Williams* v *Greatrex* [1957] 1 WLR 31.

17.4 Particular contracts

Contracts involving personal service

The court will not order specific performance of these contracts. Section 16 Trade Union and Labour Relations Act 1974 states that no court shall compel an employee to do any work by ordering specific performance of a contract of employment, or by restraining the breach of such contract by injunction.

An employer cannot be forced to employ somebody against his wishes, and the general rule is that the court will not order re-engagement of an employee, but will, instead, award compensation. In one case, however, an employer was forced to retain an employee he dismissed.

In *Hill* v *CA Parsons Ltd* [1972] Ch 305, the plaintiff was employed by the defendant for 35 years. Within two years of retirement, which would mean certain pensions etc, the defendant ordered the plaintiff to join a certain trade union, which he refused to do and got a month's notice.

HELD: the notice was wholly inadequate and a breach of contract which required six if not 12 months' notice. An interim injunction was granted so that the plaintiff's employment continued.

In all contracts involving personal service, the equitable principle applies. Thus in *Chinnock* v *Sainsbury* (1861) 30 LJ Ch 409, an agreement to allow an auctioneer to sell certain works of art could not be specifically enforced, and in *England* v *Curling* (1844) 8 Beav 129, an agreement to enter into a partnership could not be specifically enforced.

An industrial tribunal can order reinstatement or re-engagement under the provisions of the Employment Protection (Consolidation) Act 1978.

Building contracts

The general rule is that a contract to erect a building cannot be specifically enforced. Several reasons exist for this, including:

1. Damages may be an adequate remedy as the owner can engage another builder.
2. The contract may be too vague and not describe the building with sufficient certainty.
3. Specific performance may cause difficulties relating to supervision.

Where the first two reasons are not applicable, the court will in effect ignore the third and order specific performance.

In *Wolverhampton Corp* v *Emmons* [1901] 1 KB 515, the plaintiff acquired land for an improvement scheme and sold part of it to the defendant, who covenanted to demolish houses on it and build new ones. The demolition was carried out and plans for new houses approved.

HELD: specific performance would be ordered since the defendant's obligations were precisely defined by the plans, and damages would be inadequate because the defendant had possession of the site, and the plaintiff could not get the work done by employing another contractor.

Entire and severable contracts

Where the court cannot grant specific performance of a contract as a whole, it will not interfere to compel specific performance of part of that contract. Where parts of a contract are severable, specific performance of each part can be separately granted. See *Odessa Tramway* v *Mendel* (1878) 8 Ch D 235.

17.5   Specific performance and third parties

In *Beswick* v *Beswick* (above), the House of Lords granted specific performance of a contract for the benefit of a third party. Three points were stressed in that case as forming the basis of the decision:

1. The promisee's remedy at law was inadequate. The damages he could recover would only be nominal.
2. The promisor had received the entire consideration for his promise.
3. The contract could have been specifically enforced by the promisor if the promisee had failed to perform his part of transferring the business.

Specific performance could be ordered of a promise to pay a single lump sum to a third party. See *Gurtner* v *Circuit* [1968] 2 QB 587. The equitable remedy need not have been available in a similar two-party case. It is sufficient if there was a common law remedy available in such a two-party case.

17.6   Injunction: introduction

A court may be able to restrain a party from committing a breach of contract by injunction. The remedy is most appropriate where the contract contains a negative stipulation, by which the defendant precludes himself from acting in a manner inconsistent with his positive contractual obligations.

17.7   Types of injunction

There are three types of injunction commonly available.

1. *Interlocutory injunction* – this is designed to regulate the position of the parties pending a hearing.
2. *Prohibitory injunction* – this orders the defendant not to do something, for example, X contracts with Y to obtain all the beer for his pub from Y. A prohibitory injunction could be issued to prevent him buying from Z.
3. *Mandatory injunction* – this orders the defendant to undo something he has agreed not to do.

Unlike specific performance, the defendant cannot resist a prohibitory injunction on the ground that it is burdensome to him.

Interlocutory injunctions

These could possibly be used to prevent a breach of contract by the defendant before it actually occurs. The circumstances in which this is likely to occur are hard to envisage, but the rules governing the grant of such an injunction were laid down by the House of Lords in *American Cyanamid* v *Ethicon* [1975] 1 All ER 504. The basis of this case is that the plaintiff must show there is a serious issue to be tried at the trial, and that the balance of convenience is in his favour in granting the injunction. See also *Fellowes* v *Fisher* [1976] QB 122, where the subject matter of a contract is in danger of being moved out of the jurisdiction in a case where a claim for damages or for an agreed sum is being heard and the sale of that subject matter is likely to be used to pay the damages, then it would appear that the plaintiff can apply for an interlocutory injunction to restrain the defendant from removing the subject matter from the jurisdiction. Such injunctions are known as 'Mareva' injunctions. See also *Mareva Compania Naviera* v *International Bulk Carriers* [1980] 1 All ER 213.

Prohibitory and mandatory injunctions

These will not be granted if the effect is to directly or indirectly compel the defendant to do acts for which the plaintiff could not have specific performance. Thus an employee cannot be restrained from committing a breach of his positive obligation to work (s16 TULRA 1974, above).

A service contract may, however, contain certain express negative obligations, which can be enforced by injunction without compelling the defendant to work or infringing the rule that the plaintiff could not have obtained specific performance.

In *Lumley* v *Wagner* (1852) 1 De GM & G 604, the defendant contracted to sing for the plaintiff in his theatre for three months and, at the same time, not to sing elsewhere during this time without the plaintiff's consent. A third party, one Gye, offered the defendant a larger sum to sing for him.

HELD: there was no power to make the defendant sing or encourage her to sing at plaintiff's theatre. However, the court could persuade her to do so by preventing her singing elsewhere by imposing an injunction to the effect.

Lumley v Wagner has been criticised, particularly as regard the perilous position in which it puts those who have agreed, and later refuse to perform, personal contracts. In *Giles v Morris* [1972] 1 WLR 307, Megarry J pointed out that if an artist was ordered to sing and did it badly or wilfully, he would be in contempt of court. If it was not wilful, then there would be no contempt of court. As it is exceedingly difficult to define wilful and unwilful, the defendant is thus given the benefit of the doubt. An injunction may well put so much economic pressure on the defendant that he decides to perform and to perform badly as above.

Since an injunction can put so much economic pressure on the defendant in certain cases, it is tantamount to making him perform the positive part of the contract.

In *Warner Bros v Nelson* [1937] 1 KB 209, the defendant, an actress, agreed to act for the plaintiff and, at the same time, not to act or sing for anybody else for two years without the plaintiff's written consent, and no other employment could be taken up during this period without the plaintiff's consent.

HELD: the defendant could be restrained by injunction from breaking this undertaking. She would not be forced to act for the plaintiff because she could earn a living by doing other work.

The law seems to be moving away from this rule in the *Warner Bros* case and it appears that an injunction will not now be granted unless it leaves the defendant with some reasonable alternative means of earning a living.

In *Page One Records v Britton* [1968] 1 WLR 157, The Troggs, a pop group, contracted to appoint the plaintiff their sole agent and manager for five years, and agreed not to act themselves in such capacity and not to appoint any other person for that time. They fell out with the manager and wanted to replace him. The plaintiff sought an injunction.

HELD: that an injunction must be refused because to grant it would, in effect, compel The Troggs to continue to employ the plaintiff, and thus would amount to enforcing the performance by the plaintiff of a contract for personal services.

The above principles have been applied in cases where contracts of employment have included clauses requiring the employee not to work for competitors or set up in competition for a certain period after he has left the employment. In these cases, an added complication exists, for the court will not grant an injunction if the clause in the contract is too wide.

In *The Littlewoods Organisation v Harris* [1978] 1 All ER 1026, the plaintiff, was a large mail order firm who employed the defendant as a divisional director to plan their catalogues in advance. The defendant's contract of service included a clause which provided 'in the event of the determination of this Agreement ... the (defendant) shall not at any time within 12 months after such determination enter into a contract of service with Great Universal Stores'. Great Universal Stores was the plaintiff's only rival in the mail order business, but they also had, like the plaintiff, a chain of shops. The defendant resigned from the plaintiff on the offer of a job by Great Universal Stores. The plaintiff sought an injunction. The defendant argued it should not be granted as it was wider than necessary to protect the plaintiff's business.

HELD: such a covenant, although drafted in general terms, could be construed in a sense that was not unreasonably wide, and the court should construe it in that sense to render it valid and enforceable. In the circumstances, it was clear the clause was intended to protect confidential information and trade secrets and it would be limited as such.

In *Evening Standard* v *Henderson* (1986) The Times 15 November CA, the defendant had undertaken not to work for his employer's competitors during the duration of his employment. In breach of contract, he gave his employer two months' notice of termination, instead of the required twelve months. The plaintiffs offered to pay him his wages for the remaining ten months and successively claimed an injunction to prevent him from working for a rival newspaper for that period.

A sole distributorship agreement may also be enforced by injunction. In *Decro-Wall International* v *Practitioners in Marketing* [1971] 1 WLR 361, a manufacturer was restrained from breaching a 'sole distributorship' agreement in that he was prevented from disposing of the goods in any other way. However, the court would not order him to keep up the positive part of the convenant to keep up the distributor's supplies.

Lastly, it seems that the court will not grant an injunction, if the negative stipulation is not expressed. See *Mortimer* v *Beckett* [1920] 1 Ch 571. An apparent exception is *Hivac* v *Park Royal Scientific Instruments* [1946] Ch 169, but that can also be explained on the basis that the court was seeking to prevent breach of an employee's duty of confidentiality which is implied by law.

17.8   Damages in lieu of specific performance or injunction

Damages were originally only available at common law. However, s2 Chancery Amendment Act 1858 gave the Court of Chancery the power to award damages in lieu of specific performance (now s50 Supreme Court Act 1981) commonly referred to as Lord Cairns' Act.

See s50 Supreme Court Act 1981, where the Court of Appeal or High Court has jurisdiction to entertain an application for an injunction or specific performance, it may award damages in addition to, or in substitution for, an injunction or specific performance.

In contractual cases, other than those concerning land, there is little point invoking s50 SCA 1981 where there is a valid contract and a breach of this is proved. However, the plaintiff may invoke the Act on two occasions:

1. Damages may be awarded under the Act even though there is no completed

cause of action. See *Leeds Industrial Co-operative Society* v *Slack* [1924] AC 851. In such cases, it would not be possible to get damages at common law, for example, damages in lieu of a quia timet injunction and damages for breach of a restrictive covenant to which the defendant was not a party.

2. Damages awarded to the plaintiff may be greater under the Act than at common law. Damages under the Act are assessed in the same manner as at common law. But, where damages are awarded at common law, the principle is that such damages are normally assessed as at the date of the breach, a principle which is recognised and embodied in s51 Sale of Goods Act 1979.

This is not an absolute rule and if 'it would give rise to injustice, the court has power to fix such other date as may be appropriate in the circumstances' (per Lord Wilberforce in *Johnson* v *Agnew* [1980] AC 367). The plaintiff obtained a decree of specific performance on a contract for the sale of a house to the defendant. The plaintiff had bought a new house in the meantime and he could not keep up the mortgage instalments on the house he had sold to the defendant. The mortgagee took possession and sold the house making specific performance impossible. The plaintiff then claimed to have the specific performance decree cancelled and damages in lieu of specific performance requested. The date of breach of the contract was about 21 January 1974, the decree of specific performance was drawn up and entered on 26 November 1974, and specific performance became impossible on 3 April 1975, when the mortgagee took possession and sold. The Court of Appeal fixed the date of assessment of damages at 26 November 1974, but in the House of Lords:

HELD: damages should be assessed as at 3 April 1975.

'As the vendors acted reasonably in pursuing the remedy of specific performance the date on which that remedy became aborted (not being the vendor's fault) should logically be fixed as the date on which damages should be assessed' (per Lord Wilberforce).

Damages may often be awarded in addition to specific performance but, again, the only clear examples of use of this are in contracts for the sale of land.

In *Grant* v *Dawkins* [1973] 1 WLR 1406, the vendor's title to land was subject to an encumbrance which amounted to a breach of contract. The plaintiff, it was held, could get specific performance of what title the defendant had, plus damages based on the cost of discharging the encumbrance.

18

Quasi-contract

18.1 Introduction

18.2 Action for money had and received

18.3 Action for money paid

18.4 Liability to account

18.5 Quantum meruit

18.1 Introduction

Quasi-contract is also called restitution. It has been described by Lord Wright in *Fibrosa Spolka Akcynja* v *Fairbairn Lawson Combe Barbour Ltd* [1943] AC 32 in the following terms:

> 'It is clear that any civilised system of law is bound to provide remedies for what has been called unjust enrichment or unjust benefit, that is, to prevent a man from retaining the money of, or some benefit derived from, another which it is against his conscience he should keep. Such remedies in English law are generically different from remedies in contract or in tort, and are now recognised to fall within a third category of the common law which has been called quasi-contract or restitution.'

As to what constitutes 'unjust enrichment', see the recent case of *Barclays Bank* v *Hammersmith and Fulham LBC* (1991) The Times 27 November in which the Court of Appeal decided that it was proper to look at the state of mind of both payer and payee at the time the payments were made.

In a leading text, *The Law of Restitution* by Goff and Jones J, it is argued that these exceptional decisions should be classified under a category separate from contract or tort, namely restitution. The approach would bring the English law of obligations more in line with the Roman classification, the latter having a well-defined law of restitution. Goff and Jones's book has been cited with approval by the courts.

However, as quasi-contract has traditionally been viewed as part of the law of contract (see Theories, below) – and is often associated with the subject in practice – it is necessary to examine the topic in outline.

There are three main quasi-contractual actions: the action for money had and received; the action for money paid; and a quantum meruit claim.

339

Cases concerning quasi-contract do not come before the courts very often. The recent New Zealand case, *Meates* v *Westpac Banking Corporation* (1990) The Times 5 July, is therefore interesting.

The government of New Zealand had issued a number of formal documents as part of a project to establish new industries. The project never came into effect, but the appellants claimed that as a result of conversations, press statements and so on, they had understood that the government was prepared to indemnify them. They had incurred considerable expenses.

HELD: as a general rule, governments and large corporations intend ultimately to be bound only by formal written documents. Any *implied* undertaking made verbally, therefore, in the face of the written documents' express terms, could not be enforced. No quasi-contractual obligation existed.

18.2   Action for money had and received

This is an old common law action that, in many ways, resembled the equitable trust remedy. It was gradually extended to cover situations where money was paid by mistake or under a consideration that had totally failed. The action is usually available in the situations below.

Money paid under a mistake of fact

The classic test was formulated by Bramwell B in *Aiken* v *Short* (1856) 1 H & N 210:

> 'In order to entitle a person to recover back money paid under a mistake of fact, the mistake must be as to a fact which, if true, would make the person paying liable to pay the money; not where, if true, it would merely make it desirable that he should pay the money.'

This test may, however, be too narrow. In *Kerrison* v *Glyn, Mills, Currie & Co* (1912) 81 LJKB 465, the House of Lords permitted recovery of money mistakenly paid in anticipation of a future liability.

In *Morgan* v *Ashcroft* [1938] 1 KB 49, Greene MR sought to confine the law to 'cases where the only mistake is as to the nature of the transaction', although the test of Bramwell B was criticised as being too narrow.

In *Larner* v *LCC* [1949] 2 KB 683, payments made by a local authority in the mistaken belief that it was under a moral obligation to pay were recovered. The authority had voluntarily promised 'until further order' to pay all their employees on war service the difference between their service pay and their civilian pay. Larner was overpaid because he did not tell the authority that he had had increases in his service pay. He defended the action on the basis that the payments were voluntary.

HELD: the payments were not voluntary, even though there was no legal obligation to pay. The local authority had 'for good reasons of national policy, made a promise to the men which they were in honour bound to fulfil. The payments were not mere gratuities. They were made as a matter of duty.'

The nature of the mistake

The general view seems to be that a person can recover for a mistake which is less grave than the mistake required before a contract may be rescinded, so that mistakes as to creditworthiness and arithmetic have not prevented recovery. See *Kerrison* v *Glyn, Mills, Currie* (above) and *Weld-Blundell* v *Synott* [1940] 2 KB 107.

Mistake as the cause of payment

Notably in *Barclays Bank* v *Simms & Cooke* [1980] QB 677, Goff J preferred the test of whether the mistake *caused* the payment to any test relating to the nature of the mistake made. He went on to say that there were, however, three circumstances in which no recovery would be possible.

1. Where the payer intends that the payee shall have the money in any event, and is deemed in law so to intend.
2. Where the payment is made for good consideration – especially the discharge of a debt from payer to payee.
3. Where the payee has, or is deemed in law to have, changed his position in good faith as a result of the payment.

Other limitations on the power to recover

1. In submission to a claim or under a compromise of a claim.
2. Where recovery would be contrary to public policy. In *Morgan* v *Ashcroft* (above), the plaintiff, a bookmaker, overpaid the defendant on a betting account. He sued to recover the amount of the over-payment.

    HELD: the court would not recognise wagering contracts as giving rise to legal and enforceable obligations.
3. Where the plaintiff has not asked for repayment before commencing proceedings. This may, alternatively, only go to the issue of costs, but see *Kelly* v *Solari* (1841) 9 M & W 54 at p58.
4. Where there is only a mistake of law and not a mistake as to private rights. See *Cooper* v *Phibbs* (1867) LR 2 HL 149, *Solle* v *Butcher* [1950] 1 KB 671 and *Kiriri Cotton* v *Dewani* [1960] AC 192.

    In the latter case, Lord Denning MR may have thrown some doubt on the general proposition by saying that:

'The true proposition is that money paid under a mistake of law, by itself and without more, cannot be recovered back ... If there is something more in addition to a mistake of law – if there is something in the defendant's conduct which shows that of the two of them, he is the one primarily responsible for the mistake – then it may be recovered back.'

There is some indication that this may be true where money has been paid under compulsion, but the broadest sense of this dictum has not been followed.

5. Where the payee can show that the payer is estopped he has to show three things:
   a) that the payer was either under a duty to give accurate information, which he failed to do or gave inaccurate information, or that the payer made a clear misrepresentation;
   b) that the inaccurate information led him to believe that the money could be treated as his own;
   c) that he has, as a result, changed his position, so that it would be inequitable for the payer to be able to recover the money.

Failure of consideration

Most of the cases are concerned with contracts where consideration is provided on one side, but not furnished on the other. For example, where a party 'sells' a car to which the seller has no title, to a purchaser, no title can pass. There is, accordingly, a total failure of consideration for the price of the car. This will still be a total failure of consideration even though the 'purchaser' has had the use of the car.

In *Butterworth* v *Kingsway Motors* [1954] 1 WLR 1286, a 'purchaser' had a car for nearly a year, during which time it had depreciated in value nearly £500.

HELD: he was, nevertheless, entitled to recover the full purchase price on a total failure of consideration. See also *Rowland* v *Divall* [1923] 2 KB 500 (below) and *Karflex* v *Poole* [1933] 2 KB 251.

There must, however, be a total failure of consideration. A partial failure is not sufficient. So, where goods are merely defective or an insufficient quantity is supplied, there will only be a partial failure of consideration and the action for money had and received will fail.

Returnable and non-returnable benefits

1. If the plaintiff has received only a partial or a defective performance, then he may be entitled to rescind the contract. If, in these circumstances, he is able to return to the defendant what he has received under the contract, then this will work a total failure of consideration and allow the plaintiff to recover any money he has paid. See *Baldry* v *Marshall* [1925] 1 KB 260.
2. The requirement that the plaintiff must restore what he has received in this case is inapplicable where the defect in the goods is an inability to restore them, for example, where the defendant had not title to them, and the true owner took them off the plaintiff.
3. If the plaintiff has used the subject matter of the contract so as to derive a benefit from it, then there is no failure of consideration and he cannot use this method. In *Hunt* v *Silk* (1804) 5 East 449, an agreement for a lease provided that the plaintiff was to get immediate possession. The defendant, the landlord, was to do

certain repairs, and the lease was to be executed in 10 days with £10 payable by the plaintiff on execution. The plaintiff took possession and paid the £10 in advance, but the defendant failed to repair. The plaintiff as a result, vacated the premises.

HELD: the plaintiff could not claim his £10 on total failure of consideration. He had received benefits under the contract already.

Benefits different in kind

1. If the plaintiff receives a benefit different in kind to that he bargained for, then he will not be held to have received consideration, but rather a total failure of consideration is presumed and he is entitled to have his money back.

   In *Rowland v Divall* [1923] 2 KB 500, the plaintiff, a car dealer, bought a car from the defendant for £334, repainted it and resold it for £400. The car was, in fact, stolen, which was unknown to any of the parties and the police seized it. The plaintiff repaid his customer £400 and sued the defendant for £334. The insurance company which took the car sold it to the plaintiff for £260, and the defendant, relying on this, paid £260 into court on the basis this was the limit of his liability.

   HELD: the plaintiff could recover the £334 as there had been a total failure of consideration. He did not get what he paid for, viz a car with good title, and as the plaintiff was a dealer, he bought with a view to resale and title was essential to him.

2. The principle in *Rowland v Divall* has, however, also been applied in cases where the car was bought for private use.

   In *Butterworth v Kingsway Motors* (above), the plaintiff bought a car off the defendant for £1,275 and used it for almost a year. It, in fact, belonged to a finance company under a hire-purchase agreement, and they claimed its return. The plaintiff immediately claimed his £1,275, but 10 days after this the hire-purchase instalments were paid up, so that a good title could have been fed to the plaintiff.

   HELD: the question whether there was a total failure of consideration was determined at the time the plaintiff asked for his money back, and not later when the writ was issued. Thus the plaintiff was entitled to succeed, even though he had a year's use of the car for nothing.

3. Unlike *Rowland v Divall*, the purchaser in *Butterworth's* case was purchasing a car for his own use; this he bargained for and obtained. It is hard to conclude that title was of paramount importance to him. The decision has been heavily criticised.

4. In both of the above cases, the unfairness of restitution is evident. The defendant had to return the purchase price in full and no set-off was allowed in respect of the plaintiff's use. In damages, the plaintiff would have brought such benefits into account, but it appears restitution is often a bounty for the plaintiff.

Restitution and damages

Because it is often difficult to quantify the plaintiff's precise loss, it has become common in contracts for the sale of goods to use the price paid as the figure at which damages are assessed for the sake of convenience.

In *Harling* v *Eddy* [1951] 2 KB 739, the defendant sold a cow which was warranted healthy but was, in fact, diseased, and later died. The plaintiff recovered the price paid as one of the items of damages for breach of warranty.

Void contracts

If the plaintiff pays money under a void contract, then this can be recovered by him, but not if it is merely illegal.

Money paid under compulsion

The categories under which restitution may be ordered are broader than those for which rescission of contract is available, and cover, for example, money paid as a result of wrongful demands which are not accompanied by threats of violence.

18.3   Action for money paid

This action lies for money paid by the plaintiff to a third party for the defendant's benefit. Originally, the payment had to be at the defendant's request, but the law was later prepared to imply such a request in certain circumstances. The action is usually available in the following situations:

Compulsory discharge of another's liability

'Where the plaintiff has been compelled by the law to pay, or being compellable by law, has paid, money which the defendant was ultimately liable to pay, so that the latter obtains the benefit of the payment by the discharge of his liability; under such circumstances the defendant is held indebted to the plaintiff in the amount' (per Cockburn CJ in *Moule* v *Garrett* (1872) LR 7 Ex 101).

Recovery is subject to three main conditions:

1. The plaintiff's payment must have been compulsory in the sense that he must be under an immediate or ultimate obligation to make the payment. See *Exall* v *Partridge* (1799) 8 TR 308 and *Brook's Wharf & Bull Wharf* v *Goodman Bros* [1937] 1 KB 534.
2. The plaintiff must not have officiously exposed himself to the liability in making the payment. See *England* v *Marsden* (1886) LR 1 CP 529 and *Owen* v *Tate* [1975] 2 All ER 129.

3. The plaintiff's payment must have discharged a liability of the defendant. See *Receiver for Metropolitan Police District v Croydon Corporation* [1957] 2 QB 154.

Necessitous intervention

Roman law allowed a quasi-contractual action to a person who intervened to protect another's property in an emergency: English law, however, has traditionally refused such an action. See *Falcke v Scottish Imperial Insurance Co* (1886) 34 Ch D 234. Certain exceptions can be found, for example, agency of necessity, and a general principle may be emerging: *Sims v Midland Ry* [1913] 1 KB 103, *Poland v John Parr* [1917] 1 KB 236 per Scrutton LJ, *Re Rhodes* (1890) 44 Ch D 94 and *Owen v Tate* (above) per Scarman LJ.

18.4   Liability to account

A liability to account may arise:

1. where the defendant is under an obligation to pay money or property to the plaintiff which has been received from a third party; or
2. where the plaintiff is entitled to be subrogated to (placed in the shoes of) another against a third party.

Defendant acknowledging that he will pay the plaintiff at the request of the third party whose funds he holds

The nature of the legal obligation is explained in *Griffin v Weatherby* (1868) LR 3 QB 753 by Blackburn LJ:

> 'Even since the case of *Walker v Rostron* it has been considered as settled law that where a person transfers to a creditor on account of a debt, whether due or not, a fund actually existing or accruing in the hands of a third person, and notifies the transfer to the holder of the fund, although there is no legal obligation on the holder to pay the amount of the debt to the transferee, yet the holder of the fund may, and if he does promise to pay to the transferee, then that which was merely an equitable right becomes a legal right where indicated in the transferee, founded on the promise; and the money becomes a fund received or to be received for and payable to the transferee, and when it has been received an action for money had and received to the use of the transferee lies at his suit against the holder.'

This principle was applied and extended in *Shamia v Joory* [1958] 1 QB 448. The defendant owed more than £1,300 to Y. Y requested the defendant to pay £500 to Y's brother. The plaintiff later received a cheque for £500. The cheque was not met. The defendant failed to write another, although he promised to do so.

HELD: the plaintiff could recover under the principle in *Griffin v Weatherby*; the defendant had in his hands 'a fund' from which the money could be paid, because he had a monetary liability to another.

Question: to what extent may this be an equitable route around the doctrine of privity?

Question: is 'a monetary liability' a realistic description of 'a fund'?

Question: how is the principle in this case distinct from the equitable assignment of a chose in action?

Stakeholders

A stakeholder is an agent who holds money on instructions to make payment of the money lodged when instructed to do so. If he makes payment before he is instructed to do so, he will be liable to his principal.

Agent or employee receiving a secret bribe or profit

The principal or employer is entitled to claim any secret bribe or commission which is received by his agent or employee. Evidence of a corrupt motive on the part of the agent or employee is not necessary. Also, where a person wrongfully usurps an office belonging to the plaintiff, the plaintiff is entitled to all the fees and profits obtained by the usurper.

Constructive trusts

The law on constructive trusts is sometimes said to be an equitable restitutionary remedy.

Subrogation

Subrogation is the stepping 'into the shoes of' another, that is, assuming the legal rights and liabilities by displacement of that other. It is a restitutionary remedy which arises principally in contracts of insurance so as to allow an insurer who pays a claim under a policy of indemnity to enforce the rights of the insured person arising out of that loss against any third party. The right to be subrogated may also lie under contracts of guarantee; in an indorser of a Bill of Exchange; under a loan to an infant for necessaries in respect of sums so spent; or under an irrecoverable loan (sometimes).

18.5   Quantum meruit

Where a contract is terminated by breach

In *Planché* v *Colburn* (1831) 8 Bing 14, the plaintiff contracted with the defendants to write a volume for publication in 'The Juvenile Library'. After he had started, the defendants withdrew the series.

HELD: the plaintiff could recover reasonable remuneration for work already done.

What happens where damages for breach of the contract are less than would be recovered under a quantum meruit? Is the innocent party entitled to choose his remedy, or should the claim to quantum meruit be adjusted to reflect the value of damages for breach?

When a contract is void

In *Craven-Ellis* v *Canons Ltd* [1936] 2 KB 403, the plaintiff was entitled to recover quantum meruit even though he had been appointed managing director under a void contract. Greer LJ said that the obligation to pay was imposed by a rule of law and not by contract. It is, therefore, restitutionary in nature.

Quantum meruit to fix a price or remuneration

It has already been seen that quantum meruit is implied where the parties fail to fix a contract price or remuneration. See *Foley* v *Classique Coaches* [1934] 2 KB 1.

19

Agency

19.1 Introduction

19.2 Appointment of an agent

19.3 Authority of an agent

19.4 Relationship of principal and agent

19.5 Principal and agent and third parties

19.6 Termination of agency

19.7 Factors

19.1 Introduction

An agent (A) is a person appointed by a principal (P) to bring the principal into a contractual relationship with third parties (T). The agent is merely the instrument used in forming the contract; he is not a party to it and need not have contractual capacity. The principal becomes a party to the contract and must have contractual capacity.

The agent may be one of the following:

1. A universal agent: appointed to act for the principal with no limitation on powers.
2. A general agent: appointed to act in transactions of a class - a banker, a solicitor
3. A special agent: appointed for one particular purpose.

Note that the agency relationship may bear some resemblance to other types of relationship. In *Comet Group plc* v *British Sky Broadcasting* [1991] TLR 211 it was held that a promotion contract was not the same as the agency relationship. A contract between British Satellite Broadcasting and Comet, whereby Comet would promote BSB's equipment, operated until BSB's merger with Sky Television in 1990. At that point BSB instructed Comet to suspend all further sales of BSB equipment. The contract made provision expressly for the period until February 1991. The action taken by BSB in November 1990 represented a considerable

348

financial loss to Comet. BSB attempted to argue that the promotion contract was a form of agency and cited cases such as *Rhodes* v *Forwood* (1876) 1 App Cas 256 and *Hamlyn* v *Wood* [1891] 2 QB 488, all of which had in common that the court had declined to imply into the contract a term that the principal would continue in business until the expiry of the term agreed. Comet argued that the contract was not one of agency and that BSB's conduct amounted to a repudiation of the contract giving rise to an action for damages.

The court agreed with the latter argument, holding that the contract differed from agency in a number of respects, most notably in that Comet were required to purchase at the outset £13m of equipment.

19.2   Appointment of an agent

The agent is usually appointed by a contract between himself and his principal; here the agent must have contractual capacity if this contract is to be enforceable between principal and agent. The appointment may be:

Express

Generally, this may be in any form, but if A is to be authorised to contract under seal, his appointment must be by a deed which is called a 'power of attorney'.

Implied

This form of authority usually arises out of an express appointment and covers: acts necessary for the performance of the express agency; and acts in the ordinary course of the agent's business. See *Ryan* v *Pilkington* [1959] 1 WLR 403. The owners of a hotel instructed an estate agent to find a purchaser for a private hotel. He accepted a deposit from a prospective purchaser 'as agent' of the owners.

HELD: the estate agent acted within the ostensible scope of his authority, he was not expressly authorised to accept deposits.

Note the special example of the wife who, during cohabitation, is presumed to have her husband's authority to pledge his credit for necessaries suitable to their system of living, unless the husband instructed the trader not to supply goods on credit to his wife; or the husband forbade his wife to pledge his credit; or the wife had an adequate allowance to cover the purchase of necessaries. See *Miss Gray Ltd* v *Cathcart* (1922) 38 TLR 562. A trader sued a husband for £215 being the price of clothing supplied to his wife.

HELD: that the husband was not liable since he gave his wife an allowance of £960 a year. The household was sufficiently supplied with the goods in question.

Ratification

A form of retrospective appointment by way of adoption or confirmation; if at the time of the transaction A has no authority, either because he is not an agent or is an agent but is exceeding his authority, P may subsequently adopt the contract, and A is then treated as having been authorised to enter into it from the very beginning, for example, *Bolton Partners* v *Lambert* (1889) 41 Ch D 295.

Ratification is only possible if:

1. A is contracted as an agent for a named principal. See *Keighley, Maxsted & Co* v *Durant* [1901] AC 240. R was authorised by K & Co to buy wheat at an agreed price from D. R exceeded his authority and purchased at a higher price in his own name, but intending to buy for K & Co. Later, K & Co agreed to buy the wheat at the higher price, but then refused to take delivery.

   HELD: that K & Co were not liable to D since R's contract had not been ratified by K & Co. Where a person contracts on his own behalf, with an undisclosed intention to benefit another, that other person cannot ratify the contract so as to make himself liable on it.

2. P had contractual capacity when the contract was made and also at the time of ratification. See *Kelner* v *Baxter* (1866) LR 2 CP 174. A company was in the process of being formed to buy a hotel. A contract was made 'on behalf' of the company, by three promoters of the scheme, to buy wine for £900 from K. The company was eventually formed, the wine was consumed, but the company went into liquidation before payment for the wine.

   HELD: the promoters were personally liable on the contract, not the company. A principal did not exist at the time of contracting, consequently, the contract was inoperative unless binding on the promoters who signed it.

3. Ratification is of the whole contract.

4. Ratification takes place within a reasonable time.

5. P has full knowledge of all material terms or intends to ratify whatever those terms may be.

By operation of law ('agency of necessity')

This arises without any agreement where A is compelled by some emergency to act on behalf of P. It usually arises when A is in possession of property of P, and has to act to preserve that property, for example, *GNR* v *Swaffield* (1874) LR 9 Exch 132. S sent a horse by train. It arrived at its destination without anyone meeting it. The station master put the horse in a livery stable and claimed reimbursement of charges from S.

HELD: S was liable to pay. Being unaware of S's identity or his address, the station master was obliged to make suitable arrangements for the horse.

A can only act when it is impossible to obtain instructions from P; compare *Springer* v *Great Western Rail Co* [1921] 1 KB 257. The railway company agreed to carry tomatoes from Jersey to London for S. The ship arrived late in Weymouth and the railway employees were on strike. The tomatoes were sold since the railway company feared that they would not be in saleable condition on eventual arrival in London.

There must be an actual and definite commercial necessity for the creation of the contract. See *Prager v Blatspiel, Stamp & Heacock Ltd* [1924] 1 KB 566. P, a fur dealer in Bucharest, asked B Ltd, London dealers, to buy and deliver skins worth £19,000. P paid the purchase price, but delivery was prevented by the First World War. B Ltd sold the skins.

HELD: B Ltd were liable for conversion. The skins were not likely to deteriorate if properly stored, consequently, there was no necessity for the sale.

Note that, because of improved communications, agency of necessity is rare nowadays. The whole question of agency of necessity needs review as a matter of some urgency, in the light of modern conditions.

The case of *The Choko Star* [1990] 1 Lloyd's Rep 516 raised the question as to whether the master of a ship had authority to sign a Lloyd's Open Form for cargo (as opposed to salvage of the ship itself). In the initial hearing, the court held that there was implied (and hence apparent) authority to do so stemming from the authority vested in the mastership from the owners and/or shippers.

HELD: on appeal, the Court of Appeal held that there was no such implied authority and only the ancient rules as to agency of necessity might apply. The doctrine of agency of necessity confers, usually on shipmasters, certain authority by operation of law given certain conditions relating to emergency. Of those conditions, the requirement that consultation between ship's master and owners/shippers should not be possible gives most difficulty in these days of virtually instantaneous communications.

The Court of Appeal reached the decision that the doctrine of agency of necessity would apply here, given certain circumstances.

By estoppel ('holding out')

This is not really an appointment at all; it involves a representation made by P to T by which T is led to believe that P has appointed A as his agent; if T acts on that belief, P is estopped from denying the fact of agency.

In *Spiro v Lintern* [1973] 1 WLR 1002, L's wife arranged for estate agents to sell his house. She entered into a written contract with S to sell it to him. The wife lacked authority to make such a contract. L led S to believe that he was to be the purchaser by allowing S to buy L's furniture and instruct an architect to carry out repairs. The wife eventually sold the house for a higher price by exercising L's power of attorney recently executed by him in her favour.

HELD: that S was entitled to specific performance of the contract of sale and possession from the present occupier. L had represented by his conduct that his wife had proper authority to act as she did towards S. The representations were so precise and unequivocal as to amount to an estoppel.

19.3   Authority of an agent

Actual authority

P is bound by any act which he has expressly or impliedly authorised A to do on his behalf.

Ostensible (or apparent) authority

This includes the implied powers of a general agent to bind P by any act in the ordinary course of A's business (even though this has been expressly prohibited by P – unless T knows this – see *Watteau* v *Fenwick*) and authority conferred by P holding out A as his agent to T, although A has not been appointed as such. T usually has to rely on A's ostensible authority, as he is not normally in a position to know the actual terms of the appointment.

In *Watteau* v *Fenwick* [1893] 1 QB 346, H was the owner of an hotel and later the manager for its new owner. H was forbidden to buy cigars on credit. W supplied cigars on credit at H's request believing him still to be owner of the hotel.

HELD: H was acting within the scope of his usual authority as manager. F was liable to pay W for the cigars. F could not, as against W, set up any secret limitation of H's usual authority.

19.4   Relationship of principal and agent

Duties of agent to principal

These are:

To carry out the terms of the agency, including:

1. The exercise of reasonable care and skill; probably a higher standard of care is imposed upon a paid agent that upon a gratuitous agent.
2. Disclosure of any relevant information to P. In *Keppell* v *Wheeler* [1927] 1 KB 577, K employed W to sell a house. W failed to inform K of a higher offer that was made after K had provisionally agreed to sell to another 'subject to contract'.

    HELD: W was liable to pay K the difference between the sale price and the higher price not communicated.

    Unlike ordinary agency, estate agents, who by their very nature act for numerous principals, several of whom might be competing and whose interests would conflict, do not have such an extensive fiduciary duty. Failure to inform the plaintiff of what might seem important material information was not a breach of the estate agent's fiduciary duty.

    In *Kelly* v *Cooper* [1992] 3 WLR 936, the plaintiff instructed the defendant, an estate agent, to sell his house and the terms were a percentage of the selling price as commission. The estate agent had also been approached by the owner of an adjoining property to sell his house for him. The agent showed both properties to a prospective purchaser who purchased the adjoining house immediately. The agent did not inform the plaintiff of this and when approached sold at the first asking price. Had he been alerted by the agent to the fact that the purchaser had already bought the property next door and wanted to link the two properties he could probably have got far more. He refused to pay the agent's commission. The Privy Council held that the agent had acted properly in the circumstances and his commission could not be withheld.

3. Disclosure of any personal interest in the contract to P. In *Armstrong* v *Jackson* [1917] 2 KB 822, A employed J, a stockbroker, to buy some shares for him. J sold some of his own shares to A and sent A a false contract note suggesting a purchase on the open market from a third party.

    HELD: that J had failed to carry out his proper duties as agent, consequently, A could rescind the contract of sale.

4. Not to disclose confidential information to third parties.

5. Not to delegate his authority unless this is authorised, customary or necessary. Note that if a valid delegation is effected, A still remains personally liable to P for proper performance of the contract.

To account for all money and other property received for P, and to keep proper accounts of all transactions.

Not to make any secret profit out of the agency, not to take a bribe from T; if he does, P may:

1. Recover the profit from A.
2. Refuse to pay commission or other remuneration.
3. Dismiss A without notice.
4. Repudiate the contract out of which the profit arose. In *Shipway* v *Broadwood* [1899] 1 QB 369, B agreed to buy a pair of horses from S provided P, a veterinary surgeon, examined them and found no faults. P was bribed by S to give a certificate of soundness. After purchase, B discovered that the horses were not sound. He returned them and stopped payment of a cheque given to S.

    HELD: that B was not liable on the cheque. He could rescind the contract because of S's bribery. It was unnecessary to determine whether P had been biased as a result of receiving the bribe.

5. Sue A or T for damages for any loss suffered; the damages are awarded without deduction of the amount of the secret payment recovered by P. In *Salford Corporation* v *Lever* [1891] 1 QB 168, L, a coal merchant who supplied coal to the S Corporation from time to time, was induced by H, the corporation's gas manager, to charge 1*s.* a ton extra and hand over the money secured to H personally, otherwise supplies would be taken from elsewhere. The corporation recovered this bribe, which amounted to £2,329, from H, and now sued to recover the same amount from L as the excess over and above the proper price that should have been charged.

HELD: that L was guilty of fraud which was separate and distinct from H's fraud. Both L and H were separately liable to pay the corporation money secured by their individual frauds.

6. Prosecute A or T or both under Prevention of Corruption Act 1906.

Rights of agent against principal

These are:

1. To be remunerated for his services, if expressly or impliedly agreed by P.
2. To be indemnified by P for any expenses properly incurred. In *Christophorides* v *Terry* [1924] AC 566, C employed T to buy cotton. C failed to settle his account, so T sold the cotton at a loss of over £6,000. T had to pay the sellers of the cotton out of his own pocket.

   HELD: C must indemnify T for losses suffered by acting on C's behalf lawfully and in execution of his authority.

   In *Davison* v *Fernandes* (1889) 6 TLR 73, F told his stockbroker D to sell some shares believing the price quoted to him by D to be Ex Div, that is, F could keep dividend recently paid by the company. In fact, the price quoted was Cum Div, that is, D had to hand over a sum equal to the dividend to the purchaser.

3. To a lien on any goods of P in his possession for the amount due to him from P.
4. To stop goods in transit to P if he is personally liable for the price.

19.5   Principal and agent and third parties

Contracts for disclosed principal

If A indicates to T that he is contracting only as the agent, whether he names his principal or not, the contract is between P and T, and T will not normally be liable on it.

A may be liable, however:

1. if he expressly or impliedly assumes personal liability;
2. if he signs a written contract in his own name;
3. by trade usage or custom;
4. on a bill of exchange, under s26 Bills of Exchange Act 1882 or s108 Cheques Act 1948;
5. if he is actually contracting on his own behalf;
6. if he executes a deed in his own name, unless he is acting under a power of attorney for a named principal;
7. if acting as a receiver for debenture holders, s369 Cheques Act 1948;
8. if, acting for an unnamed principal, he refuses to identify P.

For example, see *Foalquest Ltd* v *Roberts* [1990] 21 EG 156. A financial consultant claimed various items of remuneration for services rendered. Whether he was so entitled depended on the true liability of the agent acting for the company with which he had dealt. The agent claimed to have acted throughout as agent for a disclosed principal and never to have assumed or accepted personal liability.

HELD: the court had looked to the objective intention of both parties, examining the form and terms of the contract and the surrounding circumstances. The Court of Appeal felt that in this case there was no reason to overturn the initial assessment of the position. There was no evidence to indicate that the agent purported to bind himself personally.

To a large extent the agent's personal liability (or lack) of it is a matter of determining the parties' intentions. In *Badgerhill Properties* v *Cottrell* (1991) The Independent 12 June, in making contracts for work with the defendant, T, the director of the plaintiff company, drew up contracts on headed notepaper bearing the company name. Against his own name on this paper T had written 'director' in brackets. The company sued the defendant for non-payment for work done, while the defendants counter-claimed that the work was defective. The question arose as to whether T was personally liable, whether he had been acting on his own behalf or that of the principal company.

The Court of Appeal held that whether T was acting on his own behalf depended to some degree on the intention of the parties. The language of the contract, the fact that the company name appeared on the headed paper, the fact that the company's trading name appeared in the contract all seemed to indicate that the defendant was trading with whoever called themselves by the trade name of the company. The fact that the word agent did not appear was not enough to prevent the contract's being construed as a contract of agency.

Contracts for undisclosed principal

Here the fact of agency is concealed altogether. T has an option: he can sue A on the contract or he can sue P when he discovers his existence; but he must make an election and is bound by it: he cannot sue one and then, having obtained judgment, sue the other, for example, *Clarkson, Booker Ltd* v *Andjel* [1964] 2 QB 775. A booked airline tickets through C Ltd, a firm of travel agents. Later, P & M Ltd claimed that the booking was made on their behalf, so C Ltd asked them for payment. Further correspondence indicated that C Ltd regarded both A and P & M Ltd as being liable. After issuing a writ against P & M Ltd, the company became insolvent. Proceedings were then commenced against A.

HELD: C Ltd had not unequivocally elected to sue only P & M Ltd with full knowledge of all the relevant facts. They had not lost their right to sue A.

P can enforce the contract against T unless:

1. A had no authority at the time of contracting.

2. A's identity was material to the contract.
3. P allowed A to contract on terms incompatible with agency, for example, as 'owner'. T can set up against P any defences he had against A before he discovered the existence of P.

Unauthorised acts of agent

Two situations may arise:

1. If A, although not in fact authorised, acts within his ostensible authority, P is liable on the contract. A is not (but he may be liable to P for breach of duty).
2. If the act is outside A's actual and ostensible authority, P is not liable, but A is liable to T for breach of warranty of authority, even though A acted in good faith, believing he had authority, for example, *Yonge* v *Toynbee* [1910] 1 KB 215. T instructed the solicitors (W) to defend an action for libel against him brought by Y. T went insane before commencement of the action, thereby revoking the solicitors' authority to act. W being unaware of this event delivered a defence to the action. Y asked for the claim to be struck out and costs against W because W acted without authority.

   HELD: that W had impliedly warranted that they had authority to act when this was not so, thus they were personally liable for Y's costs.

   Note: insanity of a principal revokes the agent's authority, but that principal is liable on a contract made with a third party who had no notice of the insanity. See *Drew* v *Nunn* (1879) 4 QBD 661.

19.6   Termination of agency

By act of parties

The termination of agency by act of parties may arise where:

1. the transaction is completed;
2. there is mutual agreement between A and P;
3. A renounces his appointment;
4. P revokes the appointment, except in those cases where A's authority is irrevocable, as where A's authority is 'coupled with an interest', such as a debt due from P to A, the authority being given as security, or where a power of attorney is expressed to be irrevocable and is given to secure a proprietary interest of A or the performance of an obligation owed to A; the power cannot be revoked without A's consent so long as A has that interest or is owed that obligation. Section 4 Powers of Attorney Act 1971.

By operation of law

The termination of agency by operation of law may arise where:

1. P dies, or becomes bankrupt or insane (in case of insanity, notice of termination must be given to T).

    In *Drew* v *Nunn* (above), N permitted his wife to buy boots and shoes from D over a period of time. N went insane in 1873 but recovered by 1877. During this period, D supplied goods to N's wife on credit, unaware of D's condition.

    HELD: N's insanity had not revoked his wife's authority to purchase from D, thus N was liable to pay for them.

2. Supervening illegality or frustration, for example, by destruction of subject matter; death or insanity of A.

    In *Stevenson & Sons* v *Cartonnagen Industrie* [1918] AC 239 A, an English company, contracted with a Germany company, C, to be their sole agents in Britain and their partners here for the manufacture of certain goods.

    HELD: that the contract of agency had been terminated by the outbreak of war between the two countries in 1914. The partnership between the two companies was dissolved.

3. By lapse of time without agency being performed.

19.7 Factors

A factor is defined as a mercantile agent having in the customary course of his business as such agent, authority either to sell goods, or to consign goods for the purpose of sale, or to buy goods or to raise money on the security of goods (s1 Factors Act 1889). This definition should be known and also the circumstances in which, under s2 of that Act, a factor can pass a good title in goods although not authorised to do so by the owner.

Definition of factor

Lord Denning said in *Rolls Razor Ltd* v *Cox* [1967] 1 QB 552, that a factor is:

> 'an agent:
> i) entrusted with the *possession* of goods of several principals, or sometimes only one principal,
> ii) for the purpose of sale *in his own name* without disclosing the name of his principal, and
> iii) he is remunerated by a commission.'

It is the first two of these characteristics that distinguish factors from *brokers*. Moreover, since a factor has possession of his principal's goods, he has a lien on them for the balance of his account with the principal; the broker has no such lien.

Transfer of title by factor

A person claiming a title to goods under s2 must show:

1. that the owner of the goods consented to the factor having possession as such;
2. that the factor was acting in the ordinary course of his business; and
3. that he (the buyer) acted in good faith in buying the goods without notice of any lack of authority on the part of the factor, for example, *Folkes* v *King* [1923] 1 KB 282.

H, a mercantile agent, was instructed by a car owner, F, to sell it for at least £575. He sold it to K for £340 and misappropriated the money.

HELD: F was not entitled to recover the car from K. H had possession of the car in order to sell it with F's permission, and K acquired a good title by purchasing it in good faith and without notice of any fraud.

20

Sale of Goods, Consumer Credit and Supply of Goods and Services

20.1   Sale of goods: definitions

'Contract of sale' – a contract whereby the seller transfers, or agrees to transfer, the property in goods to the buyer, for a money consideration called the price, s2(1) Sale of Goods Act 1979. All section references to this part of the book are to sections of this Act unless otherwise stated.

'Sale' – a contract of sale whereby the property in the goods is transferred at once.

'Agreement to sell' – a contract of sale under which the transfer of the property is to take place at a future time or subject to a condition, s2(5).

'Property' – the right of ownership (also referred to as 'title').

'Goods' – all chattels personal other than things in action and money, s61(1).

'Specific goods' – goods identified and agreed upon at the time a contract of sale is made, s61(1), for example, 'that 1976 Rover 3500'.

'Unascertained goods' – existing goods not specifically identified but referred to by description, for example, 'one of the Rover 3500 cars in your showroom' or '500 tons of wheat out of the cargo of 1,000 tons on board the SS Mars'. See *Re Wait* [1927] 1 Ch 606.

'Ascertained goods' – goods which are identified in accordance with the agreement after the contract is made.

'Existing goods' – goods actually in existence when the contract is made.

'Future goods' – goods to be manufactured or acquired by the seller after the making of the contract of sale, s5(1).

20.2   Formation of the contract

The general rules of contract apply (see, for example, s3 as to capacity). No particular form is required, s4.

20.3   Perishing of the goods

In the case of a contract for the sale of *specific* goods:

1. If, without the knowledge of the seller, the goods have perished *at the time the contract is made*, the contract is void, s6.
2. If, without the fault of either party, the goods *subsequently* perish, the contract is void if the risk has not yet passed to the buyer, s7; if the risk has passed, the buyer bears the loss.

The risk passes with the property, except where otherwise agreed; or where delivery has been delayed through the fault of either party, in which case, the goods are at the risk of the party at fault in respect of any loss that might not have occurred but for such fault, s20. In *Sterns v Vickers* [1923] 1 KB 78, 120,000 gallons of spirit out of 200,000 in a tank was sold. A delivery warrant for the 120,000 gallons was given to the buyer who failed to act upon it, consequently the spirit deteriorated.

HELD: the risk lay with the buyer as the deterioration was his fault in that he had not collected the spirit as he should have done.

Goods have 'perished' if, through damage or deterioration, they have ceased to answer to the contract description, for example, *Asfar & Co v Blundell*, or if the goods have been stolen; even a partial loss is enough if the sale was of an indivisible parcel of specific goods, for example, *Barrow, Lane and Ballard Ltd v Phillip Phillips & Co Ltd*.

In *Asfar & Co v Blundell* [1896] 1 QB 123, a load of dates was impregnated with sewage unknown to the parties at the time of sale.

HELD: the goods had perished.

In *Barrow, Lane & Ballard Ltd v Phillip Phillips & Co Ltd* [1929] 1 KB 574 at the time of a contract to sell 700 bags of Chinese nuts, some 109 of the bags had been stolen.

HELD: the entire consignment had perished since the 700 bags were for the purpose of the contract indivisible.

20.4   The price

The price must be paid wholly or partly in money; it may be fixed in the contract or in an agreed manner, for example, by a third party, s9, or by the course of dealing between the parties; otherwise the buyer must pay a reasonable price, s8.

20.5   Time of payment

Stipulations as to the time of payment are not of the essence, unless otherwise agreed, s10(1). Failure to pay by the agreed date, if any, does not therefore release the seller from his own obligations under the contract.

20.6   Implied terms

Conditions and warranties

In addition to the *express* terms of the contract, certain terms relating to the goods are *implied* in the contract of sale by the SGA 1979. These terms may be either conditions or warranties. A *condition* is a term which goes to the root of the contract, breach of which entitles the buyer to reject the goods and treat the contract as repudiated, in addition to claiming damages.

A *warranty* is a collateral term, the breach of which gives rise to an action for damages, but does not release the buyer from his own obligations.

Whether a term is a condition or a warranty depends upon the construction of the contract. The buyer may elect to treat a breach of condition as a breach of warranty only, and he must do so if the contract is not severable and he has accepted any part of the goods, s1(4).

The implied terms are as follows :

As to title, s12

A *condition* that the seller has a right to sell, for example, *Rowland* v *Divall*, and *warranties* of quiet possession and freedom from encumbrances.

In *Rowland* v *Divall*, the plaintiff 'bought' a car from the defendant who, it transpired, was not the owner. The true owner recovered the car.

HELD: the plaintiff could recover the price he had paid from the defendant.

As to sales by description, s13

A *condition* that the goods supplied shall correspond with the description; this section is applied very strictly in favour of the buyer. See *Re Moore & Co* and *Landauer & Co*. Where the buyer has not seen the goods, but relies on the description, it will be a sale by description (even if the goods are specific goods, for example, *Varley* v *Whipp*); but it may be a sale by description even where the buyer has seen the goods, for example, *Beale* v *Taylor*; and if the sale is by sample as well as by description there is a further implied condition that the bulk corresponds both with the sample and with the description.

In *Re Moore and Landauer & Co* [1921] 2 KB 519, a consignment of canned fruit was ordered to be delivered in boxes of 30 tins. Some of the boxes supplied contained only 24 tins.

HELD: the consignment did not conform to the description.

In *Varley* v *Whipp* [1900] 1 QB 513, a reaping machine was ordered by a buyer, the machine having been described by the seller as new the previous year. In fact, it was much older.

HELD: the machine did not comply with the description.

In *Beale* v *Taylor* [1967] 1 WLR 1193, the subject matter of this contract was described as a 1961 Triumph Herald convertible. The plaintiff saw the car and bought it. In fact, it turned out to be two different cars joined together.

HELD: the car did not comply with the description.

As to quality, s14

A *condition* that the goods are of merchantable quality if the seller sells the goods in the course of a business. This implied term will not apply to defects specifically drawn to the buyer's attention before the contract is made, nor will it apply if the buyer has examined the goods before the contract is made as regards defects which that examination ought to have revealed. In *Thornett and Fehr* v *Beers & Sons* [1919] 1 KB 486, a buyer of barrels of glue inspected the outside of the barrels. Had he looked inside the barrels he would have seen there was a defect in the glue.

HELD: because of the examination, the seller was under no responsibility for the defect.

Goods are merchantable if they are as fit for a purpose for which goods of that kind are commonly bought as it is reasonable to expect having regard to any description applied to them, the price, and all other relevant circumstances; compare *BS Brown & Sons Ltd* v *Craiks Ltd* [1970] 1 WLR 752. A buyer ordered cloth at 36p per yard. The cloth supplied was not suitable for dressmaking which was the buyer's particular purpose, though it was perfectly suitable for industrial purposes. The price of industrial cloth was only 30p per yard.

HELD: the difference of 6p per yard did not make the goods unmerchantable.

As to fitness for purpose

A *condition* that goods sold in the course of a business are reasonably fit for the purpose expressly or by implication made known to the seller by the buyer. Thus the buyer need not expressly state the purpose for which the goods are required if it is obvious, for example, *Frost* v *Aylesbury Dairy Co Ltd* [1905] 1 KB 608 where milk contained typhoid germs.

HELD: it was not fit for its purposes, for example, drinking – even though it had not been stated by the buyer that the milk would be drunk.

But this condition will not be implied if the circumstances show that the buyer did not rely, or that it would have been unreasonable for him to rely, on the seller's skill or judgment.

As to sales by samples, s15

A *condition* that the bulk will correspond with the sample in quality; a *condition* that the buyer will have a reasonable opportunity of comparing the bulk with the sample, and a *condition* that the goods shall be free from any latent defect rendering them unmerchantable.

Exemption clauses

Normally, the implied terms may be varied or negatived by express agreement or by trade usage. But:

1. An express term does not negate an implied term unless it is inconsistent therewith.
2. Any express term exempting the seller from all or any of the implied obligations as to title in s12 (see above) shall be void (s6(1) UCTA).

3. In a consumer sale, any term of the contract which purports to exclude or restrict the operation of ss13–15 Sale of Goods Act, is void. A consumer sale is defined as:

> '... a sale of goods (other than a sale by auction or by competitive tender) by a seller in the course of a business where the goods are of a type ordinarily bought for private use or consumption and are sold to a person who does not buy or hold himself out as buying them in the course of business'.

The onus is on the seller to prove that a particular sale is not a consumer sale (s6(2); s12 UCTA).

4. In the case of 'non-consumer sales', for example, where the buyer is in business to re-sell, an exemption clause is not enforceable to the extent that the buyer satisfies the court that it would not be fair and reasonable for the seller to rely on that term (s6(3); s11(2); s11(5) UCTA).

20.7   Passing of the property

The property passes at the time the parties intend it to pass, s17; but the property in *unascertained* goods cannot pass until they have been ascertained, s16.

In the absence of evidence to the contrary, the property is deemed to pass in accordance with the following rules, s18:

1 *Unconditional* contract for sale of *specific* goods in a *deliverable* state; the property passes when the contract is made, even though the time of payment or of delivery is postponed. In *Tarling* v *Baxter* [1827] 6 B & C 360, the buyer bought a haystack. Before he took it away it was destroyed by fire.

  HELD: property had passed and so the loss fell on the buyer.

  Goods are in a 'deliverable state' when they are in such a state that the buyer would be bound to take delivery of them under the contract, s61.

2. Contract for sale of *specific* goods, still to be put in a deliverable state; the property does not pass until this has been done and the buyer has notice thereof.

3. Contract for sale of *specific* goods in a deliverable state, the price to be ascertained by the seller weighing, measuring, etc; the property does not pass until this is done and the buyer has notice thereof;

4. Goods delivered on *approval* or *sale or return* or similar terms; the property passes when the buyer:
   a) signifies his approval or acceptance to seller; or
   b) does any other act adopting the transaction; or
   c) retains the goods without giving notice of rejection within a fixed or reasonable time.

5. Contract for sale of *unascertained* or *future* goods sold by description; the property passes when goods of that description and in a deliverable state are *unconditionally appropriated* to the contract by one party with the consent of the

other, for example, by the seller delivering the goods to the buyer or to a carrier on his behalf, without reserving the right of disposal. The buyer's assent to the appropriation may be given either before or after the appropriation, and may be implied. In *Pignatoro* v *Gilroy* [1919] 1 KB 459, a buyer ordered some bags of rice which he was to collect when they were ready from the seller. The seller informed him the bags were ready. The buyer, however, did nothing for three weeks. The bags were stolen during this time.

HELD: the buyer had by his action assented to the appropriation and thus the property in the goods and the risk of loss had passed to him.

20.8   Transfer of title

The general rule is nemo dat quod non habet: no one can transfer title to goods except the true owner or his authorised agent. Exceptions:

Estoppel

Where the owner is *estopped* by his conduct from denying the seller's authority to sell, for example, by 'holding out' a person as his agent, s21(1).

Sale by factor

Where goods are sold by a factor to a person taking in good faith without notice of any lack of authority, s21(2)(a); also see Chapter 19.

Sale under common law or statutory power

Where goods are sold under a common law or statutory power of sale or under a court order, s21(2)(b), for example, by a pawnbroker or sheriff.

Sale in market overt

Where goods are sold in market overt to a person taking in good faith without notice of any defect in title, s22(1); this is the case where goods are sold in any shop in the City of London (which deals in goods of the kind in question), during business hours on business days, or elsewhere at a recognised market or fair. In *Bishopgate Motor Finance Corporation* v *Transport Brakes Ltd* [1949] 1 KB 322, a hirer of a car under a hire-purchase agreement took it to Maidstone market where he tried to sell it by auction and failed. He then sold it privately within the precincts of the market.

HELD: the buyer got a good title.

See also *Reid* v *Metropolitan Police Commissioner* [1973] QB 551. A sale of a stolen candelabra in the New Caledonian Market, Southwark, took place at 4.00 am.

HELD: the sale did not take place in market overt, since it did not occur between sunrise and sunset, therefore, the purchaser did not acquire a good title.

Sale under voidable title

Where goods held under a voidable contract are sold to a person taking in good faith without notice of the defect before the seller's title has been avoided, s23; this section applies, for instance, where the contract is voidable for fraud, for example, *Lewis* v *Averay* but not where it is void, or example, *Cundy* v *Lindsay*. For these cases, see Chapter 13.

Sale by buyer or seller in possession

Where the buyer or seller is, with the consent of the other party, in possession of the goods, or of the documents of title to the goods, and he sells the goods to a third person who takes them in good faith without notice of the claims of the other party, the third person will obtain a good title, s25; a change in the nature of the seller's possession, for instance, from possession as owner to possession as a bailee or even as a trespasser, does not affect the operation of the rule.

Sale by hirer of motor vehicles

Where the hirer or buyer of a motor vehicle under a hire-purchase or condition sale agreement sells the vehicle to a *private* purchaser who takes it in good faith without notice of the agreement; similar protection is afforded to the first private purchaser from a trade or finance purchaser ss27-9 Hire Purchase Act 1965.

20.9   Performance of the contract

The basic duties imposed by a contract of sale are *delivery* of possession of the goods by the seller, and *acceptance* and payment by the buyer, s27; unless otherwise agreed, delivery and payment are concurrent conditions, s28. Whether the buyer is to collect the goods or the seller is to send them to the buyer is to be determined by the terms, express or implied, of the contract between them, s29(1).

Delivery

Unless otherwise agreed, the place of delivery is the seller's place of business or residence. If the seller has agreed to send the goods to the buyer, he must do so within a reasonable time, at a reasonable hour, and at his own expense, s29; moreover, a seller who is required to deliver at the buyer's premises will be discharged if the goods are delivered to a person having apparent authority to receive them. In *Galbraith & Grant Ltd* v *Block* [1922] 2 KB 155, sellers were contractually bound to deliver a crate of champagne to the buyer's house. There it was received by a respectable looking and apparently authorised person. The champagne was never seen again.

HELD: the sellers were entitled to the price from the buyers.

If the seller delivers more or less than the quantity contracted for, or delivers goods of the contract description mixed with other goods, the buyer may reject the whole of the goods or that part which does not conform with the terms of the contract, s30. The buyer cannot accept those goods that do not conform, unless the parties agree.

The buyer need not accept delivery by instalments, unless he has agreed to do so. In the latter event, if the goods are to be paid for separately, and there is a failure to make or take delivery of one or more instalments, the breach may constitute the repudiation of the whole contract, or a severable breach giving rise to a claim for damages only, depending upon the circumstances, s31. The test is the quantity of goods involved in relation to the contract as a whole and the likelihood of repetition of the breach. In *Maple Flock Co Ltd* v *Universal Furniture Products Ltd* [1934] 1 KB 148, a contract was made for the delivery of 100 tons of rag flock at a rate of three loads per week. The first 15 deliveries were satisfactory, the 16th was not, but the buyer nevertheless accepted a further four loads, all of which were satisfactory. The buyers then refused to take any further deliveries.

HELD: they were not entitled to do this. There was little likelihood of the breach being repeated.

Delivery of the goods to a carrier is prima facie a delivery of the goods to the buyer, but the buyer may decline to treat if the seller has failed to make a reasonable contract of carriage and the goods are lost or damaged in the course of transit, s32.

Acceptance

The buyer is deemed to have accepted the goods when (s35) he intimates his acceptance to the seller; or the goods have been delivered to him and he does any act in relation to them inconsistent with the seller's ownership; or he retains the goods longer than is reasonable without intimating to the seller that he has rejected them.

But he is not deemed to have accepted them, where he has not previously examined them, until he has had a reasonable opportunity of examining them, and the seller must afford him this opportunity on tendering delivery if so requested, s34.

If the buyer properly refuses to accept the goods, he is not bound to return them to the seller, s36; an unjustified refusal renders him liable to the seller for any loss thereby caused, s37.

20.10 Remedies of the unpaid seller

In the event of non-payment, the seller has remedies against the goods and against the buyer.

Remedies against goods

An unpaid seller has the following rights over the goods:

1. A lien on the goods, if the property has passed and the seller is still in possession. If credit has been given, no lien can exist until the period of credit has expired, or the buyer is insolvent, s41.

   The right may be lost by waiver, for example, by assenting to a sub-sale, or loss of possession, s43;

2. *A right to stop the goods in transit* (stoppage in transit) and retake delivery while they are in the possession of a carrier if the buyer becomes insolvent, s44. The goods are still in transit if the buyer rejects them and the carrier continues in possession of them; but the goods cease to be in transit if the buyer takes delivery before they reach their destination, or where the carrier either acknowledges to the buyer that he holds the goods on his behalf, or where he wrongfully refuses to deliver the goods to the buyer, s45;

3. A right to *withhold delivery*, co-existent with the above rights, if the property has not passed to the buyer, s39(2). (Note, that this is not a lien – no one can have a lien over his own goods.)

4. An unpaid seller who has exercised his right of lien or stoppage in transit has a right of *resale* only if:
   a) the goods are of a perishable nature; or
   b) the seller gives notice of his intention to resell, and the buyer does not tender the price within a reasonable time thereof; or
   c) the right of resale is expressly reserved in the contract, s48.

   The effect of resale is to rescind the original contract and the whole of the proceeds belong to the unpaid seller.

   The unpaid seller's rights of lien or stoppage in transit against the goods are not affected by any sale or other disposition thereof by the buyer unless:
   a) the seller has assented to it; or
   b) a document of title to the goods has been transferred to the buyer, and the buyer has further transferred it to a person taking it in good faith and for value, s47.

Remedies against the buyer

Action for the price

The seller can sue the buyer for the price if the property has passed to the buyer; or a date for payment, irrespective of delivery, has been agreed, even though the property has not passed, s49.

Action for damages for non-acceptance

If an action for the price is not available, the seller may claim damages if the buyer wrongfully refuses to accept and pay for the goods. The measure of damages is the estimated loss directly and naturally resulting in the ordinary course of events from the buyer's breach of contract. Where there is an available market for the goods in question, the measure of damages is prima facie to be ascertained by the difference between the contract price and the market price at the date of the breach, s50. However, if there is no available market, then the seller is entitled to damages for the loss of his bargain, and this depends on the state of demand for the goods. See *WL Thompson Ltd* v *Robinson (Gunmakers) Ltd*; contrast *Charter* v *Sullivan*.

In *WL Thompson Ltd* v *Robinson (Gunmakers) Ltd* [1955] Ch 177, the defendants contracted to buy a Standard Vanguard car from the plaintiffs. However, they refused to take delivery of the car. At the time there was no available market for this type of car.

HELD: the measure of damages claimable by the plaintiffs was the loss of profit on the sale.

In *Charter* v *Sullivan* [1957] 2 QB 117, a buyer failed to take delivery of a Hillman Minx car in circumstances where demand outstripped supply.

HELD: the measure of damages was purely nominal since there was no difficulty in finding another buyer for the car.

20.11 Remedies of the buyer

The buyer may have one or more of the following remedies in the event of a breach of contract by the seller.

Remedies for damages for non-delivery

This is available if the seller wrongfully neglects or refuses to deliver the goods, s51. The damages are calculated in the same manner as in 'Action for damages for non-acceptance' (above).

Specific performance

Such an order may be made if the contract is for specific or ascertained goods, and the court thinks that this is an appropriate remedy, s52.

Action for breach of warranty

On a breach of warranty, or of a condition which the buyer chooses or is required to treat as a breach of warranty, the buyer may set off his claim for damages against the purchase price, or bring an action against the seller for damages for the breach, or both, s53.

A breach of condition, which can be treated as such, enables the buyer to reject the goods and to claim damages for the breach.

20.12   Cif and fob contracts

These terms relate to contracts for the sale of goods to be carried by sea. 'Cif' means 'costs, insurance and freight'; 'fob' means 'free on board'. In a cif contract, the seller pays insurance and freight, while in an fob contract, he delivers the goods to the vessel and the buyer is responsible for insurance and freight from that time on.

Cif contracts

Under a cif contract, the seller undertakes to ship the goods at his own expense to the port of destination and to insure them during the voyage; the property normally passes when the shipping documents are tendered to the buyer, though the risk passes when the goods have been lifted over the ship's rail; thus, if the goods are lost at sea, the buyer must still pay the price against tender of the documents.

Fob contracts

Under an fob contract, carriage and insurance are arranged by the buyer, the seller's duty being merely to delivery the goods on board an appointed ship; the seller must give the buyer sufficient information to enable him to insure the goods, s32(3). The risk and property usually pass to the buyer when the goods cross the ship's rail.

20.13   Hire-purchase, credit sale and conditional sale agreements

These types of agreement are governed by the Consumer Credit Act 1974, provided that they constitute what is known as a 'consumer credit agreement'. A consumer credit agreement for the purpose of the Act must be for an individual, and for credit not exceeding £5,000.

Hire-purchase agreements, conditional sale agreements and credit sale agreements may all qualify as 'consumer credit agreements'.

Hire-purchase agreements

A hire-purchase agreement is an agreement by an owner of goods to hire them out to a bailee, and to give the bailee an option to purchase conditional on his completing the necessary payments for the goods and complying with the terms of the agreement.

Conditional sale agreement

A conditional sale agreement is an agreement for the sale of goods under which the purchase price or part of it is payable by instalments, and the property in the goods or land is to remain in the seller (notwithstanding that the buyer is to be in possession of the goods) until such conditions as to the payment of instalments or otherwise, as may be specified in the agreement, are fulfilled.

Credit sale agreements

A credit sale agreement is an agreement for the sale of goods, under which the purchase price or part of it is payable by instalments, but which is not a conditional sale agreement. The ownership in the goods therefore passes immediately to the buyer.

The Consumer Credit Act

Under the Consumer Credit Act, a licence issued by the Director-General of Fair Trading must be obtained by a person wishing to carry on a consumer credit business. If a consumer credit agreement is entered into by an unlicensed creditor, the agreement is unenforceable against the debtor, unless the Director-General makes an order that agreements made during a certain period by the creditor are to be treated as though he had been licensed.

Powers are conferred on the Secretary of State to make regulations as to the form and content of the documents embodying consumer credit agreements. The object of the regulations is to ensure that the debtor is made aware of his rights and duties, the amount and rate of the total charge for credit, the protection and remedies available to him under the Act, and any other matters which in the opinion of the Secretary of State it is desirable for him to know about concerning the agreement. In every form of consumer credit agreement, the consumer must be left with a copy of the entire agreement for his own information.

Where the antecedent negotiations included oral representations made by the dealer or on his behalf in the presence of the debtor, then the debtor has the benefit of a 'cooling off' period, unless the agreement was signed by him at the creditor's or dealer's business premises. The right to cancel may be exercised by the debtor serving a notice of cancellation at any time between his signing the agreement and the fifth day following the day on which he received his copy of the executed agreement. The effect of cancellation is that the cancelled agreement is treated as if it had never existed. Any sum paid by the debtor under or in contemplation of the agreement is repayable. Subject to a lien for the repayment of any sums owing, the debtor must restore any goods he has in his possession to the person from whom he acquired possession, and take reasonable care of the goods. He need not return the goods to the owner, though he must allow the owner to collect them himself. If the owner has not collected them within 21 days, the buyer is under no further duty to take care of them.

The Supply of Goods (Implied Terms) Act 1973

By virtue of the Supply of Goods (Implied Terms) Act 1973, substantially the same terms are implied in the case of all hire-purchase agreement as are implied in contracts for the sale of goods (see 20.6 with appropriate changes in terminology, for example, 'owner' is substituted for 'seller' and 'hirer' is substituted for 'buyer').

Again, the implied terms can only be excluded in substantially the same circumstances as in a sale of goods (see 20.6, 'Exemption Clauses').

The debtor under a hire-purchase or conditional sale agreement is entitled to terminate the agreement at any time before the final instalment. Unless the agreement provides for some smaller payment, the debtor is liable to pay to the creditor the amount (if any) by which one-half of the total price exceeds the aggregate of the sums paid and the sums due in respect of the total price immediately before the termination. The creditor cannot exercise any right of termination or repossession granted by the agreement unless he serves a 'default notice' upon the debtor. The default notice must specify the nature of the alleged breach; if the breach is capable of remedy, what action is required to remedy it and the date by which that action is to be taken; and if the breach is not capable of remedy, the sum (if any) required to be paid as compensation for the breach and the date by which it is to be paid. The date specified must be not less than seven days after the date of service of the default notice.

After one-third of the total price has been paid or tendered, the creditor cannot enforce any right to recover possession of the goods otherwise than by legal action. Contravention releases the hirer or buyer from all liability, and entitles him to recover all sums paid under the agreement. This provision does not apply if the hirer consents to repossession. The court on hearing the application for possession may order:

1. specific delivery of all the goods to the owner or seller; or
2. as in (1), but the operation of the order to be postponed on condition that the hirer or buyer or any guarantor pays the unpaid balance of the price at such times, and in such amounts, either as agreed by the parties or as the court thinks just; or
3. specific delivery of a part of the goods to the owner or seller, and for the transfer to the hirer or buyer of the title of the owner or seller to the remainder of the goods.

The limits on the creditor's right of termination or repossession do not apply to credit sale agreements because, under such an agreement, ownership in the goods has passed and the concept of termination or repossession does not arise.

20.14 Supply of goods and services

The Sale of Goods Act 1979 and the Supply of Goods (Implied Terms) Act 1973 cover, as we have seen, sale and hire-purchase agreements. Prior to the introduction of the Supply of Goods and Services Act, the supply of services and some transfers of property in goods outside the then current statutory control were covered by the common law. To remedy the lacunae and embody the law as a code, the Supply of Goods and Services Act 1982 was enacted. The Act is divided into two major parts: Part I governing the supply of goods and, in particular, covering contracts for the transfer of property in goods and contracts for the hire of goods; Part II is exclusively concerned with the supply of services. All section references in this part of the book refer, unless otherwise stated, to the Supply of Goods and Services Act 1982.

20.15 Contracts for the transfer of property in goods

'Section 1(1) In this Act a "contract for the transfer of goods" means a contract under which one person transfers or agrees to transfer to another the property in goods, other than an excepted contract.

(2) For the purposes of this section an excepted contract means any of the following:

a) a contract of sale of goods;

b) a hire-purchase agreement;

c) a contract under which the property in goods is (or is to be) transferred in exchange for trading stamps or their redemption;

d) a transfer or agreement to transfer which is made by deed and for which there is no consideration other than presumed consideration imported by the deed;

e) a contract intended to operate by way of mortgage, pledge, charge or other security.

(3) For the purposes of this Act a contract is a contract for the transfer of goods whether or not services are also provided or to be provided under the contract, and (subject to subsection (2) above) whatever is the nature of the consideration for the transfer or agreement to transfer.'

Section 1(1) includes contracts where property is transferred, or it is to be transferred, on the fulfilment of a condition.

'Property' is defined in s18(1) of the 1982 Act as 'the general property in "goods" ... and not merely a special property'. This reflects the definition in s61(1) Sale of Goods Act 1979; general property broadly meaning ownership.

By s1(2) of the 1982 Act, certain contracts are excepted from the operation of the Act:

Sale of Goods: the 1979 statute governs the sale of goods and transactions within that statute and are not within the scope of the 1982 legislation.

Hire-purchase agreements: hire-purchase agreements as defined in s189(1) Consumer Credit Act 1974 are outside the ambit of the section.

The other excepted contracts under s1(2)(c), (d) and (e) are less important for the purpose of this course.

20.16 Agreements within the 1982 Act

Section 1(3) of the 1982 Act is an important provision, stating that a contract which transfers property as defined in the Act remains within the Act, whether or not services are also provided or to be provided under the contract. The second limb of s1(3) brings within the ambit of the statute contracts regardless of whether the consideration is money consideration or otherwise. Accordingly, barter and exchange contracts, which fall outside the 1979 Act, are covered by the 1982 Act.

For example, the case of *Esso Petroleum Co Ltd* v *Commissioners of Customs and Excise* [1976] 1 All ER 117 where medallions were given to buyers of a certain quantity of petrol, although not sales of goods, would be transfers of property for the purposes of the 1982 Act.

More importantly, contracts for skill and labour or work and materials are within the 1982 Act if general property in goods passes.

In *Robinson* v *Graves* [1935] 1 KB 579, a contract for an artist to paint a portrait was a contract for skill and labour, not one of the supply of goods. The 1982 Act would now cover the contract.

Consequently, contracts under which goods and services are supplied, in so far as the essence of the contract is one for service and labour, will be subject to the 1982 Act. Contracts for the installation of central heating, plumbing and electrics will normally be within this part of the 1982 Act if property in goods passes.

Note: the essence of the contract must not be for the passing of property in goods (where the Sale of Goods Act 1979 will govern).

See and compare the following cases: *GH Myers and Co* v *Brent Cross Services Co* [1934] 1 KB 46, *Lee* v *Griffin* (1861) 30 LJ QB 252, *Cammell Laird & Co Ltd* v *Manganese Bronze and Brass* [1934] AC 402 and *Young & Marten Ltd* v *McManus Childs Ltd* [1969] 1 AC 454.

20.17 Implied conditions and warranties

All contracts within the scope of s1 of the Act have implied into them the conditions and warranties stipulated in ss2–5 of the 1982 Act. The distinction between condition and warranties has already been covered in depth, and students are referred back to the relevant parts of the course material.

Title

'Section 2(1) In a contract for the transfer of goods, other than one to which subsection (3) below applies, there is an implied condition on the part of the transferor that in the case of a transfer of the property in the goods he has a right to transfer the property and in the case of an agreement to transfer the property in the goods he will have such a right at the time when the property is to be transferred.

(2) In a contract for the transfer of goods, other than one to which subsection (3) below applies, there is also an implied warranty that:

a) the goods are free and will remain free until the time when the property is to be transferred, from any charge or encumbrance not disclosed or known to the transferee before the contract is made, and

b) the transferee will enjoy quiet possession of the goods except so far as it may be disturbed by the owner or other person entitled to the benefit of any charge or encumbrance so disclosed or known.

(3) This subsection applies to a contract for the transfer of goods in the case of which there appears from the contract or is to be inferred from its circumstances an intention that the transferor should transfer only such title as he or a third person may have.

(4) In a contract to which subsection (3) above applies there is an implied warranty that all charges or encumbrances known to the transferor and not known to the transferee have been disclosed to the transferee before the contract is made.

(5) In a contract to which subsection (3) above applies there is also an implied warranty that none of the following will disturb the transferee's quiet possession of the goods, namely:

a) the transferor;

b) in a case where the parties to the contract intend that the transferor should transfer only such title as a third person may have, that person:

c) anyone claiming through or under the transferor or that third person otherwise than under a charge or encumbrance disclosed or known to the transferee before the contract is made.'

Section 2 of the 1982 Act is identical to s12 of the 1979 Act save in so far as it applies to the transfer, rather than the sale, of goods. Both sections contain one condition and two warranties. See *Rowland* v *Divall*, 18.2.

Correspondence with description

Section 3 of the 1982 Act provides:

'(1) This section applies where, under a contract for the transfer of goods, the transferor transfers or agrees to transfer the property in goods by description.

(2) In such a case there is an implied condition that the goods will correspond with the description.

(3) If the transferor transfers or agrees to transfer the property in the goods by sample as well as by description it is not sufficient that the bulk of the goods corresponds with the sample of the goods if the goods do not also correspond with the description.

(4) A contract is not prevented from falling within subsection (1) above by reason only that, being exposed for supply, the goods are selected by the transferee.'

Section 3 of the 1982 Act is adapted from s13 of the 1979 Act. The case law relevant to the development of that provision, and the decisions upon the old 1893

Sale of Goods Act, are applicable mutatis mutandis. See *Beale* v *Taylor* [1967] 3 All
ER 253, *Grant* v *Australian Knitting Mills* [1936] AC 85, *Ashington Piggeries* v
Christopher Hill [1972] AC 441 and *Arcos* v *Ronaasen* [1933] AC 470.

Merchantable quality

Section 4 of the 1982 Act provides:

'(1) Except as provided by this section and s5 below and subject to the provisions of any
other enactment, there is no implied condition or warranty about the quality or fitness for
any particular purpose of goods supplied under a contract for the transfer of goods.
(2) Where, under such a contract, the transferor transfers the property in goods in the
course of a business, there is (subject to subsection (3) below) an implied condition that
the goods supplied under the contract are of merchantable quality.
(3) There is no such condition as is mentioned in subs(2) above:
a) as regards defects specifically drawn to the transferee's attention before the contract is
made; or
b) if the transferee examines the goods before the contract is made, as regards defects
which that examination ought to reveal.
... (9) Goods of any kind are of merchantable quality within the meaning of subsection (2)
above if they are as fit for the purpose or purposes for which goods of that kind are
commonly supplied as it is reasonable to expect having regard to any description applied
to them, the price (if relevant) and all the other relevant circumstances.'

Section 18(1) defines 'business' as including 'a profession and the activities of any
government department or local or public authority'.

'Quality' as defined in s18(1) includes the 'state or condition' of goods.

In all respects, s4(2), (3) and (9) mirror s14(2), (3) and (6) of the Sale of Goods
Act 1979. The cases discussed under s14 SGA should be referred to.

Note:

1. For this condition to be implied in to the contract, the transferor *must* transfer
property in the course of business.
2. As RG Lawson points out in his *Practical Guide to the Act*:

'The implied condition as to merchantable quality refers to the goods supplied "under"
the contract of transfer, thus encompassing more than just the goods, the property in
which is to pass pursuant to the contract. For instance if a firm installs central heating
fired by oil, any oil provided by the contractors will have to meet the requirement as to
merchantable quality even though it is not provided as part of the agreement but as part of
an initial test to determine the satisfactory working of the equipment.'

Fitness for purpose

'Section 4(4) subs (5) below applies where, under a contract for the transfer of goods, the
transferor transfers the property in goods to the course of a business and the transferee,
expressly or by implication, makes known:
a) to the transferor, or
b) where the consideration or part of the consideration for the transfer is a sum payable by

instalment and the goods were previously sold by a credit-broker to the transferor, to that credit-broker,

any particular purpose for which the goods are being acquired.

(5) In that case there is (subject to subsection (6) below) an implied condition that the goods supplied under the contract are reasonably fit for that purpose, whether or not that is a purpose for which such goods are commonly supplied.

(6) Subsection (5) above does not apply where the circumstances show that the transferee does not rely, or that it is unreasonable for him to rely, on the skill or judgment of the transferor or creditbroker.

(7) An implied condition or warranty about quality or fitness for a particular purpose may be annexed by usage to a contract for the transfer of goods.

(8) The preceding provisions of this section apply to a transfer by a person who in the course of a business is acting as agent for another as they apply to a transfer by a principal in the course of a business, except where that other is not transferring in the course of a business and either the transferee knows that fact or reasonable steps are taken to bring it to the transferee's notice before the contract concerned is made.'

Again, the 1982 Act follows the provisions of s14(3) of the 1979 Act.

Section 4(8) corresponds with s14(5) of the 1979 Act; and s4(7) with s14(4) of the 1979 Act. See *Peter Darlington Partners Ltd* v *Gosho Co Ltd* [1964] 1 Lloyd's Rep 149.

Transfer by sample

Section 15 Sale of Goods Act 1979 is the basis upon which s5 of the 1982 Act was drafted.

Section 5 provides:

'(1) This section applies where, under a contract for the transfer of goods, the transferor transfers or agrees to transfer the property in the goods by reference to a sample.

(2) In such a case there is an implied condition:

a) that the bulk will correspond with the sample in quality; and

b) that the transferee will have a reasonable opportunity of comparing the bulk with the sample; and

c) that the goods will be free from any defect, rendering them unmerchantable, which would not be apparent on reasonable examination of the sample.

(3) In subsection (2)(c) above "unmerchantable" is to be construed in accordance with section 4(9) above.

(4) For the purposes of this section a transferor transfers or agrees to transfer the property in goods by reference to a sample where there is an express or implied term to that effect in the contract concerned.'

20.18   Contracts for the hire of goods

Prior to the 1982 Act, simple hire or leasing agreements were outside the scope of the statutory implied terms appertaining to hire-purchase, conditional sale or ordinary sale contracts.

Sections 6 to 10 of the 1982 Act introduce the regime mutatis mutandi to hire agreements.

'Section 6 defined the contracts concerned.'

'(1) In this Act a "contract of the hire of goods" means a contract under which one person bails or agrees to bail goods to another by way of hire, other than an excepted contract.

(2) For the purposes of this section an excepted contract means any of the following:

a) a hire-purchase agreement;

b) a contract under which goods are (or are to be) bailed in exchange for trading stamps on their redemption.

(3) For the purposes of this Act a contract is a contract for the hire of goods whether or not services are also provided or to be provided under the contract, and (subject to subsection (2) above) whatever is the nature of the consideration for the bailment or agreement to bail by way of hire.'

Hire-purchase agreements are, of course, excluded from the operation of the 1982 Act, being governed already by the Supply of Goods (Implied Terms) Act 1973.

Note that although services may be provided under the hire contract as well as the goods, the provisions of this part of Part I of the 1982 Act still apply. For example, the contract for a hire of a car may include charges in respect of maintenance which the hirer is obliged to undertake with the owner.

A contract for the hire of goods encompasses contracts where goods are bailed by way of hire; viz the delivery of goods by one to another without title in the goods being transferred. The bailee, therefore, must have possession of the goods before the 1982 Act applies. Hire or leasing agreements are accordingly the main categories of agreement falling within s6 of the 1982 Act.

20.19 Implied conditions and warranties in hire contracts

The right to transfer possession

Section 7

'(1) In a contract for the hire of goods there is an implied condition on the part of the bailor that in the case of a bailment he has a right to transfer possession of the goods by way of hire for the period of the bailment and in the case of an agreement to bail he will have such a right at the time of the bailment.

(2) In a contract for the hire of goods there is also an implied warranty that the bailee will enjoy quiet possession of the goods for the period of the bailment except so far as the possession may be disturbed by the owner or other person entitled to the benefit or any charge or encumbrance disclosed or known to the bailee before the contract is made.

(3) The preceding provisions of this section do not affect the right of the bailor to repossess the goods under an express or implied term of the contract.'

Note:

1. Section 7(1): the bailor must have a right to transfer possession. (He need not be the owner of the goods.)

2. Section 7(2): the warranty follows the analogous provision in the 1979 Act.

However, there is no statutory warranty that goods are free from any undisclosed charge or encumbrance.

3. Hire agreements may be regulated agreements within the Consumer Credit Act 1974 and, if so, either the free and voluntary consent of the bailee must be given at the time the bailor wishes to repossess or the order of the court is required.

By s8:

'(1) This section applies where, under a contract for the hire of goods, the bailor bails or agrees to bail the goods by description.
(2) In such a case there is an implied condition that the goods will correspond with the description.
(3) If under the contract the bailor bails or agrees to bail the goods by reference to a sample as well as a description it is not sufficient that the bulk of the goods corresponds with the sample if the goods do not also correspond with the description.
(4) A contract is not prevented from falling within subsection (1) above by reason only that, being exposed for supply, the goods are selected by the bailee.'

The section is analogous to the 1979 Act.

Merchantable quality

Section 9 of the 1982 Act provides:

'(1) Except as provided by this section and s10 below and subject to the provisions of any other enactment, there is no implied condition or warranty about the quality or fitness for any particular purpose of goods bailed under a contract for the hire of goods.
(2) Where, under such a contract, the bailor bails goods in the course of a business, there is (subject to subsection (3) below) an implied condition that the goods supplied under the contract are of merchantable quality.
(3) There is no such condition as is mentioned in subsection (2) above:
a) as regards defects specifically drawn to the bailee's attention before the contract is made; or
b) if the bailee examines the goods before the contract is made, as regards defects which that examination ought to reveal.'
... (9) Goods of any kind are of merchantable quality within the meaning of subsection (2) above if they are as fit for the purpose or purposes for which goods of that kind are commonly supplied as it is reasonable to expect having regard to any description applied to them, the consideration for the bailment (if relevant) and all the other relevant circumstances.'

See discussion above.

Fitness for purpose

By s9:

'(4) Subsection (5) below applies where, under a contract for the hire of goods, the bailor bails goods in the course of a business and the bailee, expressly or by implication, makes known:

a) to the bailor in the course of negotiations conducted by him in relation to the making of the contract, or

b) to a credit-broker in the course of negotiations conducted by that broker in relation to the making of the contract, or any particular purpose for which the goods are being bailed.

(5) In that case there is (subject to subsection (6) below) an implied condition that the goods supplied under the contract are reasonably fit for that purpose, whether or not that is a purpose for which such goods are commonly supplied.

(6) Subsection (5) above does not apply where the circumstances show that the bailee does not rely, or that it is unreasonable for him to rely, on the skill or judgment of the transferor or creditbroker.'

These provisions again follow the Sale of Goods Act 1979 model. The only difference is the noticeable inclusion of the words 'in the course of negotiation'. It is doubted whether this adds anything to the interpretation of this section as compared to the previous statutory wording.

Hire by sample

Section 10(1) applies where, under a contract for the hire of goods, the bailor bails or agrees to bail the goods by reference to a sample.

'(2) In such a case there is an implied condition:

a) that the bulk will correspond with the sample in quality; and

b) that the bailee will have a reasonable opportunity of comparing the bulk with the sample; and

c) that the goods will be free from any defect, rendering them unmerchantable, which would not be apparent on reasonable examination of the sample.

(3) In subsection (2)(c) above "unmerchantable" is to be construed in accordance with section 9(9) above.

(4) For the purposes of this section a bailor bails or agrees to bail goods by reference to a sample where there is an express or implied term to that effect in the contract concerned.'

Exclusion of liability

The basic rule, which reflects s55 of the 1979 Act is confirmed in s11 of the 1982 Act.

By s11:

'(1) Where a right, duty or liability would arise under a contract for the transfer of goods or a contract for the hire of goods by implication of law, it may (subject to subsection (2) below and the 1977 Unfair Contract Terms Act) be negatived or varied by express agreement, or by the course of dealing between the parties, or by such usage as binds both parties to the contract.

(2) An express condition or warranty does not negative a condition or warranty implied by the preceding provisions of this Act unless inconsistent with it.

(3) Nothing in the preceding provisions of this Act prejudices the operation of any other enactment or any rule of law whereby any condition or warranty (other than one relating to quality or fitness) is to be implied in a contract for the transfer of goods or a contract for the hire of goods.'

The Unfair Contract Terms Act 1977 is expressly referred to in s11(1) of the 1972 Act, and the referment provision of that Act is s7.

Section 7 of the UCTA 1977 controls attempts to exclude liability where the possession or ownership of goods passed under or in pursuance of a contract not governed by the law of sale of goods and hire purchase.

To title

Unlike s6 of UCTA 1977, however, s7 permits the exclusion of terms (if any) as to title save in so far as the reasonableness test is satisfied. In Hire Purchase and Sale of Goods Act cases, s6 expressly forbids the exclusion of terms as to title.

Section 17(2) of Part III of the 1982 Act, however, adds a new s7(3A) to UCTA 1977, providing:

> '(2) The following subsection shall be inserted after s7(3) of the 1977 Act:
> (3A) Liability for breach of the obligations arising under s2 of the Supply of Goods and Services Act 1982 (implied terms about title etc in certain contracts for the transfer of the property in goods) cannot be excluded or restricted by reference to any such term.
> (3) In consequence of subsection (2) above, in s7(4) of the 1977 Act, after "cannot" there shall be inserted "(in a case to which subsection (3A) above does not apply)".'

Although s2 of the 1982 Act is covered, the test of reasonableness must still be applied in relation to hire contracts under s7 of the 1982 Act.

Furthermore, the Consumer Transactions (Restrictions on Statements) Order 1976 (SI 1976 No 1813), which makes it unlawful to attempt to exclude terms implied by the Sale of Goods Act 1979, does not apply to s7 UCTA 1977 exclusions.

Correspondence with description, merchantable quality and fitness for purpose

Section 7(2) of UCTA 1977 only deals with consumer contracts as defined in s12 of UCTA 1977 (see back to course materials). In respect of contracts falling within s7(2), and the implied terms as to correspondence with description or sample, merchantable quality and fitness for purposes, terms cannot be excluded or restricted by contract.

In respect of non-consumer contracts, s7(3) of UCTA 1977 permits exclusion or restriction of the implied terms in so far as the clause is reasonable.

Note:

1. Section 3 of UCTA 1977 which applies as is relevant to contracts within the 1982 Act.
2. For what is reasonable see s11 and Schedule 2 of UCTA 1977 and the previous discussion.

20.20   Contracts for the supply of services

By s12:

'(1) In this Act a "contract for the supply of a service" means, subject to subsection (2) below, a contract under which a person ("the supplier") agrees to carry out a service.

(2) For the purposes of this Act, a contract of service or apprenticeship is not a contract for the supply of a service.

(3) Subject to subsection (2) above, a contract is a contract for the supply of a service for the purposes of this Act whetheµr or not goods are also:

a) transferred or to be transferred, or

b) bailed or to be bailed by way of hire,

under a contract, and whatever is the nature of the consideration for which the service is to be carried out.

(4) The Secretary of State may by order provide that one or more of ss13 to 15 below shall not apply to services of a description specified in the order, and such an order may make different provision for different circumstances.

(5) The power to make an order under subsection (4) above shall be exercisable by statutory instrument subject to annulment in pursuance of a resolution of either House of Parliament.'

Note that by subsection (3), contracts for the supply of a service are still governed by Part II of the Act notwithstanding that goods are transferred or to be transferred under the contract or that goods are bailed by way of hire. A hire-purchase agreement which involves the provision of a service, although unusual, would be governed by Part II of the 1982 Act.

Note that services provided by builders, architects, surveyors, estate agents, barbers, etc, are all within Part II, as are services provided by lawyers. The latter category may be exempted from the operation of the Act by the Secretary of State, who is empowered to do so by subsection (4) of s12.

Remember that a contract may come within s1(3) or s6(3) as well as s12(3) of the 1982 Act.

Section 12(2) of the 1982 Act expressly excludes a contract of service or apprenticeship from the provisions.

20.21   Implied terms in contracts for the supply of services

In this part of the Act, the reference is to implied terms as a general group; conditions and warranties are not distinguished.

Implied term about care and skill

Section 13:

'In a contract for the supply of a service where the supplier is acting in the course of a business, there is an implied term that the supplier will carry out the service with reasonable care and skill.'

Section 13 merely enacts the common law. In the important case of *Greaves & Co (Contractors) Ltd* v *Baynham Meikle and Partners* [1975] 3 All ER 99, Lord Denning in the Court of Appeal thought:

> 'The law does not usually imply a warranty that the professional man will achieve the desired result, but only a term that he will use reasonable care and skill. The surgeon does not warrant that he will cure the patient. Nor does the solicitor warrant that he will win the case. But, when a dentist agrees to make a set of false teeth for a patient, there is an implied warranty that they will fit his gums: see *Samuels* v *Davis* [1943] 2 All ER 3.'

See the recent case of *Wilson* v *Best Travel Ltd* [1993] 1 All ER 353, in which it was made clear that s13 – that the supplier will carry out the service with reasonable care and skill – was – duty to do only what was reasonably practicable in the circumstances. In this case, when a tourist was injured abroad, the travel agents' duty extended only to checking that the hotel complied with all local safety standards. It could not be expected to insist on higher standards than that; it would be impractical to expect it.

Note that s13 of the 1982 Act only implies terms into a *contract*. Where no contract exists, reliance will have to be had on the tortious principles enunciated in *Hedley Byrne & Co Ltd* v *Heller & Partners Ltd* [1964] AC 465.

Implied term about time for performance

Section 14 of the 1982 Act provides:

> '(1) Where, under a contract for the supply of a service by a supplier acting in the course of a business, the time for the service to be carried out is not fixed by the contract, left to be fixed in a manner agreed by the contract or determined by the course of dealing between the parties, there is an implied term that the supplier will carry out the service within a reasonable time.
> (2) What is a reasonable time is a question of fact.'

This, again, is a codification of the common law. See *Rickards* v *Oppenheim* [1950] 1 KB 616.

Note, the section does not state whether the term is a condition or warranty. That must be inferred from whether the parties intend time to be of the essence. In most commercial contracts, time is of the essence and, therefore, a condition. If, however, a commercial contract did not stipulate dates, it could be argued that the parties could not have intended time to be of prime consideration.

Implied term about consideration

Section 15:

> '(1) Where, under a contract for the supply of a service, the consideration for the service is not determined by the contract, left to be determined in a manner agreed by the contract or determined by the course of dealing between the parties, there is an implied term that the party contracting with the supplier will pay a reasonable charge.
> (2) What is a reasonable charge is a question of fact.'

Note, that only if consideration is not agreed prior to or concurrent with the entering into the contract, does s15 apply. Quotations given by a tradesman are fixed price contracts, and are not variable upwards or downwards, s15 does not apply. Estimates, however, are just that and if the final charge exceeds the estimate, the receiver of the services is bound only to pay a reasonable price.

Exclusion of implied terms

Section 16:

> '(1) Where a right, duty or liability would arise under a contract for the supply of a service by virtue of this part of this Act, it may (subject to subsection (2) below and the 1977 Act) be negatived or varied by express agreement, or by the course of dealing between the parties, or by such usage as bind both parties to the contract.
> (2) An express term does not negative a term implied by this Part of this Act unless inconsistent with it.
> (3) Nothing in this Part of this Act prejudices:
> a) any rule of law which imposes on the supplier a duty stricter than that imposed by section 13 or 14 above; or
> b) subject to paragraph (a) above, any rule of law whereby any term not inconsistent with this Part of this Act is to be implied in a contract for the supply of a service.
> (4) This Part of this Act has effect subject to any other enactment which defines or restrict the rights, duties or liabilities arising in connection with a service of any description.'

Section 16 is self-explanatory. Note that s3 of UCTA 1977 is the provision which concerns Part II of the 1982 Act.

Stewart Gill Ltd v *Horatio Myer & Co Ltd* [1992] 2 WLR 721 shows that if a party seeks to rely on an exclusion clause in a contract for supply of goods and services, then the burden of proof is on that party to show the reasonableness of that exclusion.

21

Assignment

21.1   Introduction

It is a general rule of common law that a contract between two persons cannot confer rights or duties on a stranger to that contract. However, it is possible for one of the parties to the contract to transfer the benefits of that contract to another person by the process of assignment.

For example, A agrees to sell a car to B for £5,000. A may then assign to X the right to receive the money from B. Once the assignment has been effected, X may sue B if he refuses to pay him.

Contractual rights belong to a category of property law known as choses in action.

' "Chose in action" is a known legal expression used to describe all personal rights of property which can only be claimed or enforced by action, and not by taking possession.'
(*Torkington* v *Magee* [1902] 2 KB 427 at 430, per Channell J.)

Choses in action may be legal or equitable, dependent upon whether they were created by legal or equitable rules:

1. Legal choses in action include proprietary rights, such as debts and other contractual rights, policies of insurance, patents, copyrights and bills of lading.
2. Equitable choses in action include rights under a trust and legacies.

21.2   Methods of assignment

The historical evolution of the English law had a profound effect on the development of assignments. Thus it is important to examine the topic under three separate heads, which are common law; equity; statute law.

Common law

Although the common law recognised the right to transfer choses in possession, things that could be physically seized, it did not recognise assignments of choses in action.

At common law it was not possible for A to assign his contractual right against B to X. It was stated that such assignments would lead to 'officious intermeddling' in litigation, which used to constitute a wrong known as maintenance (not to be confused with the right of a divorced spouse to receive financial support from the other partner which also bears the same name).

There were a number of exceptions to this general common law prohibition, the most significant being negotiable instruments (see 21.5).

There were also a number of alternative methods by which someone who is not a party to the original contract could obtain the right to sue the debtor under the contract.

Power of attorney

The original creditor could make the third party his agent for the purposes of suing the debtor on his behalf. However, this involved a complicated procedure that suffered a number of shortcomings.

Novation

If A wished to transfer his contractual right against B to X, all three of the parties could enter into a new contract, which entirely replaced the original contract, whereby it was agreed that the debt would no longer be owed to A but to X. X had to provide valuable consideration for this contract.

Note that novation requires the agreement of all three of the parties including the debtor, whereas an assignment does not require the agreement of the debtor.

Equity

The failure of common law to recognise assignments of choses in action, particularly contractual rights, was remedied by equity. Equity recognised such assignments and, furthermore, it did not require assignment to be carried out by formal methods — as long as there was a definite intention to carry out an assignment, equity could regard the transaction as valid.

Equity looks to intention rather than to form. However, there was one major exception to this equitable maxim: assignments of equitable interests, such as rights under trusts or legacies, had been in writing. This is now enshrined in s53(1)(c) Law of Property Act 1925.

It is important to determine whether the purported equitable assignment is of an absolute or non-absolute nature:

1. If an assignment is to be absolute, the assignor must transfer the totality of his interest in the chose in action.

2. A non-absolute assignment is where the assignor reserves aspects of the right in the property to himself after the transfer, such as:

    a) co-assignment of part, but not all, of the debt to the assignee. Thus the assignment of only £4,000 of the £5,000 debt will not be an absolute assignment;

    b) a conditional assignment of the debt, whereby it is agreed at the outset that if specified, but unpredictable, events occur, either the assignment will take place, or the assignment will cease, and the rights will be returned to the assignor;

    c) an assignment by way of charge, which does not transfer the whole of the specific fund to the assignee, but merely entitles him to a payment out of a fund.

Although notice of the equitable assignment need not be given to the debtor in order to secure the assignee's rights, it is expedient for the assignee to make certain that such notice has been given. The giving of notice is particularly important if there are a number of competing claims by several purported assignees since, under the rule in *Dearle* v *Hall* (1828), priorities are established according to the chronological order in which these assignees gave notice to the debtor. Thus failure or delay in giving notice may prejudice an assignee's claim.

Furthermore, the giving of consideration by the assignee to the assignor may have an important bearing on the assignment. If the assignor promises to transfer the chose in action to the assignee, but the assignee gives nothing in return this is, in common parlance, a promise to make a gift. Gifts are unenforceable unless they are complete or perfected. Thus until the gift is perfected the donor can change his mind and refuse to make the gift. If the assignee has provided consideration for the promise by the assignor, then the assignment will be as binding as any other contract.

An assignee takes 'subject to equities'. This means that the debtor may use the same defences, whether legal or equitable, against the assignee as would have been available against the assignor. Thus A, a garage owner, undertakes work on B's car; A subsequently assigns the right to collect the money to X. When B is sued for non-payment by X, he may successfully defer the action by pleading that the work performed by A was defective. A claim by a debtor for an unliquidated sum is a counter-claim, a claim by a debtor concerning a liquidated sum is a set-off. Other forms of defence, such as mistake, misrepresentation and defect of title, are also capable of being pleaded by the debtor.

From the above information several propositions may be made:

1. Equitable assignments of equitable choses in action: the assignee can sue in his own name, without joining the assignor. The assignment is subject to equities. Consideration is necessary unless the assignment is complete and perfect.

2. Equitable assignments of legal choses in action: intention to assign is the determining factor:

a) the assignment is subject to equities;

b) the assignee must joint the assignor in an action he takes against the debtor, either as co-plaintiff or, if he refuses to be co-plaintiff, as co-defendant;

c) the assignee must have given consideration to the assignor.

Statute law

The Judicature Act of 1873 removed many of the conflicts between the old style Courts of Common Law and those of Equity. The new High Court administered both systems concurrently. Thus an assignee could sue in the High Court whether the chose was legal or equitable. A general method for assignments was created. This was re-enacted in s13(b)(1) Law of Property Act 1925 which provides:

> 'Any absolute agreement by writing under the hand of the assignor (not purporting to be by way of charge only) of any debt or other legal thing in action, of which express notice in writing has been given to the debtor, trustee or other person from whom the assignor would have been entitled to claim such a debt or thing in action, is effectual in law (subject to equities having priority over the right of the assignee) to pass and transfer from the date of such notice:
> a) the legal right to such a debt or thing in action;
> b) the legal and other remedies for the same; and
> c) the power to give good discharge for the same without the concurrence of the assignor.'

Therefore, three conditions must be satisfied if the assignment is to be regarded as valid under statute law: it must be absolute; it must be written; and written notice must be given to the debtor.

However, great formality is not required, thus incorrect statements or omissions of the date of the assignment do not invalidate the transaction. Neither is the giving of consideration considered to be a vital essential of a statutory assignment.

It should be noted that equitable assignments may still be possible if the transaction fails to meet all the requirements of s13(b)(1), for example, it is oral, or no written notice has been given to the debtor, or because it is a non-absolute assignment.

21.3   Limits of assignability

Rights cannot be assigned if they offend public policy or if they prejudice the debtor.

Public policy prevents valid assignments of certain contractual rights.

A wife cannot assign maintenance or other payments ordered pursuant to matrimonial proceedings if so doing would leave her without any means of support. See *Watkins v Watkins* [1896] P 222. A public officer cannot assign his salary. See

Liverpool Corporation v *Wright* (1859) 28 LJ Ch 868. Other statutory provisions prevent assignment of payments, such as child benefit or social security payments.

Prejudice to the debtor may invalidate an assignment

Personal contracts

In many contracts, particularly involving simple debt, it makes little difference to the debtor whether he pays the original creditor or the creditor's assignee. However, certain contracts are considered to be 'personal' to the debtor insofar that he will only be required to perform them in favour of his creditor but to no one else, such as the purported assignee of the creditor. It is, for example, the right of the employee to decide who he wishes to work for. See *Noakes* v *Doncaster Amalgamated Collieries Ltd* [1940] AC 1014.

Even contracts for sale of goods may be considered personal since the supplier may carefully choose who he wishes to supply – due to reputation, financial standing or a wealth of similar reasons. Indeed, it is recognised that the contracting parties may even make it a term of their contract that the rights under that contract shall be unassignable.

Maintenance and champerty

Maintenance of a person, by giving them financial assistance to commence an action, and champerty, offering assistance in return for a percentage of any subsequent award of damages, were, until the Criminal Law Act 1967, crimes or torts. However, this Act removed tortious and criminal liability from such actions, but still preserved its contractual implication. Thus if an assignment will, in fact, lead to an 'officious intermeddling in litigation' by someone who should more correctly leave such issues to the original parties to the contract, then the courts may regard this as a bare right to sue, and will refuse to enforce the assignee's rights. The right will be 'bare' if it is not assigned along with some other property right to which it is connected. If, for example, A assigns the right to sue for damages for breach of covenant committed by a tenant to X, but retains the property and lease for himself, such an assignment would be void.

21.4 Assignment by operation of law

The assignments that have been considered are all voluntary assignments of rights by the party's own volition. However, an involuntary assignment of the right to a chose in action may be brought about by operation of law on the death or bankruptcy of one of the contracting parties.

Assignment on death

As a general rule, all contractual rights and duties are transferred to the personal representatives of a deceased's estate. Those personal representatives may sue or be sued on any contract to which the deceased was a party. This rule does not apply to contracts for personal services.

Assignment as a bankruptcy/insolvency

When a debtor is adjudicated bankrupt, his property is vested in the trustee in bankruptcy who must endeavour to secure a fair distribution of the debtor's assets between the creditors of the bankrupt.

21.5   Negotiable instruments: a special case

The process of assignability can be a cumbersome and time-consuming process that is particularly unsuitable if a rapid succession of transactions is to be achieved by using the same chose in action to establish, for example, a long line of credit between, say, merchant bank, commercial bank, customer and subsequent users of the item in question. In order to allow speedy and reliable transactions, the negotiable instrument evolved primarily through the old Law Merchant, and this was readily accepted into the principles of common law and equity.

The more important types of negotiable instrument are:

A bill of exchange

A bill of exchange is an unconditional order in writing, addressed by one person to another, signed by the person giving it requiring the person to whom it is addressed to pay on demand a sum certain in money to, or to the order of, a specified person, or to bearer, s3(1) Bills of Exchange Act 1882. Bills of exchange are often used to fund international trade transactions.

A cheque

A cheque is a bill of exchange drawn on a banker payable on demand, s73 Bills of Exchange Act 1882.

Promissory notes

These are defined by s83 Bills of Exchange Act 1882, as an unconditional promise, in writing, made by one person to another, signed by the maker, engaging to pay on demand, or at a fixed time or determinable time in the future, a sum certain in money to or to the order of a specified person or to the bearer.

It differs from a bill of exchange in that the maker stands in place of the drawer.

Meaning of negotiability

Negotiable instruments possess special qualities not accorded to transactions that are regulated by the laws pertaining to assignments, namely:

Transfer of ownership
The rights of ownership of a negotiable instrument are transferred:

1. where the instrument is drawn payable to order, or is specially indorsed 'pay Smith or order', ownership is transferred by indorsement and delivery to the transferee; and
2. where the instrument is payable to bearer, a bank note, for example, or indorsed in blank by a mere signature on its reverse side, ownership is transferred by mere delivery.

Free from equities
When a negotiable instrument is negotiated, the transferee takes the rights of ownership freed from equities, as long as he is a holder in due course.

Holder may sue in his own name
In the event of the negotiable instrument being dishonoured through non-acceptance or non-payment, the holder may sue all previous parties to the instrument be they the drawer, acceptor or indorsers of the bills who transferred the indorsement and delivery.

It is surprising that although the common law refused to accept assignment due to the prospect of officious intermeddling in litigation, it readily accepted the speedier and more refined process of negotiability – largely due to the necessity of commercial practice.

22

Contract – an Overview

22.1 Introduction

22.2 Agreement

22.3 Consideration

22.4 Contents of a contract

22.5 Exclusion clauses

22.6 Misrepresentation

22.7 Illegality and inequality

22.8 Privity and remedies

22.9 Conclusion

22.1   Introduction

In the preceding chapters we have seen how a contract is made, and the sort of tests the court will apply to ascertain whether a contract exists, the presence of an intention to create a legal relationship on the part of the parties, a definite offer and acceptance which is unconditional, the presence of consideration, and so on.

Certain elements which might serve to vitiate the validity of a contract, mistake, misrepresentation, duress and undue influence, have been examined. We have looked at the ways in which a contract may be discharged and remedies for breach. We have also looked very briefly at certain special sorts of contracts, such as those for the sale of goods which are largely governed by statute rather than the more usual common law. Most people, having become familiar with the law of contract in these various 'compartments', go no further. All their working lives they will think of contract in these neat and handy chunks, and the law for them will stay permanently compartmentalised, not to say crystallised.

In fact, armed with the information contained in these foregoing chapters, it is now possible to go further and begin to look at the law of contract from some rather unconventional viewpoints.

22.2   Agreement

Because this is a topic dealt with in the very early stages of most contract courses, it is often dealt with in a rather simplistic way. Certain basic themes underlie the whole concept of contractual agreement. Supposedly, contractual rules are based on the intentions of the parties: the courts in assessing whether or not a valid contract exists attempt to give effect to the wishes of the parties. In reality, this rather idealistic view cannot always be upheld. It must be remembered that it is the cases where there is a dispute between the parties which are litigated. This may appear to be stating the obvious, but is well worth bearing in mind when trying to assess the parties' intentions. Clearly, if there were a consensus ad idem the case would not be before the courts! Consequently, for purely practical reasons, the courts have to adopt an objective approach. They are not concerned with the subjective mental state of the parties.

In *Felthouse* v *Bindley* (1862) 11 CBNS 869, for example, it is to be noted that the nephew instructed the auctioneer that the horse was sold. It is clear, therefore, that in his own mind he had a contract with his uncle. But because of other external factors, the court decided that there was no contract.

Note as well that the objective test as the courts apply it here is mainly concerned with how things appear to each party – not, as with some objective tests, how they appear to a fictitious 'reasonable man'.

When assessing whether agreement exists, in applying this objective test referred to above, what do the courts look for?

Traditionally, the courts have taken the process of reaching agreement in certain well-defined stages, and checked whether each stage has been satisfactorily completed before proceeding to the next. Is there intention, a valid offer, a definite acceptance, and so on?

More recently, however, a new, more liberal approach, as suggested by Lord Denning MR in *Butler Machine Tool Co Ltd* v *Ex-Cell-O Corp* [1979] 1 WLR 401 and *Gibson* v *Manchester City Council* [1979] 1 WLR 294, has arrived on the scene.

While this has not been seized on with wholehearted enthusiasm by the rest of the judiciary, this new 'holistic' approach certainly represents a possible alternative to the more orthodox methods of analysis of agreement. Given the fact that a number of other judges apart from Denning have expressed their unease (see, for example, Lord Diplock's comments in *New Zealand Shipping* v *Satterthwaite* [1975] AC 154), it seems increasingly likely that, sooner or later, the traditional offer/acceptance/consideration analysis will be overturned and replaced by something else, even if it is not Denning's proposal.

When looking at contract in general, and agreement in particular, bear in mind that though apparently governed by numerous fixed rules, 'the rule of offer and acceptance', 'the postal rules' and so on, that these rules do not *always* apply.

Rules are subject to exceptions, sometimes so many exceptions that they overwhelm the rule. See, for example, the comment of Lord Wilberforce in

Brinkibon v *Stahag Stahl* [1983] 2 AC 34, when in dealing with acceptance by telex he said

> '... no universal rule can cover all such cases; they must be resolved by reference to the intentions of the parties, by sound business practice, and in some cases by a judgment where the risks should lie'.

This tends to be true, not just of the particular case, but of contractual law generally.

22.3   Consideration

There is no real agreement about the basis of consideration. It has been suggested that mutual exchange of money, goods or, at the very least, promises, is the factor which marks out an enforceable contract from a contract which, though perhaps theoretically valid, is unenforceable in the court of law.

A promise which is gratuitous or made without consideration has always been unenforceable except when made under seal. However, in less formal contracts, those in writing but not sealed, or made verbally, or even by contract, it has become a cornerstone of contractual law that a party seeking to enforce a contract must provide evidence of an exchange of things of value.

Note that to talk of an 'exchange of consideration' is potentially misleading, since in practical terms each party provides consideration – really there are two lots of consideration; not one item being passed back and forth.

It is the *mutuality* of consideration which is important. In *Combe* v *Combe* [1951] 2 KB 215, for example, the defendant's promise to pay £100 pa to his ex-wife in reliance of which she did not apply for maintenance was held not to amount to consideration on the part of the ex-wife. This was despite the fact that she had deliberately refrained from applying to the divorce courts for maintenance and had, undeniably, suffered detriment. The important factor was that she had not refrained as part of a bargain, or at the request of her ex-husband; there was no mutuality, no element of bargain, and thus her 'detriment' was not valid consideration capable of sustaining an action at law.

This element of bargaining is expressed most clearly in the American Restatement (the original 1932 version), which states that consideration is the 'price for which the promise of the other party is bought'. Consideration as a doctrine is governed by some seemingly arbitrary rules.

In a sense, it impinges on both remedies and on the question of illegality. The basic approach for all contractual remedies at common law is to put the plaintiff in a position as though the contract had been performed. This is known as the expectation interest: what did the plaintiff expect to obtain under the contract? Thus it is logical to look at consideration: what did the plaintiff do, in return for what promise, what did he expect the defendant to do as his part of the bargain? Often the plaintiff is seeking no more, no less than the agreed consideration – usually a sum of money. See *Stilk* v *Myrick* (1809) 2 Camp 317, *Shadwell* v *Shadwell* (1860) 9 CBNS 159, *Tweddle* v *Atkinson* (1861) 1 B & S 393 and *Combe* v *Combe* (above), and numerous similar cases.

Sometimes, the plaintiff will opt for the more limited remedy known as the reliance interest; that is, the extent to which the plaintiff is worse off as a result of relying on the defendant's promise. Here the main question is not what the plaintiff expected by way of consideration from the defendant, but what the plaintiff himself furnished as consideration which is the governing factor.

Illegality has some relevance here, because the law is always changing slightly as to what the courts are prepared to see as valid consideration.

22.4   Contents of a contract

When we talk about contents of a contract, it is normally assumed that this concerns, first and foremost, conditions. The word 'condition' is itself notoriously ambiguous: it can, of course, mean some event on which the starting point or the end of the contract is based – conditions precedent and subsequent. Used in this context, the word 'condition' is not a condition (or term) of the contract at all, a fact which provides a very confusing start for those studying this aspect of contract!

'Condition' is perhaps best described as a term of the contract which, if broken, is considered so important it automatically gives rise to the right on the part of the injured party to repudiate the contract. But there are also warranties and innominate terms. Problems of classification arise when the courts are trying to decide the most appropriate remedy. If the only remedy required is damages there is really no difficulty. Such a remedy is available for breaches of warranty and condition alike. There is no *need* to classify the term in question. But if the injured party decides that damages are not sufficient, that he wants to end the contract there and then, whether he will be permitted to do so will depend on how the courts classify the term – only if the term is a condition will there be a right to terminate. One drawback that stems from this rather arbitrary mode of classification is that sometimes a breach of condition does not do all that much harm, yet the injured party will still opt to terminate. See *Reardon Smith* v *Hansen-Tangen* [1976] 3 All ER 570. This was one of several reasons for the introduction of the concept of innominate terms (in *Hong Kong Fir Shipping* v *Kawasaki* [1962] 2 QB 26).

It is true that, so far, most of the reported cases have concerned innominate terms whose breach has resulted in comparatively minor severity and thus led to an award of damages. However, innominate terms could in theory be such that to break them would result in damage of such severity that termination would be the only feasible option available to an innocent party.

Certainly, the orthodox view, that terms are neatly divided into conditions and warranties, would appear to be crumbling around the edges. While still reflected in legislation, for example, the Sale of Goods Act 1979 clearly designates certain implied terms as either conditions or warranties and depicts clearly and precisely the remedies for breach of each – this two-fold division may no longer be uniformly applied. The classification of terms is of particular importance in cases where the form of contract is one which is likely to be frequently used. Thus, in cases like *The Mihalis Angelos* [1971] 1 QB 164 and a decade later, *Bunge Corporation* v *Tradax Export SA* [1981] 2 All ER 513, when the terms in question formed part of a standardised commercial shipping contract, a decision by the courts as to whether a term is a condition, warranty or innominate term can be expected to have far reaching repercussions.

It has been argued, by Treitel in particular, that it is in any event irrelevant what the term is called – the important thing is to assess what harm breach is likely to cause.

The distinction between conditions and warranties, or between innominate terms and warranties, at the moment has some importance, because it allows an injured party to assess with some degree of certainty what his remedies are.

There is an increasingly vocal argument (see Ormrod LJ in *The Hansa Nord* [1976] QB 44) for regarding the two- or three-fold distinction between warranties and other terms as of no practical use any more. It is frequently argued now, that even for warranties there should be an option to terminate available to injured parties when the breach is particularly blatant.

22.5   Exclusion clauses

This is one of the very few areas of contractual law in which common law and statute (the Unfair Contract Terms Act 1977) stand side by side and are equally important. Indeed, the UCTA 1977 may be slowly overhauling the common law, but until statute is all-embracing and covers every type of contract (which, of course, it does not at present), then common law will continue to be of importance.

As things stand at present, although there is quite a mass of case law on exemption clauses arising out of common law, the Act itself has little illustrative case law. While one may draw certain analagous conclusions about the relationship between common law and statute, there is little explanatory case law on the Act. This is very much a developing area of law with a number of, to a variable degree, largely unresolved questions.

For example, the courts have recently begun to explore more fully the differences between total exclusion and limitation clauses. See *Ailsa Craig Fishing Co* v *Malvern Fishing Co* [1983] 1 WLR 964 and *George Mitchell Ltd* v *Finney Lock Seeds* [1983] 2 AC 803. This different treatment of limitation clauses, interpreting them more leniently than exclusion clauses, is of considerable importance in the USA, and is now beginning to be considered by the courts here.

Another issue that has arisen concerns privity and the extent to which a third party can take the benefit of an exclusion clause. The courts have not – while emphasising that, in theory, this cannot happen – been slow to find that an apparent third party is not really a third party at all by virtue of some consideration or other furnished by him. See *New Zealand Shipping Co* v *Satterthwaite & Co* [1975] AC 154.

The exact status of an exclusion clause has been subject to much discussion. Coote's *Exception Clauses* and Yates' *Exclusion Clauses* are probably the best known authorities on the subject. Lord Diplock, in *Photo Production Ltd* v *Securicor Transport Ltd* [1980] AC 827, examined the status of such clauses at length. The most commonly held theory at common law would certainly seem to be that an exemption clause is of no importance save as a defence to breach. However, an alternative view, that though a negative term, an exclusion clause *is* a term like all others and helps to define the extent of the parties' obligations, is expounded in Coote, and appears to be gaining strength in its support.

22.6 Misrepresentation

The law relating to misrepresentation occupies a central place in English common law. It is no longer a rapidly developing area like exclusion clauses. The important decade for misrepresentation was the 1960s, when a number of important changes in the law took place. The introduction of the Misrepresentation Act 1967 meant that, for the first time, damages were available for innocent misrepresentation while *Hedley Byrne* v *Heller & Partners* [1964] AC 465 resulted in the introduction of damages for negligent misstatements.

To identify the remedies available in any given case, it is necessary to distinguish between the different forms of misrepresentation: fraudulent, negligent, and innocent. Since the remedy of rescission is available for *any* form of misrepresentation, if this is what the injured party seeks by way of redress, it will not in theory be necessary to go further and start classifying the form the misrepresentation takes. However, there are a number of different rights to damages according to the form the misrepresentation takes. Thus if the injured party seeks a remedy other than, or in addition to, rescission, it becomes necessary to analyse the form the misrepresentation takes.

While these changes have undoubtedly improved the availability of remedies, there is now almost a surfeit with all the associated problems of knowing which remedy to claim, and which will be most advantageous to the injured party. The relationship between the various remedies is also not entirely clear. Atiyah and Treitel (1967 30 MLR 369) listed exhaustively the uncertainties created, in part by poor drafting, by the 1967 Act; for example, it was not clear whether the power to award damages in lieu of rescission exists where the right to rescind was itself barred; nor was the exact measure of damages under s2(2) defined. Twenty-three years on, most of the uncertainties listed in the article remain unresolved.

ıts to damages in misrepresentation are essentially tortious in nature,
re so than in any other area of contract. It has been suggested that the
ı remedies making damages available for misrepresentation in effect
the distinction, so carefully built up by the courts, between representations
ms. (See in New Zealand, the NZ Contractual Remedies Act 1979, which to
all intents and purposes abolishes the distinction.)

However, in English law fault is still a criterion in misrepresentation, where
damages are assessed, as has been stated, on tortious principles. Fault or blame is,
however, not normally of relevance in breaches of terms of contract; to that extent a
distinction between representations and terms is preserved.

22.7   Illegality and inequality

These are two areas which are usually studied separately. However, there are many
different ways in which the courts take into account unfairness and public policy
generally. Lord Denning, in *Lloyds Bank* v *Bundy* [1975] QB 326, tried to enunciate a
'doctrine of unfairness', criticising the lack of precision in doctrines such as undue
influence and unconscionable bargains, and the test of reasonableness in restraint
cases or as applied to the UCTA 1977. However, given the fact that these remarks
were obiter and the fact that the idea has been considerably criticised, it seems
unlikely that there will be much judicial suppoort for Denning's suggestions. It seems
for one thing that mention of unconscionable bargains has been linked with the much
more generalised US doctrine of unconscionability. Almost certainly, though
influenced by the US concept, Denning had in mind a principle narrower and more
specific.

Scarman LJ, for example, in *National Westminster Bank* v *Morgan* [1985] 1 All
ER 821, declared that he thought it was for Parliament (not the judiciary) to impose
such restrictions on contracts.

With regard to illegal contracts, there is little agreement about how best the
different types of illegality should be classified. It is probably simplest to divide
illegal contracts into those which are truly illegal, and those which are merely void
or unenforceable. It should be pointed out, however, that there is no consistency in
terminology; even the courts themselves use the expressions 'illegal', 'void' and
'unenforceable' as though they all meant the same thing and were interchangeable.

Cheshire and Fifoot and other major authorites agree with this two–fold division,
but it is criticised by Treitel as being likely to lead to over-simplification.

With regard to the distinction, the courts' attitude toward contracts which are
merely void is more liberal than that towards illegal contracts, which are regarded as
tainted beyond redemption. It is to be remembered also that although the courts'
attitude towards illegal contracts is best summed up in the maxim: 'the loss lies
where it falls', a plaintiff can always recover property transferred under an illegal
contract if he can prove that he has a right which arises without relying either on

the terms of the illegal contract or, conversely, on the fact of its being illegal. Note, for example, *Bowmakers Ltd* v *Barnet Instruments Ltd* [1945] KB 65, where the plaintiffs leased out machine tools on hire-purchase to the defendants who sold some of them to a third party before completing the instalments. The court held that, regardless of whether the HP contract was illegal (which was in some doubt), the plaintiffs could succeed in conversion by relying on their original title.

22.8 Privity and remedies

As with the preceding section these are topics more usually treated separately but, in fact, they overlap to a considerable degree.

Privity is largely concerned with *who* is entitled to a remedy, whilst the law relating to remedies is concerned with the form those remedies may take.

The doctrine of privity is most concerned with the question of benefit: who can sue on or take the benefit of a contract? But there is also the contrary side of the question, viz the extent to which a contract may impose a burden on a third party.

As long ago as 1937, the Law Revision Committee proposed amendments to the doctrine of privity, among which they proposed a right to sue for a third party where 'a contract by its *express terms* purports to confer a benefit on a third party'. This proposal has never been acted upon, though in *Woodar Investment Development* v *Wimpey Construction UK* [1980] 1 All ER 571, the House of Lords gave clear signs that the courts might be preparing to 'go it alone' in adjusting the doctrine of privity to protect third parties. Specific performance has been available (subject to limitations) in such cases, and makes an ideal remedy. In effect, it orders that the contract be performed as originally envisaged to confer a benefit on the third party. But, of course, it is of little use in cases where the contract has been performed, but badly (*Jackson* v *Horizon Holidays* [1975] 1 WLR 1468).

The actual substance of remedies has been sufficiently discussed in Chapters 16 and 17, and it is not proposed to go into further detail here. It should be noted, however, that the whole question of remedies is of fundamental importance. It is only by noting consequences when things go wrong that it is possible fully to understand the workings of a *valid* contract.

22.9 Conclusion

The foregoing paragraphs do not in any way represent a complete range of topics which may be thus analysed; but they may, perhaps, serve as a pointer to illustrate one or two possible approaches.

It is always useful having finished the syllabus to see how different subjects within the syllabus fit together and, of course, examination questions will often span several subject areas. It is not, perhaps, to be recommended at an earlier stage of the course;

for one thing, the student will not have all the information necessary for this cross-referring, and may find it a confusing rather than helpful exercise. But, after the first run through the course, the more the relationships between different contractual themes are studied, the more intriguing the student will (hopefully) find them.

Completion of any syllabus is often a signal for the student to embark on a massive programme of memorising large chunks of the relevant subject matter. In so doing, he or she will often find that his or her perception of the subject deteriorates rather than improves. Nowhere is this more true than of contract. The more the subject is approached from a general viewpoint, the more the student should begin to see how topics, originally studied in isolation, link up together. Obviously, different sections of the syllabus need to be studied in detail and equally obviously a student needs a basic working knowledge of all matters contractual. A superficial awareness is *not* what is being advocated here! But, once armed with this basic information, the student may approach the contract syllabus both creatively and critically, examining common themes and relationships between issues, seeking out defects in the existing law, and sensing possible reforms to come. Such constructive study is much more useful (and more interesting) than simply confining oneself to learning 'parrot-fashion' long sections of the syllabus. One hopes it is more rewarding too, for the student, not only in examination performance, but in his or her future professional life.

Index

Programming
Active
Server
Pages

**Scot Hillier and
Daniel Mezick**

Microsoft Press

PUBLISHED BY
Microsoft Press
A Division of Microsoft Corporation
One Microsoft Way
Redmond, Washington 98052-6399

Library of Congress Cataloging-in-Publication Data
Hillier, Scot.
    Programming Active Server Pages / Scot Hillier, Daniel Mezick.
        p.   cm.
    Includes index.
    ISBN 1-57231-700-0
    1. Internet programming.   2. ActiveX.   3. Web servers.
    I. Mezick, Daniel.   II. Title.
    QA76.625.H55   1997
    005.2'76--dc21   97-42103
                                                               CIP

Printed and bound in the United States of America.

1 2 3 4 5 6 7 8 9   QMQM   2 1 0 9 8 7

Distributed to the book trade in Canada by Macmillan of Canada, a division of Canada Publishing Corporation.

A CIP catalogue record for this book is available from the British Library.

Microsoft Press books are available through booksellers and distributors worldwide. For further information about international editions, contact your local Microsoft Corporation office. Or contact Microsoft Press International directly at fax (425) 936-7329. Visit our Web site at mspress.microsoft.com.

Macintosh is a registered trademark of Apple Computer, Inc. Intel is a registered trademark of Intel Corporation. FoxPro, FrontPage, Microsoft, Microsoft Press, Visual Basic, Visual C++, Windows, and Windows NT are registered trademarks and ActiveX, Outlook, Visual InterDev, Visual J++, and Visual Studio are trademarks of Microsoft Corporation. Other product and company names mentioned herein may be the trademarks of their respective owners.

Acquisitions Editor: Stephen Guty
Project Editor: Patricia N. Wagner

This book is dedicated to the staff of New Technology Solutions, whose work makes us a success.

TABLE OF CONTENTS

Foreword

What a wonderful time to be in the world of programming. The popularity of the Internet has increased the importance of developers who understand today's technology and have the ability to create Internet-enabled applications. A developer in today's environment faces many challenges in trying to decipher what are real solutions and what are just marketing promises. Advertising, events, publications, television, and movies have all adopted the Internet as the hot button, and as it becomes a mainstream source of communication and commerce, the role that developers play becomes more important. Interestingly enough, it's actually "cool" to be a developer in today's society, and those who can stay ahead of the technology curve are the ones who will achieve the greatest success. Thus, information and education are the keys to maintaining the competitive advantage—not to mention staying cool!

One of the greatest positives of the Web is also one of its biggest negatives—the flow of information. Online banners, white papers, ezines, downloadable code, list servers, and newsgroups are consistently hitting the developer community with a barrage of information about the latest technology. Because everyone is working at "Internet time" (a new term for breakneck speed), the products, strategies, and names (and acronyms!) are changing at such a rapid pace that developers spend a great deal of energy simply filtering information. This book, *Programming Active Server Pages*, helps simplify the exercise of understanding Internet development through the vision of Microsoft's developer strategy—a strategy that combines today's most popular tools and technologies with industry standards for the Internet.

Microsoft uses the word *active* to describe the experience people can have both using and building software that is truly dynamic and rich. In the early days of Internet development, most of the work was accomplished in text editors that created Web sites and with applications that were nothing more than electronic brochures. By taking advantage of Microsoft Windows NT, Visual Basic Scripting Edition, Dynamic HTML, and Internet Explorer 4.0, developers can build Web applications that truly bond together the core components of Microsoft's Active Platform strategy and make the experience more beneficial to the customer and end user.

Active is also a word that truly describes Dan Mezick and Scot Hillier, the coauthors of this book. As an active member of the business community, their company, New Technology Solutions, Inc., of New Haven, Connecticut, has offered training in Microsoft development tools, platforms, and technologies for the past four years. I was first introduced to Dan in Las Vegas at the 1991 Comdex Trade Show, and it was apparent to me then that this was a person with a passion for Microsoft technology and a pride in teaching it. Since then, Microsoft's relationship with Dan and Scot has progressed to the point where they are two of our most respected and active (there is that word again!) leaders in the worldwide developer community. These partners give their blood, sweat, and endless energy to a number of activities, including many of our events, conferences, product reviews, user group meetings, advisory councils, and technology briefings. I like to think of Dan and Scot as "human scripting languages" who tie all of the super technology, support, training, and product components together to make a very "Active Community."

As you read this book and learn how to apply technologies such as ActiveX Controls, Dynamic HTML, and COM, Dan and Scot will be right there with you each step of the way. They have, in fact, been there for the thousands of developers who have been trained via their award winning Boot Camp training series and via the Microsoft Developer Days program, of which they are Microsoft regional directors. I invite you to continue to use this resource to guide your development, and to tip your hat to Dan and Scot for "activating" once again, on behalf of Microsoft, to assist developers.

Michael Werner
Lead Product Manager,
Microsoft Developer Relations Group
Microsoft Corporation
Mikewe@microsoft.com

PREFACE

As we travel the country training developers in cutting-edge technology, we have noticed a widening gap between the "haves" and "have-nots" of the development community. Specifically, many developers are having trouble keeping pace with the latest innovations. Only a few years ago, programmers could easily specialize in a narrow area without regard for other disciplines. Visual Basic developers stayed away from everything except the front end of an application, while database administrators handled the back end. C++ programmers often contributed component technology but didn't have to be concerned with the larger picture. All of that has changed.

In today's programming environment, developers must not only be aware of new technologies but must have at least an intermediate understanding of them. The emerging role of Windows NT as a serious enterprise environment has wrenched placid developers from their roles as front-end or component developers and forced them to think about all tiers. The Internet compounds the problem. Developers need to master client/server technologies, and they must also respond to growing customer demand for Web access to information applications.

This book was written for developers who want to use the latest Internet technology to create dynamic content for the World Wide Web. Much of this technology is an extension of client/server programming, and we assume that developers reading the book will bring a basic understanding of programming principles, client/server relations, and Web development in general.

We also assume that readers are familiar with the two languages featured in this book: Hypertext Markup Language (HTML) and Microsoft Visual Basic, Scripting Edition (VBScript). We have not attempted to teach the fundamentals of either of these languages past the short introduction in Chapter 1 and a quick reference in Appendix A. If you need more information on syntax and code structures, consult the reference sections in Microsoft Visual InterDev, the primary development tool we used in preparing this book.

We have included many code samples, exercises, and projects to help readers master the development techniques presented. In order to work with the examples, you need access to Visual InterDev, Visual Basic 5.0, Microsoft Transaction Server, and Microsoft Exchange Server 5.0. Other tools that you will need, such as Microsoft Internet Information Server 3.0 and Microsoft Internet Explorer 4.0, are provided on the companion CD-ROM. (See the README.TXT file for a complete listing of the companion CD-ROM's contents.) If you don't want to work the exercises, you will also find complete code on the accompanying CD-ROM and you can view project results in Visual InterDev.

Although we have certainly made every effort to keep the book up-to-date, readers should understand that this work was created using the Preview 2 version of Internet Explorer 4.0. Writing books using beta software is not ideal by any means, but the pace of change demands that books be produced earlier in the software product cycle in order to reach the market. With this in mind, we want to point out some potential trouble areas. First, the Class IDs for ActiveX controls presented in the book will certainly change before the final version of IE 4.0 is available. You can solve this by using Visual InterDev to insert ActiveX controls in your Web page. Second, the actual feature set of IE 4.0 might change. While writing the book, we were forced to revise code as IE 4.0 moved from Preview 1 to Preview 2. This could be a concern when IE 4.0 finally ships. Finally, the Microsoft Agent control was at beta 3 when the text was written. Be aware that changes might occur in the Microsoft Agent examples when the final release ships.

As Active Server Pages and Dynamic HTML evolve, we plan to be there and provide updates. You can follow our continuing work on Web development by visiting our home page at www.vb-bootcamp.com or by visiting the Microsoft Press site at www.microsoft.com/mspress/. We hope you enjoy reading this book as much as we enjoyed creating it.

Scot Hillier and Daniel Mezick
New Technology Solutions, Incorporated
August 1997

Acknowledgments

Although many people helped us create this book, we are profoundly grateful foremost to our families. Our work includes not only books, but also a significant amount of travel as we chase new technology around the country. No one can achieve success without the support of those around them. We would especially like to thank our wives, Nancy and Roberta, who have never wavered in their support of our dreams.

New Technology Solutions is an exciting and busy place to work. Occasionally, it is a frustrating and stressful place to work. For that reason, we are also thankful to the entire staff at NTSI who have worked diligently to make the company a success. We are blessed to know so many great professionals.

We are also lucky to work with many excellent people at Microsoft. There are indeed far too many to mention, but we would like to call out both Mike Werner and Kostas Mallios. They have been key to our success with Microsoft in general and the Developer Days program in particular. Thank you.

At Microsoft Press, we were once again given a wonderful team to create this book. The thanks begin with Steve Guty, who acquired the work for Microsoft Press. Our editor, Patricia Wagner, did an excellent job of managing our nerves throughout the accelerated publishing schedule and headed up the publishing team. The manuscript was edited by Deborah Long, who did a fantastic job twisting our passive voice back to an intelligible active version.

In addition, we would like to thank proofreaders Richard Carey, Roger LeBlanc, and Teri Kieffer. The principal compositor was Elizabeth Hansford, with help from Linda Robinson, Paula Gorelick, Anne Kim, Dan Hale, and Steven Hopster. And finally, the artist was Joel Panchot.

Thanks to everyone.

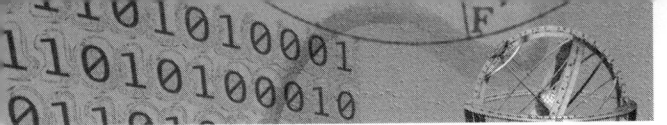

Introducing Active Content

What a difference one product cycle can make! Not long ago, conventional wisdom had Microsoft dead at the hands of the Internet. Today it isn't news to anyone that Microsoft has successfully recast itself as an ally of the Internet. But what continues to amaze is the magnitude of the consequences for developers. When Microsoft first responded to the demand for Internet development tools, products were primitive by any stretch of the imagination. In fact, Web developers joked that their favorite development tool was "Visual Notepad." Now, however, no one is joking. The suite of tools released in Microsoft Visual Studio 97 represents a firm commitment to the Internet, and the next generation of tools is on its way. This is a great time to be a Web developer.

Hypertext Markup Language

Internet development over the last few years has moved from static content to dynamic content. Just a short time ago, creating state-of-the-art Web pages required little more than mastery of Hypertext Markup Language, or HTML. HTML is a simple, text-based language that uses a series of *tags* to create a document that can be viewed by a browser. The HTML code in Listing 1-1, for example, renders the simple Web page shown in Figure 1-1 on the following page.

```
<HTML>
<HEAD>
<TITLE>My First Web Page</TITLE>
</HEAD>

<BODY BGCOLOR="WHITE">
<H2><CENTER>Welcome to My First Web Page!</CENTER></H2>
</BODY>
</HTML>
```

Listing 1-1.
HTML code for a simple Web page.

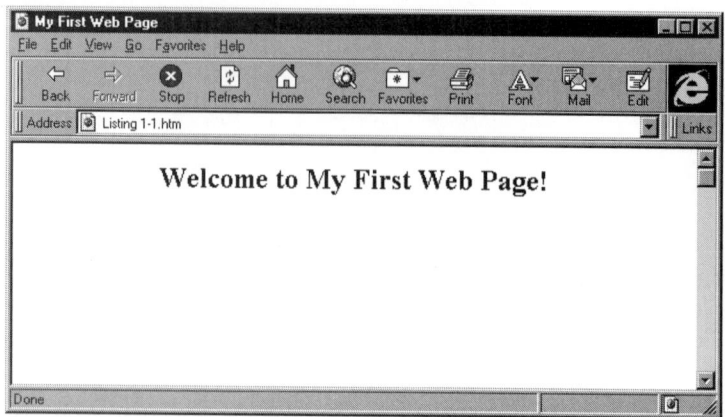

Figure 1-1.
A simple Web page.

HTML is not really a language in the same sense as C++ or Microsoft Visual Basic; it's more like a formatting syntax for documents that use escape codes. In fact, we often liken HTML coding to creating a Microsoft Word document by typing formatting codes directly into Notepad. You can expect very little functionality.

HTML is a poor language from a programming perspective for a variety of reasons. First, consider the *hyperlink,* those underlined blue words that you click to go to another page. The hyperlink is essentially a glorified GOTO statement that provides a hard-coded jump to some location in the application. Reams of articles have been written about the GOTO statement and its evils. Hard-coded links, you see, create unmaintainable code, and if you've written HTML code for any period of time, you already know how hard it is to revise or reuse.

Second, HTML provides no real way to persist data throughout an application. In fact, it's difficult to even define an application on the Web. Each page represents a stateless transaction with the server, so how do you determine when an application begins and ends? Compare this with a typical client/server application, where the beginning is signaled by double-clicking an icon and the ending is determined by selecting Exit from the File menu.

Third, HTML allows limited interactivity. Standard HTML yields static Web pages with text, images, and hyperlinks to other pages. You might hear these sites referred to as the World Wide Yellow Pages because their format is pretty much the same as that of a phone book.

Admittedly, HTML can provide some interactivity through the use of *intrinsic controls,* the input devices you generally see in HTML forms. Simple data forms can be generated with tags such as <INPUT>. The <INPUT> tag allows creation of text boxes and check boxes as well as radio buttons and push buttons. Listing 1-2 creates an HTML form that displays text boxes for a name, a telephone number, and an e-mail address, as shown in Figure 1-2.

```
<HTML>
<HEAD>
<TITLE>Simple HTML Form</TITLE>
</HEAD>

<BODY BGCOLOR="WHITE">
<FORM>
<INPUT TYPE="TEXT" NAME="txtName">Name<P>
<INPUT TYPE="TEXT" NAME="txtPhone">Phone<P>
<INPUT TYPE="TEXT" NAME="txtEMail">E-Mail<P>
</FORM>
</BODY>
</HTML>
```

Listing 1-2.
Code for an HTML form.

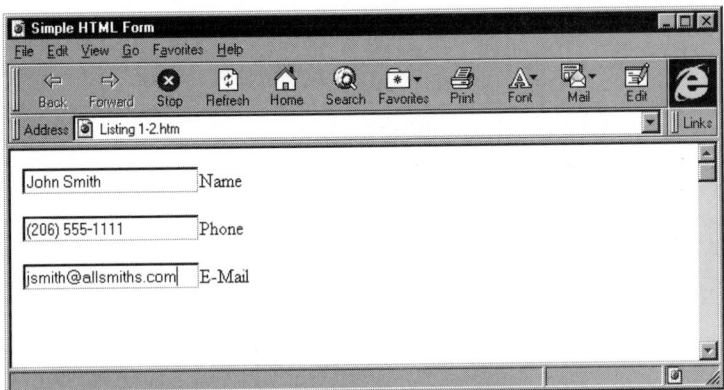

Figure 1-2.
A simple HTML form.

Forms represent the primary means of interaction in HTML. A user fills out a series of forms, which are then submitted to the back-end server. This submission process arranges the data from an HTML form in a predefined format and sends it as text to an executable file on the server. The server process can then manipulate the submitted data for the purpose of accessing a database, sending mail, or performing some other function.

HTML is created in plain text, so originally most HTML developers wrote their code directly in a text editor such as Notepad. As time went on, companies produced graphical development tools such as Microsoft FrontPage, which were designed to allow Web page creation without explicit knowledge of HTML. These graphical editors allow direct manipulation of the Web page with no laborious tag writing effort. Unfortunately, the strength of graphical editors is also their biggest drawback: they give developers the impression that they don't have to learn HTML syntax and tags—and nothing could be further from the truth. If you take one thing away from this introduction to HTML, remember this: you *must* know HTML to be a successful Web developer. Editing a page directly in text is a skill that will allow you to create exactly the effect you want whether or not it is directly supported by your favorite graphical editor. HTML is still the foundation of Internet development and will not be fully replaced anytime soon. In fact, attempts to enhance Web page development have made a thorough knowledge of HTML even more critical.

Client-Side Scripting

In an early effort to increase the interactivity of HTML Web pages, some developers turned to *scripting,* adding code-based functionality by combining a programming language with HTML. This approach often results in a strange hybrid of code and tags that once again takes developers back to the text editor. In scripting, the <SCRIPT> tag is introduced to define a code section in the Web page. Listing 1-3 uses VBScript to create a "Hello, World!" example, as shown in Figure 1-3.

```
<HTML>
<HEAD>
<META NAME="GENERATOR" Content="Microsoft Developer Studio">
<META HTTP-EQUIV="Content-Type" content="text/html;
    charset=iso-8859-1">
<TITLE>Yet Another Hello, World! Example</TITLE>

<SCRIPT LANGUAGE="VBScript">
<!--

    Sub cmdClickMe_OnClick()
        MsgBox "Hello, World!"
    End Sub

-->
```

Listing 1-3.
VBScript code for "Hello, World!"

(continued)

Listing 1-3 *continued*

```
</SCRIPT>

</HEAD>

<BODY BGCOLOR="WHITE">
<FORM>
<INPUT TYPE="BUTTON" NAME="cmdClickMe" VALUE="Click Me!">
</FORM>
</BODY>
</HTML>
```

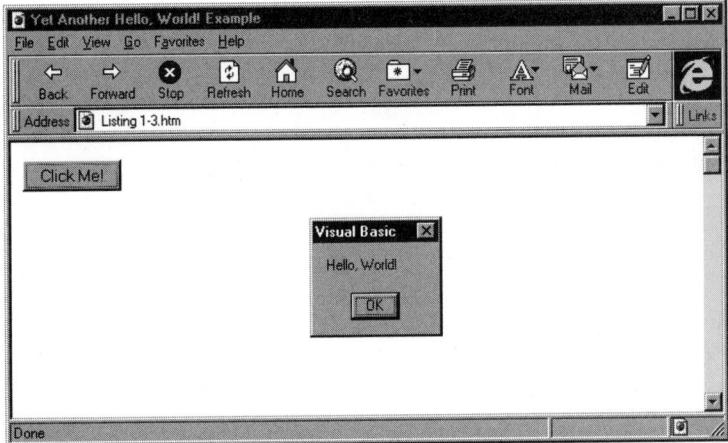

Figure 1-3.
"Hello, World!" created using VBScript.

VBScript is a scripting language based on Microsoft's popular Visual Basic for Applications (VBA), a language found in products such as Microsoft's Office 97. VBScript is not a complete version of VBA but rather a subset that keeps many of the key features of VBA while removing features that might make the language unnecessarily bulky or unsafe. For example, VBScript does not support data types—every variable defined is a Variant.

Like its big brother, VBA, VBScript is an event-driven language. This means that the code you write is executed in response to an *event,* a user interaction with a graphical user interface, or GUI. For our purposes, the GUI is the Web page. So, in the example above, when the user interacts with the GUI by clicking the Click Me! button, the action fires the OnClick event. This event is mapped to the VBScript code by way of an event-handling subroutine. A subroutine is named *ControlName_EventName* for any control and event

5

combination. The only caveat here is that some events can also be generated by the browser itself. For example, when a Web page completes a load into the browser, the Window_OnLoad event fires, independent of any user interaction with the page.

Although scripting represents an advancement in interactivity, it has its limitations. For example, not all browsers recognize scripting. Among those that do, not all use the same language. Chief among these is Netscape Navigator 3.0, which does not recognize VBScript but instead recognizes JavaScript, a scripting language originally created for Netscape Navigator. JavaScript is similar in function to VBScript but is very different in syntax. Unlike VBScript, JavaScript does not support the concept of an event-handling subroutine. All routines in JavaScript are functions, which are called by virtue of event attributes that reside in the HTML tag. Listing 1-4 is the JavaScript version of the previous VBScript example.

```
<HTML>
<HEAD>
<META NAME="GENERATOR" Content="Microsoft Developer Studio">
<META HTTP-EQUIV="Content-Type" content="text/html;
    charset=iso-8859-1">
<TITLE>JavaScript Hello, World! Example</TITLE>

<SCRIPT LANGUAGE="JavaScript">
<!--

    function clickme()
    {
        alert("Hello, World!");
        return true;
    }

-->
</SCRIPT>

</HEAD>

<BODY BGCOLOR="WHITE">
<FORM>
<INPUT TYPE="BUTTON" NAME="cmdClickMe"
    VALUE="Click Me!" OnClick="var rtn=clickme();">
</FORM>
</BODY>
</HTML>
```

Listing 1-4.
JavaScript code for "Hello, World!"

Not only does support for scripting vary by browser, but scripting does not provide the mature functionality programmers expect in a language. Scripting offers a subset of the language features developers normally use, a subset that limits structures and operators to fundamental looping and decision making. In fact, scripting alone is generally useful only for performing client-side data validation prior to submitting the form to a server.

Once scripting is added to the mix, platform complications abound. Obviously, if a scripting language is not universal, it cannot be adequately deployed on the Internet, and consequently all of the advertised advantages of platform independence on the Web come to nothing. For many Webmasters and developers, the constant battle between browsers for market share has resulted in the need to maintain three versions of each Web site: one for Microsoft Internet Explorer, one for Netscape Navigator, and one for old browsers such as Mosaic that can't understand any of the new technology.

ActiveX Components

As browser technology improved, additional platform dependence was introduced through ActiveX components, a technology based on Microsoft's Component Object Model (COM). ActiveX components range in style from fancy controls such as spinners and sliders to nonvisual components that allow data access or e-mail capability. These components make pages in Internet Explorer both attractive and functional but are nearly useless in environments that don't support ActiveX, such as Netscape Navigator.

An ActiveX component is added to a Web page through the <OBJECT> tag, which uniquely identifies the component to the browser. The following code uses an <OBJECT> tag to add an ActiveX label control to the Web page shown in Figure 1-4 on the following page:

```
<OBJECT ID="IeLabel3" WIDTH=148 HEIGHT=40
    CLASSID="CLSID:99B42120-6EC7-11CF-A6C7-00AA00A47DD2"
    CODEBASE="http://www.microsoft.com/activex/controls/ielabel.ocx">
    <PARAM NAME="_ExtentX" VALUE="3916">
    <PARAM NAME="_ExtentY" VALUE="1058">
    <PARAM NAME="Caption" VALUE="Label3">
    <PARAM NAME="Angle" VALUE="0">
    <PARAM NAME="Alignment" VALUE="4">
    <PARAM NAME="Mode" VALUE="1">
    <PARAM NAME="FillStyle" VALUE="0">
    <PARAM NAME="ForeColor" VALUE="#000000">
    <PARAM NAME="BackColor" VALUE="#C0C0C0">
    <PARAM NAME="FontName" VALUE="Arial">
```

(continued)

7

continued

```
        <PARAM NAME="FontSize" VALUE="12">
        <PARAM NAME="FontItalic" VALUE="0">
        <PARAM NAME="FontBold" VALUE="0">
        <PARAM NAME="FontUnderline" VALUE="0">
        <PARAM NAME="FontStrikeout" VALUE="0">
        <PARAM NAME="TopPoints" VALUE="0">
        <PARAM NAME="BotPoints" VALUE="0">
</OBJECT>
```

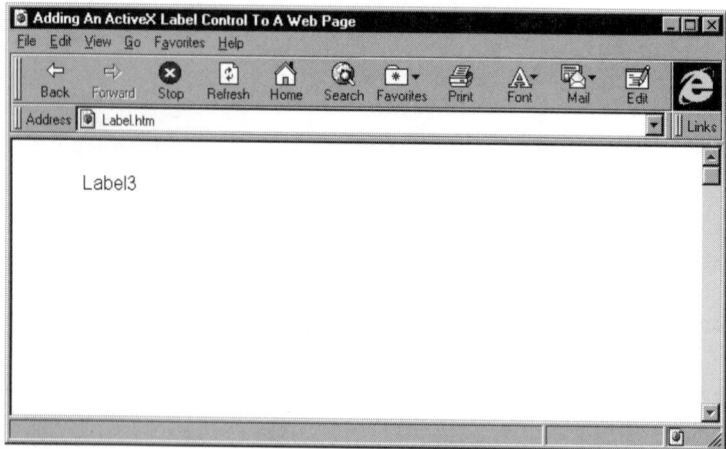

Figure 1-4.
An ActiveX label control displayed on a Web page.

The <OBJECT> tag consists of several key parts that determine how an ActiveX component is displayed on the page. The ID attribute names the control. Once named, the control can be accessed through scripting code, and all the properties, events, and methods of the control are available to the page.

Perhaps the least understood attributes are CLSID and CODEBASE. CLSID is an alphanumeric serial number that uniquely represents an ActiveX component among all others. This serial number, known as a Globally Unique Identifier, or GUID, is not used by any other ActiveX component. Internet Explorer uses the GUID to locate the ActiveX component and create it in the page.

GUID numbers are tracked on any operating system through the *registry*, a centralized database that is responsible for maintaining information about software objects used by applications. When Internet Explorer encounters an <OBJECT> tag, it goes to the registry and matches the CLSID attribute with the GUID. When the GUID is located, the registry provides additional information that locates the file for the ActiveX control. Figure 1-5 shows one of the registry entries for the Calendar ActiveX control, as viewed with the Registry Editor.

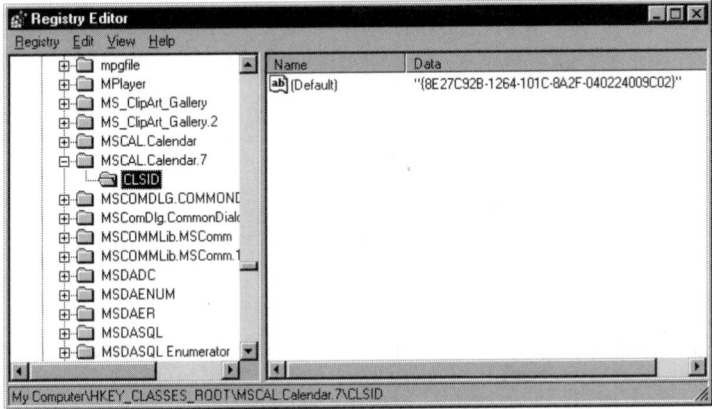

Figure 1-5.
Registry entry for the Calendar ActiveX control.

If the ActiveX control is not on the client machine, Internet Explorer uses the CODEBASE attribute to locate the ActiveX control on the server. The files for the control are downloaded via the CODEBASE attribute, and the ActiveX component is installed on the client machine. Once installed, Internet Explorer can use the control.

Accessing ActiveX components via the <OBJECT> tag is not restricted to controls. An <OBJECT> tag can activate *any* ActiveX component. This includes components you create with languages such as Visual Basic, J++, C++, and Microsoft FoxPro. In fact, you can easily extend the functionality afforded to the client by writing your own ActiveX components and downloading the components to the browser.

Supplying data to any component is accomplished with the <PARAM> tag. The <PARAM> tag uses the attributes NAME and VALUE to pass initial property value information to the ActiveX component when it is first created in the Web page. After the initial values are set, the properties can easily be changed at run time by using scripting calls.

ActiveX Documents

With the release of the latest version of Visual Basic, developers acquired another set of tools for creating dynamic content. Visual Basic 5.0 supports the creation of ActiveX controls as well as a new project type known as ActiveX documents. ActiveX documents are software objects that can be downloaded and run inside an ActiveX container such as Internet Explorer. ActiveX documents allow Visual Basic developers to immediately leverage their expertise in Visual Basic to create applications for the Internet. Essentially, ActiveX documents provide access to most of the key features of Visual Basic in a downloadable format.

Java

And don't forget about Java! This language has gained popularity quickly and is supported by both Internet Explorer and Netscape Navigator. Applets created in Java with a tool such as Microsoft Visual J++ are very similar to ActiveX components: they are self-contained, downloadable chunks of content that can be rendered in a Web page. And like ActiveX components, applets get their own special tag. The <APPLET> tag tells a browser to download Java code and run it. The following code runs an applet in a Web page:

```
<APPLET CODE="DBLBULB.CLASS" HEIGHT=35 WIDTH=26>
</APPLET>
```

The CODE attribute of the <APPLET> tag identifies the source code of the Java applet in much the same way that the CODEBASE attribute identifies the source for an ActiveX component. Applets can also have <PARAM> tags that specify initial values. In many ways, applets are the functional equivalent of ActiveX controls. In fact, scripting languages can access the public functions in applets just as they can access the methods of ActiveX components.

Dynamic HTML

Well, platform considerations are not getting any less complicated for Web developers. With the introduction of Internet Explorer version 4.0, Microsoft added a new twist to client-side functionality: Dynamic HTML, which allows tags to be programmatically changed through scripting. This is incredibly powerful. Consider the code in Listing 1-5, which uses VBScript to detect when the mouse is over some text on the Web page and then changes the text color and size.

```
<HTML>
<HEAD>
<META NAME="GENERATOR" Content="Microsoft Developer Studio">
<META HTTP-EQUIV="Content-Type" content="text/html;
    charset=iso-8859-1">
<TITLE>Dynamic HTML</TITLE>
```

Listing 1-5.   *(continued)*
Dynamic HTML.

Listing 1-5 *continued*

```
<SCRIPT LANGUAGE="VBScript">
<!--

    Function MyFont_OnMouseOver()
        MyFont.Color = "Red"
        MyFont.Size = "5"
    End Function

    Function MyFont_OnMouseOut()
        MyFont.Color = "Blue"
        MyFont.Size = "4"
    End Function

-->
</SCRIPT>
</HEAD>

<BODY BGCOLOR="WHITE">
<FONT ID="MyFont" FACE="ARIAL" SIZE="4" COLOR="BLUE">
Hey, put your mouse here!
</BODY>
</HTML>
```

Dynamic HTML defines a series of events that can be associated with HTML tags. This expands the event-driven paradigm of VBScript to include every element in the page—HTML tags, ActiveX controls, and even the browser itself have events. If you had any lingering doubt that you needed a thorough knowledge of HTML to effectively create Web pages, the preceding example should convince you. In the example, the VBScript code dynamically changes the COLOR and SIZE attributes of the <FONT> tag when mouse activity is detected. You cannot write this code unless you know exactly what the <FONT> tag is and understand its COLOR and SIZE attributes. So long, graphical editors!

Dynamic HTML adds a wealth of power and interactivity to the Web client not only through dynamic style manipulation but through other features as well. Dynamic HTML understands how to position elements on the Web page. You can, for example, translate an image by changing the attributes of a simple <IMG> tag. You can also add or delete tags from the page to create changing content. Finally, Internet Explorer 4.0 also supports the data binding of form fields. This means that a database on the server can be wired directly to a form field on the browser for rapid updates and edits. All of this makes

Dynamic HTML a powerful tool worthy of your time. This book dedicates a significant number of pages to understanding and using Dynamic HTML, but remember one thing: Dynamic HTML is currently available only to Internet Explorer 4.0, despite Microsoft's efforts to create it as an open standard.

Active Server Pages

Another milestone technology—one discussed extensively in this book—is Active Server Pages, or ASP. In many ways, ASP is the most exciting of all the new Internet technologies because it allows you to create great, platform-independent content that can be used in any browser. Or, if you want to take maximum advantage of platform-specific technologies such as Dynamic HTML, you can create ASP pages that speak directly to Internet Explorer 4.0.

At its most fundamental, ASP is scripting done on the server. This scripting code is evaluated dynamically when the page is requested, and the resulting HTML is passed to the calling browser. Consider the code in Listing 1-6, which uses ASP to generate six successive lines of text that get increasingly larger.

```
<%@SCRIPT LANGUAGE="VBSCRIPT"%>
<HTML>
<HEAD>
<META NAME="GENERATOR" Content="Microsoft Developer Studio">
<META HTTP-EQUIV="Content-Type" content="text/html;
    charset=iso-8859-1">
<TITLE>ASP Example</TITLE>
</HEAD>

<BODY BGCOLOR="WHITE">

<%For x = 1 to 6%>
    <FONT FACE="ARIAL" SIZE=<%=x%>>
    ActiveX Is Cool!
    </FONT>
    <P>
<%Next%>

</BODY>
</HTML>
```

Listing 1-6.
An ASP Web page.

The sample code includes a <SCRIPT> tag, but notice that percent signs appear inside the brackets. This syntax indicates that the code is to be executed on the server before the page is downloaded to the client. In fact, notice the percent signs that surround all the code in the page. This code is all evaluated before the browser receives the page. The resulting HTML code looks like this:

```
<HTML>
<HEAD>
<META NAME="GENERATOR" Content="Microsoft Developer Studio">
<META HTTP-EQUIV="Content-Type" content="text/html;
    charset=iso-8859-1">
<TITLE>ASP Example</TITLE>
</HEAD>

<BODY BGCOLOR="WHITE">

<FONT FACE="ARIAL" SIZE=1>
ActiveX Is Cool!
</FONT>
<P>

<FONT FACE="ARIAL" SIZE=2>
ActiveX Is Cool!
</FONT>
<P>

<FONT FACE="ARIAL" SIZE=3>
ActiveX Is Cool!
</FONT>
<P>

<FONT FACE="ARIAL" SIZE=4>
ActiveX Is Cool!
</FONT>
<P>

<FONT FACE="ARIAL" SIZE=5>
ActiveX Is Cool!
</FONT>
<P>

<FONT FACE="ARIAL" SIZE=6>
ActiveX Is Cool!
</FONT>
<P>

</BODY>
</HTML>
```

13

In the resulting HTML lies the beauty of Active Server Pages. ASP output can be limited strictly to HTML—understandable by any browser! This makes ASP an ideal choice for applications that must run on the Internet, where any browser can view a page. ASP is not limited to the lowest common denominator, however, and you can freely add client script, ActiveX controls, and Dynamic HTML to the output of ASP. ASP pages are therefore as flexible as you want them to be.

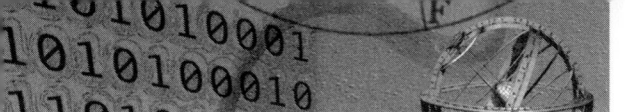

CHAPTER TWO

Web Services

The heart and soul of any good Web site is the back-end server. The Web server can provide static Web pages in the form of HTML documents, but it can also execute applications that significantly enhance the content of a site. The idea of executing content on a Web server is not new. In past implementations, a Web server used the Common Gateway Interface, or CGI, to execute content. CGI is a technology that allows a Web server to start an executable and use that process to accomplish tasks such as sending e-mail. CGI applications add much-needed functionality to Web sites, but they are typically slow because a CGI application runs as a separate process. Since the Web server and the CGI application must exchange data across processes, communication between them is slowed down considerably.

Internet Information Server

Microsoft Internet Information Server, or IIS, is the primary Web server for sites constructed on Microsoft Windows NT technology, and it represents a vast improvement over servers that simply use CGI to create content. IIS supports a new set of applications that use the Internet Server Application Programming Interface, or ISAPI. ISAPI applications can be executed by IIS in a fashion similar to CGI, but they run in the same memory space as the Web server. In fact, ISAPI applications are constructed as dynamic-link libraries that can run as much as twenty times faster than equivalent CGI applications. Microsoft Active Server Pages, or ASP, is an example of an ISAPI application. In order to understand how ASP creates dynamic content, you must first understand how IIS works with Windows NT to create a Web site. The following pages cover the fundamentals of installing and administering IIS and setting up the system to publish dynamic content.

Installing IIS

Internet Information Server is available for both the Server and Workstation versions of Windows NT. Although IIS is nearly identical under these two platforms, its installation process differs. However, neither setup is particularly difficult or time consuming.

Under Windows NT Server, IIS is used as a primary publishing mechanism. The complete version of IIS ships with Windows NT Server version 4.0 and can easily be installed during the Windows NT setup process. If you want your Windows NT Server to act as a Web server, all you have to do is install the IIS administrator when you set up the server. Figure 2-1 shows the setup dialog box for IIS.

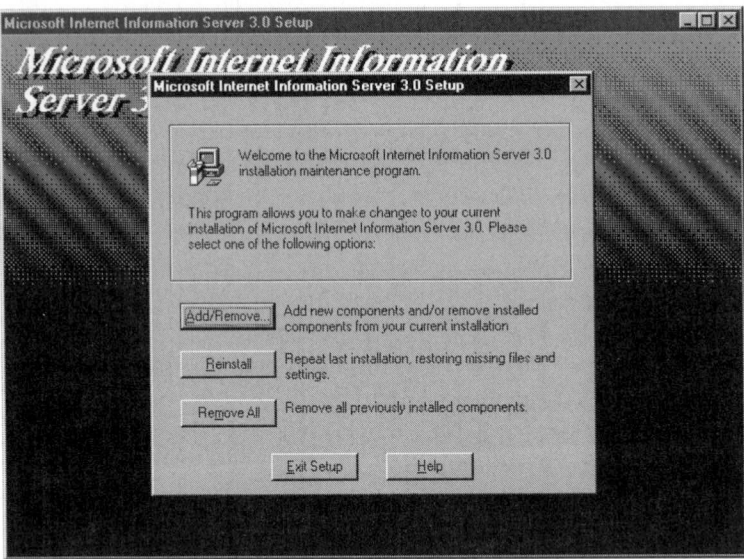

Figure 2-1.
IIS installation dialog box under Windows NT Server 4.0.

IIS running under Windows NT Server is officially regarded as version 2.0 because it does not ship with the Active Server Pages technology. ASP must be installed separately after IIS is installed. When ASP features are added to IIS, the version of IIS is automatically upgraded to version 3.0. Upgrading to 3.0 does not fundamentally change the Web server; it simply adds the ability to run Active Server Pages. You can find the ASP core on the same CD-ROM as Microsoft Visual InterDev.

At this writing, IIS version 4.0 is available in a Beta release. Under the Beta implementation, setup is straightforward and works well with all the technologies discussed in this book. The sample code provided on the CD-ROM has been fully tested with IIS 4.0 Beta.

IIS is also available for Windows NT Workstation version 4.0. When run under NT Workstation, IIS is known as Microsoft Peer Web Services. Peer Web Services is exactly the same Web server as IIS except that Peer Web Services has a 10-user connection limit. In order to install the Web server on NT Workstation, you must use the Network applet in the Control Panel. On the Services tab of the Network applet, you can install Peer Web Services as a new service, as shown in Figure 2-2.

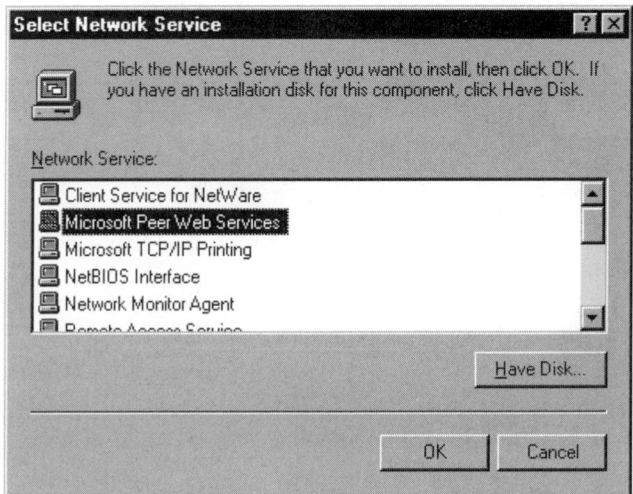

Figure 2-2.
Adding Peer Web Services.

A typical setup scenario for IIS is to create a Web site under Windows NT Server for use on an intranet while installing Peer Web Services on Windows NT Workstation for development. Visual InterDev provides the necessary tools for developing sites locally and then deploying the completed and debugged versions to IIS on a server. This setup prevents moving untested pages into production.

During the installation process, you will be prompted to provide a directory for your Web pages. Typically, this directory is named \WWWROOT. All references to your site begin with this directory name. The root directory maps directly to the name of your site. The site name is determined by the name of the host computer, which can be found by using the Network applet in the Control Panel, as shown in Figure 2-3.

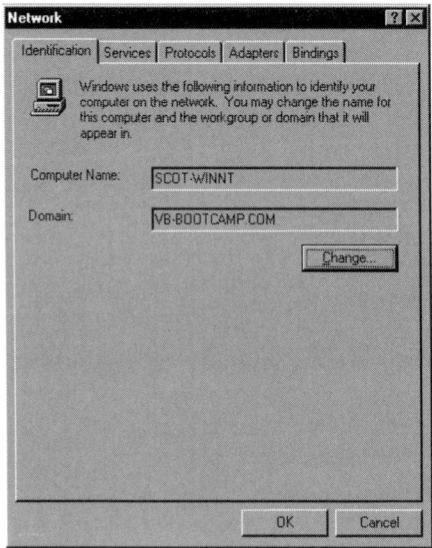

Figure 2-3.
The host computer name.

To understand how IIS uses the name of the host computer, suppose you have a Windows NT Server called NT_SERVER. This name becomes the name of the site and can be accessed by Microsoft Internet Explorer from any machine on the network. When the user explores the Uniform Resource Locator (URL) http://NT_SERVER, IIS is invoked and directs the browser to a special Web page located in \WWWROOT. Typically, this is a page named DEFAULT.HTM, but it can be any page you want.

Administering the WWW Service

When installed, IIS provides three primary services: File Transfer Protocol (FTP) and Gopher, which are file transfer services; and World Wide Web (WWW), which delivers Web pages to browsers and allows access to the functionality of Active Server Pages. For the purposes of Web development, WWW is the most important of the three services.

Administering IIS in general and the WWW service in particular is critical for the success of your site. In order to administer the WWW service, select Programs/Microsoft Internet Server/Internet Service Manager from the Start menu. Internet Service Manager lists available services, as shown in Figure 2-4.

Properties button

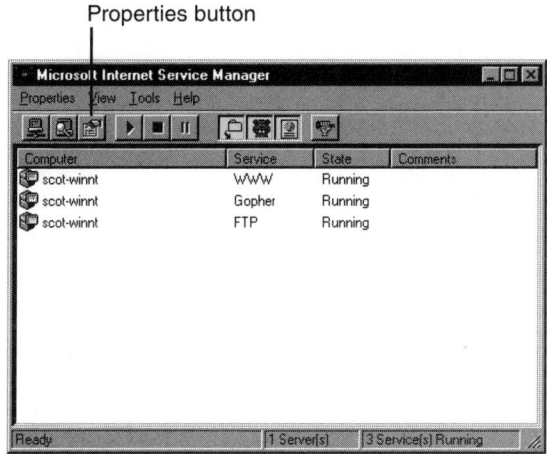

Figure 2-4.
Internet Service Manager.

When you select a service in the list and click the Properties button, a tabbed dialog box appears that presents all the features of the service. The tabs allow you to handle security features, directory locations, and logging activity. Each of these areas contains information that helps you maintain a strong site.

Under IIS 4.0 Beta, the interface for managing IIS has changed radically. Gone is the familiar Internet Service Manager, which has been replaced by Microsoft Management Console, or MMC. MMC provides an Explorer-style view of Internet services and is intended to be a centralized management system for enterprise services on Windows NT. It supports the addition of *snap-ins* that allow products such as Microsoft Transaction Server to use the MMC interface. Figure 2-5 on the following page shows the MMC interface.

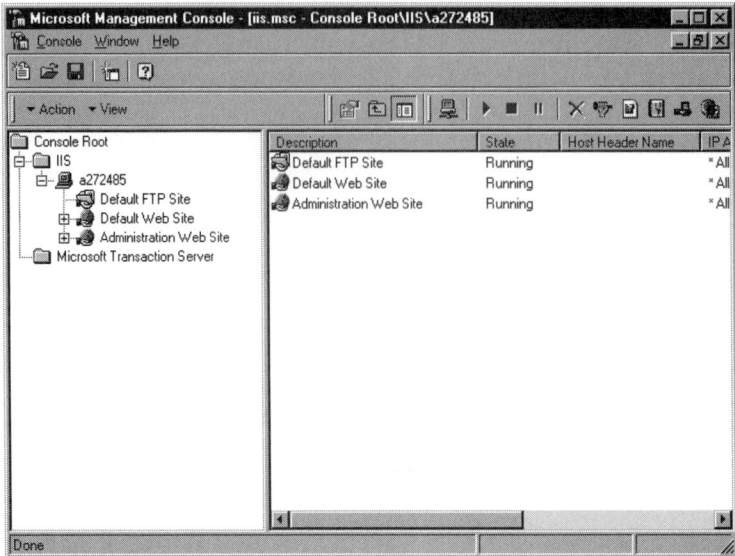

Figure 2-5.
Microsoft Management Console.

Security Issues

Security is certainly a major concern on any Web site. Many well-publicized security breaches have contributed to a general feeling of vulnerability regarding Internet systems. Fortunately, IIS is a secure server. Its security system is closely linked to Windows NT security, and together IIS and Windows NT provide a number of security layers through which a user must pass before gaining access to your site.

The first matter to consider in site security is accounts. IIS uses the same user accounts that Windows NT uses to allow access. In fact, logging on to IIS isn't much different from logging on to Windows NT. A user attempting to connect to your Web site must have a valid user ID and password for the domain.

Because Windows NT requires that all users have a user ID and a password, no one can gain access to IIS without an account. But how do you assign an account to the millions of people who might want to visit your site? The answer is to provide an anonymous logon account. An anonymous account can handle any user who does not have a real user ID and password for the Windows NT domain that is hosting your IIS server.

When IIS is installed, it automatically establishes an account for anonymous logons. This account is given a special user ID that is derived from the name of the machine. Specifically, IIS creates an anonymous account called IUSR_*MachineName*, where *MachineName* is the name of the Windows NT server. So, for example, if your server is named MyServer, your anonymous logon account is IUSR_MyServer.

Anonymous logons are allowed when you check the Allow Anonymous option found on the Service tab in the Service Properties dialog box. (See Figure 2-6.) Normally, anonymous logons are treated as domain guests, so it is vital that you check the permissions assigned to guests on your network to verify that anonymous logons are not given inappropriate authority. Any permissions assigned to guests are assigned to anonymous logons. So if you make all guests administrators on the system, anyone who browses your site will also be an administrator!

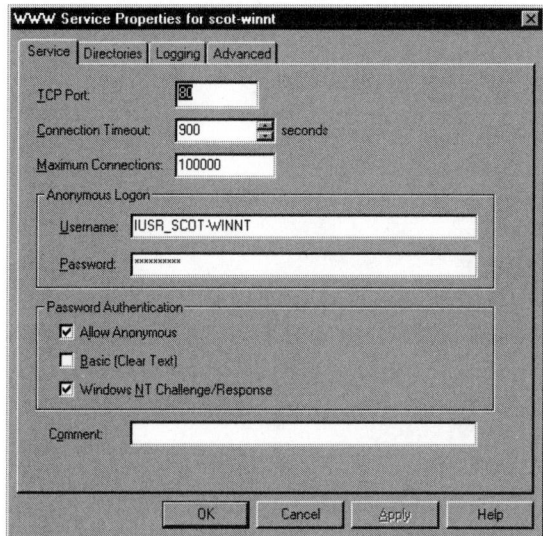

Figure 2-6.
The Service tab.

IIS also allows you to specify that users who have actual accounts on the network should be logged on under those accounts. This is done by checking the Basic (Clear Text) or the Windows NT Challenge/Response option on the Service tab. The difference between the two options has to do with the way the password is transmitted. Under Basic (Clear Text) authentication, the password can be sent over the Internet in clear (unencrypted) text. Sending a clear text password over the Internet is a potential security problem because clear text might be intercepted during the transfer, compromising the account. Most browsers, however, support the Basic (Clear Text) authentication scheme.

Windows NT Challenge/Response provides a more secure logon by encrypting the password before sending it to the server. This functionality is supported by Internet Explorer version 2.0 and later. At first, you might think that Windows NT Challenge/Response represents the most secure setup you can have, but that is not necessarily true. If your server is an Internet server, the most secure setup is to select only the Allow Anonymous option. This is true because if you allow only anonymous logons, you can easily control the permissions of every user through the anonymous account established by IIS. You can never guarantee that a user account hasn't been compromised, so anonymous logons might actually be more secure.

Under IIS 4.0, you have the same security options that you have under IIS 3.0, but you are able to set security properties for each subdirectory on the site. Select the site subdirectory through MMC, and select Properties to display the Properties dialog box. In the Properties dialog box, click the Directory Security tab and click the Edit button for the password authentication method. The resulting dialog box, shown in Figure 2-7, gives you the familiar Allow Anonymous, Basic Authentication, and Windows NT Challenge/Response options.

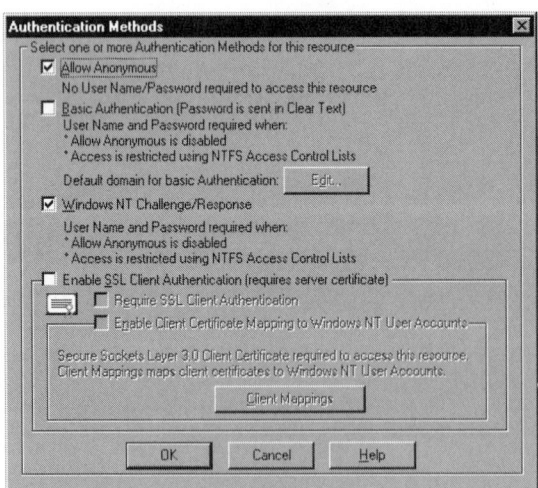

Figure 2-7.
Setting security for IIS 4.0.

Virtual Directories

IIS supports *virtual directories,* aliases for hard-coded paths on the server. Virtual directories are administered through the Directories tab in the Service Properties dialog box. (See Figure 2-8.) On the Directories tab, you can view the one-to-one relationship between hard-coded paths and virtual directories.

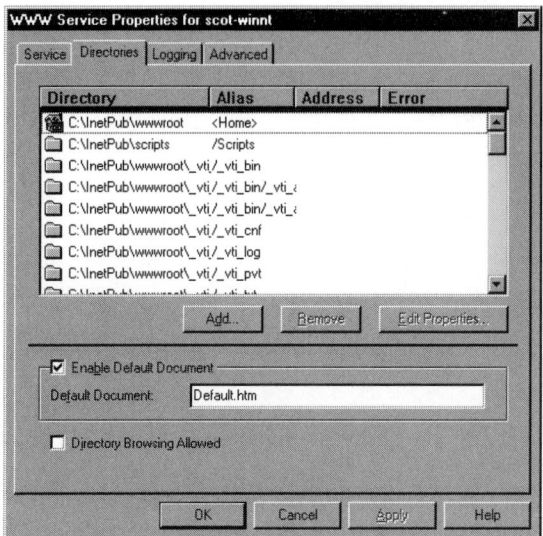

Figure 2-8.
The Directories tab.

Virtual directories offer several advantages in site development. The first is that virtual directories hide important information about the directory structures of your site. In a Web browser, the user can always view the source for any Web page by selecting Source from the View menu. If you use hard-coded paths in your Web page, you are exposing important information regarding your site's directory structure. This might aid someone in attacking your system.

The second advantage of virtual directories is more important for developers. Virtual directories allow Web pages to be moved from one machine to another without changing any code in the pages. Both machines must have the same virtual directories, although each machine would have different hard-coded paths for those directories.

Adding, deleting, and editing virtual directories is also done through the Directories tab. To add a virtual directory, click the Add button and enter the appropriate information (such as the hard-coded path and the designated alias) in the Directory Properties dialog box. (See Figure 2-9.) To delete a virtual directory, select the directory and click the Remove button. To edit an existing virtual directory, select it and click the Edit Properties button to display the Directory Properties dialog box.

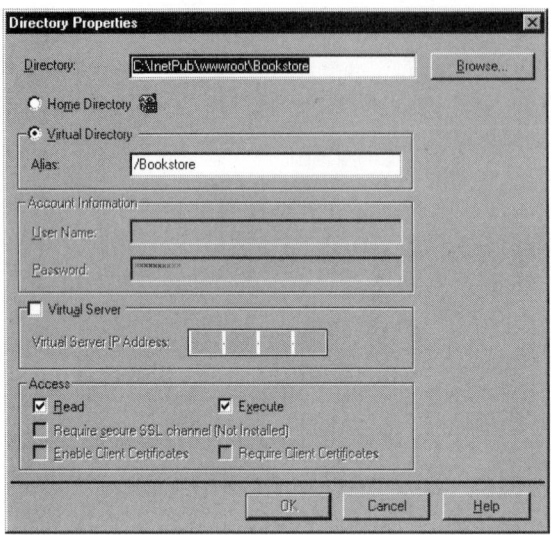

Figure 2-9.
The Directory Properties dialog box.

In the Directory Properties dialog box, you must also specify the access method for the virtual directory: Read, Execute, or both. Read access means that content in the directory can be passed from IIS to the browser. Execute access means that executable content can be run from within the directory. In practical terms, regular HTML pages require Read access while ASP pages need Execute access. In general, you should segregate Read and Execute content. This is usually done by establishing separate subdirectories on your site for HTML pages and ASP pages. The HTML subdirectory should be designated as Read but not Execute. The ASP subdirectory should be Execute but not Read.

Under IIS 4.0, you can create a new virtual directory inside MMC by right-clicking one of the Web Site icons. When the pop-up menu appears, simply choose Create New/Virtual Directory. Then use the New Virtual Directory wizard, shown in Figure 2-10. A series of dialog boxes maps the alias to the selected directory path.

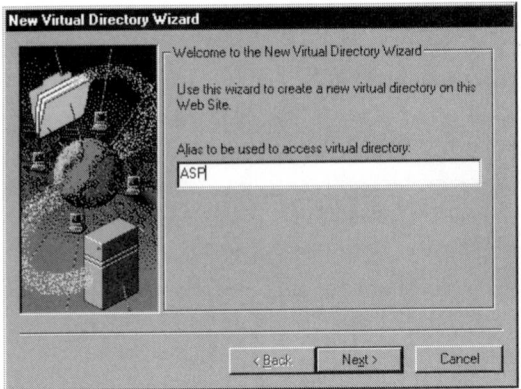

Figure 2-10.
The New Virtual Directory wizard.

Logging Activity

IIS has the capability to log user activity on the site. This is an important feature that you should utilize regularly. Logging user activity can help you identify potential security threats from outside users. On the Logging tab in the Service Properties dialog box, shown in Figure 2-11, you can choose to log to a text file or to a SQL Server database.

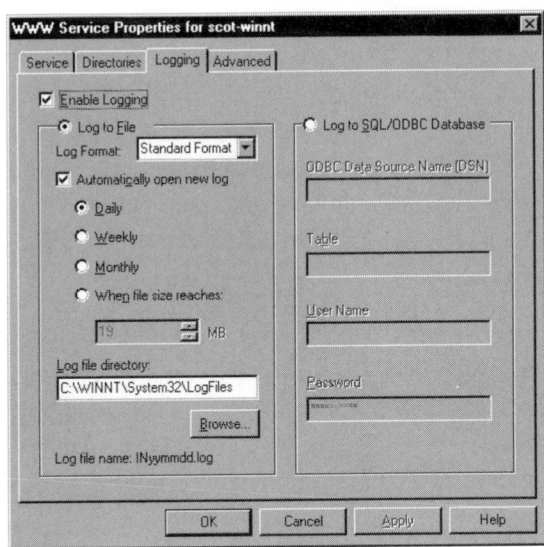

Figure 2-11.
The Logging tab.

Advanced IIS Features

On the Advanced tab in the Service Properties dialog box, shown in Figure 2-12, you can specify access to your server by Internet Protocol (IP) address; you can specify a pool of addresses for access or a pool to be denied access; and you can specify individual addresses for access. This is extremely useful for intranet systems, where you might want to restrict access by department. For example, you could limit the Accounts Receivable intranet to members of the department whose IP addresses are in the range 100.100.100.50 through 100.100.100.70. You can also manage access by IP address under IIS 4.0, but you control it by virtual directory. This allows you to establish security differently for different directories.

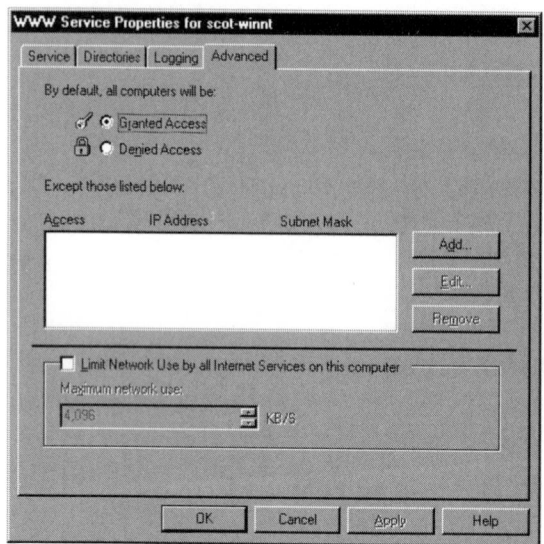

Figure 2-12.
The Advanced tab.

Personal Web Server

Personal Web Server, or PWS, is a server designed for use with Microsoft Windows 95. This is the ideal server for developing sites off line. In fact, Personal Web Server supports many of the features seen in the full version of IIS, including virtual directories and Active Server Pages. PWS ships with Visual InterDev and is typically used with Visual InterDev to create sites.

When installed, PWS can be identified as a small earth-and-computer icon located in the taskbar. Server administration is straightforward and simple—much like administration of its larger counterpart. To begin, simply double-click the earth-and-computer icon to view the Personal Web Server Properties dialog box, shown in Figure 2-13.

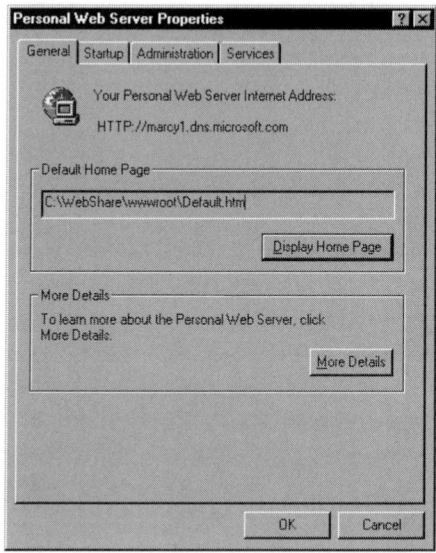

Figure 2-13.
The Personal Web Server Properties dialog box.

On the General tab, you can set the default home page for the server. The Startup tab allows you to start and stop the server and determine whether the server starts automatically when the computer is booted. The Administration tab is used to access administrative capabilities, including password authentication, virtual directories, and site logging. Note that unlike IIS administration, which is dialog-based, PWS administration is Web-based. (See Figure 2-14 on the following page.)

The Services tab of the Personal Web Server Properties dialog box reveals the two services that PWS supports: HTTP and FTP. (PWS does not provide the Gopher service available in IIS.) On the Services tab, you can control which of the services is currently running. To publish Web pages, you will need to run the HTTP service.

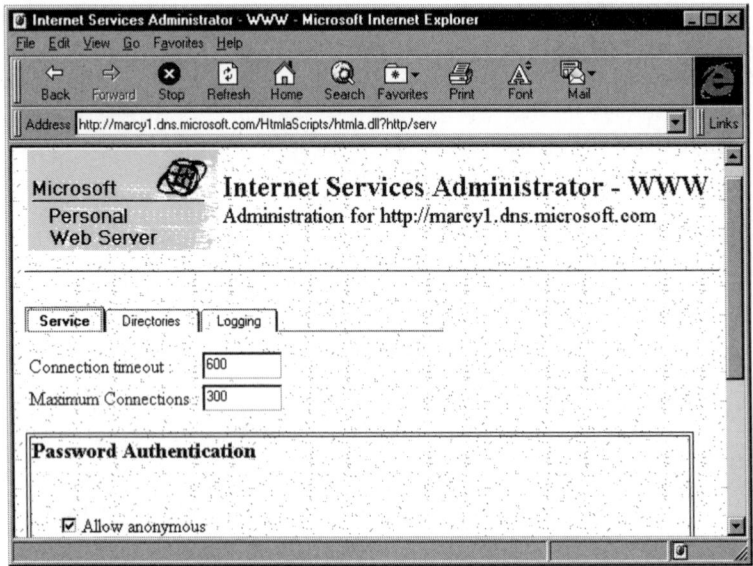

Figure 2-14.
PWS Web-based administration.

FrontPage Server Extensions

FrontPage server extensions play a valuable role when you develop content using Visual InterDev and Microsoft FrontPage. FrontPage server extensions are a set of programs and scripts that allow Visual InterDev and FrontPage to communicate with your Web server. This is important because these tools use the extensions to create new projects or to load existing ones. Normally, the extensions are installed when the server is installed, but this might not be true for all servers. Therefore, FrontPage ships with a utility called FrontPage Server Administrator, which allows you to manually install and maintain the extensions on a server. (See Figure 2-15.)

In this utility, you can specify which server receives the extensions and you can provide additional information such as the port for installation. Generally, all you need to do is select the server and click the Install button—the administrator takes care of the rest. If you later encounter difficulties locating your server with either Visual InterDev or FrontPage, you can use FrontPage Server Administrator to verify that the server extensions are properly installed on your Web server.

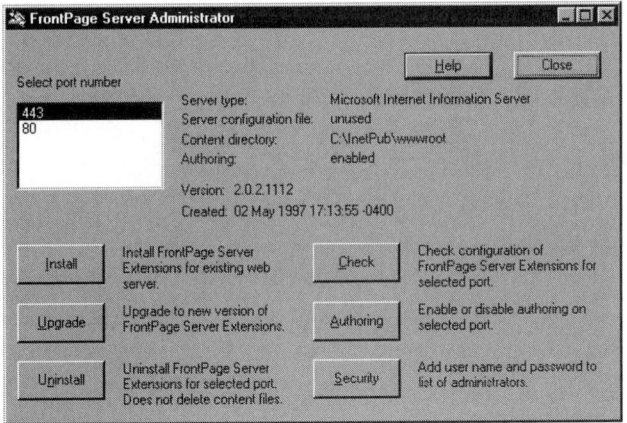

Figure 2-15.
FrontPage Server Administrator.

Additional Web Services

In addition to the standard services supported by IIS, you can take advantage of a number of services that ship as separate products. These products allow IIS to scale from a simple intranet server all the way to a high-volume public Web site or a membership service. The following items are particularly useful.

Microsoft Index Server indexes the content on your site, enables keyword searches through a search page, and returns a list of hyperlinks that map to the resulting pages.

Microsoft Proxy Server enables IIS to act as a proxy for internal clients accessing the Internet. Using a proxy server is an excellent way to enhance security on a site that does not have its own firewall. A proxy server provides a pool of TCP/IP addresses for clients to use when they access the Internet. The pooled addresses help preserve bandwidth and mask the true TCP/IP addresses of clients so that they cannot be attacked from outside.

Microsoft Merchant Server is used to create online shopping services, including online catalogs and buying services. Merchant Server has the ability to accept secure credit card transactions.

Microsoft Commercial Internet System is intended for Internet Service Providers (ISPs). It is a full-service suite that includes Simple Mail Transfer Protocol (SMTP) services, Network News Transport Protocol (NNTP) services, membership verification, and chat rooms. This system allows you to use IIS as the backbone of a full-featured online service.

A final note: IIS 4.0 ships with several new Web services, including support for the SMTP protocol and the NNTP protocol. Using MMC, you can manage a local mail server and a news server.

Using ODBC Data Sources

Because the Web server plays a key role in database publishing, it must be able to access a variety of data. All the tools used by IIS to publish data rely on Open Database Connectivity (ODBC) data sources. ODBC is a database-independent technology for accessing data. ODBC is particularly useful in Web applications and simplifies development by allowing Web pages to utilize standard Structured Query Language (SQL) syntax to interact with a database.

Before you can access a database with ODBC, you must set up an ODBC data source. Data sources are established using ODBC Data Source Administrator, an applet identified as the ODBC icon in the Control Panel. The administrator window is shown in Figure 2-16.

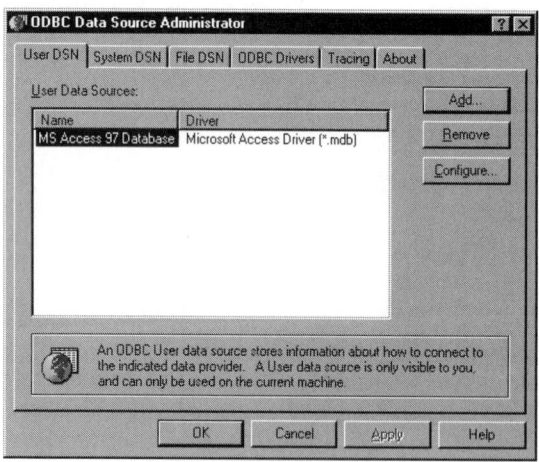

Figure 2-16.
ODBC Data Source Administrator.

Once inside ODBC Data Source Administrator, you can set up a new data source or modify an existing one. ODBC version 3.0 supports three different types of data sources: User, System, and File. A User data source is available only to the user who creates it and can be run only from the machine where it is defined. A System data source is available to all users of, and services running on, the current machine. A File data source is available to users across the enterprise, provided they have the necessary ODBC drivers installed on their machines.

ODBC drivers are middleware that is able to convert SQL syntax to proprietary formats required by individual database engines. ODBC drivers are the primary component in ODBC that provides the database independence. Each driver is responsible for mapping the common functionality of SQL to the specific functionality of any database engine.

Establishing an ODBC data source is an important first step in any Web development effort. The data source you set up should be appropriate for its intended use. You select a User, System, or File source based on the degree of availability you require for the data source. Typically, you would use a System data source for most Internet applications.

When you establish an ODBC data source, you are required to provide key information that allows the ODBC driver to access the data source. In all cases, you must first provide a name for the data source. The name is arbitrary and can be anything you want; it will be used by your script code to access the data source through ODBC. Depending on the driver, you might also have to provide additional information. For example, if you set up a SQL Server data source, you must tell the driver which machine on the enterprise has the SQL Server data and the name of the database on the machine that you want to connect with. The setup dialog box is shown in Figure 2-17.

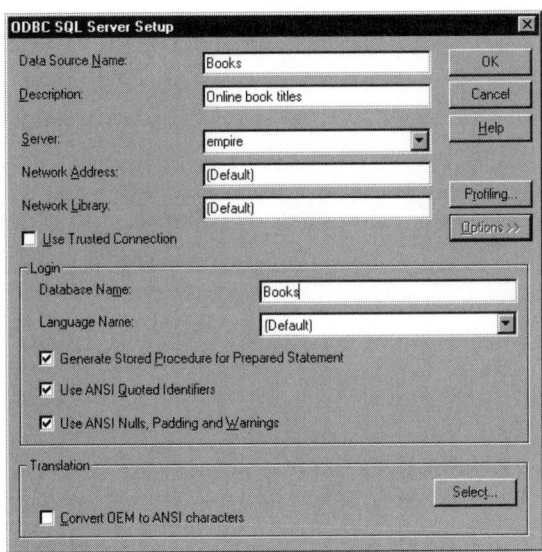

Figure 2-17.
The ODBC SQL Server Setup dialog box.

Once the required information is entered, you can close the dialog box and the data source is available for use. In most Web applications you create, you will want to make the ODBC connection available to your site through Visual InterDev. Adding an ODBC data source to Visual InterDev is accomplished by choosing Add To Project/Data Connection from the Project menu. A data connection allows Visual InterDev to recognize an ODBC data source and to help you manage it. When a data connection is added to a Visual InterDev project, a new tab, Data View, appears in the project window. (See Figure 2-18.) This tab gives you access to some sophisticated data tools that allow you to add, edit, update, and delete database records. You can even change the table structure directly in Visual InterDev. Throughout your projects, you will make extensive use of these tools. In many ways, they are superior to some of the tools that actually ship with many databases!

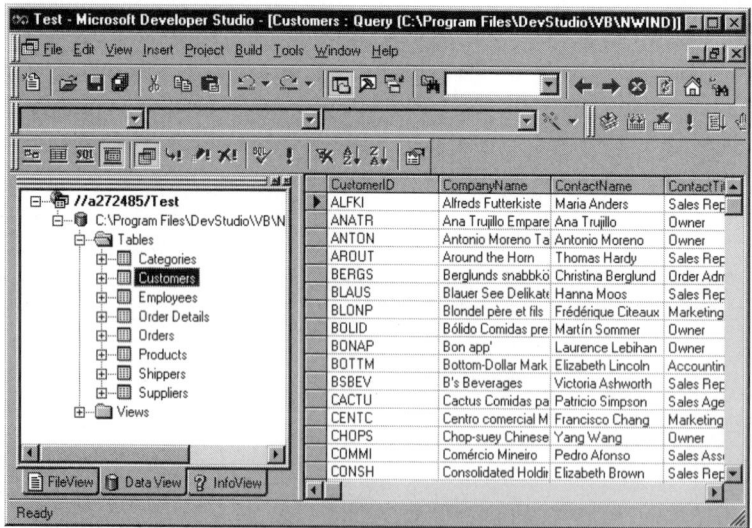

Figure 2-18.
The Data View tab in Visual InterDev.

CHAPTER THREE

Internet Explorer 4.0

Internet Explorer (IE) version 4.0 is Microsoft's latest Web browser. This version comes packed with enhancements that greatly improve the Internet experience. Many of these features, such as Active Desktop, are targeted at the end user, but other features are specifically placed to assist content developers. In order to create great content for sites that will host IE 4.0, designers and programmers must understand the full impact of the client-side features.

Active Desktop

Active Desktop is the name given to the complete integration of the operating system shell with Internet Explorer 4.0. This integration allows you to customize the desktop with elements from any Web page. Essentially, the Web page replaces your wallpaper and gives you a constant view of the Internet. (See Figure 3-1 on the following page.)

Active Desktop is controlled through the Display Properties dialog box, which is accessed by clicking the desktop with the right mouse button and choosing Properties. This is the same action you would take to alter the desktop under the normal Microsoft Windows shell. When the dialog box appears, however, you'll notice that a Web tab has been added. (See Figure 3-2 on the following page.)

The Web tab provides new ways of customizing the desktop. First, you can add new individual Web sites to your desktop. These sites can contain any component that can be rendered in IE 4.0, including ActiveX controls, Java applets, and HTML pages. To add a new site, simply click the New button and enter the site's URL in the New Active Desktop Item dialog box. Each new site you add appears on the desktop as a scrolling frame. Second, you can specify a local HTML page to use as your desktop. This is a great feature for network administrators who want to provide hyperlink access to network facilities through corporate intranets. A complete intranet site directory can be established as a local HTML page that gives users single-click access to forms,

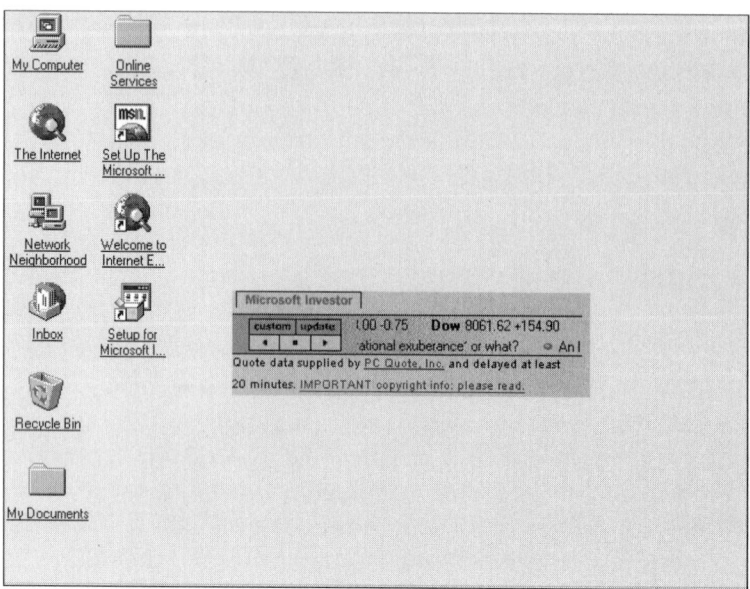

Figure 3-1.
Active Desktop.

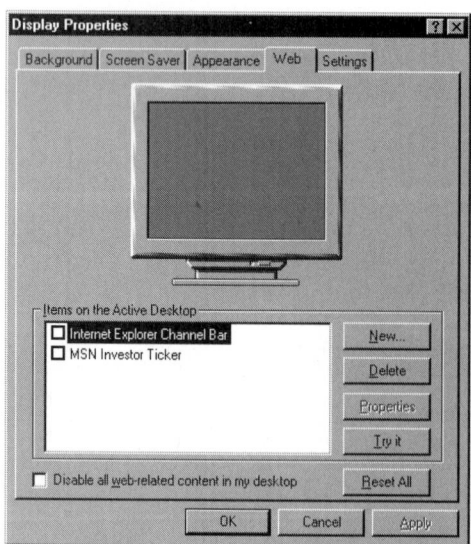

Figure 3-2.
The Display Properties dialog box.

information requests, databases, and schedules. Finally, if you don't like any of the displays, you can return to the standard desktop by simply checking Disable All Web-Related Content In My Desktop in the Display Properties dialog box.

Channels

Internet Explorer 4.0 now supports server *push,* or Internet broadcasting to a Web client. A Web site that offers content push as a service can broadcast Web content through a channel created through a Channel Definition File, or CDF. A CDF contains key information about the site and its content, including content use and update frequency.

When a channel is available to the Web client, it appears on the desktop as a logo icon in the Channel Bar. The Channel Bar contains a list of all Web sites connected to CDFs, enabling you to switch easily between the sites. Once a channel is established, IE 4.0 automatically monitors the site and downloads new content as necessary. The broadcast is enhanced by a television-style view of the site (shown in Figure 3-3), which is created by running IE 4.0 in full-screen mode.

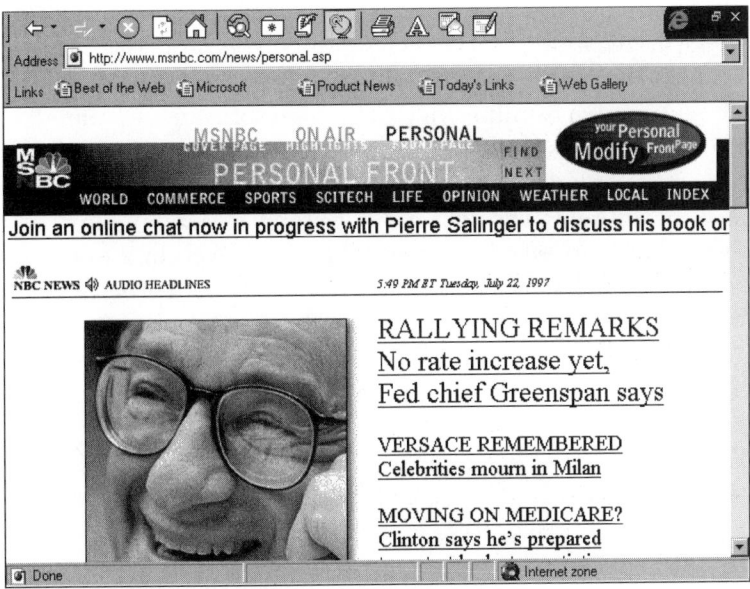

Figure 3-3.
Viewing a channel.

Subscriptions

For any site, even one that does not accommodate channels, Internet Explorer 4.0 will support a *subscription*. A subscription sets up an automatic download of a site on a periodic basis. A subscription is fundamentally different from a channel because the browser checks the site as opposed to the site broadcasting to the browser. This means that you can ask IE 4.0 to check a given site for new content and download at regular intervals. If the computer must use dial-up networking, a subscription can be established so that the modem is used automatically.

The Object Model

Although many new features of Internet Explorer 4.0 are designed to enhance the user experience, improved browsing depends entirely on improved content. To that end, IE 4.0 provides a number of new features for content developers. Most of these features, including Dynamic HTML, are covered in later chapters of this book, but all content development depends on a strong understanding of the IE 4.0 architecture. This architecture takes the form of an object model.

The concept of constructing software from objects is certainly not new. Most of the applications that you know well—Microsoft Word, Microsoft Excel, Microsoft PowerPoint, and Internet Explorer—are constructed of objects. These applications are built from well-defined software modules that provide data through variables known as *properties* and provide services through function calls known as *methods*. Properties and methods perform useful functions for a piece of software. The collection of properties and methods that define an object is called an *interface*. An interface is invoked by a user through the toolbar and menus, but it can also be called directly by a programmer through code. In fact, virtually anything a user can do with an application can be done by a programmer who makes calls to the objects. This is an extremely powerful mechanism for manipulating applications that have rich object models, such as IE 4.0.

Microsoft's object models are based on a technology known as the Component Object Model (COM), a specification that defines how objects communicate for the purpose of sharing services. Sharing services gives object models power and flexibility.

Suppose you are building an application that requires the use of tabular data. Your application needs to store data in a flat table and perform arithmetic functions on that data. Sounds like a spreadsheet, right? Well, you could build your own spreadsheet, or you could borrow the services of an existing spread-sheet such as Excel. Excel has an object model, and because COM is the technology underlying Excel, the services provided by any Excel object can be shared with any application that knows how to implement COM. All of Microsoft's development tools know how to access COM objects, so you are free to call the functions of an Excel spreadsheet from code that you wrote in Microsoft Visual Basic, Visual C++, Visual J++, Visual InterDev, or Visual FoxPro. And that is an important key: COM is language independent.

Let's imagine that you want to use the services of the Excel spreadsheet from Visual InterDev. In order to access the object, you must first review the application's object model. A partial examination of Excel's large and complex object model reveals objects named Application, Workbook, and Worksheet. (See Figure 3-4.) These objects are arranged in hierarchical order in a "has a" type of relationship: the Excel Application "has a" Workbook, and a Workbook "has a" Worksheet.

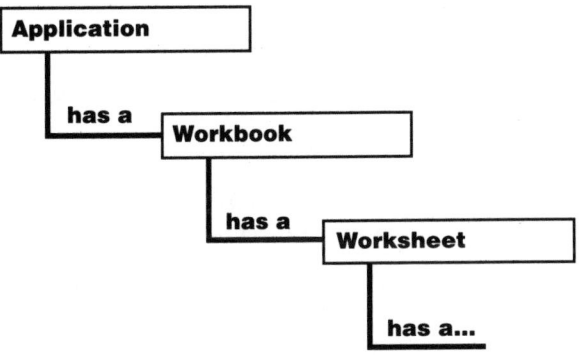

Figure 3-4.
Part of the Excel object model.

Once the object model is understood, you can programmatically access an object and its associated services. Accessing services is typically done by creating an *instance* of the object you need. An instance is a copy of the object that is created in memory and contains all of the functionality defined for the object and its services. In Visual InterDev, an instance of any COM object can be created by using the CreateObject method. The following code establishes a variable named MyWorksheet as a pointer to an instance of the COM object Worksheet contained in the application Excel:

```
Set MyWorksheet = Server.CreateObject("Excel.Worksheet")
```

Once this worksheet is created, all the services available through the object can be invoked from code. For example, a worksheet knows how to perform a spelling check on all the data contained in its cells. This service can be invoked using the CheckSpelling method. The following code does the job:

```
MyWorksheet.CheckSpelling
```

You might also find that additional objects exist under the current object. Worksheets have cells in them, so, not surprisingly, you can find a Cell object under the Worksheet object. Using the Cell object, you can access any cell in the worksheet. In fact, every cell in the worksheet is actually a member of the Cells collection. This collection allows easy access to any cell. The following code reads the value of cell A1 into a variable named MyData:

```
MyData = MyWorksheet.Cells(1, 1)
```

In a similar manner, all the objects in Internet Explorer are arranged hierarchically and are accessible from code. This code access could easily be written in a language such as Visual Basic (or any other language that supports COM). Visual InterDev, however, supports an additional access method: client-side scripting. Using languages such as VBScript or JavaScript, you can access any of the objects in IE 4.0 from script. This is a powerful technique that enables all of the client-side programming features discussed in this book.

As we continue through this book, we will add more and more capability to our Web pages by accessing the IE 4.0 object model. The complete model is shown in Figure 3-5 and provides a valuable reference. A complete object reference is also included on the CD-ROM that accompanies this book. But for now, let's take a look at some of the key objects found in the model and how to exploit them.

Window

As the top-level object in the Internet Explorer 4.0 hierarchy, the Window object represents the entire browser. When you address the Window object in script, you are directly manipulating IE 4.0. The Window object's properties, methods, and events (described in Appendix D) allow you to achieve interesting effects.

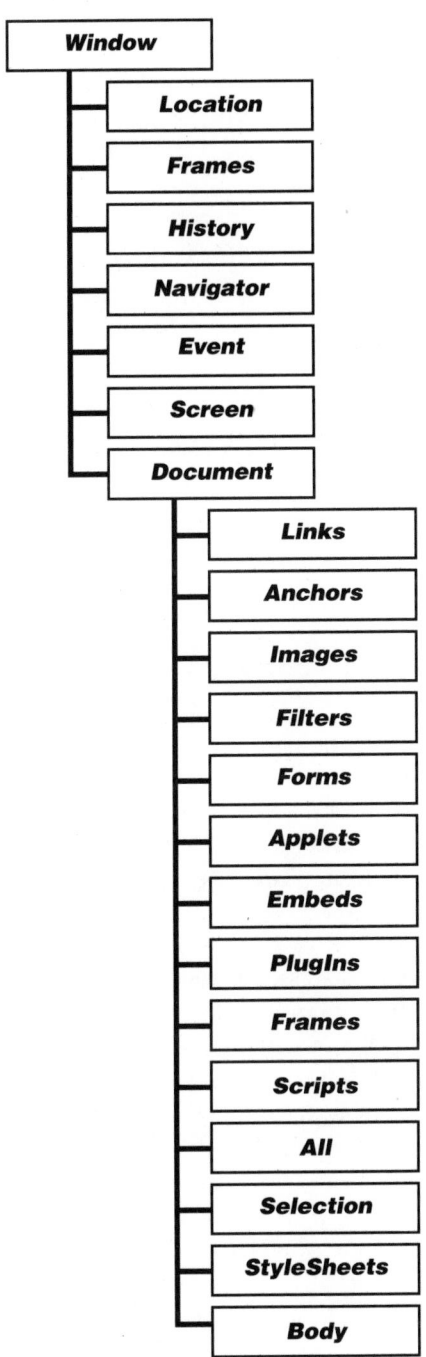

Figure 3-5.
The IE 4.0 object model.

As an example of what is possible using the Window object, let's construct a sample that creates a status bar marquee, a special effect that rolls a text message across the browser status bar. (See Figure 3-6.) You can create this effect by using properties, methods, and events of the Window object.

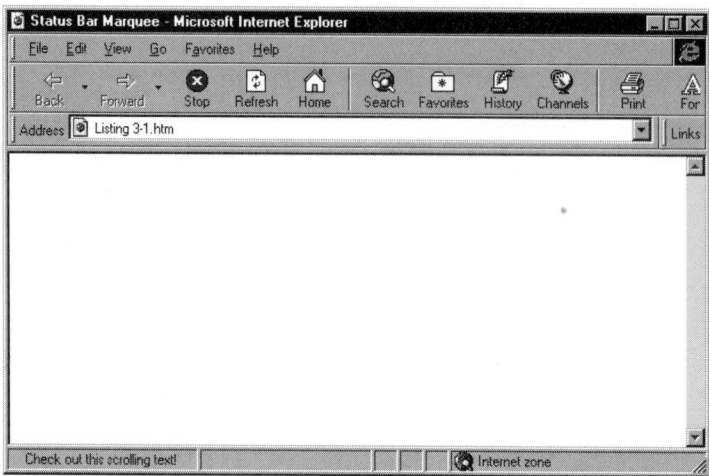

Figure 3-6.
A status bar marquee.

The Window object exposes several properties of the browser. One of these properties is Status, which allows you direct access to the text that appears on the status bar. The following code places a simple message in the status bar:

```
Window.Status = "Here is a message!"
```

Notice how the Window object is addressed directly in code. This syntax is used whenever you want to access the features of the object. Because Window is the main object in the hierarchy, it will also allow you to address its properties and methods implicitly—that is, without actually typing *Window*. Hence, the following code works just as well:

```
Status = "Here is a message!"
```

Making the text scroll is a simple matter of padding the message with spaces and reducing the number of spaces over time. In order to move the message, you need some sort of function with a periodic call that manages the position of the text in the status bar. A periodic function call can be made with the SetTimeout method of the Window object. SetTimeout allows you to specify a routine to call and a period of time to wait between calls. The timeout is identified by a variable you define. If you wanted, for example, to call a routine named Scroll every 100 milliseconds, you could write the following code:

```
Dim MyTimeout
MyTimeout = SetTimeout("Scroll", 100)
```

Using the SetTimeout method and the Status property, you can set up a routine to scroll text across the status bar. The only question is when to start the scrolling. You need an event to trigger the scrolling routine. In this case, you want to begin scrolling as soon as the page finishes loading. You can detect when a page is fully rendered in the browser by using the OnLoad event of the Window object. OnLoad fires when the page is loaded, so you can use it to establish the initial call to SetTimeout. The following code makes it happen:

```
Public MyTimeout

Sub Window_OnLoad()
    MyTimeout = SetTimeout("Scroll", 100)
End Sub
```

Note that the variable is declared Public, which makes it available to all the script in the page. This is important because you will use the variable in other routines.

Listing 3-1 shows how these pieces together—the OnLoad event, the Status property, and the SetTimeout method—create the status bar marquee.

```
<HTML>
<HEAD>
<META NAME="GENERATOR" Content="Microsoft Developer Studio">
<META HTTP-EQUIV="Content-Type" content="text/html;
    charset=iso-8859-1">
<TITLE>Status Bar Marquee</TITLE>

<SCRIPT LANGUAGE="VBScript">
<!--

    ' Script-level variables
    Public strMessage
    Public intSpaces
    Public intTimeout
```

Listing 3-1.   *(continued)*
The status bar marquee.

Listing 3-1 *continued*

```
    Sub Window_OnLoad()
        ' Initialize the variables when the page is fully loaded
        strMessage = "Check out this scrolling text!"
        intSpaces = 100
        intTimeout = Window.SetTimeout("Scroll", 100)
    End Sub

    Sub Scroll()
        ' Call this routine every 100 milliseconds
        Dim strTemp, i

        ' Scroll right to left
        intSpaces = intSpaces - 1
        If intSpaces = 0 Then intSpaces = 100

        ' Pad with spaces
        For i = 1 to intSpaces
            strTemp = strTemp & " "
        Next

        ' Write message
        Window.Status = strTemp & strMessage

        ' Reset timer
        intTimeout = Window.SetTimeout("Scroll", 100)
    End Sub
-->
</SCRIPT>

</HEAD>
<BODY>


</BODY>
</HTML>
```

This book contains examples that can be run properly only under Internet Explorer 4.0. The problem of cross-platform support has not gone away, and many of IE 4.0's new features simply exacerbate the problem. Therefore, you need a surefire methodology for identifying when your HTML is being run on IE 4.0. Fortunately, you can create a feature to examine the *user agent string* in a JavaScript function named Version. The user agent string is a special string that identifies the browser. User agent strings can be cryptic and quite confusing to humans, but if you know what to expect, they can be useful. Here is the user agent string for IE 4.0:

Mozilla/4.0 (compatible; MSIE 4.0; Windows 95)

This string can be parsed to retrieve the information that identifies the browser as an IE 4.0 browser. JavaScript is used to ensure support from the widest array of browsers. Listing 3-2 shows the function in action in a simple Web page.

```
<HTML>
<HEAD>
<META NAME="GENERATOR" Content="Microsoft Developer Studio">
<META HTTP-EQUIV="Content-Type" content="text/html;
    charset=iso-8859-1">
<TITLE>Browser Type</TITLE>

<SCRIPT LANGUAGE=JavaScript>
<!--

    function browserType()
    {
        // Define new properties for the
        // Window object, and assign them
        // using the Version function

        window.Version = Version();
        if (window.Version >= 4) window.IE4 = true;

        // Test the new properties here
        if (window.IE4 == true)
            alert("Congratulations! You are running IE 4.0!");
        else
            alert("Oh, no! Please get IE 4.0 now!");
    }

    function Version()
    {
        // Get the user agent string
        var strAgent = window.navigator.userAgent;
        var intIndex = strAgent.indexOf("MSIE ");
```

Listing 3-2.   *(continued)*
Browser detection.

43

Listing 3-2 *continued*

```
            // Display the user agent string
            alert(strAgent);

            // Parse the string to find the version number
            if (intIndex > 0)
                return parseInt(strAgent.substring(intIndex + 5,
                             strAgent.indexOf(".", intIndex)));
            else
                return 0;
    }

-->
</SCRIPT>

</HEAD>
<BODY>

<H1>Are you using IE 4.0?</H1><P>

<FORM>
<INPUT TYPE="BUTTON" VALUE="Find out!"
Name="cmdBrowser" OnClick="var rtn=browserType();">
</FORM>

</BODY>
</HTML>
```

Location

The Location object provides information about the current Internet location. It allows you to retrieve the address of the current location through the HRef property or retrieve portions of the address through the properties Hash, Host, Hostname, Pathname, Port, Protocol, and Search.

Frames

The Frames collection allows access to all the frames in the browser. The collection provides a mechanism for programmatically manipulating one frame from script running in another frame. Normally, the collection is accessed using an index number that begins with zero, but you can access the windows by name if you have provided names for them. (When you provide names for windows, you should ensure that all windows have unique names since the Frames collection will return only the first window with the specified name.) The following code declares a set of frames and gives them names:

```
<FRAMESET COLS="27%,73%">
    <FRAME SRC="/Demos/toolbar.htm" NAME="TOOLBAR" SCROLLING="Yes">
    <FRAMESET ROWS="25%,75%">
        <FRAME SRC="/Demos/banner.htm" NAME="BANNER" SCROLLING="No">
        <FRAME SRC="/Demos/home.htm" NAME="MAIN" SCROLLING="Yes">
    </FRAMESET>
    <NOFRAMES>
        <BODY BGCOLOR="FFFFFF">
        <H3>Your browser does not support frames</H3><BR>
        <H4>You're missing the show!!</H4><P>
        Get the <A HREF="http://www.microsoft.com/ie/">Internet
        Explorer</A>
    </NOFRAMES>
</FRAMESET>
```

Once the frames are defined inside a frame set, you can use the Frames collection to access any of the existing frames. In the preceding example, three frames were designated: Toolbar, Banner, and Main. Manipulating the Main window from the Toolbar window can be accomplished with the following code:

```
window.parent.frames("MAIN").navigate "http://www.microsoft.com"
```

Navigator

The Navigator object represents the entire browser. This object is useful in an environment where the browser is supporting multiple frames. A single-frame Web page has only one Window object, so the Window object and the browser can be considered one and the same. A multiple-frame Web page, however, has a separate Window object for each frame, so the only way to access the browser as a whole is through the Navigator object.

Event

The Event object supports all the events that occur in Internet Explorer. This object is extremely important in Dynamic HTML and is discussed in detail in Chapter 4.

Screen

The Screen object represents the client screen and returns information about its capabilities. Perhaps the most useful of the Screen properties are Height and Width, which return the screen resolution for the client in pixels. This information can then be used to accurately reposition elements on a Web page based on the screen resolution.

Document

The Document object represents the document currently loaded in the browser. It is perhaps the most important of all the objects in the hierarchy because it acts as the gateway to every aspect of the document, from the background color to each and every individual tag located in the document. In fact, Dynamic HTML relies heavily on accessing HTML tags through the Document object. (See Appendix D for a description of the object's properties, methods, and events.)

As a simple exercise, let's use the Document object to generate a fade-in effect that causes the browser background to gradually change from black to white. This is an interesting effect that adds some simple action to a page. (It also requires the use of the SetTimeout method of the Window object.)

The Document object gives you access to many of the HTML attributes that define the <BODY> tag. Using the BGColor property of the Document object, you can read and write to the BGCOLOR attribute, which takes as an argument the color for the page background in RGB format. This means that you must provide the color as six hexadecimal digits: the first two digits represent red, the second two represent green, and the last two represent blue. Black is 000000, and white is FFFFFF. The fade-in example will change the color from black to white over time using the SetTimeout method.

Changing the color is simple but has just one trick. You must be sure to properly format the BGColor property in code, or you will not get the intended results. Correct formatting is done with the VBScript Hex function, which takes a number as an argument and returns the hexadecimal equivalent as text. This is exactly what the BGColor property expects.

In the example, you define a variable for the background color, retrieve the existing color, and modify it. Let's say you just want to read the existing color and change it to white in only one step. The following code would work:

```
Dim lngBGColor
lngBGCOLOR = Document.BGColor
lngBGCOLOR = &HFFFFFF
Document.BGColor = Hex(lngBGColor)
```

This reading and writing is simple enough and can be done at any time from script. In order to get the fade-in effect, you must increment the background color value periodically until the background is completely white. If the fade-in code is written as a separate routine, you can use SetTimeout to call the routine at regular intervals. Here is the code:

```
lngBGColor = lngBGColor + &H111111
Document.BGColor = lngBGColor
```

The complete code for the example is shown in Listing 3-3 and simply expands this idea.

```
<HTML>
<HEAD>
<META NAME="GENERATOR" Content="Microsoft Developer Studio">
<META HTTP-EQUIV="Content-Type" content="text/html;
    charset=iso-8859-1">
<TITLE>Fade-In</TITLE>

<SCRIPT LANGUAGE="VBScript">
<!--

    ' Color constants
    Const ntsBGStart = &H0
    Const ntsBGStep = &H111111
    Const ntsBGEnd = &HFFFFFF
    Const ntsTimerStep = 10

    ' Variable for background color
    Public lngBGColor

    Sub Window_OnLoad()
        ' Set timer
        intTimeout = Window.SetTimeout("Fade", ntsTimerStep)

        ' Initialize background color
        lngBGColor = ntsBGStart
        Document.BGColor = Hex(lngBGColor)
    End Sub

    Sub Fade()
        ' Fade in
        lngBGColor = lngBGColor + ntsBGStep
        Document.BGColor = Hex(lngBGColor)

        ' Keep going until white
        If lngBGColor < ntsBGEnd Then
            intTimeout = Window.SetTimeout("Fade", ntsTimerStep)
        End If
    End Sub

-->
</SCRIPT>
```

Listing 3-3.   *(continued)*
The fade-in effect.

Listing 3-3 *continued*

```
</HEAD>
<BODY>

<CENTER><H1>Welcome to My Web Page!</H2></CENTER>

</BODY>
</HTML>
```

Document Collections

The Document object allows access to many page elements besides the background color. Accessing these elements is typically done through a *collection*, a special kind of object in the Internet Explorer object model. A collection represents a group of objects that are of the same class. It allows easy access to every member of the class. For example, using the Forms collection, you can access and perform functions on any form or every form in the document. These functions can include field validation and form submittal. Accessing controls is done through the form that contains them. In general, any property or method of a control contained on a form can be accessed through the Document and Form objects as follows:

Document.*FormName.ControlName.Property[Method]*

To practice using forms and controls in VBScript, let's create a simple form with client-side validation. In this example, assume you have a form named frmValidate with two text boxes in an HTML table. One of the text boxes, txtDate, is used to input a date.

Because there are so many different ways of entering a date, you want to validate the date before submission. In this case, use a simple HTML button to call the validation routine in the OnClick event handler. In the OnClick event handler, use the VBScript IsDate function. The IsDate function returns True if the entry in the text box is a valid date. Listing 3-4 provides complete code.

```
<HTML>
<HEAD>
<META NAME="GENERATOR" Content="Microsoft Developer Studio">
<META HTTP-EQUIV="Content-Type" content="text/html;
    charset=iso-8859-1">
<TITLE>Data Validation</TITLE>

<SCRIPT LANGUAGE="VBScript">
```

Listing 3-4.
Field validation in a form.

(continued)

Listing 3-4 *continued*

```
<!--

    Sub cmdValidate_OnClick()
        ' Validate the date
        If Not (IsDate(Document.frmValidate.txtDate.Value)) Then
            MsgBox "Not a valid date!"
        End If
    End Sub

-->
</SCRIPT>

</HEAD>
<BODY>

<FORM NAME="frmValidate">

<TABLE>
    <TR>
        <TH>
        Name
        </TH>
        <TD>
        <INPUT NAME="txtName">
        </TD>
    </TR>
    <TR>
        <TH>
        Date
        </TH>
        <TD>
        <INPUT NAME="txtDate">
        </TD>
    </TR>
    <TR>
        <TD COLSPAN=2>
        <INPUT TYPE="BUTTON" NAME="cmdValidate" VALUE="Go!">
        </TD>
        <TD>
        </TD>
    </TR>
</TABLE>

</FORM>

</BODY>
</HTML>
```

IE 4.0 supports collections for many other objects, including Links, Anchors, Images, Filters, Forms, Applets, Embeds, PlugIns, Frames, Scripts, and StyleSheets. These collections allow you to access every aspect of an HTML page and the core of Dynamic HTML.

Netscape Navigator

When you create scripts for both Internet Explorer version 4.0 and Netscape Navigator version 3.0, you will encounter differences in object models and case sensitivity. Like IE 4.0, Navigator has an object model. In fact, the two object models share many of the same base objects, including Window and Document; but the Netscape objects might have only a subset of the properties and methods found in IE 4.0.

Case sensitivity for object names in Internet Explorer is not a major concern when you use VBScript as your scripting language. However, Netscape Navigator and JavaScript are both case sensitive. This means that if you address the Window object in JavaScript, Navigator expects the W to be lowercase. Window with a capital W is not understood by Navigator. This book follows the convention that major words in objects are initial capped (e.g., Window, Document, Frames) because the text is more readable, but you can use all lowercase if you prefer.

Dynamic HTML, Data Binding, and ActiveX Controls

Although client-side scripting adds flexibility to standard HTML, it is used for little more than validating data in a form prior to submission. The limitation of scripting lies in the very nature of HTML itself: HTML is a *streaming* language. That means that HTML actually enters the browser one character at a time and the Web page is built by the browser as the data stream enters the client. Once the data has finished entering the browser, the stream is closed; and once the stream is closed, the HTML page cannot be changed.

A browser can, to a limited degree, modify the HTML stream while it is actually entering the browser. Microsoft Internet Explorer's Document object supports a method named Write, which allows VBScript code to modify the HTML stream. Because this stream modification must occur while the page is loading, you must create your VBScript code outside the boundaries of a procedure. When code is executed outside a procedure, the code runs immediately when the page is loaded—a technique appropriately called *immediate execution*. The following code uses immediate execution to add HTML content to the stream:

```
<SCRIPT LANGUAGE="VBScript">
<!--
    Document.Write "<H1>New HTML Content</H1>"
-->
</SCRIPT>
```

Notice that the code is written directly under the SCRIPT section and is not enclosed in any Sub or Function procedure. This is the key to immediate execution. Remember that if the page is fully loaded, the stream is closed and cannot be modified.

As an example, consider a Web site that offers books for sale. You want this site to present a new special offer to customers each month. In order to change the special, you can use the Write method of the Document object. Use the VBScript Now function to get the current date, and then apply the Month function to determine the month. Specials can be displayed using the Write method based on the month. Listing 4-1 contains the complete code for this exercise.

```
<HTML>
<HEAD>
<META NAME="GENERATOR" Content="Microsoft Developer Studio">
<META HTTP-EQUIV="Content-Type" content="text/html; charset=iso-8859-1">
<TITLE>Immediate Execution</TITLE>

</HEAD>
<BODY>
<H1>Here's the monthly special</H1><P>

<SCRIPT LANGUAGE="VBScript">
<!--

    Dim strSpecial

    ' Pick a special based on the month of the year
    Select Case Month(Now)
        Case 1
            strSpecial = "dBASE III: A Practical Guide"
        Case 2
            strSpecial = "The dBASE Programming Language"
        Case 3
            strSpecial = "dBASE III Plus"
        Case 4
            strSpecial = "Database Management: Developing Application "
            strSpecial = strSpecial & "Systems Using Oracle"
        Case 5
            strSpecial = "Wordstar 4.0-6.0 Quick Reference Guide"
        Case 6
            strSpecial = "Oracle Triggers and Stored Procedure "
            strSpecial = strSpecial & "Programming"
```

Listing 4-1.
Immediate execution.

(continued)

Listing 4-1 *continued*

```
        Case 7
            strSpecial = "Programming in Clipper"
        Case 8
            strSpecial = "Inside Macintosh"
        Case 9
            strSpecial = "Omni Online Database Directory"
        Case 10
            strSpecial = "Structured C for Engineering and Technology/"
            strSpecial = strSpecial & "Book and Disk"
        Case 11
            strSpecial = "An Introduction to Assembly Language "
            strSpecial = strSpecial & "Programming for the Intel "
            strSpecial = strSpecial & "8088 Microprocessor"
        Case 12
            strSpecial = "Applied Calculus with Linear Programming: "
            strSpecial = strSpecial & "For Business, Economics, Life "
            strSpecial = strSpecial & "Sciences, and Social Sciences"
    End Select

    Document.Write "<H4>" & strSpecial & "</H4>"

-->
</SCRIPT>

</BODY>
</HTML>
```

Dynamic HTML Fundamentals

The inherent limitation of HTML, the closing of data streams, triggered the development of Dynamic HTML. Dynamic HTML allows the HTML in a Web page to be altered by VBScript code *after* the data stream is closed. This is accomplished by treating every tag in the document as an object with properties. These properties are available to VBScript code throughout the life of the Web page.

Dynamic HTML builds on the foundation of VBScript by providing an expanded Internet Explorer object model along with new events. Dynamic HTML, like scripting in general, follows an event-driven programming paradigm. Code that you write is executed in response to user interaction with the Web page. The difference is that under Dynamic HTML, every element of the page is capable of supporting user interaction.

Listing 4-2 produces a simple Dynamic HTML page that changes the text's font color from black to red when the mouse passes over the text. The program is a good example of dynamically changing the HTML content of a page even after the input stream is closed. Notice that the fade effect is produced by the SetTimeout method of the Window object.

```
<HTML>
<HEAD>
<META NAME="GENERATOR" Content="Microsoft Developer Studio">
<META HTTP-EQUIV="Content-Type" content="text/html;
    charset=iso-8859-1">
<TITLE>Fading Text</TITLE>

<SCRIPT LANGUAGE="VBScript">
<!--

    Public intTimeout
    Public lngColor

    Sub htmlFade_OnMouseOver()
        lngColor = 0
        intTimeout = SetTimeout("FadeText(-1)", 50)
    End Sub

    Sub htmlFade_OnMouseOut()
        lngColor = &HFF0000
        intTimeout = SetTimeout("FadeText(0)", 50)
    End Sub

    Sub FadeText(blnDirection)
        ' Call this routine periodically to fade
        ' the text over time

        If blnDirection = 0 Then
            lngColor = lngColor - &H110000
            If lngColor < 0 Then
                lngColor = 0
            Else
                intTimeout = SetTimeout("FadeText(0)", 50)
            End If
        Else
            lngColor = lngColor + &H110000
```

Listing 4-2.

Fading text.

(continued)

Listing 4-2 *continued*

```
            If lngColor > &HFF0000 Then
                lngColor = &HFF0000
            Else
                intTimeout = SetTimeout("FadeText(-1)", 50)
            End If
        End If

        htmlFade.Color = Hex(lngColor)
    End Sub
-->
</SCRIPT>

</HEAD>

<BODY>

<B><FONT FACE="ARIAL" SIZE=6 COLOR="000000" ID="htmlFade">
Fading Text
</FONT></B>

</BODY>
</HTML>
```

The key to dynamically changing HTML content lies in treating each tag as a separate object. To that end, you need to give your tags names so that they can be addressed in code. In the fading text example, a name is given to the <FONT> tag to allow you to change attributes of the tag at run time. The name of the tag is designated by the ID attribute as follows:

```
<FONT...ID="htmlFade">
```

Once the ID is defined, you can map events that occur on the tag to code that you write in VBScript. Dynamic HTML supports a wide variety of events, including familiar ones such as Click, DblClick, and KeyPress. In this example, you use the OnMouseOver and OnMouseOut events, which detect when the mouse is passing over or has left the text that is contained in the <FONT> tags. When the appropriate event is trapped, an animation loop is established using the SetTimeout method to fade the text to red or black.

Dynamic HTML processes events at many levels, allowing containing elements to receive notification when tags within them fire events. This process of notifying containers about events occurring inside them is known as *event bubbling*. Event bubbling allows you to specify in a single location an event handler for the majority of tags in a Web page and also to specify particular behavior for any individual tag. Bubbling occurs automatically and can be trapped by each object in a hierarchy. When a tag receives an event, the Document object automatically receives that event when the tag is finished handling it. Listing 4-3 provides a simple example of event bubbling. The page consists of three pieces of text contained in <FONT> tags. The tags specify various attributes for the contained text.

```
<HTML>
<HEAD>
<META NAME="GENERATOR" Content="Microsoft Developer Studio">
<META HTTP-EQUIV="Content-Type" content="text/html;
    charset=iso-8859-1">
<TITLE>Event Bubbling</TITLE>

<SCRIPT LANGUAGE="VBScript">
<!--

    Sub Document_OnClick()
        ' Color any font tag when the mouse clicks on it
        Dim objElement
        Set objElement = Window.Event.SrcElement

        If objElement.TagName = "FONT" Then
            objElement.Color = "Red"
        End If
    End Sub


    Sub fntCancel_OnClick()
        ' Handle the Click event and cancel the bubble
        ' to the Document object

        fntCancel.Size = "6"
        Window.Event.CancelBubble = True
    End Sub

-->
</SCRIPT>

</HEAD>
<BODY>
```

Listing 4-3.
Event bubbling.

(continued)

Listing 4-3 *continued*

```
<!-- Bubble the Click event for these tags -->
<FONT FACE="ARIAL" SIZE=5>Bubble the Click event!</FONT><P>
<FONT FACE="ARIAL" SIZE=5>Bubble this one too!</FONT><P>

<!-- Handle this event separately -->
<FONT FACE="TIMES NEW ROMAN" SIZE=4 COLOR="BLUE" ID="fntCancel">
Cancel this bubble.
</FONT><P>

</BODY>
</HTML>
```

When text is clicked, the event is normally received at the document level because most of the tags in the page do not have VBScript event handlers written for their respective OnClick events. Once inside the event handler, your program checks to make sure that the tag clicked is a <FONT> tag; the code then alters the attributes of the tag to reflect the click. In this case, the color changes.

Identifying the actual tag that is clicked is the domain of the Event object. The Event object, accessed through the Window object, has properties that allow you to identify which element is involved in an event and to handle event bubbling. For each event that occurs in Dynamic HTML, you can access properties of the fired event through the Event object.

To identify the element that is clicked, you use the SrcElement property of the Event object. SrcElement can be stored in a variable, thus giving you access to all the attributes of the tag. When you assign an object reference to a variable in VBScript, the language requires use of the Set keyword. Use the following code:

```
Dim objElement
Set objElement = Window.Event.SrcElement
```

Once the element is identified, make sure it is a <FONT> tag by checking the TagName property of the Element object. If the TagName property has the value FONT, you can easily change the color of the clicked font. This happens for every <FONT> tag in the Document object, with one exception. The <FONT> tag identified as fntCancel has a separate event handler for the OnClick event. In this case, you change the size of the font, as opposed to the color, and then set the CancelBubble property of the Event object to True (−1) to prevent the Document_OnClick event handler from being executed.

57

Cascading Style Sheets

Cascading style sheets are an important part of Web development and have expanded significance in the world of Dynamic HTML. Cascading style sheets specify the layout of a Web page in a format that is separate from the actual Web page content. Separating the style from the content makes a Web site easier to maintain. In Dynamic HTML, style sheets can also be changed dynamically, allowing for special effects such as dynamic styles and dynamic layouts.

Style sheets came into use with the release of Internet Explorer 3.0. Under IE 3.0, developers of Web content could specify additional formatting such as font size and color for various portions of a page and could factor out the styles for easier maintenance of the site. Style sheets are described as *cascading* because they can be implemented at different levels of the content and can override styles defined at higher levels. You can choose to implement styles in one of three ways: linked style sheets, embedded styles, and inline styles.

Linked Style Sheets

Linked style sheets are the most global of all style sheet implementations. In this scenario, you can define a style sheet as a separate document and *link* its style to one or more Web pages. This provides a way of setting up a thematic style for your site—one that is inherited by all pages.

Linked style sheets are constructed as plain text in a file with a CSS extension. In the CSS file, you must provide one or more style definitions, which are used to format the linked page. A style definition is an HTML tag accompanied by a list of tag attributes in curly braces. Each attribute is named and followed by a colon and the attribute's value. Multiple attributes can be specified by using a semicolon to separate the attribute/value pairs. The following code defines a style for the <H1> tag:

```
H1 {font-size: 20pt; color: red}
```

You can specify as many tags as you want in one style sheet and then link them to a Web page. Linking to a Web page is accomplished by using the <LINK> tag, which is placed directly in the page where the styles are to be applied. The tag is placed in the HEAD section so that it's available before the page is rendered. As an example, suppose you have a style sheet named MYSTYLE.CSS and you want to link it to a Web page. In the HEAD section of the page, you use the following HTML:

```
<LINK REL=STYLESHEET HREF="MYSTYLE.CSS">
```

The HREF attribute of the <LINK> tag points to the URL where the style sheet can be found. The definitions provided in the style sheet are then applied universally throughout the Web page. If you want to change the styles in all of the linked Web pages, you have only to change the definitions in the style sheet. Listing 4-4 shows a typical style sheet.

```
BODY {
        margin-left:50px;
        font:9pt/11pt "Arial";
        color:black;
        text-align:left;
        background:transparent;
        }
P {
        margin-left:0px;
        font:9pt/11pt "Arial";
        color:black;
        }

H1 {
        margin-left:0px;
        font:18pt/18pt "Times New Roman";
        color:black;
        font-weight:bold;
        }
```

Listing 4-4.
A partial style sheet.

Embedded Styles

In addition to linking a Web page to a style sheet, you can choose to embed styles directly in the page's HTML. Embedded styles are created using the <STYLE> tag. In the tag, style definitions are coded in the same format as in the linked style sheet:

```
<STYLE>
<!--
    H1 {font-size:20pt; color:red}
-->
</STYLE>
```

The styles applied in the embedded section will override any styles defined in a linked style sheet. Notice also that embedded styles use HTML comment marks (<!-- -->) to hide the style definitions from old browsers that do not recognize the <STYLE> tag. (Hiding code is a common practice when new tags are involved. The technique is used with the <SCRIPT> tag, for example, to hide script code from old browsers.) Listing 4-5 provides complete code for a Web page with embedded styles.

```
<HTML>
<HEAD>
<META NAME="GENERATOR" Content="Microsoft Developer Studio">
<META HTTP-EQUIV="Content-Type" content="text/html;
    charset=iso-8859-1">
<TITLE>Embedded Styles</TITLE>

<STYLE TYPE="text/css">
<!--
    BODY {font:10pt "Arial"}
    H1   {font:15pt/17pt "Stencil"}
    P    {font:10pt "Arial"}
-->
</STYLE>
</HEAD>

<BODY>

<H1>This is the H1 style</H1>
<P>This is the P style</P>

</BODY>
</HTML>
```

Listing 4-5.
Embedded styles.

Inline Styles

If you want to define styles for a particular tag or to override styles created by linked or embedded styles, you can use inline styles. Inline styles are created by using the STYLE attribute of a tag. This attribute and its values are placed directly in the tag:

```
<H1 STYLE="font-size:20pt; color:red">Welcome!</H1>
```

Inline styles allow changes to an individual tag, embedded styles affect a whole page, and linked style sheets can be applied to the site. But what if you need to change just one section of a Web page? The answer is to use the <DIV>

tag to define a *division* in the page. A division in a Web page is similar to a section in any Microsoft Word document: it's used to specify that part of the document be treated as one unit. The <DIV> tag allows you to specify styles that apply to only a section of the page. Listing 4-6 contains sample code for styles in a division.

```
<HTML>
<HEAD>
<META NAME="GENERATOR" Content="Microsoft Developer Studio">
<META HTTP-EQUIV="Content-Type" content="text/html;
    charset=iso-8859-1">
<TITLE>A Division in a Web Page</TITLE>
</HEAD>
<BODY>

This line is outside the division
<DIV STYLE="font-size:18pt; color:red">
This line is inside the division
</DIV>
This line is outside the division

</BODY>
</HTML>
```

Listing 4-6.
Styles in a division.

Style Definition Techniques

Style sheets can be implemented through several coding techniques that simplify the use of styles. One technique for declaring styles is to use a style *class*, a predefined style that can be applied at the tag level. A style class is defined in a manner similar to a regular style, but you can name the style. The following code creates three style classes—Normal, Military, and Fancy—for the <H1> tag:

```
<STYLE>
<!--
H1.Normal {font-size:12pt; font-family:arial;}
H1.Military {font-size:20pt; font-family:stencil}
H1.Fancy {font-size:14pt; font-family:courier; font-style:italic}
-->
</STYLE>
```

Using the style class becomes a matter of invoking the class name through the CLASS attribute of a tag. The style class works as if you had defined the complete style for the class in the STYLE attribute of the affected tag. The following code shows a style class applied to an individual tag as well as to a division in the page:

```
<H1 CLASS=Military>This is the Military class</H1>
```

Another technique available for style definition is to use a style *group,* a set of tags that share similar styles and are grouped together for easy definition. For example, suppose you want to share similar styles across all of your header tags. The following code simplifies the definitions:

```
H1 H2 H3 H4 H5 H6 H7 {font-family:arial}
```

A complete style reference for Internet Explorer 4.0 is included on the CD-ROM that accompanies this book.

Dynamic Styles

Styles play a vital role not only in standard HTML but in Dynamic HTML as well. In Dynamic HTML, all styles in the Document object are available as Style objects. Style objects can be manipulated through VBScript code, resulting in comprehensive changes to a page while requiring less code. These manipulations are known as *dynamic styles.*

Dynamic styles can be coded at the same levels that styles are applied—through linking, embedding, and inline styles—and can be used for everything, from allowing users to customize Web pages to adding subtle effects when the mouse passes over key text. You can manipulate styles across an entire page by dynamically changing the style sheet that is linked to the page. As an example, let's customize a feedback form for using two different style sheets. Listing 4-7 shows the complete feedback form and customization script. The style sheets offer a choice between a red theme and a blue theme. The style can be set dynamically at run time, but initially the page is linked to the blue theme:

```
<LINK ID="LinkStyle" REL=STYLESHEET HREF="BLUE.CSS">
```

Notice that the <LINK> tag has an ID attribute so that it can be addressed in code later. On the page, two option buttons allow the selection of a red or blue theme. These are standard HTML option buttons in a form. When an option is checked, the selected theme is sent to a VBScript routine, which changes the linked style sheet by addressing the <LINK> tag through its ID attribute.

```
<HTML>
<HEAD>
<TITLE>Feedback Form</TITLE>
<LINK ID="LinkStyle" REL=STYLESHEET HREF="BLUE.CSS">

<SCRIPT LANGUAGE="VBScript">
<!--

    Sub ChangeStyle(strStyle)
        LinkStyle.HRef = strStyle & ".CSS"
    End Sub

-->
</SCRIPT>

</HEAD>

<BODY>

<H1>Feedback Form</H1>
<HR>
<!-- This form changes the page style -->
<H2>Pick a page style!</H2>
<FORM NAME="frmStyle">
<INPUT TYPE="RADIO" NAME="optStyle"
    OnClick="ChangeStyle('BLUE')"CHECKED>Blue Style<P>
<INPUT TYPE="RADIO" NAME="optStyle"
    OnClick="ChangeStyle('RED')">Red Style<P>
</FORM>

<!-- The rest of the HTML is just for the
Web page content -->

<P>
Tell us what you think about our Web site, our products,
our organization, or anything else that comes to mind. We
welcome all of your comments and suggestions.
</P>

<FORM>

<P><STRONG>
What kind of comment would you like to send?
</STRONG></P>
```

Listing 4-7.   *(continued)*
Changing a style sheet dynamically.

Listing 4-7 *continued*

```
<DL><DD>
    <INPUT TYPE="radio" NAME="MessageType"
        VALUE="Complaint">Complaint
    <INPUT TYPE="radio" NAME="MessageType"
        VALUE="Problem">Problem
    <INPUT TYPE="radio" CHECKED NAME="MessageType"
        VALUE="Suggestion">Suggestion
    <INPUT TYPE="radio" NAME="MessageType"
        VALUE="Praise">Praise
</DD></DL>

<P><STRONG>
What about us do you want to comment on?
</STRONG></P>

<DL><DD>
    <SELECT NAME="Subject" SIZE="1">
        <OPTION SELECTED>Web Site</OPTION>
        <OPTION>Company</OPTION>
        <OPTION>Products</OPTION>
        <OPTION>Store</OPTION>
        <OPTION>Employee</OPTION>
        <OPTION>(Other)</OPTION>
    </SELECT>
    Other:
    <INPUT TYPE="text" SIZE="26"
        MAXLENGTH="256" NAME="SubjectOther">
</DD></DL>

<P><STRONG>
Enter your comments in the space provided below:
</STRONG></P>

<DL><DD>
    <TEXTAREA NAME="Comments" ROWS="5" COLS="42">
    </TEXTAREA>
</DD></DL>

<P><STRONG>
Tell us how to get in touch with you:
</STRONG></P>
```

(continued)

Listing 4-7 *continued*

```
<DL><DD><PRE>
Name    <INPUT TYPE="text" SIZE="35" MAXLENGTH="256"
          NAME="UserName">
E-mail <INPUT TYPE="text" SIZE="35" MAXLENGTH="256"
          NAME="UserEmail">
Tel     <INPUT TYPE="text" SIZE="35" MAXLENGTH="256"
          NAME="UserTel">
FAX     <INPUT TYPE="text" SIZE="35" MAXLENGTH="256"
          NAME="UserFAX">
</PRE></DD></DL>

<DL><DD>
    <INPUT TYPE="checkbox" NAME="ContactRequested"
      VALUE="ContactRequested">Please contact me as
      soon as possible regarding this matter.
</DD></DL>

<P>
    <INPUT TYPE="submit" VALUE="Submit Comments">
    <INPUT TYPE="reset" VALUE="Clear Form">
</P>

</FORM>

<HR>
<H5>
New Technology Solutions, Incorporated<BR>
Copyright © 1997. All rights reserved.<BR>
</H5>
</BODY>
</HTML>
```

Changing styles globally is useful for personalizing a site, but dynamic style changes on a smaller scale can be useful for achieving limited effects with very little code. Consider the code in Listing 4-8 on the following page, which displays text that changes color when the mouse passes over it. This example uses style classes to simplify the coding. The classes are defined independently of any particular tag by using a dot before the class name in an embedded style block. Defining generic classes in this way allows easy reuse of common functionality such as color change.

```
<HTML>
<HEAD>
<META NAME="GENERATOR" Content="Microsoft Developer Studio">
<META HTTP-EQUIV="Content-Type" content="text/html;
    charset=iso-8859-1">
<TITLE>Embedded Styles</TITLE>

<STYLE>
<!--
    .Red {color:red}
    .Blue {color:blue}
-->
</STYLE>

</HEAD>

<BODY>

<SCRIPT LANGUAGE="VBScript">
<!--

    Sub eleH2_OnMouseOver()
        Dim header
        Set header = Window.Event.SrcElement
        header.ClassName = "Red"
    End Sub
    Sub eleH2_OnMouseOut()
        Dim header
        Set header = Window.Event.SrcElement
        header.ClassName = "Blue"
    End Sub

-->
</SCRIPT>

<H2 CLASS="Blue" ID="eleH2">
Visit the VB Bootcamp!
</H2>

</BODY>
</HTML>
```

Listing 4-8.
Dynamic styles with classes.

Dynamic Layouts

Perhaps the most powerful use of style sheets in Internet Explorer 4.0 is the creation of dynamic layouts, a capability new in version 4.0. Style sheets implemented in IE 3.0 do not support layouts. In fact, in version 3.0, layouts are done without style sheets by using a special ActiveX control known as the HTML Layout control. The HTML Layout control is an invisible ActiveX control that sits on top of a Web page and acts as a container for other ActiveX controls. You actually position the other ActiveX controls inside the HTML Layout control. This technique is limiting, however, because it relies on the use of ActiveX controls for placement of elements and does not work directly with the HTML in the page. Consequently, the HTML Layout control does not blend well with the page's existing HTML. In order to create layouts, you often need to mimic regular HTML characteristics in ActiveX label controls, which requires more work to implement. Additionally, ActiveX controls must be downloaded to the client and can take significantly longer to render in the browser than does plain HTML.

Dynamic layouts with cascading style sheets eliminate the problems presented by the HTML Layout control. Dynamic layouts allow complete integration with existing HTML and do not require the download of any ActiveX controls. Therefore, dynamic layouts are faster and easier to maintain than equivalent Web pages created with the HTML Layout control.

Like dynamic styles, dynamic layouts are created through Style objects. The difference is that dynamic layouts take advantage of new additions to the cascading style sheet specification utilized by IE 4.0. These new style parameters— top, left, height, width, and z-index—allow complete control of the X, Y, Z placement of various elements on the page.

Elements on the Web page can be positioned in one of three modes: static, relative, and absolute. Static positions are unaffected by the top and left style parameters; these elements are simply positioned by the browser as if no position style were assigned. Relative positions reflect top and left alignment relative to the existing static content on the page. Absolute positions use the top and left parameters for positioning by pixel, regardless of the existing content on the page. As the author of the Web page, you can specify any of these positioning schemes. The code in Listing 4-9 on the following page positions three images on a Web page: one image is positioned statically, one relatively, and one absolutely. Note that in the code each image is assigned the same top parameter for the style, but the results are decidedly different, as you can see in Figure 4-1, also on the following page.

```
<HTML>
<HEAD>
<META NAME="GENERATOR" Content="Microsoft Developer Studio">
<META HTTP-EQUIV="Content-Type" content="text/html;
    charset=iso-8859-1">
<TITLE>Position Types</TITLE>
</HEAD>
<BODY>

<!-- These images show how each position type
affects the display of HTML elements -->
<IMG SRC="STATIC.GIF"
    STYLE="position:static; top:100px"><P>
<IMG SRC="ABSOLUTE.GIF"
    STYLE="position:absolute; top:100px">
<IMG SRC="RELATIVE.GIF"
    STYLE="position:relative; top:100px">

</BODY>
</HTML>
```

Listing 4-9.
Static, relative, and absolute positions.

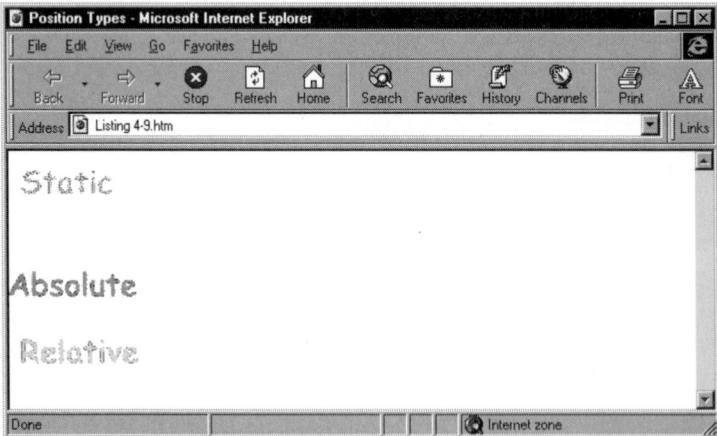

Figure 4-1.
Static, relative, and absolute positions.

Using absolute positioning, you can easily create dynamic pages that are not limited to rigidly defined rectangular sections of the page. For example, Listing 4-10 creates an animated page with dynamic styles—in this case, a simple home page for an online floral shop. The home page, shown in Figure 4-2 on page 71, displays a butterfly and a flower. The butterfly, which flaps its wings, is actually an animated GIF file. This is another appealing feature of styles with <IMG> tags: you don't have to manage the animation frames if you use animated GIFs. Animating the butterfly is a matter of changing the STYLE attribute of the <IMG> tag governing the animated GIF. This is done through periodic calls to the Fly function. Fly tracks the current top and left parameters for the style and adjusts them accordingly. The animation is controlled through the SetTimeout method, which eliminates the need to download an ActiveX Timer control.

As a background, the page uses a flower centered in the browser. Centering the image is accomplished by retrieving the browser's horizontal and vertical screen resolution, which is accessed through the Screen object. The following code repositions the flower image in the Window_OnLoad event handler:

```
' Center the flower
imgFlower.Style.Top = _
    Int((Window.Screen.Height - 412) / 2)
imgFlower.Style.Left = _
    Int((Window.Screen.Width - 384) / 2)
```

```
<HTML>
<HEAD>
<META NAME="GENERATOR" Content="Microsoft Developer Studio">
<META HTTP-EQUIV="Content-Type" content="text/html;
    charset=iso-8859-1">
<TITLE>Virtual Florist</TITLE>

<SCRIPT LANGUAGE="VBScript">
<!--

    Public intTimeout
    Public intX
    Public intY
```

Listing 4-10.   *(continued)*

An animated home page.

Listing 4-10 *continued*

```
    Sub Window_OnLoad()
        ' Center the flower
        imgFlower.Style.Top = _
            Int((Window.Screen.Height - 412) / 2)
        imgFlower.Style.Left = _
            Int((Window.Screen.Width - 384) / 2)

        ' Position the butterfly
        intY = Window.Screen.Height - 77
        intX = 77
        imgBFly.Style.Top = intY
        imgBFly.Style.Left = intX

        ' Begin the animation
        intTimeout = Window.SetTimeout("Fly", 750)
    End Sub

    Sub Fly()
        ' Get new coordinates
        intX = intX + 37
        intY = intY - 37

        If intX > Window.Screen.Width - 77 Then intX = 77
        If intY < 0 Then intY = Window.Screen.Height - 77

        ' Position the image
        imgBFly.Style.Left = intX
        imgBFly.Style.Top = intY

        ' Reset the timeout
        intTimeout = Window.SetTimeout("Fly", 750)
    End Sub
-->
</SCRIPT>

</HEAD>
<BODY>

<CENTER><H1 STYLE="font:arial bold 20; color:blue">
Welcome to the Virtual Florist!
</H1></CENTER>
```

(continued)

Listing 4-10 *continued*

```
<IMG ID="imgFlower" SRC="FLOWER.GIF"
    STYLE="position:absolute; width:384px; height:412px">
<IMG ID="imgBFly"   SRC="ANIMATED_BFLY.GIF"
    STYLE="position:absolute; width:77px; height:77px">

</BODY>
</HTML>
```

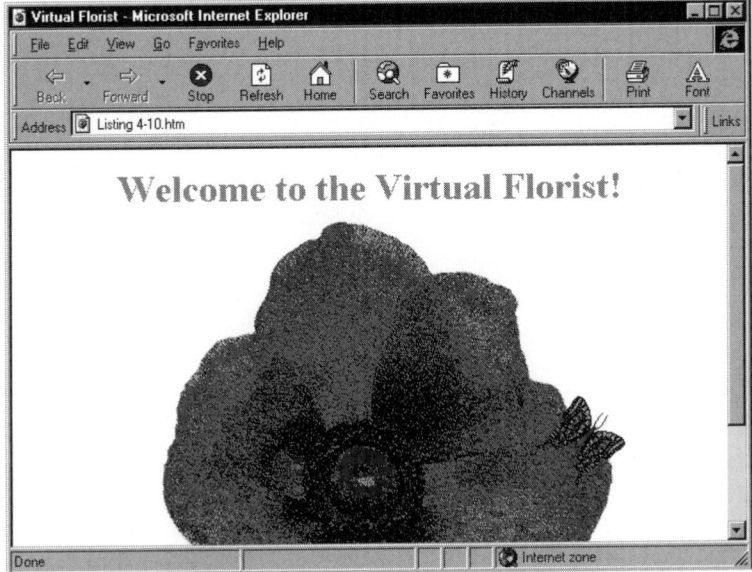

Figure 4-2.
The Virtual Florist.

Dynamic layouts can be used to create not only animated pages but also sophisticated graphical user interfaces. Listing 4-11 on the following page produces a GUI with dynamic layout that simulates the Microsoft Outlook user interface. The result is pictured in Figure 4-3 on page 75.

This Web page provides a tabbed toolbar that allows the user to click a tab to reveal a new toolbar, an effect that depends primarily on causing the images of the various toolbars to appear and disappear when the appropriate tab is clicked. The code element that allows an <IMG> tag to become visible

71

or invisible is the Display argument of the STYLE attribute. The following code causes an <IMG> tag named MyGIF to appear or disappear:

```
MyGIF.Style.Display = "none"      ' Make GIF invisible
MyGIF.Style.Display = ""          ' Make GIF visible
```

```
<HTML>
<HEAD>
<META NAME="GENERATOR" Content="Microsoft Developer Studio">
<META HTTP-EQUIV="Content-Type" content="text/html;
    charset=iso-8859-1">
<TITLE>Outlook Toolbar</TITLE>

<SCRIPT LANGUAGE="VBScript">
<!--

    Sub RollBar(intIndex)
        Call OutlookBarVisible("none")
        Call MailBarVisible("none")
        Call OtherBarVisible("none")

        Select Case intIndex
            Case 1 ' Outlook
                cmdOutlook.Style.Top = "0"
                cmdMail.Style.Top = "350"
                cmdOther.Style.Top = "375"
                Call OutlookBarVisible("")
            Case 2 ' Mail
                If cmdMail.Style.Top = "25px" Then
                    cmdOutlook.Style.Top = "0"
                    cmdMail.Style.Top = "350"
                    cmdOther.Style.Top = "375"
                    Call OutlookBarVisible("")
                Else
                    cmdOutlook.Style.Top = "0"
                    cmdMail.Style.Top = "25"
                    cmdOther.Style.Top = "375"
                    Call MailBarVisible("")
                End If
            Case 3 ' Other
                If cmdOther.Style.Top = "50px" Then
                    cmdOutlook.Style.Top = "0"
                    cmdMail.Style.Top = "25"
                    cmdOther.Style.Top = "375"
```

Listing 4-11.

The Outlook toolbar page.

(continued)

Listing 4-11 *continued*

```
                    ,Call MailBarVisible("")
              Else
                    cmdOutlook.Style.Top = "0"
                    cmdMail.Style.Top = "25"
                    cmdOther.Style.Top = "50"
                    Call OtherBarVisible("")
              End If
        End Select
    End Sub

    Sub OutlookBarVisible(strDisplay)
        imgOutlook1.Style.Display = strDisplay
        imgOutlook2.Style.Display = strDisplay
        imgOutlook3.Style.Display = strDisplay
        imgOutlook4.Style.Display = strDisplay
        imgOutlook5.Style.Display = strDisplay
    End Sub

    Sub MailBarVisible(strDisplay)
        imgMail1.Style.Display = strDisplay
        imgMail2.Style.Display = strDisplay
        imgMail3.Style.Display = strDisplay
        imgMail4.Style.Display = strDisplay
    End Sub

    Sub OtherBarVisible(strDisplay)
        imgOther1.Style.Display = strDisplay
        imgOther2.Style.Display = strDisplay
        imgOther3.Style.Display = strDisplay
    End Sub

-->
</SCRIPT>

</HEAD>

<BODY>
<DIV STYLE="position:absolute; width:100; height:400;">

<!-- Buttons -->
<INPUT STYLE="position:absolute; top:0; width:100;"
    TYPE="BUTTON" NAME="cmdOutlook" VALUE="Outlook"
    OnClick="Call RollBar(1)">
```

(continued)

73

Listing 4-11 *continued*

```
<INPUT STYLE="position:absolute; top:350; width:100;"
    TYPE="BUTTON" NAME="cmdMail" VALUE="Mail"
    OnClick="Call RollBar(2)">

<INPUT STYLE="position:absolute; top:375; width:100;"
    TYPE="BUTTON" NAME="cmdOther" VALUE="Other"
    OnClick="Call RollBar(3)">

<!-- Outlook bar images -->
<IMG SRC="INBOX.GIF"    ID="imgOutlook1"
    STYLE="position:absolute; left:32; top:80">
<IMG SRC="CALENDAR.GIF" ID="imgOutlook2"
    STYLE="position:absolute; left:32; top:125">
<IMG SRC="CONTACTS.GIF" ID="imgOutlook3"
    STYLE="position:absolute; left:32; top:170">
<IMG SRC="TASKS.GIF"    ID="imgOutlook4"
    STYLE="position:absolute; left:32; top:215">
<IMG SRC="JOURNAL.GIF"  ID="imgOutlook5"
    STYLE="position:absolute; left:32; top:260">

<!-- Mail bar images -->
<IMG SRC="INBOX.GIF"    ID="imgMail1"
    STYLE="position:absolute; left:32; top:80; display:none">
<IMG SRC="SENTITEMS.GIF"ID="imgMail2"
    STYLE="position:absolute; left:32; top:125; display:none">
<IMG SRC="OUTBOX.GIF"   ID="imgMail3"
    STYLE="position:absolute; left:32; top:170; display:none">
<IMG SRC="DELETED.GIF"  ID="imgMail4"
    STYLE="position:absolute; left:32; top:215; display:none">

<!-- Other bar images -->
<IMG SRC="MYCOMPUTER.GIF"ID="imgOther1"
    STYLE="position:absolute; left:32; top:80; display:none">
<IMG SRC="FOLDER.GIF"    ID="imgOther2"
    STYLE="position:absolute; left:32; top:125; display:none">
<IMG SRC="NOTES.GIF"     ID="imgOther3"
    STYLE="position:absolute; left:32; top:170; display:none">

</DIV>
</BODY>
</HTML>
```

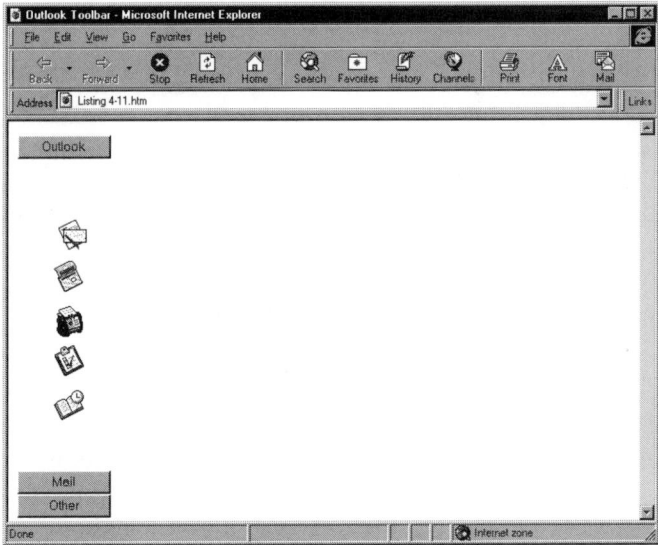

Figure 4-3.
An Outlook-type interface.

Data Binding

Database publishing is by far the most common use of Internet technology today. While client-side scripting is useful for validating data input fields and while Dynamic HTML contributes considerably to the quality of the user interface, no real business problem can be solved without allowing data access. In the past, data access on the Web depended on the server querying the database and formatting a Web page with the resulting records. The outstanding feature of the methodology is a constant string of round-trips to the server for each new query on the database. Although this method is functional, it does present problems. Making many trips to the server is slow going, and the updating of pages can be affected by many factors other than the speed of the query, resulting in an unsatisfying user experience.

Internet Explorer 4.0 changes the very nature of data access on the Web by supporting *current-record data binding*. Binding data on the client means that a view of data from the data source can be browsed and edited without the client having to return to the server for an update. Web pages created with binding respond more quickly than their server-side counterparts, resulting in a superior user interface and application.

In order to bind data to an object, IE 4.0 introduces two new HTML attributes: DATASRC and DATAFLD. These two attributes are used to bind an HTML element to a particular column in a recordset. DATASRC and DATAFLD can be used with the following tags: <TABLE>, <SPAN>, <DIV>, <OBJECT>, <PARAM>, <SELECT>, <TEXTAREA>, <IMG>, and <MARQUEE>. DATASRC represents a recordset that is generated as a result of executing a Structured Query Language (SQL) statement on a data source. DATAFLD is used to map one of the fields in the recordset to an individual element such as a text box.

Creating a recordset that can be bound to an element requires the use of an ActiveX control. IE 4.0 ships with two ActiveX controls capable of creating recordsets from various data sources: the Tabular Data Control (TDC) and Remote Data Services (RDS). The TDC is used to access delimited data in a text file, while RDS is used to access data in an ODBC data source.

Tabular Data Control

The Tabular Data Control (TDC) is an ActiveX control specifically designed to access data kept in a delimited text file. The control is fairly simple to use and requires setting only a few properties. (Appendix D contains a complete listing of properties and methods supported by the TDC.)

The TDC is inserted in a Web page by using the <OBJECT> tag. As with all ActiveX objects, IE 4.0 checks the CLASSID attribute to uniquely identify the control. The following code places the TDC in a Web page:

```
<OBJECT ID="Data1" WIDTH=0 HEIGHT=0 BORDER="0"
    CLASSID="CLSID:333C7BC4-460F-11D0-BC04-0080C7055A83">
    <PARAM NAME="DataURL" VALUE="DATA.TXT">
    <PARAM NAME="UseHeader" VALUE="True">
</OBJECT>
```

Once the TDC is in a Web page, you can bind an appropriate HTML element to any field in the data source. Listing 4-12 shows a complete example in which the data from a text file is bound to text boxes in the page. The result is pictured in Figure 4-4 on page 78.

The example utilizes the first row of data in the text file as the field designations. Setting the UseHeader property to True tells IE 4.0 to use the first row of data as the column names. These column names can then be used to bind a particular element. For example, the following code binds a text box with the Supplier field:

```
DATASRC=#Data1 DATAFLD="Supplier"
```

DATASRC is set to the name of the TDC as defined in the ID attribute
of the <OBJECT> tag. Note the pound sign (#) placed before the name in the
DATASRC attribute. This syntax is a required part of the data binding specification. DATAFLD is then set to the name of the field in the text file.

```
<HTML>
<HEAD>
<META NAME="GENERATOR" Content="Microsoft Visual InterDev 1.0">
<META HTTP-EQUIV="Content-Type" content="text/html;
    charset=iso-8859-1">
<TITLE>Tabular Data Control</TITLE>

<SCRIPT LANGUAGE="VBScript">
<!--

    Sub cmdNext_OnClick
        ' The TDC has a RecordSet property that
        ' allows access to the data in the text file
        Document.frmData.Data1.Recordset.MoveNext

        If Document.frmData.Data1.Recordset.EOF Then
            Document.frmData.Data1.Recordset.MoveLast
        End If
    End Sub

    Sub cmdPrev_OnClick
        Document.frmData.Data1.Recordset.MovePrevious

        If Document.frmData.Data1.Recordset.BOF Then
            Document.frmData.Data1.Recordset.MoveFirst
        End If
    End Sub

-->
</SCRIPT>

</HEAD>
<BODY>

<FORM NAME="frmData">
```

Listing 4-12.   *(continued)*
Using the Tabular Data Control.

Listing 4-12 *continued*

```
<!-- The Tabular Data Control -->
<OBJECT ID="Data1" WIDTH=0 HEIGHT=0 BORDER="0"
    CLASSID="CLSID:333C7BC4-460F-11D0-BC04-0080C7055A83">
    <PARAM NAME="DataURL" VALUE="DATA.TXT">
    <PARAM NAME="UseHeader" VALUE="True">
</OBJECT>

<!-- The following fields are bound to the data
source using DATASRC and DATAFLD -->
<INPUT ID="lngProductID" TYPE="TEXT" SIZE=2
    DATASRC=#Data1 DATAFLD="ProductID"><P>
<INPUT ID="strSupplier" TYPE="TEXT" SIZE=50
    DATASRC=#Data1 DATAFLD="Supplier"><P>

<INPUT ID="strManufacturer" TYPE="TEXT" SIZE=50
    DATASRC=#Data1 DATAFLD="Manufacturer"><P>

<INPUT TYPE="BUTTON" NAME="cmdNext" VALUE="Next">
<INPUT TYPE="BUTTON" NAME="cmdPrev" VALUE="Prev">

</FORM>

</BODY>
</HTML>
```

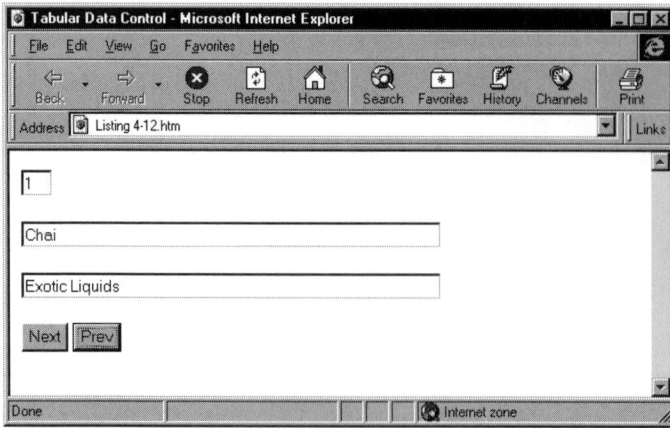

Figure 4-4.
The Tabular Data Control.

Remote Data Services

Although binding to delimited text files can be useful, most business data is maintained in relational databases. Accessing these databases is the job of Remote Data Services (RDS). RDS is capable of creating recordsets from any ODBC data source running on the server and bringing that data to the client.

Normally, accessing an ODBC data source by the client requires that the client have the appropriate ODBC driver installed. This scenario generally requires a substantial client setup process to access the data. However, any setup at all on the Web is virtually impossible given the fact that a client cannot be controlled on the Internet in the same manner that a typical client/server setup might be controlled by a developer. So without any guarantee that an ODBC driver is present on the client, how can a recordset from the server be made available to the client?

The answer is that RDS uses a proxy/stub system. Proxies and stubs are not new. In fact, proxy/stub pairs are at the core of all remote communication between distributed objects. In a proxy/stub pair, data is packed by the stub on the server side and sent to the proxy on the client side; once the client receives the data, it is unpacked and presented for display. This method of packing and unpacking data across a distance is called *marshaling*. Marshaling is used extensively not only by RDS but also by such technologies as the Component Object Model (COM), which is the heart of ActiveX technology.

RDS depends on a server-side component to pack the data. In fact, you must install the server-side portion of RDS in order to use client-side data binding. The proxy cannot work without the stub. Fortunately, installing the server-side portion of RDS is a minor task. You can find the setup for RDS on the CD-ROM that accompanies this book.

Once the server is set up, you can use the client-side portion of RDS known as the Advanced Data Control (ADC). The ADC is as simple to use as the Tabular Data Control. Listing 4-13 on the following page shows a complete example of binding data to a grid control in a Web page. When utilizing the ADC, you have to set only three properties to get a simple connection: Connect, Server, and SQL. The Connect property is the ODBC connection string for the data source. Server is generally the name of the Web server where the data source is located (and where the server-side portion of the ADC resides). SQL is simply the Structured Query Language statement to run. (Appendix D lists all the properties and methods for the ADC.)

Once the ADC is in a Web page, data binding is accomplished in the same fashion that it is with the Tabular Data Control. This means that you can use the DATASRC and DATAFLD attributes to bind to the same elements that are supported by the TDC. The sample code binds to a grid where all of the fields are displayed at once, so only the DATASRC attribute is set for the grid.

```
<HTML>
<HEAD>
<META NAME="GENERATOR" Content="Microsoft Developer Studio">
<META HTTP-EQUIV="Content-Type" content="text/html;
    charset=iso-8859-1">
<TITLE>Advanced Data Control</TITLE>
</HEAD>
<BODY>

<FORM>

<!-- NOTE: In this example, you must define an
ODBC data source named Biblio. See Chapter 2
for help.-->

<!-- The Advanced Data Control -->
<OBJECT ID="Data1" HEIGHT=10 WIDTH=10
    CLASSID="CLSID:BD96C556-65A3-11D0-983A-00C04FC29E33">
    <PARAM NAME="SQL" VALUE="SELECT * FROM Publishers">
    <PARAM NAME="SERVER" VALUE="http://scot-winnt">
    <PARAM NAME="CONNECT" VALUE="DSN=Biblio">
</OBJECT>

<!-- A data-bound grid -->
<OBJECT ID="MSFlexGrid1" WIDTH=548 HEIGHT=180 DATASRC="#Data1"
    CLASSID="CLSID:6262D3A0-531B-11CF-91F6-C2863C385E30">
    <PARAM NAME="_ExtentX" VALUE="14499">
    <PARAM NAME="_ExtentY" VALUE="4763">
    <PARAM NAME="_Version" VALUE="327680">
</OBJECT>

</FORM>

</BODY>
</HTML>
```

Listing 4-13.
Using the Advanced Data Control.

ActiveX Controls

In addition to the data binding provided by new ActiveX controls, Internet Explorer 4.0 also supports impressive multimedia features through ActiveX controls. The multimedia controls that ship with IE 4.0 are intended to create fast, capable graphics and sound without the long download times typically associated with multimedia Web content. This section briefly examines the new multimedia controls and their uses. Look for a complete reference to these controls on the CD-ROM that accompanies this book.

Structured Graphics Control

The Structured Graphics control is an ActiveX control used for creating graphics from simple vectors. Using the control, you can create an image as a series of lines and shapes. The image can be as complex as you like, but you must specify exactly how to draw it. The specification is delivered through a set of <PARAM> tags associated with the control. Each <PARAM> tag specifies an instruction such as the color or the shape of the drawing. The following code generates a rectangle:

```
<OBJECT ID="MyShape"
    CLASSID="CLSID:5FD6A143-372A-11D0-A521-0080C78FEE85">
    <PARAM NAME="Line0001" VALUE="Rect(0,0,50,20,0)">
</OBJECT>
```

A <PARAM> tag for the control always specifies a line number for the NAME attribute and a drawing instruction for the VALUE attribute. The lines must begin with 0001 and increase by one for each new instruction. Failing to sequence the lines correctly causes the drawing to stop.

Path Control

The Path control is an ActiveX control that defines a sequence of *x,y* coordinates. Once the path is defined, you can specify another ActiveX control or HTML element that will follow the path. In this way, you can create a complicated animation path and have images and controls follow the path on the Web page. Defining the path is a simple matter of using two <PARAM> tags to specify the set of *x* coordinates and matching *y* coordinates referenced to an interval of time, or tick. For example, if you want to define a path that moves an image from the lower left corner of the browser to the upper right corner, you can use the following <OBJECT> tag:

```
<OBJECT ID="pthSquare"
    CLASSID="CLSID:E0E3CC60-6A80-11D0-9B40-00A0C903AA7F">
    <PARAM NAME="AutoStart" VALUE=-1>
    <PARAM NAME="XSeries" VALUE="0,0;100,640">
    <PARAM NAME="YSeries" VALUE="0,480;100,0">
    <PARAM NAME="EdgeAction" VALUE="2">
    <PARAM NAME="TickInterval" VALUE=10>
</OBJECT>
```

Note how the XSeries and YSeries properties use a tick/coordinate pair to define the position of an object. With such pairs, you can simply define key positions at key moments and the Path control takes care of interpolating the position of the object at intermediate ticks. TickInterval is used to specify the duration of a tick. This example takes 1 second to cross the browser because a single tick occurs every 10 milliseconds and it takes 100 ticks to complete the animation. The AutoStart property determines whether the path animation occurs immediately after the page is loaded, and EdgeAction defines behavior after the path is complete. In this case, the animation begins immediately and keeps looping. Listing 4-14 shows the Path control and the Structured Graphics control creating a bouncing ball.

```
<HTML>
<HEAD>
<META NAME="GENERATOR" Content="Microsoft Developer Studio">
<META HTTP-EQUIV="Content-Type" content="text/html;
    charset=iso-8859-1">
<TITLE>Bouncing Ball</TITLE>

<SCRIPT LANGUAGE="VBScript">
<!--

    Sub Window_OnLoad()
        pathBall.Target = objBall.Style
    End Sub

-->
</SCRIPT>

</HEAD>

<BODY BGCOLOR="BLACK" TEXT="RED">
```

Listing 4-14.   *(continued)*
A bouncing ball created with the Path control.

Listing 4-14 *continued*

```
<!-- Structured Graphics control -->
<OBJECT ID="objBall"
STYLE="position:absolute;height:70;width:110;top:0;left:0;zindex:0"
    CLASSID="CLSID:5FD6A143-372A-11D0-A521-0080C78FEE85">
    <PARAM NAME="Line0001" VALUE="SetLineColor(255,255,255)">
    <PARAM NAME="Line0002" VALUE="SetFillColor(255,0,0,0,0,255)">
    <PARAM NAME="Line0003" VALUE="SetFillSTYLE(1)">
    <PARAM NAME="Line0004" VALUE="SetLineSTYLE(1)">
    <PARAM NAME="Line0005" VALUE="Oval(0,-25,50,50,0)">
</OBJECT>

<!-- Path control -->
<OBJECT ID="pathBall"
    CLASSID="CLSID:E0E3CC60-6A80-11D0-9B40-00A0C903AA7F">
    <PARAM NAME=AutoStart VALUE=-1>
    <PARAM NAME=XSeries VALUE="0,0;30,0;45,0;52,0;55,0">
    <PARAM NAME=YSeries VALUE="0,0;30,80;45,160;52,240;55,320">
    <PARAM NAME=EdgeAction VALUE="1">
    <PARAM NAME=TickInterval VALUE=10>
</OBJECT>

</BODY>
</HTML>
```

Sequencer Control

The Sequencer control is an ActiveX control that you can use to sequence a series of actions. These actions can include calling VBScript functions, manipulating ActiveX control properties and methods, and accessing intrinsic HTML controls. The Sequencer control allows you to synchronize behavior among scripts and objects by defining a set of actions to occur across the page.

Just as the Structured Graphics control uses a series of <PARAM> tags to define a vector graphic, the Sequencer control uses a series of <PARAM> tags to define a series of actions. Here is the basic syntax for the Sequencer control:

```
<OBJECT ID=object
    CLASSID="CLSID:37992B41-F5E3-11CF-97DF-00A0C90FEE54">
    <PARAM NAME="Actionx"
        VALUE="AT Time, RepeatCount, RepeatRate Action, TieBreak">
```

Action*x* is the NAME attribute of the <PARAM> tag and is structured as an integer beginning with 0001. The actions specified by the Sequencer control must be in order as <PARAM> tags starting with 0001. The VALUE attribute specifies which action to take. *Time* is when to take the action, specified in minutes:seconds:milliseconds after the sequence begins. *RepeatCount* is the number of times to repeat the action, where −1 is an infinite loop. *RepeatRate* defines the interval at which the action should be repeated, specified in the minutes:seconds:milliseconds format. *Action* is the act performed by the Sequencer, and *TieBreak* is a priority number assigned to the action in case two actions conflict. For example, the following code calls a VBScript function named Animate every second in an infinite loop:

```
<OBJECT ID="Sequencer1"
    CLASSID="CLSID:37992B41-F5E3-11CF-97DF-00A0C90FEE54">
    <PARAM NAME="Action0001"
        VALUE="AT 00:00:00, -1, 00:01:00 Animate(), 1">
```

Sprite Control

The Sprite control is an ActiveX control that provides frame-based animation for your Web page. To use the control, you must define a series of images that will create the frames of an animated sequence. Once the images are defined, you can control when and how the animation plays. This makes the Sprite control superior to both an animated GIF, which cannot be controlled, and a movie, which generally takes longer to download. The Sprite control can also use an associated Sprite Frame Source object, which allows you to create animated frames as a grid of images. This means, for example, that you can download a single GIF file that contains all of the animation frames, structured in a grid format that the Sprite Frame Source object can provide as discrete frames to the Sprite control.

Listing 4-15 shows a complete example using a series of GIF images of the earth. The images are stored together in a single file named EARTHGRID.GIF. (See Figure 4-5.) The file contains 18 images in total, arranged in two columns of 9 images.

```
<HTML>
<HEAD>
<META NAME="GENERATOR" Content="Microsoft Visual InterDev 1.0">
<META HTTP-EQUIV="Content-Type" content="text/html;
    charset=iso-8859-1">
<TITLE>The Sprite Control</TITLE>
```

Listing 4-15.   *(continued)*

The Sprite control.

84

Listing 4-15 *continued*

```
</HEAD>
<BODY>

<!-- The Sprite control -->
<OBJECT ID="Earth" HEIGHT=50 WIDTH=50
CLASSID="CLSID:FD179533-D86E-11D0-89D6-00A0C90833E6">
    <PARAM NAME="Repeat" VALUE=-1>
    <PARAM NAME="PlayRate" VALUE=1>
    <PARAM NAME="InitialFrame" VALUE=1>
    <PARAM NAME="FrameMap"
        VALUE="1,100,,;2,100,,;3,100,,;4,100,,;
            5,100,,;6,100,,;7,100,,;8,100,,;9,100,,;
            10,100,,;11,100,,;12,100,,;13,100,,;14,100,,;
            15,100,,;16,100,,;17,100,,;18,100,,;">
    <PARAM NAME="NumFrames" VALUE=18>
    <PARAM NAME="NumFramesAcross" VALUE=9>
    <PARAM NAME="NumFramesDown" VALUE=2>
    <PARAM NAME="SourceURL" VALUE="EARTHGRID.GIF">
    <PARAM NAME="MouseEventsEnabled" VALUE="False">
    <PARAM NAME="AutoStart" VALUE=-1>
</OBJECT>

</BODY>
</HTML>
```

Figure 4-5.
EARTHGRID.GIF.

Transitions Control

The Transitions control is an ActiveX control that can create professional fades, wipes, and cuts between visible objects on the Web page. The control is placed in a page utilizing an <OBJECT> tag that specifies the type of transition. You connect the control to a particular object by intercepting the

85

painting functions of the object you want to affect. For example, to apply a Transitions control named MyTrans to an <IMG> tag named MyGIF, you could use the following code:

```
MyGIF.StopPainting(MyTrans)
MyGIF.StartPainting(100)
```

The StopPainting method ties the Transitions control to the selected element. The StartPainting method starts the transition. The duration of the transition is determined by the value passed to StartPainting. The value represents the speed of the transition in milliseconds. Listing 4-16 shows a simple example of a transition applied to text on a Web page.

```
<HTML>
<HEAD>
<META NAME="GENERATOR" Content="Microsoft Developer Studio">
<META HTTP-EQUIV="Content-Type" content="text/html;
    charset=iso-8859-1">
<TITLE>Transitions Control</TITLE>

<SCRIPT LANGUAGE="VBScript">
<!--

    Sub Window_OnLoad
        ' Intercept the painting process
        txtDivision.StopPainting(Transition1)

        ' Set the text color
        txtHeader.Style.Color = "Black"

        ' Start the transition
        txtDivision.StartPainting(2000)
    End Sub

-->
</SCRIPT>

</HEAD>
<BODY>

<!-- Transitions control -->
<OBJECT ID="Transition1" WIDTH=11 HEIGHT=11
    CLASSID="CLSID:EEE70103-6A8F-11D0-BD28-00A0C908DB96">
```

Listing 4-16.   *(continued)*
Transition of text on a Web page.

Listing 4-16 *continued*

```
        <PARAM NAME="Clsid"
            VALUE="{EB8F50E2-85D1-11D0-9D9D-00A0C908DB96}">
        <PARAM NAME="TransitionStyle" VALUE="1">
</OBJECT>

<!-- The text to transition -->
<DIV ID="txtDivision"
     STYLE="position:relative; height:100; width:200;">
<H1 ID="txtHeader" STYLE="color:white;">Text Transition</H1>
</DIV>

</BODY>
</HTML>
```

Visual Filter Control

The Visual Filter control is an ActiveX control that applies effects such as shadows, flips, and lights to visible elements on the Web page. Multiple effects can be grouped under a single ActiveX control through the use of <PARAM> tags. Each series of tags designates an effect that you identify with a unique integer. The following code shows how to create a light source on the page:

```
<OBJECT ID="objLight"
    CLASSID="CLSID:DA9E9D23-3661-11D0-BDC2-00A0C908DB96">
    <PARAM NAME="Effect0.Clsid"
        VALUE="{F1631E43-47F8-11D0-80D4-00AA006EC537}">
</OBJECT>
```

Once the effect is created, you must apply it to an element on the page by setting the Filter property of the element. <DIV>, <IMG>, and <OBJECT> tags support the Filter property. Listing 4-17 shows a complete example.

```
<HTML>
<HEAD>
<SCRIPT LANGUAGE="VBScript">

<!--

    Sub Window_OnLoad
        ' Add a point of light
```

Listing 4-17.
The Visual Filter control.

(continued)

Listing 4-17 *continued*

```
        Call objLight(0).AddPoint(0, 0, 250, _
                                    255, 0, 0, 90)


        ' Set the filter on the object
        txtDivision.Filter = objLight
        objLight.Refresh
    End Sub

    Sub Document_OnMouseMove()
        ' Move the light source
        Call objLight(0).MoveLight(0, Window.Event.x, _
                                    Window.Event.y, 250, -1)
        objLight.Refresh
    End Sub

-->
</SCRIPT>

<BODY BGCOLOR="BLACK">
<!-- The Visual Filter control -->
<OBJECT ID="objLight" WIDTH=11 HEIGHT=11
    CLASSID="CLSID:DA9E9D23-3661-11D0-BDC2-00A0C908DB96">
    <PARAM NAME="Effect0.Clsid"
        VALUE="{F1631E43-47F8-11D0-80D4-00AA006EC537}">
    <PARAM NAME="Effect0.ID" VALUE="Filter1">
    <PARAM NAME="Effect0.Enabled" VALUE="-1">
    <PARAM NAME="Effect0.LightsAmount" VALUE="100">
</OBJECT>

<!-- The text to light up -->
<DIV ID="txtDivision"
    STYLE="position:relative; width:100%;
    height:100%; left:0; top:0">

<CENTER>
<FONT COLOR="WHITE" FACE="Verdana" SIZE="100pt">
Lights
</FONT>
</CENTER>

</DIV>
</BODY>
</HTML>
```

Mixer Control

With all the great visual multimedia effects to experiment with, don't forget audio! The Mixer control is an ActiveX control that mixes together different sound wave files. You can play individual wave files or combine wave files inside channels. The control uses both Sound and Channel objects to handle the WAV files and associated channels. Adding a sound to the control is a matter of using the NewSound method. Sounds can easily be played using the Play method of the Sound object. Listing 4-18 produces an example that plays a familiar WAV file when a Web page is loaded.

```
<HTML>
<HEAD>
<META NAME="GENERATOR" Content="Microsoft Developer Studio">
<META HTTP-EQUIV="Content-Type" content="text/html;
    charset=iso-8859-1">
<TITLE>Mixer Control</TITLE>

<SCRIPT LANGUAGE="VBScript">
<!--

    ' Variable for Sound object
    Public Wave

    Sub Window_OnLoad
        ' Declare Sound object
        Set Wave = objSound.NewSound("URLWav")

        ' Load wave file
        Wave.LoadMedia "The Microsoft Sound.wav", 2

        ' Play wave file
        Wave.Play
    End Sub
-->
</SCRIPT>

</HEAD>
<BODY>
<H1>Try leaving and returning to this page!</H1>
```

Listing 4-18. *(continued)*

The Mixer control.

Listing 4-18 *continued*

```
<!-- The Mixer control -->
<OBJECT ID="objSound"
    CLASSID="CLSID:9A7D63C1-5391-11D0-8BB6-0000F803A803">
</OBJECT>

</BODY>
</HTML>
```

The Microsoft Agent

Using a browser to explore the Internet is simple. The challenge is to find what you want when you arrive at a Web site. Web sites are usually designed with creative considerations, not standardization, in mind, so each presents a unique landscape to the bewildered user. Even familiar sites can be updated frequently. The result of this confusion is that most people resort to simply using search services and blindly following hyperlinks until they stumble upon some useful information.

The Microsoft Agent is an ActiveX control that provides a friendly assistant to help explore Internet sites. This assistant can be programmed by the site developer to help users find information. In the current version, a developer can choose from three different standard characters or create a new character.

Programming a Web page to host the Agent is as simple as placing any ActiveX control in a page. Simply use the <OBJECT> tag with the appropriate CLASSID attribute, and the Agent is available. Because the Agent ships with IE 4.0, you are guaranteed that it will always be available on the client machine. The following code shows the <OBJECT> tag for the Agent:

```
<OBJECT ID="Agent1" WIDTH=32 HEIGHT=32
    CLASSID="CLSID:F5BE8BD2-7DE6-11D0-91FE-00C04FD701A5">
</OBJECT>
```

When the control is available, you must load the selected character before it can be displayed. You can load more than one character into the Agent control, and they will all be managed as members of the Characters collection. When loading a character, you simply provide the filename and a name for the character to use in the Characters collection.

Once loaded, the Agent can be displayed by calling the Show method. The Agent supports speech and movement to present the personality. It can speak any text string provided to the Speak method and can move to any pixel location specified in the MoveTo method. Listing 4-19 shows a complete example that allows you to display, move, and converse with the standard Agent characters shown in Figure 4-6 on page 93.

The Agent can do more than simply move and speak. It can also receive voice or mouse input and can perform tasks such as navigating to a desired Web page. These features are explored in detail in the project in Chapter 7.

```
<HTML>
<HEAD>
<META NAME="GENERATOR" Content="Microsoft Developer Studio">
<META HTTP-EQUIV="Content-Type" content="text/html;
    charset=iso-8859-1">
<TITLE>Document Title</TITLE>

<SCRIPT LANGUAGE="VBScript">
<!--
    Sub Window_OnLoad
        ' Dimension variables
        Dim Agents
        Dim AgentPath

        ' Set variables
        Set Agents = Document.frmAgent.Agent1.Characters
        AgentPath = "c:\program files\microsoft agent\characters\"

        ' Load characters
        Agents.Load "GENIE", AgentPath & "Genie.acs"
        Agents.Load "ROBOT", AgentPath & "Robby.acs"
        Agents.Load "WIZARD", AgentPath & "Merlin.acs"
    End Sub

    Sub cmdSpeech_OnClick()
        ' Declare variables
        Dim MyAgent
        Dim MyForm
        Dim AgentName
```

Listing 4-19.   *(continued)*
Using the Microsoft Agent.

Listing 4-19 *continued*

```
        ' Get data
        Set MyForm = Document.frmAgent
        Set MyAgent = Document.frmAgent.Agent1
        AgentName = MyForm.lstAgents.Value

        MyAgent.Characters(AgentName).Show
        MyAgent.Characters(AgentName).Speak MyForm.txtSpeech.Value

        Window.Event.CancelBubble = True
    End Sub

    Sub Document_OnClick()
        ' Declare variables
        Dim MyAgent
        Dim AgentName

        ' Get data
        Set MyForm = Document.frmAgent
        Set MyAgent = Document.frmAgent.Agent1
        AgentName = MyForm.lstAgents.Value
        MyAgent.Characters(AgentName).MoveTo Window.Event.X, _
                                            Window.Event.Y

    End Sub
-->
</SCRIPT>
</HEAD>
<BODY>

<FORM NAME="frmAgent">
<!-- The Microsoft Agent -->
<OBJECT ID="Agent1" WIDTH=32 HEIGHT=32
    CLASSID="CLSID:F5BE8BD2-7DE6-11D0-91FE-00C04FD701A5">
</OBJECT>

<P>

<INPUT TYPE="TEXT" NAME="txtSpeech" VALUE="Dynamic HTML is Cool!">
<INPUT TYPE="BUTTON" NAME="cmdSpeech" VALUE="Speak!">
</P>
```

(continued)

Listing 4-19 *continued*

```
<SELECT NAME="lstAgents" SIZE=3>
    <OPTION VALUE="GENIE" SELECTED>Genie
    <OPTION VALUE="WIZARD">Merlin
    <OPTION VALUE="ROBOT">Robby
</SELECT>

</FORM>

</BODY>
</HTML>
```

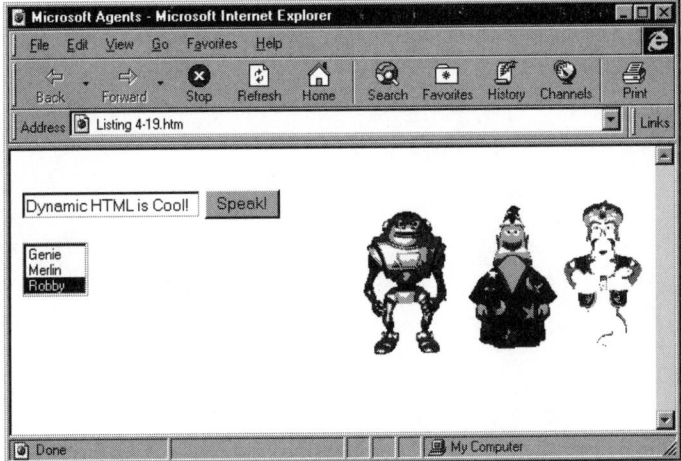

Figure 4-6.
The Microsoft Agent.

Active Server Pages

Dynamic HTML provides the primary client-side programming tool for Microsoft Internet Explorer version 4.0. But Dynamic HTML is not supported by browsers such as Netscape Navigator. In fact, very little of the client-side functionality supported by various browsers can be considered truly cross-platform.

If you want to design an Internet site accessible to a number of different browsers, you need to move the programming from the client to the server. Microsoft Active Server Pages (ASP) allows you to create server-side applications that can be used by a variety of browsers. ASP is essentially nothing more than VBScript that runs on the server. The script code generates HTML when a page is requested. That is the key to ASP: a client never sees your code—only the resulting HTML, which can be recognized by any browser.

Active Server Pages Fundamentals

Listing 5-1 produces a simple ASP page that generates a greeting based on the time of day. In this example, the hour of the day is determined by using the code *Hour(Now)*, where Now is a VBScript function that returns the current date/time stamp. If the hour is less than 12, a variable is assigned the greeting "Good Morning!" From noon to 6 PM, the message is "Good Afternoon!" and after 6 PM, "Good Evening!"

```
<%@ LANGUAGE="VBSCRIPT"%>
<!DOCTYPE HTML PUBLIC "-//IETF//DTD HTML//EN">
<HTML>

<HEAD>
<META HTTP-EQUIV="Content-Type"
    CONTENT="text/html; CHARSET=iso-8859-1">
```

Listing 5-1. *(continued)*
A simple ASP example.

Listing 5-1 *continued*

```
<META NAME="GENERATOR"
    CONTENT="Microsoft FrontPage 2.0">
<TITLE>Simple ASP Example</TITLE>
</HEAD>

<BODY BGCOLOR="#FFFFFF">
<%
Dim strGreeting

If Hour(Now) < 12 Then
    strGreeting = "Good Morning!"
ElseIf Hour(Now) > 11 And Hour(Now) < 18 Then
    strGreeting = "Good Afternoon!"
ElseIf Hour(Now) > 17 Then
    strGreeting = "Good Evening!"
End If
%>
<H1><%=strGreeting%></H1>
</BODY>
</HTML>
```

Notice that the code structure in the listing is surrounded by special characters—angle brackets and percent signs (<%...%>). These symbols designate the code as server-side code, which means that the code will be evaluated before the page is actually sent to the browser. In fact, if you were to view the resulting HTML from Listing 5-1 in Internet Explorer, you would see the following (assuming it's afternoon, of course!):

```
<!DOCTYPE HTML PUBLIC "-//IETF//DTD HTML//EN">
<HTML>

<HEAD>
<META HTTP-EQUIV="Content-Type"
    CONTENT="text/html; CHARSET=iso-8859-1">
<META NAME="GENERATOR"
    CONTENT="Microsoft FrontPage 2.0">
<TITLE>Simple ASP Example</TITLE>
</HEAD>
<BODY BGCOLOR="#FFFFFF">

<H1>Good Afternoon!</H1>
</BODY>
</HTML>
```

This is the point of using ASP. The result of the code is simply HTML! This page is visible in any browser and will work in Netscape Navigator as well as in Internet Explorer. ASP provides true platform independence for the Internet developer.

Listing 5-1 contains a few other features that are worth mentioning. Notice the line of code at the top of the page—the code that specifies the language that will be used for the page:

```
<%@ LANGUAGE="VBSCRIPT"%>
```

Normally, you would use VBScript as the language, but ASP also supports JavaScript. Unlike client-side scripting, the choice of language here has no impact on browser compatibility since the code is all executed on the server. You simply code using the language that makes you comfortable.

Also notice the line of code where the HTML is actually generated. The code uses the variable to write the greeting, as follows:

```
<H1><%=strGreeting%></H1>
```

The variable strGreeting is enclosed by the angle brackets and percent signs used in the rest of the server-side code, but it is also preceded by an equal sign. The equal sign plays an important role in ASP, telling ASP to insert the actual value of the variable in the page as HTML. Therefore, the value of the greeting is inserted at this point and is seen in the browser as text content.

Objects and Components

At the simplest level, creating an ASP page is nothing more than writing server-side code to produce the result you have in mind. VBScript, however, is not a fully functional language, and it falters when you try to create more complex pages. For example, VBScript has no intrinsic functions to allow data access, nor can it open text files. In fact, VBScript has no intrinsic functions that allow access to any external data sources. How, then, can you use ASP to perform advanced functions such as data access? The answer is that you supplement VBScript with ASP *objects* and *components.*

ASP objects and components are nothing more than ActiveX components, like any ActiveX DLLs you might use in Microsoft Visual Basic. The difference between ASP objects and ASP components lies in the way they are packaged. ASP objects are ActiveX elements that are always available to VBScript. You do not have to explicitly create ASP objects for your use. ASP supports the Application, Session, Request, Response, and Server objects. ASP components, on the other hand, are DLLs that exist outside the ASP framework. These components can be created in any language, but Microsoft has packaged several useful ASP components with Visual InterDev. ASP components are not available unless they are specifically created in code. ASP supports the Database Access, File Access, Browser Capabilities, Ad Rotator, and Content Linking components.

The GLOBAL.ASA File

One of the biggest concerns facing Internet developers, regardless of the technology they use, is the difficulty of creating a true *application* on the Internet. The interaction between a browser and a Web server is basically a stateless transaction in which the server hands a Web page to the client and then forgets that the client even exists. When the client subsequently asks for another Web page, the server has no memory of the first request. The essential problem for all Web applications is this: How do you define an application?

Defining an application in the Microsoft Windows environment is simple. The application starts when the icon is double-clicked, and the application ends when Exit is chosen from the File menu. In between these two events, data can easily be remembered in variables. However, this is not true for Internet applications. How can you determine when an application begins and ends? If a user comes to a site and views a page, you might say that the application has started. But what if the user jumps to another site and returns five minutes later? Is the application still live? What if the user leaves for an hour? Two hours?

This problem of defining the beginning and ending of an application affects the ability to correctly manage variables and work flow. Fortunately, Active Server Pages provides a solution. ASP uses a special file, named GLOBAL.ASA, to define the beginning and ending of an application as well as the beginning and ending of an individual user's session. GLOBAL.ASA is responsible for detecting four key events in your site: Application_OnStart, Application_OnEnd, Session_OnStart, and Session_OnEnd. Listing 5-2 shows a typical GLOBAL.ASA file.

```
<SCRIPT LANGUAGE="VBSCRIPT" RUNAT="Server">

' You can add special event handlers in this file, which
' will be run automatically when special Active Server
' Pages events occur. To create these handlers, add
' a subroutine with a name from the list below that
```

Listing 5-2.   *(continued)*
GLOBAL.ASA.

Listing 5-2 *continued*

```
' corresponds to the event you want to use. For example,
' to create an event handler for Session_OnStart, you would
' put the following code into this file (without the
' comments):
'
' Sub Session_OnStart
'      **Put your code here **
' End Sub

' EventName                Description
' Session_OnStart          Runs the first time a
'                          user runs any page in
'                          your application
' Session_OnEnd            Runs when a user's session
'                          times out or quits your
'                          application
' Application_OnStart      Runs once when the first
'                          page of your application
'                          is run for the first time
'                          by any user
' Application_OnEnd        Runs once when the Web
'                          server shuts down

</SCRIPT>

<SCRIPT LANGUAGE=VBScript RUNAT=Server>
    Sub Session_OnStart

    End Sub

    Sub Session_OnEnd

    End Sub

    Sub Application_OnStart

    End Sub

    Sub Application_OnEnd

    End Sub

</SCRIPT>
```

99

GLOBAL.ASA contains <SCRIPT> tags to designate scripting sections. These tags contain a special attribute named RUNAT=Server, which specifies that the contained VBScript should run on the server, not on the client. RUNAT=Server is similar in functionality to the angle bracket/percent sign symbols used in the Web page to designate server-side scripting. The events in GLOBAL.ASA can be trapped on the server side using standard syntax. For example, trapping the start of an application is accomplished with the following code:

```
<SCRIPT LANGUAGE=VBScript RUNAT=Server>
    Sub Application_OnStart
        ' Application-specific code
    End Sub
</SCRIPT>
```

Although the GLOBAL.ASA file uses events to mark the beginning and ending of an application, it is still not clear what constitutes an application. One working definition, offered by Microsoft, defines an Internet application as a virtual directory and all of its pages. If a user requests a Web page from a virtual directory named Bookstore, the user has started the Bookstore application and the Application_OnStart and Session_OnStart events will fire in GLOBAL.ASA.

By this definition, an application can be used by many browsers at the same time. The Application_OnStart event fires only once—when the first user requests a Web page from the virtual directory. When other users then request pages from the same directory, only the Session_OnStart event fires.

While *application* can refer to multiple browsers accessing the same set of Web pages, *session* refers to an individual browser accessing the same Web pages. A session for an individual browser lasts as long as the user continues to request Web pages from the virtual directory. If the user stops requesting additional Web pages for 20 minutes, the session ends and the Session_OnEnd event fires. When all user sessions in the virtual directory have ended, the Application_OnEnd event fires.

As an example, consider the following scenario. Two users are about to access the Magazine application on a Web site. User1 accesses first and requests the Web page DEFAULT.ASP. At this moment, the Application_OnStart and Session_OnStart events fire.

Just 5 minutes later, User2 accesses the same application. Because User1 has been active in the last 20 minutes, the Magazine application is still live. Therefore, only the Session_OnStart event fires, signaling the beginning of a second user session. Additionally, the site will now require that both the User1 and User2 sessions end before the application can be closed.

During the next 15 minutes, User1 does not access any pages in the Magazine application. Because User1 has been inactive for 20 minutes, ASP concludes that the session for User1 has ended and the Session_OnEnd event fires. The application is still active, however, because User2 has requested a page in the last 20 minutes.

User2 remains active for an hour, reading magazine articles by requesting Web pages. Finally, though, User2 shuts down the computer, and 20 minutes after User2 leaves the site, the Session_OnEnd event fires. Because User2 is the last user of the application, the application terminates and the Application_OnEnd event fires.

Active Server Pages Objects

ASP hosts a number of built-in objects that are available to the developer. These objects help manage everything from variables to form submission. The objects are simple to use and can be called directly from code without any special syntax. In this section, we examine the ASP objects available in Visual InterDev for the Internet developer. Properties and methods supported by these objects are described in Appendix D.

Application Object

The Application object allows you to create *application variables,* variables that are available to all users of an application. All users who request Web pages from the same virtual directory can share any application variables defined in those pages.

Listing 5-3 shows a code sample that uses the Application object. In this example, an application variable is used to track the last time the page was visited.

```
<%@ LANGUAGE="VBSCRIPT"%>
<HTML>
<HEAD>
<TITLE>Application Variables</TITLE>
</HEAD>

<BODY BGCOLOR="FFFFFF">

This page was last visited on <%=Application("Time")%>
```

Listing 5-3.   *(continued)*

The Application object.

Listing 5-3 *continued*

```
<%Application.Lock%>
<%Application("Time") = Now%>
<%Application.Unlock%>

</BODY>
</HTML>
```

Creating an application variable is a simple matter of addressing the Application object with the name of the new variable you want to create. For example, the following code produces an application variable named Company and sets its value to NewTech:

```
Application("Company") = "NewTech"
```

The name is arbitrary, and the variable can contain any kind of information, whether numbers or text.

Because the variable is available to a number of users simultaneously, you must deal with concurrency; that is, you cannot guarantee that two users will not try to set the variable to different values at the same time. To deal with this situation, the Application object supports Lock and Unlock methods. The Lock method locks the entire Application object, not just the variable you are changing, so always unlock the Application object immediately after changing a variable value:

```
Application.Lock
Application("Company") = "NewTech"
Application.Unlock
```

Although application variables are useful for temporary storage of data, they can't be used to store data permanently. The data in an application variable is destroyed when the Application_OnEnd event fires. Be sure to move application variables to permanent storage, such as a database, if you want to save the values after the application terminates.

Session Object

In programming applications, developers are often less concerned about data shared by many users and more concerned about data related to an individual user. ASP supports variables for individual users through the Session object, which allows you to create *session variables* for use by individuals.

Listing 5-4 shows how to define some session variables in the GLOBAL.ASA file. Defining session variables is just as simple as defining application variables.

the name of the variable you
ation and session variables is
e user and last as long as the
questing pages from a given

file, which
ive Server
rs, add
ow that
For example,
Start, you would
thout the

```
      **Put your code here
' End Sub

' EventName              Description
' Session_OnStart        Runs the first time a
'                        user runs any page in
'                        your application
' Session_OnEnd          Runs when a user's session
'                        times out or quits your
'                        application
' Application_OnStart    Runs once when the first
'                        page of your application
'                        is run for the first time
'                        by any user
' Application_OnEnd      Runs once when the Web
'                        server shuts down

</SCRIPT>

<SCRIPT LANGUAGE=VBScript RUNAT=Server>
    Sub Session_OnStart
        Session("Company") = "NewTech"
        Session("EMail") = "info@vb-bootcamp.com"
    End Sub
</SCRIPT>
```

Listing 5-4.
Creating session variables.

Session variables can be created in any Web page or GLOBAL.ASA file, and they can be accessed from any Web page in the application where the variables were originally defined. You can retrieve the values of session variables by reading them out of the Session object. The following code reads the session variables established in Listing 5-4 and displays them in text fields:

```
<FORM>
<P><INPUT VALUE=<%=Session("Company")%>>Company</P>
<P><INPUT VALUE=<%=Session("EMail")%>>E-Mail</P>
</FORM>
```

Earlier in this chapter, Internet applications were described as stateless transactions between a Web server and a browser. If Internet applications are stateless, how does ASP remember session variables for each user of an application? The answer is that the session variables are saved on the server for each client. The browser itself receives a unique identifier that tells the server which set of data belongs to that client. The client stores the identifier, called a Globally Unique Identifier (GUID), and uses it later to retrieve the data stored by the server. Thus, each client can have individual data for each application used on the Internet.

Request Object

An Internet application certainly differs in many ways from a typical client/server application, but they are similar in that the application absolutely depends upon the transfer of data between client and server. When a Web server wants to send data to a client, it does so by creating a Web page and sending it. When a client wants to return data to the Web server, the browser relies on the process of *form submission.*

To send data to a Web server, a client utilizes a form with <FORM> tags, which contain data input fields such as text boxes. The client packages the entered data into the data fields and subsequently submits the package to the back end.

The process of submitting a form is controlled by two attributes of the <FORM> tag: METHOD and ACTION. The METHOD attribute of the <FORM> tag determines how the data is sent to the server. This attribute has two possible values: POST and GET. POST tells the browser to package all data inside the form and send it to the server. GET, on the other hand, sends the data as an integral part of the Uniform Resource Locator for the target page. The ACTION attribute specifies the target page for the submitted data. The following code, for example, sends all data from the text fields to a page named DATA.ASP by the POST method:

```
<FORM METHOD="POST"
    ACTION="http://www.vb-bootcamp.com/data.asp">
<P><INPUT TYPE="TEXT" NAME="txtName"></P>
<P><INPUT TYPE="TEXT" NAME="txtEMail"></P>
<P><INPUT TYPE="SUBMIT"></P>
</FORM>
```

The special control designated in the form as TYPE="SUBMIT" is a button that is clicked by the user when the form is ready for submission. Clicking the button causes the browser to package the data in the text fields and submit it. The format of the submitted data is strictly defined so that the server knows what to expect from the client. The data takes the form of Field=Value pairs sent to the server in clear text format. If, in the preceding example, you typed *NewTech* into the txtName field and *Info* into the txtEMail field, the following text would be sent to the page DATA.ASP:

```
txtName=NewTech&txtEMail=Info
```

On the server side, this data could then be parsed back into fields and values and used by the server for any purpose, including data access or creating and sending e-mail. This is where the Request object comes in. The Request object is used by ASP to parse submitted data received from a client. To use the Request object, simply provide the name of the field you would like to examine, and the Request object returns the value. For example, the following code would return the value NewTech:

```
<%=Request.Form("txtName")%>
```

Request.Form is used anytime you want to examine the contents of a form submitted to an ASP page. The Request object is available only to ASP pages and can return data only from a form submitted directly to your page. You cannot access data from forms that were not submitted to your page.

Many Internet applications use sequential form submission to accomplish a task such as drilling into a database. However, there are times when a user does not need to fill out a form and submit it and would rather simply click a hyperlink to view data. This too can be accomplished by using the Request object.

Creating a hyperlink that is capable of submitting data requires an anchor, or <A>, tag. The anchor tag uses the HREF attribute to designate a target page and to carry data to the target page when the user clicks the link.

A question mark (?) separates the target page and the data. Consider the example in which the form submitted txtName and txtEMail fields. If you wanted to submit the same data using a hyperlink, you might write this code:

```
<A HREF=
"http://www.vb-bootcamp.com/data.asp?txtName=NewTech&txtEMail=Info">
Click here to submit data!
</A>
```

Notice how the data attached to the hyperlink takes the format Field=Value, just as it does in a submitted form. As long as you provide the data in this format, the Request object will be able to parse it. Strangely, you cannot use the syntax Request.Form on data submitted through a hyperlink. Instead, you must use Request.QueryString, which works in the same way as Request.Form but is used on data submitted by a hyperlink. Thus, the following code returns the value NewTech from the hyperlink:

```
<%=Request.QueryString("txtName")%>
```

The Request object has several other uses as well. You can, for example, use Request to retrieve all kinds of information about the client. You can access everything from cookies sent with the client's request to the user agent string of the browser. Listing 5-5 shows a simple example of using the ServerVariables collection of the Request object to determine the Microsoft Windows NT account that the client is logged on to.

```
<%@ LANGUAGE="VBSCRIPT"%>

<HTML>
<HEAD>
<META NAME="GENERATOR" Content="Microsoft Visual InterDev 1.0">
<META HTTP-EQUIV="Content-Type" content="text/html;
    charset=iso-8859-1">
<TITLE>Server Variables</TITLE>
</HEAD>
<BODY BGCOLOR="WHITE">

<H1>
You are logged in under <%=Request.ServerVariables("LOGON_USER")%>
</H1>

</BODY>
</HTML>
```

Listing 5-5.
Determining the Windows NT logon account.

Server variables provide a wide range of information about the client and the Web server. Complete documentation of all variables supported in this collection can be found in Visual InterDev, but accessing any particular variable is simply a matter of reading the collection. For example, the following code returns the user agent string of the client browser:

```
<%=Request.ServerVariables("HTTP_USER_AGENT")%>
```

Response Object

The Response object manages the content returned to a browser by ASP. In fact, although you might not realize it, you use the Response object in every ASP page. When you use the angle bracket/percent sign/equal sign combination (*<%=variable%>*) to return ASP-generated content, the equal sign is actually shorthand for the Write method of the Response object. Therefore, the following two lines of code are equivalent:

```
<%="NewTech"%>
<%Response.Write "NewTech"%>
```

Because the Response object is used so frequently in ASP, the equal sign shorthand makes a lot of sense. Otherwise, you would have to type countless iterations of *Response.Write* into every ASP page.

Another useful feature of the Response object is the Expires property. Response.Expires specifies the time in minutes before the current page expires. If this property is set to zero, the Web page expires the moment it is downloaded and Internet Explorer will not cache the page.

Caching in Internet Explorer version 4.0 affects many development efforts and can prevent your site from behaving correctly. IE 4.0 actually caches pages in two ways: to disk and to memory. Most developers and users are familiar with page caching to disk and expect this to occur, but most people do not realize that IE 4.0 also caches pages to memory. In fact, IE 4.0 remembers in RAM the last five pages that were viewed. This can have a significant impact on the way your application behaves. Consider the following simple code to show a date/time stamp in a Web page:

```
<H1>The time is now <%Response.Write Now%>
```

Under normal conditions, IE 4.0 requests this page and the server script is run, causing the current time to appear on the page. However, if the browser moves to another page and then back to the page with the date/time stamp, the time will not change. This is because IE 4.0 has cached the results of the

ASP page in RAM and does not request a new page when the browser returns. This behavior will continue until the user visits five different pages, after which the first page is flushed from the RAM cache.

You can prevent this caching behavior by setting the Expires property of the Response object to 0, forcing the Web page to expire. The complete code in Listing 5-6 displays the correct time whenever the page is visible—regardless of whether it is in the RAM cache.

RAM caching can cause strange effects at design time as well. Developers often make changes to a Web page in Visual InterDev, browse it, and wonder why the changes do not appear in the new page. This usually happens because the old version of the page is still in the RAM cache and IE 4.0 does not load the changed page. Therefore, when developing pages in Visual InterDev, always reload your page into the browser after making changes.

```
<%@ LANGUAGE="VBSCRIPT"%>
<%Response.Expires = 0%>
<HTML>
<HEAD>
<META NAME="GENERATOR" Content="Microsoft Visual InterDev 1.0">
<META HTTP-EQUIV="Content-Type" content="text/html;
    charset=iso-8859-1">
<TITLE>Forcing a Page to Expire</TITLE>
</HEAD>
<BODY BGCOLOR="white">
<H1>The time is now <%Response.Write Now%>

</BODY>
</HTML>
```

Listing 5-6.
Forcing a page to expire.

Server Object

The Server object is a sort of catchall object, providing functions that are not related to each other in any way except that they are useful to the Internet developer.

Perhaps the most important of all the Server object functions is the CreateObject method, which creates an instance of an ActiveX component. The component can be either a built-in component that ships with Visual InterDev (discussed in the next section) or a component you make yourself in any language. In any case, using a server-side ActiveX component requires the CreateObject method.

CreateObject takes as an argument the ProgID of the ActiveX component that you want to use. A ProgID is a descriptive name for a component such as Excel.Sheet or Word.Basic. The following code shows how you could use the CreateObject method to generate an instance of an e-mail component that has a ProgID of Mail.Connector.

```
Set MyObject = Server.CreateObject("Mail.Connector")
```

Active Server Pages Components

ASP components are really just ActiveX components—like any you might create in Visual Basic, Visual C++, or even Visual J++. These special components, however, are written by Microsoft and ship with Visual InterDev. They are designed to perform useful, generic tasks for Web sites, including data access. You create these components in your Web page by using the CreateObject method of the Server object. Once they are created, you can access their properties and methods to perform functions in your site.

Database Access Component (ActiveX Data Objects)

The most useful of all the ASP components has to be the Database Access component, also called the ActiveX Data Objects, or ADO. Database publishing on the Web utilizes this component, and the objects contained in it, to read and write to Open Database Connectivity (ODBC) data sources. (See Appendix D for a complete list of ActiveX Data Objects.)

The Connection object is created through the CreateObject method of the Server object and uses a variable to receive the object reference. Once the Connection object is created, it can be used to open a connection to any ODBC data source. The following code establishes a connection to a SQL Server ODBC source named Publications:

```
<%
    ' Declare a variable
    Dim objConnection

    ' Create the Connection object
    Set objConnection = Server.CreateObject("ADODB.Connection")

    ' Open the data source connection
    objConnection.Open "Publications", "sa", ""
%>
```

In this code, objConnection is the variable used as an object reference to the instance of the Connection object. This reference can access all the properties and methods of the Connection object. The Open method establishes the data source connection and has three arguments: data source name, user ID, and password.

When the data source connection is open, you can use a Recordset object to retrieve information from the data source. The Recordset object allows you to run an SQL SELECT statement and returns a set of records matching the statement. Like the Connection object, the Recordset object is created by using the Server object. In the following example, the program runs an SQL SELECT statement on the data source represented by the variable objConnection:

```
<%
    ' Declare a variable
    Dim objRecordset

    ' Create the Recordset object
    Set objRecordset = Server.CreateObject("ADODB.Recordset")

    ' Run the SQL query
    objRecordset.Open "SELECT *", objConnection
%>
```

After the records are retrieved, you can use the MoveFirst, MoveLast, MoveNext, and MovePrevious methods to navigate the records. The Write method of the Response object can place the data onto a Web page, which is then passed to a browser. Listing 5-7 shows a complete sample ASP page that builds a list box of publishing companies contained in a Publications data source.

```
<%@ LANGUAGE="VBSCRIPT"%>

<HTML>
<HEAD>
<META NAME="GENERATOR" Content="Microsoft Visual InterDev 1.0">
<META HTTP-EQUIV="Content-Type" content="text/html;
    charset=iso-8859-1">
<TITLE>Using ADO</TITLE>
</HEAD>
<BODY>
```

Listing 5-7. *(continued)*
Building a data list with ADO.

Listing 5-7 *continued*

```
<%
    ' Declare variables
    Dim objConnection
    Dim objRecordset
    ' Create objects
    Set objConnection = Server.CreateObject("ADODB.Connection")
    Set objRecordset = Server.CreateObject("ADODB.Recordset")

    ' Open connection and run query
    objConnection.Open "Publications", "sa", ""
    objRecordset.Open "SELECT pub_name FROM Publishers", objConnection
%>

<!-- Build SELECT list from recordset -->
<SELECT SIZE=8>
<%
    Do While Not ObjRecordset.EOF
%>

<!-- Create each entry in the list -->
<OPTION><%=objRecordset("pub_name")%></OPTION>

<%
        objRecordset.MoveNext
    Loop
%>
</SELECT>

</BODY>
</HTML>
```

Managing the information in a Recordset object is one of the primary programming tasks in any data-driven Web application. Often a simple query returns many more rows of data than can be reasonably displayed. For example, consider what happens when you use any Internet search engine. The engine accepts a keyword and then returns links to sites with references to the requested topic. Many times, however, there are thousands of Internet sites that contain the requested keyword. Showing all the sites at once on a single Web page is obviously impossible.

The answer to large query-result sets is *paging*. Paging is used by all search engines to return a portion of the query results—say, 10 records at a time—

so that the user can effectively manage the information returned. ADO supports paging through several properties of the Recordset object: PageSize, PageCount, and AbsolutePage.

When you use ADO to retrieve a recordset, you can specify that the records be divided into pages. Setting a value for the PageSize property specifies the number of rows from the recordset that will constitute a page. Then you can determine the total number of pages in a recordset through the PageCount property. Accessing any given page is accomplished with the AbsolutePage property.

Listing 5-8 provides a complete paging example that allows a user to browse records 10 at a time. In this example, a session variable named CurrentPage is used to track the page currently in use. The user can click two hyperlinks to navigate to the previous set or next set of 10 records.

```
<%@ LANGUAGE="VBSCRIPT"%>
<%Response.Expires = 0%>
<HTML>
<HEAD>
<META NAME="GENERATOR" Content="Microsoft Visual InterDev 1.0">
<META HTTP-EQUIV="Content-Type" content="text/html;
    charset=iso-8859-1">
<TITLE>Paging Records</TITLE>
</HEAD>
<BODY>
<%

    ' What page are we on?
    Select Case Request.QueryString("Direction")
        Case ""
            Session("CurrentPage") = 1
        Case "Next"
            Session("CurrentPage") = Session("CurrentPage") + 1
        Case "Previous"
            Session("CurrentPage") = Session("CurrentPage") - 1
    End Select

    ' Constants
    Const adOpenKeyset = 1

    ' Declare variables
    Dim objConnection
    Dim objRecordset
```

Listing 5-8.   *(continued)*
Paging with ADO.

Listing 5-8 *continued*

```
    ' Open database
    Set objConnection = Server.CreateObject("ADODB.Connection")
    objConnection.Open "Biblio", "", ""

    ' Create the SQL statement
    Dim strSQL
    strSQL = strSQL & "SELECT Authors.Author, Titles.Title, "
    strSQL = strSQL & "Publishers.`Company Name` FROM Authors, "
    strSQL = strSQL & "`Title Author`, Titles, Publishers "
    strSQL = strSQL & "WHERE Authors.Au_ID = `Title Author`.Au_ID "
    strSQL = strSQL & "AND `Title Author`.ISBN = Titles.ISBN "
    strSQL = strSQL & "AND (Publishers.`Company Name` LIKE "
    strSQL = strSQL & "'%Microsoft%') ORDER BY Authors.Author"

    ' Create recordset
    Set objRecordset = Server.CreateObject("ADODB.Recordset")
    objRecordset.PageSize = 10
    objRecordset.Open strSQL, objConnection, adOpenKeyset
    objRecordset.AbsolutePage = CLng(Session("CurrentPage"))

    ' Show the results
%>

<P>Page <%=Session("CurrentPage")%> of <%=objRecordset.PageCount%>
</P>

<TABLE BORDER>
        <TR>
        <TH>
        Author
        </TH>
        <TH>
        Title
        </TH>
        <TH>
        Publisher
        </TH>
        </TR>
<%
    Dim i
    For i = 1 To objRecordset.PageSize
%>
```

(continued)

Listing 5-8 *continued*

```
        <TR>
        <TD>
        <%=objRecordset("Author")%>
        </TD>
        <TD>
        <%=objRecordset("Title")%>
        </TD>
        <TD>
        <%=objRecordset("Company Name")%>
        </TD>
        </TR>
<%
        objRecordset.MoveNext
    Next
%>
</TABLE>

<!-- NEXT hyperlink -->
<%If CLng(Session("CurrentPage")) < objRecordset.PageCount Then %>
<P><A HREF="paging.asp?Direction=Next">Next Page</A></P>
<%End If%>

<!-- PREVIOUS hyperlink -->
<%If CLng(Session("CurrentPage")) > 1 Then %>
<P><A HREF="paging.asp?Direction=Prev">Previous Page</A></P>
<%End If%>

<%
    ' Close database
    objRecordset.Close
    objConnection.Close
    Set objRecordset = Nothing
    Set objConnection = Nothing
%>

</BODY>
</HTML>
```

The example utilizes several techniques that are worth discussing. Notice first that the program requires only a single ASP file to accomplish the entire paging process. The same ASP file is called again and again for each page of data. Normally, when a page is called, Internet Explorer provides the page from RAM, if available. In the example, the page will always be in RAM because it is called recursively.

The problem with retrieving a page from RAM, however, is that your query will not be executed unless you run the server-side code. You have to prevent IE 4.0 from using the ASP file already in RAM. To force a return to the server, set the Expires property of the Response object to zero. This code forces a refresh of the file on each request and results in the proper behavior.

Also note that the code runs the same query each time the page is called, changing only the AbsolutePage property. Running the same query over and over might seem wasteful, but it requires far fewer resources than storing large Recordset objects in session variables and trying to persist them across pages. Imagine a site with thousands of users, each with a Recordset object in a session variable. This would quickly eat up server-side resources.

Using ADO, you can perform data access on the server side by using any SQL statement. Queries can be retrieved using SQL server stored procedures or through hard-coded SQL SELECT statements. Updates are performed using SQL UPDATE statements and the Execute method of the Connection object. You can also use ADO on the client side in combination with the Advanced Data Control (ADC), covered in Chapter 4. In fact, the ADC is little more than an ActiveX control wrapper for much of the functionality of ADO. The ADC provides access to many of these features through its Recordset property.

File Access Component

The File Access component allows access to text files on your Web site. The component actually consists of two separate objects: the FileSystem object, which is used to open and close files; and the TextStream object, which is used to read and write.

To open a file for access, first create a FileSystem object with the CreateObject method of the Server object. Once the FileSystem object is instantiated, you can use the CreateTextFile method to create a new file or the OpenTextFile method to open an existing file. In either case, the result is a TextStream object that allows reading or writing. The following code shows how to use the objects to access a file named DATA.TXT:

```
Set objFile = Server.CreateObject("Scripting.FileSystemObject")
Set objStream = objFile.OpenTextFile("DATA.TXT")
```

After the TextStream object is created, you can use any number of available methods to read or write to the file. Keep in mind, however, that a file is usually opened only for reading or writing, not for both simultaneously. This can greatly affect the code in your ASP page, occasionally requiring a file to be opened, closed, and then reopened for different operations.

In addition to simple reading and writing, the File Access component is also useful for creating dynamic content. Try creating a tip-of-the-day effect, which displays a different tip or message on the page each time the page is accessed. Listing 5-9 shows a complete example that provides Visual Basic programming hints. The key to generating tips is to create a text file that has a single line for each tip. The tips are then accessed randomly by using the ReadLine method of the TextStream object. A single line is placed on the page by using the Write method of the Response object.

```
<!DOCTYPE HTML PUBLIC "-//IETF//DTD HTML//EN">
<HTML>

<HEAD>
<META HTTP-EQUIV="Content-Type" content="text/html;
    charset=iso-8859-1">
<META NAME="GENERATOR" content="Microsoft FrontPage 2.0">
<TITLE>VB Tips</TITLE>
</HEAD>

<BODY BGCOLOR="#FFFFFF">
<%

    ' Declare variables
    Dim objFile
    Dim objStream

    ' Open file
    Set objFile = _
        Server.CreateObject("Scripting.FileSystemObject")
    Set objStream = _
        objFile.OpenTextFile(Server.MapPath("/ASP") & _
                        "\Chap05\Listing 5-9\tips.txt")

    Randomize Timer
    intLine = Int(Rnd * 19)
```

Listing 5-9.   *(continued)*
Generating a tip of the day.

Listing 5-9 *continued*

```
    For i = 0 to intLine
        objStream.SkipLine
    Next

    strText = objStream.ReadLine
    objStream.Close
    Set objStream = Nothing
    Set objFile = Nothing

%>
<CENTER><H1>VB Tip of the Day</H1></CENTER>
<%=strText%>

</BODY>
</HTML>
```

Browser Capabilities Component

The Browser Capabilities component identifies the browser that is currently accessing the site and provides programmatic access to the list of features supported by the browser. This component is a tremendous asset to Web developers who are targeting both Internet Explorer and Netscape Navigator. Using this component, you can tailor the Web page to a particular browser.

The Browser Capabilities component relies on the browser's user agent string to identify the browser type. The user agent string (discussed in detail in Chapter 3) is passed by the browser to the server each time a Web page is requested. For example, the user agent string for IE 4.0 looks like this:

Mozilla 4.0 (compatible; MSIE 4.0; Windows 95)

In order to determine the supported features of a particular browser, the Browser Capabilities component attempts to match the browser's user agent string to entries in a special initialization file named BROWSCAP.INI. When the Browser Capabilities component matches a user agent string, all of the features listed for that browser are immediately accessible as properties of the component. Listing 5-10 on the following page shows the portion of BROWSCAP.INI that corresponds to IE 4.0.

```
[Mozilla/4.0 (compatible; MSIE 4.0; Windows 95)]
browser=IE
Version=4.0
majorver=#4
minorver=#0
frames=TRUE
tables=TRUE
cookies=TRUE
backgroundsounds=TRUE
vbscript=TRUE
javascript=TRUE
javaapplets=TRUE
ActiveXControls=TRUE
Win16=False
beta=False
AK=False
SK=False
AOL=False
crawler=False
```

Listing 5-10.
BROWSCAP.INI entry for IE 4.0.

Using the Browser Capabilities component is similar to providing a conditional compilation statement in your ASP page. You can construct simple If...Then statements that greatly affect the final content. For example, Listing 5-11 sends an <OBJECT> tag to a browser that supports ActiveX controls, an <APPLET> tag to a Java-capable browser, or a text message to browsers that have neither feature.

```
<%@ LANGUAGE="VBSCRIPT"%>
<%Response.Expires = 0%>
<HTML>
<HEAD>
<META NAME="GENERATOR" Content="Microsoft Visual InterDev 1.0">
<META HTTP-EQUIV="Content-Type" content="text/html;
    charset=iso-8859-1">
<TITLE>Browser Capabilities</TITLE>
</HEAD>
<BODY>
<CENTER>
```

Listing 5-11.   *(continued)*
Detecting browser capabilities.

Listing 5-11 *continued*

```
<%

    ' Create Browser Capabilities component
    Dim objBrowser
    Set objBrowser = _
        Server.CreateObject("MSWC.BrowserType")

    ' Find out what features are supported
%>
<%
    If objBrowser.ActiveXControls Then
%>

<H1>ActiveX Controls</H1>

<SCRIPT LANGUAGE="VBScript">
<!--

    Sub Window_OnLoad()
        pathBall.Target = objBall.Style
    End Sub

-->
</SCRIPT>

<!-- Structured Graphics control -->
<OBJECT ID="objBall"
    STYLE="POSITION:ABSOLUTE;HEIGHT:70;
        WIDTH:110;TOP:0;LEFT:0;ZINDEX:0"
    CLASSID=
        "CLSID:5FD6A143-372A-11D0-A521-0080C78FEE85">
    <PARAM NAME="Line0001"
        VALUE="SetLineColor(255,255,255)">
    <PARAM NAME="Line0002"
        VALUE="SetFillColor(255,0,0,0,0,255)">
    <PARAM NAME="Line0003"
        VALUE="SetFillSTYLE(1)">
    <PARAM NAME="Line0004"
        VALUE="SetLineSTYLE(1)">
    <PARAM NAME="Line0005"
        VALUE="Oval(0,-25,50,50,0)">
</OBJECT>
```

(continued)

119

Listing 5-11 *continued*

```
<!-- Path control -->
<OBJECT ID="pathBall"
    CLASSID=
        "CLSID:E0E3CC60-6A80-11D0-9B40-00A0C903AA7F">
    <PARAM NAME=AutoStart VALUE=-1>
    <PARAM NAME=XSeries
        VALUE="0,0;30,0;45,0;52,0;55,0">
    <PARAM NAME=YSeries
        VALUE="0,0;30,80;45,160;52,240;55,320">
    <PARAM NAME=EdgeAction VALUE="1">
    <PARAM NAME=TickInterval VALUE=10>
</OBJECT>


<%ElseIf objBrowser.JavaApplets Then%>

<H1>Java Applet</H1>
<APPLET CODE="marquee.class" HEIGHT=40 WIDTH=400>
    <PARAM NAME="CAPTION" VALUE="Java is Cool!">
</APPLET>

<%Else%>

<!-- Text-only browser -->
<H1>No Components Supported!</H1>

<%End If%>
</CENTER>
</BODY>
</HTML>
```

Ad Rotator Component

The Ad Rotator component is designed specifically for sites that are renting advertising space. The component provides a way of controlling the rotation of advertising images in a site. It reads information regarding advertisements from a special text file that directs which ad to show and for how long. Using the Ad Rotator is a simple matter of creating the component and reading the text file. Here is the code:

```
<%
    Dim Ad
    Set Ad = Server.CreateObject("MSWC.AdRotator")
    Response.Write Ad.GetAdvertisement("ADS.TXT")
%>
```

The text file read by the Ad Rotator has a well-defined structure that determines the image to display, specifies the percentage of time to show the image, and provides a hyperlink that is activated when the advertisement is clicked. You simply construct the text file in the appropriate format, and the component does the rest.

Content Linking Component

The Content Linking component is designed for publication of online magazines and newspapers. The component links separate Web pages together, allowing them to be scrolled. Chapter 8 provides a complete project that uses the Content Linking component.

Like the Ad Rotator, the Content Linking component depends on a text file to create the publication. The file, known as the Content Linking List, provides a listing of the linked Web pages and a description of each. Using the Content Linking component simply requires creating the component and reading the associated text file. Here is the code:

```
<%Set objLinker = Server.CreateObject("MSWC.NextLink")%>
```

Once the publication is created, you can use methods such as GetNextURL and GetPreviousURL to navigate the pages. Descriptions of individual pages are retrieved through the GetNextDescription and GetPreviousDescription methods. These values can be used to generate hyperlinks to other pages in the publication. Here is the code:

```
<A HREF="<%=objLinker.GetNextURL%>">
    <%=objLinker.GetNextDescription%>
</A>
```

Using Other ActiveX Components

In addition to using all of the components provided by Visual InterDev, you can create your own ActiveX components for ASP. The project in Chapter 9 features a custom component created with Visual Basic 5.0 to send Internet e-mail.

Once a custom component is created, it can be accessed in the same way as any other component—through the CreateObject method of the Server object. All you have to do is provide the ProgID for the custom component. This feature is a powerful tool that allows you to extend ASP to include any functions you need.

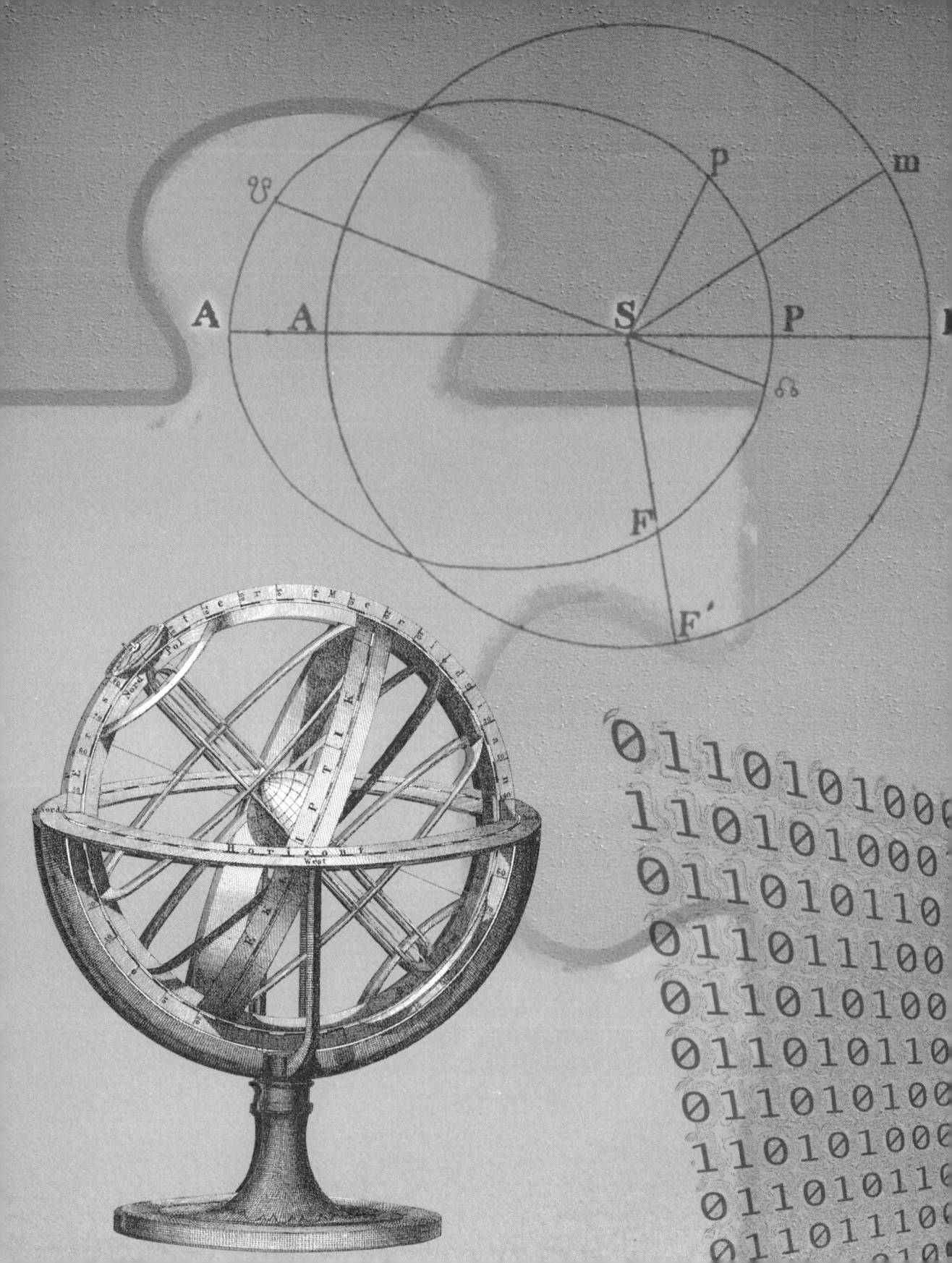

An Online Bookstore

This project creates a virtual bookstore using Microsoft Active Server Pages (ASP) technology. You will construct several pages that advertise books and take orders. The primary component of the project is the Connection component, which uses ActiveX Data Objects (ADO) to access ODBC data sources.

Requirements

1. Microsoft Visual InterDev 1.0

2. Microsoft Internet Information Server 3.0 (or Microsoft Personal Web Server) with Active Server Pages installed

3. Microsoft Internet Explorer 4.0

4. Remote Data Services (RDO) installed on the server

5. Microsoft Agent control

6. Bookstore project files

Completing this exercise depends on the correct setup of the Microsoft Agent control. Although Internet Explorer 4.0 ships with the final version of the Agent control, this exercise was created with the beta 3 version of the control. This means that you should not install the Agent control that ships with IE 4.0, but rather install the beta 3 version from the CD-ROM that accompanies this book.

As an alternative, you can examine the documentation for the IE 4.0 Agent control and determine whether the code in this exercise is acceptable. You might also choose to modify some of the code where appropriate.

Part I: Setting Up a New Web Project

Step 1

To begin a new Web project, start Visual InterDev and choose New from the
File menu. When the New dialog box appears (Figure 6-1), click the Projects
tab and choose the Web Project wizard. Then specify a location for your project
files in the Location box, give your project the name Bookstore, and click OK.

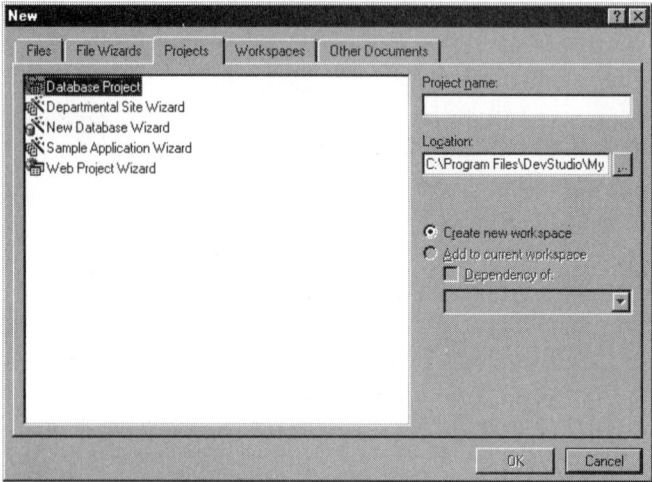

Figure 6-1.
The New dialog box.

The Web Project wizard (Figure 6-2) will ask you for the name of the Web
server on which the new project will be created. If this text box contains an
entry, you can accept it; if the box is empty, type the name of the machine that
is running Internet Information Server (or Personal Web Server). (If you don't
know the correct name of your Web server, look up the Identification information by using the Network applet in the Control Panel.) Click Next.

The Web Project wizard will contact the selected Web server and present
you with the step 2 dialog box. Choose the option Create A New Web. Make
sure the name of the web is Bookstore. Check the option to enable full-text
searching of the site, and click Finish.

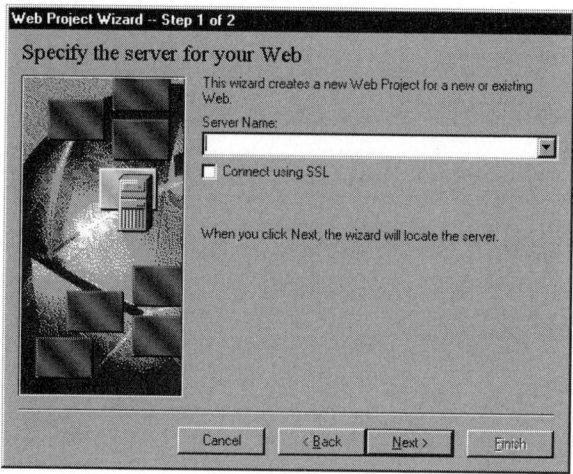

Figure 6-2.
The Web Project wizard.

Key Point

In Visual InterDev parlance, a *web* refers to a set of Web pages that are actually under the control of Internet Information Server. A *project*, on the other hand, is a set of files created and maintained by Visual InterDev.

The Web Project wizard will create your new web and open the project.

Step 2

When the Web Project wizard creates your web, several elements are provided by default. You can examine these files by clicking the FileView tab, which lists files named GLOBAL.ASA and SEARCH.HTM and a directory named IMAGES. These filenames might appear gray because they exist on the Web server but not in your working directory. Select the files in the FileView tab, and then choose Web Project/Get Working Copy from the Project menu to update your working files.

Double-click GLOBAL.ASA. This is a special file that Visual InterDev uses to track the beginning and end of user sessions. Global information regarding data access passwords can also be saved here. Visual InterDev will use this file later to initialize a data connection.

Right-click SEARCH.HTM. Choose Preview In Browser from the pop-up menu. Visual InterDev shows you the Internet Explorer search form, which is used to perform full-text searches of your Web site.

Close the open files by choosing Close All from the Window menu.

Step 3

This project utilizes a Microsoft Access database named BIBLIO.MDB to provide the online database of books, publishers, and authors. This database ships with many Microsoft development tools, including Visual Basic. In order to access this database, you must establish an ODBC data source on your machine.

Minimize Visual InterDev. You will now be working with the ODBC Data Source Administrator to create your new data source. Open the Control Panel by choosing Settings/Control Panel from the Start menu. In the Control Panel, locate the icon labeled ODBC. Double-click this icon to open the ODBC Data Source Administrator (Figure 6-3).

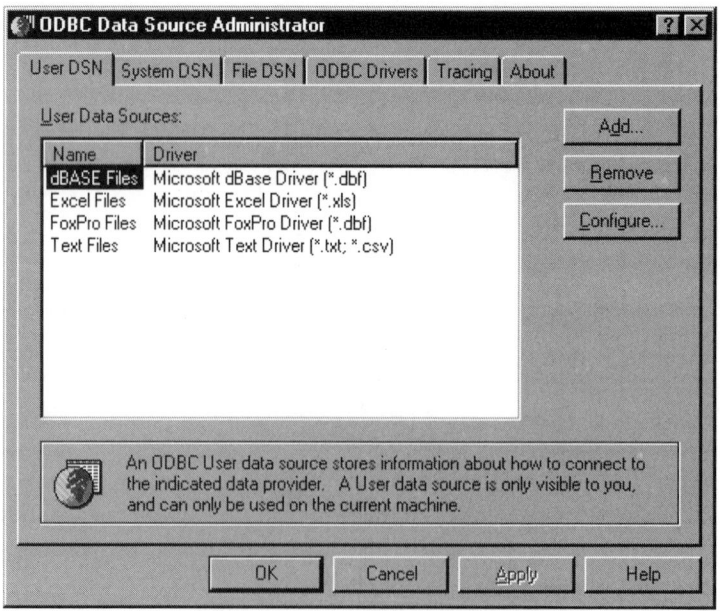

Figure 6-3.
The ODBC Data Source Administrator.

The ODBC Data Source Administrator converts existing databases to ODBC data sources. Data sources that you create for use with Visual InterDev should be System DSN or File DSN sources. Click the System DSN tab, and click the Add button.

In the Create New Data Source dialog box, select Microsoft Access Driver and click Finish. The ODBC Data Source Administrator will display the setup dialog box for Access data sources.

In the Data Source Name text box, type *WebPages* for the data source. This is the ODBC alias you will use to access the database. Click the Select button, and navigate to the file BIBLIO.MDB. (You can find a copy of BIBLIO.MDB in the \CODE\DATABASES directory on the companion CD-ROM.) This will associate the database with the alias WebPages through the ODBC Data Source Administrator. Click OK. The data source is now established, and you can exit the ODBC Data Source Administrator.

Step 4

Maximize Visual InterDev again. Now you will add the data source to your web project. On the FileView tab, click the project title, and then choose Add To Project/Data Connection from the Project menu. When the Select Data Source dialog box appears, click the Machine Data Source tab, select the WebPages data source, and click the OK button.

Visual InterDev will add a new data connection to your web project based on the WebPages data source. This is the database that you will use to display books for sale on the site.

Note that Visual InterDev has added a new tab to your project window, the Data View tab. Click this tab, and you can view the database structure. If you double-click any table, Visual InterDev even allows you to view and edit the data.

Part II: Creating the Home Page

In this part, you will create a home page for the bookstore. Before you begin, however, you must add some graphics files to your site.

Step 1

If you don't already have the Bookstore web open in Visual InterDev, open it now. Click the IMAGES directory, and choose Add To Project/Files from the Project menu. Navigate the \CODE\CHAP06\IMAGES directory on the companion CD-ROM to find the following files, and add them to your project:

BANNER.GIF
HOTLIST.GIF
ORDER.GIF
SEARCH.GIF

Step 2

To add a new Web page to your project, choose New from the File menu. When the New dialog box appears, click the Files tab and then click HTML Page. In the File Name box, type *DEFAULT.HTM*, and click OK. Visual InterDev will automatically add the new Web page to your site.

> ### Key Point
>
> While Internet Information Server is not case sensitive, other servers (UNIX, for example) do distinguish between names such as DE-FAULT.HTM and default.htm.

Step 3

Visual InterDev ships with a special edition of Microsoft FrontPage, a graphical editing tool for creating Web pages. You will use this tool to create a simple home page for the Bookstore site. The page will consist of some text, graphics, and links to other pages.

Right-click DEFAULT.HTM, and choose Open With from the pop-up menu. In the Open With dialog box, open the file with Microsoft FrontPage Editor. FrontPage should present a blank Web page.

Start by adding a banner to the top of the home page welcoming people to the site. In FrontPage, you can add an image to the site by choosing Image from the Insert menu. In the Image dialog box, choose to insert an image by specifying the location of the image in the From Location text box:

/BOOKSTORE/IMAGES/BANNER.GIF

Click the OK button, and the banner will appear on the page. Center the banner by clicking the Center button on the toolbar.

> **WARNING:** Graphics do not always display properly in Microsoft FrontPage, even when you have specified a legitimate file location. This is normally not a problem, and the graphics will appear in the final page under Internet Explorer.

At this point, your home page has a black-and-white image on a gray background—not very attractive. You can easily change the background color by choosing Background from the Format menu. In the Page Properties dialog box, list boxes present color selections for the background and text. Change the background color to white, and click the OK button.

Save your work by choosing Save from the File menu.

Step 4

Start a new line by pressing the Enter key on your keyboard—the same as you would do with any word processor. Left-justify this line by clicking the Left button on the toolbar.

Now add some simple text, and turn the text into a hyperlink. This link will allow the user to access the full-text search capabilities of the site. Type *Search This Site,* highlight all the text you typed, and select the Arial font from the font formatting toolbar. Keep the text highlighted, and add a link to the full-text search page by choosing Hyperlink from the Insert menu. In the Hyperlink dialog box, type *SEARCH.HTM* in the URL text box and click OK. This will link the text to the search page. Save your work.

Your home page should now look like the example in Figure 6-4 on the following page.

Step 5

Right-click the new link you created, and choose Follow Hyperlink from the pop-up menu. The full-text search page that was generated by the Web Project wizard at the beginning of the exercise will be loaded into FrontPage. Using the techniques introduced in this exercise, change the background color of the page to white and customize the generic text to fit the Bookstore home page. Be careful not to change the text boxes or buttons in any way.

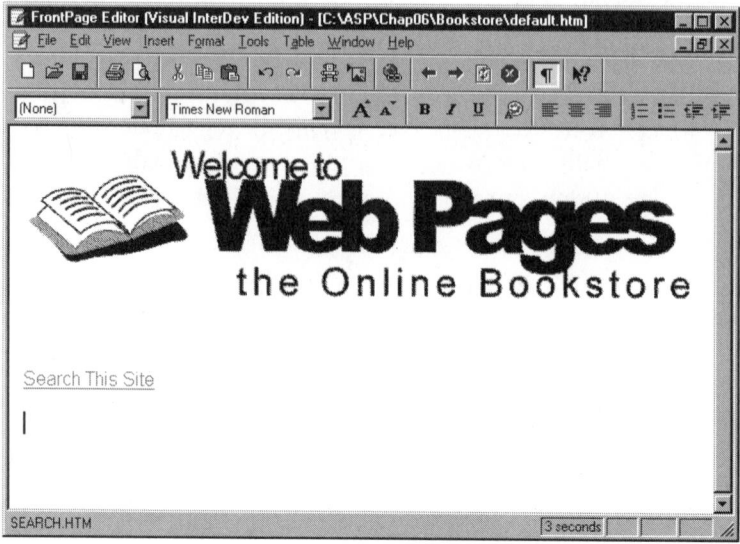

Figure 6-4.
The Bookstore home page.

Step 6

After you save all your changes, close FrontPage Editor and return to Visual InterDev. Browse your new site by selecting DEFAULT.HTM and choosing Preview In Browser from the File menu. Try out the hyperlink and full-text search capabilities.

Part III: Using Dynamic HTML

In this part of the project, you will use Dynamic HTML to create some interesting client-side effects.

Step 1

If you don't already have the Bookstore web project open in Visual InterDev, open it now. Right-click the DEFAULT.HTM file. Choose Open With from the pop-up menu, and open the file with FrontPage Editor. Insert a new line above the hyperlink that connects to the site search page. On this new line, insert a table by choosing Insert Table from the Table menu. In the Insert Table dialog box, set the number of columns to two and the number of rows to two, set the width of the table to 100 percent, and click the OK button.

In the first cell of the table, insert an image by choosing Image from the Insert menu. In the Image dialog box, type the following URL:

```
/BOOKSTORE/IMAGES/HOTLIST.GIF
```

To insert a horizontal dividing line above and below the table, choose Horizontal Line from the Insert menu. Save your work, and exit FrontPage Editor.

Step 2

Return to Visual InterDev, and open DEFAULT.HTM in the text editor. Identify the table that you inserted in FrontPage by locating the following HTML code in the Web page:

```
<TABLE BORDER="0" WIDTH="100%">
    <TR>
        <TD WIDTH="50%"><IMG
        SRC="../Bookstore/images/hotlist.gif" WIDTH="153"
        HEIGHT="48"></TD>
        <TD WIDTH="50%"> </TD>
    </TR>
    <TR>
        <TD WIDTH="50"%> </TD>
        <TD WIDTH="50"%> </TD>
    </TR>
</TABLE>
```

The <TR> tags identify new rows in the table, while the <TD> tags designate cells in the table. You need to break the table at the beginning of the first cell in the second row. In this cell, add a <FONT> tag manually by simply typing in the code. The final result should look like this:

```
<TABLE BORDER="0" WIDTH="100%">
    <TR>
        <TD WIDTH="50%"><IMG
        SRC="../Bookstore/images/hotlist.gif" WIDTH="153"
        HEIGHT="48"></TD>
        <TD WIDTH="50%"> </TD>
    </TR>
    <TR>
        <TD WIDTH="50"%><FONT ID="txtSpecial" COLOR="BLUE" SIZE="4">
        Learn Dynamic HTML</FONT></TD>
        <TD WIDTH="50"%> </TD>
    </TR>
</TABLE>
```

Step 3

In the HEAD section, create a SCRIPT section and add some code that uses Dynamic HTML to draw attention to the specials. Insert the following code between the <SCRIPT> tags:

```
Sub txtSpecial_OnMouseOver()
    txtSpecial.Size = "5"
    txtSpecial.Color = "Red"
End Sub

Sub txtSpecial_OnMouseOut()
    txtSpecial.Size = "4"
    txtSpecial.Color = "Blue"
End Sub
```

Step 4

Save the file, and preview it in the browser by selecting Preview In Browser from the File menu. You should see a monthly special appear below the Hot List image on the page, as shown in Figure 6-5. Now try passing your mouse over the special.

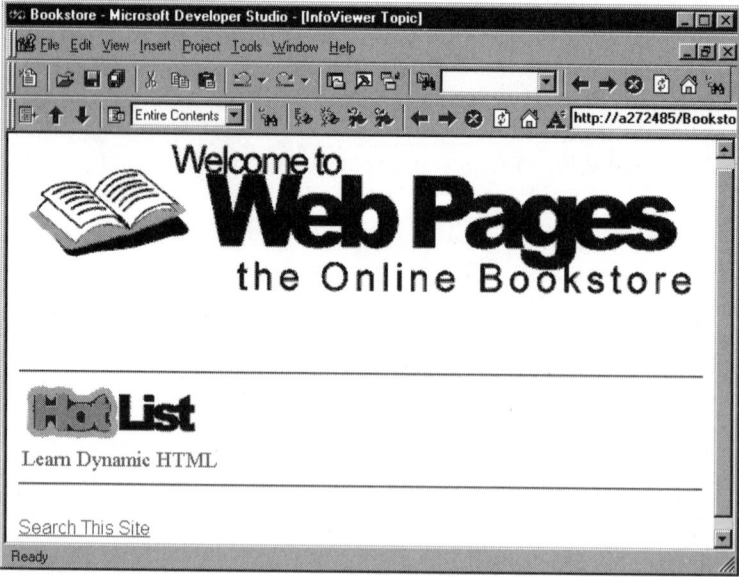

Figure 6-5.
A monthly special.

Step 5

Now that you have generated some Dynamic HTML, use the Window object to create a scrolling message track that appears in the status bar of the Internet Explorer browser. Return to Visual InterDev, and make sure that DEFAULT.HTM is open in the text editor. In the SCRIPT section, add the following code to create a scrolling marquee in the status bar of the browser:

```
' Script-level variables
Public strMessage
Public intSpaces
Public intTimeout

Sub Window_OnLoad()
    ' Initialize the variables when the page
    ' is fully loaded
    strMessage = "Check out this scrolling text!"
    intSpaces = 100
    intTimeout = Window.SetTimeout("Scroll", 100)
End Sub

Sub Scroll()
    ' Call this routine
    ' every 100 milliseconds

    Dim strTemp, i
    strTemp = ""

    ' Scroll right to left
    intSpaces = intSpaces - 1
    If intSpaces = 0 Then intSpaces = 100

    ' Create padding of spaces
    For i = 1 To intSpaces
        strTemp = strTemp & " "
    Next

    ' Write message
    Window.Status = strTemp & strMessage

    ' Reset timer
    intTimeout = Window.SetTimeout("Scroll", 100)
End Sub
```

Step 6

Save your page by choosing Save from the Visual InterDev File menu. Right-click DEFAULT.HTM, and view it with Internet Explorer. You should see the scrolling message on the status bar.

Part IV: Using ActiveX Controls

In this part of the project, you will insert an ActiveX control, the Microsoft Agent, into the DEFAULT.HTM file. The Agent control presents an animated character that can help users navigate your site. In this exercise, the Agent control will provide help in locating and ordering a book.

Step 1

Before you can use the Agent control, you must install it on your machine. Run the setup program provided on the CD-ROM that accompanies this book. Place the control in a directory named C:\PROGRAM FILES\MICROSOFT AGENT. Once installed, the Agent is just like any other ActiveX control you might use.

Step 2

If you don't already have the Bookstore project open, open it now. Open DEFAULT.HTM in the Visual InterDev text editor. Locate the beginning of the Web page body, as indicated by the <BODY> tag. Create a new line below the <BODY> tag, and place your cursor there. This is where you will insert the code to render the Agent.

Insert the Agent control by selecting Into HTML/ActiveX Control from the Insert menu. In the ActiveX Control dialog box, locate the Microsoft Agent control, select the control, and click the OK button. Visual InterDev will display an icon representing the Agent control and a Properties dialog box.

Click the All tab, and examine all the properties of the Agent control. Change its ID property to Wizard. If you were to actually use this control in a Web site, you would also have to set the CodeBase property of the Agent to refer to the location where the files for the ActiveX control were kept. This allows a client browser to download the Agent control automatically if it is not installed on the client's machine. Internet Explorer 4.0 ships with the Agent control, so no CODEBASE attribute is required.

Return to the code by closing the Properties window and the Graphical Layout window. You should see the following code added by Visual InterDev:

```
<OBJECT ID="Wizard" WIDTH=100 HEIGHT=51
    CLASSID="CLSID:F5BE8BD2-7DE6-11D0-91FE-00C04FD701A5">
</OBJECT>
```

The <OBJECT> tag is used to insert an ActiveX control in the Web page. Internet Explorer determines which control to insert based on the CLSID attribute, which is a unique serial number for the requested control. The <OBJECT> tag is sufficient to address the ActiveX control, but the Agent control has no visible interface until you load one of the character files that contain the animations for the Agent.

The Agent character should be loaded when the page is first loaded into the browser. This can be accomplished with the Window_OnLoad event. In the same SCRIPT section where you created the monthly special, add the following code:

```
Sub Window_OnLoad()
End Sub
```

You will load the Agent animation files in the OnLoad event. These files exist as ACS files, which are typically loaded during the setup process for the Microsoft Agent. This exercise assumes that you have installed the Agent in the directory C:\PROGRAM FILES\MICROSOFT AGENT and also assumes that the character files are located in C:\PROGRAM FILES\MICROSOFT AGENT\CHARACTERS. If you have installed the files in a different location, you must modify the code accordingly.

Add the following code to the OnLoad event to load the Agent character:

```
' Initialize the variables when the page
' is fully loaded

' Dimension variables
Dim Agents
Dim AgentPath

' Set variables
Set Agents = Wizard.Characters
AgentPath = "c:\program files\microsoft agent\characters\"

' Load character
Agents.Load "WIZARD", AgentPath & "Merlin.acs"
```

Save your work, and preview DEFAULT.HTM by selecting Preview In Browser from the File menu. The Agent should be visible.

Step 3

Now you can add some functionality to the Agent. The Agent control supports custom commands, which you can assign to the Agent as soon as the entire Web page is loaded. The custom commands are displayed whenever the user right-clicks the Agent. Use the OnLoad event of the Window object to create the custom commands. Here is the code:

```
' Create custom commands
Agents("WIZARD").Commands.Caption = "Custom Commands"

' Name, Caption, Voice Command, Enabled, Visible
Agents("WIZARD").Commands.Add "Search", "Search", "Search", True, True
Agents("WIZARD").Commands.Add "Find Book", "Find Book", "Find Book", _
                             True, True

' Show Agent
Agents("WIZARD").Show
Agents("WIZARD").Play "Surprised"
Agents("WIZARD").Speak "Welcome to WebPages!"
```

Place the following code in the SCRIPT section to hide the Agent when the user exits the current page:

```
Sub Window_OnUnload()
    Wizard.Characters("WIZARD").Hide
End Sub
```

Step 4

When a user right-clicks the Agent and chooses a custom command, the Agent control fires the Command event and the Command event performs the function appropriate to the menu item. In this step of the exercise, you will direct the browser to the SEARCH.HTM page whenever the Search item is selected from the Agent menu. Add the following code to a new SCRIPT section to handle the Command event:

```
<SCRIPT LANGUAGE="VBScript">
<!--

Sub Wizard_Command(UserInput)
    ' Set variables
    Dim Agent
    Set Agent = Wizard.Characters("WIZARD")
```

```
' Go to search page
If UserInput.Voice = "Search" Or UserInput.Name = "Search" Then
    Window.Navigate "search.htm"
End If
End Sub

-->
</SCRIPT>
```

When your program navigates to the search page, the Agent will reappear through the use of an <OBJECT> tag. Although the Agent is actually hiding between pages, it seems to be present throughout the site.

Step 5

Save your work, and open DEFAULT.HTM in Internet Explorer. When the page opens and the Agent becomes visible (Figure 6-6), right-click the Agent and choose Search from the pop-up menu. The Agent navigates to the search page and gives you some instructions. If you have a multimedia computer with a working microphone, try speaking a command to the Agent!

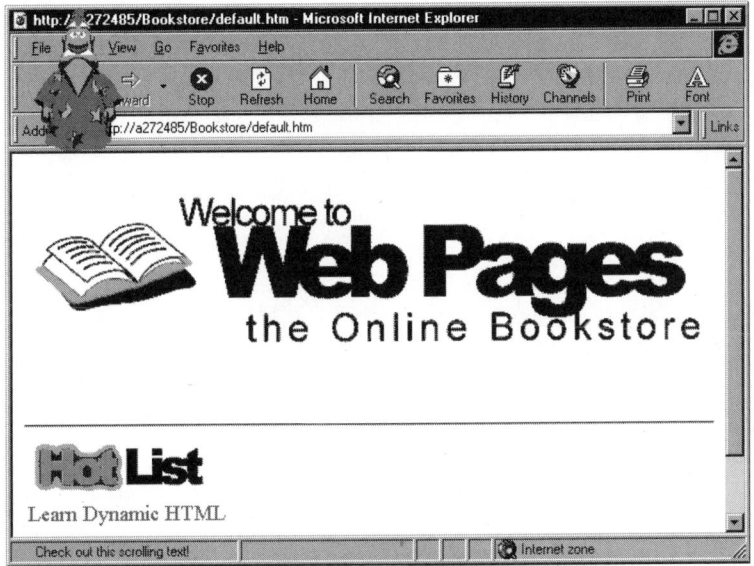

Figure 6-6.
The Agent control.

Step 6

Open SEARCH.HTM in Visual InterDev. You need to add functionality to the Agent, enabling it to respond when a user navigates to the search page either by using the hyperlink on the home page or by commanding the Agent.

Insert the Agent control into SEARCH.HTM just as you did for the home page. Add a SCRIPT section to your code to load the character animations and to take action when the page is loaded. Use the following code:

```
<SCRIPT LANGUAGE="VBScript">
<!--

    Sub Window_OnLoad()
        ' Dimension variables
        Dim Agents
        Dim AgentPath

        ' Set variables
        Set Agents = Wizard.Characters
        AgentPath = "c:\program files\microsoft agent\characters\"

        ' Load character
        Agents.Load "WIZARD", AgentPath & "Merlin.acs"

        ' Show Agent
        Agents("WIZARD").Show

        ' Move Agent
        Agents("WIZARD").MoveTo 0, 0

        ' Give instructions
        Agents("WIZARD").Speak _
            "Use this page to perform full text searches."

        ' Move again
        Agents("WIZARD").MoveTo Window.Screen.Width - 100, 0
    End Sub

    Sub Window_OnUnload()
        Wizard.Characters("WIZARD").Hide
    End Sub

-->
</SCRIPT>
```

Part V: Publishing the Database

In this part of the exercise, you will publish the Bookstore database by allowing a user to search the database for a book by title, author, or publisher. You will build a form on the home page for searching and publish the results on a separate page.

Step 1

If you don't already have the Bookstore project open, open it now. To start building the form, right-click the file DEFAULT.HTM and choose Open With from the pop-up menu. Open the file in Microsoft FrontPage Editor.

In the table where you inserted HOTLIST.GIF, insert the search image into the top cell of the right-hand column by choosing Image from the Insert menu. In the From Location text box, specify this location:

/BOOKSTORE/IMAGES/SEARCH.GIF

To create a bookmark to the new image, select the entire image and choose Bookmark from the Edit menu. Name the new bookmark Find Book. The Agent will use this bookmark later to display the form to the user.

WARNING: When inserting a bookmark for the image, you must be careful to select, or highlight, the entire image. If the image is not completely highlighted, the bookmark menu will be unavailable.

Step 2

In the cell below the search image, build a table to allow searches. Place three text boxes in the cell by choosing Form Field/One-Line Text Box from the Insert menu for each text box. Use text to label the boxes Title, Author, and Publisher, respectively.

To name the controls for the text boxes, right-click each box and choose Form Field Properties from the pop-up menu. In the Text Box Properties dialog box, name the controls txtTitle, txtAuthor, and txtPublisher.

After creating the text boxes, add Submit and Reset buttons to the form by choosing Form Field/Push Button from the Insert menu. Right-click the first button, and choose Form Field Properties from the pop-up menu. Change the value of the button to *Go!* Click OK, and right-click the second button to change its properties. Change the button type for the second button to *Reset.* Click OK, and save your work.

Step 3

Now that the form is created, you need to change the form attributes to submit the form data to your search engine. Right-click the form in the Web page, and choose Form Properties from the pop-up menu. In the Form Properties dialog box, name the form frmLocate. Be sure that the form handler option is set to Custom ISAPI, NSAPI, Or CGI Script, the appropriate setting for sending the form data to an ASP page.

Click the Settings button to change the target for the form. In the Action text box in the Settings For Custom Form Handler dialog box, enter */BOOK-STORE/LOCATE.ASP*, which is the name of the ASP page that will publish the database. You have not yet created LOCATE.ASP, but you will shortly. Click OK in both dialog boxes, and save your work.

Step 4

Leave FrontPage Editor, and return to Visual InterDev. To add a new file, click the project title on the FileView tab and then choose New from the File menu. In the New dialog box, create a new ASP page, name it LOCATE.ASP, and click the OK button.

In the BODY section of LOCATE.ASP, create some VBScript code that runs a query on the database and returns the results to the browser. Start by clicking the Data View tab in the project window. On the tab, double-click the Authors table, which should become visible in the work area of Visual InterDev.

You should also see the Query toolbar floating over the work area. Click the Show Diagram Pane button to view table relationships, and drag the Titles, Publishers, and Title Author tables from the project window to the work area.

These data tools can help create a query by selecting fields and specifying criteria. Start by clearing all the check marks in the tables you dragged to the work area. Next carefully check the Author, Title, and Company Name boxes in the Authors, Titles, and Publishers tables.

Now click the Show SQL Pane button on the Query toolbar to view the resulting SQL statement. The statement should look like this:

```
SELECT Authors.Author, Titles.Title, Publishers.`Company Name`
FROM Authors, `Title Author`, Titles, Publishers
WHERE Authors.Au_ID = `Title Author`.Au_ID AND
`Title Author`.ISBN = Titles.ISBN
```

This SQL statement is not the complete statement, but you can use it as a starting point for modifying your Web page. Add the following code to the BODY section to run the query and format the result:

> NOTE: This SQL statement can be tricky to create. The code is designed to concatenate pieces to produce one complete SQL statement. In this construction, you will find strange characters such as the back accent (`) and the single quote('). Don't confuse the two!

```
<%

Public dbBooks
Public rsBooks
Dim strSQL

' Open a connection to Biblio
Set dbBooks = Server.CreateObject("ADODB.Connection")
dbBooks.Open("WebPages")

' Build SQL statement
strSQL = "SELECT Authors.Author, Titles.Title, Publishers.`Company Name` "
strSQL = strSQL & "FROM Authors, `Title Author`, Titles, Publishers "
strSQL = strSQL & "WHERE (Authors.Au_ID = `Title Author`.Au_ID AND "
strSQL = strSQL & "`Title Author`.ISBN = Titles.ISBN AND "
strSQL = strSQL & "Titles.PubID = Publishers.PubID)"

If Request.Form("txtTitle") <> "" Then
    strSQL = strSQL & " AND Title LIKE '%" & Request.Form("txtTitle") & "%'"
End If

If Request.Form("txtAuthor") <> "" Then
    strSQL = strSQL & " AND Author LIKE '%" & _
        Request.Form("txtAuthor") & "%'"
End If

If Request.Form("txtPublisher") <> "" Then
    strSQL = strSQL & " AND `Company Name` LIKE '%" & _
        Request.Form("txtPublisher") & "%'"
End If

' Run the query
Set rsBooks = Server.CreateObject("ADODB.Recordset")
rsBooks.Open strSQL, dbBooks, 3
%>

<!-- Build the results table -->
<%
If rsBooks.BOF And rsBooks.EOF Then%>
    <H2><CENTER>Sorry, no results! Please try again!</CENTER></H2>
```

(continued)

141

continued

```
<%Else
    ' Populate the cursor
    rsBooks.MoveLast
    rsBooks.MoveFirst
End If

If rsBooks.RecordCount > 200 Then%>
    <H2><CENTER>
    Sorry, too many results. Please narrow your search
    </CENTER></H2>
<%Else%>
    <%If Not rsBooks.BOF Then%>
    <H2>Here are the results of your search:</H2>

    <TABLE BORDER>
        <TR>
        <TH>
        Author
        </TH>
        <TH>
        Title
        </TH>
        <TH>
        Publisher
        </TH>
        </TR>
    <%
    Do While Not rsBooks.EOF
    %>
        <TR>
        <TD>
        <%=rsBooks("Author")%>
        </TD>
        <TD>
        <A
    HREF=
    "/Chapter7/OrderForm.asp?Title=<%=Server.URLEncode(rsBooks("Title"))%>">
        <%=rsBooks("Title")%>
        </A>
        </TD>
        <TD>
        <%=rsBooks("Company Name")%>
        </TD>
        </TR>
    <%
```

```
        rsBooks.MoveNext
    Loop
    %>
    </TABLE>

    <%End If%>
<%End If%>

<%
' Close database
rsBooks.Close
dbBooks.Close
Set rsBooks = Nothing
Set dbBooks = Nothing
%>
```

> NOTE: Normally you would expect such an application to present result sets as pages containing sets of 10 or 20. While ADO supports paging, not all ODBC drivers do. In particular, the Access drivers used in this exercise do not support paging.

Step 5

Save your work, and run the project in Internet Explorer. Test the search form to see whether results are returned properly.

Step 6

Now add a new menu command that will automatically submit the search form for the user. Close LOCATE.ASP, and open DEFAULT.HTM in Visual InterDev Editor. Locate the Window_OnLoad event where you described the commands that the Agent would perform. Add a new command named Find Book by using the Add method of the Commands object. The following code shows the complete Window_OnLoad event for the Agent:

```
Sub Window_OnLoad()
    ' Initialize
    ' the variables when the page
    ' is fully loaded

    ' Scrolling status
    strMessage = "Welcome to Web Pages!!"
    intSpaces = 100
    intTimeout = Window.SetTimeout("Scroll", 100)
```

(continued)

continued

```
' Dimension variables
Dim Agents
Dim AgentPath

' Set variables
Set Agents = Wizard.Characters
AgentPath = "c:\program files\microsoft agent\characters\"

' Load character
Agents.Load "WIZARD", AgentPath & "Merlin.acs"

' Create custom commands
Agents("WIZARD").Commands.Caption = "Custom Commands"

' Name, Caption, Voice Command, Enabled, Visible
Agents("WIZARD").Commands.Add "Search", "Search", "Search", _
    True, True
Agents("WIZARD").Commands.Add "Find Book", "Find Book", _
    "Find Book", True, True

' Show Agent
Agents("WIZARD").Show
Agents("WIZARD").Play "Surprised"
Agents("WIZARD").Speak "Welcome to WebPages!"
End Sub
```

Step 7

When a user chooses the Find Book command, the Agent should explain how to use the search form to locate a book. This is accomplished through the Wizard_Command event, which moves the Agent and explains the form. Code for the Wizard_Command event should look like this:

```
Sub Wizard_Command(UserInput)
    ' Set variables
    Dim Agent
    Set Agent = Wizard.Characters("WIZARD")

    ' Go to search page
    If UserInput.Voice = "Search" Or _
       UserInput.Name = "Search" Then
         Window.Navigate "search.htm"
    End If
```

```
    ' Explain book search
    If UserInput.Voice = "Find Book" Or _
       UserInput.Name = "Find Book" Then
       Window.Navigate "#Find Book"

       ' Move Agent
       Agent.MoveTo Window.Screen.Width - 100,
                    Window.Screen.Height - 100

       ' Point to form
       Agent.GestureAt Int(Window.Screen.Width / 2),
                       Int(Window.Screen.Height / 2)

       ' Give instructions
       Agent.Speak "Use this form to find a book."

       ' Move again
       Agent.MoveTo 0, 0
    End If
End Sub
```

Step 8

Save your work, and run the Web site in Internet Explorer. Test the search form and the Agent functions.

Part VI: Taking the Order

In this part of the project, you will take book orders over the network by simply recording orders in a text file. If you were creating a real-life Web site, you would want to provide a secure mechanism for taking orders, but this exercise gives you experience in using the text file components of Visual InterDev.

Step 1

If you don't already have the Bookstore project open in Visual InterDev, open it now. Add a new HTML file to your project by clicking the project title and choosing New from the File menu. In the New dialog box, insert a new ASP page, name the page ORDERFORM.ASP, and click the OK button.

Right-click ORDERFORM.ASP on the FileView tab, and choose Open With from the pop-up menu. In the Open With dialog box, open the file with Microsoft FrontPage Editor. You will use FrontPage to design an order form for the Web site.

Right-click the page, and choose Page Properties from the pop-up menu. Use the dialog box to change the background of the page to white.

Step 2

Build the order form by adding form elements through the Form Field items on the Insert menu. Use the following elements:

Control Type	Control Name
One-Line TextBox	txtName
One-Line TextBox	txtAddress1
One-Line TextBox	txtAddress2
One-Line TextBox	txtCity
One-Line TextBox	txtState
One-Line TextBox	txtZip
One-Line TextBox	txtCreditCard
Scrolling TextBox	txtBookTitle
Push Button	cmdSubmit
Push Button	cmdReset

Insert each of the elements into ORDERFORM.ASP by choosing Form Field from the Insert menu. Change the name of each element by right-clicking the element and typing in the name from the table above. For the Scrolling TextBox, set Rows to 2 and Columns to 20. Change the button properties for cmdSubmit and cmdReset to Submit and Reset.

Step 3

Add an image to the top of the page by choosing Image from the Insert menu. In the From Location text box, type the following location:

```
/BOOKSTORE/IMAGES/ORDER.GIF
```

Right-click the form, and choose Form Properties from the pop-up menu. In the Form Properties dialog box, set Form Handler to Custom ISAPI, NSAPI, Or CGI Script. Click the Settings button, and enter ORDER.ASP in the Action text box. Click the OK button in both dialog boxes.

Save the page, and close FrontPage Editor.

Step 4

Open ORDERFORM.ASP in Visual InterDev. You need to add some server-side VBScript to automatically place the name of the ordered book in the form. Locate the <TEXTAREA> tag, which holds the book title, and insert the following code:

```
<P><TEXTAREA NAME="txtBookTitle" ROWS="2" COLS="20">
    <%=Request.QueryString("Title")%>
    </TEXTAREA> Book Title </P>
```

In Visual InterDev, choose New from the File menu. In the New dialog box, add a new ASP page, name the page ORDER.ASP, and click OK.

This page will acknowledge receipt of the order and print it in a text file. Use the text components of Visual InterDev to write instructions for the page. In the BODY section of ORDER.ASP, add the following code:

```
<H2><CENTER>Thanks for your order!</CENTER></H2>

<%
Dim objFile
Dim objStream

' Open ORDER.TXT for writing

Set objFile = Server.CreateObject("Scripting.FileSystemObject")
Set objStream = objFile.OpenTextFile(Server.MapPath ("/Bookstore") + _
                                "\order.txt", 8, True)


objStream.WriteLine Request.Form("txtName")
objStream.WriteLine Request.Form("txtAddress1")
objStream.WriteLine Request.Form("txtAddress2")
objStream.WriteLine Request.Form("txtCity")
objStream.WriteLine Request.Form("txtState")
objStream.WriteLine Request.Form("txtZip")
objStream.WriteLine Request.Form("txtCreditCard")
objStream.WriteLine Request.Form("txtBookTitle")

objStream.Close
Set objStream = Nothing
Set objFile = Nothing

%>
```

Step 5

Save your work, and test the order form by previewing ORDER.HTM in the Visual InterDev environment.

Step 6

Write your own code to add a hyperlink from the body of DEFAULT.HTM to ORDER.HTM. Add new commands to the Agent so that the Agent can take a user to the order form from the home page.

Save your work, and run the site. Test all the pieces.

Something to Try on Your Own

Locate the simple Dynamic HTML on the Hot List. Change this code to become an anchor tag that will fill in the search form with information from the database when the user specifies a particular title.

An Online Catalog

This project creates an online catalog named *The Home Page,* an imaginary store that offers household goods for purchase on the Web. With a few small exceptions, this project is designed completely with client-side technologies, including Dynamic HTML and current-record data binding.

Requirements

1. Microsoft Visual InterDev 1.0
2. Microsoft Internet Information Server 3.0 or later (or Microsoft Personal Web Server) with Active Server Pages installed
3. Microsoft Internet Explorer 4.0
4. Remote Data Services installed on the server
5. Catalog project files

This project makes extensive use of Remote Data Services (RDS) for accessing ODBC data sources on the Web server. You must have RDS installed on the Windows NT server where you have installed Internet Information Server. The server portion of RDS is included on the CD-ROM that accompanies this book. The client portion of RDS (known as the Advanced Data Control) ships with Internet Explorer 4.0 and does not require any additional installation.

This project was created using the Preview 2 version of IE 4.0. As a result, some parts of the exercise might require minor modifications to accommodate the final release of IE 4.0. In particular, you should be careful to note the CLSID attributes of the <OBJECT> tags in the code. Quite often CLSID attributes change between the preview and final release of a product. In most cases, any required changes should be minor.

The database used by the online catalog can also be found on the CD-ROM that accompanies this book. It is named HOME.MDB and is a Microsoft Access database. You will need to copy this file to the server where your RDS components can access the data. Later in the project, you will set up an ODBC data source for the database.

Part I: Setting Up a New Web Project

Step 1

To begin a new Web project, start Visual InterDev. Choose New from the File menu. When the New dialog box appears (Figure 7-1), click the Projects tab and choose the Web Project wizard. Specify a location for your project files in the Location text box, give your project the name Catalog, and click OK.

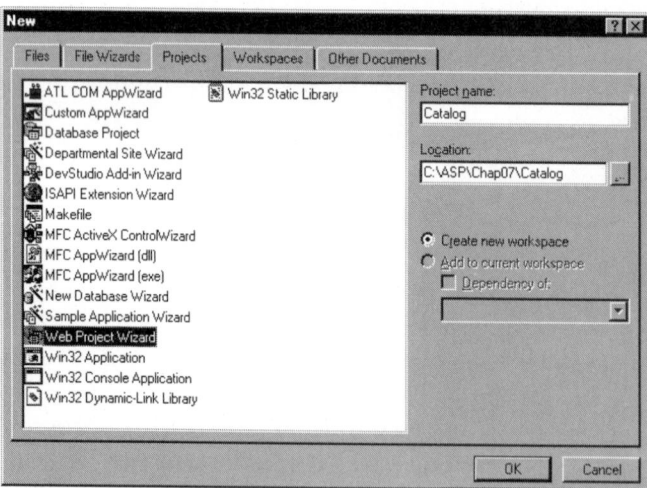

Figure 7-1.
The New dialog box.

The Web Project wizard will ask you for the name of the Web server on which the new project will be created. If this text box contains an entry, you can accept it; if the box is empty, type the name of the machine that is running

Internet Information Server (or Personal Web Server). (If you don't know the correct name of your Web server, look up the Identification information by using the Network applet in the Control Panel.) Click Next.

The Web Project wizard (Figure 7-2) will contact the selected Web server and present the step 2 dialog box. Choose the option Create A New Web. Make sure the name of the web is Catalog. Check the option to enable full-text searching of the site. Click Finish. The Web Project wizard will create your new web and open the project.

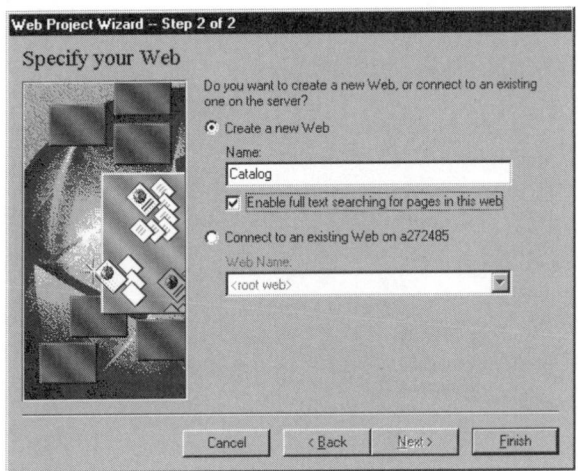

Figure 7-2.
The Web Project wizard.

Step 2

When the Web Project wizard creates your project, several elements are provided by default. You can examine these elements by clicking the FileView tab, which lists files named GLOBAL.ASA and SEARCH.HTM and a directory named IMAGES. These filenames might appear gray because they exist on the Web server but not in your working directory. Choose Web Project/Get Working Copy from the Project menu to update your working files.

Double-click GLOBAL.ASA. This is a special file that Visual InterDev uses to track the beginning and end of user sessions. Visual InterDev will use this file later to initialize a data connection.

Step 3

This project utilizes a Microsoft Access database named HOME.MDB to provide the online database of catalog items. In order to access this database, you must establish an ODBC data source on your machine.

Minimize Visual InterDev. You will now be working with the ODBC Data Source Administrator (Figure 7-3) to create your new data source. Open the Control Panel by choosing Settings/Control Panel from the Start menu. Locate the icon labeled ODBC. Double-click this icon to open the ODBC Data Source Administrator.

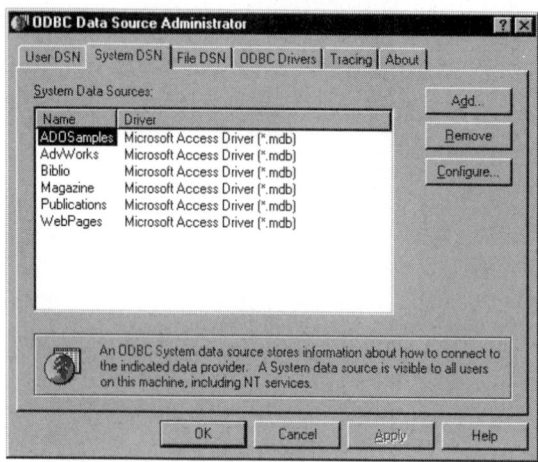

Figure 7-3.
The ODBC Data Source Administrator.

The ODBC Data Source Administrator creates ODBC data sources from existing databases. Data sources that you use with Visual InterDev must be System DSN or File DSN sources. Click the System DSN tab, and then click the Add button.

In the Create New Data Source dialog box, select Microsoft Access Driver and click Finish. The ODBC Data Source Administrator will display the setup dialog box for Access data sources.

In the Data Source Name text box, type *HomePage*. This is the ODBC alias you will use to access the database. Click the Select button, and locate the file HOME.MDB. This will associate the database with the ODBC alias HomePage. Click OK. The data source is now established, and you can exit the ODBC Data Source Administrator.

Step 4

Maximize Visual InterDev again. Now you will add the data source to your Web project. On the FileView tab, click the project title and choose Add To Project/ Data Connection from the Project menu. When the Select Data Source dialog box appears, click the Machine Data Source tab, choose the HomePage data source, and click OK. Visual InterDev will add a new data connection to your Web project based on the HomePage data source. This is the database that you will use to display items for sale on the site.

Note that Visual Interdev has added a new tab to your project window, the Data View tab. Click this tab to view the database structure. The database contains three tables—Categories, Products, and Orders—which store all the data for the online catalog.

Double-click the Categories table. The table, shown in Figure 7-4, consists of three fields: CategoryID, CategoryName, and CategoryDescription. Each category will appear on the home page. If you want to add or remove categories, you can simply change the data by using the Visual InterDev data tools, and all changes will be reflected immediately on the home page. You need not rewrite the Web site.

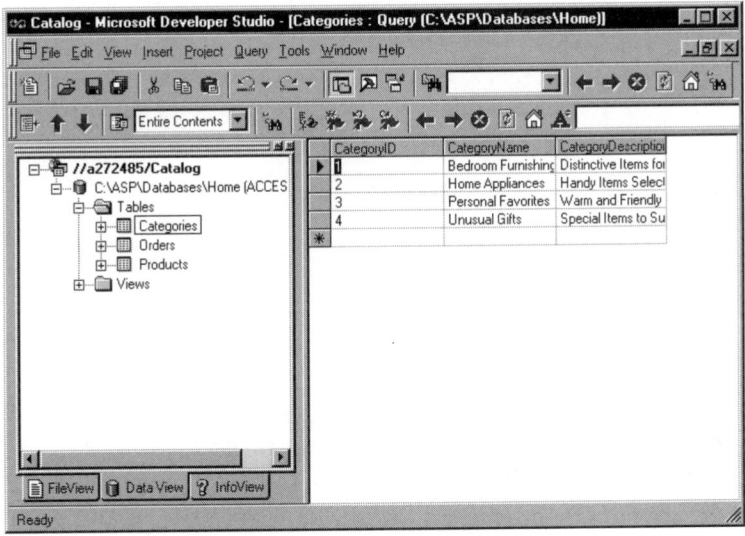

Figure 7-4.
The Categories table.

Double-click the Products table, which stores all the product information for the catalog categories. The Products table, shown in Figure 7-5, contains the following fields: ProductID, CategoryID, ProductName, ProductDescription, ProductPrice, and ProductImage. Any single product is associated with a category through the CategoryID field. You can easily add a new product to the database by entering new information and associating it with an existing CategoryID.

The ProductImage field holds the Uniform Resource Locator (URL) for the image of the product. Normally, an image is downloaded rather than stored in the database directly. The site uses the ProductImage data to dynamically load an <IMG> tag with an image.

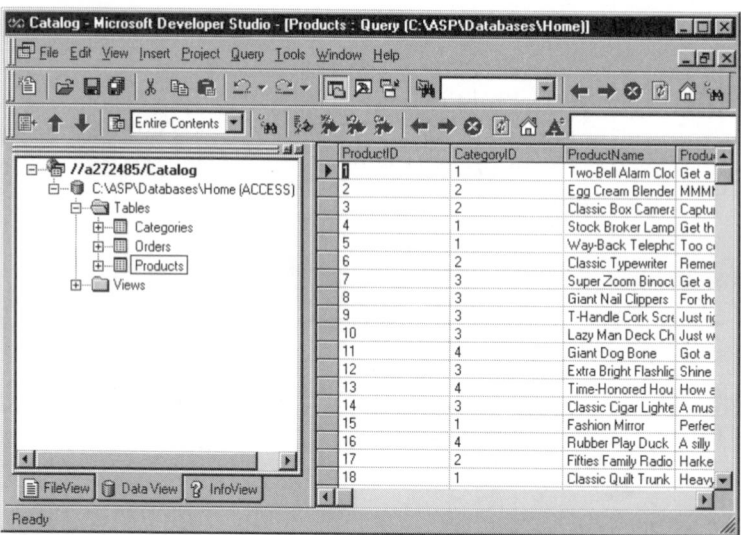

Figure 7-5.
The Products table.

Double-click the Orders table, which is used to capture order information from customers. (See Figure 7-6.) In this project, you will build an order form that populates the database with a new record for each order. You can then examine the contents to fill orders.

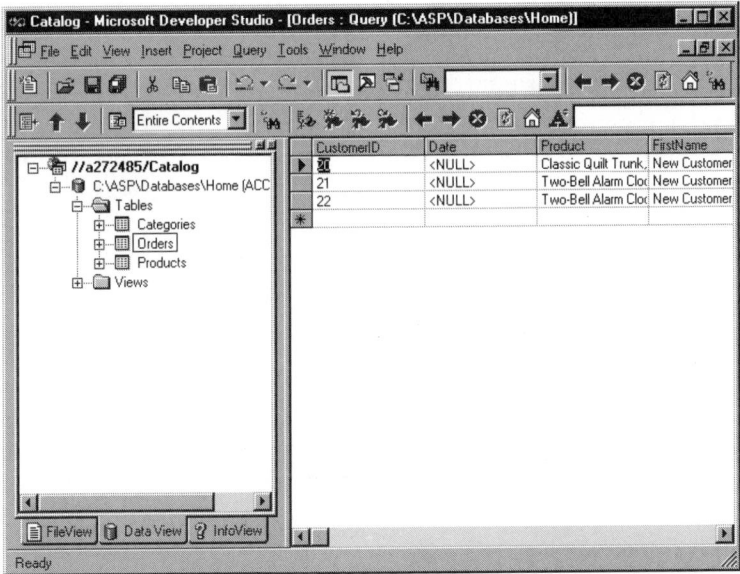

Figure 7-6.
The Orders table.

Part II: Creating the Home Page

In this part, you will create a home page for the catalog. Before you begin, however, you need to add some graphics files to your site.

Step 1

If you don't already have the Catalog web open in Visual InterDev, open it now. On the FileView tab, click the IMAGES directory and then choose Add To Project/Files from the Project menu. Add the project images from the \CODE\CHAP07\CATALOG\IMAGES directory on the CD-ROM that accompanies this book.

Step 2

Choose New from the File menu. When the New dialog box appears, click the Files tab and select HTML Page. In the File Name text box, type *DEFAULT.HTM*, and click OK. Visual InterDev will automatically add a new Web page to your site.

Step 3

Right-click the file DEFAULT.HTM in the project window. Choose Open With from the pop-up menu. In the Open With dialog box, open the file with Microsoft FrontPage Editor (Visual InterDev Edition).

In FrontPage, choose Background from the Format menu. In the Page Properties dialog box, specify white as the background color for the page and click OK.

To insert a page banner into the document, choose Image from the Insert menu. In the Image dialog box, add the new image by specifying its location. Use the following virtual directory:

```
/CATALOG/IMAGES/BANNER.JPG
```

Hit the return key once to start a new line, and insert a horizontal rule by choosing Horizontal Line from the Insert menu. Save your page in FrontPage, and return to Visual InterDev.

Step 4

In the following steps, you will use the Advanced Data Control (ADC) to build a list of product categories. The categories are kept in the database, so changes to the database will automatically update the Web page.

To begin, open DEFAULT.HTM in the text editor in Visual InterDev. In DEFAULT.HTM, locate the horizontal rule (<HR>) tag that you inserted in FrontPage. Make some space below this tag, and add the ADC to the page by inserting the following code:

```
<!-- The Advanced Data Control -->
<OBJECT ID="datCategories" HEIGHT=10 WIDTH=10
    CLASSID="CLSID:BD96C556-65A3-11D0-983A-00C04FC29E33">
    <PARAM NAME="SQL" VALUE="SELECT * FROM Categories">
    <PARAM NAME="SERVER" VALUE=[your site name]>
    <PARAM NAME="CONNECT" VALUE="DSN=HomePage">
</OBJECT>
```

WARNING: The CLASSID attribute might be different for your version of the Advanced Data Control. Check it carefully.

Step 5

Once the ADC is added, you can use it to retrieve category names, which will be placed in a special division of the Web page reserved only for categories.

Create this division with the <DIV> tag. Add the following code to the BODY section of DEFAULT.HTM, just below the <OBJECT> tag that you added for the ADC:

```
<!-- The category list is built in this division -->
<SPAN ID="divCategories"
STYLE="position:absolute;left:50;top:200;width:300;height:300;">
</SPAN>
```

Step 6

The category division will be populated in the Window_OnLoad event handler. In the code's HEAD section, create a SCRIPT section and add code for the Window_OnLoad event. Create a Range object that points to the <SPAN> tag where the categories should be inserted. Then use the PasteHTML method of the Range object to paste records from the database into the division. Here is the code:

```
<SCRIPT LANGUAGE="VBScript">
<!--

Sub Window_OnLoad
    ' ** Create the product categories **
    ' Variables
    Dim rngCategories
    Dim objRecordset
    Dim strID
    Dim strCategory
    Dim strStyle

    ' Create the Range object for
    ' adding new categories
    Set rngCategories = Document.Body.CreateTextRange()
    rngCategories.MoveToElementText(divCategories)
    If rngCategories.Text <> "" Then Exit Sub

    ' Add the categories to the Range object
    Set objRecordset = datCategories.Recordset

objRecordset.MoveFirst
Do While Not objRecordset.EOF

    ' Get category name and ID
    strCategory = objRecordset("CategoryName")
    strID = objRecordset("CategoryID")MMM
```

(continued)

continued

```
' Paste in new HTML
strStyle = "STYLE=font-style:normal; " & _
    "background-color:transparent; font-size:20;>"

rngCategories.PasteHTML _
    "<P><FONT " & "ID='Category" & Trim(strID) & _
    "' FACE=Verdana COLOR=Blue " & strStyle _
    & strCategory & "</FONT></P>"

        ' Move to next record
        objRecordset.MoveNext
    Loop
End Sub

-->
</SCRIPT>
```

Step 7

Save the page, and preview it to verify that the categories are visible. Your page should look like the one shown in Figure 7-7.

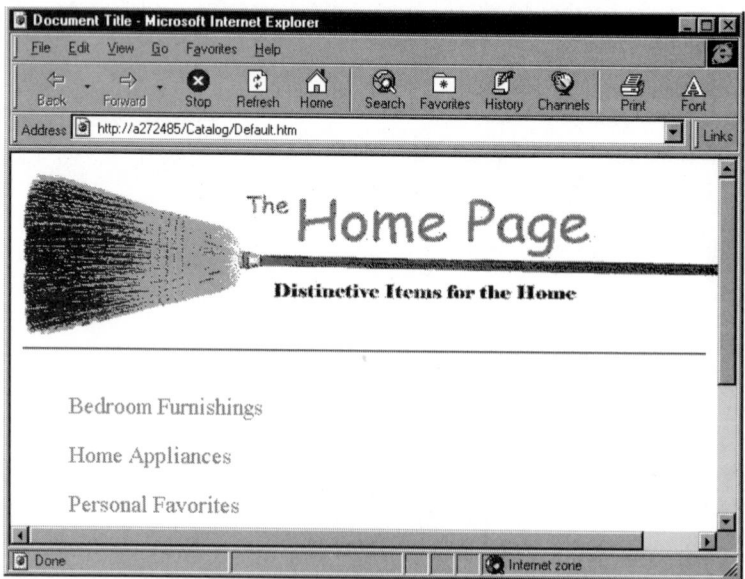

Figure 7-7.
Displaying categories.

Step 8

Now that you have the categories listed, you will want to display a description of each category when the mouse passes over its name. In order to accomplish this, create a second division in the page and write the category descriptions as hidden HTML text in the new division. Use Dynamic HTML to display a description when the mouse passes over its category title.

Begin by adding the following division below the first division:

```
<!-- The category descriptions are shown here -->
<SPAN ID="divDescriptions"
STYLE="position:absolute;left:350;top:200;width:300;height:300;">
</SPAN>
```

Because the category descriptions are part of the database, you must add them to the new division dynamically at run time. The descriptions are added in the same manner as the category names—by using a Range object. Add the following code to the Window_OnLoad event, after the code that generates the category listings:

```
' ** Create the category descriptions **

' Variables
Dim rngDescriptions
Dim strDescription

' Create the style
strStyle = "STYLE=position:container; left:0; top:0; " & _
    "visibility:hidden; font-size:16;"

' Create the Range object
Set rngDescriptions = Document.Body.CreateTextRange()
rngDescriptions.MoveToElementText(divDescriptions)
If rngDescriptions.Text <> "" Then Exit Sub

' Add the descriptions to the division
objRecordset.MoveFirst
Do While Not objRecordset.EOF
    ' Get description and ID
    strDescription = objRecordset("CategoryDescription")
    strID = objRecordset("CategoryID")
```

(continued)

continued

```
' Paste in new HTML
    rngDescriptions.PasteHTML _
    "<P><FONT FACE='Viner Hand ITC' COLOR=Purple ID='Text" _
    & Trim(strID) & "' " & strStyle & ">" & strDescription _
    & "</FONT></P>"

    'Move to next record
    objRecordset.MoveNext
Loop
```

Step 9

When the descriptions are added to the page, they are invisible. The Visibility argument of the STYLE attribute is set to hidden. You will use the OnMouse-Over and OnMouseOut events to display each description at the appropriate time—that is, when the mouse passes over its catalog name. Place the event handlers in the same SCRIPT section you used for the Window_OnLoad event, and write them at the SPAN level, which will trap all events from the items in the division. When the OnMouseOver or OnMouseOut event of the division fires, the SrcElement property will determine exactly which category received the event and will fire the transition to show the text:

```
Sub divCategories_OnMouseOver()
    ' Mouse passes over a category

    Dim objEvent
    Dim strTarget

    On Error Resume Next

    ' Get the target element
    Set objEvent = Window.Event
    strTarget = objEvent.SrcElement.ID

    If strTarget <> "divCategories" Then

        ' Change the category attributes
        objEvent.SrcElement.Style.FontStyle = "italic"
        objEvent.SrcElement.Color = "Black"

        ' Show the category description
        Select Case strTarget
```

```
                Case "Category1"
                    Text1.Style.Visibility = "visible"
                Case "Category2"
                    Text2.Style.Visibility = "visible"
                Case "Category3"
                    Text3.Style.Visibility = "visible"
                Case "Category4"
                    Text4.Style.Visibility = "visible"
            End Select
        End If
End Sub

Sub divCategories_OnMouseOut()
    ' Mouse leaves a category

    Dim objEvent
    Dim strTarget

    On Error Resume Next

    ' Get the target element
    Set objEvent = Window.Event
    strTarget = objEvent.SrcElement.ID

    If strTarget <> "divCategories" Then
        ' Change the category to normal
        objEvent.SrcElement.Style.FontStyle = "normal"
        objEvent.SrcElement.Color = "Blue"

        ' Hide the description
        Select Case strTarget
            Case "Category1"
                Text1.Style.Visibility = "hidden"
            Case "Category2"
                Text2.Style.Visibility = "hidden"
            Case "Category3"
                Text3.Style.Visibility = "hidden"
            Case "Category4"
                Text4.Style.Visibility = "hidden"
        End Select
    End If
End Sub
```

Step 10

Save your work, and view the page in Internet Explorer. You should now see the categories and descriptions. The result should look like the page shown in Figure 7-8.

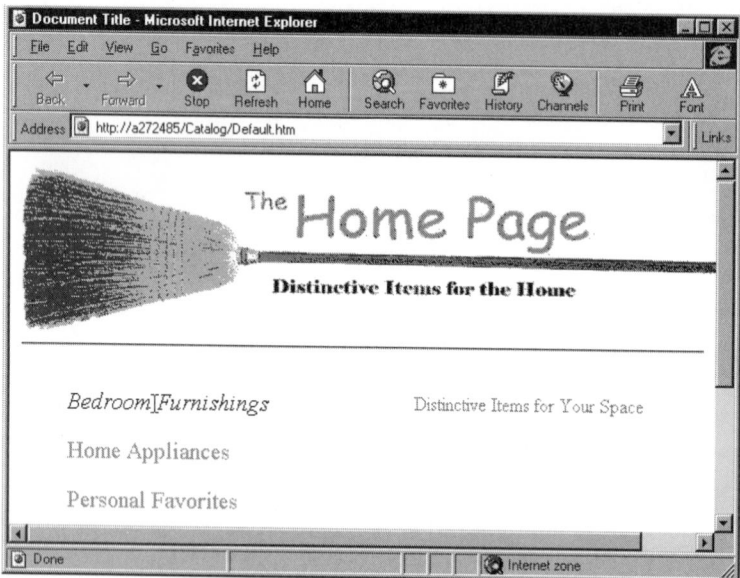

Figure 7-8.
Displaying category descriptions.

Part III: Browsing the Catalog

In this part, you will create the Web page that displays the catalog items for the selected category. The display includes photos and text descriptions of the catalog items.

Step 1

If you don't already have the Catalog project open, open it now. Open the file DEFAULT.HTM. Add the code on the facing page to the SCRIPT section of the page to trap the OnClick event for a category. When a user clicks a category, your program will display a page featuring the items in that category.

```
Sub divCategories_OnClick()
    ' User selects a category

    ' Variables
    Dim objEvent
    Dim strTarget
    Dim strQuery

    On Error Resume Next

    ' Get target element
    Set objEvent = Window.Event
    strTarget = objEvent.SrcElement.ID

    ' Build query string
    If strTarget <> "divCategories" Then
        ' Build target URL
        Select Case strTarget
            Case "Category1"
                strQuery = "catalog.asp?Category=1"
            Case "Category2"
                strQuery = "catalog.asp?Category=2"
            Case "Category3"
                strQuery = "catalog.asp?Category=3"
            Case "Category4"
                strQuery = "catalog.asp?Category=4"
        End Select
    End If

    ' Navigate to the new page
    Window.Navigate strQuery
End Sub
```

Save the Web page, and close it.

Step 2

Choose New from the File menu. In the New dialog box, add an ASP page to the project, name the page CATALOG.ASP, and click OK. This is the only piece of the project that depends on server-side functionality. You will use the server side only for receiving the submitted category identifier from the home page.

Step 3

The CATALOG.ASP page is used to view all the items in a particular category. The items for the category are retrieved by using the ADC. The query run by the ADC is based on the category that received the click on the home page. Add the following lines to the BODY section of the code to insert the ADC in the page:

```
<!-- The Advanced Data Control -->
<OBJECT ID="datItems"
    CLASSID="CLSID:BD96C556-65A3-11D0-983A-00C04FC29E33"
    ALIGN="baseline" BORDER="0" WIDTH="10" HEIGHT="10">
    <PARAM NAME="SQL" VALUE=
    "SELECT * FROM Products WHERE CategoryID=<%=Request.QueryString("Category")%>">
    <PARAM NAME="SERVER" VALUE="[your site name]">
    <PARAM NAME="CONNECT" VALUE="DSN=HomePage">
</OBJECT>
```

> **WARNING:** This project was written using Preview 2 of Internet Explorer 4.0 and Remote Data Services. Verify that the CLSID for the Advanced Data Control has not changed. This can be done by selecting Into HTML/ActiveX Control from the Visual InterDev Insert menu and inserting the ADC into the Web page.

Step 4

Close CATALOG.ASP in Visual InterDev, and right-click it on the FileView tab in the project window. Choose Open With from the pop-up menu. In the Open With dialog box, open the file by using Microsoft FrontPage Editor.

In FrontPage Editor, choose Background from the Format menu. Set the page background color to white, and click OK.

Step 5

The navigation toolbar for this page will be a set of four pushbuttons in a table. To create the table, move to a new line in the page and choose Insert Table from the Table menu. In the Insert Table dialog box, select one row and four columns, set the table width to 100 percent, and click OK. Save your work, and return to Visual InterDev.

Open CATALOG.ASP in the text editor of Visual InterDev, and locate the table that you just inserted in the page. Use the <INPUT> tag to add a pushbutton to each of the four cells in the table. Here is the code:

```
<TABLE BORDER="0" WIDTH="100%">
    <TR>
        <TD WIDTH="25%">
        <INPUT TYPE="BUTTON" NAME="BtnBack"  VALUE="BACK">
        </TD>
        <TD WIDTH="25%">
        <INPUT TYPE="BUTTON" NAME="BtnNext"  VALUE="NEXT">
        </TD>
        <TD WIDTH="25%">
        <INPUT TYPE="BUTTON" NAME="BtnOrder" VALUE="ORDER">
        </TD>
        <TD WIDTH="25%">
        <INPUT TYPE="BUTTON" NAME="BtnHome"  VALUE="HOME">
        </TD>
    </TR>
</TABLE>
```

Step 6

Your page will use Dynamic HTML to display product information as the user browses the catalog. Add the following lines to the BODY section of the code to insert two product information text areas in the page:

```
<CENTER>
<P>
<!-- The item name -->
<SPAN ID="ItemName" STYLE="font-family:verdana; font-size:20;">
</SPAN>
</P>

<P>
<!-- The item description -->
<SPAN ID="ItemDescription" STYLE="font-family:verdana; font-size:12;">
</SPAN>
</P>
</CENTER>
```

Step 7

Each item description should be accompanied by a photo. To display a photo of any item in the catalog, insert an <IMG> tag between the two <SPAN> tags in the code. Here is the code for the image:

```
<!-- The item photo -->
<P><IMG ID="imgItem" SRC=""></P>
```

Step 8

You must also add some code to the page to display the information from the database. You want to show the first item in the category when the page is first loaded. You can accomplish this by creating a Window_OnLoad event in the HEAD section. Here is the code:

```
<SCRIPT LANGUAGE="VBScript">
<!--

    Sub Window_OnLoad()
        DisplayData
    End Sub

    Sub DisplayData()
        ' Variables
        Dim objRecordset
        Dim objTextRange

        ' Get objects
        Set objRecordset = datItems.Recordset

        ' Display item name
        ItemName.InnerText =
            objRecordSet("ProductName").Value & ", $" & _
            objRecordset("ProductPrice").Value

        ' Display item GIF
        imgItem.src = "/Catalog/Images/" & _
            objRecordset("ProductImage").Value

        ' Display item description
        ItemDescription.InnerText = _
            objRecordset("ProductDescription").Value & ""
    End Sub

-->
</SCRIPT>
```

Step 9

Next provide code for operating the navigation toolbar you created in step 5. This code accesses the Recordset object of the Advanced Data Control to move between the records. (The Advanced Data Control can bind to elements in a

Web page, and you will often use it for this. Chapter 4 contains examples of binding the ADC. However, in this project, you do not want to bind data; you want to use script code to read the data out and present it in a different way. The Recordset object provides a means for accessing data in the ADC when it is not functioning as a bound control.)

The Recordset object used in the ADC is closely related to the ActiveX Data Objects (ADO) used in Active Server Pages. Methods associated with ADO Recordsets can also be used with the ADC Recordset object. This allows navigation through the familiar MoveFirst, MoveLast, MoveNext, and MovePrevious methods. Accessing any individual field in the current record is done by referencing the field name in parentheses—for example, MyRecordset ("MyField").

Add the following SCRIPT section to your code so that users will be able to browse the database:

```
<SCRIPT LANGUAGE="VBScript">
<!--

    Sub btnNext_OnClick
        ' Move to next item
        datItems.Recordset.MoveNext

        If datItems.Recordset.EOF Then
            datItems.Recordset.MoveLast
        Else
            DisplayData
        End If
    End Sub

    Sub btnBack_OnClick
        ' Move to previous item
        datItems.Recordset.MovePrevious

        If datItems.Recordset.BOF Then
            datItems.Recordset.MoveFirst
        Else
            DisplayData
        End If
    End Sub
```

(continued)

continued

```
Sub btnHome_OnClick
    ' Go home
    Window.Navigate "/Catalog/default.htm"
End Sub

Sub btnOrder_OnClick
    'Go to order page
    Window.Navigate "/Catalog/orders.asp?Product=" & _
        lblName.Caption
End Sub
```

```
-->
</SCRIPT>
```

Step 10

Save your work, and test the catalog browsing features. Your Web page should look like the one in Figure 7-9.

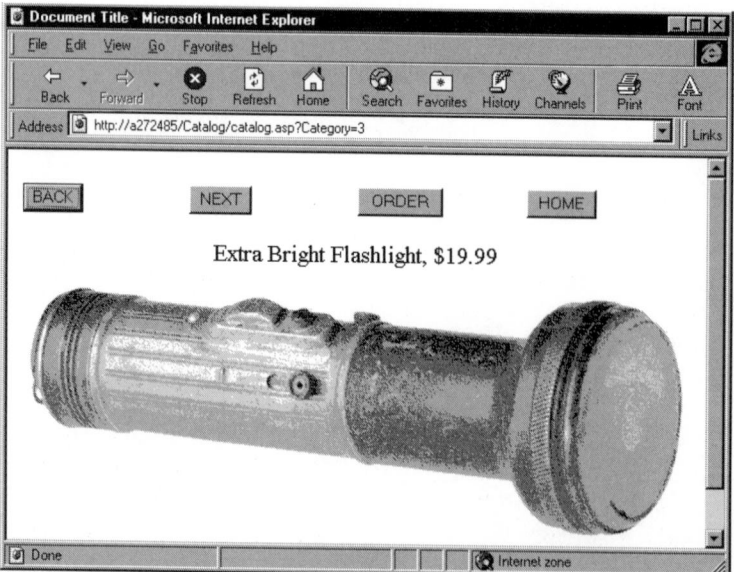

Figure 7-9.
Browsing the catalog.

Part IV: Taking Orders

In this part, you will take orders from the catalog and write them to a database by using the ADC.

Step 1

Open the Catalog project. To add a new Web page for taking product orders, choose New from the File menu. In the New dialog box, add a new ASP page, name the page ORDERS.ASP, and click OK.

Step 2

Right-click the file ORDERS.ASP in the project window, and choose Open With from the menu. In the Open With dialog box, open the file with Microsoft FrontPage Editor. Change the page's background color to white by selecting Background from the Format menu.

To insert a banner into the page, choose Image from the Insert menu. In the Image dialog box, insert the image from the following location:

`/CATALOG/IMAGES/ORDER.JPG`

Insert a horizontal rule below the image by choosing Horizontal Line from the Insert menu.

Step 3

To insert a table for the orders, choose Insert Table from the Table menu. In the Insert Table dialog box, create a table with 2 columns and 10 rows. In the first column, add text to the cells to identify the fields in the table as Date, Product, First Name, Last Name, Address1, Address2, City, State, and Zip.

Step 4

Save your work, and return to Visual InterDev. Open ORDERS.ASP in the Visual InterDev text editor. Identify the table that you inserted in FrontPage Editor, and modify the table to add text boxes and a pushbutton to the page. The finished form should look like the one pictured in Figure 7-10 on page 172. The code is shown on the following pages.

```
<TABLE BORDER="0">
    <TR>
        <TD>
        <FONT FACE="Verdana"><STRONG>Date</STRONG></FONT>
        </TD>
        <TD>
        <INPUT DATASRC="#datOrders" DATAFLD="Date" NAME="txtDate">
        </TD>
    </TR>
    <TR>
        <TD>
        <FONT FACE="Verdana"><STRONG>Product</STRONG></FONT>
        </TD>
        <TD>
        <INPUT DATASRC="#datOrders" DATAFLD="Product"
            NAME="txtProduct">
        </TD>
    </TR>
    <TR>
        <TD>
        <FONT FACE="Verdana"><STRONG>First Name</STRONG></FONT>
        </TD>
        <TD>
        <INPUT DATASRC="#datOrders" DATAFLD="FirstName"
            NAME="txtFirstName">
        </TD>
    </TR>
    <TR>
        <TD>
        <FONT FACE="Verdana"><STRONG>Last Name</STRONG></FONT>
        </TD>
        <TD>
        <INPUT DATASRC="#datOrders" DATAFLD="LastName"
            NAME="txtLastName">
        </TD>
    </TR>
    <TR>
        <TD>
        <FONT FACE="Verdana"><STRONG>Address1</STRONG></FONT>
        </TD>
        <TD>
        <INPUT DATASRC="#datOrders" DATAFLD="Address1"
            NAME="txtAddress1">
        </TD>
    </TR>
```

```
    <TR>
        <TD>
        <FONT FACE="Verdana"><STRONG>Address2</STRONG></FONT> 
        </TD>
        <TD>
        <INPUT DATASRC="#datOrders" DATAFLD="Address2"
            NAME="txtAddress2">
        </TD>
    </TR>
    <TR>
        <TD>
        <FONT FACE="Verdana"><STRONG>City</STRONG></FONT>
        </TD>
        <TD>
        <INPUT DATASRC="#datOrders" DATAFLD="City" NAME="txtCity">
        </TD>
    </TR>
    <TR>
        <TD>
        <FONT FACE="Verdana"><STRONG>State</STRONG></FONT>
        </TD>
        <TD>
        <INPUT DATASRC="#datOrders" DATAFLD="State" NAME="txtState">
        </TD>
    </TR>
    <TR>
        <TD>
        <FONT FACE="Verdana"><STRONG>Zip</STRONG></FONT>
        </TD>
        <TD>
        <INPUT DATASRC="#datOrders" DATAFLD="Zip" NAME="txtZip">
        </TD>
    </TR>
    <TR>
        <TD>
        <FONT FACE="Verdana"><STRONG></STRONG></FONT> 
        </TD>
        <TD>
        <INPUT TYPE="BUTTON" NAME="cmdOrder" VALUE="Order!">
        </TD>
    </TR>
</TABLE>
```

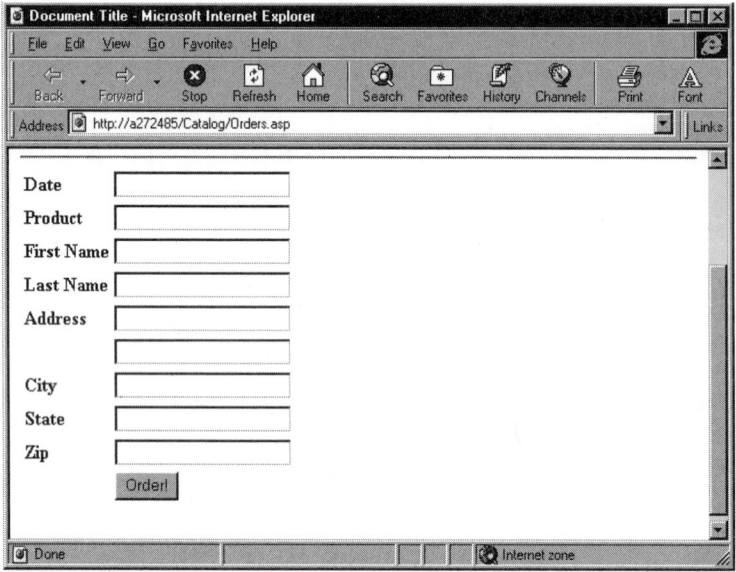

Figure 7-10.
The Orders form.

Step 5

The table you created will be filled by the ADC, which will read the Orders table from the database and store the new order information. Add the following lines to the BODY section of your code to connect to the database:

```
<!-- The Advanced Data Control -->
<OBJECT ID="datOrders"
    CLASSID="CLSID:BD96C556-65A3-11D0-983A-00C04FC29E33"
    ALIGN="baseline" BORDER="0" WIDTH="50" HEIGHT="50">
    <PARAM NAME="Connect" VALUE ="DSN=HomePage">
    <PARAM NAME ="Server" VALUE ="[your Web server]">
    <PARAM NAME ="SQL"
        VALUE="SELECT * FROM Orders WHERE FirstName='New Customer'">
</OBJECT>
```

Step 6

Although the ADC can handle recordsets on the client, it cannot add new records to the database. You will have to rely on the ActiveX Data Objects (ADO) to add new records. (You can still use the ADC to update entries.) Add the following lines to the HEAD section of your code to generate a new record:

```
<%

' Add a new blank record to the database
Set db = Server.CreateObject("ADODB.Connection")
db.Open "HomePage"

' Create SQL
strSQL = "INSERT INTO Orders (FirstName, Product) VALUES " & _
    "('New Customer','" & Request.QueryString("Product") & "')"

db.Execute strSQL

%>
```

Step 7

When all the data is filled in, you will want to save the new order in the database. However, before you allow the data to be saved, you should validate the values in the text fields. Add the following SCRIPT section to your code to perform the data validation:

```
<SCRIPT LANGUAGE="VBScript">
<!--

    Function Validate()
        Validate = True

        ' Validate date
        If Not IsDate(txtDate.Value) Then
            MsgBox "Invalid date!"
            Validate = False
        End If

        ' Validate text fields
        If txtProduct = "" Or _
            txtFirstName = "" Or _
            txtLastName = "" Or _
            txtAddress1 = "" Or _
            txtCity = "" Or _
            txtState = "" Or _
            txtZip = "" Then
            MsgBox "Please fill in all fields!"
            Validate = False
        End If
    End Function

-->
</SCRIPT>
```

Step 8

After the data has been validated, it can be saved in the database. To save the data, use the OnClick event of the cmdOrder button. Here is the code:

```
Sub cmdOrder_OnClick()
    ' Validate the data
    If Not Validate Then Exit Sub

    ' Submit the form to the Orders table
    datOrders.SubmitChanges

    ' Thank the customer
    MsgBox "Thanks for your order!"

    ' Move to the home page
    Window.Navigate "default.htm"
End Sub
```

Step 9

Save your work, and view the site in Internet Explorer 4.0.

Something to Try on Your Own

When a customer places an order, your Web page displays a message box as confirmation. Try changing the confirmation to show some Dynamic HTML on the ORDERS.ASP page. You will need to add some HTML to the page to affect the display when the order is made. Try using the Visibility argument of the STYLE attribute to show and hide the confirmation.

CHAPTER EIGHT

An Online Magazine

This project creates an online magazine using the Content Linking component of Microsoft Active Server Pages (ASP). The Content Linking component allows you to treat a series of Web pages as a linked set of pages in a magazine, newspaper, or book. You will also use a database to provide the content to the site dynamically, rather than hard-coding each new page.

Requirements

1. Microsoft Visual InterDev 1.0

2. Microsoft Internet Information Server 3.0 (or Microsoft Personal Web Server) with Active Server Pages installed

3. Microsoft Internet Explorer 4.0

4. Magazine project files

Part I: Setting Up a New Web Project

Step 1

To begin a new web project, start Visual InterDev. Choose New from the File menu. When the New dialog box appears (Figure 8-1), click the Projects tab and select the Web Project wizard. Then specify a location for your project files in the Location box, give your project the name Magazine, and click OK.

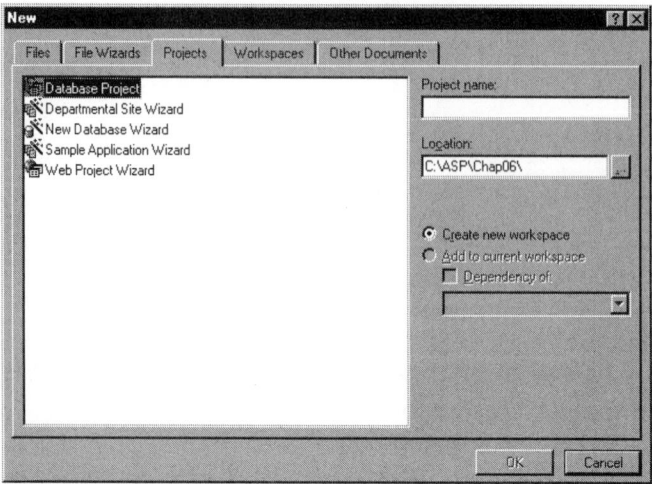

Figure 8-1.
The New dialog box.

The Web Project wizard (Figure 8-2) will ask you for the name of the Web server on which the new project will be created. If this text box contains an entry, you can accept it; if the box is empty, type the name of the machine that is running Internet Information Server (or Personal Web Server). (If you don't know the correct name of your Web server, look up the Identification information by using the Network applet in the Control Panel.) Click Next.

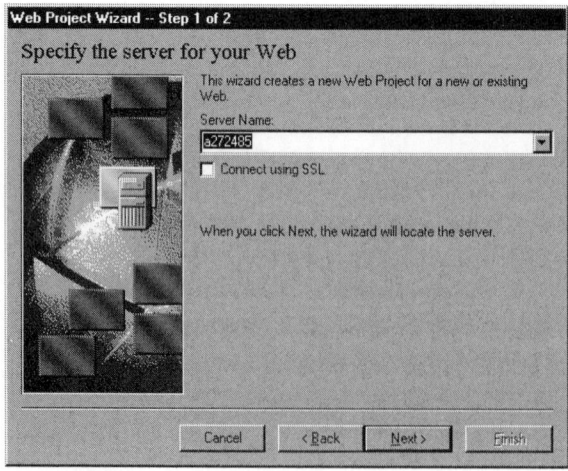

Figure 8-2.
The Web Project wizard.

The Web Project wizard will contact the selected Web server and present you with the step 2 dialog box. Choose the option Create A New Web. Make sure the name of the web is Magazine. Do *not* check the option to enable full-text searching of the site, because you will create this page yourself later. Click Finish. The Web Project wizard will create your new web and open the project.

Step 2

This project utilizes a Microsoft Access database named MAGAZINE.MDB to provide the online database of articles. In order to access this database, you must establish an ODBC data source on your machine. Set up the ODBC data source in the ODBC Data Source Administrator, and name the source Magazine.

Step 3

Return to Visual InterDev. Now you will add the data source to your web project. On the FileView tab, click the project title and then choose Add To Project/ Data Connection from the Project menu. When the Select Data Source dialog box appears, click the Machine Data Source tab, select the Magazine data source, and click the OK button. Visual InterDev will add a new data connection to your web project based on the Magazine data source.

When the Magazine data source is added to your project, Visual InterDev places a Data View tab in the project window. Click this tab to view the Magazine database structure. In the Tables folder, you will see that the Magazine data source consists of an Articles table and a Sections table. Articles contains information about the articles in the magazine, while Sections contains the actual text. Editing the magazine is a simple matter of changing entries in these database tables.

When you double-click the Articles table, Visual InterDev displays the table in the working area. The Articles table consists of the fields ArticleID, ArticleTitle, ArticleSubTitle, and ArticleNote. These fields are used to generate the table of contents for the site. (See Figure 8-3 on the following page.)

The Sections table stores the detail for each article. Every article has one or more sections, and each section has text contained in a binary field. The magazine pages are constructed using this text. (See Figure 8-4 on the following page.)

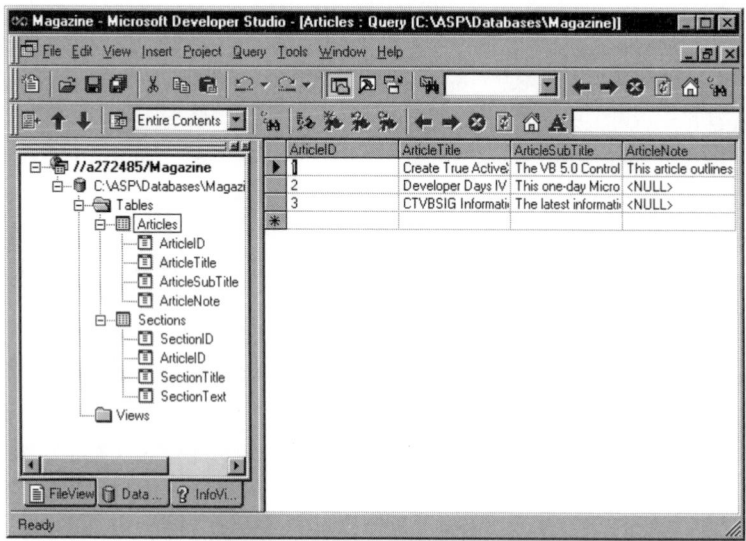

Figure 8-3.

The Articles table.

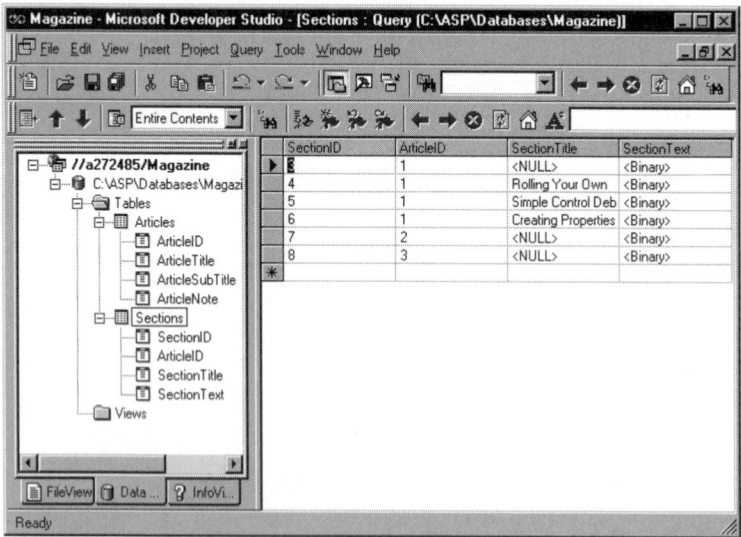

Figure 8-4.

The Sections table.

Part II: Creating the Home Page

In this part, you will create a home page for the magazine. Before you begin, however, you must add some graphics files to your site.

Step 1

If you don't already have the Magazine web open in Visual InterDev, open it now. On the FileView tab, click the IMAGES directory and choose Add To Project/Files from the Project menu. Copy the image files for this project to your site.

Step 2

To add a new Web page to your project, choose New from the File menu. When the New dialog box appears, click the Files tab and click Active Server Page. In the File Name text box, type *DEFAULT.ASP*, and click OK. Visual InterDev will automatically add the new Web page to your site.

Step 3

Close DEFAULT.ASP in Visual InterDev, and open it again by right-clicking the file on the FileView tab. Choose Open With from the pop-up menu. In the Open With dialog box, open DEFAULT.ASP with Microsoft FrontPage Editor (Visual InterDev Edition).

In FrontPage Editor, choose Background from the Format menu. In the Page Properties dialog box, change the page background color to white and then click OK.

To insert a page banner, choose Image from the Insert menu. In the Insert dialog box, add the new image by specifying its location:

```
/MAGAZINE/IMAGES/BANNER.GIF
```

Insert a horizontal rule below the banner by choosing Horizontal Line from the Insert menu. Save your work, and return to Visual InterDev.

Part III: Creating a Site Style Sheet

This project uses the Magazine data source to provide all the content for the magazine. The content is stored in the database, but the formatting is not. Formatting information in the database is limited to simple paragraph delineation using the <P> tag. The style for your magazine site will be generated using a linked style sheet.

The style sheet for the site defines styles for the header and paragraph tags, which are used for different sections of a magazine article. Articles on the site use the following tags:

Article Section	Associated HTML Tag
Article Title	<H1>
Article Subtitle	<H4>
Section Title	<H2>
Section Text	<P>

Step 1

If you don't already have the Magazine project open in Visual InterDev, open it now.

To add a new file to the site, choose New from the File menu. In the New dialog box, add a new text file, name it MAGAZINE.CSS, and click OK. This is the file for the linked style sheet. Define the styles by adding the following code to MAGAZINE.CSS:

```
BODY {
        margin-left:10px;
        font:12pt/14pt "Garamond";
        color:black;
        text-align:left;
        background:transparent;
        }

P {
        margin-left:10px;
        font:12pt/14pt "Garamond";
        color:black;
        text-align:left;
        background:transparent;
        }

H1 {
        margin-left:10px;
        font:18pt/20pt "Arial Black";
        color:black;
        text-align:left;
        background:transparent;
        }
```

```
H2 {
        margin-left:10px;
        font:12pt/14pt "Arial Black";
        color:black;
        text-align:left;
        background:gray;
        }

H3 {
        margin-left:10px;
        font:12pt/14pt "Garamond";
        color:black;
        text-align:left;
        background:transparent;
        }

H4 {
        margin-left:10px;
        font:14pt/16pt "Garamond";
        font-style:italic
        color:black;
        text-align:left;
        background:transparent;
        }
```

Step 2

Save MAGAZINE.CSS, and open DEFAULT.ASP in Visual InterDev. Attach the newly created style sheet to DEFAULT.ASP by adding the following code to the HEAD section of the page:

```
<LINK REL=STYLESHEET HREF="Magazine.css">
```

Part IV: Linking the Content

Now that you have the home page started and the style sheet defined, you are ready to use the Content Linking component to create the magazine. The Content Linking component relies on a text file that describes the Web pages contained in the online publication. These pages can be hard-coded HTML documents that you want to link together, or they can be ASP pages that generate your content dynamically. In this project, you will use the Magazine data source to generate ASP pages for your magazine content. The data source uses query string arguments to specify which article will be displayed.

Step 1

If you don't already have the Magazine project open, open it. Choose New from the File menu. In the New dialog box, add a text file and name the file MAGAZINE.TXT. This is the content linking text file, and the entries in the file are the Uniform Resource Locators (URLs) of the pages you want linked. In this project, the URL will always be the same (since content is generated by ASP), but you will pass different arguments to designate the articles. Add the following entries to MAGAZINE.TXT to set up the links:

```
/Magazine/Content.asp?ArticleID=1    Create ActiveX Controls
/Magazine/Content.asp?ArticleID=2    Developer Days Information
/Magazine/Content.asp?ArticleID=3    CTVBSIG Information
```

Save MAGAZINE.TXT, and return to DEFAULT.ASP.

Step 2

You need to produce a table of contents for the magazine. This table will appear on the home page and will be generated using the content linking text file. The Content Linking component gives you several methods for returning the contents of the text file, enabling you to find out how many entries are in the file and to access them one at a time. When you read each item, you will dynamically generate a hyperlink to the appropriate document and display the hyperlink in a table. Add the following code to the BODY section of DEFAULT.ASP, just below the <HR> tag you inserted earlier:

```
<%
' Variables
Dim objLinker
Dim i

' Create Content Linking component
Set objLinker = Server.CreateObject("MSWC.NextLink")
%>

<!-- Generate table of contents
from Content Linking list -->
<H1>Table of Contents</H1>
```

```
<TABLE>
<%
For i = 1 to objLinker.GetListCount("Magazine.txt")
%>
    <TR>
        <TD><IMG SRC="/Chapter8/Images/Bullet.gif"></TD>
        <TD><H3><A HREF="<%=objLinker.GetNthURL("Magazine.txt", i)%>">
        <%=objLinker.GetNthDescription("Magazine.txt", i)%></A></H3>
        </TD>
    </TR>
<%Next%>
</TABLE>
```

Step 3

Save your work, and preview DEFAULT.ASP in Internet Explorer by selecting Browse With from the File menu. In the Browse With dialog box, choose Internet Explorer. You should see the table of contents displayed on the home page, as shown in Figure 8-5.

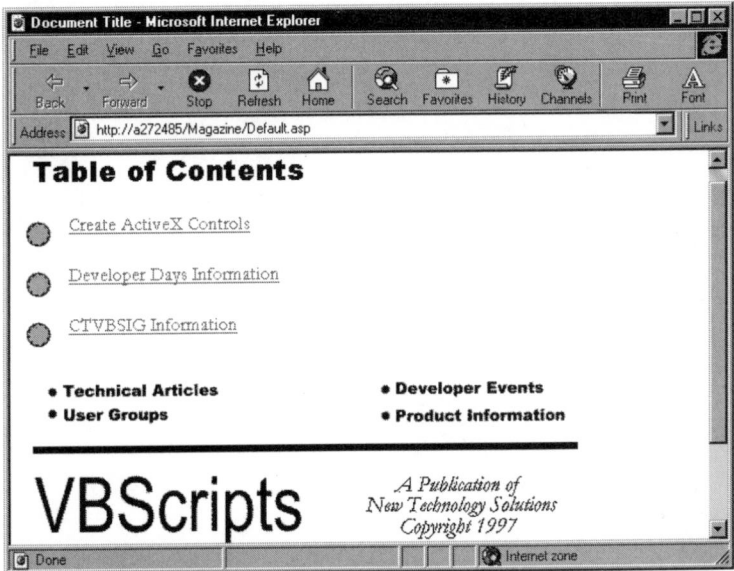

Figure 8-5.
The magazine cover page.

Part V: Creating the Magazine Articles

In this part of the project, you will create an ASP page to dynamically generate the magazine content based on the entries in the Magazine data source. ActiveX Data Objects (ADO) will read the data source and build the magazine article, and the linked style sheet will format the page.

Step 1

If you don't already have the Magazine project open, open it now. Choose New from the File menu. In the New dialog box, insert a new ASP page, name it CONTENT.ASP, and click OK.

Step 2

Creating the article page is a simple matter of reading the data out of the database and generating the article content. Add the following code to the BODY section of CONTENT.ASP:

```
<%
' Variables
Dim objConnection
Dim objRecordset
Dim strSQL

' Open data source
Set objConnection = Server.CreateObject("ADODB.Connection")
objConnection.Open "Magazine"

' Build SQL statement
strSQL = "SELECT * FROM Articles,Sections "
strSQL = strSQL & "WHERE Sections.ArticleID = Articles.ArticleID "
strSQL = strSQL & "AND Articles.ArticleID = " & _
    Request.QueryString("ArticleID")

' Get records
Set objRecordset = Server.CreateObject("ADODB.Recordset")
objRecordset.Open strSQL, objConnection

' Get article information
Dim strTitle
Dim strSubTitle
Dim strNote
```

```
strTitle = objRecordset("ArticleTitle") & ""
strSubTitle = objRecordset("ArticleSubTitle") & ""
strNote = objRecordset("ArticleNote") & ""

' Article title
If strTitle <> "" Then
%>
    <H1><%=strTitle%></H1><%
End If

' Article subtitle
If strSubTitle <> "" Then
%>
    <H4><%=strSubTitle%></H4><%
End If

' Build article body
' Variables
Dim strSection
Dim strText

Do While Not objRecordset.EOF
    ' Get section header
    strSection = objRecordset("SectionTitle") & ""
    If strSection <> "" Then
%>
        <H2><%=strSection%></H2><%
    End If

    ' Get section text
    strText = objRecordset("SectionText") & ""
    If strText <> "" Then
%>
        <%=strText%>
<%
    End if

    ' Get next section
    objRecordset.MoveNext
Loop

' Close database
objRecordset.Close
objConnection.Close
Set objRecordset = Nothing
Set objConnection = Nothing
%>
```

Step 3

The site style sheet manages font styles for the magazine articles. Add the following code to the HEAD section of CONTENT.ASP to establish a link to the style sheet:

```
<LINK REL=STYLESHEET HREF="Magazine.css">
```

Step 4

Save your work, and preview the site by right-clicking DEFAULT.ASP and selecting Browse With from the pop-up menu. In the Browse With dialog box, choose Internet Explorer. From the table of contents, select an article to view, and verify that your site is working. The result should look like the example in Figure 8-6.

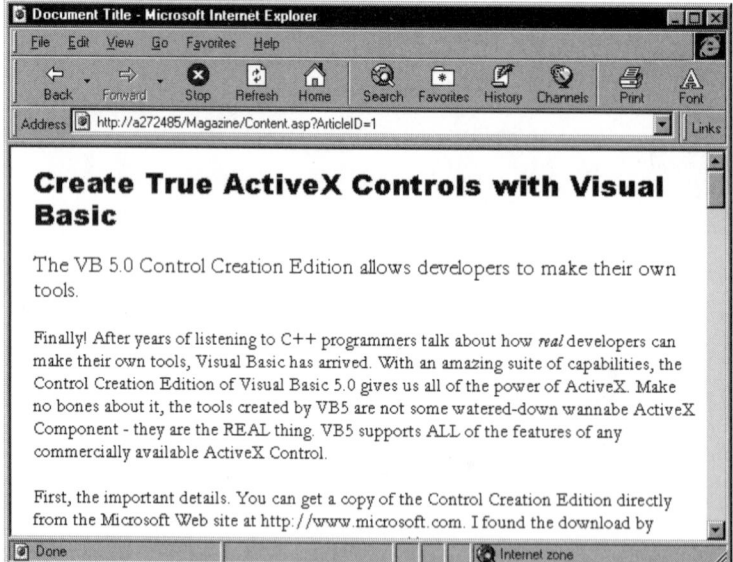

Figure 8-6.
Viewing an article.

Step 5

The Content Linking component can not only produce a table of contents, but it can also navigate through the linked pages. In this portion of the project, you will use the component to create navigational tools—two images that allow the user to move backward and forward through the linked pages. To start, change the CONTENT.ASP page attributes that display hyperlinks. In particular, change the <BODY> tag to prevent the images you use from being highlighted in the page. Use this code:

```
<BODY LINK="White" VLINK="White" ALINK="White">
```

If you use hard-coded Web pages in your content linking text file, the Content Linking component can automatically generate the next and previous links. In this project, however, you are generating content from a database, so you must perform some trickery to build the navigational tools. Add the following code to the top of the BODY section in CONTENT.ASP to create the navigational tools:

```
<%
' This code creates navigational tools for the site

' Variables
Public objLinker
Public intArticleID
Public intArticles

' Get Content Linking object info
Set objLinker = Server.CreateObject("MSWC.NextLink")

' Get ArticleID
intArticleID = CInt(Request.QueryString("ArticleID"))
intArticles = CInt(objLinker.GetListCount("Magazine.txt"))
%>

<!-- Navigational tools -->
<DIV>
<!-- Next article -->
<%If intArticleID > 1 Then%>
    <A HREF=
        <%=objLinker.GetNthURL("Magazine.txt", intArticleID - 1)%>>
    <IMG ID="imgBack" SRC="/Magazine/Images/Back.gif">
    </A>
<%End If%>

<!-- Previous article -->
<%If intArticleID < intArticles Then%>
    <A HREF=<%=objLinker.GetNthURL("Magazine.txt", intArticleID + 1)%>>
    <IMG ID="imgNext" SRC="/Magazine/Images/Next.gif">
    </A>
<%End If%>
```

Step 6

When the user passes the mouse over one of the navigational controls, the page should provide some information about the article that will be displayed if the link is activated. You can show a description of the next link by using Dynamic HTML and the information in the content linking text file. In this step, you will create two <FONT> tags that link descriptions of the articles to the Next and Back icons. Add the following code to the BODY section of the page, just below the section that generates the image controls for navigation:

```
<!-- Article descriptions -->
<%If intArticleID > 1 Then%>
    <FONT FACE="Verdana" ID="txtBack" SIZE=4
    STYLE="position:relative;visibility:hidden;color:red;margin-left:20px">
    <%=objLinker.GetNthDescription("Magazine.txt", intArticleID - 1)%>
    </FONT><BR>
<%End If%>

<%If intArticleID < intArticles Then%>
    <FONT FACE="Verdana" ID="txtNext" SIZE=4
    STYLE="position:relative;visibility:hidden;color:red;margin-left:20px">
    <%=objLinker.GetNthDescription("Magazine.txt", intArticleID + 1)%>
    </FONT>
<%End If%>
```

Step 7

In the <FONT> tags, the visibility argument of the STYLE attribute is initially set to hidden. Therefore, neither of the descriptions is visible at the start. A description will be displayed when the mouse passes over one of the images. Create a SCRIPT section in the HEAD section of the page to trap the mouse events and display the appropriate text. Here is the code:

```
<SCRIPT LANGUAGE="VBScript">
<!--

    Sub imgBack_OnMouseOver()
        txtBack.Style.Visibility = "Visible"
    End Sub
```

```
    Sub imgBack_OnMouseOut()
        txtBack.Style.Visibility = "Hidden"
    End Sub

    Sub imgNext_OnMouseOver()
        txtNext.Style.Visibility = "Visible"
    End Sub

    Sub imgNext_OnMouseOut()
        txtNext.Style.Visibility = "Hidden"
    End Sub

-->
</SCRIPT>
```

Step 8

Save your work, and test the site. Your navigational controls and descriptions should be fully functional and should look like the example shown in Figure 8-7.

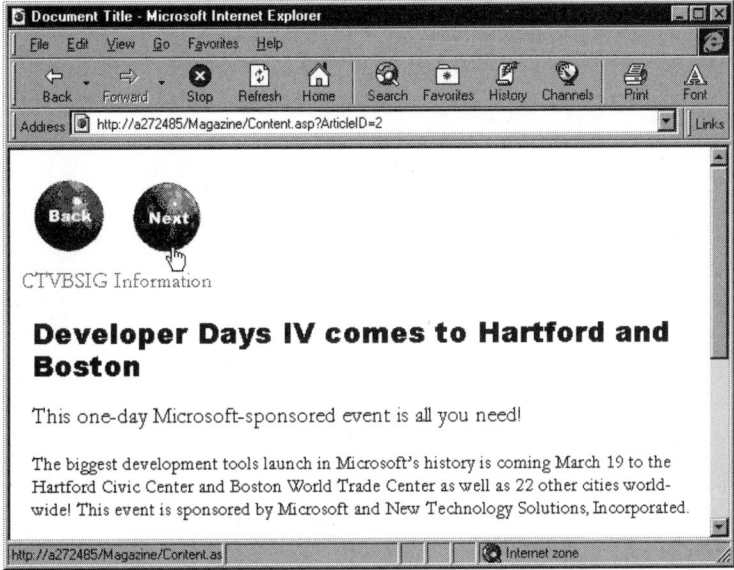

Figure 8-7.
The navigational tools.

Part VI: Searching the Site

In this part, you will create full-text search capability to provide an index for the magazine.

Step 1

If you don't already have the Magazine project open, open it now. Choose New from the File menu. In the New dialog box, create a new ASP page, name it SEARCH.ASP, and click OK.

Step 2

Open DEFAULT.ASP in Visual InterDev Editor. You need to add a form to this page to access the SEARCH.ASP page. A search string should be entered in a text field and passed to the search engine. Add the following code to the BODY section to place a hyperlink in the page:

```
<!-- Index search form -->
<DIV STYLE="position:absolute; top:250px; left:400px; width:200;">
    <CENTER>
    <IMG SRC="/Magazine/Images/Search.gif"><BR>
    <FORM ACTION="/Magazine/Search.asp" METHOD="POST">
    <INPUT NAME="SearchString"><BR>
    <INPUT TYPE="SUBMIT" VALUE="Search!">
    </FORM>
    </CENTER>
</DIV>
```

Save and close DEFAULT.ASP.

Step 3

Open SEARCH.ASP, your new search engine for the site. In this page, you will open a connection to the database, provide a text search mechanism, and build a list of hyperlinks to the appropriate documents.

Start by linking SEARCH.ASP to the site style sheet to maintain a consistent look. Add the following code to the HEAD section of SEARCH.ASP:

```
<LINK REL=STYLESHEET HREF="Magazine.css">
```

Step 4

The actual search is performed by creating a query against the database, using the keyword submitted by the user. If the keyword appears in an article's text, a hyperlink is generated in the results page. In this step, you will use ADO to run the query and show the results of the search.

NOTE: The SQL statement for this exercise can be tricky to write. Although spread out across several lines of code, an example of the final statement might look like this:

SELECT * FROM Articles, Sections WHERE Sections.ArticleID = Articles.ArticleID AND Sections.SectionText LIKE '%VBScript%'

Add the following code to the BODY section of SEARCH.ASP to complete the page:

```
<H1>Here are the results of your search...</H1>

<%
' Variables
Dim objConnection
Dim objRecordset
Dim strSQL

' Open data source
Set objConnection = Server.CreateObject("ADODB.Connection")
objConnection.Open "Magazine"

' Build SQL statement
strSQL = "SELECT * FROM Articles,Sections "
strSQL = strSQL & "WHERE Sections.ArticleID = Articles.ArticleID "
strSQL = strSQL & "AND Sections.SectionText LIKE '%" & _
    Request.Form("SearchString") & "%'"
' Get records
Set objRecordset = Server.CreateObject("ADODB.Recordset")
objRecordset.Open strSQL, objConnection%>

<TABLE>
<%
Do While Not objRecordset.EOF
%>
    <TR>
        <TD>
        <A HREF="Content.asp?ArticleID=<%=objRecordset("ArticleID")%>">
        <H3><%=objRecordset("ArticleTitle")%></H3>
        </A>
        </TD>
    </TR>
<%
    ' Get next record
    objRecordset.MoveNext
Loop
%>
</TABLE>
```

Step 5

Save your work, and test the site. Try searching for a keyword. Your result should look like Figure 8-8.

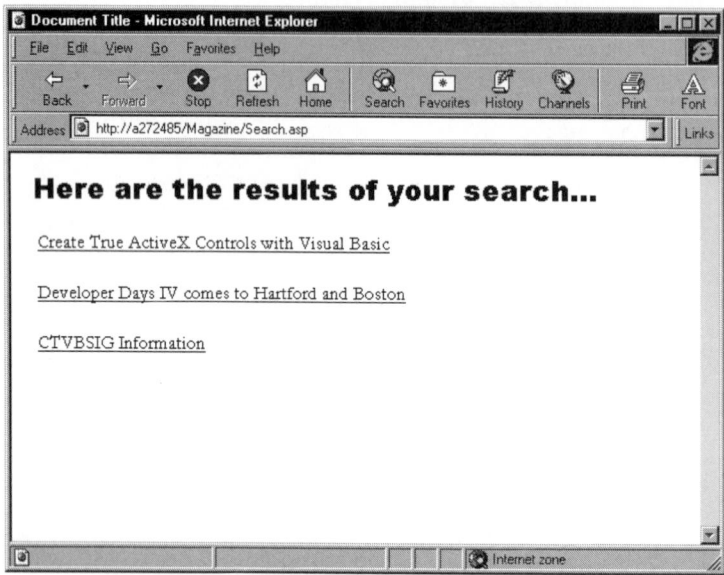

Figure 8-8.
Search results.

Part VII: Tip of the Day

In this part, you will add a "tip of the day" feature to SEARCH.ASP, which will show a new Visual Basic tip each time a query is run. This feature uses the TextStream object of the File Access component to access a text file of tips and display one at random.

Step 1

If you don't already have the Magazine project open, open it now. Add the text file TIPS.TXT to your project from the CD-ROM that accompanies this book.

Step 2

Open TIPS.TXT, and examine the contents. Notice that the file structure has each tip on a separate line. You select a tip at random by reading a random line from the file. In SEARCH.ASP, add the following code below the </TABLE> tag to present the tips:

```
<H1>Tip of the Day...</H1>
<%
' Tip of the day

' Variables
Dim objFile
Dim objStream
Dim TextNumber
Dim i

Set objFile = Server.CreateObject("Scripting.FileSystemObject")
Set objStream = objFile.OpenTextFile(Server.MapPath ("/Magazine") _
    + "\tips.txt")

Randomize Timer
TextNumber = Int(Rnd*30)

For i = 0 to TextNumber
    objStream.SkipLine
Next

strText = objStream.ReadLine
objStream.Close
%>

<H4><%=strText%></H4>
```

Your result should look like Figure 8-9 on the following page.

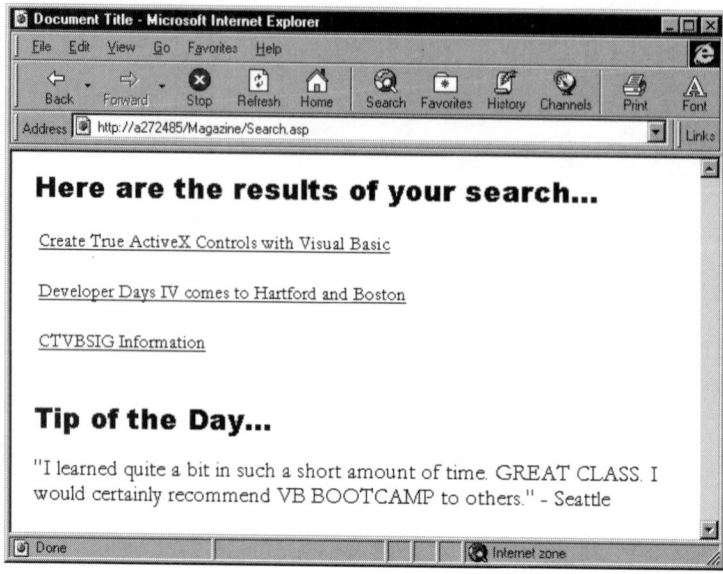

Figure 8-9.
Tip of the day.

Something to Try on Your Own

When SEARCH.ASP returns search results, include the first 100 characters of text from each document found so that users can easily decide whether they want to view the whole document.

An E-Mail Information System

This project creates an e-mail information system that allows users to receive e-mail containing detailed information about products and services available from your Web site. The system is similar to the old "fax back" systems, which returned product information to users via a fax machine. At the core of the project is the creation of an ActiveX component that is capable of sending e-mail. The component is written in Microsoft Visual Basic 5.0. This project does not teach Visual Basic but is designed to show programmers familiar with Visual Basic 5.0 how to use that knowledge with Visual InterDev.

Requirements

1. Microsoft Visual Basic 5.0

2. Microsoft Visual InterDev 1.0

3. Microsoft Internet Information Server 3.0 (or Microsoft Personal Web Server) with Active Server Pages installed

4. Microsoft Exchange Server 5.0 (or other SMTP mail server)

5. Microsoft Internet Explorer 4.0

6. E-mail project files

Part I: Learning the SMTP Protocol

Before you can create the E-mail component in this project, you must understand a little about the Simple Mail Transfer Protocol (SMTP) used to send mail on the Internet. SMTP is a clear text protocol that functions through a series of commands and responses exchanged between the e-mail client and server.

Before automating the process, investigate this protocol by sending e-mail manually, using an application named Telnet.

NOTE: You will need direct access to an SMTP server. This project assumes that you are using Exchange 5.0 as your Internet mail server. Other servers might function slightly differently.

Sending e-mail does not require a complicated piece of client software. In fact, every computer running Microsoft Windows has a built-in network client, Telnet, which allows you to interact with a server by typing in commands.

Step 1

Start Telnet by choosing Run from the Start menu and typing the command *Telnet*. The Telnet application window appears, as shown in Figure 9-1.

Figure 9-1.
The Telnet application.

Once Telnet is started, connect to your e-mail server by choosing Remote System from the Connect menu. In the Connect dialog box, provide the following information:

Host Name: *[Your Server IP Address]*
Port: 25

Click the Connect button. After a few moments, the server should respond with this message:

220 *[Your Server Name]* Microsoft Exchange Internet Mail Service
5.0.1457

Step 2

You are now communicating with the server. To see your instructions to the server, choose Preferences from the Terminal menu. In the Terminal Preferences dialog box, check the Local Echo option and click OK.

Step 3

Begin your e-mail transmission by typing the e-mail address of the sender and pressing enter:

MAIL FROM: *[Sender's E-Mail Address]*{ENTER}

The server should respond:

250 OK – mail from <*[Sender's E-Mail Address]*>

Step 4

Type the recipient's address, and press enter:

RCPT TO: *[Recipient's E-Mail Address]*{ENTER}

The server should respond:

250 OK – Recipient <*[Recipient's E-Mail Address]*>

Step 5

To tell the server that you are ready to send the body of your message, type the following:

DATA{ENTER}

The server should respond:

354 Send Data. End with CRLF.CRLF

Step 6

Type the body of your message line by line with a carriage return at the end of each line. The server recognizes that your message is complete when you send a period on a line by itself.

For example, to send a test message, type the following into Telnet:

DATE: *[Today's Date in dd/mm/yy Format]*{ENTER}
FROM: *[Sender's Name]*{ENTER}
TO: *[Recipient's Name]*{ENTER}
SUBJECT: Telnet Test!{ENTER}
{ENTER}
This is an e-mail test from Telnet!{ENTER}
.{ENTER}

Don't forget the period on the last line. The server will respond with the following:

250 OK

Step 7

Your message has been sent. Close Telnet by choosing Disconnect and then Exit from the Connect menu.

Step 8

Open your e-mail package, and check for your message!

Part II: Creating the E-Mail Component

Step 1

Using Windows Explorer, create a new directory where you can build the ActiveX E-Mail component for your e-mail information system. Name the directory \VBMAIL.

Start a new Visual Basic 5.0 ActiveX DLL project. Access the properties for your new project by choosing Project1 Properties from the Project menu. On the General tab in the Project Properties dialog box, change the project name to VBMail and change the project description to Active Server Pages E-Mail Component. Click OK.

When the project is first opened, a default class named CLASS1 is created. Change the name of this default class to Connector.

Save the project in the directory \VBMAIL.

Step 2

You can create the e-mail connector by using Winsock, an ActiveX control that ships with Visual Basic 5.0 and allows a Visual Basic component to access the Internet. With Winsock, you can automatically send e-mail.

Because Winsock is an ActiveX control, you need to add a form to your project to host the control, even though the component will not have a user interface. To add this form, choose Add Form from the Project menu and name the form frmVBMail.

Choose Components from the Project menu. In the Components dialog box, select Microsoft Winsock Control 5.0 and click OK.

Add the Winsock control to your newly created form by double-clicking the control in the Visual Basic Toolbox. Change the name of the control to sockVBMail. Save your project.

Step 3

In Active Server Pages code, the Connector class will be the primary interface for e-mail. This class must include properties that allow you to designate the sender and receiver of the mail, as well as the mail content. Add the following code to the Connector class to create the necessary properties for the E-Mail component:

```
' Variables
Private m_Sender As String
Private m_Recipient As String
Private m_SenderName As String
Private m_RecipientName As String
Private m_Subject As String
Private m_Body As String
Private m_Server As String

' Property procedures
Public Property Get Sender() As String
    Sender = m_Sender
End Property

Public Property Let Sender(strSender As String)
    m_Sender = strSender
End Property
```

(continued)

continued

```
Public Property Get Recipient() As String
    Recipient = m_Recipient
End Property

Public Property Let Recipient(strRecipient As String)
    m_Recipient = strRecipient
End Property

Public Property Get SenderName() As String
    SenderName = m_SenderName
End Property

Public Property Let SenderName(strSenderName As String)
    m_SenderName = strSenderName
End Property

Public Property Get RecipientName() As String
    RecipientName = m_RecipientName
End Property

Public Property Let RecipientName(strRecipientName As String)
    m_RecipientName = strRecipientName
End Property

Public Property Get Subject() As String
    Subject = m_Subject
End Property

Public Property Let Subject(strSubject As String)
    m_Subject = strSubject
End Property

Public Property Get Body() As String
    Body = m_Body
End Property

Public Property Let Body(strBody As String)
    m_Body = strBody
End Property

Public Property Get Server() As String
    Server = m_Server
End Property
```

```
Public Property Let Server(strServer As String)
    m_Server = strServer
End Property
```

Step 4

After all the information is provided to the component through the properties, you can call the Send method of the Connector class to send e-mail. To create the Send method, choose Add Procedure from the Tools menu. In the Add Procedure dialog box, set the following attributes:

```
Name: Send
Type: Function
Scope: Public
```

After the Send function is added, designate the return data type as Boolean. The complete function definition should appear as follows:

```
Public Function Send() As Boolean
End Function
```

You will complete the Send method shortly, but first add some supporting functionality to the component.

Step 5

Because many of the steps involved in sending e-mail require a response from the e-mail server, you need to create a routine that causes the E-Mail component to wait for the server's response. This can be accomplished with a private routine named GetResponse. Add the routine to the Connector class by choosing Insert Procedure from the Tools menu. In the Insert Procedure dialog box, set the following attributes:

```
Name: GetResponse
Type: Sub
Scope: Private
```

After the GetResponse routine is created, add the following code to force a wait for the server's response:

```
Dim strTemp As String

strTemp = ""
Do While strTemp = ""
    frmVBMail.sockVBMail.GetData  strTemp
    DoEvents
Loop
```

Step 6

In this step, you will create the code necessary to use SMTP, the protocol that allows communication between the e-mail server and the client. Although this project was originally designed to use Microsoft Exchange Server 5.0, you can use any e-mail server that supports SMTP.

Return to the Send method, and add the following code to connect to the SMTP mail server:

```
With frmVBMail.sockVBMail
    Send = True

    ' Connect to SMTP server
    If .State <> sckConnected And .State <> sckOpen Then
        .Connect Server, 25
        Do While .State <> sckConnected
            DoEvents
        Loop
    End If
```

Step 7

Once the E-Mail component is successfully connected to the e-mail server, you can construct and send a message using SMTP. The message is sent to the server in parts until each necessary piece—sender, recipient, body—is received. Then the server sends the message to the recipient. Add the following code to the Send method to build and send an e-mail message:

```
On Error GoTo SendErr

With frmVBMail.sockVBMail
    Send = True

    ' Connect to SMTP server
    If .State <> sckConnected And .State <> sckOpen Then
        .Connect Server, 25
        Do While .State <> sckConnected
            DoEvents
        Loop
    End If

    ' Create the message
    Dim strMessage As String
```

```
' The sender
strMessage = "MAIL FROM:" & Sender & vbCrLf
.SendData strMessage
GetResponse

' The recipient
strMessage = "RCPT TO:" & Recipient & vbCrLf
.SendData strMessage
GetResponse

' The body of the message
strMessage = "DATA" & vbCrLf
.SendData strMessage
GetResponse

strMessage = "DATE:" & Format$(Now, "dd/mm/yy") & vbCrLf
strMessage = strMessage & "FROM:" & SenderName & vbCrLf
strMessage = strMessage & "TO:" & RecipientName & vbCrLf
strMessage = strMessage & "SUBJECT:" & Subject & vbCrLf & vbCrLf
strMessage = strMessage & Body & vbCrLf
strMessage = strMessage & "." & vbCrLf
.SendData strMessage
GetResponse
```

Step 8

After the message is sent, you must close the connection to the e-mail server. Use the Close method of the Winsock control to close the connection and complete the Send method code:

```
' Close connection
.Close
Do While .State <> sckClosed
    DoEvents
Loop
End With

SendExit:
    Exit Function

SendErr:
    Send = False
    Resume SendExit
```

Save your project.

Step 9

Before you can use the E-Mail component in an ASP page, you must compile the DLL by choosing Make VBMail.dll from the File menu. Then save your work, and exit Visual Basic.

Part III: Setting Up a New Web Project

Step 1

Start Visual InterDev. Choose New from the File menu. When the New dialog box appears, click the Projects tab, and choose the Web Project wizard. Then specify a location for your project files in the Location text box, give your project the name EMailInfo, and click OK.

The Web Project wizard will ask you for the name of the Web server on which the new project will be created. If this text box contains an entry, you can accept it; if the box is empty, type the name of the machine that is running Internet Information Server (or Personal Web Server). (If you don't know the correct name of your Web server, look up the Identification information by using the Network applet in the Control Panel.) Click Next.

The Web Project wizard will contact the selected Web server and present you with the step 2 dialog box. Choose the option Create A New Web. Make sure the name of the web is EMailInfo.

The Web Project wizard will create your new web and open the project.

Step 2

This project utilizes a Microsoft Access database named EMAILINFO.MDB to provide the online database of information. In order to access this database, you must establish an ODBC data source on your machine. Set up the ODBC data source in the ODBC Data Source Administrator, and name the source EMailInfo.

Step 3

Return to Visual InterDev. Now you will add the data source to your web project. On the FileView tab, click the project title and then choose Add To Project/ Data Connection from the Project menu. When the Select Data Source dialog box appears, click the Machine Data Source tab and choose the EMailInfo data source. Click the OK button. Visual InterDev will add a new data connection to your web project based on the EMailInfo data source.

Part IV: Creating the Home Page

In this part of the project, you will create a home page for the e-mail information system. Before you begin, however, you must add some graphics files to your site.

Step 1

If you don't already have the EMailInfo web open in Visual InterDev, open it now. On the FileView tab, click the IMAGES directory and choose Add To Project/Files from the Project menu. Add the image files for this project to your site.

Step 2

To add a new Web page to your project, choose New from the File menu. When the New dialog box appears, click the Files tab and select Active Server Page. In the File Name box, type *DEFAULT.ASP* and click OK. Visual InterDev will automatically add the new Web page to your site.

Step 3

Open DEFAULT.ASP by right-clicking the file in the project window. Choose Open With from the pop-up menu. In the Open With dialog box, open the file with Microsoft FrontPage Editor (Visual InterDev Edition).

In FrontPage, choose Background from the Format menu. On the Background tab in the Page Properties dialog box, change the background color of the home page to white. Click OK.

Add a banner to the home page by choosing Image from the Insert menu. In the Insert dialog box, insert an image from the following location:

`/EMAILINFO/IMAGES/BANNER.JPG`

Click OK, and center the banner by clicking the Center button on the toolbar. The result should look like the page in Figure 9-2.

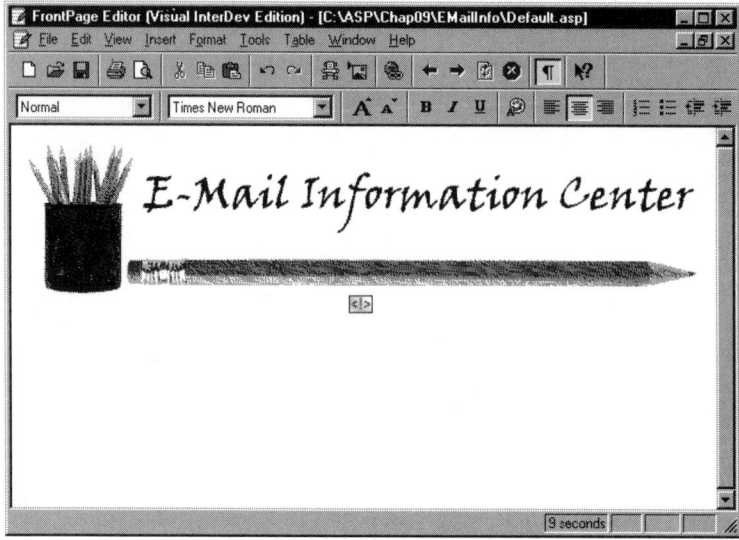

Figure 9-2.
The home page banner.

Step 4

The home page will walk the user through the steps necessary to receive information from the e-mail system. On a new line on the Web page, place the text *Step 1* to mark the first thing the user must do. Change the size to Heading 3 using the Change Style drop-down list box on the toolbar. Below this heading, type the message *Enter your personal information.*

Step 5

You will need a form to gather personal information from the user, including the user's name and e-mail address. You might also want to request other useful information, such as a mailing address.

Below *Step 1*, add a new form by choosing Form Field/Push Button from the Insert menu. A new Submit button should appear, along with a black outline designating a new form.

Step 6

To access the properties of the new form, right-click inside the black border and select Form Properties from the pop-up menu. In the Form Properties dialog box, be sure that the Form Handler box designates Custom ISAPI, NSAPI, Or CGI Script as the handler.

Click the Settings button in the Form Properties dialog box. In the Settings For Custom Form Handler dialog box, set the ACTION attribute to submit the form to the following address:

```
/EMAILINFO/MAIL.ASP
```

In the same dialog box, check that the METHOD attribute is set to POST. Click OK to exit the Settings For Custom Form Handler dialog box, and click OK again to exit the Form Properties dialog box.

Step 7

Now build the remainder of the form. Place your cursor above the Submit button, and add a new table by choosing Insert Table from the Table menu. In the Insert Table dialog box, create a table with the following attributes:

```
Rows: 8
Columns: 2
Border Size: 0
Cell Padding: 2
Cell Spacing: 2
```

Click OK to add the new table to the page.

Step 8

Add label text to the cells in the first column of the table. Use the cell labels shown below:

Row Number	Row Label
1	First Name
2	Last Name
3	E-Mail
4	Address
5	*Blank*
6	City
7	State
8	Zip

Using the Change Style drop-down list box on the toolbar, change the style for each cell to Heading 5.

Step 9

To add text fields to the cells in the second column, choose Form Field/One-Line Text Box from the Insert menu.

Change the name of each text field in the form by right-clicking the field and choosing Form Field Properties from the pop-up menu. In the Text Box Properties dialog box, type the new field name, as shown below:

Row Number	Field Name
1	txtFirstName
2	txtLastName
3	txtEMail
4	txtAddress1
5	txtAddress2
6	txtCity
7	txtState
8	txtZip

Save your work.

Step 10

Start a new line below the table and above the Submit button. On this line, type the text *Step 2*. Using the Change Style drop-down list box on the toolbar, change the style to Heading 3. Below this heading, type the message *Select a topic*.

Step 11

Below the text, add a drop-down list box by choosing Form Field/Drop-Down Menu from the Insert menu.

Change the properties for the drop-down list box by right-clicking the field and choosing Form Field Properties from the pop-up menu. In the Drop-

Down Menu Properties dialog box, change the name of the control to *lstTopic* and click OK.

Step 12

Next to the Submit button, add a new button by choosing Form Field/Push Button from the Insert menu. Right-click the new button, and choose Form Field Properties from the pop-up menu. In the Push Button Properties dialog box, change the button type to Reset and click OK.

Save your work, and exit FrontPage Editor.

Step 13

Return to Visual InterDev. Preview your page in Internet Explorer by right-clicking DEFAULT.ASP and choosing Browse With from the pop-up menu. The result should look like the page in Figure 9-3.

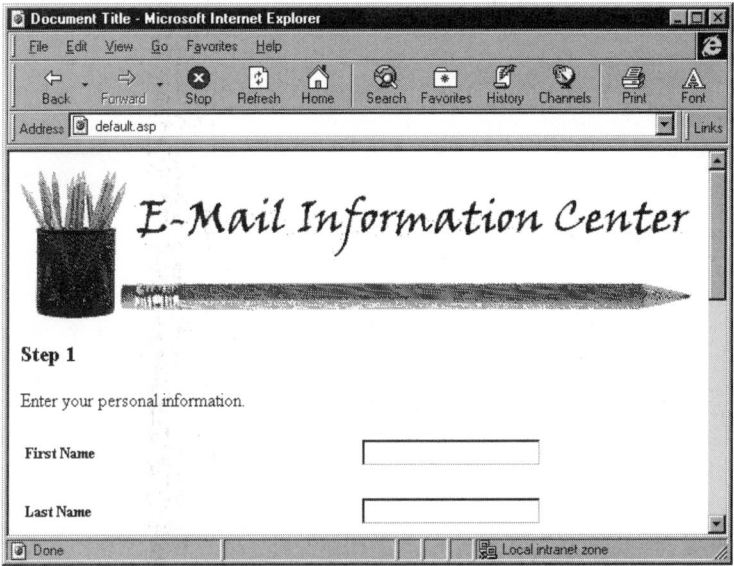

Figure 9-3.
The home page.

Part V: Building the Topic List and Sending Mail

In this part of the project, you will create the list of topics to appear in the drop-down list box on the home page. Use ADO to read the database and create the list.

Step 1

If you don't already have the EMailInfo web open in Visual InterDev, open it now. Open DEFAULT.ASP in Visual InterDev. Identify the <SELECT> tag that creates the drop-down list box.

Add an <OPTION> </OPTION> tag pair for each topic in the database. These tags are used to denote items in the list. Add the following code between the <SELECT> and </SELECT> tags:

```
<%

' Variables
Dim objConnection
Dim objRecordset

' Open a connection
Set objConnection = Server.CreateObject("ADODB.Connection")
objConnection.Open "EMailInfo"

' Get entries
Set objRecordset = Server.CreateObject("ADODB.Recordset")
objRecordset.Open _
    "SELECT ItemID, ItemDescription FROM Items", objConnection

' Build the list.
' The description is shown in the list,
' but the ItemID is returned in code
' so that you can search the database.
Do While Not objRecordset.EOF%>
    <OPTION VALUE=<%=objRecordset("ItemID")%>>
    <%=objRecordset("ItemDescription")%>
    </OPTION><%
    objRecordset.MoveNext
Loop

' Close the connection
objRecordset.Close
objConnection.Close
```

```
Set objRecordset = Nothing
Set objConnection = Nothing

%>
```

Save your work.

Step 2

Preview DEFAULT.ASP in Internet Explorer. You should see the topics in the drop-down list box, as shown in Figure 9-4.

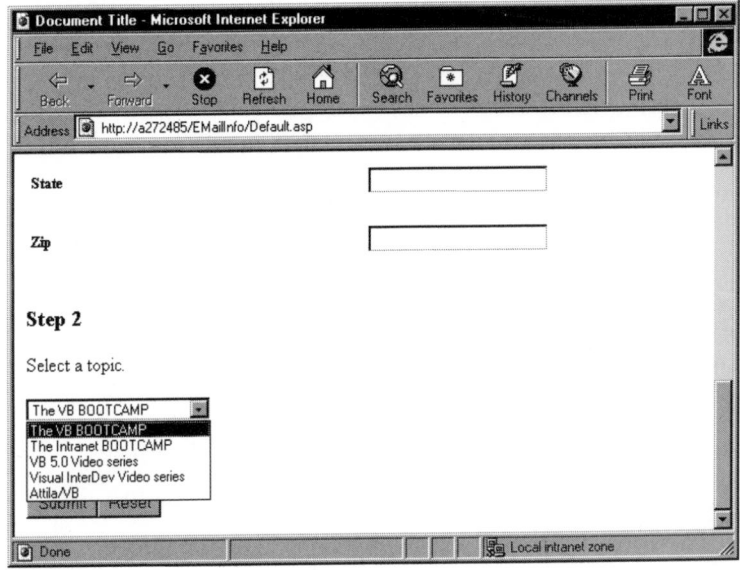

Figure 9-4.
The topic list.

Step 3

Now that the information form is complete, you are ready to send the mail. Add a new page to your project by choosing New from the File menu. In the New dialog box, add a new ASP page, name it MAIL.ASP, and click OK.

Step 4

To send the mail, use the E-Mail component you created earlier. Because the component was written in Visual Basic 5.0, it is already properly registered and ready to use. You create an instance of this component in the same way that

you create an instance of any component—by using the CreateObject method
of the Server object. Add the following code to the BODY section of MAIL.ASP
to access the E-Mail component:

```
<%

' Variables
Dim objMail
Dim objConnection
Dim objRecordset
Dim blnSuccess

blnSuccess = False

' Create the E-Mail component
Set objMail = Server.CreateObject("VBMail.Connector")

' Create database objects
Set objConnection = Server.CreateObject("ADODB.Connection")
Set objRecordset = Server.CreateObject("ADODB.Recordset")

' Get the item to send
objConnection.Open "EMailInfo"
objRecordset.Open _
    "SELECT ItemDescription, ItemText FROM Items WHERE ItemID =" _
    & Request.Form("lstTopic"), objConnection

If Not objRecordset.EOF Then
' Set data into Mail component
objMail.Sender = Application("Sender")
objMail.Recipient = Request.Form("txtEMail")
objMail.SenderName = Application("SenderName")
objMail.RecipientName = Request.Form("txtFirstName") _
    & " " & Request.Form("txtLastName")
objMail.Subject = objRecordset("ItemDescription")
objMail.Body = objRecordset("ItemText")
objMail.Server = Application("Server")

' Send mail!
blnSuccess = objMail.Send
End If

If blnSuccess Then%>
<H1>Thank You!  Your mail was sent.</H1>
<%Else%>
<H1>We're sorry!  There is a problem sending mail.
Please check your information.</H1>
<%End If%>
```

Step 5

In the code for the E-Mail component, you specified several key properties using Application variables. These variables provide a simple way of customizing the application for your e-mail server and information topics. To set up these variables in the GLOBAL.ASA file, open the file in Visual InterDev. GLOBAL.ASA traps four important events in your project: Session_OnStart, Session_OnEnd, Application_OnStart, and Application_OnEnd. Here is the code:

```
<SCRIPT LANGUAGE="VBScript" RUNAT="Server">

    Sub Application_OnStart
        Application("Sender") = "[Your Company E-Mail]"
        Application("Server") = "[Your E-Mail Server]"
        Application("SenderName") = "[Your Company Name]"
    End Sub

</SCRIPT>
```

Save your work.

Step 6

Test your application. You should now be able to send e-mail!

> **NOTE:** This application requires that all form fields be filled out! The user can crash the application by not providing information for all fields in DEFAULT.ASP. Add data validation to the form later as an extra exercise.

Part VI: Capturing Customer Data

In this part of the project, you will save the additional information provided by the user. The data can be used later for mailing lists or for list server applications. Capturing the additional data is a simple matter of using ActiveX Data Objects (ADO) to write a new record to the Customers table.

Step 1

If you don't already have the EMailInfo project open, open it now. Add the following code to the BODY section of MAIL.ASP:

> **NOTE:** The SQL string in this step can be difficult to create. Pay close attention to the use of single quotes and double quotes. Single quotes designate text in the SQL language, while double quotes are used by VBScript to create strings.

```
<%
' Add the customer data
Dim strSQL

' Build SQL string
strSQL = "INSERT INTO Customers (FirstName,LastName,Address1,"
strSQL = strSQL & "Address2,City,State,Zip,EMail)"
strSQL = strSQL & "VALUES ('" & Request.Form("txtFirstName") & "'"
strSQL = strSQL & ",'" & Request.Form("txtLastName") & "'"
strSQL = strSQL & ",'" & Request.Form("txtAddress1") & "'"
strSQL = strSQL & ",'" & Request.Form("txtAddress2") & "'"
strSQL = strSQL & ",'" & Request.Form("txtCity") & "'"
strSQL = strSQL & ",'" & Request.Form("txtState") & "'"
strSQL = strSQL & ",'" & Request.Form("txtZip") & "'"
strSQL = strSQL & ",'" & Request.Form("txtEMail") & "')"

' Execute statement
objConnection.Execute strSQL

' Destroy objects
objRecordset.Close
objConnection.Close
Set objRecordset = Nothing
Set objConnection = Nothing
%>
```

Save your project.

Step 2

Test all the aspects of your new e-mail information system.

Something to Try on Your Own

Add data validation to the input form to ensure that all fields are filled in.

CHAPTER TEN

Microsoft Transaction Server

Although stand-alone Web applications are gaining significant momentum as a business solution, browser-based products are also likely to appear as additions to existing enterprise systems. For many businesses, browser access to business systems represents a powerful new way to provide information to remote locations. These remote sites might consist of customers who need technical support, other offices within the same company that are not part of an existing wide-area network (WAN), or even employees who are telecommuting across a modem. Demand for access can easily strain existing enterprise hardware that was not originally selected with external connection in mind.

As an application begins to scale into hundreds or even thousands of users, system resources become the limiting factor. Internet lore is full of stories about sites that were unprepared for a high level of demand and had to be shut down the same day they debuted. That is where Microsoft Transaction Server (MTS) enters the picture.

MTS is designed to provide all the features necessary to efficiently use the resources of machines hosting business systems. In particular, MTS provides pooling for three key system resources: threads, objects, and ODBC connections. MTS also includes features such as transaction management, but this chapter will focus only on using MTS to scale your site.

MTS relies heavily on the creation of COM business objects to efficiently manage middle tier functionality. These COM objects can be created in any visual development tool that supports them, including Microsoft Visual Basic, Microsoft Visual C++, Microsoft Visual J++, and Microsoft Visual FoxPro, but all the business objects created in this chapter will be built in Visual Basic. The chapter does not attempt to teach the fundamentals of constructing Visual Basic business objects but focuses instead on special techniques required to use these components under MTS. Therefore, you should be familiar with the process of creating ActiveX DLL projects in Visual Basic 5.0 prior to using these techniques on your Web site.

Scaling Considerations in Active Server Pages

Scaling any application requires efficient use of system resources. Although this is easily stated, many development teams do not properly consider the impact of system resource limitations during an application's design phase.

To understand these limitations, consider a real-world analogy, a hypothetical auto repair shop. The shop starts small, with perhaps a single garage bay and a handful of customers. The small business can easily handle its limited customer load and flourishes in the community. As time goes on, the excellent work done at the shop gains a reputation, and more and more customers seek services from the business. The owners get together and decide that their business must grow. Their goal is to be flexible and expand the business automatically with each new customer. Therefore, they make the ill-fated decision to hire a new mechanic for each new customer they take on. The owners reason that because of the one-to-one relationship between mechanics and customers, every customer will be satisfied and will never have to wait for service from a mechanic.

The experiment, of course, is a failure. The garage facility is not equipped to handle dozens of mechanics working on dozens of cars at the same time. Now the owners face having to purchase a larger garage for all the new mechanics. Since they did not plan on the purchase of a new building and new equipment, the budget does not support the required growth and the business fails.

The answer to the problem is clearly to pool the resources of the garage and a few mechanics to support the load of new customers. Rather than continue to hire mechanics and build garages, the business uses the resources it has as efficiently as possible and continues to grow and prosper. But the lessons obvious in our auto repair shop example are often lost in the business of software design. Most systems face inevitable growth and require intelligent planning and careful resource allocation. Yet how many times does a business get caught having to purchase new hardware to support the latest application?

The problems of scaling software involve three key resources that are analogous to the garage and mechanics in our example. These resources are threads, objects, and ODBC connections, and their management directly affects your site's performance. Microsoft Internet Information Server (IIS) and Microsoft Active Server Pages (ASP) include built-in scaling features that assist in resource management.

Threads are execution points within the memory space of an application. IIS provides multithreading capability to manage users who come to your site simultaneously. However, this capability might or might not be extended to the COM objects called by ASP. Therefore, processing information such as data source updates can be slowed if your business objects are single-threaded—and Visual Basic typically creates only single-threaded business objects.

Object instances also require thoughtful management. Many systems create one instance of a single-threaded business object for each client who calls. This process creates a one-to-one relationship between object instances and application users. This is exactly the same as hiring a mechanic for each new customer and can result in a fatal blow to system resources. MTS solves this problem by creating a pool of object instances which can be shared by all clients.

ODBC connections must also be handled correctly. In many applications, developers open an ODBC connection at the start of a session and close it at the end. Although extremely common in Visual Basic applications, this practice is devastating when trying to scale. A system simply does not have the resources to provide every user with an individual ODBC connection. ASP helps by automatically pooling the connections made to data sources that are accessed with ActiveX Data Objects (ADO). This feature is enabled by the system registry setting shown in Appendix D.

Without the use of any special software such as MTS, Active Server Pages provides reasonable scaling features as long as you perform data access directly from the script in a Web page. This architecture supports multithreading capabilities and ODBC connection pooling, but it presents several problems.

First, ASP is script intensive. When programming data access from an ASP page with ADO, you usually write all code directly into the Web page. This script-intensive style can be terribly difficult to maintain. Script is mixed directly with HTML, potentially resulting in a pile of spaghetti code no one can understand.

Second, script is not reusable. Active Server Pages does not support anything like the binary reusability of a Visual Basic business object. Although ASP can use Visual Basic objects, it cannot create the equivalent of a class module internally. Typically, developers are limited to cut-and-paste, which promotes poor coding practices and produces bulky pages.

Third, script cannot be accessed by other applications. Because script code does not support encapsulation, it cannot be accessed by other applications that might want to perform data access on the same source with the same business rules. Therefore, if you want to access the same data source with a Visual Basic application, you would have to write a separate set of functionality for each new application. This is a terrible waste of time and effort.

In order to create an environment in which any application can access a data source, you need to factor out the common functionality of the business rules and call it from the ASP page. Removing data access from the page and transferring it to a separate business object allows other applications that support the Distributed Component Object Model (DCOM) to reuse the business logic without additional work. Under this scenario, you depend absolutely on a product such as Microsoft Transaction Server to provide the thread, object, and connection pooling necessary to scale the application.

The Transaction Server Explorer

The primary interface to MTS is Microsoft Transaction Server Explorer, which provides a way of adding, removing, and managing components under the control of MTS. MTS Explorer (Figure 10-1) is built on the same GUI metaphor as Windows Explorer.

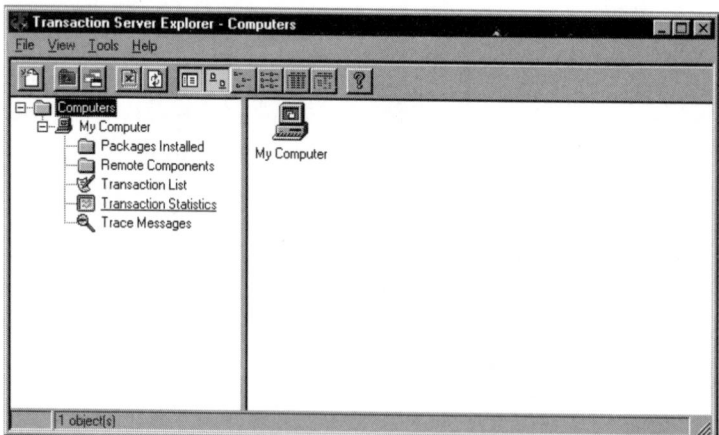

Figure 10-1.
MTS Explorer.

In MTS Explorer, you can view components that are located on any machine in the enterprise. Components placed under MTS control reside inside a *package,* an administrative grouping of components that allows them to exist in the same security context.

Placing an object under MTS control is a relatively simple process. First, you must construct an ActiveX DLL in Visual Basic. At the simplest level, the DLL need not have any special features associated with it. Simply include at least one public method in the class module. For example, the ActiveX DLL named SimpleObject has one class module, Simple, and one method, Process. The following is the complete code for SimpleObject:

```
Public Function Process() As String
    Process = "I got your call!"
End Function
```

After compiling the DLL, open MTS Explorer. Click the Packages Installed folder, and choose New from the File menu. In the Package wizard (Figure 10-2), click Create An Empty Package to define a new package for the ActiveX DLL. MTS prompts for a name and then creates the new package.

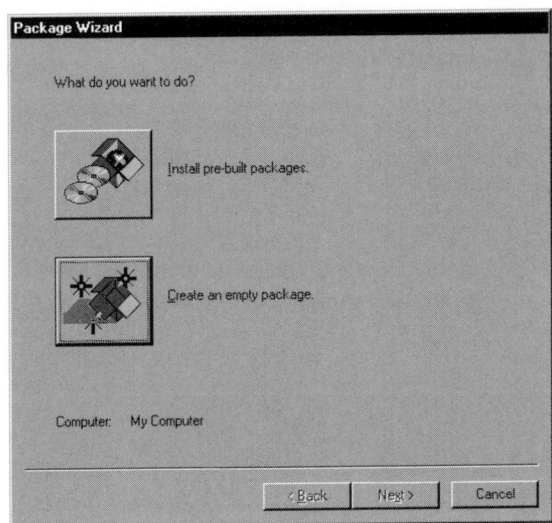

Figure 10-2.
The Package wizard.

To install the component, click the new package to open it. Inside the package, click the Components folder and choose New from the File menu. In the Component wizard (Figure 10-3), choose your new component from a list of all registered components on the machine.

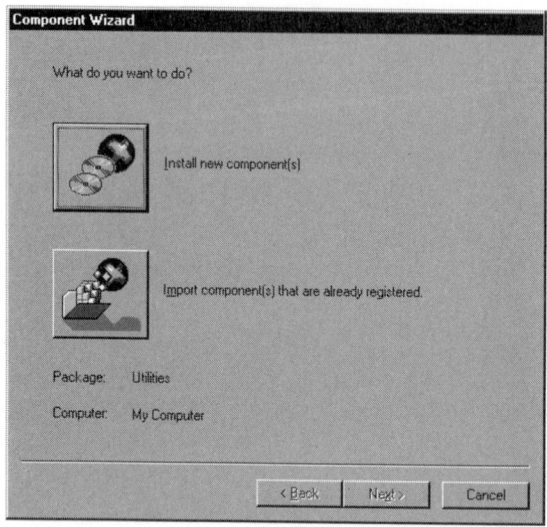

Figure 10-3.
The Component wizard.

At this point, the component is installed under MTS control. Now whenever the component is called by an ASP page or even another application over DCOM, MTS will intercept the request and process it using a pool of objects created from the SimpleObject ActiveX DLL. The object is available to all enterprise applications that support DCOM.

There is a catch here, however. MTS appears to ASP pages as an out-of-process component, a component that runs in a separate memory space from ASP. Normally, ASP does not allow the use of out-of-process components, but that can be changed using a registry setting. Table D-16 in Appendix D shows the appropriate setting for out-of-process component use in ASP. Be sure to carefully change the setting before attempting to use MTS with ASP.

After the registry setting is changed and the component is installed, you can call the component from a Web page. Use the CreateObject method of the Server object to create an instance of the object and call it. Here is the code:

```
<%
Dim objSimple
Dim strReturn

Set objSimple = Server.CreateObject("SimpleObject.Simple")

strReturn = objSimple.Process
%>

<%=strReturn%>
```

Coding your application with MTS rather than ASP alone has distinct advantages. First, simply by placing your component in MTS, you provide thread pooling automatically. Second, writing ASP code to perform even complex functions now becomes a simple matter of creating an object and calling a method. Finally, any other application can call the same objects that ASP calls, making the enterprise scalable and easier to maintain than it would be without MTS.

ODBC Connection Pooling

ODBC connection pooling is necessary for scaling sites. As stated earlier, IIS provides ODBC connection pooling automatically, based on a registry setting, but this pooling is not done when you call an out-of-process component—you have to provide the pooling as a separate feature. Fortunately, MTS includes ODBC connection pooling for modified Visual Basic code that supports it.

When creating Visual Basic applications, most developers don't concern themselves with ODBC connection pooling. Front-end components routinely open connections at the beginning of a session and leave them open until the application is terminated. Under MTS, ODBC connections are not opened by the front end or by the Web page but rather by the business object itself. Therefore, the ActiveX DLLs you create in Visual Basic must open a connection, read or write to the data source, and then close the connection. The Web page never accesses the database directly.

You might wonder how the data could appear on the page if the Web page itself never has direct access to a recordset. A Web page calling MTS objects relies on the objects to return data from a data source in a predictable format. This format can be as simple as a delimited string or as complex as a collection of objects. In any case, the business object is responsible for selecting records from the database, packaging them, and returning them to ASP.

As a simple example, Listing 10-1 shows the complete code for a Visual Basic business object that reads entries from a data source and returns them as a delimited string. The ASP page parses the returned string and places the entries in a <SELECT> tag. This is a typical technique for creating lookup lists.

```
Public Function GetPublishers() As String
On Error GoTo GetPublishersErr
    GetPublishers = ""

    ' Open connection
    Dim objConnection As RDO.rdoConnection
    Dim objResultset As RDO.rdoResultset

    Set objConnection = New RDO.rdoConnection
    objConnection.Connect = "DSN=Biblio"
    objConnection.EstablishConnection rdDriverNoPrompt, True

    ' Run query
    Set objResultset = objConnection.OpenResultset _
        ("SELECT Name FROM Publishers ORDER BY Name")

    ' Create return string
    Dim strTemp As String
    strTemp = ""

    Do While Not objResultset.EOF
        strTemp = strTemp & objResultset!Name & "|"
        objResultset.MoveNext
    Loop

    GetPublishers = strTemp

    ' Close connection
    objResultset.Close
    objConnection.Close
    Set objResultset = Nothing
    Set objConnection = Nothing

GetPublishersExit:
    Exit Function
```

Listing 10-1.
Returning a lookup list.

(continued)

Listing 10-1 *continued*

```
GetPublishersErr:
    GetPublishers = Err.Description
    Resume GetPublishersExit
End Function
```

In the example, the business object is an ActiveX DLL with one method, GetPublishers. The object uses Remote Data Objects (RDO) to access an ODBC data source created from the BIBLIO.MDB database that ships with Visual Basic. The component opens a connection to the data source and reads out all publisher names. The names are added to a string that is delimited by pipe characters (|). The component is compiled and placed in MTS Explorer. Note how the object opens a connection at the beginning of the function and closes the connection before returning the string of publishers. This coding style is required by MTS to allow ODBC connection pooling.

The string is returned to an ASP page through a call to the business object. Listing 10-2 shows the complete Web page code for building a lookup list. The publishers are parsed and added as entries to a <SELECT> tag. Other applications, such as Visual Basic front ends, can use the same object to fill a lookup list as well.

```
<%@ LANGUAGE="VBSCRIPT" %>

<HTML>
<HEAD>
<META NAME="GENERATOR" Content="Microsoft Visual InterDev 1.0">
<META HTTP-EQUIV="Content-Type" content="text/html;
    charset=iso-8859-1">
<TITLE>Document Title</TITLE>
</HEAD>
<BODY>

<%
    ' Variables
    Dim objQuery

    ' Create the business object
    Set objQuery = Server.CreateObject("QueryPublishers.List")
```

Listing 10-2.
Building a lookup list.

(continued)

Listing 10-2 *continued*

```
            ' Run the query
            Dim strReturn
            strReturn = objQuery.GetPublishers

            ' Fill the list box
            Dim intStart
            Dim intCurrent

            intStart = 1
            intCurrent = 1

            ' Parse the returned string
        %>

            <FORM>
            <SELECT SIZE=20>
        <%
            Do While intCurrent < Len(strReturn)
                intCurrent = InStr(intStart, strReturn, "|")
                If intCurrent = 0 Then Exit Do
        %>

                <OPTION>
                <%=Mid(strReturn, intStart, intCurrent - intStart)%>
                </OPTION>
        <%
                intStart = intCurrent + 1
            Loop
        %>
            </SELECT>
            </FORM>

        </BODY>
        </HTML>
```

As your site gets more complicated, you will want to return more than a simple list from a lookup table—you will want complete sets of records. This example uses an array to retrieve records and return them to the Web page. Listing 10-3 shows the code for a method that reads the BIBLIO.MDB data source and returns information about the authors contained in the database. The information is packed as entries in an array and returned to the client Web page.

The GetRows method of the Recordset object is specifically designed to create a Variant array from a Recordset. This array can be returned to the client, where it is unpacked and displayed.

```
Public Function GetAuthors(ByRef ReturnData As Variant) As Boolean
On Error GoTo GetAuthorsErr

    GetAuthors = False

    ' Open connection
    Dim objConnection As RDO.rdoConnection
    Dim objResultset As RDO.rdoResultset

    Set objConnection = New RDO.rdoConnection
    objConnection.Connect = "DSN=Biblio"
    objConnection.EstablishConnection rdDriverNoPrompt, True

    ' Run query
    Set objResultset = objConnection.OpenResultset _
        ("SELECT Author, [Year Born] FROM Authors ORDER BY Author", _
        rdOpenStatic)

    ' Evaluate the query results
    If objResultset.BOF And objResultset.EOF Then
        Err.Raise vbObjectError, "QueryAuthors", "No Records Returned!"
    End If

    ' Fill the array
    ReturnData = objResultset.GetRows(200)

    GetAuthors = True

    ' Close connection
    objResultset.Close
    objConnection.Close
    Set objResultset = Nothing
    Set objConnection = Nothing

GetAuthorsExit:
    Exit Function
```

Listing 10-3.

Returning a set of records.

(continued)

Listing 10-3 *continued*

```
GetAuthorsErr:
    GetAuthors = False
    ReDim ReturnData(0 To 1, 1 To 1)
    ReturnData(0, 1) = Err.Description
    ReturnData(1, 1) = Err.Source
    Resume GetAuthorsExit
End Function
```

When the array arrives in the Web page, ASP reads all the entries and builds an HTML table with the data. In this way, a complete set of data can be returned without having direct access to an ODBC connection in the Web page. The page can also write data back by calling methods that perform SQL Update functions inside of Visual Basic business objects. Listing 10-4 shows the complete code for building a table of records.

```
<%@ LANGUAGE="VBSCRIPT" %>

<HTML>
<HEAD>
<META NAME="GENERATOR" Content="Microsoft Visual InterDev 1.0">
<META HTTP-EQUIV="Content-Type" content="text/html;
    charset=iso-8859-1">
<TITLE>Document Title</TITLE>
</HEAD>
<BODY>

<%
    ' Create business object
    Dim blnReturn
    Dim objAuthors
    Dim varReturn
    Set objAuthors = Server.CreateObject("QueryAuthors.Table")

    ' Run query
    blnReturn = objAuthors.GetAuthors(varReturn)
%>
<H2>Here are the authors!</H2>
<TABLE BORDER>
<%
```

Listing 10-4.
Building a table of records.

(continued)

Listing 10-4 *continued*

```
' Fill the grid with first 10 rows
    For i = 0 To 9
%>
    <TR>
        <TD>
        <%=varReturn(0, i)%>
        </TD>
        <TD>
        <%=varReturn(1, i)%>
        </TD>
    </TR>
<%
    Next
%>
</TABLE>
</BODY>
</HTML>
```

Add, edit, and delete functionality can be provided through objects under MTS. The objects are subsequently available, without rewriting, to all applications on the enterprise.

Object Instance Pooling

The final concern when scaling applications is object instance pooling, which allows for the creation of a group of objects that can be shared by many applications. When a pool of objects is shared, the system has to create far fewer objects than if each user had an individual copy. Therefore, resources are used more efficiently. MTS provides object instance pooling, but you must make slight changes to your business objects in order to take full advantage of MTS.

When a business object is created under MTS, a special object named ObjectContext is created to monitor the process. The ObjectContext object monitors the resource usage of a business object and notifies MTS when the object can be returned to the pool. Normally, an object is pooled only after the client releases all references to it. However, if you change your code slightly, you can actually notify MTS directly that the object is ready to return to the pool. Cycling business objects in and out of the pool in MTS is called Just-In-Time (JIT) activation and As-Soon-As-Possible (ASAP) deactivation. JIT/ASAP pooling is the most efficient way of using system resources.

Enabling JIT/ASAP pooling requires that your business object communicate directly with the ObjectContext object assigned by MTS. This is done by using a special function named GetObjectContext, which is a member of the MTS API. To access this function, you must set a reference to MTS in the References dialog box of Visual Basic. Once the reference is set, you can use the following code to access the ObjectContext object:

```
Dim objContext As MTxAS.ObjectContext
Set objContext = GetObjectContext()
```

When your business object has a reference to the ObjectContext object, it can easily call the SetComplete method to tell MTS to recycle the object. This method causes MTS to place the business object back in the pool for reuse.

When objects are recycled in this way, MTS can use just a few objects to service many clients simultaneously. Of course, recycling objects means that any data retained in the objects is lost. Therefore, do not create business objects for permanent data storage. Instead, use Session variables to save any required data in the client that calls.

A Complete MTS Project

Microsoft Transaction Server (MTS) is designed to manage the entire overhead associated with scalable business applications. Using MTS, you can immediately gain the benefits of resource pooling and transaction processing. This exercise will show you how to use MTS to build fault-tolerant, scalable applications that run on the Internet.

Requirements:

1. Microsoft Windows NT 4.0

2. Microsoft Transaction Server

3. Microsoft Visual Basic 5.0, Enterprise Edition

4. Microsoft Visual InterDev 1.0

5. Microsoft Internet Information Server

6. Microsoft Internet Explorer 4.0

Part I: Setting Up the ODBC Data Source

Before you can use the ODBC API, you must set up an ODBC data source. In this exercise, you will interact with the Microsoft Access database NORTH-WIND.MDB, which ships with Visual Basic and which is included on the companion CD-ROM.

Establishing the data source is not a development tool function, but rather an operating system function. Setup is accomplished using the ODBC Data Source Administrator utility found in Microsoft Windows.

Step 1

In the Control Panel, locate an icon labeled ODBC. Double-click this icon to start the ODBC Data Source Administrator.

Step 2

In order to create a new data source, click the System DSN tab and then click the Add button.

Step 3

The Create New Data Source dialog box will appear, listing all the ODBC drivers available on your machine. For this exercise, you will need the Microsoft Access driver. Choose this driver from the list, and click Finish.

Step 4

When the ODBC Setup dialog box appears, you can define the new data source. First, you must provide a name. This can be any name, but for this exercise, type *NorthWind*.

Next, click the Select button and navigate the file system until you find the NORTHWIND.MDB file. Select this database file.

Click the OK button, and back out of the ODBC Data Source Administrator. You have now defined the data source.

Part II: Creating the Business Objects

Step 1

Using the File Manager, create a new directory named \MTS. Beneath this new directory, create a directory named SERVER.

Step 2

To start your new Visual Basic ActiveX DLL project, choose References from the Project menu and set references to the Microsoft Remote Data Object 2.0 component and the Microsoft Transaction Server 1.0 Type Library.

Change the properties of Project1 by choosing Project1 Properties from the Project menu. In the Project Properties dialog box, change the name of the project to MTSObject and change the description to MTS Training Exercise Objects. Click OK.

Step 3

In this part of the project, you will use a single class to query the NorthWind data source and return records and you will learn custom marshaling techniques to return data from a lookup table and records from a query.

Change the name of the Class1 class to Query.

Save the project in the \MTS\Server directory.

Step 4

Create a new method in the Query class by choosing Add Procedure from the Tools menu. In the Add Procedure dialog box, set the following attributes:

```
Name: GetCategories
Type: Function
Scope: Public
```

After inserting the new function, modify it to return a String data type. The complete function should now look like this:

```
Public Function GetCategories() As String
End Function
```

The GetCategories method returns a delimited string with all the category names. This technique is a quick way to return lookup table information to a list.

Step 5

Add the following code to the GetCategories method to read the category names from the data source and format the return string:

```
On Error GoTo GetCategoriesErr

    ' Get object context
    Dim objContext As MTxAS.ObjectContext
    Set objContext = GetObjectContext()

    Dim objConnection As RDO.rdoConnection
    Dim objResultset As RDO.rdoResultset

    ' Make connection.
    ' NOTE: Connections made to MTS must
    ' be made with the rdDriverNoPrompt option!
    Set objConnection = New RDO.rdoConnection
    objConnection.Connect = "DSN=NorthWind"
    objConnection.EstablishConnection rdDriverNoPrompt, True

    ' Run query
    Set objResultset = objConnection.OpenResultset _
        ("SELECT CategoryName FROM Categories")

    ' Build return string
    Dim strReturn As String
    strReturn = ""

Do While Not objResultset.EOF
    strReturn = strReturn & objResultset("CategoryName") & "|"
    objResultset.MoveNext
Loop

    ' Close connection to allow pooling
    objResultset.Close
    objConnection.Close
    Set objResultset = Nothing
    Set objConnection = Nothing

    ' Tell MTS we are done
    objContext.SetComplete
```

(continued)

231

continued

```
GetCategoriesExit:
    GetCategories = strReturn
    Exit Function

GetCategoriesErr:
    strReturn = Err.Description

    ' Tell MTS we failed
    objContext.SetAbort
    Resume GetCategoriesExit
```

Step 6

After the category names are returned to the front end, the user can select a category and see the associated products from the data source for that category. This is accomplished with a method named GetProducts, which returns all the products in an array to the client. The client then uses the array to fill a grid.

Add the GetProduct method by choosing Add Procedure from the Tools menu. In the Add Procedure dialog box, set the following attributes:

```
Name: GetProducts
Type: Function
Scope: Public
```

Step 7

Change the GetProducts function to accept two arguments and to return a Boolean value that indicates success or failure. The resulting function should look like this:

```
Public Function GetProducts(strCategory As String, _
    ByRef arrProducts As Variant) As Boolean

End Function
```

Step 8

GetProducts uses the category to search for products and fill an array with results. It also uses Just-In-Time activation to ensure that instances of the Query class are recycled as soon as possible. Add the following code to the GetProducts function to return an array of products to the client:

```
On Error GoTo GetProductsErr

    ' Get object context
    Dim objContext As MTxAS.ObjectContext
    Set objContext = GetObjectContext()

    ' Declare database objects
    Dim objConnection As RDO.rdoConnection
    Dim objResultset As RDO.rdoResultset

    ' Make connection
    Set objConnection = New RDO.rdoConnection
    objConnection.Connect = "DSN=NorthWind"
    objConnection.EstablishConnection rdDriverNoPrompt, True

    ' Run query
    Dim strSQL As String
    strSQL = "SELECT ProductName,CompanyName,UnitPrice "
    strSQL = strSQL & "FROM Products,Suppliers,Categories "
    strSQL = strSQL & "WHERE Products.SupplierID=Suppliers.SupplierID "
    strSQL = strSQL & "AND Products.CategoryID=Categories.CategoryID "
    strSQL = strSQL & "AND Categories.CategoryName='" & strCategory & "'"
    Set objResultset = objConnection.OpenResultset(strSQL)

    ' Build return array
    arrProducts = objResultset.GetRows(100)

    ' Close connection to allow pooling
    objResultset.Close
    objConnection.Close
    Set objResultset = Nothing
    Set objConnection = Nothing

    ' Tell MTS we are done
    GetProducts = True
    objContext.SetComplete

GetProductsExit:
    Exit Function

GetProductsErr:
    ' Tell MTS we failed
    GetProducts = False
    objContext.SetAbort
    Resume GetProductsExit
```

Step 9

Now that the business object is complete, you can compile it by choosing Make MTSObject.dll from the File menu. When the DLL is created, save your work and exit Visual Basic.

Part III: Placing the Business Object Under MTS Control

Step 1

From the Start menu, start MTS Explorer. In Explorer, choose My Computer and Packages Installed.

Add a new package to MTS by choosing New from the File menu. In the Package wizard, install a new empty package. Name the new package MTS NorthWind Exercise, and click Next.

Set the package identity to Interactive User, and click Finish.

Step 2

Double-click your new package to reveal the Components folder, and then double-click the Components folder itself. Choose New from the File menu to add a new component to your package. In the Component wizard, choose to import a component that is already registered.

Locate the component MTSObject.Query, select it, and click Finish. Your component is now registered and under the control of Microsoft Transaction Server.

Part IV: Preparing to Use MTS with IIS

Step 1

Before you can use MTS with Internet Information Server, you have to change an IIS registry setting to allow IIS to handle out-of-process ActiveX components.

NOTE: Making incorrect changes to the system registry can result in serious problems. Make the following changes carefully!

Changes to the IIS system registry are made through the registry editor. Start the editor by running Regedit from the command line in Windows.

Inside the registry, locate the following entry:

```
HKEY_LOCAL_MACHINE\SYSTEM
\CurrentControlSet
 \Services
  \W3SVC
   \ASP
    \Parameters
     \AllowOutOfProcCmpnts
```

The AllowOutOfProcCmpnts key is normally set to 0, which prevents IIS from using out-of-process components such as those in MTS. Double-click this key, and change its value to 1. This allows IIS to work with components in MTS.

Part V: Creating the Web Pages

Step 1

Start Visual InterDev. Create a new web project by choosing New from the File menu. When the New dialog box appears, click the Projects tab, and then choose the Web Project wizard. Locate your new project below the \MTS directory you created earlier, and then give your project the name NorthWind. Click OK.

Step 2

The Web Project wizard will ask you for the name of the Web server on which the new project will be created. If this text box contains an entry, you can accept it; if the box is empty, type the name of the machine that is running Internet Information Server. Click Next. If you don't know the correct name of your Web server, look up the Identification information by using the Network applet in the Control Panel.

The Web Project wizard will contact the selected Web server and present you with the step 2 dialog box. Choose the option Create A New Web. Make sure the name of the web is NorthWind. Check the option to enable full-text searching of the site, and click Finish. The Web Project wizard will create your new web and open the project.

Step 3

This project will be built in a set of browser frames. Add a new HTML page for the frames by choosing New from the File menu. In the New dialog box, add a new HTML page and name the page DEFAULT.HTM. Click OK.

Define the frame set for the application by altering the Web page to appear as follows:

```
<HTML>
<HEAD>
<TITLE>Transaction Server</TITLE>
</HEAD>
<BODY>
<FRAMESET COLS="27%,73%">
    <FRAME SRC="categories.asp" NAME="LIST" SCROLLING="No">
    <FRAME SRC="products.asp" NAME="MAIN" SCROLLING="No">
</FRAMESET>
</BODY>
</HTML>
```

Save the page.

Step 4

Add a new ASP page to the project by choosing New from the File menu. In the New dialog box, select to add a new ASP page and name the page CATE-GORIES.ASP. Click OK.

This page will present a list of product categories to the user, who can then view the products by clicking hyperlinks. Add the following code to the BODY section of the page to create the categories from the NorthWind data source:

```
<%
' Variables
Dim objQuery

' Create the business object
Set objQuery = Server.CreateObject("MTSObject.Query")

' Run the query
Dim strReturn
strReturn = objQuery.GetCategories

' Fill the list box
Dim intStart
Dim intCurrent
```

```
intStart = 1
intCurrent = 1

' Parse the returned string
Do While intCurrent < Len(strReturn)
    intCurrent = InStr(intStart, strReturn, "|")
    If intCurrent = 0 Then Exit Do
%>
<FONT FACE="Verdana" SIZE=4>
<A TARGET="MAIN"
HREF="products.asp?Product=<%=Server.URLEncode(Mid(strReturn, intStart,
                                  intCurrent - intStart))%>">
    <%=Mid(strReturn, intStart, intCurrent - intStart)%>
</A>
</FONT>
<%
    intStart = intCurrent + 1
Loop
%>
```

Step 5

Add a new ASP page to the project by choosing New from the File menu. In the New dialog box, select to add a new ASP page and name the page PRO-DUCTS.ASP. Click OK.

This page will build a table of all products from the database in the selected category. Add the following code to the BODY section to create the HTML table:

```
<%
' Create business object
Dim blnReturn
Dim objProducts
Set objProducts = Server.CreateObject("MTSObject.Query")

' Run query
Dim varReturn
blnReturn = _
    objProducts.GetProducts(Request.QueryString("product"), varReturn)
%>

<IMG SRC="banner.gif"><P>
```

(continued)

continued

```
<!-- Begin table definition -->
<TABLE BORDER WIDTH=100%>
    <TR>
    <TD>
    Product
    </TD>
    <TD>
    Company
    </TD>
    <TD>
    Price
    </TD>
    </TR>

<%
' Fill the grid
Dim i
For i = 0 To UBound(varReturn, 2)
%>
    <TR>
    <TD>
    <%=varReturn(0, i)%>
    </TD>
    <TD>
    <%=varReturn(1, i)%>
    </TD>
    <TD>
    <%=varReturn(2, i)%>
    </TD>
    </TR>
<%
Next
%>
</TABLE>
```

Step 6

Save the project, and view DEFAULT.HTM in Internet Explorer. The result should look like the page in Figure 10-4. You will access Visual Basic business objects in MTS to perform the queries.

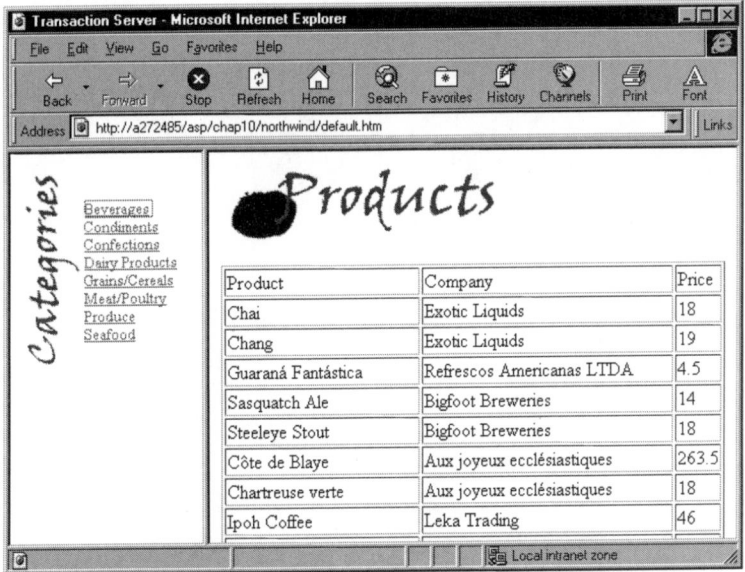

Figure 10-4.

The completed exercise.

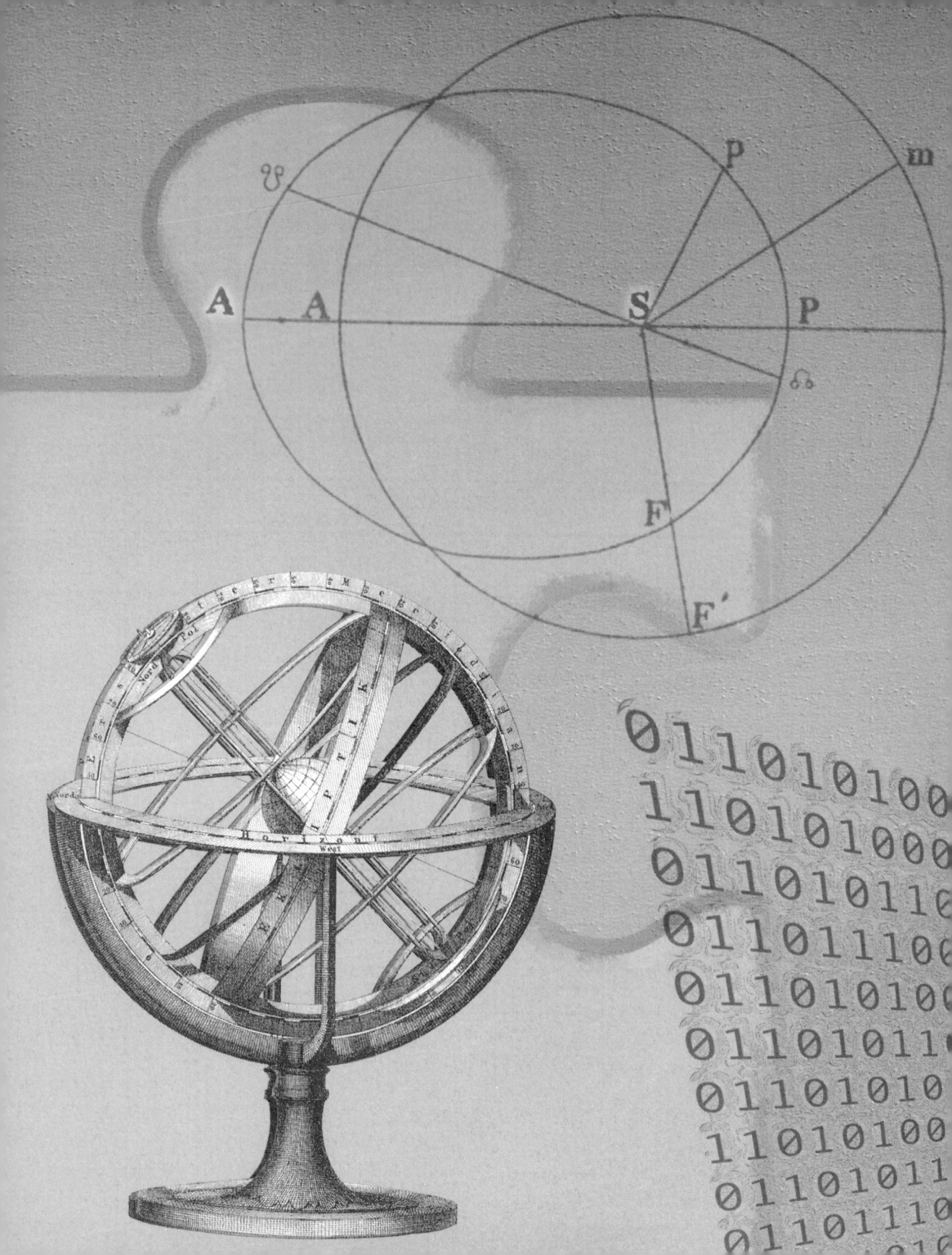

Choosing the Right Technology

If you are a Web developer, you face a bewildering number of options for creating business solutions that run in a browser. Competing technologies present a confusing picture as you try to select a suite of tools for your project. This section examines some of the key issues involved in Web-based solutions and provides guidance in the selection of technologies for creating an application.

Client Platform Considerations

Without question, the single biggest concern in technology selection is the target browser. You must identify the various browsers you will support with your solution. If the application is intended as a public Internet solution, look to the widest possible audience. That does *not* mean that you must accommodate every type of browser. If you try to do so, you are limited to simple HTML pages with no frames or tables. A solution written to the lowest common denominator offers little functionality or visual appeal.

In most cases, support for Microsoft Internet Explorer and Netscape Navigator should be sufficient to reach over 90 percent of the intended audience. However, different versions of these browsers support different technology levels. If your application has to support an earlier version of IE or NN—one prior to version 3.0—some of the newer technologies might not work. And even limiting the scope of the solution by version might not be sufficient to solve the problem. Operating systems can affect the equation as well. For example, IE 3.0 running under Microsoft Windows 3.11 does not recognize the <OBJECT> tag.

Obviously, target platforms become the primary focus of technology selection. The following table shows some popular browsers and their capabilities.

Browser	HTML	Cascading Style Sheets	Dynamic HTML	Scripting	ActiveX	Java
Internet Explorer 4.0	3.2	Complete	Yes	VBScript JScript	Complete	1.1
Internet Explorer 3.0	2	Format support only	No	VBScript JScript	Complete	1.0
Netscape Navigator 4.0 (Communicator)	3.2	Complete	Yes*	JavaScript	Active Documents	1.1**
Netscape Navigator 3.0	2	None	No	JavaScript	None	1.0
Netscape Navigator 2.0	2	None	No	JavaScript	None	1.0

 * Dynamic HTML is implemented differently in Communicator than in IE 4.0.

** Communicator supports partial implementation of Java 1.1, with complete support promised.

You could examine endless combinations of browsers and operating systems, but let's focus on the most common solutions and consider suggestions for creating wide-ranging applications. For the sake of discussion, assume that a *platform-independent solution* means an application that can be used by Internet Explorer and Netscape Navigator versions 3.0 and later. Even in this limited domain, you'll find plenty to be concerned with.

HTML Support

Within your limited field, all the browsers you are targeting support the latest HTML 3.2 standard. This does not mean that you can use *any* HTML tag. Many tags are not part of the HTML standard and are simply proprietary to a particular browser. The <LAYER> tag in Netscape Navigator 4.0 (also known as Communicator) is a good example of a tag not supported by any other browser. <LAYER> is used to create invisible layers of HTML content in the Communicator version of Dynamic HTML. However, if you limit yourself to the HTML 3.2 standard and stay away from proprietary tags, all the target browsers should support your content.

Cascading Style Sheets

Cascading Style Sheets (CSS) were introduced under Internet Explorer 3.0 and were enhanced under IE 4.0. Communicator introduced CSS support for Netscape browsers. IE 4.0 and Communicator accommodate the complete CSS specification, including positioning elements through left, top, height, width, and z-index attributes. Under IE 3.0, CSS support is limited to font attributes such as size, color, and style and does not include advanced content positioning.

Dynamic HTML Support

Dynamic HTML is, of course, a new feature of Internet Explorer 4.0 and is not supported in any previous release of IE. Netscape Communicator also supports a version of Dynamic HTML, which can lead to confusion regarding the implementation of this technology. Although Netscape uses the same name for its dynamic positioning technology, the technology itself is fundamentally different from Dynamic HTML under IE 4.0. Under Communicator, you create layers of content that can be moved and sized dynamically. These layers can be created by using a <STYLE> tag with a position attribute set to ABSOLUTE or by using the proprietary <LAYER> tag.

Although you can create effects in Communicator that are similar to effects in IE 4.0, you will have an extremely difficult time creating an application using Dynamic HTML that runs under both IE and Communicator. At this time, the World Wide Web Consortium (W3C) is considering standards for Dynamic HTML that might eventually bring the two browsers closer together, but the Dynamic HTML issue illustrates a larger truth: competition has left little motivation for companies to agree on any content generation standards. Look for this trend to continue.

Scripting Support

Here the choice is clear. If you want to use client-side scripting in both Microsoft and Netscape products, you need to use JavaScript, which is recognized by all the target browsers. Bear in mind, however, that Internet Explore's JScript does not contain the same level of case sensitivity as Navigator's JavaScript.

Internet Explorer also differs from Netscape Navigator in the implementation of its browser object model. Generally speaking, the object model of IE 4.0 is far richer than that of any other browser, but most of this model is used to tie scripting to Dynamic HTML. Therefore, if you use the browser object model beyond the simple Window, Document, and Form objects, be careful to ensure that the script runs on all target platforms.

Also note that some third parties have created plug-ins for Navigator that allow some support for VBScript. The best known of these comes from N-Compass Labs. Although a plug-in can be useful, users might not have the plug-in when they reach your site and presumably would be forced to download it prior to viewing any content that required it. Forced downloading is time-consuming.

ActiveX Support

This area might surprise you because Communicator offers some level of support for ActiveX technologies. Communicator has the ability to host documents from applications such as Microsoft Word and Microsoft Excel through Automation. The feature allows you to make documents a part of any site that targets the browser. However, any Navigator version prior to Communicator will not support ActiveX documents. Additionally, some literature advertises that Visual Basic ActiveX documents can be viewed in Communicator. At this writing, we can find no such support in the product.

Java

Java is another area where support is widespread. But note that Internet Explorer version 3.0 and Netscape Navigator version 3.0 support only version 1.0 of the Java Development Kit (JDK). The most recent release of Java, which is version 1.1, is fully supported only by IE 4.0. Communicator provides only partial support for JDK 1.1, but Netscape promises full support by the end of 1997.

After examining the difficulties confronting developers who target a wide audience, you might feel that you are left with only HTML 2.0, JavaScript, and Java 1.0. But the truth is that the best solution targets optimal features of all the target browsers. The key to optimizing any solution you create is to use the Browser Capabilities component of Active Server Pages. (The Browser Capabilities component is discussed in Chapter 5.) Finally, test your site in every version of the browser you expect to support. You absolutely cannot guarantee that the site behaves correctly without multiple-platform testing.

Server-Side Considerations

Platforms that can function as Web servers fall into three categories: Windows, non-Windows, and Internet Service Providers. The Windows platform is obviously the tool of choice for the back end of any Web application. Active Server Pages is available only from Microsoft under the Windows platform (although third parties have created versions for other systems). The problem arises when you cannot use Windows, Internet Information Server, and ASP as a back-end solution. In this case, you need to be aware of other available technology.

Even without Windows, IIS, and ASP, you can still use many of the client-side technologies described in this book. Non-Windows platforms can download client-side script in either VBScript or JavaScript. You can also use client-side ActiveX components. Even though the server might not understand the components, the browser can still request a file download, so all you have to do is make the files available on the server and Internet Explorer can use them. Java is also still effective. Once again, as long as the files are on the server, the browser can retrieve them. What you lose with non-Windows platforms is the ease and performance of Active Server Pages. You will probably be left with older, slower technology such as Common Gateway Interface (CGI).

If you are using an Internet Service Provider (ISP), client-side technologies are still available. As long as you can upload script, DLL files, and CLASS files, you can use VBScript, JavaScript, ActiveX, and Java. Some ISPs even support ASP on their server. Check with your ISP to see which technologies are used on the server and whether they are available to subscribers.

Conclusion

Selecting a technology is a function of many different factors. You must decide whether your application will run on the Internet or on an intranet. You must identify your infrastructure support and determine whether you can use ASP as a back end. You should also consider existing knowledge and code investments. If, for example, you have seasoned Visual Basic programmers at your shop, training them in Java might not make sense. Additionally, existing code can be reused in your Web solutions. You might have existing ActiveX controls that could be used in Web pages or Visual Basic forms that could be easily converted to ActiveX Documents. All in all, no simple answers exist, and the pressure of competition promises to prevent true cross-platform solutions for years to come.

VBScript and ActiveX Primer

This appendix provides a quick reference for developers who are starting to use the VBScript language and ActiveX technology to create dynamic Web pages.

Script Sections

Understanding scripting begins with <SCRIPT> tags, which designate sections of an HTML Web page where script code can be inserted. Although usually placed as the last set of tags in the HEAD section of a Web page, <SCRIPT> tags can be used anywhere in the page. A <SCRIPT> tag has the following syntax:

<SCRIPT	
CLASS	The style class for the <SCRIPT> tag
EVENT	The name of the event that the <SCRIPT> tag will handle
FOR	The name of the HTML element that triggers the handled event
ID	The identifier for the tag
LANGUAGE	The scripting language used for this section
SRC	The source file for this section
TITLE	Additional information
>	
</SCRIPT>	

VBScript is an event-driven language, and the primary purpose of a SCRIPT section is to map the code you write to a user interaction or a system response. Microsoft Internet Explorer supports many different types of events, including a full range of mouse and keyboard events. (For a complete list of supported events, see the online reference on the CD-ROM that accompanies this book.)

Mapping events to code in a SCRIPT section can be accomplished in different ways. You can choose, for example, to dedicate an entire SCRIPT section to a single event by using the EVENT and FOR attributes of the <SCRIPT> tag. The following code declares a SCRIPT section for the Window_OnLoad event:

```
<SCRIPT LANGUAGE="VBScript" FOR="Window" EVENT="OnLoad">

</SCRIPT>
```

Obviously, if you declare a SCRIPT section for just one event, you will have to create multiple sections—one for each event that you want to trap. But multiple SCRIPT sections are difficult to maintain, so you might want to combine a number of events in one section. This is accomplished by using the *Sub Object_EventName* syntax. The following code designates a single section that contains event handlers for both the OnLoad and OnUnload events of the Window object:

```
<SCRIPT LANGUAGE="VBScript">
    Sub Window_OnLoad()

    End Sub

    Sub Window_OnUnload()

    End Sub
</SCRIPT>
```

You can also choose to map events by using event-handling attributes, which are mapped directly to a tag and call a VBScript procedure written in a SCRIPT section. The following code uses an event-handling attribute to call a function for the OnLoad event of the Window object:

```
<SCRIPT LANGUAGE="VBScript">
    Sub PageStart
        MsgBox "Page Loaded!"
    End Sub
</SCRIPT>

<BODY LANGUAGE="VBScript" OnLoad="PageStart">
```

Regardless of how you choose to declare events, you must be wary of attempting to execute client-side code in a browser that does not support scripting. Browsers have an interesting response to tags they do not recognize: they simply ignore them. This has a strange effect on the code contained in a SCRIPT section. For example, you would expect the following code to show a message when the page is loaded:

```
<SCRIPT LANGUAGE="VBScript">
    Sub Window_OnLoad()
        MsgBox "Hello!"
    End Sub
</SCRIPT>
```

This code works well if the browser recognizes script. But an old Mosaic browser, which does not understand the <SCRIPT> tag, ignores the tag and sees only the following text:

```
Sub Window_OnLoad()
    MsgBox "Hello!"
End Sub
```

Because the code now appears as text, the old browser is happy to display the code as content in the body of the browser. This is not at all what you want. The solution to the problem is to surround the code with HTML comment marks, which hide the code from old browsers and prevent unwanted behavior. Newer browsers expect to see the comment marks and will ignore them.

```
<SCRIPT LANGUAGE="VBScript">
<!--
    Sub Window_OnLoad()
        MsgBox "Hello!"
    End Sub
-->
</SCRIPT>
```

Declaring Variables

VBScript supports only one data type: the Variant. A Variant is a variable that can represent any data—numbers, text, or objects. You simply declare a variable and assign the value. A Variant can, however, distinguish the kind of data stored in the variable. This distinction is known as the Variant subtype, which determines whether a value is added or concatenated (for example, when you use a + sign).

Data subtypes can lead to subtle Type Mismatch errors in your script code. For example, suppose you want to assign the Window object to a variable. You might declare a Variant with the Dim statement and assign the object, but this will fail unless you use the Set keyword required by VBScript when dealing with object data:

```
Dim MyWindow
Set MyWindow = Window
```

VBScript supports a full range of subtype conversions. Generally, these functions begin with capital C (for convert) and the subtype you want. Thus, a number can convert to a string, as follows:

```
Dim MyString
Dim MyNumber
MyNumber = 5
MyString = CStr(MyNumber)
```

Variables declared in VBScript have lifetime and scope restrictions. *Lifetime* and *scope* refer to how long the variable is available and what parts of the VBScript code can access it. VBScript supports three levels of scope through the keywords Public, Private, and Dim.

Public variables are declared inside of a SCRIPT section but outside of any procedure. When variables are declared as Public, they are available to all the scripts in the Web page. Their values persist as long as the page is loaded.

Private variables are also declared inside of a SCRIPT section and outside of any procedure. When variables are declared as Private, they are available only to the routines defined in the SCRIPT section where the variables are defined. Their values persist as long as the Web page is loaded.

Variables declared with the Dim keyword can be declared outside of routines, where they behave as Private variables. They can also be declared directly in the body of a procedure, where they are available only to the procedure code itself; no other routine can use them. When variables are declared in a procedure, their values persist only until the procedure finishes running, and then they are destroyed.

Key Language Elements

VBScript supports a number of structures designed to perform decision and looping functions in the program. These structures create the logic of the program.

The primary decision structure in VBScript is the If...Then statement, which has the following syntax:

```
If condition Then
    [statements]
[ElseIf condition-n Then
    [elseifstatements]]...
[Else
    [elsestatements]]
End If
```

If...Then structures are useful for making simple decisions but can be cumbersome if the number of cases is too large. Fortunately, VBScript supports the Select...Case statement, which provides a number of different branching tests in a single compact statement. The Select...Case statement has the following syntax:

```
Select Case testexpression
    [Case expressionlist-n
        [statements-n]]...
    [Case Else expressionlist-n
        [elsestatements-n]]
End Select
```

In addition to decision structures, VBScript supports several looping structures, which allow you to perform an operation many times or move easily through a group of objects. The primary loop structure is For...Next, which loops a fixed number of times based on the definition of a looping variable. The For...Next loop has the following syntax:

```
For counter = start To end [Step step]
    [statements]
Next
```

Although For...Next is good for simple loops, more complex loops require a richer structure. The Do loop allows looping to continue until a condition is met, supporting conditional testing at either the beginning or the end of the loop. The Do loop has the following syntax:

```
Do [{While | Until} condition]
    [statements]
Loop [{While | Until} condition]
```

If you need to move through a set of objects contained in a collection, choose the For Each...Next loop, which allows you to perform an operation on every member of a collection or an array. The For Each...Next loop has the following syntax:

```
For Each element In group
    [statements]
Next [element]
```

Using ActiveX Components

In addition to the built-in variables, functions, and structures of VBScript, you can utilize ActiveX components in constructing your Web pages. These ActiveX components can be controls found in the toolbox of a visual development tool, or they can be Automation servers that do not have a graphical user interface. In any case, VBScript accesses the functionality of an ActiveX component through the <OBJECT> tag, which defines the component to be run on the client. The <OBJECT> tag has the following syntax:

<OBJECT	
ACCESSKEY	The key to use as an accelerator with the CTRL key
ALIGN	The alignment to use with the component
CLASS	The style class of the component
CLASSID	The Globally Unique Identifier (GUID) that identifies the component
CODE	The location of the Java class file
CODEBASE	The location of the component files for downloading
CODETYPE	The Internet media-type for the component
DATA	The Internet address where the component's run-time data is located
DATAFLD	The database field to bind to the component
DATASRC	The ID of the Advanced Data Control to bind with
HEIGHT	The height of the component
ID	The identifier for the component in this page
LANGUAGE	The language to use with event attributes
NAME	The name of the component or bookmark
STYLE	The style attributes for the component
TABINDEX	The tabbing order for the component
TITLE	Additional information
TYPE	The MIME type for the scripting engine
WIDTH	The width of the component
>	
</OBJECT>	

Although the <OBJECT> tag has many attributes, only three of them are required to use a component: ID, CLASSID, and CODEBASE. ID is the name of the component. You use this attribute in VBScript to address the properties, events, and methods of the component.

The CLASSID attribute contains the GUID that uniquely identifies the component. (The GUID is a serial number unique to the component and is the same on every client machine running the component.) CLASSID is stored in the system registry for all ActiveX components. When Microsoft Internet Explorer 4.0 encounters an <OBJECT> tag, it uses the CLASSID attribute to identify the component in the system registry and create a copy of it. If the component is not in the registry, IE 4.0 can download it from the address specified by the CODEBASE attribute.

Once downloaded, the component generally sets default values for its properties. This is usually accomplished through <PARAM> tags, which identify a property of the component and a default value. A <PARAM> tag has the following syntax:

```
<PARAM
DATAFLD             The database field to bind to the component
DATAFORMATAS        Indicates whether the bound data is HTML or
                    plain text
DATASRC             The ID of the Advanced Data Control to bind with
NAME                The property name
VALUE               The default value
>
```

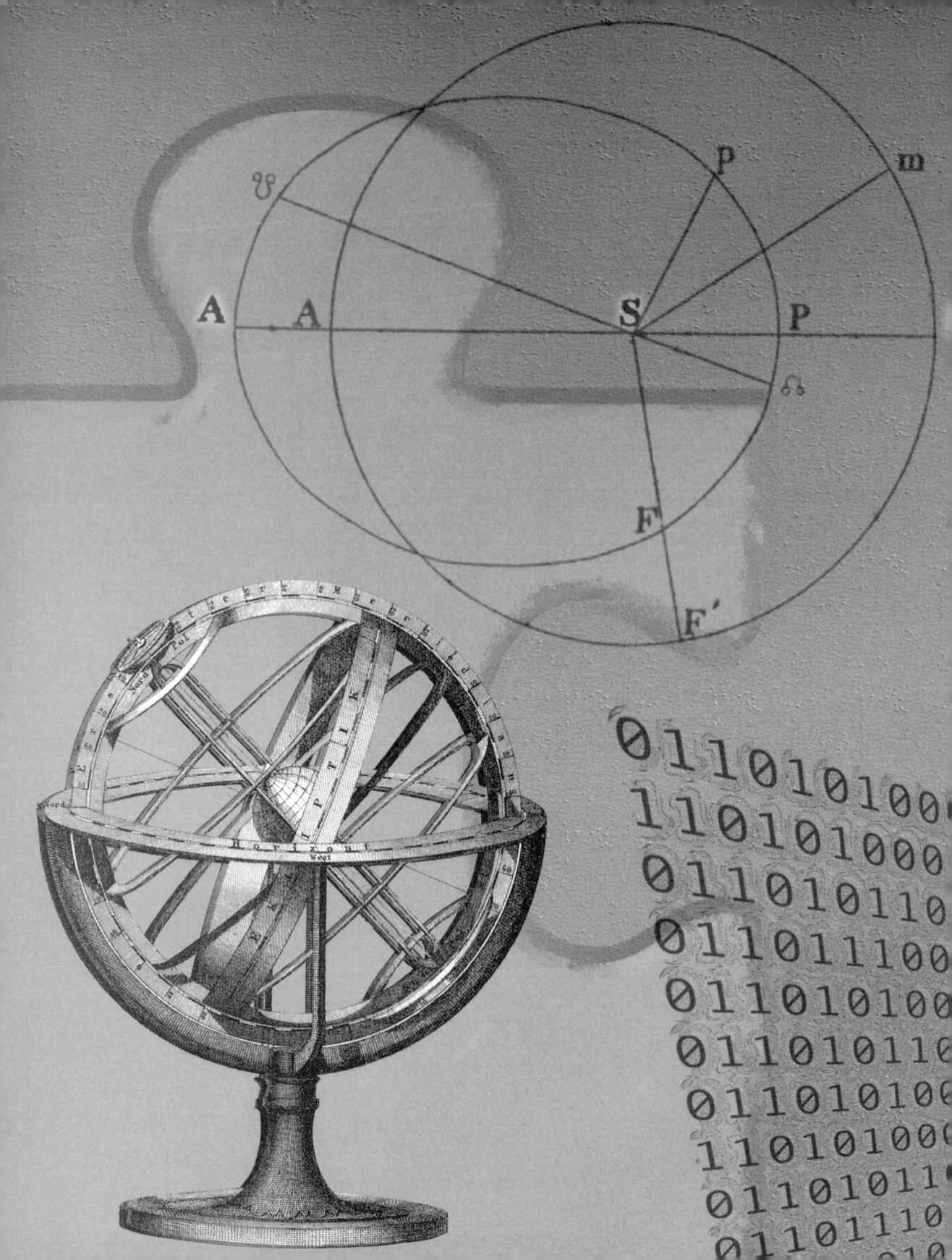

JScript and Java Primer

Most of the examples in this book use the VBScript language, but not all browsers support VBScript. In fact, only Microsoft Internet Explorer fully supports VBScript, Dynamic HTML, and ActiveX. If you are interested in creating an application that can run on both Netscape Navigator and Internet Explorer, your solution might be Active Server Pages with a little client-side script. This is an excellent approach for Internet applications that must run on the largest number of browsers. This appendix gives an overview of the JScript language, Microsoft's implementation of JavaScript, which runs on both Netscape Navigator and IE 4.0.

JScript Event Handling

The <SCRIPT> tag, discussed in detail in Appendix A, designates script code in JScript as well as in VBScript. However, mapping events to script code is done a little differently in JScript than in VBScript. In VBScript, you can choose from several techniques, but in JScript, you always use the event attribute method. The following code would be used to handle the Window OnLoad event:

```
<SCRIPT LANGUAGE="JavaScript">
<!--
    function pageStart
    {
        alert("Page Loaded!");
        return true;
    }
-->
</SCRIPT>

<BODY LANGUAGE="JavaScript" OnLoad="var rtn =pageStart();">
```

Notice that JScript has a much different syntax than VBScript. JScript looks more like C than like Basic. Every routine in JScript is a function, and the beginning and end of a function is defined by using curly braces ({}). And JScript is case sensitive! That's right, case matters. In most instances, JScript uses lowercase for all object names. So be careful when you use the Window and Document objects—they are *window* and *document* to JScript.

Declaring Variables

Like VBScript, JScript does not have any specific data types. Instead, it has only a single typeless data, which can be thought of as a Variant and which functions much like the Variant in VBScript. Also, like VBScript, JScript supports subtypes in variables. In other words, although the variable is typeless, the data inside the variable is identified by JScript as one of three types: String, Numeric, or Boolean.

The String data subtype in JScript is unique in scripting languages because it behaves as an object. Simply declaring a variable and assigning text to it creates a String object. Methods associated with the String object can be used to perform functions such as parsing or capitalization. The following code creates a String object and capitalizes all the characters in the text:

```
<SCRIPT LANGUAGE="JavaScript">
<!--
    function caps(stringData)
    {
        alert(stringData.toUpperCase());
    }
-->
</SCRIPT>
```

In addition to the String object, JScript supports several other intrinsic objects that can be used directly in the scripting language. The available objects are the Array, Date, Math, Number, and Function objects. For documentation on the properties and methods of the objects, refer to the CD-ROM that accompanies this book.

The Numeric data subtype is used to hold any numbers, and the Boolean subtype is used for true and false values. JScript recognizes the keywords true and false, but beware of case sensitivity. Declaring variables in JScript requires the var keyword—the only keyword for declaring variables.

Variables in JScript have two levels of scope: global and local. A variable declared inside the SCRIPT section but outside of functions is global and can be used by all functions. A variable declared inside a function is available only to the function in which it resides.

Custom Objects

In addition to its intrinsic objects, JScript supports custom objects in code. Creating custom objects gives your script a more object-oriented look and feel. A custom object is created by using special functions that declare properties and methods for the object. As an example, let's create an object named alien to describe a mythical extraterrestrial. To define the object, establish a function with variables for properties:

```
function alien(skincolor, numheads, antenna)
{
    //Properties
    this.skincolor = skincolor;
    this.numheads = numheads;
    this.antenna = antenna;
}
```

Notice the use of the keyword this, which refers to the object instance being created with the function. The function accepts arguments for all the properties and assigns them in turn when the alien object is created. You can also create methods for the alien object in the same way. First, declare the methods as functions in your script:

```
function eat(food)
{
    window.alert("MMMMM " + food + " was good!");
}

function changeskincolor(color)
{
    if (color == "Green" | color == "Red")
    {
        this.skincolor = color;
    }

    if (color == "Red")
    {
        this.numheads = 5;
    }
}
```

Once the functions are created for the methods, assign them to the object using the keyword this. Here is the complete function for the alien object:

```
function alien(skincolor, numheads, antenna)
{
    // Properties
    this.skincolor = skincolor;
    this.numheads = numheads;
    this.antenna = antenna;

    // Methods
    this.eat = eat;
    this.changeskincolor = changeskincolor;
}
```

Once the alien object is declared, you can create instances of it by using the keyword new. This allows you to call the associated properties and methods by using a variable. The following code shows a complete alien example:

```
<HTML>
<HEAD>
<TITLE>Aliens!!</TITLE>

<SCRIPT LANGUAGE="JavaScript">

    var MyAlien // This is the variable for the instance

    function createalien()
    {

        // Create an instance of a
        // new alien

        MyAlien = new alien("Green", 12, "Yes");
        window.alert("Alien Created!");
    }


    // Define the class

    function alien(skincolor, numheads, antenna)
    {
    // Properties
        this.skincolor = skincolor;
        this.numheads = numheads;
        this.antenna = antenna;

        // Methods
        this.eat = eat;
```

```
            this.changeskincolor = changeskincolor;
    }

    function eat(food)
    {
        window.alert("MMMMM " + food + " was good!");
    }

    function changeskincolor(color)
    {
        if (color == "Green" | color == "Red")
        {
            this.skincolor = color;
        }

        if (color == "Red")
        {
            this.numheads = 5;
        }
    }

</SCRIPT>

<BODY BGCOLOR="WHITE">
<CENTER>
<FORM NAME="frmAlien">

<!-- This button creates the alien -->
<INPUT TYPE="BUTTON" VALUE="Create Alien"
    OnClick="createalien();"><P>

<!-- This text box is for the alien's food -->
<INPUT NAME="txtFood"><P>

<!-- This button feeds the alien whatever is
in the text box -->
<INPUT TYPE="BUTTON" VALUE="Feed the Alien"
    OnClick="MyAlien.eat(document.frmAlien.txtFood.value);">
<P>

<!-- This button reads the skin color and displays it -->
<INPUT TYPE="BUTTON" VALUE="Get Skin Color"
    OnClick="window.alert(MyAlien.skincolor);">
<P>
```

(continued)

continued

```
<!-- This text box allows you to set a new color -->
<INPUT NAME="txtColor">

<!-- This button sets the new color -->
<INPUT TYPE="BUTTON" VALUE="Set Skin Color"
    OnClick="MyAlien.changeskincolor(document.frmAlien.txtColor.value);">
<P>

<!-- This button displays the number of heads -->
<INPUT TYPE="BUTTON" VALUE="Number of Heads"
    OnClick="window.alert(MyAlien.numheads);">

</FORM>
</CENTER>
</BODY>
</HTML>
```

Key Language Elements

JScript supports a number of decision and looping structures, many of which mimic the structures available in VBScript. The primary decision structure in JScript is the if statement, which is similar to the VBScript If...Then statement. The if statement uses the following syntax:

```
if (condition)
    statement1
[else
    statement2]
```

Unlike VBScript, JScript does not support a statement similar to the Select...Case statement. Instead, you use multiple lines of if statements to create complex branches. The only alternative to this is an implicit branch using a somewhat unreadable question mark structure. For information about this oddity, see the CD-ROM that accompanies this book.

JScript supports several different types of loops. The first is a statement that mimics the VBScript For...Next loop, the for statement. Here is the syntax for the for statement:

```
for (initialization; test; increment)
    statement
```

The while loop is the equivalent of the VBScript Do loop. This structure loops as long as a condition is true, giving you control over when the loop ends.

The following code shows the syntax for the while loop:

```
while (expression)
    statement
```

Like VBScript, JScript also supports a loop that allows you to perform a function on each member of a collection or an array. In JScript, this structure is called the for...in statement. Here is the syntax for the for...in statement:

```
for (variable in [object | array])
    statement
```

Using Java Applets

Many developers use Java applets in Web pages to enhance the graphical user interface. Like ActiveX components, Java applets are separately compiled, downloadable units of software that can run in a Web page. And like ActiveX components, Java applets can support events, properties, and methods. These members can be accessed by both JScript and VBScript.

Applets are placed in a Web page by using the <APPLET> tag, which has the following syntax:

<APPLET	
ALIGN	The alignment for the applet
ALT	The text to show if the browser can't execute the applet
CLASS	The style class of the applet
CODE	The name of the applet file to download and run
CODEBASE	The base address of the applet
DATAFLD	The field to bind with an applet parameter
DATASRC	The identifier of the Advanced Data Control to bind with
HEIGHT	The height of the applet
HSPACE	The horizontal margin for the applet
ID	The identifier for the applet in script
NAME	The name of the applet
SRC	The Internet address of a data file
STYLE	The style attributes of the applet
TITLE	Additional information
VSPACE	The vertical margin for the applet
WIDTH	The width of the applet
>	
</APPLET>	

Although the <APPLET> tag has many attributes, only one is really required: the CODE attribute identifies the applet to download and run. Unlike ActiveX components, Java applets do not rely on the registry to download; the file is downloaded and run each time. As in ActiveX components, however, properties can be stored in <PARAM> tags for the application to read. A <PARAM> tag has the following syntax:

<PARAM	
DATAFLD	The database field to bind to the component
DATAFORMATAS	Indicates whether the bound data is HTML or plain text
DATASRC	The ID of the Advanced Data Control to bind with
NAME	The property name
VALUE	The default value
>	

Internet Glossary of Terms

Active Desktop   The shell integration of Microsoft Internet Explorer with the Microsoft Windows operating system.

ActiveX Data Objects (ADO)   A set of ActiveX components designed to access ODBC data sources using the OLEDB standard.

ActiveX technologies   A suite of products and technologies produced by Microsoft to allow communication between software objects.

address   The location of a user on the Internet. Typically, this address is formatted as *user@host*, where *user* is the name of your account and *host* is the name of the domain you are on (e.g., fred@bedrock.com).

anonymous connection   A connection to a Web server done without an account or a password. An anonymous account allows any browser to log on but can restrict access to various functions for security purposes.

backbone   The main series of connections in a network.

bandwidth   The amount of data, measured in bits per second, that can be passed through the existing network infrastructure.

browser   A client-side application used to view information on the Internet.

Browser Capabilities component   An ActiveX component that allows you to identify the type and capabilities of a browser.

channel   A technology that allows services to push data to Microsoft Internet Explorer.

chatting   Communicating directly in real time with other users on the Internet.

client   An application or a computer that communicates with and requests information from a server.

com   An Internet address extension indicating that the Web site is a commercial site.

Component Object Model (COM)   The technology that allows software objects to communicate. All ActiveX components are based on COM.

Content Linking component   An ActiveX component used to link discreet Web pages together in a book or a magazine format.

domain   A unique alphanumeric name for an Internet site.

Domain Name System (DNS)   A system for translating alphanumeric computer names into Internet Protocol (IP) addresses.

Dynamic HTML   The technology that allows every tag in an HTML Web page to be treated as a programmable object.

edu   An Internet address extension indicating that the Web site is an educational institution.

File Access component   An ActiveX component used to access text files from script.

File Transfer Protocol (FTP)   A communications standard for transferring files between computers on the Internet. FTP is supported by Microsoft Internet Information Server.

firewall   A security measure that protects information and prevents access to a computer or network system.

gateway   A computer that connects one network with another when the two networks operate on different protocols.

Gopher   A file transfer system that allows searching with menus. Gopher is supported by Microsoft Internet Information Server.

Graphics Interchange Format (GIF)   A compressed graphics file format for distributing graphics on the Internet.

host   A Web server that users can log on to.

HyperText Markup Language (HTML)   The coding standard for creating Web pages.

HyperText Transfer Protocol (HTTP)   The communications standard for transferring Web pages between computers.

Integrated Services Digital Network (ISDN)   A data transfer mechanism that supports up to 64 Kb per second over a standard phone line.

Internet Database Connector (IDC)   A special implementation of the ISAPI interface to Microsoft Internet Information Server, designed to allow database publishing.

Internet Explorer   The Microsoft Web browser.

Internet Information Server (IIS)   A Web server designed for use with Microsoft Windows NT Server. It provides WWW, FTP, and Gopher services.

Internet Protocol (IP)   The communications standard that is the foundation of the Internet. IP allows information to be routed in packets across the Internet and to be reassembled at the destination computer.

Internet Server Application Programming Interface (ISAPI)   The set of function calls that provides access to the functionality of Microsoft Internet Information Server. Several ISAPI applications are used in IIS specifically to publish databases: the Internet Database Connector, OLEISAPI, and dbWeb.

IP address   A four-part number used to uniquely identify each computer on the Internet. Each part can be a maximum of three integers, and parts are separated by a dot. The format of the address is *xxx.xxx.xxx.xxx*; an example is 123.45.6.78.

265

local area network (LAN)   A group of networked computers, usually confined to a single office or building.

mirror site   An FTP server that has copies of the same files as another server. These servers are often used for download access to popular files.

name resolution   The process of mapping a domain name to an IP address.

Network News Transfer Protocol (NNTP)   A communications standard for distributing and retrieving news articles. The largest system of news distribution is Usenet.

OLEDB   A specification that defines a set of standard interfaces for accessing data. The ActiveX Data Objects (ADO) implement the OLEDB standard.

packet   A piece of electronic information sent over the Internet. Each packet contains the destination address, the sender's address, data, and error-handling information.

ping   A short message sent from one computer to another for the purpose of checking communications links.

Post Office Protocol (POP3)   A system allowing Internet mail to be downloaded to a client.

Remote Data Services   The service that allows thin Web access to an ODBC data source through the Advanced Data Control (ADC).

Simple Mail Transfer Protocol (SMTP)   A communications standard for sending electronic mail on the Internet.

socket   A communications link with the Internet. Many sockets can be open on a single computer at once.

subscription   The process of periodically locating Internet sites and downloading content for later use.

Transfer Control Protocol/Internet Protocol (TCP/IP)   A communications standard for all computers on the Internet.

Uniform Resource Locator (URL)   An Internet address that specifies a server or file. It typically consists of the following: a protocol, a host name, a folder structure, and a filename (for example, http://some_host.com/some_folder/some_web_page.htm).

World Wide Web Consortium (W3C)   An industry consortium that promotes standards for the Internet.

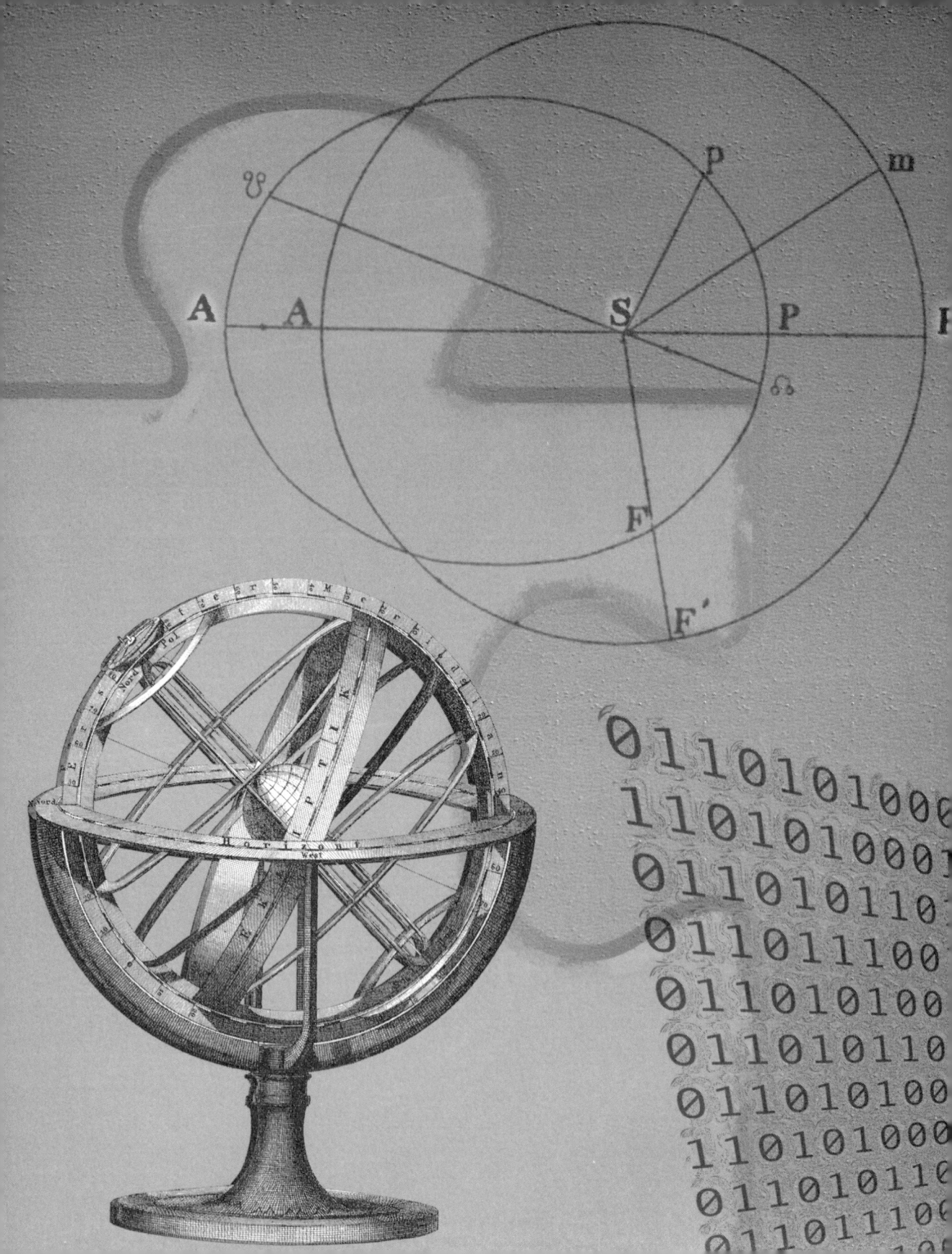

Object, Control, and Registry Reference

Table D-1
Window Object Properties

Property	Description	Syntax
Name	The window name.	*Object.***Name**
Length	The number of HTML elements in the window.	*Object.***Length**
Parent	Returns a reference to the parent hosting the window.	*Object.***Parent**
Self	Returns a reference to the Window object itself.	*Object.***Self**
Top	Returns a reference to the host of the window.	*Object.***Top**
Status	The text displayed in the status bar of the browser.	*Object.***Status** = *text* *text*: the text to display
DefaultStatus	The text displayed in the browser by default when there are no other messages to display.	*Object.***DefaultStatus** = *text* *text*: the text to display
Opener	Returns a reference to the Window object that created the current window. Occurs if code causes a new instance of IE to open.	*Object.***Opener**

(continued)

Table D-1 Window Object Properties *continued*

Property	Description	Syntax
Closed	Indicates whether the window is closed.	*variable* = *Object*.**Closed** *variable*: returns True if window is closed
Client	Returns a reference to the Navigator object.	*Object*.**Client**
DialogArguments	Returns the variable or array of variables passed into the modal dialog window. This property is read-only and applies only to windows created using the ShowModalDialog method.	*Object*.**DialogArguments**
DialogWidth, DialogHeight	Sets the width and height of a window created using the ShowModalDialog method. The default unit is pixels but can be any CSS unit.	*Object*.**DialogWidth** = *value* *Object*.**DialogHeight** = *value*
DialogTop, DialogLeft	Sets the top and left positions (relative to the upper-left corner of the desktop) of a window created using the ShowModalDialog method. The default unit is pixels but can be any CSS unit.	*Object*.**DialogTop** = *value* *Object*.**DialogLeft** = *value*
Document	Returns a reference to the Document object.	*Object*.**Document**
Event	Returns a reference to the Event object in the current event handler.	*Object*.**Event**
History	Returns a reference to the History object.	*Object*.**History**
Location	Returns a reference to the Location object.	*Object*.**Location**

Property	Description	Syntax
Navigator	Returns a reference to the Navigator object. The Navigator object contains information about the version, name, and supported features of the current browser.	*Object.***Navigator**
OffscreenBuffering	Indicates whether off-screen buffering is used.	*Object.***OffscreenBuffering** = *Boolean*
ReturnValue	Specifies the return value for a window created using the ShowModalDialog method.	*Object.***ReturnValue** = *value*
Frames	Accesses the Frames collection.	*Object.***Frames(***index***)** *index*: a string or integer specifying the frame to be accessed
Screen	Returns a reference to the Screen object.	*Object.***Screen**

Table D-2
Window Object Methods

Method	Description	Syntax
Navigate	Forces navigation to a new Uniform Resource Locator (URL).	*Object*.**Navigate** *URL* *URL*: the target address
Blur	Causes an immediate loss of focus and fires the OnBlur event.	*Object*.**Blur**
Focus	Causes the application to receive focus and fires the OnFocus event.	*Object*.**Focus**
Alert	Displays a dialog box with a message and an OK button. Similar to a MsgBox in VBScript.	*Object*.**Alert**(*text*) *text*: the message to the user
Confirm	Displays a dialog box with a message and OK/Cancel buttons. Similar to a MsgBox in VBScript. Returns True if OK is clicked.	*variable* = *Object*.**Confirm**
Prompt	Displays a dialog box prompting for text input.	*variable* = *Object*.**Prompt**(*text, default*) *text*: the message prompting the user *default*: the default response from the user
SetTimeout	Runs a routine after a specified number of milliseconds have elapsed.	*variable* = *Object*.**SetTimeout**(*procedure, milliseconds[, language]*) *procedure*: the name of the routine to run *milliseconds*: the time delay *language*: the scripting language of the procedure
ClearTimeout	Cancels a timeout that was set with the SetTimeout method.	*Object*.**ClearTimeout**(*variable*) *variable*: the return value from the SetTimeout method, which identifies the timeout to be canceled
Close	Closes the current window.	*Object*.**Close**
Open	Opens a new stream for input. This uses the Write and WriteLn methods of the Document object to generate the new page.	*Object*.**Open**(*[mimetype]*) *mimetype*: the MIME type for the new window input

Method	Description	Syntax
Scroll	Turns scroll bars on and off.	*Object.***Scroll** = **"Yes"**/**"No"**
ShowModalDialog	Displays an HTML dialog box.	*variable* = *Object.***ShowModal Dialog**(*URL[, args[, features]]*) *variable*: a reference to the new dialog box *URL*: the URL to show *args*: the arguments to display *features*: the browser features that the dialog box will support
SetInterval	Runs a routine after a specified number of milliseconds have elapsed.	*variable* = *Object.***SetInterval** (*procedure, milliseconds[, language]*) *procedure*: the name of the routine to run *milliseconds*: the time delay *language*: the scripting language of the procedure
ClearInterval	Cancels an interval that was set with the SetInterval method.	*Object.***ClearInterval**(*variable*) *variable*: the return value from the SetInterval method, which identifies the interval to be canceled.
ExecScript	Runs a routine.	*Object.***ExecScript**(*procedure[, language]*) *procedure*: the name of the routine to run *language*: the scripting language of the procedure
ShowHelp	Displays a Help file.	*Object.***ShowHelp**(*URL[, args]*) *URL*: the target address of the Help file *args*: the display arguments

Table D-3
Window Object Events

Event	Description	Syntax
OnFocus	Fires when the window receives the focus.	**Sub Window_OnFocus( )** **End Sub**
OnLoad	Fires when the current Web page has fully loaded.	**Sub Window_OnLoad( )** **End Sub**
OnUnload	Fires immediately before the current Web page is unloaded.	**Sub Window_OnUnload( )** **End Sub**
OnBlur	Fires immediately before the window loses focus.	**Sub Window_OnBlur( )** **End Sub**
OnHelp	Fires when the F1 key is hit and the window has the focus.	**Sub Window_OnHelp( )** **End Sub**

Table D-4
Document Object Properties

Property	Description	Syntax
AlinkColor	Specifies the color of an active link. An active link is created when the user has clicked a link but has not yet released the mouse button.	*Object.***AlinkColor** = *color* *color*: a string in RGB format or a designated color value (e.g., "WHITE" or "FFFFFF")
LinkColor	Specifies the color of a hyperlink that has not yet been visited.	*Object.***LinkColor** = *color* *color*: a string in RGB format or a designated color value (e.g., "WHITE" or "FFFFFF")
VlinkColor	Specifies the color of a hyperlink that has been visited.	*Object.***VlinkColor** = *color* *color*: a string in RGB format or a designated color value (e.g., "WHITE" or "FFFFFF")
Title	Sets or returns the title of the current document.	*Object.***Title** = *text* *text*: the new title text
BGColor	Sets or returns the background color of the current document.	*Object.***BGColor** = *color* *color*: a string in RGB format or a designated color value (e.g., "WHITE" or "FFFFFF")
Cookie	Reads or writes a cookie to the client. Cookies are small pieces of data stored for later use.	*Object.***Cookie**

274

Property	Description	Syntax
LastModified	Returns the date the page was last changed.	*Object.***LastModified**
Location	Returns a Location object that contains information about the current URL.	*Object.***Location**
Referrer	Returns the URL of the previous Location object.	*Object.***Referrer**
FGColor	Sets or returns the foreground color of the current document.	*Object.***FGColor** = *color* *color*: a string in RGB format or a designated color value (e.g., "WHITE" or "FFFFFF")
ActiveElement	Returns the element that currently has the focus.	*Object.***ActiveElement**
ReadyState	Returns the state of the downloading document.	*Object.***ReadyState** Possible values: 1: the object is unavailable 2: the object is loading 3: the object is available but not fully loaded 4: the object is loaded and available
Domain	Returns the host name from where the pages originated. If the domain is the same, code can access pages across frames in the browser.	*Object.***Domain**
URL	Returns the URL of the document.	*Object.***URL**
Body	Returns a reference to the Body object associated with this document.	*Object.***Body**
ParentWindow	Returns a reference to the Window object associated with this document.	*Object.***ParentWindow**
Selection	Returns a reference to the current Selection object.	*Object.***Selection**

Table D-5
Document Object Methods

Method	Description	Syntax
Close	Closes the current document.	*Object*.**Close**
Open	Opens a new stream for the Write and WriteLn methods.	*Object*.**Open**
Clear	Sets or returns a value that determines how text appears beside floating images.	*Object*.**Clear** = *variable* *variable*: specifies how text appears around floating images: 1: appears past all floating images 2: appears past left-aligned floating images 3: appears past right-aligned floating images
Write	Writes HTML to the currently open stream.	*Object*.**Write**(*text*)
WriteLn	Same as Write but adds a carriage return.	*Object*.**WriteLn**(*text*)
ExecCommand	Executes a command over the entire selection or range.	*variable* = *Object*.**ExecCommand** (*command[, value[, Boolean]]*) *command*: the command ID to execute *value*: the value to assign as a result of the command *Boolean*: specifies whether a GUI is presented when necessary (−1, True; 0, False)
QueryCommandEnabled	Returns a Boolean value indicating whether a command is available.	*variable* = *Object*. **QueryCommandEnabled** (*command*) *command*: the command ID to execute
QueryCommandValue	Returns the current value of a command.	*variable* = *Object*. **QueryCommandValue** (*command*) *command*: the command ID to query

Method	Description	Syntax
QueryCommandText	Returns the string associated with a command.	*variable = Object.***QueryCommandText** (*command*) *command*: the command ID to execute
ElementFromPoint	Returns the element for a specified *x,y* coordinate.	*variable = Object.***ElementFromPoint** (*x, y*)
QueryCommandSupported	Returns whether the current command is available.	*variable = Object.***QueryCommandSupported** (*command*) *command*: the command ID to execute
QueryCommandState	Returns the current state of a command.	*variable = Object.***QueryCommandState** (*command*) *command*: the command ID to execute
QueryCommandIndeterm	Returns whether a command is in an indeterminate state.	*variable = Object.***QueryCommandIndeterm** (*command*) *command*: the command ID to execute
CreateElement	Creates an element object of the specified tag.	*variable = Object.***CreateElement**(*tag*) *variable*: a reference to the new element *tag*: the new tag to create

Table D-6
Document Object Events

Event	Description	Syntax
OnClick	Fires when the user clicks the document.	**Sub Document_OnClick()** **End Sub**
OnMouseOver	Fires when the mouse passes over the document.	**Sub Document_OnMouseOver()** **End Sub**
OnDblClick	Fires when the user double-clicks the document.	**Sub Document_OnDblClick()** **End Sub**
OnKeyPress	Fires when a key is pressed.	**Sub Document_OnKeyPress()** **End Sub**

OnMouseDown	Fires when the mouse button is clicked and down.	**Sub Document_OnMouseDown**
		(y, x, shift, button)
		End Sub
		y,x: the coordinates of the mouse
		shift: specifies the state of the Shift, Ctrl, and Alt buttons:
		  1: Shift key
		  2: Ctrl key
		  4: Alt key
		
		button: specifies which button on the mouse was clicked:
		  1: Left button
		  2: Right button
		  4: Middle button

OnMouseMove	Fires as the mouse moves over the document.	**Sub Document_OnMouseMove**
		(y, x, shift, button)
		End Sub
		y,x: the coordinates of the mouse
		shift: specifies the state of the Shift, Ctrl, and Alt buttons:
		  1: Shift key
		  2: Ctrl key
		  4: Alt key
		button: specifies which button on the mouse was clicked:
		  1: Left button
		  2: Right button
		  4: Middle button

Event	Description	Syntax
OnMouseUp	Fires after the mouse button comes up from a click.	**Sub Document_OnMouseUp** (*y, x, shift, button*) **End Sub** *y,x*: the coordinates of the mouse *shift*: specifies the state of the Shift, Ctrl, and Alt buttons: 1: Shift key 2: Ctrl key 4: Alt key *button*: specifies which button on the mouse was clicked: 1: Left button 2: Right button 4: Middle button
OnKeyDown	Fires when a key is pressed and down.	**Sub Document_OnKeyDown** (*shift*) **End Sub** *shift*: specifies the state of the Shift, Ctrl, and Alt buttons: 1: Shift key 2: Ctrl key 4: Alt key
OnKeyUp	Fires when a key is released after being pressed.	**Sub Document_OnKeyUp**(*shift*) **End Sub** *shift*: specifies the state of the Shift, Ctrl, and Alt buttons: 1: Shift key 2: Ctrl key 4: Alt key
OnMouseOut	Fires when the mouse leaves the document.	**Sub Document_OnMouseOut( )** **End Sub**
OnReadyStateChange	Fires when the document's ready state changes. Occurs just before the OnLoad event of the window.	**Sub Document_ OnReadyStateChange( )** **End Sub**
OnHelp	Fires when F1 is pressed.	**Sub Document_OnHelp( )** **End Sub**

Table D-7
Event Object Properties

Property	Description	Syntax
KeyCode	Returns or sets the ASCII value of the pressed key that fired the event.	*Object*.**KeyCode**
FromElement	Returns the element the mouse is leaving in a MouseOut or MouseOver event.	*Object*.**FromElement**
ToElement	Returns the element the mouse is entering in a MouseOver or MouseOut event.	*Object*.**ToElement**
Button	Returns the mouse button that fired the event.	*Object*.**Button**
CancelBubble	Stops event bubbling for the event.	*Object*.**CancelBubble** = *value* *value*: −1 True, 0 False
SrcElement	Returns the element involved in the event.	*Object*.**SrcElement**
X	Specifies the *x* coordinate of the mouse.	*Object*.**X**
Y	Specifies the *y* coordinate of the mouse.	*Object*.**Y**
ShiftKey	Returns True if the Shift key is down when the event fires.	*Object*.**ShiftKey**
CtrlKey	Returns True if the Ctrl key is down when the event fires.	*Object*.**CtrlKey**
AltKey	Returns True if the Alt key is down when the event fires.	*Object*.**AltKey**
ReturnValue	Allows a return value to be passed back from an event.	*Object*.**ReturnValue** = *value* *value*: −1 True, 0 False

Table D-8
Tabular Data Control Properties and Methods

Property/Method	Description	Syntax
CharSet property	A string expression that describes the character set used for the data file. If no value is supplied, the input file is assumed to be *latin1*. If left at its default value or explicitly set to "", the Tabular Data Control will automatically sense whether the input data is a Unicode file.	*Object.***CharSet** = *value*
DataURL property	A string that specifies the Internet address of the data file.	*Object.***DataURL** = *value*
EscapeChar property	A special character that negates the effect of other characters used to perform functions such as field and column delimiting. For example, if TextQualifier is set to " (double-quote) and you set the EscapeChar property to \ (backslash), the following data file will be interpreted correctly: "This is data" "This is \"real\" data"	*Object.***EscapeChar** = *value*
FieldDelim property	The character used to mark the end of a data field. The default is a comma.	*Object.***FieldDelim** = *value*
FilterColumn property	The name of a column to filter the recordset. Used in conjunction with FilterCriterion and FilterValue properties.	*Object.***FilterColumn** = *ColumnName*
FilterCriterion property	A logical operator that determines which records are displayed. This operator can be =, <>, >, <, >=, or <=.	*Object.***FilterCriterion** = *operator*
FilterValue property	An expression used to compare with the FilterColumn property using the FilterCriterion property.	*Object.***FilterValue** = *value*

(continued)

Table D-8   Tabular Data Control Properties and Methods *continued*

Property/Method	Description	Syntax
Language property	A string that specifies the language of the text data file.	*Object.*__Language__ = *language*
RowDelim property	The character used to specify the end of a row of data. The default is a carriage return.	*Object.*__RowDelim__ = *value*
SortAscending property	A Boolean value that determines how the column specified by the SortColumn property is used to sort the data in the data file. Values are True and False.	*Object.*__SortAscending__ = __Boolean__
SortColumn property	The column to be used with the SortAscending property to sort the order of rows in the data file.	*Object.*__SortColumn__ = __ColumnName__
TextQualifier property	A character used to delineate text strings in the file. The default is a " (double quote).	*Object.*__TextQualifier__ = *value*
UseHeader Property	A Boolean value that specifies whether the first row in the data file contains names for the columns.	*Object.*__UseHeader__ = __Boolean__
Reset method	A method that causes the TDC to re-sort the data based on the new property settings.	*Object.*__Reset__

Table D-9
Advanced Data Control Properties and Methods

Property/Method	Description	Syntax
Connect property	The string used to identify the data source for the ADC.	*Object.***Connect =** **"DSN=***datasource***;UID=***userID***;** **PWD=***password***;"**
RecordSet property	A property that allows access to the underlying recordset contained in the ADC.	*Object.***Recordset**
Server property	A property that indicates the server name and protocol for accessing data.	*Object.***Server =** *value* **HTTP** **<PARAM NAME="Server"** **VALUE="http://***awebsrvr:port***">** **HTTPS** **<PARAM NAME="Server"** **VALUE="http://***awebsrvr:port***">** **DCOM** **<PARAM NAME="Server"** **VALUE="***machinename***">** **In-process** **<PARAM NAME="Server"** **VALUE="">**
SQL property	The Structured Query Language statement for the resulting recordset.	*Object.***SQL =** *value*
CancelUpdate method	A method that cancels all changes to the recordset.	*Object.***CancelUpdate**
MoveFirst, MoveLast, MoveNext, MovePrevious methods	Methods that navigate the recordset rows.	*Object.***MoveFirst** *Object.***MoveLast** *Object.***MoveNext** *Object.***MovePrevious**
Refresh method	A method that forces a requery of the data source.	*Object.***Refresh**
SubmitChanges method	A method that sends changes made to the recordset to the server for updating the database.	*Object.***SubmitChanges**

**Table D-10
Application Object Methods**

Method	Description	Syntax
Lock method	Prevents access to the Application variables collection.	**Application.Lock**
UnLock method	Allows access to the Application variables collection.	**Application.UnLock**

**Table D-11
Session Object Properties and Methods**

Property/Method	Description	Syntax
SessionID property	Returns the ID number for the current session.	**Session.SessionID**
Timeout property	Sets or returns the lifetime of the session in minutes. Defaults to 20 minutes.	**Session.Timeout**
Abandon method	Immediately terminates the session.	**Session.Abandon**

**Table D-12
Request Object Properties**

Property	Description	Syntax
ClientCertificate property	A collection of values stored in the client certificate.	**Request.ClientCertificate** (*variable*)
Cookies property	A collection of values sent as cookies with the HTTP header.	**Request.Cookies**(*variable*)
Form property	A collection of data sent with a submitted form.	**Request.Form**(*fieldname*)
QueryString property	A collection of data sent as part of a hyperlink.	**Request.QueryString** (*fieldname*)
ServerVariables property	A collection of server environment variables.	**Request.ServerVariables** (*variable*)

Table D-13
Response Object Properties and Methods

Property/Method	Description	Syntax
Buffer property	Determines whether page output is buffered.	**Response.Buffer = True|False**
ContentType property	Specifies the HTTP content type for the current response.	**Response.ContentType = "text/HTML"**
Cookies property	Allows values to be written to the client's cookies collection.	**Response.Cookies** (*cookiename*)(*key*) = *value*
Expires property	Sets the amount of time before a cached page expires. Setting to zero causes immediate expiration.	**Response.Expires =** *time*
ExpiresAbsolute property	Sets a date and time on which a cached page expires.	**Response.ExpiresAbsolute =** *#date#*
Status property	Sets the status line returned by the server. Can be used to set messages such as "401 - Not Found."	**Response.Status = "401 - Not Found"**
AddHeader method	Allows the addition of a custom header to the Web page.	**Response.AddHeader** *name, value*
AppendToLog method	Allows the addition of information to the Web server log entry for this request.	**Response.AppendToLog** *string*
BinaryWrite method	Writes binary data to a page for use by client objects.	**Response.BinaryWrite** *data*
Clear method	Erases buffered ASP output.	**Response.Clear**
End method	Stops ASP processing and sends the result to the client.	**Response.End**
Flush method	Empties the buffer and sends the result to the client.	**Response.Flush**
Redirect method	Instructs the client to connect to a different URL	**Response.Redirect** *URL*
Write method	Writes output to the HTML page. The equal sign serves as a shorthand notation.	**Response.Write** *data*

Table D-14
Server Object Properties and Methods

Property/Method	Description	Syntax
ScriptTimeout property	Sets the time that a script can run before a message appears on the client.	**Server.ScriptTimeout =** *time*
CreateObject method	Creates an instance of an ActiveX component for use in ASP.	*variable* = **Server.CreateObject** (*ProgID*)
HTMLEncode method	Provides HTML encoding for a given string.	*variable* = **Server.HTMLEncode** (*string*)
MapPath method	Returns the complete directory structure for a virtual directory name.	*path* = **Server.MapPath** (*virtualdirectory*)
URLEncode method	Provides URL encoding for a given string.	*variable* = **Server.URLEncode**(*string*)

Table D-15
ActiveX Data Objects

Object	Description
Command	Executes an operation against an ODBC data source. The operation can be an SQL statement or a stored procedure.
Connection	Establishes a connection to an ODBC data source.
Error	Returns ODBC driver errors.
Field	Allows access to a specific field inside of a set of records.
Parameter	Allows values to be passed to a Command object.
Recordset	Represents a set of records returned from a Command object.

Table D-16
Key Registry Entries

Registry Entry
```
HKEY_LOCAL_MACHINE
\SYSTEM
\CurrentControlSet
\Services
\W3SVC
\ASP
\Parameters
```

Registry Entry	Allowed Values	Description
AllowOutOfProcCmpts	0: False (default) 1: True	Determines whether ASP supports out-of-process components. Must be set to True when using Microsoft Transaction Server.
AllowSessionState	0: False 1: True (default)	Determines whether ASP can access session variables and utilize session events.
BufferingOn	0: False (default) 1: True	Determines whether ASP buffers all generated output before sending the results to a client browser.
DefaultScriptLanguage	Any string allowed VBScript (default)	The name of the default scripting language.
EnableParentPaths	0: False 1: True (default)	Determines whether ASP can use double dots (..) to access parent directories.
LogErrorRequests	0: False 1: True (default)	Determines whether ASP logs failures to the Windows NT event log.
MemFreeFactor	50–150 50 (default)	The maximum length of the free memory list as a percentage of the used memory list.
MinUsedBlocks	5–20 10 (default)	The minimum length of the used memory list before elements can be freed.
NumInitialThreads	1–10 2 (default)	The number of threads created by ASP when it starts.
ProcessorThreadMax	1–C8 10 (default)	The maximum number of threads per processor.
RequestQueueMax	1–FFFFFFFF 500 (default)	The number of requests that can wait in a queue for each thread before generating a Server Too Busy error.

(continued)

Table D-16 Key Registry Entries *continued*

Registry Entry	Allowed Values	Description
ScriptEngineCacheMax	0–FFFFFFFF 30 (default)	The number of ActiveX server engines that can exist in memory.
ScriptErrorMessage	String	The error message displayed in the browser if ScriptErrorsSentToBrowser is set to False.
ScriptErrorsSentToBrowser	0: False 1: True (default)	Determines whether ASP sends debugging error messages to the browser.
ScriptFileCacheSize	0–FFFFFFFF −1 (default)	Sets memory to be used for caching script results. −1 indicates that all pages should be cached.
ScriptFileCacheTTL	0–FFFFFFFF 300 secs (default)	The amount of time scripts will remain in memory cache.
ScriptTimeout	0–FFFFFFFF 90 secs (default)	The time allowed before a running script is terminated. (E.g., this can happen in an endless loop.)
SessionTimeout	0–FFFFFFFF 20 mins (default)	The amount of time that session variables are saved.
StartConnectionPool	0: False 1: True (default)	Turns on ODBC connection pooling for ASP. (Do not confuse this with pooling accomplished by MTS.)
ThreadCreationThreshold	0–FFFFFFFF 5 (default)	The number of waiting thread requests before a new thread is created.

INDEX

Scot Hillier

Scot Hillier, a graduate of Virginia Military Institute, is a former naval submarine officer. As a principal at New Technology Solutions, Inc., in North Haven, Connecticut, he has trained thousands of developers across the country since 1995. He is also the developer of the Visual Basic Add-In wizard AttilaVB/Pro (patent pending). Scot serves as regional director of the Microsoft Developer Days program in Hartford, Connecticut. His articles appear regularly in *Visual Basic Programmer's Journal.*

Daniel Mezick

Daniel Mezick is regional director of the Microsoft Developer Days program in Boston and the chair of The New Technology Forum, a Boston-based forum for advanced developers using Microsoft tools. He is the coauthor, with Scot Hillier, of *Visual Basic 5 Bootcamp: Everything You Need to Pass Microsoft's Visual Basic 5 Certification* from McGraw Hill. Since 1993, Dan has taught Microsoft Visual Basic to thousands of developers at New Technology Solutions, Inc., a technical training firm based in North Haven, Connecticut.

New Technology Solutions, Inc.

New Technology Solutions, in North Haven, Connecticut, provides training and tools to developers working with Microsoft Visual Basic. All of NewTech's training programs include our award-winning tools, 30 days of question-and-answer support, and access to our developers-only web site.

NewTech employees also write feature articles and columns for *Visual Basic Programmer's Journal* and are active in presenting technology topics at such conferences as VBITS and DCI's INTERNET WORLD. NewTech sponsors the Microsoft Developer Days event, in Boston and Hartford, as well as the Connecticut Visual Basic Special Interest Group, one of the largest VB user groups in the country. (You can browse http://www.microsoft.com/devdays/ for detailed information on Microsoft Developer Days.) Contact New Technology Solutions (or browse http://www.vb-bootcamp.com) to learn more about the following areas.

■ VB BOOTCAMP®

This is the flagship nationwide seminar for developers only. In just one or two days, you learn all the essentials of developing and deploying mission-critical business systems in Visual Basic.

■ INTRANET BOOTCAMP™

This course teaches you the key technologies and skills you need for deploying intranet technology using Microsoft Visual Basic, Scripting Edition (VBScript), as well as the Microsoft Internet Explorer and Microsoft Internet Information Server (IIS).

■ ON-SITE TRAINING

New Technology Solutions, Inc., offers on-site, hands-on technology training and tailors the training to your exact requirements. The company's clients include the FBI, Levi Strauss, Aetna, American Airlines, Chemical Bank, Prudential Insurance, and McDonald's. Call (203) 239-6874 to schedule training and arrange course content tailored to your needs.

■ VIDEO TRAINING

New Technology Solutions, Inc., offers the following training videos. All the tapes include source code, exercises, and a money-back guarantee. Call for pricing and availability.

- ❏ *VB BOOTCAMP/FUNDAMENTALS* (7 hours; for developers only)

- ❏ *VB BOOTCAMP/ADVANCED* (4 hours; covers advanced topics)

- ❏ *INTRANET/FUNDAMENTALS* (4 hours; covers VBScript and IIS)

- ❏ *INTRANET/ADVANCED* (4 hours; covers advanced intranets)

■ DISTANCE LEARNING PROGRAMS AND COMPUTER-BASED TRAINING

The company offers a variety of distance learning programs and CD-ROM–based training. Write for more information, or browse the New Technology Solutions web site:
http://www.vb-bootcamp.com

New Technology Solutions, Inc.
444-A Washington Avenue
North Haven, CT 06473
Phone: (203) 239-6874
Fax: (203) 239-7997
Email: info@vb-bootcamp.com
World Wide Web: http://www.vb-bootcamp.com

The manuscript for this book was prepared and submitted to Microsoft Press in electronic form. Text files were prepared using Microsoft Word 97. Pages were composed by Microsoft Press using Adobe PageMaker 6.5 for Windows, with text in New Baskerville and display type in Helvetica bold. Composed pages were delivered to the printer as electronic prepress files.

Cover Graphic Designer
Tim Girvin Design, Inc.

Cover Illustrator
Glenn Mitsui

Interior Graphic Designer
Pam Hidaka

Interior Graphic Artist
Joel Panchot

Principal Compositor
Elizabeth Hansford

Principal Proofreader/Copy Editor
Richard Carey

Indexer
Maro Riofrancos

To really **understand Dynamic HTML,**
go to the source.

U.S.A.   **$39.99**
U.K.   £37.49 [V.A.T. included]
Canada $55.99
ISBN   1-57231-686-1

Web sites developed for Microsoft® Internet Explorer 4 can offer the most advanced, most exciting interactive features, thanks to Dynamic HTML—a technology that author Scott Isaacs helped create. Now he's written the programmer's bible on this important subject. Part technical manifesto, part application sourcebook, INSIDE DYNAMIC HTML starts by laying out core concepts and tools—HTML, cascading style sheets, and scripting fundamentals. Subsequent chapters explain the object model and element collections.

But beyond presenting the technical blueprint to Dynamic HTML, this book delivers what you need most—provocative, reusable techniques that demonstrate key benefits of the new object model. What's more, the companion CD-ROM supplies you with a copy of Microsoft Internet Explorer 4.0, the Internet Client Software Development Kit (SDK), sample scripts, and more. INSIDE DYNAMIC HTML is for Web developers, sophisticated content providers, users of JavaScript and other scripting tools, and anyone else who wants the lowdown on this widely embraced approach to a livelier Web. Give your pages the power of dynamic content. Get INSIDE DYNAMIC HTML.

Microsoft Press

You work with Microsoft® **Office.**

Now you want to build a great **intranet.**

Congratulations, you're **nearly done.**

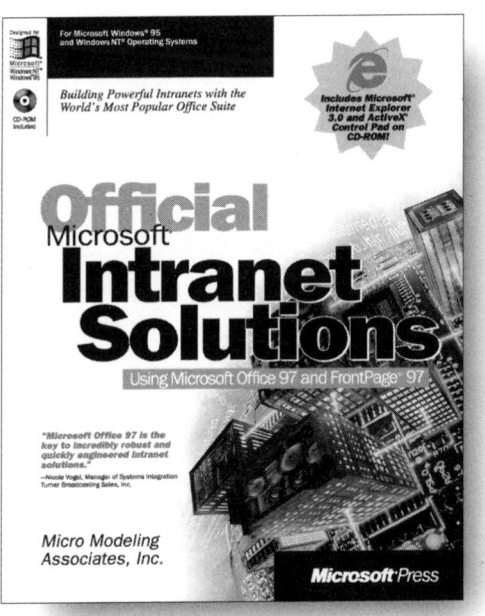

For Microsoft Windows® 95 and Windows NT® Operating Systems

CD-ROM Included

Building Powerful Intranets with the World's Most Popular Office Suite

Includes Microsoft® Internet Explorer 3.0 and ActiveX™ Control Pad on CD-ROM!

Official
Microsoft®
Intranet Solutions
Using Microsoft Office 97 and FrontPage® 97

"*Microsoft Office 97 is the key to incredibly robust and quickly engineered intranet solutions.*"
—Nicole Vogel, Manager of Systems Integration, Turner Broadcasting Sales, Inc.

Micro Modeling Associates, Inc.

Microsoft Press

You don't need to start from scratch. In fact, once you upgrade to Microsoft Office 97, all you add is Microsoft FrontPage® 97, Microsoft Internet Explorer, and this book. Here technical managers and developers can discover how to use these popular programs to quickly create awesome, full-featured intranets that are easy for everyone to use—administrators and users alike. So build on the foundation you've already put in place. To find out how, get OFFICIAL MICROSOFT INTRANET SOLUTIONS.

U.S.A.	**$39.99**
U.K.	£37.49 [V.A.T. included]
Canada	$54.99
ISBN	1-57231-509-1

Microsoft® Press

Register Today!

Return this
Programming Active Server Pages
registration card for
a Microsoft Press® catalog

U.S. and Canada addresses only. Fill in information below and mail postage-free. Please mail only the bottom half of this page.

1-57231-700-0A   *PROGRAMMING ACTIVE SERVER PAGES*   *Owner Registration Card*

_____
NAME

_____
INSTITUTION OR COMPANY NAME

_____
ADDRESS

_____
CITY   STATE   ZIP

Microsoft®*Press*
Quality Computer Books

**For a free catalog of
Microsoft Press® products, call
1-800-MSPRESS**

AIR FRYER
easy everyday

AIR
FRYER
easy everyday

140 super-simple, delicious recipes

Sam & Dom Milner
of RecipeThis

WHITE LION
PUBLISHING

Quarto

First published in 2024 by White Lion Publishing
an imprint of The Quarto Group.
One Triptych Place,
London,
SE1 9SH
United Kingdom
T (0)20 7700 6700
www.Quarto.com

A catalogue record for this book is available from the British Library.

HB ISBN 978 0 7112 9813 2
PB ISBN 978 0 7112 9814 9
Ebook ISBN 978 0 7112 9815 6

10 9 8 7 6 5 4 3 2 1

Designer: Georgie Hewitt
Project Editor & Food Stylist: Rebecca Woods
Photographer: Dan Jones
Prop Stylist: Faye Wears
Group Publishing Director: Denise Bates
Editorial Director: Nicky Hill
Senior Production Controller: Rohana Yusef
Air fryer icon illustrator: Renata Latipova
Printed in China

Key to symbols

Recipe is suitable for:

 Basket air fryer

 Dual air fryer

 Air fryer oven

Small air fryer

Notes

- All calorie counts are per serving where a recipe states "Serves" or per item when a recipe states "Makes"
- Metric and imperial measurements are given for all recipes, use one set only and not a mixture of both
- All tablespoons and teaspoons are level
- All milk should be whole/full-fat unless otherwise stated
- All eggs should be UK large eggs or US XL eggs, unless otherwise stated
- Be careful when handling raw chicken, never wash it and never use anything that has come into contact with it ie utensils and chopping boards, on cooked foods without washing them thoroughly first.
- When baking sweet treats, we recommend unsalted butter, and in savoury cooking salted butter. Unless otherwise stated, bring the butter to room temperature before using.
- Do refer to your air fryer manual, as they often operate differently and follow the manufacturer's safety guidelines.

Contents

WELCOME

We're Sam and Dom, and we love cooking with kitchen gadgets. We have been air frying for 12 years – long before it was a social media trend and long before there was the current huge range of air fryers on the market. Back then, you just had the Philips air fryer, which was much smaller than it is today, and people were using them for the basics, such as making homemade chips, warming up pastries or cooking frozen food. You couldn't cook a whole chicken in it, or any cakes larger than 15cm/6 inch. Today, people are using their air fryers for a much broader range of dishes, and there is a wider variety of air fryers to reflect the more diverse air frying community.

On meeting someone new with an air fryer, the first question is always "Which air fryer do you have?" Do you have the oven? Do you have the basket? Do you have the dual?

This got us thinking about a topic for our second air fryer cookbook. With the focus on easy everyday air fryer recipes, we decided to develop the recipes around the most popular styles of air fryers. Every recipe in this book has been tested in the basket, dual and air fryer oven, and we have provided guidance on how to adapt recipes to some other styles of air fryer.

But while the recipes will work in all the air fryers for which a symbol appears (check out the variations at the bottom of the pages), some recipes really wow us in a particular air fryer. With this in mind, you will see "hero" mentions. Look out for the hero mention for your type of air fryer, and why not start with those recipes?

We hope that you love these air fryer recipes as much as we do.

Sam & Dom x

understanding
air fryers

air fryer basics

WHAT IS AN AIR FRYER?

An air fryer is what I call my "magic machine", because every time I create a new recipe and push the air fryer to its new limits it feels like I have achieved magic. Cynics will tell you that an air fryer is just a small convection oven, but they are much more than that. Air fryers use powerful fans to circulate hot air around the food. Because they are much smaller than a standard oven, it means that they cook food much faster.

You can cook most things in an air fryer that you would usually cook in the oven, under the grill/broiler, in the microwave, the toaster, the sandwich maker, the deep fat fryer, the wok, and the cast iron casserole dish. Because air fryers replace so many other machines, you can save space in your kitchen by just having an air fryer and they can sit on your countertop.

10 REASONS WHY WE LOVE AIR FRYING

They cook more quickly Cooking the average whole chicken in the oven takes around 1¾ hours, plus a preheat. Yet the same chicken will cook in the air fryer in under an hour.

You don't need to preheat an air fryer It always feels like such an effort to preheat an oven and having to get it nice and hot before you start cooking. Yet with an air fryer it only requires a preheat on a handful of recipes, and even then it's only a couple of minutes.

There is no parboiling required I remember as a kid watching my mum cook roast potatoes. She would parboil the potatoes, before oven roasting them. The air fryer is much better; you peel and quarter the potatoes and toss them in oil and seasonings, then the air fryer does the hard work for you.

They use a lot less oil Cooking a whole chicken in the oven requires lots of butter under the skin, to stop it drying out, whereas in the air fryer a whole chicken needs just one tablespoon of olive oil.

Most are energy efficient I have a gadget attached to our smart meter that tells us how much electricity we are using. It will go red if we run the kettle and the microwave at the same time. Yet we can run four air fryers at once when recipe testing and it will stay at green.

They are easy to use I cannot think of an easier way to cook. There are so many easy recipes to follow, many with few ingredients – perfect for quickly prepping dinner, or for those who hate cooking.

They travel well Most motorhome and caravan owners we know have an air fryer. We have travelled many times with our air fryer and it makes keeping the holiday grocery costs down so much easier. (There's more about travelling with the air fryer on page 14.)

You can reduce the fat in your diet This is perfect if you are on a diet, suffer from high cholesterol or generally like eating healthily. You will find that for the average serving size for dinner in the air fryer, you will need just ¼ tablespoon of extra virgin olive oil.

You can leave the air fryer to it Imagine standing over a pan sautéing some onions. Then imagine placing them into the air fryer, leaving the room and only coming back when the air fryer beeps. In the Milner house, we love being able to put the food in the air fryer and leave it to it.

They are easier to clean than an oven Forget all those roasting tins that you have to scrub. Instead, there are plenty of accessories that make cleaning up quick and soak-free – most can just be popped in the dishwasher. Along with this, the air fryer itself just needs a quick wipe down with hot soapy water.

the air fryer range

We bought our first air fryer basket in 2012, upgraded to a bigger one in 2016, bought our first air fryer oven in 2019, also got our first multi cooker with air fryer function the same year and then jumped on the dual bandwagon in early 2023. They are like family, so we can't choose a favourite – we love them all. But if you want just one, hard-working machine, there are various things to consider.

ALL AIR FRYERS ARE DIFFERENT

This is the biggest consideration when you are deciding which air fryer to have in your kitchen. You walk into an electronics store and the salesperson tells you that you must have whichever one is popular at the time. It will either be the one that is selling best, or the one that they get a higher commission for.

And not all air fryers are the same. There are basket air fryers, some with extra-large baskets and some with tiny ones. There are dual air fryers with two drawers, or multi cookers with an air fryer function, air fryers with a crisper plate, others with a standard basket. There are air fryer ovens, or air fryer ovens with a rotisserie function, some have five shelves, some have four shelves. The combinations feel seemingly endless, and I am sure after that list I have overwhelmed you.

Well, it gets a little more complicated. Each brand will have different quirks, and some air fryers will be better than others – they all have different strengths and weaknesses. Just like choosing a television, or a phone or a washing machine, they all have pros and cons. As a result, it's not unheard of to make an inappropriate choice, hate your air fryer, then think air fryers are rubbish and wonder why everyone likes them so much!

That's why we're here to help. Throughout this chapter we are going to give you a crash course in air fryers, including the benefits of each type of air fryer, so that you can make the best choice for your first air fryer, or so that you have all the information for when you upgrade or add an extra air fryer to your kitchen.

Most importantly, we'll explain how the cooking time of your food may vary depending on which air fryer you have, and how to adapt the recipe you're following.

LET'S START WITH AIR FRYER BASKETS

The basket air fryer is the most common type of air fryer and the one that has been around the longest. First released by Philips in 2010 after a partnership with Fred Van Der Weij, continental Europe loved it! We bought our first one in 2012 and noticed at the time that only Germany and the Netherlands were taking it seriously. Today, most recipes you see online are written for cooking in the basket models.

In basket air fryers, food is placed into a perforated basket with a handle. This basket then clips into a larger drawer, which is inserted into the main unit with the heating element. The food is cooked quickly as the basket raises it up from the base of the drawer, meaning that air can circulate all around. There are usually deep indentations in the drawer base, which helps the air to circulate efficiently. To remove the food from the air fryer, you simply unclip the basket and lift it out of the drawer, then food can be tipped out of the basket directly onto plates.

When they were first introduced, air fryer baskets were much smaller and the food you could cook in them was more basic. (Forget roasting a whole chicken back in 2012.) But over the years, with many popular electronics brands competing, they have got bigger and better. For example, Philips started at about 4.2 litres/4.4 quart and now they have the XL which is 6.2 litres/ 6.5 quart and XXL which is the most powerful air fryer we have personally used and is 7.2 litres/7.6 quart, which is larger than most on the market.

but what sized air fryer basket should you get?

Cooking capacity is real area of confusion, and our readers often contact us about this. Like a slow cooker, air fryer size is given in units of

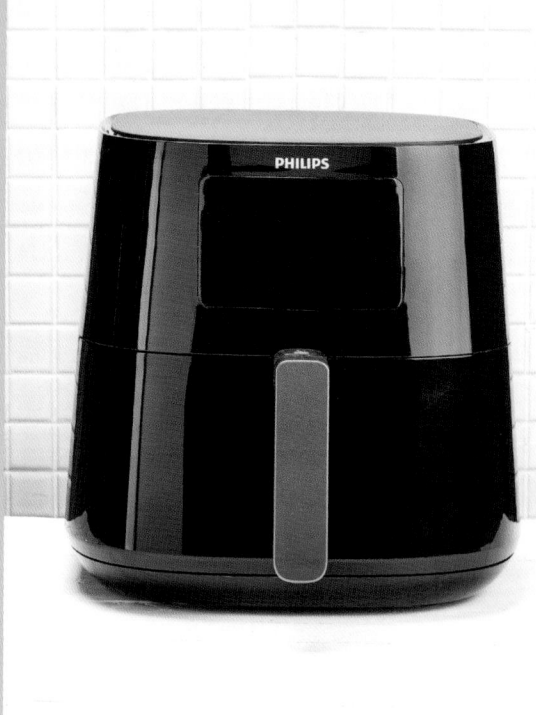

volume, not physical size. So when you read the air fryer specifications and it says 4.2 litres/4.4 quart, you may well wonder what that actually means in a real life cooking scenario.

Well, I have another way: I measure air fryers – both ones I use now and ones I have used in the past – and work out which size round baking pan will fit well in the basket. This gives me a better idea of what I can cook in the space (and helps me visualise it) and have a clearer idea about which sized air fryer I need in my kitchen. Although models do vary, I have found the below to be reasonably accurate:

2.0 litre/2.1 quart – 14cm/5½ inch
4.2 litre/4.4 quart – 16.5cm/6½ inch
5.5 litre/5.8 quart – 20cm/8 inch
6.2 litre/6.5 quart – 20cm/8 inch
7.2 litre/7.6 quart – 23cm/9 inch

You can use these baking pan sizes as a guide for buying accessories for your air fryer, such as silicone pans. We have sometimes found that the same-sized accessories fit two different sizes of air fryer because the volume difference is in the height of the basket, not the size of the base.

We find the 4.2 litre air fryer, known as "medium" is perfect for one to two people, although it won't hold a whole chicken. Instead, try our smaller piri piri poussin (see page 82).

We have both 5.5 litre and 6.2 litre XL air fryers in our home kitchen and they are perfect for two to four people – or for those who love whole chicken or want to cook a full meal in the air fryer.

The 7.2 litre XXL models are very spacious and ideal for a family of four. You can cook a larger chicken in them, as well as several portions of chips without it feeling overcrowded.

THE SINGLE DRAWER AIR FRYER

The single drawer air fryer has a similar shape and capacity to the basket models. The main difference is that instead of a perforated basket that sits inside the main drawer, these models have drawers with a flat base and a perforated crisper plate that sits inside the drawer. Like the basket, these plates raise up the food so that air can circulate underneath and food can crisp up. As there is no inset basket, the handle is attached to the drawer itself.

The bonus of this style of air fryer is the ability to remove the crisper plate so that you can cook dishes with lots of liquid (such as soups, sauces and curries) directly in the drawer, rather than having to transfer them to a silicone container, or similar. The drawer can essentially act as a saucepan, and as they are non-stick, they are easy to clean.

You can cook food with the plate (for dryer items that you want to crisp) or without (for saucier foods), or even use a combination of cooking styles by removing the crisper plate halfway through. For example, if you were cooking our root vegetable soup (see page 128), you would air fry the root vegetables with the crisper plate in place, then remove it before adding liquids. (It's worth noting that you can cook in this way in a standard basket air fryer too, but you will just need to transfer the vegetables to an air fryer accessory before adding the liquids to finish the cooking process.)

When purchasing an air fryer, opt for an air fryer with a removeable crisper plate if you plan to make a lot of recipes with liquids. And beware: if you are upgrading from a basket model to an air fryer with a crisper plate, the plate gets very hot, just like a heavy baking tray you have just removed from the oven. If you are used to tipping food straight out of the basket onto a plate, it is easy to forget that the crisper plate is loose and tip the red hot crisper plate onto your hand in the process. Use less of an angle when tipping, or use a kitchen utensil to remove the food.

For the recipes in this book, adapt as necessary. You will find that you don't have to transfer wet ingredients to silicone as you would if using the basket, and you'll likely not have to reduce the size of your accessories (or split them between drawers) as you would for the dual. And keep the crisper plate in unless directed to remove it in the recipe, because if the food is not raised up, it will take slightly longer to cook.

THE DUAL AIR FRYER

The dual air fryer has gained the most popularity in recent years and is like having two drawer air fryers in one. Forget just filling one drawer with food, you now have two, giving you much more space! Like the single drawer air fryers, the drawers have crisper plates and can be used as saucepans too when those are removed. All single drawer or basket air fryer recipes can be cooked in the dual, although the drawers are narrower and so the physical cooking spaces are smaller despite a larger capacity overall.

how does a dual air fryer differ from the others?

In terms of times and temperatures to use when air frying, the method of cooking in a dual is almost identical to single drawer or basket air fryers – you're simply cooking in two rectangular spaces rather than one square one, and you will have about 50 per cent more space, too.

The main advantage of the dual is that it gives you the scope to cook two totally different things at the same time, even at different temperatures and in different styles. For example, you can remove the crisper plate from one drawer and use it to make our saucy chicken curry (see page 191), while leaving the plate in the second drawer and using it to cook our Bombay potatoes (see page 159), which really opens up possibilities.

there are just a few considerations

The drawers are narrower than a basket so what you could fit in one basket, you might need to spread out over two drawers. For example, when cooking the lamb roast (see page 192) in a basket air fryer, we would cook the lamb in the centre of the basket, surrounded by the vegetables. In the dual drawers, you would add meat to one drawer and the veggies to the other. The time and temperature would be the same. Use personal judgement and divide food between the drawers if one seems too full.

Dividing the food may mean it cooks more quickly For example, if you are making the French fries (see page 154) and spread them between drawers, you will have less food in each drawer compared to making the full batch in one air fryer basket. Less food in each may mean it cooks more quickly, so do check the food a few minutes before the recipe states so that you don't overcook it.

Speed up the sides Sometimes when air frying, you can be cooking the main element of a dish, such as a piece of meat or fish, then waiting on the air fryer to finish before you can cook any accompaniments. With the dual, you can cook your veggies in one drawer and your meat in the other. For example, with our teriyaki duck noodles (see page 94) we can cook the veggie stir fry mix in one drawer, then the duck in the other.

The different function buttons Some dual air fryers have several functions, including air fry, bake and roast. Unless stated otherwise, recipes in this book always use the "air fry" button, as it produces the best results. But on machines with multiple functions, most "air fry" settings cook between 160–210°C/320–410°F. Therefore, if you need to cook at a lower heat (such as when melting butter or chocolate) you can use the "bake" function, which is much gentler.

"Match" is our favourite feature When we got our first dual air fryer, we fell in love with the "match" feature, which allows you to simultaneously set the same time and temperature for both drawers. It's perfect if two different foods require the same cooking time and temperature, or if you're simply dividing the same ingredients between both drawers.

"Sync" is our lazy feature If you are cooking two different foods with different cooking times, the "sync" feature let's you set the time and temperature for both drawers at the beginning, then staggers the start times so that they will finish cooking at the same time. This means that you don't need to come back into the kitchen to get the other drawer going.

Adapting is key There are so many different sized dual air fryers – from the smaller 7.6 litres/8 quart models to those with a larger 10 litre/10.5 quart capacity. You will need to buy air fryer accessories that comfortably fit the dimensions of your two drawers.

The dual air fryer is best for People who like variety. Before air frying, you would cook a soup in a saucepan, then turn the oven on for the part-baked bread rolls. Now you can cook the soup in one drawer and warm up the bread in the other.

THE FLEX DRAWER AIR FRYER

This is the rising star of air fryers – part dual, part single drawer air fryer, they offer the best of both worlds. They have one very large drawer (up to 9–10 litres/9.5–10.5 quart) with a removeable divider that can be slotted into the centre. This gives them the capability of cooking with two different temperature zones with the divider inserted, as you can in a dual. However, remove it and they become a very large version of a single drawer air fryer, with a crisper plate (or plates) that can be removed so it can serve as a very large saucepan, too. We love it for recipes like the lamb roast (see page 192) because, with the divider removed, it will accommodate a larger lamb joint.

If you are lucky enough to have one of these models, you can follow the dual instructions, because it too has a crisper plate that can be removed so you won't need to transfer wet ingredients into containers. However, you will find that you are also unlikely to need to split ingredients between two different drawers, as you will have one very large capacity drawer to use, and so cake tins, for example, will fit at the sizes stated in the recipe.

AIR FRYER OVEN

This is the third type of air fryer we primarily focus on in this book. If you like cooking with an oven, an air fryer oven is like a mini version, with shelves rather than a basket or drawer, although unlike an oven, you can cook directly on the shelves without any bakeware. If you want lots of space, they are much bigger than a basket or dual air fryer, and many models also have an amazing rotisserie accessory. We love the air fryer oven so much that we have a chapter dedicated to them, starting on page 60.

LET'S TALK SMALL AIR FRYERS

You may have seen the small basket air fryers when browsing. They look tiny beside the XL alternatives, and even smaller when beside a dual air fryer.

A small air fryer is often one-third the size of an XL air fryer or one-fifth the capacity of a large dual air fryer. Typically a small air fryer is 2 litres/2.1 quart but we have seen them smaller.

Despite their diminutive size and lower wattage, they still carry the same cook time as more powerful, larger air fryers. This is because they have a smaller volume and so require less power to warm up and there will be less food to cook.

so why would you want such a small air fryer?

Cooking for one These small air fryers were originally made for one person. The idea is that if you just want to cook a single pork steak with some vegetables, or a chicken breast rather than a whole chicken, you can.

Just for chips I have met many people who just use their small air fryer for chips. It's simply a deep fat fryer replacement and they have no interest in anything else. In which case this size is perfect.

travelling with the air fryer

A small air fryer is perfect for travelling with as it's compact and doesn't take up much room. It fits nicely in the boot of your car, is easy to take to a holiday cottage, plus its low wattage is perfect for using on campsites.

We have travelled to Spain many times with our air fryer and it makes cooking so much easier. I can buy local food, then cook it in the air fryer for dinner in our self-catering accommodation. Because we like to drive to our destination, a smaller air fryer takes up a lot less room in the car, and I can still avoid the holiday apartment oven. Plus, to save money on eating out, a small air fryer is also good for pasties, toasties and a quick portion of chips.

During the many times we have stayed at campsites, we have found that it's very easy to blow a fuse and trip the electric. Then you have to head to the campsite's reception with a sheepish look on your face, apologising as they reconnect the electric for you. This will easily happen if you use a bigger air fryer, but small 2 litre/2.1 quart air fryers are low watt and subsequently more campsite friendly. If you are worried about power supply on campsites, I recommend going for an air fryer under 1000 wattage and these are usually under 2 litres/2.1 quart in capacity.

Chicken drumsticks from air fryer to air fryer

Now that I have run through the different types of air fryers, let me talk you through cooking chicken drumsticks in different air fryers.

First we like to flavour them with one of our marinades from page 37. Then, we place the drumsticks in the air fryers as shown below.

01 **Air fryer basket (or single drawer)** Place three chicken drumsticks from left to right and one along the bottom.

02 **Air fryer dual** Instead of left to right, lay them top to bottom as the dual is narrow and tall vs a square basket. You can also double batch and cook four in each drawer.

03 **Small air fryer basket** Simply space two chicken drumsticks in the small area you have available. Or swap two medium drumsticks for four small ones to fit the air fryer size.

04 **Air fryer oven** Place four drumsticks on an air fryer oven shelf/rack. If you are cooking just one shelf of chicken drumsticks, you can use any of the shelves, because the air circulates so well it doesn't affect the cooking time.

In a basket or dual air fryer, we will cook them at 180°C/360°F for 17 minutes (turning them over after 10 minutes), or until the drumsticks reach an internal temperature of 70°C/160°F or above.

If we are cooking in an air fryer oven, preheat for 2 minutes, then cook them on a single shelf for 21 minutes (turning them over after 10 minutes), or until cooked through. If you are cooking two shelves of drumsticks, cook them for a total of 26 minutes, switching the shelves around halfway through cooking.

01
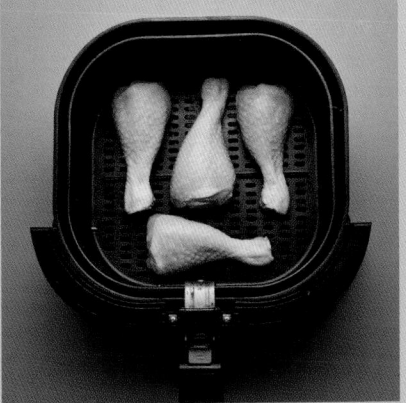

02

03

04

cooking for one

We have many air fryer readers who are cooking for one: from the older person living alone and the single professional to students heading to university and becoming independent for the first time. The first question they ask us, is "How easy are air fryer recipes to adapt for one person?" and my first response is always that the air fryer is made for YOU! Unlike a family, you don't need two air fryers or a dual for full meals, and it's easy to batch and make meals ahead so that it doesn't feel like you're cooking all the time just for yourself.

I wish the air fryer was about when my Grandma was widowed 31 years ago. She didn't like cooking and would have loved warming up her favourite meals in it. I also love watching our best mate with it, who is a single working professional who works unsociable shifts and loves how easy it is.

If you're cooking for one, how should you adapt these air fryer recipes? Which are best for one person? What freezes well, and are you stuck eating the same kind of food all the time?

how to convert recipes

For many of the recipes in this book that serve four people, you can divide the ingredients by four and make it into a recipe to serve one. I do this frequently with Bombay potatoes because the rest of my household doesn't care for Indian food. I can quarter the ingredients and keep the same time and temperature. The same goes for a meal like corned beef hash (see page 50) – I simply halve the ingredients and make it for one.

While it is often easy to reduce the quantities (in proportion) for a regular meal or side dish, if you wanted to reduce a baking recipe, we suggest that you follow our dual adaptations, which provide options for smaller cooking accessories. For example, our sprinkle cake (see page 212), can be cooked in four mini tins to fit the dual drawers, so you can simply quarter the recipe and make just one mini cake (which serves two) and enjoy it over a couple of days!

When adapting the recipes, be aware that if you have much less food in the air fryer, it may cook more quickly as the air can circulate more freely. Therefore, cooking times stated in the recipes may be slightly too long, and you'll need to keep an eye on the food, especially towards the end of the cooking time.

Top tips

Choose an XL air fryer basket (such as a 5.5 litre/5.8 quart air fryer capacity) for full meals. This is a very useful size for fitting a piece of protein, such as a turkey steak, alongside a portion of potatoes and vegetables, and cooking everything together in the same basket. (See our turkey dinner for one on page 92.)

If you have a mini air fryer (such as the 2 litre/2.1 quart) you can make our poussin recipe (see page 82) and cook the fries at the same time.

Make ahead and freeze It can get a bit boring when you are cooking for one and dinner is often a single chicken breast cooked in the air fryer. Instead, we love making chicken bags to add exciting flavours. Chicken is marinated in heavy duty freezer bags, then frozen in portions. We have a choice of seven different marinades (see page 37) so you can prepare a variety and make mealtimes more fun.

Batch cook There are lots of recipes in this book that you can batch cook and freeze in single portions, then air fry later. Some of our favourites include chilli con carne (see page 55), sweet potato and chickpea curry (see page 130), or sausages and peppers (see page 105).

Make a smaller portion See opposite for how to adapt larger recipes to serve one – or just halve a standard "serves four" recipe to serve two people so that you have lunch ready for the next day!

let's talk air fryer accessories

I have bought many air fryer accessories over the years – some have been amazing, some have been okay and some have been useless. It's a learning curve, and as you buy accessories, you will see which ones work for you. In our accessories section, I will share which types of air fryer accessories we find useful, and which of our recipes they are used in.

WHY DO YOU EVEN NEED AIR FRYER ACCESSORIES?

You need air fryer accessories just like you need accessories for a standard oven. In the oven you would cook with a range of metal, ceramic or silicone bakeware, and the same applies to cooking in the air fryer.

There is a huge range of air fryer accessories available, but we don't want you wasting money, so the ones featured here are only those that we personally used while writing the recipes for this book.

You can use any accessory brand you like, you just need to make sure that what you have fits your air fryer size and that you're not going to slow down the cooking process too much. For example, tightly wrapping food in foil, or adding foil over food too soon (to stop the browning), can slow down the cooking time, as can very using thick silicone or glass, so plan this into your cooking time.

We have found some of our favourite accessories when we were not expecting to. Charity shops that sell bric a brac, supermarkets with good "home" departments that we wander into when doing our weekly food shop, or department stores are all great sources. The bakeware aisle is a good source for small roasting tins that fit your air fryer oven, fun coloured silicone muffin cups or different sized foil trays.

WHAT ACCESSORIES CAN YOU USE IN THE AIR FRYER?

The general rule is that anything that is oven safe is fine for use in the air fryer, as long as it fits. Our favourites include silicone (such as pans and muffin cups), ceramic dishes (such as ramekins and casserole dishes), paper liners or metal bakeware.

Glass, such as Pyrex, is regularly used in ovens, but in the air fryer it really extends the cooking time, so we tend to avoid it.

accessories for every air fryer owner

Regardless of which air fryer model you own, we recommend that you have the following in your kitchen for your air fryer:

Spray bottle A spray bottle is essential for air frying. Simply fill an empty spray bottle with extra virgin olive oil, then use it to spray the top of your air fryer food for an extra crisp. Avoid commercial oil sprays, as they may include chemicals that cause damage to the air fryer.

Pastry brush These can be really handy for brushing egg wash onto your bread dough or pastry, or even for spreading liquid over ingredients to speed up the prep process such as spreading tomato purée over the pastry for our homemade sausage rolls (see page 202).

Thermometer Another air fryer essential is a thermometer. You can quickly check the internal temperature of meat to avoid overcooking, or just to get meat to your ideal doneness. We also use them to check cakes are baked through – insert it into the centre of the cake and if the probe comes out clean with no raw batter on it, it's done.

Non-scratch sponges When washing the air fryer you need to make sure to use non-scratch washing utensils so that you don't remove the non-stick coating. Softer, non-scratch ones avoid excessive wear and tear of the air fryer, especially if you're using an air fryer with a crisper plate and removing it to use the bottom.

Utensils As well as non-scratch sponges, we also recommend silicone utensils, such as spatulas and spoons, as these won't scratch the air fryer when you're stirring food during cooking.

Bakeware Any bakeware that fits the air fryer and would normally be used in the oven is perfect. We use round springform pans and standard cake tins in various sizes (10cm/4 inch for small air fryers or duals, or 18–20cm/7–8 inch ones for standard air fryer baskets). We also like to use mini metal trays in the air fryer oven, and the ones we have measure 24cm x 18cm/9½ x 7 inch (see page 63).

silicone is the air fryer's friend

If we could choose just one type of accessory to use, we would opt for silicone. It wipes clean or can just go in the dishwasher, making clean up effortless. For baking, you can just use silicone and avoid lining containers with baking parchment. It also comes in many different sizes, so you can always find something that fits your air fryer, and you can often use a size slightly bigger because it is bendy and you can easily adjust it to fit.

But shop around: some silicone is flimsy, so try to hunt out stronger products for your air fryer. When you buy better-quality silicone accessories, they last a long time and are better for the environment compared to single use paper liners or foil. Silicone also comes in lots of shapes and sizes, meaning no matter what size air fryer you have, you'll always find a favourite silicone that fits.

01 Muffin cups I use these to make our road trip muffins (see page 207) but you can also cook the sprinkle cake batter (see page 212) and make vanilla muffins with sprinkles rather than a large cake. If you are using them for muffins but want to serve them in paper liners, line the silicone cups with the paper liners and the weightier silicone will stop the paper liners from blowing around in the air fryer.

02 Silicone cake pans These come in many different sizes, so you will always find something to fit your air fryer. Look for sturdy silicone, as many that are marketed for the air fryer are quite flimsy. We use 9cm/3½ inch, 14cm/5½ inch and 19cm/7½ inch pans the most. We use the largest pan for cooking all our cakes in the air fryer, and for other baking recipes, such as flapjacks (see page 204). The medium size is great if you have a smaller air fryer size or are cooking a smaller portion, while the smallest pan is perfect for measuring out ingredients as well as for melting butter or chocolate in the air fryer.

03 Round pans with handles This is my favourite air fryer accessory of all time. It's made from sturdy silicone that lasts; I have regularly used the same pan for the last few years and it's still going strong. Thanks to the pan's handles, it's easy to move it in and out of the air fryer. It's also very deep and so it can hold a reasonable portion of food. We use it for wet foods such as chilli or our sweet potato and chickpea curry (see page 130).

04 Dual silicone with handles The same concept as the round pan but designed to fit the shape of dual air fryer drawers. We have two of these, so we can divide large portions of food between the two pans and cook one in each drawer, as we do for our moussaka (see page 182).

can you use ceramics in the air fryer?

Yes, you can use anything ceramic that fits in your air fryer. Ramekins are the most common ceramic to use in the air fryer. Four will normally fit a standard air fryer basket, while I can fit two in each drawer of a dual, or one to two in a smaller air fryer. Ramekins are popular because you can walk into a shop, buy them and just know that they will fit the air fryer. However, with casserole dishes you can be staring at the mini casserole dish on the shelf and wondering if you should take a chance on it! I recommend measuring the size of the inside of your air fryer at home, then subtracting 1cm/½ inch to avoid accessories being too tight a fit. Store these measurements on your phone in a notepad file, then when out shopping you're not guessing and you know the exact size limit.

01 **Ramekin dishes** Perfect for air fryers of any shape or size. We love them for little portions of our favourite recipes; see them being used in the seafood crumbles (see page 120) or as a small portion option for our cheesecake (see page 210).

02 **Square baking dishes** These are ideal for air fryers that have a square shape, such as basket or single drawer air fryers. We can easily fit 18cm/7 inch square dishes in our air fryer, but if your air fryer is smaller you may need to go down in size.

03 **Small rectangular dishes** Useful for dual air fryers as they have a smaller capacity, so you can fit one in each drawer.

04 **Larger rectangular dishes** If you have an air fryer with a flex drawer, you will be able to fit much larger baking dishes in it. Measure your drawer and buy the biggest that will fit to maximise the space you have.

accessories for small basket air fryer owners

If you own a small air fryer, you can use many of the same accessories, but for some you will just need to go smaller.

For example, I will use the spray bottle, pastry brush and thermometer as usual. However only one ramekin, rather than four in a standard basket, will fit the basket – perfect for feeding one. Then I need to choose silicone, ceramics and bakeware that fits the smaller air fryer size.

The best thing to do is get the tape measure out and check the size of your air fryer for what will fit. For example, with my small air fryer, I know I can use round accessories up to 14cm/5½ inches. There are a lot of shopping choices for silicone and bakeware that are smaller than this size, so it's easy to get equipped for getting started with air frying.

accessories for dual air fryer owners

If you have a dual air fryer, use the same pastry brushes, bottles, etc, but choose rectangular accessories instead of square or round ones to maximise the space in the drawers. Most useful are rectangular silicone containers with handles, which make removing the containers from narrow drawers much easier.

You also use any ceramic or metal bakeware that fits the dual baskets. However, because most dual air fryer models have removable crisper plates, you can cook items with lots of liquid directly in the bottom of the drawers, so silicone (and other) containers are used a lot less.

accessories for air fryer oven owners

If you are using an air fryer oven, you can use similar accessories as those used in basket and dual air fryers. However, the advantage is that you will be able to use wider objects, such as mini oven trays, which wouldn't fit in the other models – and which we love. (They are great for cooking two different meals, if you have a fussy partner!) Do bear in mind though that if you are cooking on more than one shelf, the depth of containers should be a consideration. Turn to our introduction to the air fryer oven on page 62 for more information.

MEAL
PREP

meal prep 101

When I first heard of meal prep, I imagined doing a bumper supermarket shop, then spending huge amounts of time making freezer meals for the whole month. But I soon learnt that meal prep could be anything you wanted it to be.

You could start with prepping some simple vegetables for the next day's dinner, or make a quiche that can be reheated when you need a snack, or marinate some meat that can make a handy base for a meal on those days when your life is crazy and you're late getting dinner cooked.

Of course, you could also do a month's meals, but it's all about what makes your life easier.

For our meal prep storage, we have a chest freezer, lots of freezer bags, and large ice cube trays (see them on page 32), but any smallish freezerproof containers will work well too.

Our main meal prep routine will include an hour or so on a Sunday prepping veggies, snacks and leftovers for the freezer to avoid food waste.

my simple sunday routine

If you want to get started with your own meal prep routine, let me introduce you to my Sunday routine. The bonus is that what I am meal prepping also becomes brunch too.

I get out my mixing bowls and favourite veggie knife (please tell me I am not the only one with a favourite knife?), then get started.

01 I start by making veggie bags (see pages 26–27), using what is left from our weekly veg box delivery to avoid any food waste. I gather the vegetables from the fridge, peel and dice them, add seasoning and oil, then bag them to use for Monday to Wednesday. If we have eaten out and have more leftover vegetables than usual, these bags can be frozen and then cooked from frozen in the air fryer without a par boil. Thanks to the oil they freeze well, and you can adjust the portion sizes in the bags to suit your household.

If you are having a Sunday lunch, you can prepare the lunch vegetables at the same time. Sometimes I will prepare the next four weeks' worth of Sunday vegetables and freeze the spare bags – it makes the next few Sundays even more stress free.

02 As I prep the veggie bags, there will be plenty of peelings, usually including parsnip, carrot and potato skins. I will have a spare bowl to collect these as they are delicious when air fried and taste just like crisps/chips (see page 28). They usually become my Sunday brunch.

03 I also like to make an impossible quiche and air fry it. It can be breakfast, a quick lunch, the basis for an evening meal, or just a snack that we can quickly reheat when we are standing in front of the fridge starving. I also love the cheat's element of this quiche that makes it very quick to prepare (see page 30).

04 I check the use-by dates on fridge supplies. This is very important if you want to save money and avoid food waste. If I have meat that is close to expiring, I will label it and freeze it. Any leftover meals that are not going to get eaten within 3 days of being made, I will freeze in portions and label them ready for another busy day.

05 If I have spare soup, sauce or curry, I will spoon it into large silicone ice cube trays. I use small ones for smaller portions; for example, leftover curry paste or marinades, or the big 240ml/1 cup version. Whichever I use, I freeze them and, once frozen, push the frozen portion out of the silicone and transfer to a freezer bag so that I can grab one from the freezer when I need it.

make-ahead rainbow veggie bags

These veggie bags are prepped and then stored in the fridge or freezer, making mealtimes even easier. As they feed one, they are perfect if you live alone and don't feel like prepping for one each day after work. Alternatively, you can double the portions to feed two, or double again to feed a family of four. They cook well from the fridge or from the freezer and perfect for busy evenings.

....

SERVES **5 BAGS**
HERO **BASKET/DUAL**
PREP **15 MINUTES**
COOK TIME **15 MINUTES**
CALORIES **205 PER BAG**

....

1½ medium butternut squashes
2 medium courgettes/zucchini
1 red (bell) pepper/capsicum
1 green (bell) pepper/capsicum
1½ tbsp extra virgin olive oil
2 tsp dried parsley
Salt and black pepper

01 Peel and dice the butternut squash into 1cm/½ inch cubes and put them in a large mixing bowl. Slice the courgette into thick slices, then quarter each slice. Deseed and dice the peppers into 1cm/½ inch chunks. Add them to the bowl with the butternut squash cubes.

02 Add your olive oil and parsley, and season with salt and pepper. Mix well with your hands until the veggies are well coated with the olive oil and seasonings.

03 Divide the seasoned veggies equally between five freezer bags and store in the fridge if using within 5 days, or freeze if you will not be using them this week.

04 When ready to air fry, tip the contents of the freezer bag (defrosted, if you have frozen it, or see below) into the air fryer basket/drawer and spread out so that they cook evenly. Set the temperature to 180°C/360°F and cook for 15 minutes, or until the butternut squash is fork tender. Or add an extra 5 minutes if you prefer crispier veggies.

Cooking from frozen If cooking rainbow veggie bags from frozen, tip a bag from the freezer into the air fryer, spread them out and cook at 160°C/320°F for 15 minutes. Shake the basket/drawer and cook for another 5 minutes at 200°C/400°F or until crispy to your liking.

Butternut squash swaps You can swap a similar quantity of sweet potato or pumpkin for the butternut squash and use the same time and temperature.

dom's simple potatoes & carrots

One of my favourite side dishes Dom makes us for lunch is potatoes and carrots. He will empty the bottom of the fridge, gather all the potatoes and carrots we have in, cook a big batch and bag up the remainder for other days. This recipe makes three bags, each serving two people – perfect for the next three days or to freeze for later.

....

MAKES **3 BAGS**
HERO **BASKET/DUAL**
PREP **15 MINUTES**
COOK TIME **20 MINUTES**
CALORIES **470 PER BAG**

....

7 medium red potatoes
6 medium carrots
2 tbsp extra virgin olive oil
1 tbsp dried thyme
1 tsp dried rosemary
½ tsp garlic powder
Salt and black pepper

01 Scrub the potatoes then cut them into 2.5cm/1 inch chunks. Peel and dice the carrots into 2cm/¾ inch slices.

02 Put the potatoes and carrots in a bowl and add the olive oil, herbs and garlic powder. Season with salt and pepper, and mix well with your hands until the potatoes and carrots are well coated with the olive oil and seasonings.

03 Divide the potatoes and carrots equally between three freezer bags and store in the fridge if using within 5 days, or freeze if you will not be using them this week.

04 When ready to air fry, tip the contents of the freezer bag (thawed, if you have frozen it, or see below) into the air fryer basket/drawer and spread out so that they cook evenly. Set the temperature to 180°C/360°F and cook for 20 minutes, or until the potatoes and carrots are fork tender. Add an extra 5 minutes if you prefer a crispier texture.

Cooking from frozen If you prefer to cook your potatoes and carrots from frozen, tip a bag from the freezer into the air fryer, spread them out and cook at 160°C/320°F for 20 minutes. Shake the basket/drawer and cook for another 5 minutes at 200°C/400°F or until crispy to your liking.

crispy curried veggie peelings

These moreish veggie snacks are made by mixing leftover vegetable peelings with olive oil and seasonings, and then they are air fried until crispy. Our favourites are using leftovers from parsnips, carrots, sweet potatoes or white potatoes, but you can mix and match any root vegetable, depending on the season.

....

SERVES **4**
HERO **BASKET/DUAL**
PREP **10 MINUTES**
COOK TIME **10–18 MINUTES**
CALORIES **111**

....

Peeled skins from 6 medium
  carrots
Peeled skins from 3 medium
  parsnips
Peeled skins from 3 medium
  white potatoes
1 tbsp extra virgin olive oil
1 heaped tsp mild curry
  powder
½ tsp ground turmeric
½ tsp garam masala
Salt and black pepper

01 Peel the vegetables as you do your meal prep, with either a knife for a thicker peeling or a peeler for a skinny peeling.

02 Add the peelings, the olive oil and spices to the bowl and season with salt and pepper. Mix well with your hands until the peelings are well coated with the olive oil and the seasonings.

03 Tip the peelings into the air fryer basket/drawer and spread out so that they cook evenly. Set the temperature to 180ºC/360ºF and cook for 10 minutes for skinny peelings or 18 minutes for thick. As air fryers differ, keep a close eye on them, and shake the drawer during cooking so that they cook evenly and don't burn.

Peeling size You can use a knife for a thicker peelings or go skinny with a vegetable peeler. The ones made with a vegetable peeler (pictured) will be crisper and more like crisps/potato chips.

cheese & tomato impossible quiche

A frittata is a quiche without any pastry, whereas an impossible quiche is a quiche with a fake pastry. You add flour to the quiche filling, then as the quiche cooks the flour drops to the bottom creating the structure of a pastry crust. It's called "impossible" because when you make it for the first time, your brain is saying "that is impossible"!

SERVES **6**
HERO **BASKET**
PREP **8 MINUTES**
COOK TIME **30 MINUTES**
CALORIES **220**

5 large eggs
120ml/4fl oz/½ cup whole/full-fat milk
2 spring onions/scallions
7 cherry tomatoes
85g/3oz/1 cup grated Cheddar cheese
2 tsp dried mixed herbs/Italian seasoning
2 tsp dried oregano
125g/4½oz/1 cup self-raising/rising-flour
Salt and black pepper

01 Crack the eggs into a mixing jug, pour in the milk and mix with a fork until combined.

02 Chop the spring onions into small chunks and halve the tomatoes. Add the spring onions, tomatoes, grated cheese and dried herbs to the jug, season with salt and pepper and mix well. Stir in the flour and mix again, making sure no flour is stuck at the bottom or down the sides.

03 Pour the mixture into a 20cm/8 inch loose-based pie tin – or a similar size that fits your air fryer. (We divide the mixture between two 10cm/4 inch pie tins in the dual air fryer). Carefully, as it will be full, transfer it to the air fryer.

04 Set the temperature to 180°C/360°F and cook for 20 minutes, then decrease the temperature to 160°C/320°F, cover with foil to avoid overbrowning on top, and cook for a further 10 minutes, or until a thermometer probe comes out clean. Allow it to sit in the air fryer basket to cool a little as the air fryer cools down, as then it's easier to remove from the air fryer. Serve the quiche warm or cold, though in the Milner house we like it cold and to take with us for picnic food.

You must try quiche bites! Sometimes leftovers taste better than the original recipe and this is one of those times. Chop leftover quiche into squares, then place into the air fryer. Air fry at 200°C/400°F for 4 minutes and you have something that can only be described as croutons meets flavoured bread. So good!

bits & bobs freezer sauce for everything

My favourite way to make a sauce is to gather up different veggies that need using up, to avoid wastage. I cook them until tender, then blend and use as base for a sauce that can be transformed into different sauces depending on what meals we are eating. We will then freeze in 240ml/ 1 cup portions which can be used when needed.

MAKES **4 FREEZER CUBES**
HERO **DUAL**
PREP **15 MINUTES**
COOK TIME **40 MINUTES**
CALORIES **373 PER CUBE**

6 medium tomatoes
3 medium carrots
1 medium courgette/zucchini
225g/8oz butternut squash, peeled and deseeded
1 tbsp extra virgin olive oil
1 tbsp dried parsley
1 garlic bulb
1 × 150g/5½oz pack garlic and herb cream cheese (we use Boursin)
2 tsp dried basil
240ml/8fl oz/1 cup whole milk/full-fat milk, plus extra if needed
Salt and black pepper

01 Quarter the tomatoes and peel and slice the carrots. Slice the courgette into 1cm/½ inch slices and then into quarters. Peel the butternut squash and chop it into 2cm/¾ inch cubes. Put all the vegetables in the air fryer drawer, removing the crisper plate first. Add the olive oil and parsley, and season generously with salt and pepper. Mix well with your hands until the vegetables are well coated with the oil and seasonings.

02 Slice the top off the garlic bulb exposing the cloves at the top. Spray with olive oil and season with salt and pepper. Wrap tightly in foil and place in the air fryer on top of the vegetables. Set the temperature to 180°C/360°F and cook for 30 minutes.

03 Remove the foil-wrapped garlic and shake the air fryer drawer to rotate the vegetables. Unwrap the cream cheese and place over the vegetables. Sprinkle half the basil over the cheese and air fry at the same temperature for a further 10 minutes.

04 Meanwhile, pour the milk into a blender or food processor. Squeeze the soft flesh out of the garlic head, discarding the papery skin, and add it to the blender. When the air fryer beeps, tip the contents of the air fryer drawer into the blender – including any juices that have collected – and add the remaining basil. Pulse until you have a creamy sauce, adding a little extra milk if it's too thick.

05 If freezing, pour the sauce into large 240ml/1 cup freezer cubes (or into small freezer-proof boxes) and allow to cool before adding the lid and freezing.

Basket sauce Combine the ingredients in a mixing bowl, then divide it between two silicone containers that fit your air fryer (ours are 20cm/8 inch) and cook one at a time, following the same time and temperature as mentioned above. I will usually do the garlic bulb in one batch and the cheese in the other.

Bits and bobs You can mix and match vegetables you have in, but try to balance naturally starchy vegetables, such as root vegetables, with vegetables with a higher water content, such as tomatoes or courgette. If you just add watery vegetables, your sauce will be too thin, and with too many root vegetables, it will be too thick.

Sauce suggestions Use the sauce as your base for:
Cheese sauce – add 225g/8oz/2½ cups grated Cheddar cheese.
Tomato sauce – swap the milk for a 400g/14oz passata.
Mexican sauce – swap the milk for 400g/14oz of salsa.

let's chop up a chicken

We first started jointing chickens when we moved into an apartment in Portugal. It was 2009 and whole chickens were often on clearance and much cheaper than buying different parts of the chicken – and perfect for buying in bulk. It gave us a choice. We could chop the legs, we could have skin-on chicken breasts, or we could collect chicken wings in a freezer bag and freeze ready for game night.

First, we're going to show you how to chop up a chicken, then we'll share with you the marinades we use with our pieces of chicken, and provide cooking times and temperatures for the different cuts. If marinated chicken is not your thing, you can freeze the chicken as it is in freezer bags, then thaw and air fry following the same cooking intructions (see page 37).

01 Place your whole chicken on a chopping board and grab your favourite sharp knife. Use one hand to hold a leg slightly away from the breast and cut through the skin at the joint. Pull the leg away from the bird and you should be able to see the joint. Cut through it to remove the leg, then repeat to remove the other leg.

02 To divide the leg into thigh and drumstick, place the leg on the board and feel for the joint. Slice the skin there so that you can see it, then take one end of the leg in each hand and bend the leg backwards until you feel it pop out. Get your knife into the loosened joint and cut down firmly to separate the pieces, then do the same again for the other chicken leg.

03 Feel for the backbone of the chicken and cut down the side of it to remove the breast. Keep your knife as close to the bone as you can as you cut the breast from the carcass so that you don't waste any chicken. Then slice all the way down to the bottom, removing the wing with the breast. Repeat to remove the other breast and wing. This is called a "supreme" and you can use it like this, but we like to remove the wings and cook those separately.

04 To remove the wing from the breast, carefully cut around the joint at the base of the breast. You will now have eight chicken pieces.

You have now chopped up a chicken: congratulations!

We now recommend deciding on what you plan to cook straight away and what you plan to freeze – and how to incorporate your various chicken pieces into your meal prep routine.

We usually chop up about four whole chickens at once so that we have plenty for our meal prep routine. We will prepare bags of just drumsticks; mixed drumsticks and thighs; full legs; and skin-on chicken breasts.

Also consider how many portions you would like to thaw and cook together. For example, cooking for our family will normally require four chicken leg portions, so we will freeze four of them together in a single heavy-duty freezer bag.

To avoid dinner boredom and not feel like you're cooking the same food everyday, you'll find our flavourful go-to marinades on the next page.

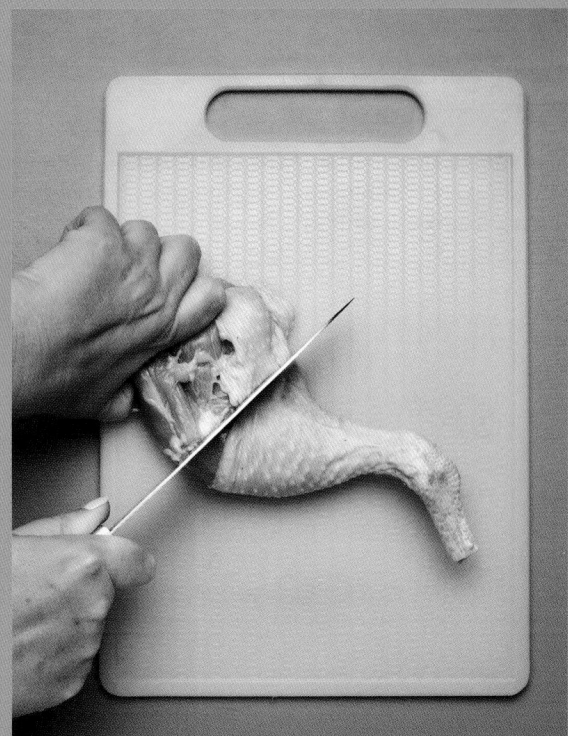

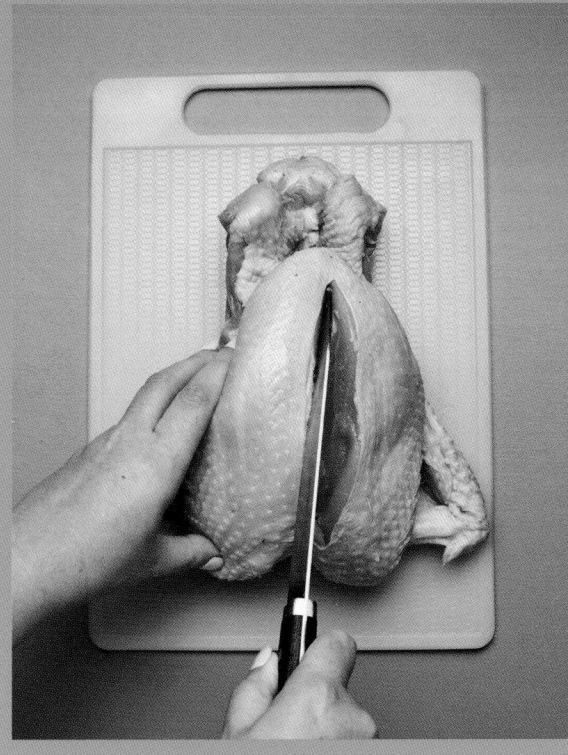

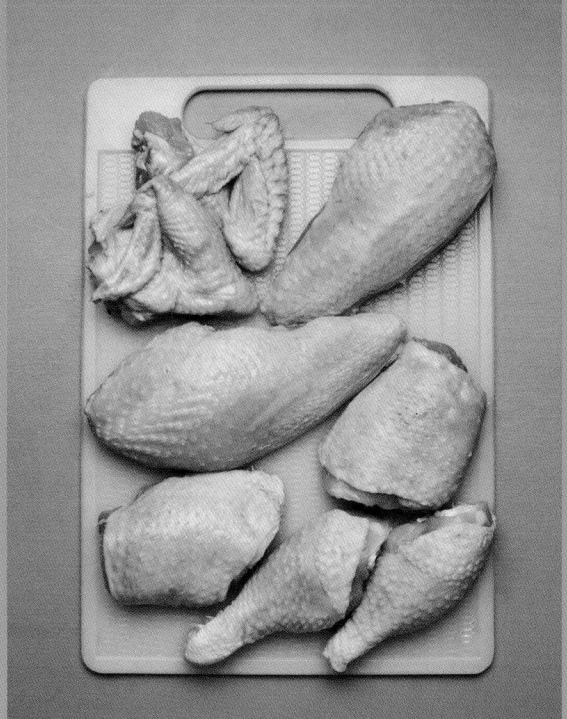

7 marinades for everything

After a long day at work, there is nothing more satisfying than grabbing a bag of marinated chicken breasts from the fridge (or freezer), placing them straight in the air fryer and putting your feet up. These seven marinades were originally created for chicken, but we also use them regularly with pork chops, fish fillets and tofu.

marinate in 5 simple steps

01 Choose your container Think of what you're using in the air fryer. If that's a foil tray/pan then choose this, or if you are air frying directly in the basket/drawer or want to save freezer space then opt for freezer bags. Though make sure that the freezer bags you use are the heavy duty ones that can handle the marinade.

02 Choose your protein We find the marinade ingredients are perfect for 750g/1lb 10oz of protein such as: 4 chicken legs, 6 chicken thighs, 8 chicken drumsticks, 8 chicken wings, 4 chicken breasts, 4 pork chops, 8 salmon fillets or 450g/1lb pressed (see page 145) tofu.

03 Choose your marinade We like to mix it up and do a variety of marinades to make mealtime more fun. Choose your favourite, or do a variety.

04 Prepare everything Set up a batch system and make the marinades first in the storage containers, then batch add the proteins and give them a good mix.

05 Fridge vs freezer If you plan to consume your marinated protein within 3 days, store in the fridge and allow to marinate for at least 2 hours before air frying. Or label and freeze for up to 3 months. Check out the tip on page 38 for how to cook from frozen.

Top tips

You don't have to batch You could use this page as your guide and simply marinate some chicken breasts for dinner.

Prepare in containers Use the container as your mixing bowl and save on washing up. You could prepare in a foil tray, freeze, thaw and air fry all in the same tray.

Reserve a little If making for tonight, you can also reserve a little marinade (1 tablespoon is a good amount) to brush over your protein just before serving. (Make sure you put it in a different bowl and don't use the marinade from the raw meat.)

Serving Once cooked, you can use your marinated chicken protein in a salad, serve with one of our vegetable recipes, or have it for sandwiches – the choice is yours. But do look out for these marinades in action throughout the book.

Paper liners We love using paper liners for marinated foods. As you can cook the food on the paper liner, you don't have a messy air fryer to deal with, and you can transfer your food from the freezer bag directly to the paper liner.

Pat's pans We love that Pat, an air fryer oven user of many years, streamlines her cooking by using foil trays/pans instead of cooking directly in the air fryer. The marinade can be mixed up in the trays, so the food can be prepped, frozen and cooked all in the same container, and then discarded after use to save on washing up too! You can do the same with the basket, or drawer air fryers – just find a pan that fits.

CORIANDER/CILANTRO LIME
2 tbsp lime juice
3 tbsp extra virgin olive oil
2 tbsp clear honey
1 tsp garlic purée
2 tbsp finely chopped fresh coriander/cilantro
Salt and black pepper

CURRY YOGHURT
1 tsp garlic purée
1 tsp ginger purée
1 tbsp extra virgin olive oil
3 tbsp Greek yoghurt
2 tsp mild curry powder
1 tsp ground turmeric
1 tsp ground cumin
1 tsp dried coriander/cilantro leaf
Salt and black pepper

GREEK KEBABS
2 tsp garlic purée
1 tbsp balsamic vinegar
1 tbsp lemon juice
1 tbsp extra virgin olive oil
2 tbsp Greek yoghurt
2 tsp dried oregano
Salt and black pepper

HAWAIIAN SUMMER
2 tbsp pineapple juice
2 tbsp barbecue sauce
1 tbsp tomato ketchup
Juice and finely grated zest of 1 lime
1 tbsp extra virgin olive oil
1 tsp garlic purée
1 tsp ginger purée
1 tsp ground cumin
1 tsp smoked paprika
Salt and black pepper

HONEY & GARLIC
1 tbsp white wine vinegar
1 tbsp extra virgin olive oil
2 tsp garlic purée
100g/3½oz/⅓ cup clear honey
¼ tsp dried parsley
Salt and black pepper

MOROCCAN SPICE
1 tsp garlic purée
1 tsp ginger purée

2 tsp tomato purée/paste
1 tsp harissa paste
4 tbsp passata
2 tbsp extra virgin olive oil
1 tsp dried coriander/cilantro leaf
1 tsp ground cumin
1 tsp smoked paprika
¼ tsp ground cinnamon
Salt and black pepper

SWEET CHILLI
240g/8½oz/¾ cup sweet chilli sauce
1 tsp garlic purée
1 tsp ginger purée
2 tsp soy sauce
¼ red (bell) pepper/capsicum, finely chopped
½ tsp Chinese 5-spice powder
Salt and black pepper

01 Choose a marinade from the list. Add the marinade ingredients to a heavy-duty freezer bag or mix them up in a foil tray/pan.

02 Add the meat, fish or tofu to the bag and mix well with your hands.

03 Transfer the container to the fridge or freezer. If you are planning on cooking it that day, allow to marinate for at least 2 hours beforehand.

04 Transfer the protein to the air fryer basket/ drawer, placing it either on a paper liner or keeping it in its foil container. Set the temperature to 180ºC/360ºF, then follow the relevant cook time below:

Chicken drumsticks – 17 minutes
Chicken thighs – 23 minutes
Chicken legs – 25 minutes
Small (140g/5oz) chicken breasts – 15 minutes
Medium (200g/7oz) chicken breasts – 20 minutes
Large (250g/9oz) chicken breasts – 25 minutes
Frozen chicken wings – 20 minutes
Pork chops – 18 minutes
Salmon fillets – 12 minutes
Tofu cubes – 12 minutes

marinated chicken snack bags

You're probably wondering what to do with marinated chicken; well, picture yourself standing in front of the fridge, wishing you had something easy to eat right now. These snack bags are full of thinly sliced marinated chicken that you can grab as you need it – it can become a sandwich, be used in salads, snack on when starving, or take with you on long walks or road trips. You can also mix and match with any of our marinades.

....

SERVES **4**
HERO **BASKET/DUAL**
PREP **2 MINUTES**
COOK TIME **20 MINUTES**
CALORIES **138 (WITHOUT MARINADE)**

....

4 medium chicken breasts in marinade (see pages 36–7), thawed
Salt and black pepper

01 Remove the chicken breasts from the freezer bag that you marinated them in and place onto a paper liner inside your air fryer basket/drawer. Pour over any remaining marinade left in the freezer bag.

02 Set the temperature to 180ºC/360ºF and cook for 20 minutes, or until the chicken breasts have reached an internal temperature of 70ºC/160ºF or above.

03 Let the chicken rest for a couple of minutes, then season with salt and pepper and cut into thin slices. Once cold, transfer to food bags and store in the fridge for snack time – they will last 2–3 days.

Freezer friendly snacking You can also store your just-cooked chicken in snack bags in the freezer. Once cool, transfer the chicken snack slices to an oven tray, then freeze for an hour on the tray to firm up. Transfer the slices to freezer bags, seal and freeze for up to 3 months. Because you have pre-frozen them spread out on the tray, the chicken slices won't stick to each other once bagged up. If you don't want to wait for them to thaw, place the slices of frozen chicken into the air fryer basket/drawer and air fry at 150ºC/300ºF for 10 minutes to defrost.

Cooking from frozen Raw chicken breasts that have been frozen in their marinade are so moist and flavourful. Simply remove them from the freezer bag and place onto a paper liner inside your air fryer basket/drawer. Alternatively, if you have frozen them in a foil tray, remove the lid from your foil tray and place the tray in the air fryer. Cook at 120ºC/250ºF for 18 minutes to defrost the chicken. Turn the chicken over with tongs and increase the temperature to 160ºC/320ºF. Cook for a further 14 minutes or until the chicken breasts have reached an internal temperature of 70ºC/160ºF or above.

BBQ shredded chicken wraps

Our favourite thing about cooking a rotisserie chicken (see page 73) is that air fryer chicken is a lot moister than oven-roasted chicken. Shredding the leftover chicken and enjoying a day or two later is amazing. After a few add-ins, you have delicious barbecue chicken wraps that are freezer friendly too.

....

MAKES **4**
HERO **BASKET/DUAL**
PREP **5 MINUTES**
COOK TIME **8 MINUTES**
CALORIES **367**

....

240g/8½oz/1½ cups shredded
  chicken from rotisserie
  chicken (see page 73)
120g/4¼oz/½ cup barbecue
  sauce
70g/2½oz/½ cup canned
  sweetcorn, drained
85g/3oz/1 cup grated
  mozzarella cheese
1 tbsp dried basil
4 mini tortilla wraps
4 tsp cream cheese
1 egg, beaten for egg wash
Salt and black pepper

01 In a mixing bowl, combine the leftover shredded rotisserie chicken, barbecue sauce, sweetcorn, grated cheese and basil. Season generously with salt and pepper, and mix with your hands until the chicken is well coated.

02 Using a butter knife, spread a wrap with a layer of cream cheese, then add 3 heaped tablespoons of the barbecue chicken. Roll up the wrap tightly, tucking the sides in as you go, to stop it coming apart, then brush the top of the wrap with egg wash. Repeat to fill and roll all the wraps.

03 Place the wraps into the air fryer basket/drawer. In our basket air fryer, we can fit four wraps in at once, while in the dual we can fit three in each drawer; do it in batches if you need to.

04 Set the temperature to 180ºC/360ºF and cook for 6 minutes. Flip the wraps over and egg wash the other sides, then cook for a final 2 minutes. Serve warm.

Wraps for the freezer The BBQ chicken wraps above are perfect for easy meal prep and for using up leftovers. You can also prep the wraps, but instead of air frying straight away, wrap them in foil and place in the freezer. Defrost when you want one and cook following the instructions above.

PANTRY

pantry ingredients

When I was 16 and had fallen on hard times, I met a lovely lady and she let me sleep on her sofa. She was on a low income and did a lot of cooking from pantry staples. She bulk bought canned and other pantry foods and would top each up to a quantity of six. Then, if she went a week without being able to afford groceries, this was her back up. Even now, almost 25 years later, I still stack my pantry in volumes of six. With the cost of living crisis, pantry foods, which can taste delicious, have made a comeback and have become very popular for cooking in the air fryer.

canned goods cooking times

Thoroughly drain your listed canned veggies and pat dry with kitchen paper. Put them in a bowl with 2 teaspoons of extra virgin olive oil and 1 teaspoon of your favourite dried seasonings. Mix well with your hands and load into the air fryer.

Whole mushrooms 180ºC/360ºF – 8 minutes

Mixed vegetables 180ºC/360ºF – 15 minutes

Baby potatoes 180ºC/360ºF – 20 minutes

Whole baby carrots 180ºC/360ºF – 20 minutes

Sliced baby carrots 180ºC/360ºF – 15 minutes

Peas 180ºC/360ºF – 6 minutes

Sweetcorn 180ºC/360ºF – 6 minutes

7 pantry ingredients we always have in

Canned tomatoes and/or passata Chopped tomatoes are fantastic for making sauces, and you can blend them if you prefer a smooth sauce. Or if you prefer smooth sauces without any blending, swap canned tomatoes for passata.

Canned tuna I always buy it in brine rather than oil. It's perfect for a last minute tuna melt or a salad.

Canned sweetcorn The can of many uses: tuna melts, salads, air fried into a crispy snack, or use it for bulking up recipes to feed more mouths.

Canned chickpeas If I have a favourite meal in the air fryer it is my sweet potato and chickpea curry (see page 130). Chickpeas, like sweetcorn, are also ideal for salads, snacking on and bulking up meals.

Canned taco beans mix I love these cans of Mexican deliciousness. Instead of mixing up lots of different cans, these combinations of various types of bean in a spicy tomato sauce are a fantastic add in. We use them in quesadillas (see page 52), or in place of the red kidney beans in a chilli con carne (see page 55).

Canned brown lentils Forget dried lentils, with the air fryer cans of brown lentils are a fast solution. Try them toasted (page 58).

Canned whole potatoes These have become a very popular pantry staple for the air fryer and OMG these are delicious and now a Milner mealtime favourite.

Because we like to practise what we preach, you will find all these canned ingredients used throughout the book.

other supplies you will always find in our pantry

- Coconut milk
- Pineapple
- Beans: black, black-eyed, baked
- Extra virgin olive oil
- Balsamic vinegar
- Worcestershire sauce
- Honey
- Maple syrup
- Wholegrain mustard
- Tomato purée/paste
- Garlic purée
- Ginger purée
- Cocoa powder
- Sugar: icing/confectioner's, light brown, granulated
- Flour: self-raising/self-rising, plain/all-purpose

10 herbs and spices we use the most

We much prefer to use dried herbs and spices because they are easy to store, making everyday cooking so much easier. They also travel well, so we pack them to add instant flavour to our holiday meals. Below are the ones we use the most at home (and therefore in these recipes), along with salt and pepper:

- Mixed herbs/Italian seasoning
- Oregano
- Basil
- Thyme
- Rosemary
- Mint
- Dill
- Smoked paprika or sweet paprika
- Mixed spice or pumpkin spice
- Cumin

brilliant breadcrumbs

Homemade breadcrumbs don't cook as well as shop-bought crumbs in the air fryer. They struggle to crisp up and can look pale. Instead, choose from these three pantry staples:

Panko breadcrumbs These will give you the crisp on your food that in texture will be very similar to breaded food you normally eat, and a good golden colour.

Golden breadcrumbs These are popular in the UK and have a deep golden colour, reminiscent to that on fish fingers/fish sticks.

Shake 'N Bake These are the US favourite. You can get them in different flavours, which means they are useful for mixing and matching flavours depending on what you are coating.

how to start your own pantry

If you have never stocked a pantry before, you can start slow, check out special deals and build it up over time.

We notice, when shopping, that the best deals will be in your eyeline so that the shop can bring them to your attention – or they might also be on prominent end-of-aisle displays. Pantry staples are often on 'buy one get one free' deals so you can stock up whenever items are on offer. Soon you will have a pantry stocked for easy everyday recipes.

20-minute herby canned potatoes

I hadn't eaten a canned potato in more than 20 years, yet here I was, trying them in the air fryer after a reader asked for them. I was pleasantly surprised by how delicious this simple staple tasted and now I have a pantry stocked with canned potatoes!

....

SERVES **2**
HERO **BASKET/DUAL**
PREP **8 MINUTES**
COOK TIME **20 MINUTES**
CALORIES **176**

....

1 × 540g/19oz can potatoes
½ tbsp extra virgin olive oil
½ tsp dried parsley
A pinch of dried rosemary
A pinch of garlic powder
Extra virgin olive oil spray
Salt and black pepper

01 Drain the potatoes, then gently place them onto a piece of kitchen paper/paper towel. Let the potatoes sit for 5 minutes to soak up the extra moisture.

02 Very gently place the potatoes into a bowl; try not to be heavy-handed as the potatoes are pre-cooked and preserved in water and can break easily. Add the olive oil, herbs and garlic powder and season with salt and pepper. Mix with your hands until the potatoes are well coated.

03 Tip the potatoes into the air fryer basket/drawer and spread them out. Set the temperature to 180ºC/360ºF and cook for 15 minutes. When the air fryer beeps, the potatoes will be almost golden. To create a crisper texture, spray the potatoes with olive oil, increase the temperature to 200ºC/400ºF and air fry for an extra 5 minutes before serving.

Slices are even better Whilst I love whole canned potatoes, cutting each baby potato into slices really adds a wow factor – the crisp is better and it's like a crunchy feast. Follow the technique above, but after patting dry, slice each potato into 5mm/¼ inch slices. Add the same amount of oil and seasonings and air fry the sliced potatoes for the same time and temperature as above. We use these in our Monday pie recipe (see page 180).

Add canned baby carrots We love that canned potatoes and baby carrots carry the same cook time. Simply follow the baby potatoes recipe, but also drain and pat dry a **300g/10½oz can of baby carrots**. Add 50 per cent more of the oil and seasonings to the bowl to give the carrots and potatoes a great taste, and continue with the recipe as above.

dom's stuffed tuna melts

If there is one pantry staple we always have in, its canned tuna. Dom makes tuna melts in the air fryer from his favourite shop-bought cheesy bread, filled with onion, sweetcorn, mayo and plenty of cheese. They're so delicious.

....

SERVES **4**
HERO **BASKET/DUAL**
PREP **8 MINUTES**
COOK TIME **8 MINUTES**
CALORIES **699**

....

2 × 145g/5oz cans tuna in brine
1 × 160g/5½oz can sweetcorn
¼ medium red onion, peeled
  and finely diced
1 tbsp cream cheese
5 tbsp mayonnaise
½ tsp wholegrain mustard
1 tsp dried parsley
1 tsp dried oregano
115g/4oz/1¼ cups grated
  mature/sharp Cheddar
  cheese
2 cheese cob loaves or
  4 individual rolls
Salt and black pepper

01 Drain the tuna and sweetcorn and tip them both into a mixing bowl. To the bowl, add the onion, cream cheese, mayonnaise, mustard, parsley, oregano and three-quarters of the Cheddar. Season with salt and pepper, mix well, then set aside.

02 Next, use a serrated knife to cut the crust off the top of the bread. Cut out the fluffy insides of the bread, going just halfway down the loaf so that there is a hollow at the top, but a thick layer of bread at the base to create a bread boat. Add one-quarter of the removed bread pieces to the tuna bowl.

03 Mix the bread chunks into the tuna mixture before using a spoon to distribute the filling between the two bread boats. Press down to fit more into each bread cob. Sprinkle with the remaining Cheddar on top and press the cheese down to stop it escaping when being air fried.

04 Place the tuna melts into the air fryer basket, or place one in each drawer. Set the temperature to 180°C/360°F and cook for 8 minutes. When the air fryer beeps the cheese will be melted and golden and the bread will be starting to get crispy.

corned beef hash

I love corned beef hash and it takes me back to my childhood. My Grandma would always talk about how corned beef was the hero ingredient during Second World War rationing and how the local soldiers would give her their corned beef ration to feed her young daughters. Corned beef hash is one of those old-fashioned greats that is just perfect cooked in the air fryer.

....

SERVES **2**
HERO **BASKET/DUAL**
PREP **8 MINUTES**
COOK TIME **36 MINUTES**
CALORIES **857**

....

4 medium white potatoes
2 large carrots
2 tsp mixed herbs/Italian
  seasoning
1 tbsp extra virgin olive oil
1 small onion
1 × 340g/11¾oz can corned
  beef
Salt and black pepper
1 × 400g/14oz can baked
  beans, to serve (optional)

01 Scrub the potatoes, then dice them into 1cm/½in cubes. Peel and dice the carrots into a cubes of a similar size. Put the potatoes, carrots, mixed herbs and olive oil in a bowl, season with salt and pepper, and mix well with your hands.

02 Tip the potato and carrot mixture into the air fryer basket/drawer and spread out for an even cook. Set the temperature to 180°C/360°F and cook for 20 minutes.

03 Meanwhile, peel and finely slice the onion and, when the air fryer beeps, add it to the air fryer. Shake the basket/drawer to combine everything, then air fry at the same temperature for a further 8 minutes.

04 Whilst the potatoes, carrots and onion are cooking, open a can of corned beef and cut it into 2cm/¾ inch chunks. When the air fryer beeps, shake the air fryer and add the corned beef chunks on top. If you are serving your corned beef hash with baked beans, divide them between two ramekins. Find a space in the air fryer for the ramekins.

05 Cook the hash and the beans for 8 minutes until the corned beef is crisping up and the beans are heated through, then serve your corned beef hash with the beans.

taco bean & cheese quesadillas

If I close my eyes and enjoy a quick daydream, I am back in Mexico eating the most delicious quesadillas. If you are having a pantry clear out, that can of taco beans and those wraps you forgot about are ideal for a quick taste of Mexico.

SERVES **2**
HERO **BASKET**
PREP **8 MINUTES**
COOK TIME **8 MINUTES**
CALORIES **893**

4 small tortilla wraps
2 tbsp sour cream
3 tbsp extra virgin olive oil
1 tsp frozen chopped garlic
1 tsp dried coriander/cilantro leaf
1 × 400g/14oz can mixed taco beans in tomato sauce
1 spring onion/scallion, finely sliced
1 tsp taco seasoning
4 tbsp salsa
85g/3oz/1 cup grated Cheddar cheese
Salt and black pepper

01 Place the four mini wraps on a worktop and spread sour cream over two of them, spreading it close to the edge, as it will work like egg wash for keeping the wraps in place as they air fry.

02 Mix together the olive oil, garlic and coriander in a bowl, then brush it over the tops of the other two wraps.

03 Drain the can of taco beans and tip the beans into a mixing bowl; reserve the tomato sauce in a separate dish. Add the spring onion, taco seasoning and 1 tablespoon of the salsa to the beans, and mix well. Season with salt and pepper, then spoon the bean mixture over the sour cream coated wraps. Sprinkle over the grated cheese and top with the other wraps, oil side up, and press down to seal.

04 Gently place a quesadilla into the air fryer basket, set the temperature to 180ºC/360ºF and cook for 8 minutes, or until the tortilla is crispy and the cheese has melted. Repeat to cook the second quesadilla, if necessary.

05 While the quesadillas are air frying, mix the reserved sauce from the beans with the remaining salsa. When the air fryer beeps, serve the quesadillas with the salsa dip.

Dual quesadillas To make quesadillas that fit into the dual drawers, we use half the amount of filling in one wrap, spreading it over one half of the tortilla, then fold the tortilla over to make a semi-circular quesadilla, like you would a pasty. You can use the same time and temperature and put one folded quesadilla in each drawer. Then when it's time to serve, slice them in half instead of into quarters.

cook-once eat-twice chilli con carne

Known in the UK as 'chilli con carne' and in the USA simply as 'chili', this is a delicious dish when cooked in the air fryer. It can be stretched to feed more mouths thanks to the pantry staples that bulk up this famous one pot dinner. Serve with quesadillas for the ultimate pantry dinner, or why not load up the chilli con carne over some homemade flatbread from page 196.

....

SERVES **4**
HERO **DUAL**
PREP **5 MINUTES**
COOK TIME **39 MINUTES**
CALORIES **443**

....

450g/1lb minced beef/ground beef
1 medium carrot, peeled and finely diced
1 medium white onion, diced
1 × 500g/1lb 2oz jar chilli sauce
1 × 400g/14oz can kidney beans, drained
1 × 400g/14oz can chopped tomatoes
1 tbsp mixed herbs/Italian seasoning
1 heaped tsp cayenne pepper, or to taste
2 tsp smoked paprika
Salt and black pepper

01 Remove the crisper plate from your dual air fryer and place the minced beef directly into the bottom of the air fryer, or into a silicone dish if using an air fryer basket. Sprinkle the carrot and onion over the mince.

02 Set the temperature to 180ºC/360ºF and cook for 5 minutes, then use a wooden spoon to break up the mince. Cook for another 4 minutes.

03 When the air fryer beeps, add the remaining ingredients, season with salt and pepper, and mix well. If you like a spicier chilli, increase the cayenne pepper to suit your taste buds.

04 Air fry the chilli for a further 30 minutes at the same temperature, or until the chilli is piping hot throughout. We recommend a quick stir halfway through the cooking time to prevent the kidney beans becoming overly crispy on top.

Leftover-chilli dogs Chilli dogs (in photo, left) are perfect for using up a little leftover chilli – and, made in the air fryer with melted cheese, even better. Simply cook **4 frankfurters/large hotdogs** at 180ºC/360ºF for 8 minutes, until cooked through. Load them into **4 hotdog buns**, then spoon **leftover chilli** over each one. Top each with **a sprinkling of Cheddar cheese** and load them back into the air fryer. Cook at the same temperature for another 8 minutes to heat the chilli and melt the cheese, before serving. Sprinkle with **sliced fresh chilli** and **spring onions/scallions** to serve, if you like.

hawaiian chicken salad

SERVES **4**
HERO **BASKET/DUAL**
PREP **15 MINUTES, PLUS MARINATING**
COOK TIME **23 MINUTES**
CALORIES **499**

4 medium chicken breasts
1 recipe quantity Hawaiian
   Summer Marinade
   (see page 37)

FOR THE CHICKEN BREADING
45g/1½oz/1 cup panko
   breadcrumbs
20g/¾oz/¼ cup desiccated/
   dried shredded coconut
2 tsp smoked paprika
A pinch of garlic powder

FOR THE SALAD
1 little gem lettuce
¼ red onion
8 cherry tomatoes
1 medium avocado
1 red (bell) pepper/capsicum
4 slices canned pineapple
   (in juice)
70g/2½oz/½ cup drained
   canned sweetcorn

FOR THE DRESSING
2 tbsp extra virgin olive oil
3 tbsp pineapple juice (from
   the can of sliced pineapple)
½ tsp garlic purée
½ tsp ginger purée
2 tbsp maple syrup
A squeeze of lime juice
A pinch of smoked paprika
Salt and black pepper

This Hawaiian chicken salad is my summer clear-out recipe, with lots of bits and bobs going in: spare salad items, marinated chicken from the freezer, along with lots of favourite canned staples. This is brilliant for your next barbecue.

01 Put the chicken and the marinade in a bowl and mix well with your hands, then cover with cling film/plastic wrap. Leave to marinate in the fridge for at least 2 hours, or you can leave it overnight if you prefer.

02 When ready to cook, combine the breading ingredients on a large plate and mix well. Roll each marinated chicken breast in the breading until well coated, shaking to remove any excess.

03 Place the chicken breasts in the air fryer basket, spreading them out; if using the dual air fryer, place two breasts in each drawer. Set the temperature to 180ºC/360ºF and cook for 15 minutes. When the air fryer beeps, increase the temperature to 200ºC/400ºF and air fry for a further 8 minutes, or until the chicken reaches an internal temperature of 70ºC/160ºF or above.

04 Whilst the chicken is cooking, prepare the salad. Wash and shred the lettuce, peel and slice the red onion and slice the cherry tomatoes in half. Stone and peel, then slice the avocado, and deseed and dice the red pepper. Slice the pineapple into chunks, then drain the canned sweetcorn. Layer up your salad on a serving plate, starting with the lettuce, then set aside.

05 When the air fryer beeps, remove the chicken from the air fryer and place on a chopping board. While it rests, combine your salad dressing ingredients in a jug, season with salt and pepper, and mix with a fork.

06 Slice the chicken and add to the salad, then finish with a drizzle of your salad dressing.

toasted lentils

I love draining cans of pantry staples, such as chickpeas and sweetcorn, then making them crispy and yummy in the air fryer. Toasted lentils are my new favourite. They are perfect for sprinkling on salads or soups, or make a guilt-free evening snack.

....

SERVES **4**
HERO **DUAL/BASKET**
PREP **5 MINUTES**
COOK TIME **8 MINUTES**
CALORIES **101**

....

1 × 400g/14oz can brown
  lentils
1 tbsp extra virgin olive oil
1 tbsp dried oregano
Salt and black pepper

01 Thoroughly drain the can of lentils, then tip them onto a couple of pieces of kitchen towel/paper towel to dry them further and soak up all the excess moisture.

02 Transfer the lentils to a bowl and add the olive oil and oregano, along with a generous seasoning of salt and pepper. Mix well with your hands.

03 Tip the lentils into the air fryer basket/drawer and spread out. If using an air fryer with a crisper plate, remove the plate and cook them directly in the bottom. Set the temperature to 200ºC/400ºF and cook for 8 minutes, or until crispy to your liking.

Waste not If using a basket, some of the toasted lentils may have escaped the basket into the bottom of the air fryer. Simply remove the basket and tip these extra-crispy lentils into your serving bowl with the others – they will also be delicious.

Mix up the flavours If oregano is not your thing, swap the 1 tablespoon of oregano for the same quantity of curry powder, taco seasoning, Southern Fried seasoning, piri piri or Cajun spice mix. Or try ½ tablespoon each of dried parsley and dill together, or team up smoked paprika and ground cumin.

Crispy cumin chickpeas Try switching the lentils for a can of chickpeas and swapping the oregano for cumin to make crispy cumin chickpeas. We use these on top of hummus for our mezze (see page 185).

crispy dill pickle chips

I have lost count of the times I have ordered a quarter pounder at a fast-food chain and asked for extra gherkins/pickles. But it wasn't until I first visited the US that I realised there was a much better way to enjoy gherkins and that was in a delicious breading. With this crispy dill pickle chips recipe, they are so easy to re-create in your air fryer.

....

SERVES **4**
HERO **BASKET/DUAL**
PREP **10 MINUTES**
COOK TIME **8 MINUTES**
CALORIES **97**

....

1 × 340g/12oz jar sliced
   gherkins/pickles
35g/1¼oz/¼ cup plain flour/
   all-purpose flour
1 large egg
28g/1oz/½ cup panko
   breadcrumbs
1 tbsp dried dill
2 pinches of cayenne pepper
2 pinches of garlic powder
Salt and black pepper

01 Thoroughly drain the gherkins, then place them on a couple of pieces of kitchen towel/paper towel to dry them further and soak up all the excess extra moisture. Drain them again on some fresh kitchen paper, as gherkins do carry a lot of liquid.

02 Set up your production line for the breading. Put the flour in a shallow bowl. Crack the egg into another bowl, season with salt and pepper, then beat the egg with a fork and set aside. Put the breadcrumbs in a third shallow bowl, add the dill, cayenne pepper and garlic powder, season with salt and pepper, and stir with a fork. You're now ready to bread your gherkins.

03 One at a time, place the gherkins into the flour, turning to coat, then drench in the egg. Finally, roll them in the breadcrumb mixture to give them a good coating.

04 Place the gherkin chips in the air fryer basket/drawer and spread out. If you're using a dual air fryer you can spread them out over two drawers. Set the temperature to 200ºC/400ºF and cook for 6 minutes, then turn them over and cook for a further 2 minutes until golden and crispy to your liking.

Reserve the pickle juices Those juices from a jar of gherkins are amazing for using in sauces or marinades. Our favourite is in the burger sauce on page 108, as part of our burger in a bowl.

AIR FRYER
OVEN

getting to know your air fryer oven

WHAT IS AN AIR FRYER OVEN?

Air fryer ovens use the same cooking technology as the basket or drawer models, but are more similar in appearance to a standard oven, although much smaller in size. Like an oven, they come with shelves which slot into grooves at the sides, although in an air fryer oven you can cook food directly on the shelves.

The main benefit of air fryer ovens is their size. They are usually about 10 litres – giving them twice the capacity of standard basket models. This means that you can cook the same amount of food as in two air fryer baskets or the same as in one dual. You are also not as restricted in accessory size as there is more space on the shelves to use mini oven trays, for example, which wouldn't be possible in other models.

Another huge bonus of air fryer ovens is the rotisserie that comes with most models, which is brilliant for rotating your favourite roasting meats, as well as for kebabs. I can never decide between gyros (see page 77) or Brazilian barbecue (see page 70) for the best thing to make with it.

There are some benefits of standard air fryers which the oven models miss out on. Firstly, if you are buying an air fryer to save on energy bills, it's not as good an option. Because it's like a mini oven, we find it costs a lot more to run compared to other air fryers we own.

Additionally, as they are much bigger than standard air fryers, they don't heat up as quickly and so will need preheating. (We recommend a preheat of 2 minutes before adding your food.) Food also does not cook as quickly in the oven models as it does in basket or drawer models.

The air fryer oven is best for people who prefer traybakes, or who are looking for a smaller version of the oven. It's also great for those who love entertaining, as the rotisserie is an appealing function for wowing your friends. They are also good if you want a larger air fryer to cook a greater volume of food.

air fryer oven shelves

In air fryer communities, "rack" is the name often given to the shelves in an air fryer oven, because they look similar to cooling racks. They are also sometimes numbered in air fryer recipes, so the top shelf would be "shelf one", the next down "shelf two" and so on.

But not all air fryer oven models are equal – some will have three shelves and some will have four, or even five. To make things simple in this book, we like to describe them as "top", "middle" or "bottom" shelf. (You can see these racks on page 15, loaded with chicken drumsticks.)

can you cook directly on the racks?

Yes, you can. Think of the racks like an air fryer basket: ingredients to be air fried are often prepared in a bowl, then transferred to the basket. Instead, transfer the food to a rack, spreading it out so that it cooks evenly, and placing it at the top of the air fryer oven. Then, if an air fryer recipe asks you to "shake the basket", you would turn the food on the rack over with tongs instead.

If an air fryer basket recipe calls for using a silicone container, paper liner, foil or casserole dish, for example, because of the mess it makes, you can simply use a similar accessory and place the food on the rack in its container. As air fryer ovens are bigger, the advantage is that you can easily fit a 23cm/9 inch square container on a shelf in the oven, while in the air fryer basket the maximum you'll be able to fit is 18cm/7 inches.

air fryer oven accessories

Anything that you would use in the oven can be used in an air fryer oven, it will sometimes just need to be a bit smaller. Everything we have featured in this book for the basket or drawer can be used in the oven, but our favourite accessory for the oven is the mini oven tray. The ones we have measure 24cm x 18cm/9½ x 7 inches and we have used them in both the pork tenderloin traybake (see page 64) and the shrimp boil tray-bake (see page 66).

Not only are they great fun when used for one-person traybakes, but mini trays are also more convenient than many other accessories. Because the gap between the shelves isn't very high, if cooking on two shelves you sometimes won't be able to fit two foil trays in at once. The same issue would apply to casserole dishes, and deeper silicone pans, but the trays have low sides so prevent this being a problem.

the 20 per cent rule

After experimenting with the recipes from this book, we have found that air fryer ovens, on average, cook 20 per cent slower than basket or dual models. We cooked the same recipes in the basket or drawer air fryers at the same time as the oven and found that the food in the oven was not quite there – it wasn't generally as cooked or crispy and would need a little longer.

While the recipes in this chapter have been written for the oven and so no adjustments are necessary, if you would like to cook any of the other recipes in this book in an oven model, you will need to add about 20 per cent more cooking time. For example, if a basket recipe states 20 minutes, you will need to preheat the air fryer oven for 2 minutes, then cook the food on the rack for 25 minutes. Similarly, 8 minutes becomes 10 minutes, or 12 minutes becomes 15 minutes, and so on.

for even cooking

If you are only cooking enough food to fill one shelf, it doesn't matter where in the oven that shelf is situated. This is because the air fryer oven is small and the heat circulates very well.

But if you have a full layer of food on the top shelf (especially if it's on a tray or in a container), and wish to cook more on the middle or bottom shelf, any food below the top shelf will cook more slowly. The solution is to switch the shelves around during cooking, so that the food on both shelves is exposed to the heat at the top – see our pork tenderloin and shrimp boil recipes, where each tray gets time on the top shelf and you don't have a problem with uneven cooking. If you want foods to crisp up more, make sure they are at the top.

let's convert a recipe for the air fryer oven

If you are cooking a basket or dual recipe in the air fryer oven, follow the tips below for the best results:

- If you can cook food directly on the rack rather than using a container, do this, as the air will circulate more freely and not slow the cooking time of the food below as much (and may even add tasty cooking juices to the food below!).
- If everything will fit on one shelf, just use one shelf so that nothing is placed below.
- Preheat the air fryer oven for a couple of minutes before you add your food.
- If you are cooking one shelf of food, add 20 per cent of the cook time.
- If you are cooking two shelves of food, remember to switch them around during cooking so that the food on both the trays can crisp up, and add a little more cooking time on top of the 20 per cent.

Next, we are going to share with you how to cook a traybake in the air fryer oven, then introduce you to our favourite air fryer oven feature – the rotisserie.

pork tenderloin traybake

This is one of the first recipes we made using the air fryer oven. We loaded one mini oven tray with pork tenderloin and skin-on apples and pears, then the other with cubed root vegetables. Because the vegetables are cubed, it speeds up the cooking time.

SERVES **2**
HERO **OVEN**
PREP **10 MINUTES**
COOK TIME **55 MINUTES**
CALORIES **892**

1 × 450g/1lb pork tenderloin
1 red apple
1 pear
2 tbsp clear honey
1 tbsp wholegrain mustard
1 tsp garlic purée
2 tsp balsamic vinegar

FOR THE VEGETABLES
2 medium white potatoes
2 medium carrots
1 medium parsnip
140g/5oz Brussels sprouts
1 tbsp extra virgin olive oil
2 tsp dried thyme
Salt and black pepper

01 Scrub and peel the potatoes, carrots and parsnip, then dice them into 2cm/¾ inch cubes. Halve the spouts if large, or leave them whole if smaller. Put the vegetables in a bowl and add the olive oil and thyme. Add a generous seasoning of salt and pepper, and mix well with your hands.

02 Spread the root vegetables across one of the mini baking trays – leaving the sprouts in the bowl – and place on the top shelf of the air fryer oven. Set the temperature to 180ºC/360ºF and cook for 15 minutes. Add your sprouts and mix into the other vegetables, then cook for a further 10 minutes.

03 While the veg are cooking, place the pork tenderloin on the other baking tray, laying it diagonally so that it fits, and season generously with salt and pepper. Slice the apple and pear into wedges, discarding the cores. Spread the fruit out around the pork.

04 Put the honey, mustard, garlic purée and vinegar in a small bowl and mix with a tablespoon. Pour half the mixture over the pork and fruit, creating a glaze over the tops.

05 When the air fryer beeps, move the vegetable tray to a lower shelf and add the tray with the pork and fruit to the top shelf. Set the temperature to 180ºC/360ºF and cook for 30 minutes, or until the pork reaches an internal temperature of 70ºC/160ºF or above. Brush the pork with the remaining marinade, then serve the pork with the fruity wedges and the vegetables.

Dual or basket tenderloin If you are using the basket, you can add the pork tenderloin to the centre, then spread the fruit and veggies around the meat. Or if using a dual, you can place the pork tenderloin and fruit in one drawer and the vegetables in the other. Cook at 180ºC/360ºF for 28 minutes (matching the drawers if using a dual), adding the sprouts after the first 8 minutes.

Which trays? We use mini oven trays – you can see these on page 66, but you can use any tray that fits your air fryer oven.

shrimp boil traybake

A shrimp boil is a great simple traybake for your air fryer oven. If it's new to you, shrimp boil comes from the Deep South of the USA. It varies, but usually includes king prawns/jumbo shrimp, smoked sausage, baby potatoes and mini corn on the cob. The Cajun seasoning and Cajun butter give it its wow factor.

SERVES **2**
HERO **OVEN**
PREP **15 MINUTES**
COOK TIME **39 MINUTES**
CALORIES **673**

....

4 frozen mini corn on the cob
1 large red onion
2 frankfurters/smoked
   sausages
4 baby potatoes
5 tsp Cajun seasoning
2 tsp garlic purée
Juice of ½ lemon
1 tbsp extra virgin olive oil
175g/6oz frozen raw peeled
   king prawns/shrimp
Salt and black pepper
 Fresh thyme leaves, for
   sprinkling
Lemon wedges, to serve

FOR THE CAJUN BUTTER SAUCE
55g/2oz/¼ cup salted butter
1 tsp Cajun seasoning
2 tsp garlic purée
1 tsp dried thyme
Juice of 1 lemon

01 Find yourself two air fryer oven trays (see page 63) and place two frozen corn on the cobs on each tray. Slice the red onion into slim wedges and divide them between the trays.

02 Slice the sausages and potatoes into quarters and put them in a mixing bowl. Add 3 teaspoons of the Cajun seasoning, the garlic purée, lemon juice and olive oil. Mix well, then arrange on the trays, drizzling any seasoned oil left in the bowl over the trays, too.

03 Put the trays in the air fryer oven, placing them on the top and bottom shelves, set the temperature to 180°C/360°F and cook for 10 minutes. Swap the trays around, and cook for another 10 minutes so that everything is evenly browned.

04 Remove the trays from the oven and scatter on the frozen prawns, spreading them evenly between the two trays. Sprinkle a teaspoon of the remaining Cajun seasoning over each tray, along with a generous seasoning of salt and pepper. Place the two trays back into the air fryer oven and cook at the same temperature for 16 minutes, swapping the trays around halfway through cooking, then remove the trays from the air fryer and set aside.

05 Add all the Cajun butter sauce ingredients to a ramekin. Place it in the oven and cook at the same temperature for 3 minutes, or until the butter has melted. Stir the sauce ingredients together, then pour it into two little sauce dishes and place a dish on each tray.

06 To serve, pour half the sauce over the ingredients on each tray, creating a delicious garlic sauce. Roll your corn on the cob in some of the butter and reserve the remaining sauce for dunking. Finish by sprinkling with fresh thyme and slicing two lemons into quarters creating lemon wedges and adding to the trays.

Basket or dual shrimp boil If using a basket or dual air fryer, the process is much quicker. First, cook the sausages and potatoes at 180°C/360°F for 10 minutes, then add the corn and the red onion and cook for another 10 minutes. Add the frozen prawns, stir, and cook for a final 10 minutes. If using the dual, split the ingredients between the two drawers for an even cook. We recommend cooking in a foil tray/pan so that it's easy to mix in the garlic butter and easier to serve.

let's learn all about the rotisserie

For many, the attraction of an air fryer oven is the rotisserie – and the ability to recreate your favourite rotisserie meat at home. A rod goes through the meat and clamps secure it in place so that the meat can constantly rotate. This means it's very juicy and never gets dry. You can use your imagination and do many combinations of meat, plus kebabs are also perfect this way.

honey mustard gammon

Whether you call it gammon or ham, it's our all-time favourite meat to cook using the rotisserie, and is a great rotisserie starting point.

1.2kg/2lb 10oz boneless
  gammon/ham joint
½ tsp black pepper
2 tsp dried parsley
2 tsp wholegrain mustard
2 tsp clear honey

SERVES **6**
HERO **OVEN**
PREP **5 MINUTES**
COOK TIME **65 MINUTES**
CALORIES **288**

01 Score both the fat side and lean side of the gammon with a knife going in by about 1cm/½in. This creates pockets to hold the seasonings to make your gammon more flavoursome.

02 Add the pepper, parsley, mustard and honey to a small bowl and mix with a fork. Using a pastry brush, brush the marinade all over the gammon, making sure it goes into the cuts you have made.

03 Push the rod all the way through the gammon joint until it comes out the other side.

04 Feed a clamp onto the rod, as far as it will go until the spikes of the clamp are firmly skewering the gammon. Repeat for the opposite end so that the gammon is clamped in place.

05 Position the gammon so that it is in the middle of the rod, then tighten the screws to finger tight.

06 Carefully place the gammon in the air fryer oven, positioning the rod in the rotisserie socket. Make sure that it is hooked in properly on both sides and that it won't fall off.

07 Set the temperature to 180ºC/360ºF and air fry the gammon for 65 minutes, or until the gammon reaches an internal temperature of 70ºC/160ºF or above.

Top tips

I'm watching you As you start the rotisserie, we recommend that you turn the light on and watch it for the first 2 minutes. This is to make sure that the rod is rotating properly in the socket.

Weight matters Because you're securing the meat on a rod that is rotating, it can't be too heavy or the meat will fall off. Aim for a joint that's between 800g/1¾lb and 1.3kg/3lb.

Attach to the meat When using the rotisserie, it's important that the spikes on the clamp are inserted firmly into the meat. This stops the meat from moving about and keeps it in position as it rotates.

Seasoning variety You can use any dried seasonings on your rotisserie meats; we recommend 1 tablespoon per whole chicken, or per roasting joint. Instead of 1 tablespoon of mixed herbs, you could add the same amount of Cajun seasoning, Chinese 5-spice, or why not make a piri piri chicken?

Mix a marinade If you would like to marinade your rotisserie meat, why not try one of the 7 marinades from page 37. You can prepare them ahead of time too, then cook when you are ready.

Rest, then remove We recommend removing the meat from the air fryer oven with oven gloves, then allow it to rest before removing the clamps and rod.

Love leftovers These rotisserie recipes will feed 4–6 people. Keep any leftovers in an airtight container in your fridge, then use the air fryer shelves to warm them up the next day. Or why not try the gammon in sandwiches, like we do in our afternoon tea on page 218?

brazilian picanha barbecue

If I could just eat one type of meat for the rest of my life, it would be the Brazilian picanha. Famous at Brazilian barbecue buffet restaurants, it is carved at your table and you just know you're going to ask the waiter for another slice. Back at home, the picanha can be recreated using the rotisserie.

....

SERVES **6**
HERO **OVEN**
PREP **5 MINUTES**
COOK TIME **35 MINUTES, PLUS RESTING**
CALORIES **388**

....

1.3kg/3lb rump beef (with fat cap attached)
Extra virgin olive oil spray
2 tsp garlic purée
2 tsp smoked paprika
1 tsp dried parsley
¼ tsp light brown sugar
¼ tsp onion powder
A pinch of cayenne pepper
1 tsp sea salt
1 tsp black pepper

01 Slice the rump in half, creating two separate pieces both with a piece of the rump cap attached. Thread the rod through the top of a rump piece, then bend the piece round and thread the rod back through the bottom of the piece too, to create a 'C' shape with the meat with the fat on the outside. Repeat for the second piece of rump, pushing them close together so that the two fit on the rod.

02 Lay the rod flat on a clean chopping board and spray the top half of the rump with olive oil, then smother with half the garlic purée, rubbing it into the olive oil with your fingertips.

03 Combine the paprika, parsley, sugar, onion powder, cayenne pepper, salt and black pepper in a small bowl, then sprinkle half over the top of the rump and rub it in with your hands. Turn the rump over and do the same again, spraying with the olive oil, smothering with the remaining garlic purée, then coating with the remaining rub and seasoning.

04 Feed a clamp through the end of the rod, as far as it will go until the spikes of the clamp are firmly skewering the beef. Repeat to add a clamp on the opposite side, so that the rump is secured in place.

05 Position the rump steaks so that they are in the middle of the rod. Once in the middle, tighten the screws to finger tight.

06 Carefully place the rump in the air fryer oven, positioning the rod in the rotisserie socket. Make sure that it is hooked in properly on both sides and that it won't fall off.

07 Set the temperature to 180ºC/360ºF and air fry the rump beef for 35 minutes for medium-rare. Remove from the air fryer oven with oven gloves, then allow it to rest for 5 minutes before serving.

Dual or basket Brazilian beef Half this rump will fit in an air fryer basket – just halve the seaosning mix – or you can fit one half in each drawer of a dual. Place each half on a metal kebab skewer and spread half the seasoning across each piece of rump. Cook at 180ºC/360ºF for 30 minutes.

Brazilian barbecue cook times
Cook at 180ºC/360ºF for:
25 minutes – rare
35 minutes – medium–rare
40 minutes – medium
50 minutes – medium–well done
60 minutes – well done

apple cider pork shoulder

We always associate pork shoulder with the slow cooker and pulled pork. But a delicious plan B is to use the rotisserie to air fry pork shoulder. When carved, it's a delicious pork roast that is perfect for your next roast dinner.

SERVES **6**
HERO **OVEN**
PREP **5 MINUTES**
COOK TIME **60 MINUTES**
CALORIES **490**

1.2kg/2lb 10oz boneless pork shoulder
440ml/15½fl oz/1¾ cups sweet (hard) apple cider
1 tbsp extra virgin olive oil
1 tbsp sweet paprika
Salt and black pepper

01 Place the pork shoulder in a large mixing bowl and pour over the apple cider. Cover with cling film/plastic wrap and place in the fridge to marinate for at least 2 hours, although you can leave it overnight if you prefer.

02 After marinating, remove the pork shoulder from the cider, then use kitchen paper/paper towel to pat it dry. Drizzle the olive oil over the shoulder, sprinkle with sweet paprika and season with salt and pepper. Use your hands to rub the olive oil and seasonings into the pork.

03 Push the rod all the way through the pork shoulder until it comes out the other side.

04 Feed a clamp onto the rod, as far as it will go until the spikes of the clamp are firmly skewering the pork. Then repeat for the opposite end so that the pork is clamped in place.

05 Position the pork so that it is in the middle of the rod. Once in the middle, tighten the screws to finger tight.

06 Carefully place the pork in the air fryer oven, positioning the rod in the rotisserie socket. Make sure that it is hooked in properly on both sides and that it won't fall off.

07 Set the temperature to 180°C/360°F and air fry the pork for 60 minutes, or until the pork reaches an internal temperature of 70°C/160°F or above.

Basket or dual pork If you don't have an air fryer with a rotisserie function, you can follow the recipe above for pork (or the gammon recipe on page 68) and convert it for cooking in an air fryer basket or in a dual air fryer. Prepare the pork as above, but instead of a rod and clamps, place the joint into the air fryer basket (or drawer). Set the temperature to 180°C/360°F and air fry for 25 minutes. Turn the pork over and air fry at the same temperature for another 25 minutes, or until cooked through.

rotisserie chicken

I have lost count of the amount of times I have queued in the supermarket for a rotisserie chicken. The excitement when they pass you the bag with the warm chicken inside! But I have not bought a single one since I got an air fryer XL. I buy a chicken from my local butcher and can cook the whole chicken in the basket or watch it rotate on the rotisserie

....

SERVES **4**
HERO **OVEN**
PREP **5 MINUTES**
COOK TIME **50 MINUTES**
CALORIES **470**

....

1.3kg/3lb medium whole
   chicken
1 tbsp extra virgin olive oil
1 tbsp mixed herbs/Italian
   seasoning
Salt and black pepper

01 Place the whole chicken on a clean chopping board. Drizzle with olive oil and sprinkle over the mixed herbs and a generous seasoning of salt and pepper. Use your hands to rub the olive oil and seasonings all over the chicken.

02 Tie the chicken legs with string, then push the rod all the way through the chicken until it comes out the other side.

03 Feed a clamp onto the rod, as far as it will go until the spikes of the clamp are firmly skewering the chicken. Repeat for the opposite end so that the bird is clamped in place. Make sure the clamp is attached to chicken meat, not the bone.

04 Position the chicken so that it is in the middle of the rod. Once in the middle, tighten the screws to finger tight.

05 Carefully place the chicken in the air fryer oven, positioning the rod in the rotisserie socket. Make sure that it is hooked in properly on both sides and that it won't fall off.

06 Set the temperature to 180ºC/360ºF and air fry the chicken for 50 minutes, or until the chicken reaches an internal temperature of 70ºC/160ºF or above.

Basket or dual chicken Prepare the chicken as above. But instead of a rod and clamps, place the chicken directly into the air fryer basket/drawer, breast side down. Set the temperature to 180ºC/360ºF and air fry for 25 minutes. Turn the chicken over and air fry at the same temperature for another 25 minutes, or until the chicken reaches an internal temperature of 70ºC/160ºF or above. You can also do the same with the roast duck and other similar-sized birds, although if you like your duck a little pink, reduce the cook time by 10 minutes.

Pair of poussins Another favourite trick of ours is air frying two poussins together using the rotisserie. Known in the USA as a Cornish hen, they are small spring chickens and they air fry so well. You can do just one, or two like we do. Simply follow the rotisserie chicken recipe above, but divide the oil and seasonings between two 450g/1lb poussins, then feed them both onto the rod. Use the same temperature, but because they are much smaller air fry for 25 minutes, or until the chicken reaches an internal temperature of 70ºC/160ºF or above.

crispy duck & pancakes

The first food I ever tried at a Chinese restaurant was crispy duck and pancakes. It's now my go-to when I order a Chinese takeaway, but you can do it at home – much cheaper – in the air fryer.

SERVES **4**
HERO **OVEN**
PREP **5 MINUTES**
COOK TIME **45 MINUTES**
CALORIES **302**

1 tsp garlic purée
½ tsp ginger purée
2 tbsp clear honey
½ tbsp soy sauce
3 tbsp oyster sauce
1.2kg/2lb 10oz whole duck
1 tbsp extra virgin olive oil
1 tbsp Chinese 5-spice powder
12 Chinese pancakes
½ cucumber
a few spring onions/scallions
Salt and black pepper

01 In a small bowl, combine the garlic and ginger purées, honey, soy sauce and oyster sauce. Set half aside in another bowl for serving.

02 Use a knife to create score slashes across the skin of the duck breast, cutting through the fat but making sure you don't pierce the flesh so it stays juicy. Drizzle the duck with olive oil, sprinkle with the Chinese 5-spice and season with salt and pepper. Rub the seasonings into the duck with your hands until it's evenly coated.

03 Next, coat the duck with the sauce using a pastry brush, making sure you cover it completely.

04 Tie up the duck legs with string, then push the rod all the way through the duck until it comes out the other side. Feed a clamp onto the rod until the spikes of the clamp are firmly skewering the duck. Repeat for the opposite end so that the bird is clamped in place. Make sure the clamp is attached to duck meat, not the bone.

05 Position the duck so that it is in the middle of the rod. Once in the middle, tighten the screws. Carefully place the duck in the air fryer oven, positioning the rod in the rotisserie socket. Make sure that it is hooked in properly on both sides and that it won't fall off.

06 Set the temperature to 180°C/360°F and air fry the duck for 45 minutes, or until the duck reaches an internal temperature of 60°C/140°F or above, depending how you like your duck. Remove the duck from the rod and allow it to cool before carving.

07 While the duck is resting, make your crispy duck platter. Add the reserved sauce to a bowl, get out your pancakes and slice your cucumber and spring onion into thin matchsticks.

08 Once the duck is cool enough to handle, shred the duck. Pile it onto a serving platter with the pancakes, cucumber and spring onion and serve with the sauce on the side. Everyone can help themselves, filling the pancakes with a layer of the sauce, shredded duck, cucumber and spring onion, then an extra drizzle of the sauce.

Crispy duck After cooking the duck, you're likely to be shredding the duck for pancakes. The skin will be nice and crispy, but if you want the meat crispy too, this can be done quickly in the air fryer. After shredding, spray the meat with olive oil and add it to the top shelf of the air fryer oven, or put it in the air fryer basket, and air fry at 200°C/400°F for 8 minutes. You can also do the same with your duck leftovers.

Save the duck fat As the duck rotates, the lovely fat will drip down into the drip tray at the bottom of the air fryer oven. When the air fryer is cool enough to handle, carefully remove the drip tray and tip the duck fat into a mesh strainer set over an airtight container (with a lid). Strain the fat into the container, then pop on the lid and keep in the fridge, ready for your next batch of air fried potatoes.

greek gyros

One of the rotisserie's magic tricks is kebabs. Because it is rotating, you never have to worry about the meat getting dry. Let's start with these yummy gyros, served in flatbreads with French fries and plenty of Greek sauce.

SERVES **6**
HERO **OVEN**
PREP **15 MINUTES, PLUS MARINATING**
COOK TIME **60 MINUTES**
CALORIES **642**

900g/2lb boneless skinless chicken thighs

FOR THE GYRO MARINADE
2 tsp garlic purée
1 tbsp balsamic vinegar
1 tbsp lemon juice
1 tbsp extra virgin olive oil
2 tbsp thick Greek yoghurt
2 tsp dried oregano
Salt and black pepper

FOR THE GREEK SAUCE
Juice of 1 small lemon
½ tsp garlic purée
5 tbsp thick Greek yoghurt
A pinch of dried parsley

TO SERVE
6 Saskia's Flatbreads (see page 196), warmed
1 recipe quantity French Fries (see page 154)
Shredded lettuce
1 medium cucumber, diced
1 large tomato, chopped

01 Put the marinade ingredients in a bowl and mix well. Add the chicken thighs and mix well with your hands. Cover the bowl with cling film/plastic wrap and place in the fridge to marinate for at least 2 hours, but overnight is best.

02 After marinating, remove the cling film and feed all the chicken thighs onto the rod. You will have to push them down close to each other for them all to fit.

03 Feed a clamp onto the rod, as far as it will go until the spikes of the clamp are firmly skewering the chicken meat. Then repeat for the opposite end so that all the chicken is clamped in place.

04 Position the chicken so that it is centred in the middle of the rod and not too close to the edges. Once in the middle, tighten the screws to finger tight.

05 Carefully place the marinated chicken in the air fryer oven, positioning the rod in the rotisserie socket. Make sure that it is hooked in properly on both sides and that it won't fall off.

06 Set the temperature to 180°C/360°F and air fry the chicken for 30 minutes. Reduce the temperature to 160°C/320°F and air fry for another 30 minutes or until the chicken reaches an internal temperature of 70°C/160°F or above. Use oven gloves to remove the chicken rod from the air fryer oven.

07 Whilst the gyro meat is air frying, put the Greek sauce ingredients in a bowl, mix to combine and set aside.

08 Once the gyro meat has rested, you can slice it directly from the rod and it will slice like a kebab from the takeaway. Pile the gyro meat into warm flatbreads along with fries and salad, and finish with a drizzle of the Greek sauce.

Basket or dual gyros Using a metal kebab holder that fits the size of your air fryer, place half the gyro meat on the rod and place in the air fryer basket. Set the temperature to 180°C/360°F and air fry for 20 minutes. Turn the kebab over and cook at the lower temperature of 160°C/320°F for another 20 minutes. Repeat for the remaining gyro meat, or if you have a dual fryer you can do one in each drawer.

rotisserie kebabs (three ways)

Beyond using the rod and clamps you also have a kebab holder. We recommend cooking five kebabs at once. They rotate like a rotisserie, and we love to mix and match between the kebabs below. If cooking in batches, start tucking into one while the next is cooking.

tofu kebabs

Tofu cubes, courgette and cherry tomatoes with a delicious dried Greek rub make an easy vegan alternative to our gyros from page 77.

....

MAKES **5**
HERO **OVEN**
PREP **5 MINUTES**
COOK TIME **15 MINUTES**
CALORIES **113**

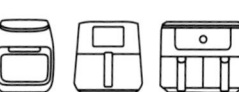

....

¾ medium courgette/zucchini
225g/8oz block of tofu, pressed (see page 145)
170g/6oz cherry tomatoes
1 tbsp extra virgin olive oil
1 tbsp balsamic vinegar
1 tsp lemon juice
2 tsp dried oregano
½ tsp dried rosemary
1 tsp mixed herbs/Italian seasoning
½ tsp garlic powder
Salt and black pepper

01 Slice the courgette into 2cm/¾ inch thick slices, then cut the slices in half. Cut the tofu into 2cm/¾ inch cubes and put them in a bowl with the cherry tomatoes and courgette. Add the olive oil, balsamic vinegar, lemon juice, dried herbs and garlic powder. Season generously with salt and pepper, then mix well with your hands.

02 Very gently thread the cubed tofu, sliced courgette and whole cherry tomatoes onto the kebab skewers, dividing the different elements equally between the five skewers. Attach the kebab holder to the rotisserie rod and hook the skewers onto the kebab holder. Position the

rod in the rotisserie socket, making sure that it is hooked in properly on both sides and that it won't fall off.

03 Set the temperature to 180°C/360°F and cook for 15 minutes, or until crispy to your liking. Or if you prefer crispier tofu, add an extra 5 minutes of cooking time at the same temperature.

Pork and halloumi souvlaki Pork steak with halloumi and Greek seasoning also makes a delicious summery air fryer kebab. Put **340g/12oz pork steak** and **175g/6oz halloumi cheese** (both diced into 2.5cm/1 inch cubes) into a bowl. Add **1 tbsp white wine vinegar, 2 tbsp extra virgin olive oil, 2 tsp lemon juice, 2 tsp garlic purée, 2 tsp wholegrain mustard, 2 tsp dried rosemary, 2 tsp dried oregano and 2 tsp sweet paprika**, season with **salt and black pepper** and mix well. Gently thread the halloumi and pork onto the kebab skewers. Cook at 180°C/360°F for 18 minutes, or until the pork is cooked through and the halloumi is turning light golden.

Surf and turf This is my all-time favourite kebab, combining steak with prawns/shrimp. Make as the kebabs above, but instead of tofu, slice **310g/11oz steak** into chunks, then thaw **225g/8oz raw king prawns/shrimp**. Add both to a bowl with **1 teaspoon steak seasoning** and **1 tablespoon extra virgin olive oil** and season well with **salt and pepper**. Mix well with your hands and feed onto the kebab skewers. Air fry at 180°C/360°F for 8 minutes.

Basket or dual kebabs Thread the tofu, pork, halloumi or prawns/shrimp onto smaller metal skewers, which will fit in the air fryer basket or into the drawers. Set the temperature to 180°C/360°F and air fry for 12 minutes, turning halfway through, until cooked through.

POULTRY

Let's air fry a poussin

One of the biggest mistakes people make when buying an air fryer is getting one that is too small. The assumption is that if you are feeding one to two people, you just need a small one. Then you realise how amazing it would be to cook a whole chicken in it and realise you went too small.

That is when a poussin (known in the USA as a Cornish hen) becomes a wonderful plan B.

They weigh on average between 450g/1lb and 650g/1lb 7oz, making them a third of the weight – and a much smaller size – than a standard chicken. This means that they cook much faster in the air fryer, as well as being a perfect fit for the tiny air fryer, or for those with a smaller appetite.

piri piri poussin with fries

In Portugal, the famous piri piri chicken is always made with small chickens, served with French fries and a side salad or rice. We're going to show you how to do this with a poussin and how you can combine the poussin with the fries in a small air fryer basket.

1 tbsp dried piri piri seasoning
½ tbsp lemon juice
½ tbsp garlic purée
2 tbsp extra virgin olive oil
1 × 450/1lb poussin/Cornish hen

FOR THE FRENCH FRIES
2 medium white potatoes
2 tsp extra virgin olive oil
1 tsp dried coriander/cilantro leaf
Salt and black pepper

SERVES **1**
HERO **SMALL BASKET**
PREP **10 MINUTES**
COOK TIME **40 MINUTES**
CALORIES **1253**

....

01 Put the piri piri seasoning, lemon juice, garlic purée and olive oil in a small bowl and mix with a spoon. Place the poussin, breast side down, on a chopping board, then smoother half the marinade mixture over any visible skin.

02 Next, slice the potatoes into French fries, leaving the skins on. Put them in a bowl and add the olive oil, coriander and a generous seasoning of salt and pepper. Mix with your hands until the fries are well coated, then scatter the fries into the air fryer basket, adding them to the gaps around the outside of the poussin. Set the temperature to 180ºC/360ºF and air fry for 20 minutes.

03 When the air fryer beeps, turn the poussin over by positioning a fork inside its cavity and flipping it. Use a pastry brush to brush the remaining marinade over the other half of the poussin, again covering all visible skin.

04 Continue air frying at the same temperature for a further 15 minutes, or until the poussin reaches an internal temperature of 70ºC/160ºF or above. Remove the poussin from the basket and put it to one side to rest.

05 Shake the air fryer basket and the juices from the poussin will mix with the French fries for a lovely flavour. Air fry at the same temperature for an extra 5 minutes to make the fries crispier.

06 When the air fryer beeps, quarter the poussin, creating four pieces of poultry, and serve with the fries.

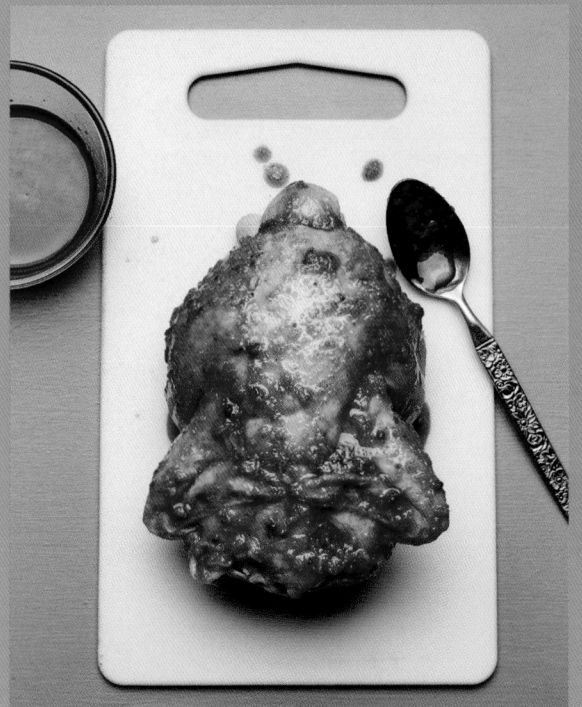

Top tips

Have a bigger air fryer? The beauty of the poussin is that you can fit one in a small air fryer and two in a bigger air fryer, whilst keeping the same time and temperature. If you have a dual, you can cook a poussin in one drawer, then fries in the other, or why not try two poussins on the rotisserie? (See page 73.)

Don't like piri piri? Swap the piri piri for 1 tablespoon of another favourite dried seasoning.

Add a salad The Portuguese make a delicious salad to go with their piri piri baby chickens, with little gem lettuce and sliced cucumber, onion and tomato. They toss it in a dressing of 2 teaspoons each of honey, olive oil, balsamic vinegar and white wine vinegar.

hunter's chicken

What is not to love about hunter's chicken? This classic dish of chicken breast, wrapped in bacon, smothered in barbecue sauce, and topped with melted cheese is made so easy with the air fryer. We use a silicone container to avoid a big clean up, or you can use paper liners.

....

SERVES **4**
HERO **BASKET/DUAL**
PREP **5 MINUTES**
COOK TIME **33 MINUTES**
CALORIES **539**

....

4 medium chicken breasts
8 rashers smoked back bacon
55g/2oz/heaped ½ cup
  grated mature/sharp Cheddar
  cheese
55g/2oz/½ cup grated
  mozzarella cheese
Salt and black pepper

FOR THE BARBECUE SAUCE
240ml/8fl oz/1 cup barbecue
  sauce
4 tbsp clear honey
1 tsp garlic purée
2 tsp sweet paprika

01 Put your chicken breasts onto a chopping board and season generously with salt and pepper. Tightly wrap two slices of bacon around each chicken breast, covering it well. Secure the bacon with cocktail sticks/toothpicks to stop it flying off during air frying.

02 Gently place the bacon-wrapped chicken breasts in the air fryer basket/drawer. Set the temperature to 180ºC/360ºF and air fry for 28 minutes, or until the chicken reads an internal temperature of 70ºC/160ºF or above.

03 While the chicken is air frying, add all the barbecue sauce ingredients to an air fryer-safe dish or silicone pan, and mix with a fork.

04 When the air fryer beeps, remove the chicken from the air fryer and remove the cocktail sticks that have held the bacon in place.

05 Place the chicken in the dish so that it's sitting in the barbecue sauce, then sprinkle both the grated cheeses over the chicken.

06 Air fry the hunter's chicken at 180ºC/360ºF for a final 5 minutes to melt the cheese and warm up the barbecue sauce before serving.

sweet chilli chicken breasts with cucumber noodles

We love sweet chilli chicken. Because of the sweet chilli marinade the chicken gets a slightly chargrilled look and tastes so flavoursome. Serve with cucumber noodles and it's a delicious light summer meal.

....

SERVES **2**
HERO **BASKET/DUAL**
PREP **8 MINUTES**
COOK TIME **20 MINUTES**
CALORIES **404**

....

2 Sweet Chilli marinated
   medium chicken breasts
   (see page 37)
1 cucumber
¼ tsp Chinese 5-spice powder
1 tbsp extra virgin olive oil
1 tsp garlic purée
½ tsp ginger purée
½ tsp lemongrass purée
Salt and black pepper
Sliced red chilli, to serve
   (optional)

01 Line the air fryer basket/drawer with a paper liner or a foil tray, then add the marinated sweet chilli chicken breasts. Pour any extra marinade from the bag over the chicken, too. Set the temperature to 180ºC/360ºF and cook for 20 minutes.

02 Whilst the chicken is cooking, make your cucumber noodles. Peel the cucumber with a potato peeler or julienne peeler to make thin ribbons or noodles. Squeeze the cucumber between your hands to release excess moisture, then place in a bowl and add all the remaining ingredients. Mix well to coat the cucumber noodles in the dressing, then split the noodles between two dinner plates.

03 When the air fryer beeps, use a thermometer to check if the chicken is 70ºC/160ºF or above. If not, cook for an extra 4 minutes and check again. Allow it to rest for a few minutes, then slice it and serve with the cucumber noodles, scattered with red chilli if you like some extra heat.

sofia's dorito wings

MAKES **8**
HERO **BASKET/DUAL**
PREP **8 MINUTES**
COOK TIME **20 MINUTES**
CALORIES **340**

....

1 × 180g/6¼oz Doritos, or other
   tortilla chips
2 large eggs
35g/1¼oz/¼ cup plain/all-
   purpose flour
8 large chicken wings
1 tbsp sweet paprika
1 tsp garlic powder
Extra virgin olive oil spray
Salt and black pepper
Sour cream and chive dip, to
   serve (optional)

Crispy air-fried chicken wings are delicious and there are so many different ways to coat them. This wings recipe was made by Sofia, who loved bashing the bag of Doritos into the perfect crumb.

....

01 Thoroughly bash the bag of Doritos with a rolling pin until they are in fine crumbs, then transfer them to a bowl.

02 Crack the eggs into another bowl and season with salt and pepper, then beat the eggs with a fork. Put the flour in a third bowl. Arrange the bowls in a production line, starting with the flour, then the egg, then the Dorito crumbs.

03 Place the chicken wings on a chopping board and season generously with salt and pepper. Sprinkle the paprika and garlic powder evenly onto the wings and use your hands to rub the seasonings all over them.

04 One at a time, dunk the wings first into the flour, then drench in the egg, then roll them in the Dorito crumbs, making sure the wings get a good coating from each.

05 Place the wings in the air fryer basket/drawer and spread out. If using a dual fryer, you can spread them out over two drawers. You may need to cook them in two batches. Set the temperature to 180°C/360°F and cook for 20 minutes until golden and crispy, spraying with olive oil halfway through for a better crisp, then serve – with sour cream and chive dip, if you like.

apricot chicken dinner for two

The clever "sync" feature on the dual means that different foods will be ready at the same time, even if they have different cooking times. We will be cooking the marinated vegetables in one drawer and the chicken legs in the other for a lovely dinner in for two.

SERVES **2**
HERO **DUAL**
PREP **8 MINUTES**
COOK TIME **25 MINUTES**
CALORIES **726**

½ yellow (bell) pepper/capsicum
½ orange (bell) pepper/ capsicum
1 medium courgette/zucchini
6 dried apricots
175g/6oz cherry tomatoes
½ x 400g/14oz can chickpeas, drained
2 heaped tsp ground cumin
2 tsp smoked paprika
2 medium chicken legs
Salt and black pepper
fresh coriander/cilantro leaves, to serve

FOR THE APRICOT MARINADE
145g/5oz/½ cup apricot jam
1 tbsp white wine vinegar
1 tbsp extra virgin olive oil
2 tsp garlic purée
2 tsp ginger purée
2 tsp harissa paste
2 tsp ground cumin
1 tbsp dried coriander/cilantro leaf

01 Put all the apricot marinade ingredients in a bowl and mix well. If you have a really thick jam, use the back of the spoon to break it down. Set aside.

02 Dice the peppers into 2cm/¾ inch chunks. Slice the courgette into 2cm/¾ inch thick slices, then cut the slices into quarters. Slice the dried apricots into quarters. Put the pepper, courgette, apricots and cherry tomatoes into a bowl. Add the chickpeas, cumin and smoked paprika, along with three-quarters of the apricot marinade, and mix everything together well with your hands. Place the vegetables in one drawer of your dual without the crisper plate.

03 Season the chicken legs generously with salt and pepper, then coat them in the remaining marinade. Place the chicken legs in the second drawer, leaving the crisper plate in this time.

04 Once you have a drawer ready with the vegetables and a second drawer with the chicken, it's time to sync your air fryer drawers. Press "sync" then set the vegetable drawer to air fry at 180ºC/360ºF for 25 minutes, then set the chicken drawer to the same temperature for 20 minutes. The chicken will start cooking once 5 minutes has passed, so that they will both be ready at the same time. Though, for an even cook, we recommend for the last 5 minutes that you use tongs to turn the chicken over.

05 Transfer the vegetables to a serving platter and top with the chicken, then scatter with coriander leaves and serve.

Apricot chicken in a basket To cook in the basket simply use a container that will fit your air fryer and keep the same time and temperature. Then place the chicken over the vegetables and it can all cook together.

Plan ahead If you prefer to make ahead, you can place the chicken into the bowl over the vegetables, wrap in cling film/plastic wrap and leave to marinate in the fridge until you're ready to cook.

turkey dinner for one

At Christmas, Thanksgiving and Easter, everyone prepares massive meals, but what if you're just cooking for one? For this hearty turkey dinner, we use a single turkey steak, serving it with a stuffing ball, pigs in blankets, roast potatoes and veggie fries. Rather than buying large packs from the supermarket, we purchase meat from our local butchers and vegetables from the greengrocer, which means we can order smaller portions – perfect for feeding one.

....

SERVES **1**
HERO **BASKET/DUAL**
PREP **10 MINUTES**
COOK TIME **34 MINUTES**
CALORIES **984**

....

1 medium parsnip
1 medium turnip
1 medium carrot
1 medium white potato
1 tbsp extra virgin olive oil
1 heaped tsp dried parsley
225g/8oz turkey steak
1 tsp dried thyme
1 sage and onion stuffing ball
  (see tip opposite)
2 pigs in blankets (mini
  sausages wrapped in streaky
  bacon)
240ml (8fl oz/1 cup) turkey gravy
Salt and black pepper
Cranberry sauce, to serve
  (optional)

01 Peel the parsnip, turnip and carrots, then slice them into vegetable sticks. Peel the potato and cut it into quarters. Put all the veg in a mixing bowl and season generously with salt and pepper. Add the olive oil and parsley, and mix well with your hands so that they are well coated in the oil and seasonings.

02 Remove the potatoes from the bowl and put them into the air fryer basket/drawer. Set the temperature to 180°C/360°F and air fry for 5 minutes to give the potatoes a head-start. Once the 5 minutes is up, add the remaining vegetables and cook for a further 15 minutes.

03 When the air fryer beeps, shake, and do a fork test – skewer a carrot or two with a fork and if it feels like they are almost tender, it's time to add the meat. Move the potatoes and vegetables to one side of the basket to make room for the turkey. If you are using a dual fryer, use the second drawer for the meat.

04 Season the turkey steak with salt and pepper and sprinkle the thyme over it. Add it to the air fryer and find another gap for the stuffing ball and the pigs in blankets. Air fry at the same temperature for another 12 minutes, flipping the steak after 8 minutes.

05 Add the turkey steak, potatoes and vegetables to a dinner plate. Tip the gravy into a ramekin and place this into the gap you've just made in the air fryer. Air fry at 200°C/400°F for 2 minutes; this will crisp up the pigs in blankets and the stuffing ball, as well as heating the gravy through. Add the remaining items to your plate and serve. We love to add a generous spoonful of cranberry sauce to compliment the turkey.

Single stuffing balls Many butchers will sell you an individual stuffing ball, but if you can't get them, simply buy a pack, remove one and freeze the remainder. Then, when you are cooking a Sunday roast for one in the future, you can just remove another from the freezer as you need it.

teriyaki duck noodles

One of our go-to air fryer ingredients is egg noodles. Compared to pasta or rice, they are fast cooking in the air fryer. You can combine your favourite protein (in this recipe we are using duck breast) with a simple sticky Asian sauce and a stir fry vegetable mix. Super-simple and perfect for busy weeknights.

....

SERVES **2**
HERO **BASKET/DUAL**
PREP **8 MINUTES**
COOK TIME **25 MINUTES**
CALORIES **1450**

....

2 × 225g/8oz skin-on duck
  breasts
1 tbsp extra virgin olive oil
½ tsp Chinese 5-spice powder
Salt and black pepper

FOR THE TERIYAKI SAUCE
2 × 120g/4¼oz pouches thick
  teriyaki sauce
1 tsp ginger purée
2 tsp garlic purée
A splash of soy sauce

FOR THE STIR FRY
2 spring onions/scallions
300g/10½oz stir fry vegetable
  mix (we use a mix with carrot,
  green cabbage, bean sprouts,
  red (bell) pepper/capsicum
  and water chestnuts)
1 tsp Chinese 5-spice powder
1 tbsp extra virgin olive oil
½ x 275g/9¾oz pack of fresh
  egg noodles

01 Place the duck breasts, skin-side down, into the air fryer basket/drawer. Rub the tops of the duck with half the olive oil, sprinkle with the Chinese 5-spice powder, and season generously with salt and pepper. Set the temperature to 180ºC/360ºF and air fry for 5 minutes.

02 Mix all the teriyaki sauce ingredients together in a small bowl. When the air fryer beeps, flip the duck over with tongs and season the skin side with salt and pepper. Brush about ½ tablespoon of the teriyaki sauce over each duck breast using a pastry brush. Air fry the duck at the same temperature for a further 7 minutes, then remove it from the air fryer and allow it to rest.

03 For the stir fry, slice the spring onions and set the green parts aside. Put the spring onions whites and the stir fry vegetables in a mixing bowl and add the Chinese 5-spice powder and the olive oil. Season with salt and pepper and mix well with your hands. Tip the stir fry mix into the air fryer basket/drawer and spread it out. Air fry at 180ºC/360ºF for 8 minutes, or until the stir fry mix is starting to get crispy.

04 Put the remaining teriyaki sauce and the egg noodles into a silicone pan with handles. Once done, add the stir fry vegetables and use a fork to mix everything together so that the noodles and veggies are evenly coated in the sauce.

05 Place the silicone pan into the air fryer basket and air fry at 180ºC/360ºF for a final 5 minutes, or until the egg noodles are heated through.

06 Slice the duck breasts and serve them on top of the stir fried teriyaki noodles, sprinkled with the spring onion greens.

Dual noodles If you have the dual air fryer, speed up the cook time by cooking the stir fry mix in one drawer and the duck breasts in the other drawer.

MEAT

Let's air fry a beef wellington

Succulent fillet of beef surrounded by a flavoursome layer of prosciutto, pâté and garlic mushrooms, all covered with crisp, golden pastry is the ultimate dinner party favourite. It first became popular to cook beef Wellington's in the air fryer back in 2018, and it's easier than you think to prepare, but before you start, see our tips on page 100.

special occasion beef wellington

SERVES **6**
HERO **BASKET**
PREP **20 MINUTES**
COOK TIME **84 MINUTES**
CALORIES **523**

....

900g/2lb beef fillet
Extra virgin olive oil spray
2 tsp dried thyme
2 tsp dried parsley
250g/9oz chestnut (cremini) mushrooms
A pinch of garlic powder
Plain (all-purpose) flour, for dusting
1 × 500g/1lb 2oz pack of puff pastry
100g/3½oz prosciutto slices
180g/6¼oz Brussels pâté
1 egg, beaten
Salt and black pepper

01 Place your fillet on a chopping board, spray with olive oil, then rub the herbs and salt and pepper all over the fillet. Air fry at 180ºC/360ºF for 5 minutes, flip over and cook at the same temperature for another 5 minutes. Allow to rest and, once cool, wrap in foil and put in the fridge overnight. The next day, remove the fillet from the fridge, unwrap the foil and pat it dry with kitchen paper/paper towel.

02 Slice the mushrooms into 5mm/¼ inch slices and tip them into the air fryer basket. Spray with olive oil and season with salt, pepper and garlic powder. Set the temperature to 180ºC/360ºF and cook for 9 minutes. Tip the mushrooms onto a plate to cool.

03 Flour a clean worktop and your rolling pin, and roll out the puff pastry to a large rectangle measuring about 35 × 28cm/14 × 11 inches. Lay your prosciutto slices over the pastry, leaving a 1cm/½ inch border around the edge, then spread an even layer of pâté over the prosciutto. Add a layer of the cold sliced mushrooms over the pâté, overlapping them so that there are no gaps. Place the fillet of beef over the mushrooms in the centre of the pastry sheet. Using a pastry brush, brush a layer of egg wash over the border around the edge of the pastry. Carefully roll the pastry over to create a tight log, tucking in the pastry at the sides as you go.

04 Poke holes in a paper air fryer liner so that the air can circulate (this is important so that it doesn't slow down the cooking time) and place the liner in the air fryer basket. Carefully place the Wellington into the air fryer basket over the paper liner, with the seal side upwards (and best side down – you'll flip it later), and brush the top with egg wash. Cook at 180ºC/360ºF for 20 minutes.

05 Use the sides of the paper liner as handles to help you lift the Wellington out of the air fryer onto a worktop. Carefully roll it over, so that it's now the right way up and place back onto the paper liner. Cut small slits in the pastry along the top of the Wellington to let the steam escape so that the pastry won't go soggy. Use the liner again to carefully place the Wellington back into the air fryer basket and brush the top and sides with extra egg wash. Set the temperature to 180ºC/360ºF and air fry for 45 minutes, or until the centre of the beef reads a temperature of 52ºC/125ºF for medium rare or 57ºC/134ºF for medium. Remove the Wellington from the air fryer basket, and allow to rest for 5 minutes before slicing.

Top tips

Slice your mushrooms thinly too thick and your beef Wellington will end up too wide once rolled and will be too big for the air fryer.

Aim for a maximum size of 900g/2lb beef fillet so that the Wellington will fit in the air fryer.

Prosciutto or pancakes? These are both popular ingredients for layering into the Wellington to help prevent soggy pastry. We prefer to use prosciutto as it adds extra flavour to the beef.

Go diagonal If you have a smaller air fryer, you may struggle to move the Wellington. By placing it diagonally in an air fryer basket, it will be easier to get it in and out of the air fryer.

Add a non-stick layer It's important to use a paper liner or place a sheet of baking parchment under your beef Wellington to stop it sticking. Use a knife to poke air holes in the paper so that the air can still circulate and you will avoid an uncooked base. The excess paper at the sides will also give you "handles" to help you lower the Wellington in, and lift it out, of the fryer.

Flipping the beef Wellington This is important as air fryers cook from the top, so to make sure our Wellington doesn't have a soggy bottom, we turn it during cooking. Cook the bottom of the Wellington first, pastry seal up, then flip it over and then cook the top. Remember our tip for the paper liner above? Well that also makes it easier to flip.

Don't overcook your beef! Remember that beef Wellington will continue cooking for a little while once it comes out of the air fryer. Aim for 52°C/125°F for medium rare, and it will finish at 55°C/131°F once it is done resting.

Start small When we first made a beef Wellington, we were very aware of the cost involved. Therefore, we made two mini Wellingtons out of **two 170g/6oz fillet steaks**. It was the perfect portion for the two of us. To do this, sear the steaks and assemble as in the recipe, but decrease the other main ingredient quantities and use: **85g/3oz mushrooms**; **300g/10½oz pastry**; **60g/2oz pâté**; **60g/2oz prosciutto**. Cook, pastry seal up, at 180°C/360°F for 10 minutes, then flip it over and cook at 200°C/400°F for another 10 minutes.

Adjust for your air fryer size If you have a smaller air fryer, you could also make a smaller Wellington with a **675g/1½lb beef fillet**. When going smaller, reduce the main ingredients to the following: **85g/3oz mushrooms**; **250g/9oz pastry**; **60g/2oz pâté**; **60g/2oz prosciutto**. Cook at 180°C/360°F for 15 minutes, then flip it over and cook for another 18 minutes for medium rare or another 22 minutes for medium. A Wellington this size will still feed four people (rather than six from a big one), so it is still a great choice.

Dual air fryer if you have a dual air fryer, you are likely to have a problem fitting a full-sized Wellington into the air fryer drawer. If this is you, we recommend doing two smaller ones, as mentioned above.

everyday meatloaf wellington

While a classic beef wellington is great for special occasions, the everyday version is a meatloaf wellington, using minced beef instead. This tastes so good, I could eat it every Sunday, forever!

....

SERVES **6**
HERO **BASKET**
PREP **15 MINUTES**
COOK TIME **35 MINUTES**
CALORIES **608**

....

1 small white onion
450g/1lb minced/ground beef
1 tsp garlic purée
2 tsp tomato purée/paste
1 tsp dried parsley
2 tsp sweet paprika
2 tsp mixed herbs/Italian
  seasoning
1 tbsp Worcestershire sauce
1 large egg, plus 1 beaten egg,
  to glaze
28g/1oz/½ cup panko
  breadcrumbs
Plain/all-purpose flour, for
  dusting
½ x 500g/1lb 2oz block of puff
  pastry
85g/3oz/1 cup grated
  Cheddar cheese
Salt and black pepper

FOR THE KETCHUP GLAZE
1 tbsp tomato ketchup
1 tbsp barbecue sauce
1 tsp smoked paprika
1 tsp garlic purée

01 Peel and finely dice the onion. Tip it into a bowl and add the beef, garlic and tomato purées, parsley, sweet paprika, mixed herbs, Worcestershire sauce, egg and breadcrumbs. Season well with salt and pepper, and mix well with your hands until well combined, then shape the mixture into a loaf shape.

02 Flour a clean worktop and your rolling pin, and roll out the puff pastry to a large rectangle measuring about 33 × 23cm/13 × 9 inches. In a ramekin, combine all the glaze ingredients, then brush an even layer over the pastry using a pastry brush, leaving a 1cm/½ inch border around the edge for the egg wash.

03 Sprinkle the cheese over the glaze to create an even layer, then place the meatloaf in the centre.

04 Brush a layer of egg wash over the border around the edge of the pastry. Carefully roll the pastry over the meatloaf to create a tight parcel, tucking in the pastry at the sides as you go.

05 Poke holes in a paper air fryer liner so that the air can circulate and place the liner in the air fryer basket. Carefully place the Wellington in the air fryer basket over the paper liner, with the seal side upwards (and best side down – you'll flip it later), and brush the top with egg wash. Cook at 180ºC/360ºF for 15 minutes.

06 Use the sides of the paper liner as handles to help you lift the Wellington out of the air fryer onto a worktop. Carefully roll it over, so it's now the right way up and place back onto the paper liner. Cut small slits in the pastry along the top of the Wellington to let the steam escape so that the pastry won't go soggy. Use the liner again to carefully place the Wellington back into the air fryer basket and brush the top and sides with egg wash. Cook for a further 20 minutes, or until the centre of the beef reads an internal temperature of 70ºC/160ºF or above. Remove the meatloaf Wellington from the air fryer basket and allow to rest for 5 minutes before slicing.

Feeding one but love Wellington? Follow the meatloaf Wellington recipe above, but instead of making a loaf, form the meat mixture into 10 meatballs. Roll out the pastry, add the glaze and the cheese, then cut the pastry into 10 equal-sized squares. Place a meatball in each square and fold it into a neat parcel, then brush with the egg wash. You can then cook yourself three for dinner, and freeze the remainder for later. Air fry at 180ºC/360ºF for 20 minutes.

Use low-fat meat This is important when making a meatloaf Wellington. We used a 5 per cent fat minced/ground beef; go higher and the fat will cause the pastry of the wellington to go soggy.

joan's quick pork bites & veggies

I met a lovely lady called Joan as I gave a demo on how to cook my rainbow vegetables in the air fryer (see page 26). She mentioned she had just purchased a pork steak and asked if she could add it to the mix. This pork bite and veggie recipe is dedicated to you, Joan, and is also perfect for one.

....

SERVES **1**
HERO **BASKET/DUAL**
PREP **5 MINUTES**
COOK TIME **15 MINUTES**
CALORIES **452**

....

1 × 225g/8oz pork steak
A pinch of dried thyme
1 Rainbow Veggie Bag (see page 26)
Salt and black pepper

01 Chop your pork steak into bite-sized chunks and put them in a mixing bowl. Add the thyme, season with salt and pepper, and mix with your hands to coat.

02 Add your veggie bag to the bowl and mix well with your hands until the veggies and pork bites are mixed together.

03 Tip the pork and veggies into the air fryer basket/drawer. Set the temperature to 180ºC/360ºF and cook for 15 minutes, or until the pork reaches an internal temperature of 70ºC/160ºF or above and the butternut squash is fork tender.

Swap pork for chicken We also love buying pre-diced chicken breast and using that instead of pork. Just add 5 minutes to the cooking time.

20-minute weeknight sausage dinner (two ways)

Sausages are one of our favourite foods to prepare in the air fryer. They cook quickly, are cheap compared to most other meats, and are perfect for easy weeknight dinners. Here are two of our favourite recipes.

sausage & rainbow peppers

Sausages are cooked with different coloured peppers, red onion and some simple seasonings all at the same time.

....

SERVES **2**
HERO **BASKET/DUAL**
PREP **8 MINUTES**
COOK TIME **20 MINUTES**
CALORIES **667**

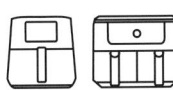

....

3 (bell) peppers/capsicums (in any colour
   combination of red, yellow, green)
1 red onion
6 thick sausages
2 tsp extra virgin olive oil
2 tsp dried oregano
Salt and black pepper

01 Deseed the peppers and chop them into strips, and peel and finely slice the red onion. Put the peppers and onion in a bowl and add the sausages, olive oil and oregano. Season with salt and pepper, and mix well with your hands.

02 Tip the sausages, onion and peppers into the air fryer basket/drawer. Set the temperature to 180ºC/360ºF and cook for 15 minutes. Give the basket or drawer a good shake, then cook for a further 5 minutes until the sausages are brown to your liking and the peppers and onion are nice and crispy.

Summer sausage traybake If you love a sausage traybake, ring the changes with this summery version. Peel **2 sweet potatoes** and dice them into 2cm/¾ inch cubes. Chop **1 courgette/zucchini** and **1 red (bell) pepper** the same size. Put the chopped veg into a bowl and add **6 thick sausages, 1 tablespoon extra virgin olive oil, 2 teaspoons garlic purée, 2 teaspoons dried oregano** and **1 teaspoon dried thyme**. Season well with **salt and black pepper** and mix well with your hands. Cook at 180ºC/360ºF for 13 minutes, then add **170g/6oz cherry tomatoes**, halved, give everything a shake, and cook for another 7 minutes or until the sweet potatoes are fork tender and the sausages are brown to your liking.

the ultimate doner kebab fakeaway

When we lived in Portugal, Kyle and I truly missed our doner kebabs, so we recreated them for the air fryer.

....

SERVES **4**
HERO **BASKET/DUAL**
PREP **10 MINUTES**
COOK TIME **50 MINUTES, PLUS RESTING**
CALORIES **691**

....

900g/2lb lean minced/ground lamb
Saskia's Flatbread (see page 196)

FOR THE DONER SEASONING
1 tbsp dried oregano
1 tbsp dried thyme
1 tbsp mixed herbs/Italian seasoning
1 tbsp dried coriander/cilantro
1 tbsp ground cumin
1 tbsp sweet paprika
1 tsp onion powder
1 tsp cayenne pepper
Salt and black pepper

FOR THE GARLIC SAUCE
240ml (8fl oz/1 cup) fat-free Greek yoghurt
1 garlic clove, minced
1 tsp dried parsley

FOR THE KEBAB SALAD
2 medium tomatoes
¼ medium cucumber
¼ medium white onion
A small chunk of red cabbage

01 Combine all the ingredients for the doner kebab seasoning in a bowl, add a good amount of salt and pepper, and mix well.

02 Add the lamb to the bowl with the seasoning and mix well with your hands. Form the spiced lamb mixture into a log the shape of a meatloaf.

03 Lay a large sheet of foil (big enough to wrap the kebab in) out on your worktop. Place the doner loaf in the centre and wrap it tightly with the foil. Place the wrapped doner kebab in the air fryer basket/drawer, with the foil seal up. Set the temperature to 160ºC/320ºF and cook for 25 minutes.

04 When the air fryer beeps, open up the foil carefully, to create a layer of foil in the bottom of the air fryer which will hold the juices but expose the meat. Increase the temperature to 180ºC/360ºF and air fry for a further 25 minutes, or until the lamb is fully cooked.

05 In the meantime, mix the garlic sauce ingredients together in a small serving bowl, then put to one side.

06 For the salad, slice the tomatoes and cucumber and finely slice the onion. Shred the cabbage and sprinkle them over a platter.

07 When the doner meat is cooked, allow it to rest for 30 minutes, then it will slice better, like true doner meat. Whilst you are waiting, you can prepare and air fry the flatbreads.

08 Once rested, slice your doner into thin slices or use a vegetable peeler for a perfect slice. Serve the doner meat with salad, warm flatbread and garlic sauce.

Batch prepare your seasoning Combining all the elements for the seasoning takes a while, so we make it in large batches – usually five times the mix above – and store it in a plastic container so that it's ready for future kebabs.

Got a dual air fryer? Then for the ultimate fakeaway, cook the doner kebab in one drawer and the French fries (see page 154) in the other.

dom's burger in a bowl

In the summer, when we have some minced/ground beef in the fridge, I will smile at Dom and ask for a burger in a bowl for lunch. This recipe uses the typical ingredients of a burger, minus the bread. Instead, it is served like a salad and is delicious and perfect for the summer diet.

....

SERVES **2**
HERO **BASKET/DUAL**
PREP **10 MINUTES**
COOK TIME **20 MINUTES**
CALORIES **418**

....

FOR THE BURGERS
225g/½lb lean minced/ground
   beef
1 tsp mustard powder
2 tsp dried basil
1 tsp lightest cream cheese
1 tbsp grated Cheddar cheese
Salt and black pepper

FOR THE BURGER SALAD
1 small lettuce (such as baby
   gem)
1 large tomato
¼ medium white onion
10 gherkin/pickle slices

FOR THE BURGER SAUCE
1 tsp tomato ketchup
2 tbsp mayonnaise
2 tbsp fat-free Greek yoghurt
1 tsp gherkin/pickle juice
½ tsp English mustard
¼ tsp smoked paprika

01 Put all the ingredients for the burgers in a bowl, season with salt and pepper, and mix well with your hands. Divide the mixture into two equal portions and form each into a burger patty.

02 Put the burger patties in the air fryer basket/drawer, making sure that they are spread out and not on top of each other. Set the temperature to 180ºC/360ºF and cook for 20 minutes.

03 In the meantime, make the salad. Shred the lettuce and put it in a large salad dish. Slice the tomato and finely slice the onion, then scatter both over the lettuce. Finish with a layer of gherkin slices.

04 Next, make the burger sauce by combining all the sauce ingredients in a small bowl, then put to one side.

05 When the air fryer beeps, chop the burgers into bite-sized chunks and scatter them over the prepared salad. Finish the salad by drizzling the burger sauce over the top.

12-minute lamb koftas

I often buy extra minced/ ground lamb from the butcher's just to make koftas. These koftas are one of the easiest kebabs to make in the air fryer and can be made with or without skewers. We usually have them as an alternative to doner kebabs (see page 106) and will serve them with the same doner kebab salad and sauce, and then enjoy them with homemade flatbreads (see page 196).

....

SERVES **2**
HERO **BASKET/DUAL**
PREP **5 MINUTES**
COOK TIME **12 MINUTES**
CALORIES **475**

....

¼ medium white onion
450g/1lb minced/ground lamb
1 tsp garlic purée
1 tbsp dried coriander/cilantro
  leaf
2 tsp ground cumin
¼ tsp cayenne pepper
1 tsp ground coriander
1 tsp tandoori powder
A pinch of ground cinnamon
Salt and black pepper

01 Peel and finely dice the onion. Put it in a bowl and add the lamb, garlic purée, coriander and dried spices. Season well with salt and pepper and mix everything together well.

02 Divide the mixture into six equal portions and shape them into koftas – which are the shape of fat sausages. If using kebab skewers, thread a skewer through the length of each kofta.

03 Place as many koftas as will fit in your air fryer basket/drawers in a single layer – you may need to cook them in batches. Set the temperature to 180ºC/360ºF and cook for 12 minutes, or until cooked through.

FISH

let's air fry parmesan crusted cod

We call this our "last-minute fish for dinner" recipe as it is prepared and cooked in 20 minutes! This can be done with many different fish fillets, but we love it most with cod.

Instead of classic breading with flour, egg and breadcrumbs, you spread a sticky layer on the top of your fish, then press it upside down into the Parmesan crumb. It creates a crispy crumb on top of your fish fillets.

Top tips

Fish fillets cook fast in the air fryer Keep an eye on them until you get used to your air fryer, as it's easy to overcook them, leaving them dry.

Vary the flavours We have used our honey marinade here, but you can mix and match with any of the marinades from page 37. In the Milner house, we cook the most with the coriander and lime marinade.

Go for the underdog to save the £££ Whilst I love cod, haddock and salmon, basa, coley, and pollock are much cheaper and taste just as good.

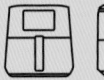 

SERVES **2**
HERO **BASKET/DUAL**
PREP **8 MINUTES**
COOK TIME **12 MINUTES**
CALORIES **280**

....

2 × 110g/3¾oz skin-on cod fish fillets
1 tsp dried parsley
½ recipe quantity of Honey and Garlic Marinade (see page 37)
1 tbsp wholegrain mustard
15g/½oz/⅓ cup panko breadcrumbs
1 tsp dried oregano
2 pinches of garlic powder
1 tbsp finely grated Parmesan cheese
Salt and black pepper

01 Pat the cod fillets dry, then season them generously with salt and pepper, and sprinkle the parsley over.

02 In a bowl, mix together the marinade and the mustard, then brush it over the cod, covering the tops and sides.

03 Combine the breadcrumbs, oregano, garlic powder and Parmesan on a dinner plate, season with salt and pepper, and use your hands to mix everything together. Place the cod fillets, skin-side up, into the crumb. Push them down firmly and move them about a bit, to create a generous coating. Then flip the cod fillets back over.

04 Place the cod fillets side by side in the air fryer basket/drawer and set the temperature to 180ºC/360ºF. Cook for 12 minutes, or until the cod is crispy to your liking and cooked through.

Bacon-wrapped cod fillets Instead of adding the Parmesan crumb, you can cover the fillets with bacon instead. Simply follow steps 1 and 2, then wrap each cod fillet in **3 slices of back bacon**, until fully covered – the bacon will stay in place thanks to the marinade. Air fry at 180ºC/360ºF for 14 minutes, or until your fish is cooked and the bacon is nice and crispy.

sofia & jorge's fish fingers, chips & beans

Sofia and Jorge love their school dinners. They have a school menu printed out and the night before school they will proudly mention what they are having. Fish Friday is their favourite and every third Friday is fish fingers/sticks. Here is their homemade version that they always have served on their favourite blue fish themed plates.

SERVES **2**
HERO **DUAL**
PREP **10 MINUTES**
COOK TIME **23 MINUTES**
CALORIES **628**

2 medium potatoes
2 tsp extra virgin olive oil
1 tsp dried oregano
35g/1¼oz/¼ cup plain/all-
   purpose flour
1 tsp dried dill
1 medium egg
1 tsp lemon juice
55g/2oz/½ cup golden
   breadcrumbs
1 tsp dried parsley
2 × 110g/3¾oz fish fillets
   thawed
½ x 400g/14oz can of baked
   beans
Salt and black pepper

01 To prepare the chips, peel the potatoes and slice them into chunky chips/fries. Put them in a bowl with the olive oil, oregano and a generous seasoning of salt and pepper. Mix with your hands and tip them into an air fryer drawer, spreading them out so that they cook evenly. Cook the chips at 160°C/320°F for 10 minutes.

02 Meanwhile, make the fish fingers. Set up a production line. Put the flour in a shallow bowl and stir in the dill. Crack the egg into another bowl, beat it, then stir in the lemon juice. Put the breadcrumbs in a third bowl and add the parsley. Give each bowl a generous seasoning of salt and pepper, and also season the fish fillets with salt and pepper too.

03 Slice each fish fillet into two or three fish fingers. To coat, first, turn the fish fingers over in the flour to fully coat, then drench them in the egg. Finish with a double coating of the breadcrumbs. Place the fish fingers in the other drawer of the dual air fryer.

04 After the 10 minutes are up, shake the chips, then match the air fryer drawers and cook the chips and fish fingers together at 180°C/360°F for 8 minutes.

05 The fish fingers should now be cooked – just check that they are crispy enough and piping hot, then remove them from the drawer onto the kids' plates. Pour the beans into two ramekins and place them into the now empty drawer.

06 Cook the chips and beans at the same temperature for another 5 minutes, or until they are crispy and the beans are piping hot. Then serve the fish fingers, chips and beans together.

Basket fish fingers If cooking in a basket, it's a little slower because the food is not as spread out. Air fry the chips for 15 minutes at 180°C/360°F. Make some room in the basket and add the fish fingers, then air fry for another 5 minutes. Add the beans and cook everything for 5 minutes, then serve.

marinated salmon (two ways)

On page 37 we shared our marinade recipes; this is how to use them with salmon fillets to take your salmon to the next level.

hawaiian salmon with mango salsa

You will love Hawaiian salmon. Using our Hawaiian marinade and serving with a quick homemade mango salsa (which stores in the fridge perfectly) it is perfect for a summer salmon fix.

....

SERVES **2**
HERO **BASKET/DUAL**
PREP **8 MINUTES, PLUS MARINATING**
COOK TIME **14 MINUTES**
CALORIES **542**

....

2 × 110g/3¾oz salmon fillets
1 recipe quantity Hawaiian Summer marinade (see page 37)
Lemon wedges, to serve

FOR THE MANGO SALSA
2 canned pineapple rings
½ avocado
½ mango
¼ red onion
½ red chilli
1 tbsp finely chopped fresh parsley
Juice of 1 lime
1 tbsp clear honey

01 Place the salmon in a freezer bag, add the marinade and shake to get a good coating of the marinade all over the salmon. Place into the fridge to marinate for at least 2 hours.

02 Tip the salmon fillets and their marinade into a foil tray/pan and place into the air fryer basket/drawer. Set the temperature to 180ºC/360ºF and air fry for 14 minutes, or until the salmon flakes on touch.

03 While the salmon cooks, make the salsa. Chop the pineapple into chunks, peel and dice the avocado and mango, and peel and finely chop the red onion. Deseed and very finely dice the red chilli. Put everything into a mixing bowl and add the parsley, lime juice and honey. Stir everything together, then serve it with the salmon and lemon wedges for squeezing over.

Make curried salmon Place **2–4 salmon fillets** into a freezer bag with the **curry yoghurt marinade** from page 37 and shake about to mix. Marinate in the fridge for at least 2 hours, then place onto a paper liner. Place in the air fryer basket/drawer, set the temperature to 180ºC/360ºF and cook for 14 minutes, or until cooked through.

Frozen salmon If you prefer, you can prep the marinated salmon and it can go in the freezer raw for up to 3 months. Using our dual air fryer, we love to match the drawers and cook the salmon (from frozen) in one drawer and frozen rainbow veggies (see page 26) in the other drawer. They both need 160ºC/320ºF for 20 minutes.

smoked haddock with baby potatoes & green beans

Sue, our pescatarian reader, asked for fish fillets with potatoes and veg for dinner. To avoid washing up and to use everyday ingredients that can be mixed and matched, we created this recipe!

....

SERVES **2**
HERO **BASKET/DUAL**
PREP **8 MINUTES**
COOK TIME **25 MINUTES**
CALORIES **330**

....

285g/10oz baby potatoes, scrubbed
2 tbsp extra virgin olive oil
2 tsp dried parsley
140g/5oz green beans, trimmed
1 tbsp dried mixed herbs
2 × 110g/3¾oz smoked haddock fillets
A squeeze of lemon juice
Salt and black pepper
Lemon wedges and fresh dill, to serve (optional)

01 Quarter the baby potatoes and put them in a 18 × 18cm/7 × 7 inch foil tray/pan (or a size compatible with your air fryer). Season the potatoes with salt and pepper, add 1 tablespoon of the olive oil and the parsley, and mix with your hands until the potatoes are well coated.

02 Place the tray into the air fryer basket/drawer, set the temperature to 180°C/360°F and cook for 10 minutes.

03 When the air fryer beeps, shake the potatoes and add the green beans. Drizzle with the remaining olive oil and sprinkle in the dried herbs. Use a spatula to mix everything together, then air fry at the same temperature for another 5 minutes, or until the potatoes are fork tender.

04 Give the potatoes and green beans a shake. Place the haddock fillets on top of the veg and drizzle with lemon juice. Using the same temperature, cook for a further 10 minutes, or until the fish is fully cooked and flakes on touch. Transfer the haddock to dinner plates, then shake the tray to mix the potatoes and green beans in the flavoursome oil. Spoon the veg onto the plates, drizzling any oil from the bottom of the tray over the potatoes. We love to serve this with lemon wedges and a sprinkling of fresh dil.

Mix and match Thanks to fish fillets and vegetables with similar cook times it's easy to mix and match:

- Swap smoked haddock for similar-sized salmon, seabass, cod, hake or tuna fillets.
- Swap green beans for asparagus, broccolini, peppers, tomatoes or baby corn.

15-minute catfish and broccolini We mixed and matched the haddock recipe above, switching the haddock for **basa/catfish** and the veg for broccolini. Add **230g/8½oz of broccolini** to the foil tray, drizzle over **1 tablespoon olive oil**, and sprinkle with **1 teaspoon dried parsley**, then season with salt and pepper. Shake the tray to coat everything, then cook at 180°C/360°F for 5 minutes. Add the fish fillets on top, season them with salt and pepper, add **a squeeze of lemon juice** and cook for another 10 minutes until the fish is cooked through.

20-minute seafood crumble pots

These individual crumbles are perfect for smaller air fryer baskets. A crumble can also be savoury and these use frozen seafood bags, reducing the prep and are perfect for an effortless seafood starter.

SERVES **4**
HERO **BASKET/DUAL**
PREP **8 MINUTES**
COOK TIME **20 MINUTES**
CALORIES **616**

1 × 350g/12oz bag raw frozen seafood mix
Juice of 1 lemon
1 × 150g/5½oz pack of garlic and herb cream cheese (we use Boursin)
1 tbsp chopped fresh parsley
2 tsp dried thyme
2 tsp wholegrain mustard
2 tbsp grated Parmesan cheese
125g/4½oz/1 cup frozen peas
4 tbsp white wine
Salt and black pepper

FOR THE CRUMBLE TOPPING
125g/4½oz/1 cup self-raising/self-rising flour
60g/2oz/¼ cup unsalted butter, softened and diced
28g/1oz/⅓ cup porridge oats/oatmeal
2 tsp dried thyme
28g/1oz/⅓ cup grated Parmesan cheese
2 tsp English mustard powder (such as Colman's)

01 Put the frozen seafood and lemon juice into a silicone container and add a generous seasoning of salt and pepper. Unwrap the block of cream cheese and find a spot for it in the centre of the container. Transfer the container to the air fryer basket/drawer. Set the temperature to 180ºC/360ºF and cook for 10 minutes, or until the prawns/shrimp are pink and cooked through.

02 Whilst the seafood is cooking, make the crumble topping. Put all the crumble ingredients into a mixing bowl. Stir everything together, then rub the fat into the flour and oat mixture until you have a crumble topping. Season the crumble with salt and pepper.

03 Remove the container from the air fryer and add the parsley, thyme, mustard, Parmesan, frozen peas and white wine to the seafood. Mix everything together well.

04 Divide the creamy seafood filling between four ramekins (about 200ml/7fl oz/¾ cup) until three-quarters full. We find the easiest way to stop spillages is to use a ladle. Sprinkle the crumble mixture over the tops, dividing it equally among the ramekins.

05 Place the ramekins into the air fryer basket. If using the dual, you will need to divide the ramekins between the two drawers. Set the temperature to 180ºC/360ºF and cook for 10 minutes, or until golden on top and piping hot throughout.

garlic butter prawns with white wine

One of my favourite Spanish tapas dishes is prawns with garlic butter and white wine. Using frozen king prawns/shrimp it's so easy to make using the air fryer. Your guests will think you have made a great effort when you haven't.

SERVES **2**
HERO **BASKET/DUAL**
PREP **5 MINUTES**
COOK TIME **12 MINUTES**
CALORIES **240**

2 tbsp salted butter, diced
¼ medium red onion, finely chopped
4 garlic cloves, peeled and finely sliced
4 tbsp white wine
240g/8½oz frozen raw peeled king prawns/shrimp
1 tbsp finely chopped fresh parsley
A squeeze of lemon juice
Salt and black pepper

01 Put the butter, red onion, garlic and white wine in a container suitable for the air fryer basket/drawer. Set the temperature to 120ºC/250ºF and cook for 4 minutes.

02 Stir the melted butter and wine mixture, then add the frozen prawns. Increase the temperature to 180ºC/360ºF and cook for 8 minutes (or 10 minutes if your prawns are jumbo sized), or until the prawns are pink and cooked through.

03 Transfer everything to a tapas dish, including the delicious garlic wine butter, stir in parsley and season with salt and pepper. Add a squeeze of lemon juice and serve.

Serving suggestion We love to cook part-baked bread in the air fryer to dunk into the wonderful garlic and white wine cooking juices. Place four part-baked rolls into the air fryer whilst you are dishing up the prawns and air fry for 5 minutes at 180ºC/360ºF.

frozen prawns & avocado salsa

Inspired by a meal at a Peruvian restaurant whilst in Mexico, we air fry the king prawns/shrimp whilst we prep this quick avocado salsa. This recipe is brilliant for bringing to parties, or stuff it into a flatbread and it's perfect for when you have lots of salad items in and are looking for something different to make. This also travels well for something healthy to take to work with you.

....

SERVES **2**
HERO **BASKET/DUAL**
PREP **8 MINUTES**
COOK TIME **8 MINUTES**
CALORIES **224**

....

240g/8½oz frozen raw peeled
  king prawns/shrimp
Juice of 3 limes
¼ cucumber
½ medium avocado
175g/6oz cherry tomatoes
¼ medium red onion
a few sprigs of fresh coriander/
  cilantro
Salt and black pepper

01 Place the frozen prawns in an air fryer friendly container inside your air fryer basket/drawer. Squeeze the juice of two limes over them and season well with salt and pepper. Set the temperature to 180°C/360°F and cook for 8 minutes, or for 10 minutes for jumbo prawns.

02 In the meantime prepare the remaining ingredients, adding them to a salad dish as you prep them. Slice the cucumber into 1cm/½ inch thick slices, then quarter each slice, and chop the avocado into 1cm/½ inch cubes. Quarter the cherry tomatoes, and peel and finely chop the onion. Then finely chop the coriander. Stir everything together in the salad dish.

03 When the air fryer beeps, allow the prawns to cool, then place them on a chopping board and cut into 1cm/½ inch chunks. Add the prawns to the salad, season with salt and pepper and squeeze in the remaining lime. Mix with a spoon and serve.

VEGETARIAN & VEGAN

let's air fry a warm salad

Throughout this chapter we will be sharing simple recipes for air-fried veggies. But what about combining some of your vegetables into a warm salad? We make warm salads in autumn and winter, and for enjoying the last of the root vegetables in spring before summer arrives.

best of autumn maple salad with toasted lentils

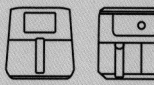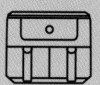

SERVES **2**
HERO **BASKET/DUAL**
PREP **12 MINUTES**
COOK TIME **33 MINUTES**
CALORIES **507**

225g/8oz butternut squash
  (prepared weight, see method)
225g/8oz sweet potatoes
2 tbsp extra virgin olive oil
½ tsp sweet paprika
1 tsp pumpkin spice
225g/8oz Brussels sprouts
2 tsp maple syrup
2 tsp balsamic vinegar
½ x 400g/14oz can brown lentils,
  drained
60g/2oz rocket/arugula leaves
Salt and black pepper

FOR THE SALAD DRESSING
1 tbsp balsamic vinegar
1 tbsp maple syrup
1 tbsp extra virgin olive oil
1 garlic clove, minced

This is our vegan autumn salad that we make when our favourite fall foods are in season. It's loaded with butternut squash, sweet potatoes and Brussels sprouts, all flavoured with a maple–balsamic glaze. Mix with rocket and toasted lentils for the wow factor.

01 Peel the butternut squash and sweet potato, and dice into 2cm/¾ inch cubes. Put them in a mixing bowl with 1 tablespoon of the olive oil, the sweet paprika, and half the pumpkin spice. Mix well with your hands. Tip into the air fryer basket/drawer and spread out so that they cook evenly. Set the temperature to 180ºC/360ºF and cook for 10 minutes.

02 In the meantime, prepare the sprouts. Slice them in half and put in a bowl with 2 teaspoons of the olive oil, and the maple syrup and balsamic vinegar. Season generously with salt and pepper, then mix with your hands. When the air fryer beeps, add the sprouts and shake the basket/drawer to allow the sprouts to mix well with the butternut squash and sweet potatoes. Air fry at the same temperature for a further 15 minutes.

03 While the air fryer is busy, prepare the lentils in the same bowl as you did the sprouts. Add the lentils, the remaining 1 teaspoon of olive oil and the remaining pumpkin spice. Season with salt and pepper and mix with your hands, then put to one side.

04 To prepare the salad dressing, put all the dressing ingredients in a jug, season with salt and pepper and mix with a fork, then set side.

05 When the air fryer beeps, toss the rocket leaves into the roasted autumn vegetables and divide between two serving plates. Add the lentils to the air fryer basket/drawer and air fry at 200ºC/400ºF for 8 minutes, or until toasted. Sprinkle the toasted lentils over the salad and drizzle with the salad dressing before serving.

creamy root vegetable soup

When we arrived in Finland to visit Santa last Christmas, it was -8°C/-17°F and we were tired from travelling. The hotel served us the most amazing warm and comforting root vegetable soup and I vowed there and then to recreate it in the air fryer. I have added coconut milk and ginger to make it creamy and for some winter spice.

SERVES **4**
HERO **DUAL**
PREP **8 MINUTES**
COOK TIME **30 MINUTES**
CALORIES **549**

2 medium carrots
1 large sweet potato (about 450g/1lb)
2 medium parsnips
1 tbsp extra virgin olive oil, plus an optional drizzle for the top
1 tbsp mixed herbs/Italian seasoning
½ tbsp dried rosemary
½ tbsp dried thyme
1 × 150g/5½oz pack garlic and herb cream cheese (we use Boursin)
1 × 400g/14oz can full-fat coconut milk
1½ tbsp ground ginger
Salt and black pepper

01 Peel the carrots, sweet potato and parsnips, and dice them all into 2cm/¾ inch cubes. Put them in a bowl with the olive oil, mixed herbs, rosemary and thyme. Season with salt and pepper, and mix well with your hands.

02 Tip the root vegetables into the air fryer basket, or spread out between two dual drawers. Set the temperature to 160°C/320°F and cook for 15 minutes.

03 When the air fryer beeps, shake the air fryer basket/drawers. Take the top foil off your cheese and place the cheese in the centre of the air fryer, on top of the vegetables. Increase the temperature to 180°C/360°F and cook for a further 10 minutes.

04 Add a can of coconut milk to a blender, then refill the coconut can and scrape the edges, getting every last bit of coconut that is stuck to the sides. Add the roast vegetables, reserving a few of the vegetables for serving over your soup. Scoop the cheese out of the rest of the foil and add it to the blender along with the ground ginger, and pulse until you have a smooth soup. Taste and adjust the seasoning with salt and pepper. The soup will now be warm, but not piping hot. If you would like it hotter, pour it into an air fryer container (or into the drawer of the dual without the crisper plate) and air fry at 180°C/360°F for another 4–5 minutes.

05 Divide the soup among four bowls, top each one with a few of the reserved roasted vegetables and finish with an optional extra drizzle of olive oil.

Freezer friendly This soup freezes well. Pour into your favourite freezer container and freeze for up to 3 months, or it will keep for up to 3 days in the fridge.

sweet potato & chickpea curry

The process of making an air fryer curry is a simple one. You air fry your dry ingredients first (your sweet potato and chickpeas), before creating your curry sauce. We like to serve it with our homemade garlic and coriander naan bread (see box below).

SERVES **4**
HERO **BASKET/DUAL**
PREP **8 MINUTES**
COOK TIME **35 MINUTES**
CALORIES **807**

2 medium sweet potatoes
1 tbsp extra virgin olive oil
1 tsp dried coriander/cilantro leaf
¼ tsp mild curry powder
¼ tsp ground turmeric
1¼ tsp garam masala
1 × 400g/14oz can chickpeas, drained
Salt and black pepper
Garlic and Coriander Naans (see opposite), to serve

FOR THE CURRY SAUCE
4 frozen spinach blocks, thawed
1 × 400ml/14oz can coconut milk
240ml/8fl oz/1 cup passata
4 tsp tikka paste
2 tsp ginger purée
2 tsp dried coriander/cilantro leaf
1 tsp ground cumin

01 Peel the sweet potatoes and dice them into 2cm/¾ inch cubes. Put them in a mixing bowl and add the olive oil, coriander leaf, curry powder, turmeric and ¼ teaspoon of the garam masala. Season generously with salt and pepper, mix with your hands and tip into the air fryer basket/drawer.

02 Set the temperature to 180ºC/360ºF and cook for 20 minutes. Add the chickpeas to the air fryer with the sweet potatoes and sprinkle the remaining garam masala over the top. Mix well with a spatula for an even coating, then cook at the same temperature for another 5 minutes.

03 Put all the curry sauce ingredients in a silicone container that fits into your air fryer and mix well with a spatula. When the air fryer beeps, transfer the sweet potatoes and chickpeas to the container and stir in.

04 Place the silicone container into the air fryer basket and air fry at the same temperature for another 10 minutes. Your curry will now be piping hot and ready for serving, along with some naan.

Dual curry Instead of a silicone container, when it's time to mix the curry sauce with the other ingredients, remove the crisp plate and cook directly in the bottom of the drawer. If serving with naan bread, have a curry in one drawer and naan in the other.

Garlic and coriander naan This naan bread is made with our air fryer flatbread dough and is delicious served with our sweet potato and chickpea curry above. Simply make a portion of **Saskia's two-ingredient yoghurt dough** on page 196, swapping the plain/all-purpose flour for self-raising/self-rising flour. As you knead the dough, incorporate **2 teaspoons garlic purée** and **1 tablespoon dried coriander/cilantro leaf**. Cook the naan at 180ºC/360ºF for 4 minutes. While the breads are cooking, in a bowl combine **2 tablespoons olive oil**, **1 teaspoon dried coriander leaf** (or use **1 tablespoon finely chopped fresh coriander**) and **1 teaspoon garlic purée**. Brush the naans with the flavoured oil and cook for another 4 minutes at the same temperature.

vegan falafel subs

We love falafel in the air fryer. Mainly because they are quick cooking, but also because of how crispy they go without needing extra oil. Take them to the next level by serving in a vegan sub.

....

SERVES **4**
HERO **BASKET/DUAL**
PREP **10 MINUTES**
COOK TIME **25 MINUTES**
CALORIES **456**

....

2 vegan part-baked baguettes
115g/4oz vegan cheese, grated

FOR THE FALAFEL BALLS
1 × 400g/14oz can chickpeas
1 tsp extra virgin olive oil
2 tsp ground cumin
1 red (bell) pepper/capsicum
¼ red onion
1 tsp ground coriander
1 tsp smoked paprika
1 tsp garlic purée
½ tsp ground ginger
¼ tsp cayenne pepper
1 tbsp dried parsley
Plain/all-purpose flour, for your hands

FOR THE TOMATO SAUCE
6 tbsp passata
1 tbsp tomato purée/paste
2 tsp garlic purée
2 tsp dried basil
2 tsp dried oregano
Salt and black pepper

01 Drain the chickpeas and add them to a mixing bowl. Add the olive oil and half the cumin, and mix with your hands. Tip into the air fryer basket/drawer and cook for 2 minutes at 180ºC/360ºF. This will help to dry the excess moisture from the chickpeas and make them easier to bind. Transfer your chickpeas to a blender/food processor.

02 Slice the pepper into 2cm/¾ inch squares and put them in the same bowl you used for the chickpeas. Season with salt and pepper and the remaining cumin and mix with your hands, then tip into the air fryer. Cook for 5 minutes at 200ºC/400ºF.

03 When the air fryer beeps, tip the pepper into the blender with the chickpeas and add the remaining falafel ingredients. Blitz until everything comes together into a thick paste.

04 Form the blended mixture into 12 falafel balls, flouring your hands as you need to stop them sticking. Place the balls into the air fryer basket, or spread between two drawers if using a dual. Cook at 180ºC/360ºF for 12 minutes, or until the falafels are nice and golden, and piping hot.

05 In the meantime, in a small bowl, mix together the tomato sauce ingredients, then set aside.

06 When the air fryer beeps, slice open the part baked baguettes and slice in half creating two smaller baguettes from each one. Spread a layer of the tomato sauce over each, then add three falafel balls to each one and coat with more tomato sauce. Divide the grated cheese between the subs and place them in the air fryer. I can fit all four in a standard sized air fryer, or two in each dual drawer. Air fry at 160ºC/320ºF for 6 minutes, until the cheese is melted and the sauce is piping hot.

Vegan cheese We have found that some vegan cheeses struggle to melt quickly in the air fryer. You can either melt the cheese fast in the microwave (20 seconds full power) or leave the subs in the air fryer to stay warm for an extra 5 minutes, as the heat will help with the melting.

Part-baked bread We love using part-baked bread in the air fryer and it averages half the cook time of the oven instructions on the packaging. You can use baguettes and slice them in half like we have done above, or use small crusty rolls.

baked macaroni cheese

This macaroni cheese is a brilliant concept. Every ingredient is loaded into a foil container in one go – no adding ingredients bit by bit – making it very fast to prep. It's similar to baked mac and cheese, and thanks to using cream cheese there is no separate cheese sauce to make.

....

SERVES **4**
HERO **BASKET**
PREP **5 MINUTES**
COOK TIME **40 MINUTES**
CALORIES **781**

....

250g/9oz dried macaroni pasta
375g/13oz/4 cups grated mature/sharp Cheddar cheese
600ml/21fl oz/2½ cups whole/full-fat milk
2 tsp garlic purée
2 tsp English mustard
1 tbsp dried oregano
1 × 150g/5½oz pack garlic and herb cream cheese (we use Boursin)
Salt and black pepper

FOR THE CRISPY TOPPING
1 tbsp panko breadcrumbs
1 tbsp grated Parmesan cheese
1 tsp dried basil

01 Put all the ingredients except the cream cheese into a 18cm/7 inch square foil tray/pan and stir together, then make a space in the middle and place the cream cheese block in it.

02 Place the foil container carefully into the air fryer basket. Set the temperature to 180ºC/360ºF and cook for 35 minutes, stirring every 9 minutes to avoid clumping together. (We usually set the timer for 9 minutes at a time to remind ourselves to stir!) As you stir, the cream cheese will be mixed in and you will have a creamy macaroni cheese. At first it will not resemble mac and cheese, but have patience and when the liquid is fully absorbed by the pasta in the last few minutes of the cooking time, it will come together.

03 Once the time is up, do a taste test (the best job!), double checking the pasta is soft and it's nice and cheesy, and adding more salt and pepper if needed.

04 Combine the ingredients for the crispy topping in a small bowl. Sprinkle it over the top of the mac and cheese and cook for a few more minutes at 200ºC/400ºF, or until light golden, then serve.

Dual mac and cheese You can choose a foil container that fits the dual, or make the macaroni cheese directly in the drawer, removing the crisper plate first. If using the bottom, add an extra 10 minutes at 180ºC/360ºF.

Dishes We have made this mac and cheese in a casserole dish (as photographed), in a foil container, direct in the bottom of our dual, and in silicone. You can keep the same cook times and just go with whichever container you prefer.

easy-prep vegetarian enchiladas

These vegetable and taco bean enchiladas are so good that I will make two batches: one for dinner tonight, the other for the freezer (see tip).

SERVES **2**
HERO **BASKET/DUAL**
PREP **10 MINUTES**
COOK TIME **30 MINUTES**
CALORIES **599**

1 × 300g/10½oz jar of tomato salsa
4 small tortilla wraps
Extra virgin olive oil spray
115g/4oz/1¼ cups grated Cheddar cheese

FOR THE FILLING
½ red (bell) pepper/capsicum
¼ aubergine/eggplant
¼ medium red onion
½ tbsp extra virgin olive oil
2 tsp ground cumin
2 tsp ground coriander
½ tsp dried oregano
½ tsp smoked paprika
½ × 400g/14oz can mixed taco beans in tomato sauce
½ tbsp sour cream
40g/1½oz/½ cup grated Cheddar cheese
1 tbsp jalapeño slices from a jar
35g/1¼oz/¼ cup sweetcorn
Salt and black pepper

TO SERVE (ALL OPTIONAL)
Sliced avocado
Fresh coriander/cilantro
Sour cream

01 Chop the pepper and the aubergine into 2cm/¾ inch cubes. Slice the red onion into 1cm/½ inch thick slices. Put the chopped vegetables in a bowl and add the olive oil, ½ teaspoon of the cumin, ½ teaspoon of the coriander, the oregano and paprika, and a generous seasoning of salt and pepper. Mix well with your hands, then tip into the air fryer basket/drawer. Air fry at 180°C/360°F for 15 minutes or until the peppers have a barbecue-style grilled look.

02 Whilst the veggies are cooking, put all the remaining filling ingredients in a mixing bowl and add half the jar of salsa. When the veggies are cooked, add them to the bowl and stir.

03 Divide the filling evenly among the tortilla wraps. Roll each one up tightly, tucking in the top and bottom as you roll, like you're preparing a burrito. Place the enchiladas, side by side, in an 18cm/7 inch square foil tray/pan – or a ceramic dish, paper liner or silicone container will also work well. Push them close together in the tray to keep them in place.

04 Spray the tops of the enchiladas with olive oil to help them crisp up, then place the tray in the air fryer basket. Air fry at 180°C/360°F for 8 minutes, or until they are crisp and not soggy at all.

05 Spoon over enough of the remaining salsa to cover the wraps, then sprinkle the Cheddar over the top. Continue to air fry at 160°C/320°F for 7 minutes, or until the salsa is piping hot and the cheese has melted.

06 Serve the enchiladas with your choice of toppings, such as avocado, coriander and/or sour cream.

Dual enchiladas You can choose a foil container that fits the dual, or we prefer to use the bottom of the dual from step 3.

Make a double batch We'll often make a double batch of the filling, then fill and roll eight tortilla wraps rather than four. That way we can place four in the freezer, ready to pull out and cook when needed.

Non-stick Add a dessertspoon of salsa to the bottom of your container. It will stop the wraps from sticking and make them easier to remove once cooked.

Bowl leftovers If you have spare filling mix, you can combine it with the salsa for the topping. We found when we scraped the bowl we had about 2 teaspoons leftover to use up.

creamed spinach & butternut squash tart

As a former vegetarian, I always hated only having the choice of a nut roast or mushrooms when eating out for Christmas lunch. I also know other vegetarian's whose pet peeve is cheese being in everything. This tart is nut free, mushroom free and cheese free. You will also love our hack for cooking the squash and blind baking the pie crust at the same time.

SERVES **6**
HERO **BASKET**
PREP **10 MINUTES**
COOK TIME **35 MINUTES**
CALORIES **374**

180g/6¼oz/⅓ cups plain/all-purpose flour, plus extra for dusting
90g/3¼oz/6 tbsp salted butter
225g/8oz butternut squash (prepared weight)
2 tsp extra virgin olive oil
3 tsp dried parsley
¼ red onion
200g/7oz frozen spinach (about 5 blocks), thawed
240ml/8½oz/1 cup sour cream
1 large egg, beaten
1 tbsp garlic purée
2 tsp dried oregano
A handful of fresh basil leaves, shredded
Salt and black pepper

01 Put the flour in a mixing bowl and add the butter, cubing it as you add it. Rub the fat into the flour using your fingertips until the mixture resembles breadcrumbs. Gradually add about 3 tablespoons water and mix with your hands until everything comes together and you have a soft pastry dough. Lightly flour your kitchen worktop and a rolling pin, and roll out the pastry until 3mm/⅛in thick and large enough to line a 20cm/8 inch loose-bottomed pie tin. Lift the pastry with the rolling pin and use it to line the tin.

02 Peel the butternut squash and chop it into 1cm/½ inch cubes. Put them in a mixing bowl with the olive oil and 1 teaspoon of the parsley, season with salt and pepper and mix well with your hands. Arrange the cubes in a single layer over the pastry. Place the pie tin in the air fryer, set the temperature to 180ºC/360ºF and cook for 15 minutes.

03 In the meantime, make your creamed spinach filling. Peel and finely slice the red onion and put it in a mixing bowl. Squeeze any excess moisture out of the spinach, then add that to the bowl, along with the sour cream, beaten egg, garlic purée, oregano, finely chopped basil and the remaining parsley. Mix everything together well.

04 When the air fryer beeps, carefully remove the squash from the pastry case and put to one side. Spoon the creamed spinach into the pastry case, then scatter the roasted butternut squash over the top of the tart.

05 Air fry the tart at 180ºC/360ºF for 20 minutes, or until the pie crust is golden, the creamed spinach is heated through and your butternut squash is getting crispy. Leave the tart in the air fryer to cool for 5 minutes, then remove the tin from the air fryer. Slice into 6 wedges and serve warm.

Dual mini tarts Instead of using one large pie tin, you can also make the tart in two 10cm/4 inch pie tins. Divide the ingredients between the two and cook one in each drawer. Because they are smaller, the final cook time is just 15 minutes.

moroccan lentil-loaded sweet potato steaks

Sweet potato steaks are delicious and a fun vegan food that are perfect when sweet potatoes are in season. A gigantic sweet potato will make two large steaks, which we pair with delicious Moroccan-spiced lentils.

SERVES **2**
HERO **BASKET/DUAL**
PREP **8 MINUTES**
COOK TIME **42 MINUTES**
CALORIES **798**

1 gigantic sweet potato
  (800g–1kg/1¾–2¼lb)
Extra virgin olive oil spray
1 tsp ground cumin
1 tsp smoked paprika
Salt and black pepper
Vegan sour cream or thick
  yoghurt, to serve

FOR THE LOADED LENTILS
1 recipe quantity Moroccan
  Marinade (see page 37)
1 × 400g/14oz can chopped
  tomatoes
1 × 400g/14oz can of brown
  lentils, drained
1 small white onion, finely diced
2 tsp ground cumin
2 tbsp finely chopped
  coriander/cilantro

01 Peel the sweet potato, then stand it up and slice through it to create two large slices, each about 3.5cm/1½ inches thick. Trim to make two 225g/8oz sweet potato steaks that measure approximately 12cm/4½ inches in length and 8cm/3¼ inches wide. (Or if your sweet potato is smaller you can make 175g/6oz steaks – see tip below.)

02 Spray the steaks with olive oil and sprinkle with the cumin and a good seasoning of salt and pepper. Place them in the air fryer basket, side by side, or put one in each dual drawer. Set the temperature to 160°C/320°F and cook for 30 minutes. Turn the sweet potato steaks over with tongs and spray with olive oil again. Add a sprinkle of smoked paprika and cook at 200°C/400°F for a further 4 minutes.

03 In the meantime, put the Moroccan marinade in a silicone container. Add the tomatoes, brown lentils, onion, cumin, coriander and a generous seasoning of salt and pepper. Mix well and set aside.

04 When the air fryer beeps, remove the steaks and add the container with the lentils to the air fryer (or put them directly in the drawer without the crisper plate, if using a dual). Cook at 180°C/360°F for 8 minutes, or until piping hot. Pour the Moroccan lentils over the sweet potato steaks, and serve with a dollop of vegan sour cream or yoghurt.

Smaller steaks If you're cooking smaller 175g/6oz sweet potato steaks, reduce the cook time to 20 minutes at 160°C/320°F, with the same 4 minutes at 200°C/400°F.

Trimmings We love to use the sweet potato trimmings to make some crisps/chips, then transform them into our sweet potato nachos from page 150.

Swap steaks for baked potatoes Make our lentil recipe above, but instead serve it with the baked sweet potatoes from page 153.

Vegetarian lentil wraps Any leftover lentils can be used to fill wraps for a quick lunch. Spread a wrap with **cream cheese**, then add **3 heaped tablespoons of Moroccan lentils**, sprinkle with **28g/1oz/ ⅓ cup grated mozzarella cheese** and wrap it tightly. Brush the top with **beaten egg**, then air fry at 180°C/360°F for 6 minutes. Flip the wrap over, brush the top with egg, and air fry at the same temperature for a further 2 minutes.

famous feta (three ways)

Blocks of feta cheese are like magic in the air fryer, because they cook fast and work with a lot of different recipes. They have become famous across social media, especially combined with cherry tomatoes. Here are three of our favourite feta recipes, including the famous pasta sauce.

greek baked feta

If you have ever visited Greece, the chances are you have enjoyed baked feta. This recipe takes just 8 minutes to cook and shouts out simplicity.

SERVES **2**
HERO **BASKET/DUAL**
PREP **5 MINUTES**
COOK TIME **8 MINUTES**
CALORIES **325**

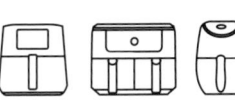

1 × 200g/7oz block of feta cheese
225g/8oz cherry tomatoes
2 tsp extra virgin olive oil
2 tsp dried oregano
1 tsp dried thyme
Crusty bread, to serve

01 Put the block of feta into an air fryer-safe dish or silicone air fryer container. Scatter the tomatoes into the dish around the feta, then drizzle with the olive oil and sprinkle with the dried herbs.

02 Place the silicone container in the air fryer basket/drawer. Set the temperature to 180ºC/360ºF and cook for 8 minutes, or until lightly baked. Serve with crusty bread.

Feta pasta sauce If you cook the feta and cherry tomatoes for longer and stir, it's like a creamy tomato sauce and is perfect for pasta, casseroles and many other similar recipes. To do this, simply follow the recipe opposite but cook for 15 minutes instead of 8 minutes. Tip the contents of the container into a blender or food processor, add **1 teaspoon minced garlic** and **2 tablespoons fat-free Greek yoghurt** and blend for a smooth creamy sauce. Or, for a Tuscan-style sauce, just stir rather than blending and the tomatoes will have a similar texture to sun-dried tomatoes.

Feta cheese & chive dip Make the pasta sauce above and leave it in the fridge to chill for at least 2 hours and it will thicken like a Mediterranean dip. You can then flavour your dip and serve it with your favourite bread or crackers. We like to add the following to ours: **1 finely chopped small red onion, 85g/3oz/1 cup grated mature/sharp Cheddar cheese, 2 tablespoons finely chopped fresh chives** and **1 tablespoon dried basil**. If you'd like your dip warm, air fry at 160ºC/320ºF for 6 minutes, or until warmed through.

ravioli bites

We first fell in love with these ravioli bites 8 years ago. The idea is simple: fresh, prepared ravioli is breaded and air fried. They are perfect for an easy appetiser.

....

SERVES **2**
HERO **BASKET/DUAL**
PREP **8 MINUTES**
COOK TIME **6 MINUTES**
CALORIES **583**

....

1 large egg
35g/1¼oz/¼ cup plain flour/
   all-purpose flour
28g/1oz/½ cup panko
   breadcrumbs
2 tbsp grated Parmesan cheese
2 tsp dried oregano
A pinch of garlic powder
175g/6oz fresh prepared
   vegetarian ravioli
Salt and black pepper
Feta Cheese and Chive Dip
   (see page 143), to serve
   (optional)

01 Crack the egg into a bowl, then beat with a fork. Put the flour in another shallow bowl. Put the breadcrumbs in a third bowl, add the Parmesan, oregano, garlic powder and a generous seasoning of salt and pepper, and stir with a fork. Your bowls are now ready for breading.

02 Coat the ravioli first in the flour, then dredge in the egg and finish with a thorough coating of the breadcrumbs.

03 Gently place the breaded ravioli into the air fryer basket/drawer spreading them out, so that they cook evenly. Set the temperature to 200ºC/400ºF and cook for 6 minutes, or until crispy, then serve with the dip, if making.

avocado wedges

SERVES **2**
HERO **BASKET/DUAL**
PREP **8 MINUTES**
COOK TIME **8 MINUTES**
CALORIES **412**

....

2 medium avocados, not too ripe
1 large egg
35g/1¼oz/¼ cup plain flour/
  all-purpose flour
28g/1oz/½ cup panko
  breadcrumbs
2 tsp taco seasoning
A pinch of garlic powder
Salt and black pepper

Avocados are sliced into wedges and breaded with panko crumbs flavoured with taco seasoning – perfect for using up your avocados.

01 Peel the avocados, remove the stones and slice into wedges. We usually get 8 wedges per avocado.

02 Crack the egg into a bowl, then beat with a fork. Put the flour in another shallow bowl. Put the breadcrumbs in a third bowl, add the taco seasoning, garlic powder and a generous seasoning of salt and pepper, and stir with a fork. Your bowls are now ready for breading.

03 Gently turn the avocado wedges over in the flour to coat, then dredge in the egg and finish with a thorough coating of the breadcrumbs.

04 Gently place the breaded avocado wedges into the air fryer basket/drawer spreading them out so that they cook evenly. Set the temperature to 200ºC/400ºF and cook for 8 minutes, or until crispy.

salt & pepper tofu

SERVES **2**
HERO **BASKET /DUAL**
PREP **8 MINUTES**
COOK TIME **16 MINUTES**
CALORIES **205**

....

½ red (bell) pepper/capsicum
½ green (bell) pepper/capsicum
½ medium red onion
1 red chilli
250g/9oz tofu, pressed
1 tbsp extra virgin olive oil
4 tsp Chinese 5-spice powder
Salt and black pepper

Move aside salt and pepper chips/fries. This is how to make the Chinese takeaway classic using tofu.

01 Slice the peppers into strips, and slice the red onion. Slice the red chilli, discarding the seeds (or keep them in if you like the heat). Slice the tofu into thick strips, like chunky chips/fries.

02 Put everything in a bowl and add the olive oil and 5-spice powder. Season with salt and pepper and mix well with your hands, but be gentle, as you don't want the tofu to break.

03 Transfer everything to the air fryer basket/drawer and set the temperature to 200ºC/400ºF. Cook for 16 minutes, or until the peppers are tender and the tofu has got a crisp to it.

Press your tofu This will help it crisp up. Place the tofu block on a plate between two clean tea towels/dish towels. Place something heavy (such as a heavy pan) on top and let it sit for an hour to squeeze out any excess moisture before using in recipes.

POTATOES

let's air fry crisps

Air fryers make light work of making your own crisps (or potato chips, as you might call them). Potatoes are sliced super thin on a mandolin, then tossed in extra virgin olive oil. Season them with your favourite dried seasonings, then after a quick mix with your hands, the crisps/chips are ready for the air fryer.

They are perfect for a quick snack, or why not use them to make our sweet potato nachos (see page 150)

SERVES **2**
HERO **BASKET/DUAL**
PREP **10 MINUTES**
COOK TIME **13 MINUTES**
CALORIES **531**

....

4 medium white potatoes
3 tbsp extra virgin olive oil
2 tsp mixed herbs/Italian
   seasoning
A pinch of garlic powder
Salt and black pepper

01 Preheat the air fryer to 200ºC/400ºF. Peel the potatoes, then using a mandolin on a 2mm/¹⁄₁₆ inch setting, slice the potatoes into very thin discs. Discard any ends that are not a uniform circle shape.

02 Put the potato slices in a bowl and add the olive oil, herbs and garlic powder. Season with salt and pepper, and mix well with your hands.

03 Arrange the sliced potatoes in the air fryer basket or spread out over two dual drawers, making sure that they are in a single layer (you will need to cook them in batches). Keep the temperature at 200ºC/400ºF and cook for 7 minutes. Use tongs to flip the crisps over and cook at the same temperature for another 6 minutes, or until crispy and light golden.

Sweet potato crisps We prefer to use white potatoes because it's quicker to get them nice and crispy in the air fryer, and also easier to get white potatoes in a uniform shape. If you would rather do sweet potatoes, follow the recipe above but use **425g/15oz sweet potatoes** and slice them across the width so that you get nice round crisps and not long floppy oval ones. Add an extra 1 minute of cooking time on each side, and if you feel some are still not crispy enough, add a couple of extra minutes, but remove the cooked ones first.

Top tips

Use what you have You can use white, red or sweet potatoes as they all have a similar cook time. Avoid small potatoes because the size of crisp will be too small.

Don't scrimp on the oil Compared to other air fryer potato recipes, you need more olive oil for crisps, to create the perfect crispy texture.

Keep a close eye on them As they are so thin, they can burn quickly, so we keep an eye on them and give them a check after 10 minutes, and if they need to be crispier (they may still feel soggy on touch), give them a little longer.

Choose your flavour Try our mixed herb crisps (opposite), or add 2 teaspoons of your favourite dried seasonings. This can be a combination of seasoning or just one. Why not try:

- Salt and black pepper
- Smoked paprika and ground cumin
- Curry powder
- Chinese 5-spice powder
- Dried basil
- Cajun seasoning
- Fajita seasoning
- Shawarma seasoning

Love apples and pears? Using your mandolin, cut thin slices of apple and/or pear to make fruit crisps instead. Cook them at the same time and temperature as the potato crisps. Instead of the delicious flavour options above, you can dust them with pumpkin spice, ground cinnamon, or a mixture of the two. They make a fantastic snack and are great for putting in your kids lunch boxes.

sweet potato nachos

I love nachos and the more loaded they are, the better. I want sour cream, guacamole, avocado, melted cheese and plenty of beans. We use a loose-based pan, because it makes transferring the nachos to a serving plate easier.

SERVES **2**
HERO **BASKET**
PREP **10 MINUTES**
COOK TIME **8 MINUTES**
CALORIES **978**

1 recipe quantity Sweet Potato
   Crisps (see page 148)
1 x can 400g/14oz taco beans
   in tomato sauce
1 tsp ground coriander
1 tsp garlic powder
1 tsp sweet paprika
140g/5oz/1 cup frozen
   sweetcorn
170g/6oz/2 scant cups grated
   mature/sharp Cheddar
   cheese
6 pickled jalapeños, sliced, plus
   extra to sprinkle
Salt and black pepper

TO SERVE (ALL OPTIONAL)
2 tbsp sour cream
2 tbsp guacamole
Fresh coriander/cilantro

01 Create a layer of sweet potato crisps/chips in the bottom of a 20cm/8 inch dish.

02 Drain the mixed taco beans, and put them in a mixing bowl. Add the ground coriander, garlic powder, sweet paprika and frozen sweetcorn, then season with salt and pepper and mix well.

03 Sprinkle half the grated cheese over the sweet potato crisps, then add the taco bean mixture, followed by the remaining cheese. Finish by sprinkling over the sliced jalapeños. As you layer up, don't take the toppings right to the edges – you will then have some crisps/chips that are bare at the edges and can be grabbed easily when the nachos are cooked.

04 Place the dish in the air fryer basket. Set the temperature to 180ºC/360ºF and cook for 8 minutes, or until the beans are heated through and the cheese is melted.

05 Remove the dish from the air fryer with oven gloves as it will be hot. Use a spatula to get underneath and remove the nachos from the base, transferring them to a serving platter. We like to serve them with sour cream and guacamole, and sprinkled with fresh coriander leaves and more jalapeños, but it's up to you!

Dual nachos When making this in the dual air fryer, we swap the dish for two rectangular ones that perfectly fitted the dual drawers, then divide the ingredients equally between them.

Lighten the load If you have a night of nachos in front of the TV planned and you prefer to be free of washing up, you can make these in a foil tray instead.

baked sweet potatoes

I love cooking sweet potatoes in the air fryer. But one question that comes up time and time again is, 'How long do sweet potatoes take?" Or 'Why are my potatoes still hard and yours aren't?' The easiest way to avoid sweet potatoes with uncooked (or overcooked) centres is to refer to our chart with the cooking times of various sizes of sweet potatoes, which you can refer back to when you need it.

....

SERVES **2**
HERO **BASKET/DUAL**
PREP **3 MINUTES**
COOK TIME **45 MINUTES**
CALORIES **337**

....

Extra virgin olive oil spray
2 large sweet potatoes
  (approximately 450g/1lb
  each), scrubbed
Salt and black pepper
Your choice of fillings, to serve

01 Spray a dinner plate with olive oil and season it generously with salt and pepper.

02 Roll the sweet potatoes in the olive oil and seasoning until they are well coated.

03 Place the sweet potatoes in a single layer in the air fryer basket/drawer. Set the temperature to 180°C/360°F and cook for 45 minutes, or until the sweet potatoes are fork tender.

04 To serve, place a sweet potato on a dinner plate, slice in half and load it up with your favourite toppings.

Sweet potato cooking times This is our guide for how to adapt cooking times for different sizes of potatoes (arranged by size in the photo, left). Whether you are cooking one potato or four, the cook time doesn't change.

- 150g/5½oz (small) – 20 minutes
- 300g/10½oz (medium) – 25 minutes
- 450g/1lb (large) – 45 minutes
- 550g/1¼lb (extra large) – 55 minutes
- 700g/1lb 9oz (extra extra large) – 60 minutes
- 900g/2lb (gigantic) – 75 minutes

simply the best skin-on seasoned french fries

In the Milner house, we just love to recreate fast-food-style fries in the air fryer. We love the way they are cooked in their skin, with just the right amount of seasoning. Because they are thin cut, they cook quicker and, thanks to the skin and seasoning, they are so wonderfully crispy.

....

SERVES **2**
HERO **BASKET/DUAL**
PREP **5 MINUTES**
COOK TIME **20 MINUTES**
CALORIES **349**

....

3 medium potatoes
4 tsp extra virgin olive oil
2 tsp dried oregano
Salt and black pepper

01 Scrub the potatoes, then using a knife or a potato chipper, cut the potatoes into French fries.

02 Put the fries in a bowl and add the olive oil and oregano. Season with salt and pepper, and mix well with your hands.

03 Tip the potatoes into the air fryer basket/drawer and spread them out so that they cook evenly. Set the temperature to 160ºC/320ºF and cook for 15 minutes. Shake the basket, then increase the temperature to 200ºC/400ºF and cook for a further 5 minutes, or until crispy to your liking.

Go sweet potato If you're like Jorge and prefer sweet potatoes, you can swap like for like and keep the same time and temperature.

garlic parmesan hasselback potatoes

We love baby potatoes in the air fryer. Cooked whole, they go so crispy and are fork tender in a third of the time of large potatoes. One way to take them to the next level is to prepare hasselback potatoes, which we make taste even better with garlic and Parmesan.

....

SERVES **2**
HERO **BASKET/DUAL**
PREP **10 MINUTES**
COOK TIME **25 MINUTES**
CALORIES **377**

....

675g/1½lb baby potatoes
1 tbsp extra virgin olive oil
1 tbsp dried oregano
1 tbsp garlic purée
28g/1oz/½ cup grated
  Parmesan cheese
Salt and black pepper

01 To create hasselback potatoes, slice each potato at 2–3mm/¹⁄₁₆th inch intervals, only taking the knife three-quarters of the way down so that the slices are still joined at the base and the potato is still in one piece.

02 Put the sliced potatoes in a mixing bowl and add the olive oil and oregano. Season with salt and pepper, and mix well with your hands. Add the garlic purée and mix again – the garlic will create a sticky coating on the potatoes. Add the Parmesan to the bowl and mix a final time to create a Parmesan coating over the potatoes.

03 Carefully tip the potatoes into the air fryer basket/drawer and spread them out so that they cook evenly. Set the temperature to 180ºC/360ºF and cook for 25 minutes, or until the hasselback potatoes are crispy and fork tender.

Cutting tip When slicing these, it's easy to go a little hard on the knife and cut all the way through the potato. To stop this happening, insert a metal skewer lengthways into the potato, about 5mm/¼ inch up from the base. The knife will hit the skewer each time you cut down and stop you cutting all the way through.

baby potatoes (three ways)

If I could choose one favourite potato, it would be baby. They are so versatile – from slicing to cubing to quartering, or just keeping them whole. Also, because the skin tastes so good, you have no peeling to do, which speeds up your prep time. Below you will find our three favourite ways to cook them – from Spanish potatoes, to a hearty breakfast version, to spiced Bombay potatoes to serve with your curry.

spanish chorizo & pepper potatoes

We love these Spanish potatoes. Quartered baby potatoes are loaded up with red peppers, onion and chorizo, and seasoned with paprika.

SERVES **4**
HERO **BASKET/DUAL**
PREP **10 MINUTES**
COOK TIME **25 MINUTES**
CALORIES **290**

675g/1½lb baby potatoes
1 red (bell) pepper/capsicum
1 small red onion
2 tbsp extra virgin olive oil
1 tsp smoked paprika
1 tsp dried oregano
1 tsp dried coriander/cilantro leaf
1 tsp garlic purée
85g/3oz chorizo, diced
Salt and black pepper
Oregano leaves, to garnish (optional)

01 Scrub the baby potatoes, then cut them into quarters. Slice the red pepper and onion into a similar shape. Put the potatoes, peppers and onion in a mixing bowl and add all the remaining ingredients apart from the chorizo. Season with salt and pepper, and mix well with your hands.

02 Tip the potatoes into the air fryer basket/drawer and spread them out so that they cook evenly. Set the temperature to 180ºC/360ºF and cook for 20 minutes.

03 When the air fryer beeps, shake the potatoes, then add the chorizo to the air fryer basket over the potatoes. Increase the temperature to 200ºC/400ºF and cook for a further 5 minutes, or until the potatoes are crispy and fork tender, and the chorizo is nice and crispy too.

04 Serve the potatoes hot – as they are, or they are lovely sprinkled with oregano leaves.

Breakfast potatoes These are similar to Spanish potatoes and carry the same cook time and temperature. Swap the chorizo for the same quantity of **bacon bits**, then swap out the paprika, coriander and garlic for **1 tablespoon dried parsley** and increase to **1 tablespoon dried oregano**.

Make-ahead Bombay potatoes When we are having a curry night (see page 191), we prep the Bombay potatoes ahead and then cook the potatoes at the same time as the curry to save time and make dinner even easier. Simply prep the same amount of potatoes, as in the recipe above. Put them in a mixing bowl and, instead of the additions above, add **1 tablespoon extra virgin olive oil, 1 teaspoon ground coriander, 1 teaspoon garam masala, 1 teaspoon mild curry powder, 1 teaspoon garlic purée** and **1 teaspoon ginger purée**, and season with **salt and black pepper**. You can now continue to cook them at the same time and temperature as above.

VEGETABLES

quick-cook sunday vegetables

This is a brilliant and effortless way of cooking your favourite Sunday dinner vegetables in the air fryer. Potatoes, parsnips, carrots and Brussels sprouts come together in one air fryer basket, ready for serving alongside your favourite Sunday roast.

....

SERVES **4**
HERO **BASKET/DUAL**
PREP **10 MINUTES**
COOK TIME **30 MINUTES**
CALORIES **262**

....

3 medium white potatoes
4 large carrots
1 large parsnip
2 tbsp extra virgin olive oil
1 tsp dried rosemary
1 tsp dried thyme
225g/8oz Brussels sprouts
1 tbsp balsamic vinegar
1 tbsp dried parsley
salt and black pepper

01 Scrub and peel the potatoes, carrots and parsnip, then dice them into 2cm/¾ inch cubes. Put the vegetables in a bowl and add the olive oil, rosemary and thyme. Add a generous seasoning of salt and pepper, and mix well with your hands.

02 Tip the veg into the air fryer basket/drawer and spread out so that they cook evenly. Set the temperature to 160ºC/320ºF and cook for 10 minutes.

03 In the meantime, prepare the sprouts. Clean and chop them in half, then put them in the bowl. Drizzle with balsamic vinegar, add the parsley, season with salt and pepper and mix with your hands. Once the root vegetables have been cooking for 10 minutes, tip the prepared sprouts into the air fryer and use a spatula to mix everything together. Continue air frying for another 10 minutes.

04 When the air fryer beeps, shake the air fryer basket/drawer, increase the temperature to 180ºC/360ºF and cook for a further 10 minutes, or until the root vegetables are fork tender.

simply the easiest cauliflower cheese

We have some simple tricks to make this creamy cauliflower cheese even easier. Combining frozen cauliflower with a leftover veggie cheese sauce, this is perfect for Sunday dinners, Christmas or just a simple dinner side dish.

....

SERVES **4**
HERO **BASKET/DUAL**
PREP **5 MINUTES**
COOK TIME **25 MINUTES**
CALORIES **767**

....

675g/1½lb frozen cauliflower
   florets
1 tsp dried oregano
1 tsp dried mixed herbs/Italian
   seasoning
1 recipe quantity Bits and Bobs
   Cheese Sauce (see page 33)
85g/3oz/1 cup grated mature/
   sharp Cheddar cheese, for
   sprinkling
Salt and black pepper

01 Place the frozen cauliflower florets into the air fryer basket/ drawer and spread out so that they cook evenly. Set the temperature to 180ºC/360ºF and cook for 15 minutes.

02 When the air fryer beeps, transfer the just-cooked cauliflower to a silicone pan or casserole dish with handles. (If using a dual, you can use two smaller dishes and cook one in each drawer.) Sprinkle the herbs over the cauliflower and season with salt and pepper. Pour over the cheese sauce and sprinkle grated cheese over the top.

03 Place the dish into the air fryer basket/drawer, set the temperature to 180ºC/360ºF and air fry for 10 minutes, or until the cheese sauce is heated through and the cheese on top has melted.

Why do we use frozen cauliflower? Frozen cauliflower cooks quickly in the air fryer, doesn't go hard like fresh and, of course, saves you on prep time.

everyday air fryer veggies

If you are looking for simple everyday veggies in the air fryer, you will love these. Each recipe needs only five ingredients or less, making them perfect for weeknights, and choices include leeks, spring greens, aubergine and cauliflower.

crispy leeks

Do you ever have one leek leftover and wonder what to do with it? Let me introduce you to crispy leeks; shredded leek, simple seasoning and olive oil work like a dream. Enjoy it as a side, or sprinkle it over soups.

SERVES **2**
HERO **BASKET/DUAL**
PREP **5 MINUTES**
COOK TIME **14 MINUTES**
CALORIES **34**

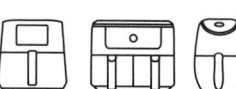

1 large leek
Extra virgin olive oil spray
1 tsp dried oregano
Salt and black pepper

01 Slice the leek in half, then slice each half into 1cm/½ inch slices, to create a shredded look. Using a sieve, wash the leek under cold water, then pat dry with kitchen towel/paper towel.

02 Tip the shredded leek into the air fryer basket/drawer and spread it out so that it cooks evenly. Set the temperature to 160ºC/320ºF and cook for 8 minutes.

03 Shake the shredded leeks, generously spray with olive oil, sprinkle with oregano, and season with salt and pepper. Air fry at 200ºC/400ºF for a further 6 minutes, or until crispy to your liking.

shredded spring greens

I look forward to when spring greens are in my weekly vegetable box. You can quickly shred them (or buy them sliced) and toss in oil and seasoning and they taste so good when air fried.

SERVES **2**
HERO **BASKET/DUAL**
PREP **5 MINUTES**
COOK TIME **10 MINUTES**
CALORIES **104**

 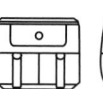

225g/8oz sliced spring greens
1 tbsp extra virgin olive oil
1 tbsp dried parsley
Salt and black pepper

01 Place the sliced spring greens in a bowl and add the olive oil and the parsley. Season generously with salt and pepper and mix with your hands until they are evenly coated.

02 Tip the spring greens into the air fryer basket/drawer and spread them out so that they cook evenly.

03 Set the temperature to 180ºC/360ºF and cook for 10 minutes, or until the edges are starting to crisp and are cooked to your liking.

parmesan-coated aubergine slices

My aunt, when visiting from the USA, would take me shopping for 'eggplant'. It wasn't until I was a grown up that I realised eggplant was what us Brits call 'aubergine'. They are still a favourite and are delicious sliced and air fried with Parmesan.

SERVES **2**
HERO **BASKET/DUAL**
PREP **5 MINUTES**
COOK TIME **13 MINUTES**
(PER BATCH)
CALORIES **107**

1 large aubergine/eggplant
Extra virgin olive oil spray
28g/1oz/⅓ cup grated Parmesan cheese
Salt and black pepper

01 Slice the aubergine into 1cm/½ inch thick slices. Arrange the aubergine slices in your air fryer basket/drawers, adding as many as you can fit in a single layer – we usually need to cook our aubergine in three batches.

02 Spray the tops with the olive oil spray and season with salt and pepper. Set the temperature to 180ºC/360ºF and cook for 10 minutes, or until the aubergine is crispy and fork tender.

03 When the air fryer beeps, sprinkle the tops of the aubergine slices with Parmesan and air fry at the same temperature for 3 minutes to melt the cheese. If necessary, repeat the process to cook the remaining aubergine.

cauliflower steaks

This is crispy cauliflower with less prep. Simply slice a cauliflower into thick steak-like slices and you're ready to air fry.

SERVES **4**
HERO **BASKET/DUAL**
PREP **5 MINUTES**
COOK TIME **18 MINUTES**
CALORIES **61**

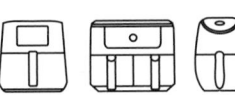

1 large cauliflower
Extra virgin olive oil spray
2 tsp taco seasoning
Salt and black pepper

01 Place the cauliflower on a chopping board, stalk side down, and slice the cauliflower into 2.5cm/1 inch thick slices. You can usually get four good sized steaks from a large cauliflower – they will each need a bit of the core to help hold them together, so any slices from the ends that fall apart can be used for another recipe.

02 Place the cauliflower steaks in the air fryer basket/drawer and spread them out so that they cook evenly. Spray the tops with the olive oil spray and sprinkle evenly with the taco seasoning and salt and pepper.

03 Set the temperature to 180ºC/360ºF and cook for 12 minutes. When the air fryer beeps, adjust the temperature to 160ºC/320ºF and air fry for a further 6 minutes, or until fork tender and crispy to your liking.

jalapeño poppers

If there is a party food you must air fry, it is jalapeño poppers. They are quick to prepare, taste delicious and travel well for taking to a gathering.

....

MAKES **32**
HERO **BASKET/DUAL**
PREP **8 MINUTES**
COOK TIME **12 MINUTES**
CALORIES **43**

....

1 tbsp salted butter
16 jalapeño chillies
165g/5¾oz/¾ cup cream cheese
115g/4oz/1¼ cups grated mature/sharp Cheddar cheese
1 tsp garlic purée
1 spring onion/scallion, thinly sliced
4 tsp dried coriander/cilantro leaf
28g/1oz/½ cup panko breadcrumbs
Salt and black pepper

01 Put the butter in a ramekin and place the ramekin in the air fryer. Set the temperature to 120°C/250°F and air fry for 4 minutes, or until the butter is melted.

02 Slice the jalapeños lengthways and remove the seeds. Discard the seeds and wash your hands; there is nothing worse than touching your face, especially your eyes, after touching the spicy peppers.

03 Put the cream cheese, Cheddar cheese, garlic purée, spring onion, and half the dried coriander into a mixing bowl. Season with salt and pepper and mix well with a spoon. Spoon the mixture into the jalapeños.

04 In another bowl, combine the breadcrumbs, melted butter and the remaining coriander, and mix with a fork. Grab one filled jalapeño at a time and push it, cream cheese down, into the breadcrumbs. The breading will stick to the cheese filling to create a crust. Repeat for all the jalapeño halves until they all have a crust.

05 Carefully place the jalapeños into the air fryer basket/drawer, set the temperature to 180°C/360°F and cook for 8 minutes, or until crispy to your liking.

Bacon-wrapped jalapeño poppers I often get asked for party food ideas for gluten-free guests, or for those that eat low-carb. These bacon wrapped poppers are ideal. Simply skip the breaded crust and wrap each popper in **half a slice of streaky bacon** instead. Give them an extra 2 minutes of cooking time to really crisp up the bacon.

seriously crispy corn

SERVES **2**
HERO **DUAL/BASKET**
PREP **2 MINUTES**
COOK TIME **12 MINUTES**
CALORIES **140**

280g/10oz/2 cups frozen
  sweetcorn
1 tsp extra virgin olive oil
1 heaped tsp smoked paprika
Salt and black pepper

With nut allergies in the house, we're always looking for a delicious snack that has a similarly nutty, satisfying texture. This crispy corn is it! You can mix it up with different dried seasonings and it has a similar texture to crisps/chips.

01 Put the frozen sweetcorn in a mixing bowl, add the olive oil and paprika, and season generously with salt and pepper. Mix well with your hands until the sweetcorn is well seasoned.

02 Tip the sweetcorn into the air fryer basket/drawer. Set the temperature to 180°C/360°F and cook for 8 minutes. Shake the sweetcorn to help it crisp up evenly, then increase the temperature to 200°C/400°F and cook for a further 4 minutes, or until crispy to your liking. A fun thing to do to check it's cooked is to shake the air fryer basket/drawer – when it's ready you will hear the crunchy corn rattle in the air fryer.

Crispy peas You can also make crispy peas in the same way, keeping the same cook time and temperature. Or why not mix and match and make crispy corn and peas?

three-ingredient creamed corn

SERVES **2**
HERO **BASKET/DUAL**
PREP **2 MINUTES**
COOK TIME **12 MINUTES**
CALORIES **387**

1 × 150g/5½oz pack of garlic
  and herb cream cheese (we
  use Boursin)
210g/7½oz/1½ cups frozen
  sweetcorn
1 tsp dried basil

If there is a food that Kyle would have me cooking for him 24/7, it would be creamed corn. He loves the creamy sauce and the warm corn. But there are often lots of ingredients. This easy cheat's version has just three ingredients!

01 Unwrap the cream cheese and place it in the centre of a silicone container, then place the container in the air fryer basket/drawer. Set the temperature to 180°C/360°F and cook for 5 minutes.

02 When the air fryer beeps, add the frozen sweetcorn around the block of cheese. Then sprinkle the basil over the cheese and sweetcorn. Air fry at the same temperature for a further 7 minutes.

03 When the air fryer beeps, the cheese will have a really soft texture. Stir with a silicone spatula until you have a creamy corn, before serving.

avoid-the-waste broccoli ends

SERVES **1**
HERO **BASKET/DUAL**
PREP **6 MINUTES**
COOK TIME **12 MINUTES**
CALORIES **108**

Stems from 2 large broccoli
  heads
extra virgin olive oil spray
1 tsp dried coriander/cilantro
  leaf
Salt and black pepper

Try our broccoli ends and you'll be surprised by how something so simple – made with something you usually throw out – can taste so good. Made from the chunky stems of broccoli heads and sliced like vegetable fries, they will become your new air fryer go-to.

01 Peel the broccoli stems, then slice them into sticks the size of French fries. Put them in a bowl, spray with olive oil and sprinkle with coriander. Season generously with salt and pepper, and mix well with your hands.

02 Tip into the air fryer basket/drawer and spread out so that they cook evenly. Set the temperature to 180ºC/360ºF and cook for 10 minutes, or until fork tender.

03 Spray the fries again with olive oil, then increase the temperature to 200ºC/400ºF and cook for a further 2 minutes, or until starting to get crispy.

Save those ends For a bigger batch, each time you use a broccoli head, slice off the stem and freeze it in a freezer bag. Once you have six, you will be able to make a good-sized portion. If you're making a big batch, cook for 15 minutes instead of 10.

12-minute broccolini

SERVES **2**
HERO **BASKET/DUAL**
PREP **2 MINUTES**
COOK TIME **12 MINUTES**
CALORIES **63**

200g/7oz long-stem broccoli/
  broccolini
extra virgin olive oil spray
2 pinches of dried coriander/
  cilantro leaf
Salt and black pepper

Long-stem broccoli is much easier to air fry than regular broccoli florets. This is because the leafy tops of regular florets get overcooked whilst the stem is still not fork tender. Thanks to the shape and size of broccolini, it cooks much more evenly. If the stems of your broccolini are quite chunky, halve them lengthways so that they cook more evenly. (Pictured on page 173)

01 Place the broccolini into the air fryer basket/drawer and spread out so that it cooks evenly. Spray with the olive oil and sprinkle with coriander, then season generously with salt and pepper.

02 Set the temperature to 160ºC/320ºF and cook for 12 minutes, or until the leafy tops are crispy and the stem is fork tender.

oregano-crusted beetroot wedges

I had to live in Portugal to appreciate how delicious beetroot is. Over there, it sits proudly next to the broccoli and carrots, and is most loved by the locals when it's roasted and added to salad. Adding extra oregano creates a crispy crust. If you have not cooked raw beetroot before, this is a fun alternative to potato wedges that you must try.

SERVES **4**
HERO **BASKET/DUAL**
PREP **8 MINUTES**
COOK TIME **25 MINUTES**
CALORIES **84**

6 medium raw beetroots/ beets
1 tbsp extra virgin olive oil
1 tbsp white wine vinegar
4 tsp dried oregano
Salt and black pepper

01 Peel and slice your beetroot into wedges – we usually get eight wedges from a medium beetroot. If they are out of season and a bit smaller, quartering them usually works well.

02 Put the beetroot wedges in a bowl, add the olive oil, vinegar and oregano, and season generously with salt and pepper. Mix well with your hands.

03 Tip the beetroot wedges into the air fryer basket/drawer and shake the air fryer basket/drawer to naturally spread them out. Set the temperature to 180°C/360°F and cook for 25 minutes, or until the beetroot is fork tender and the oregano is crispy. If your wedges are large, we recommend adding another 5 minutes cooking time at the same temperature.

'But beetroot is messy' This is the most common response I receive whenever I say I love peeling, chopping and air frying beetroot. Yes, your chopping board and bowl will be a little red after prep, and your hands will go pinker, but after two washes, they will all be perfect again. Although I recommend avoiding a white board and bowl, as it will show up a lot more on these.

butternut squash for everything

Butternut squash is so versatile. It can be transformed from simple roasted squash to a purée, a mash, or a curry sauce with some simple hacks.

....

SERVES **2**
HERO **BASKET/DUAL**
PREP **5 MINUTES**
COOK TIME **40 MINUTES**
CALORIES **171**

....

1 medium whole butternut
  squash
Extra virgin olive oil spray
¼ tsp dried parsley
Salt and black pepper

01 Cut a slice off the base of the butternut squash to make a flat, stable surface, then stand it up and slice through it lengthways to create two halves. Use a spoon to scoop out the seeds.

02 Spray the flesh of the butternut squash with olive oil, then sprinkle with parsley and season generously with salt and pepper.

03 Place the butternut squash halves in the air fryer basket, or if using a dual, place a squash half in each drawer. Set the temperature to 180°C/360°F and cook for 40 minutes, or until the butternut flesh is fork tender.

Butternut squash mash Follow the roasted butternut squash recipe, but wrap **2 peeled garlic cloves** in foil and cook in the air fryer with the squash. Scoop the cooked flesh out of the squash and add it to a bowl with the soft cooked garlic and a generous sprinkling of **salt and pepper**. Mash with a potato masher before serving.

Butternut squash purée To transform into a purée, air fry the squash for another 10 minutes at the same temperature until it is super soft. Remove the squash flesh from the skin and tip into a bowl. Use a hand blender to mix until you have a creamy purée. The purée is perfect for baby food, to use as a base for a creamy sauce, or for adding hidden veggies to your kids' meals.

Butternut squash curry sauce Make as the purée recipe above, but wrap **3 peeled garlic cloves** in foil and cook in the air fryer with the squash. Then after puréeing add **1 tablespoon thick Greek yoghurt**, **1 teaspoon ground cumin** and **1 teaspoon garam masala** along with a sprinkling of **salt and pepper**. Stir well.

Freezer cubes Once cool, my favourite option is to spoon the curry sauce into large ice cube trays (we use ones that are 240ml/8½fl oz/1 cup volume) and place in the freezer. Once frozen, move the ice cubes to a freezer bag, then you can just grab one (or more) when you need it. Defrost in a silicone pan in the air fryer at 160°C/320°F for 5 minutes. You can use it as a base for air fryer curry and it's delicious. (See our Chicken Tikka Masala on page 191.)

crispy courgette fries

After the jalapeño poppers on page 168, the best vegetable for breading is courgette. Because these were popular in the US first, I always find myself saying 'zucchini fries'.

We air fry the courgette first, which reduces its watery texture then bread it and crisp up in the air fryer.

....

SERVES **2**
HERO **BASKET/DUAL**
PREP **8 MINUTES**
COOK TIME **20 MINUTES**
CALORIES **229**

....

1 medium courgette/zucchini
2 tsp dried oregano
35g/1¼oz/¼ cup plain flour/
  all-purpose flour
1 large egg
45g/1½oz/1 cup panko
  breadcrumbs
1 tsp dried thyme
1 tsp dried basil
Extra virgin olive oil spray
Salt and black pepper
Burger sauce (see page 108),
  for dunking (optional)

01 Slice the courgette into fries, put them in a bowl and add the oregano and a generous seasoning of salt and pepper. Mix to evenly coat, then tip them into the air fryer basket/drawer. Set the temperature to 200ºC/400ºF and cook for 12 minutes.

02 In the meantime, put the flour into a shallow bowl. Crack the egg into another bowl and beat with the fork. Put the breadcrumbs into a final bowl, add the thyme and basil, season generously with salt and pepper, and mix with a fork.

03 When the air fryer beeps, toss the courgette/zucchini fries, a few at a time, first in the flour, then drench them in the egg, then roll them in the breadcrumbs to thoroughly coat.

04 Place the courgette/zucchini fries back into the air fryer basket/drawer and spread out so that they cook evenly. If using a dual, you can spread them between the two drawers. Spray the tops with olive oil. Set the temperature to 200ºC/400ºF and cook for 8 minutes, or until crispy to your liking. We like to serve them with burger sauce for dunking!

7 DAYS OF DINNERS

make-ahead monday: simple leftovers pie

After a roast dinner on a Sunday, Dom will do the dishes while I prepare the Monday pie, a leftover tradition we have had for more than 15 years. We love having the Monday pie prepared in the fridge, so that the next day's dinner just needs reheating.

If you've not experienced the delights of Monday pie, the filling is made from leftover roast dinner meat, baked beans, passata and bacon, and can also include other vegetables. It is topped with sliced potatoes.

....

SERVES **4**
HERO **BASKET/DUAL**
PREP **10 MINUTES**
COOK TIME **50 MINUTES**
CALORIES **419**

....

1 white onion
4 back bacon slices/rashers
Extra virgin olive oil spray
225g/8oz leftover roast lamb (see page 192, or see tip)
1 × 400g/14oz can baked beans
400g/14oz/1½ cups passata
4 tbsp gravy
1 tbsp Worcestershire sauce
1 tbsp dried thyme
1 tsp sweet paprika
½ x 540g/1lb 3oz can whole potatoes
½ tbsp extra virgin olive oil
½ tsp dried parsley
Salt and black pepper

01 Peel and slice the onion, then slice the bacon into 1cm/½ inch squares. Put the onion and bacon into your air fryer basket/drawer, spreading them out so that they cook evenly. Spray with olive oil spray, set the temperature to 180ºC/360ºF and air fry for 10 minutes, or until the bacon is crispy.

02 In the meantime, chop the lamb into 1cm/½ inch chunks. Add the lamb to a mixing bowl, add the baked beans, passata, gravy, Worcestershire sauce, thyme and paprika, and stir everything together.

03 When the air fryer beeps, stir the crispy bacon and onion into the pie filling, season with salt and pepper, and mix well.

04 Slice the canned potatoes into 5mm/¼ inch thick slices and put them in a bowl. Add the olive oil and parsley and season well with salt and pepper. Mix well with your hands until they are evenly coated.

05 Find a casserole dish that fits your air fryer and tip the filling into it. (If using the dual, I will spread the mixture between two small casserole dishes or enamel pie tins.) Place the potato slices over the top of the pie filling, overlapping and making sure there are no gaps.

06 Carefully place the dish into the air fryer basket/drawer, set the temperature to 180ºC/360ºF and cook for 40 minutes, or until the pie is warmed through and the potatoes are golden and crispy.

Tip You can use any leftover meat for this pie. We used leftover lamb from the Sunday roast lamb dinner, but pork, chicken, beef and gammon/ham also work well.

Freezer friendly To make ahead for the freezer, make this pie filling, leaving off the potatoes, then freeze in a foil tray/pan. The night before air frying, transfer from the freezer to fridge to defrost, then add the sliced potatoes just before air frying.

hectic tuesday:
make-ahead moussaka

We call Tuesday 'Hectic Tuesday' because, like most parents, it's the night when your kids need to be everywhere: Jorge is at cooking class, 90 minutes later Sofia is at cooking class, then an hour later Kyle is at football practice. This make-ahead moussaka can be made the day before and simply reheated in those few minutes you have available.

....

SERVES **4**
HERO **DUAL**
PREP **15 MINUTES**
COOK TIME **27 MINUTES**
CALORIES **1145**

....

1 large aubergine/eggplant
Extra virgin olive oil spray
675g/1½lb minced/ground lamb
1 small onion, peeled and diced
1 tbsp dried oregano
250g/9oz/1 cup passata
1 tbsp mixed herbs/Italian seasoning
2 tsp dried thyme
2 tsp dried basil
2 tsp garlic purée
2 tsp tomato purée/paste
1 recipe quantity Bits and Bobs Sauce for Everything (see page 33)
85g/3oz/1 cup grated mature/sharp Cheddar cheese
28g/1oz/½ cup grated Parmesan
Salt and black pepper
1 recipe quantity of Saskia's Flatbreads (see page 196), to serve

01 Slice the aubergine into 5mm/¼ inch thick slices. Arrange the aubergine slices in your air fryer drawers, adding as many as you can fit in a single layer – you may have to cook them in batches. Spray the tops with the olive oil spray and season generously with salt and pepper. Set the temperature to 180ºC/360ºF and cook for 10 minutes, or until the aubergine is crispy and fork tender, then remove from the air fryer.

02 Put the lamb in the bottom of the air fryer drawer (removing the crisper plate first) and spread it out. Sprinkle the onion and oregano over the meat, and season with salt and pepper. Set the temperature to 180ºC/360ºF and cook for 5 minutes. Use a silicone spatula to break up the meat, then cook for a further 4 minutes.

03 When the air fryer beeps, stir the lamb again and add the passata, all the dried herbs and the garlic and tomato purées. Taste to check the seasoning, then tip it all into a bowl.

04 Dividing the mixture between two silicone containers that fit the dual drawers, start building up the moussaka layers. Start with a layer of sliced aubergine, a layer of the meat sauce (use it all), then another layer of aubergine.

05 Put the Bits and Bobs sauce in a mixing jug and add the grated Cheddar. Pour the sauce over the final layer of aubergine slices and sprinkle the top of the moussaka with the grated Parmesan. Place a crisper plate into each drawer and add a moussaka to each. Air fry for 8 minutes at 200ºC/400ºF, then serve with the flatbreads.

Basket moussaka Cook the aubergine/eggplant and meat sauce in the air fryer basket, then layer them up in a 20cm/8 inch round silicone container for the final cook.

Make ahead If making ahead, skip the 8 minute final cook time. Instead, layer up the moussaka in a silicone container and place in the fridge for up to 3 days. When ready to reheat, set the temperature to 160ºC/320ºF and cook for 30 minutes in the container, or until piping hot in the centre.

mezze wednesday: seriously good greek mezze

This is our go-to in the summer for a fun Greek tapas spread. We find that we often have many of the ingredients already, then we can prep whilst the air fryer cooks and get creative in putting together our mezze.

Plus, we have designed the mezze prep in a way that some items can be made ahead, so that it's not all to be done at once.

SERVES **4**
HERO **DUAL**
PREP **20 MINUTES**
COOK TIME **33 MINUTES**
CALORIES **819**

1 pot of shop-bought hummus
A few crispy chickpeas (see page 58)
1 recipe quantity Feta Cheese and Chive Dip (see page 143)
2 Saskia's Flatbreads (see page 196)
Extra virgin olive oil spray

FOR THE LAMB MEATBALLS
250g/9oz minced/ground lamb
¼ red onion, finely diced
1 tsp dried oregano, plus a sprinkling for the flatbreads
6 mint leaves, shredded
1 tsp garlic purée
2 tbsp panko breadcrumbs
1 small egg

FOR THE ROASTED VEGETABLES
1 red (bell) pepper/capsicum
½ aubergine/eggplant
¼ courgette/zucchini
1 tbsp extra virgin olive oil

1 tsp dried oregano
Salt and black pepper

FOR THE GREEK SALAD
85g/3oz/13 pitted mixed olives
¼ cucumber, sliced
¼ red onion, sliced
175g/6oz cherry tomatoes, halved
1 tbsp shredded fresh basil
1 tbsp extra virgin olive oil
1 tbsp white wine vinegar

01 Put all the meatball ingredients in a bowl, season with salt and pepper, and mix well with your hands, then divide it into 8 equal portions and roll them into meatballs (these can be prepped up to 3 days ahead).

02 The day you want to serve your mezze, transfer the meatballs straight from the fridge into the air fryer basket/drawer. Set the temperature to 180°C/360°F and cook for 14 minutes.

03 As your meatballs air fry, prepare your roasted vegetables. Chop the peppers into thick strips and put them in a mixing bowl. Cut the aubergine and courgette into 2cm/¾ inch dice and add to the bowl. Add the olive oil, oregano and a generous seasoning of salt and pepper, and mix with your hands.

04 When the air fryer beeps, remove the meatballs from the fryer. Tip the vegetables into the air fryer and, using the same temperature, cook for 15 minutes, or until the peppers look like they have been on the barbecue.

05 Meanwhile, put all the ingredients for the Greek salad in a bowl and mix well.

06 Start building your mezze spread. Put the hummus in a small serving bowl and top with a few crispy chickpeas, then put the feta dip in another small bowl. Put the meatballs and the roasted vegetables each in their own bowl.

07 For a finishing touch, slice the flatbreads into 3cm/1¼ inch wide strips. Spray with olive oil, sprinkle with dried oregano and air fry at 200°C/400°F for 4 minutes. Add to the selection and serve.

throwback thursday: toad in the hole

If there is a comfort food I love the most, it is toad in the hole. Thick pork sausages are cooked in a Yorkshire pudding batter and are even easier and quicker thanks to the air fryer. We prefer our toad in the hole cooked in the dual air fryer because it makes a more traditional dish – and you can make one in each drawer. But it is also easily adapted to the air fryer basket (see our tip below).

....

SERVES **4**
HERO **DUAL**
PREP **5 MINUTES, PLUS RESTING**
COOK TIME **29 MINUTES**
CALORIES **743**

....

125g/4½oz/1 cup plain/all-purpose flour
2 large eggs
240ml/8fl oz/1 cup whole/full-fat milk
12 thick pork sausages
200ml/7fl oz/¾ cup beef gravy
225g/8oz frozen green beans
Salt and black pepper

01 Make the Yorkshire pudding batter 15 minutes before you place the sausages in the air fryer, because the batter needs to sit for at least 20 minutes. Put the flour in a mixing bowl and season with salt and pepper. Make a well in the centre of the flour and crack the eggs into the well, then mix with a fork until well combined. Gradually add the milk, mixing until bubbles form in your batter and it's a similar consistency to pancake batter. Put it to one side and let it rest for 15 minutes.

02 Remove the crisper plate from the two air fryer drawers and divide the sausages between the drawers, placing six in each. Cook at 200°C/400°F for 8 minutes. When the air fryer beeps, turn the sausages over with tongs, then quickly pour the Yorkshire pudding batter over the sausages. Air fry at the same temperature for a further 8 minutes.

03 When the air fryer beeps, use a plate to flip both the toad in the holes over – this will help the bottoms to crisp up. Air fry at 200°C/400°F for another 5 minutes, or until golden to your liking.

04 When the air fryer beeps, remove the toad in the holes from each drawer and add the crisper plates back in. Pour your gravy into a ramekin and put it in one of the drawers, then add the frozen green beans to the other drawer. Match the air fryer drawers and cook at 180°C/360°F for 8 minutes or until the green beans and gravy are piping hot.

05 Slice each toad in the hole in half so that there are three sausages in each portion, then serve with green beans and gravy.

Toad in the basket Divide the ingredients between two 20cm/8 inch silicone containers, each 5cm/2 inches deep. Cook them one at a time following the times and temperatures above.

Fatty sausages It's important that you use full fat sausages and avoid low-fat varieties. This is because the fat from the sausages is what helps the toad in the hole to cook.

friday fish supper: dom's fish burgers

These fish burgers are delicious – they're like having crispy breaded fish in a burger bun. It adds something different to your Friday night fakeaway. Serve them with our skin-on French fries (see page 154) for a proper burger and chips weekend spread.

SERVES **2**
HERO **BASKET/DUAL**
PREP **10 MINUTES**
COOK TIME **8 MINUTES**
CALORIES **786**

35g/1¼oz/¼ cup plain/all-purpose flour
1 tbsp dried basil
1 large egg, beaten
2 tsp lemon juice
55g/2oz/½ cup golden breadcrumbs
1 tbsp dried parsley
2 × 110g/3¾oz white fish fillets
1 tbsp dried dill
2 brioche bread buns or rolls, sliced in half
A few lettuce leaves
2 slices processed burger cheese
½ tomato, sliced
Salt and black pepper

FOR THE DILL SAUCE
2 tsp finely chopped fresh dill
2 tbsp mayonnaise
½ tsp garlic purée
4 tbsp Greek yoghurt
2 tsp lemon juice

01 First set up a production line. Put the flour in a shallow bowl and stir in the basil. Put the beaten egg in another bowl and stir in the lemon juice. Put the breadcrumbs in a third bowl and add the parsley. Give each bowl a generous seasoning of salt and pepper, and also season the fish fillets with salt and pepper too. Add a sprinkling of dill to both sides of the fish fillets, then you're ready for breading.

02 First, turn the fish over in the flour to fully coat, then drench them in the egg. Finish with a double coating in the breadcrumbs.

03 Place the breaded fish fillets into the air fryer basket/drawer, set the temperature to 180°C/360°F and cook for 8 minutes, or until cooked through.

04 In the meantime, mix together the dill sauce ingredients in a small bowl.

05 When the air fryer beeps, you can assemble the burgers. Spread a thick layer of dill sauce over the bottom halves of the buns, then add some shredded lettuce and a fish fillet. Top the fish with a slice of cheese, then add a couple of tomato slices before putting the bun lids on top and serving straight away.

Frugal fakeaway Frozen fish fillets are usually cheaper than fresh ones. We use frozen pollock that we thaw before following the recipe above. Other great choices include filleted basa/catfish and tilapia. If using frozen, pat dry with kitchen paper/paper towel first.

saturday fakeaway: chicken tikka masala with bombay potatoes & naan

This chicken curry tastes amazing, it is easy to prepare, includes a hidden veggie curry sauce and is freezer friendly too. Best of all, it takes just 18 minutes to air fry.

SERVES **2**
HERO **BASKET/DUAL**
PREP **10 MINUTES**
COOK TIME **18 MINUTES**
CALORIES **1175**

675g/1½ lb boneless skinless chicken thighs
Extra virgin olive oil spray
2 tsp ground cumin
½ tsp ground turmeric
2 tsp ground coriander
2 tsp smoked paprika
½ tsp ground ginger
½ tsp garlic powder
Salt and black pepper

FOR TIKKA MASALA SAUCE
1 recipe quantity Butternut Squash Curry Sauce
  (see page 175)
1 tbsp tikka masala curry paste
2 tbsp passata
1 tsp tomato purée/paste
1 tsp garlic purée
1 tsp ginger purée

TO SERVE
Make-ahead Bombay Potatoes (see page 159)
Garlic and Coriander Naan (see page 130)
Thick yoghurt (optional)

01 Slice the chicken thighs into quarters, creating large chunks of chicken. Spray them with olive oil to create a sticky texture, then put them into a mixing bowl. Add all the dried spices, season generously with salt and pepper, and mix well with your hands.

02 Place the seasoned chicken into the air fryer basket/drawer. Set the temperature to 180ºC/360ºF and cook for 12 minutes, or until the chicken reaches an internal temperature of 70ºC/160ºF or above.

03 Put the butternut squash curry sauce in a mixing bowl and add the tikka masala paste, passata and the tomato, garlic and ginger purées. Stir everything together well.

04 Transfer the cooked chicken to the curry sauce bowl and toss to coat. Transfer to the dual drawer (without the crisper plate) or if you are using a basket air fryer, tip it into a silicone container. Cook at the same temperature for a further 6 minutes, or until the sauce is heated through and has slightly reduced.

05 Serve the chicken tikka masala with the Bombay potatoes, and warm naan bread – and yoghurt, if you like.

Don't want to make naan bread? You can reheat shop bought naan bread in the air fryer. Cook from frozen at 200ºC/400ºF for 4 minutes, or from room temperature at 180ºC/360ºF for 3 minutes for a quick warm through.

sunday roast:
rosemary leg of lamb with carrots, potatoes & peas

For the ultimate Sunday roast dinner, this lamb roast ticks all the boxes. Made with a small bone-in leg of lamb, goose fat roast potatoes, thyme flavoured carrots and minted peas, it looks amazing, yet is as simple as you can get.

....

SERVES **4**
HERO **BASKET/DUAL**
PREP **15 MINUTES**
COOK TIME **65 MINUTES**
CALORIES **604**

....

1.3kg/3lb bone-in leg of lamb
Extra virgin olive oil spray
2 tsp dried rosemary
1 garlic bulb
6 medium potatoes
2 tsp goose fat/duck fat
1 tbsp dried thyme
4 medium carrots
1 tsp extra virgin olive oil
1 tbsp mixed herbs/Italian seasoning
200g/7oz/1½ cups frozen garden peas
5 mint leaves, thinly shredded
1 tsp mint sauce
1 tsp salted butter
Salt and black pepper

01 Spray the lamb leg with olive oil, then rub the dried rosemary and a generous seasoning of salt and pepper all over the lamb. Carefully place the lamb leg into the air fryer basket/drawer. Slice the top off your garlic bulb and then spray

a little olive oil on top and sprinkle with salt and pepper. Wrap the garlic in foil and place in the air fryer basket/drawer with the lamb leg. Cook at 180ºC/360ºF for 25 minutes.

02 While the lamb is cooking, prepare the sides. For the potatoes, peel, then slice each in half. Put the potatoes in a bowl and add the goose fat and the dried thyme, season with salt and pepper and mix with your hands. Put it to one side.

03 Next, peel and slice the carrots into quarters – we find slicing them diagonally works well for an even cook. Put the carrots into a mixing bowl with the olive oil, and dried mixed herbs. Season with salt and pepper and mix well with your hands.

04 When the air fryer beeps, turn the the lamb over. Remove the garlic bulb from the foil and squeeze the soft cloves out of the skin. Add half the garlic to each bowl of veggies and mix both with your hands. Scatter the potatoes and carrots into the gaps around the lamb (or into the second drawer if using a dual). Keep the temperature at 180ºC/360ºF and air fry for a further 25 minutes.

05 When the air fryer beeps, check the internal temperature (see tip below), then remove the lamb, place it on a plate and cover with foil to allow it to rest. In the meantime, spread the carrots and potatoes out in the air fryer basket/drawer and air fry for a further 10 minutes.

06 While waiting on the carrots and potatoes, put the frozen peas, fresh mint, mint sauce and butter into a silicone container. Season with salt and pepper, and mix with a spoon.

07 When the air fryer beeps, swap the potatoes and carrots for the peas and air fry at the same temperature for 5 minutes, or until the peas are heated through and the butter has melted. Your lamb leg dinner is now ready for serving.

Use a thermometer This is important to avoid overcooking your lamb. For "medium" you need an internal temperature to 53ºC/127ºF. This is medium-rare, but as the lamb rests, it will continue to cook in the residual heat for a short time and will increase by 9ºC/48ºF.

BAKING

let's air fry flatbread

Known as two-ingredient yoghurt dough in the air fryer communities, this flatbread-style dough is perfect for the many different air fryer recipes where you need a simple dough to use in multiple ways. Master this flatbread dough, then with the recipes in this book, make bagels, pasties and – our personal favourite – naan bread. This dough also freezes well.

saskia's flatbreads (& two-ingredient dough)

SERVES **4 FLATBREADS**
HERO **BASKET/DUAL**
PREP **10 MINUTES**
COOK TIME **6 MINUTES**
CALORIES **252**

225g/8oz/1¾ cups plain flour/all-purpose flour, plus extra for dusting
250g/9oz/1 cup fat-free Greek yoghurt

I first tried recipes for this two-ingredient dough six years ago when it became an air fryer trend. I hated it; either the dough was too dry from too much flour, or too wet from too much yoghurt. Then Saskia, my baking teacher, taught me the perfect ratio of 90 per cent flour to yoghurt, and since then it's been my go-to dough. Thank you Saskia. Once you've mastered the basic dough, you can also add any flavourings you wish – see our tip box opposite.

01 Sift the flour into a mixing bowl and add the yoghurt. Use the back of a wooden spoon to press the yoghurt into the flour to help combine the two ingredients, then stir together with the wooden spoon until coming together into a dough.

02 Flour a clean worktop, your hands, and your rolling pin, then tip the dough onto your worktop. With your floured hands, knead the dough for a couple of minutes, gathering in any little bits of mixture that haven't combined as you knead, until you have a smooth dough.

03 Divide the dough into four equal portions and roll one out at a time to an oval shape of a flatbread (or if you have a small air fryer, just roll it to the size and shape that will fit in your fryer).

04 Carefully place a flatbread into the air fryer basket, or you can place one in each drawer if you have a dual. Set the temperature to 180°C/360°F and cook for 4 minutes, then flip over and cook for another 2 minutes, or until the flatbread is golden to your liking. Repeat to cook the rest of the flatbreads. Note that they will puff up slightly as they cook and will naturally flatten after a couple of minutes resting time.

Just the dough If a recipe in the book calls for Saskia's Two-Ingredient Dough, prepare it following steps 1 and 2, then continue as directed in the recipe.

Top tips

Naturally sticky dough Because it's a combo of yoghurt and flour, the dough is naturally sticky. This is okay, but you just need to be patient when handling the dough – make sure your hands are floured to stop them sticking and avoid the temptation to over-flour your dough.

Flavour your flatbread After starting with just two ingredients, the dough can be any flavour you want it to be. We recommend a teaspoon of garlic purée along with a teaspoon of any favourite dried herb or spice. Or why not use half a teaspoon each of two favourites, such as dried basil and dried oregano?

Freezing the dough This flatbread dough freezes perfectly and is ideal for when you expect to have leftover dough or you want it ready-made for next time. Simply roll out the flatbreads as above, then freeze on an oven tray that is laid flat in the freezer. (Freezing flat before bagging like this stops the dough sticking together.) Once frozen, load the raw flatbreads into freezer bags.

Saskia's pinch pot At baking class, Saskia has what she calls a flour pinch pot. This is brilliant for baking with sticky dough as you can flour your sticky hands without having to put them into your clean flour bag. Simply fill a small bowl with flour and have it on the worktop next to you for quick access.

Self-raising flour swap If you want your dough to rise, such as for the bagels (see page 198), swap the plain/all-purpose flour for self-raising/self-rising flour.

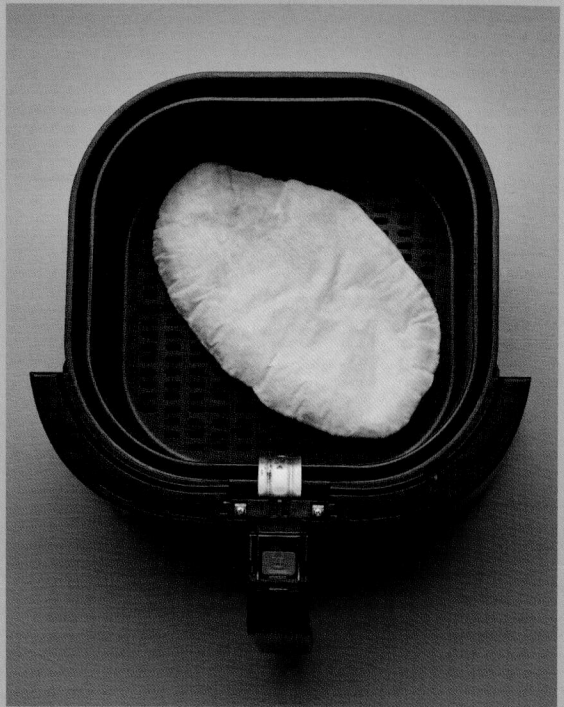

the easiest bagels recipe ever

Love warm bagels? Then transform a batch of this yoghurt dough into bagels, mixing and matching with your favourite toppings and fillings.

....

MAKES **4**
HERO **BASKET/DUAL**
PREP **5 MINUTES**
COOK TIME **16 MINUTES**
CALORIES **266**

....

Plain/all-purpose flour, for dusting
1 recipe quantity Saskia's Two-Ingredient Dough (see page 196), made using self-raising/self-rising flour, at room temperature
1 small egg, beaten
2 tsp bagel seasoning

01 Dust a clean worktop with flour, and lightly dust your rolling pin. Flour your hands, too, to stop the dough sticking to them.

02 Knead the dough, then divide it into four equal portions and shape them into balls. Stick your finger in the flour to dust it, then insert it into the centre of one of the balls and wiggle it around firmly until you have a large hole, about 3cm/1¼ inch wide. You could also use a small cookie cutter for this, if you prefer. Repeat until you have shaped all four bagels.

03 Brush the tops of the bagels with the beaten egg, then sprinkle with the bagel seasoning.

04 Place the bagels into the air fryer – you should be able to fit all four in one air fryer basket or, if you have a dual fryer, place two in each drawer. Set the temperature to 180°C/360°F and cook for 8 minutes.

05 When the air fryer beeps, reduce the temperature to 160°C/320°F and cook for a further 8 minutes. They should be cooked, but If the bottoms aren't firm, flip them over and cook for another 2 minutes to crisp up the bases. Serve warm with your favourite fillings.

Bagel bites If you are using a small cookie cutter to create your bagel shapes, you can make little bagel bites from your leftover bagel holes. Brush them with egg wash, then put them in the air fryer, spreading them out for an even cook, and air fry at 180°C/360°F for 5 minutes.

cheese, onion & potato pasties

As a kid, I loved visiting the local bakery. The sausage rolls, flapjacks and warm cheese and potato pasties always caught my eye. Clearly, they made a lasting impression as all three are in this chapter! We are using the yoghurt dough as an easy method for recreating those pasties in the air fryer.

MAKES **4**
HERO **BASKET/DUAL**
PREP **10 MINUTES**
COOK TIME **28 MINUTES**
CALORIES **562**

1 large baking potato
1 spring onion/scallion
2 tsp extra virgin olive oil
¼ tsp mustard powder
2 tsp mixed herbs/Italian seasoning
1 recipe quantity Saskia's Two-Ingredient Dough (see page 196), at room temperature
Plain/all-purpose flour, for dusting
4 tbsp sour cream
115g/4oz/1¼ cups grated mature/sharp Cheddar cheese
1 egg, beaten
Salt and black pepper

01 Peel the potato and dice it into 1cm/½ inch cubes. Clean and slice the spring onion. Put both into a bowl and add the olive oil and half each of the mustard and the mixed herbs. Season with salt and pepper, and mix with your hands until the potato and onion are well coated in the oil and seasonings. Transfer just the potato cubes to the air fryer basket/drawer, set the temperature to 180°C/360°F and cook for 10 minutes. Then tip the onion into the air fryer with the potatoes and cook for a further 8 minutes.

02 In the meantime get your pasty dough ready. Dust a clean worktop with flour, and lightly dust your rolling pin. Flour your hands, too, to stop the dough sticking to them. Roll the dough to a sheet 5mm/¼ inch thick. Use the back of a pasty maker to make four dough circles. You will need to gather up the scraps and re-roll the dough to make the fourth circle.

03 When the air fryer beeps, tip the potato and onion into a mixing bowl. Add the sour cream, cheese, and the remaining seasonings and mix well with a spoon.

04 Flour the dough discs on both sides, then also flour the pasty maker to prevent sticking. Add a dough round to the pasty maker, then add one-quarter of the filling. Use the pasty maker to fold one side of the dough over to make a semi-circular pasty, then gently remove it from the pasty maker. Repeat the process to fill the other three pasties.

05 Using a pastry brush, egg wash the tops of your pasties. Place two pasties into the air fryer basket, or one in each drawer if using the dual air fryer. Set the temperature to 180°C/360°F and cook for 10 minutes, or until piping hot throughout. Repeat to cook the remaining two pasties and serve warm.

Use a cookie cutter If you don't have a pasty maker, you can still make these. Simply roll out the dough and cut out the rounds with a 15cm/6 inch cookie cutter. Add a spoonful of filling to the dough round and fold over to create a semi-circular pasty, then crimp the edges with a fork to seal.

Cooking from frozen If you prefer air frying raw pasties from frozen (shop-bought or your own), add them to the air fryer basket/drawer still frozen and air fry at 160°C/320°F for 6 minutes, followed by 200°C/400°F for 4 minutes, or until piping hot.

homemade sausage rolls

Sausage rolls in the air fryer are a must. You can make full sized sausage rolls like the bakery, or make smaller mini sausage rolls for parties. We love to have them in the summer for picnics, for afternoon tea or as a midmorning snack on Christmas Day.

....

MAKES **4**
HERO **BASKET/DUAL**
PREP **8 MINUTES**
COOK TIME **13 MINUTES**
CALORIES **482**

....

Plain/all-purpose flour, for dusting
½ x 500g/1lb 2oz block of puff pastry (freeze the rest for another day)
1 tbsp tomato purée/paste
1 tsp dried thyme
325g/11½oz seasoned sausage meat (or remove the skin from pork sausages)
1 egg, beaten for egg wash
Ketchup, to serve (optional)

01 Dust a clean worktop and a rolling pin with flour. Roll out the puff pastry into a large rectangle measuring 30 × 20cm/12 × 8 inches. Cut the rectangle in half lengthways to create two long pastry strips.

02 Spread a layer of tomato purée over the centre pastry strips (we find this is easiest to do with a pastry brush), leaving a 1cm/½ inch gap around the edges of each for the egg wash. Sprinkle the dried thyme over the purée.

03 Divide the sausagemeat into two portions and roll each one out into a sausage shape 30cm/12 inches long. Place a sausage down the length of each pastry strip.

04 Brush egg wash around the bare edge of the dough, then fold the dough over to make a long sausage roll. Crimp down the edge of the log with a fork to seal it, then repeat to fold the other roll. Use a sharp knife to cut each sausage roll in half to make four large sausage rolls, then make a number of small slashes across the top of the rolls so that the steam can escape during cooking.

05 Carefully place the sausage rolls into the air fryer basket/drawer, spreading them out. I can normally fit four sausage rolls in a basket, or two in each dual drawer. Brush the tops of the rolls with egg wash.

06 Set the temperature to 180ºC/360ºF and cook for 10 minutes. Brush them with a little more egg wash, then cook for another 3 minutes, or until cooked through and golden. Serve warm or cold – they are delicious with ketchup.

Make party rolls If you want smaller sausage rolls for a party, simply cut them smaller. Once you have cut them into four, cut each one into quarters, so that you have 16 party-sized rolls. If cooking party sausage rolls, a total cook time of 8 minutes will be perfect.

golden syrup flapjacks

Whether you live in the UK and call them flapjacks or live in the USA and call them granola bars, they are one of the easiest air fryer recipes. If you don't like golden syrup, you can swap it for the same quantity of maple syrup or honey.

....

SERVES **8**
HERO **BASKET**
PREP **8 MINUTES**
COOK TIME **24 MINUTES**
CALORIES **303**

....

115g/4oz/½ cup unsalted
  butter
2 tbsp golden syrup/light corn
  syrup
100g/3½oz/½ cup light brown
  sugar
250g/9oz/2½ cups porridge/
  rolled oats

01 Put the butter into a 20cm/8 inch silicone pan, cutting it into bite-sized cubes as you add it. Add the golden syrup, then transfer the pan to the air fryer basket. Set the temperature to 120ºC/250ºF and cook for 4 minutes, or until the butter has melted.

02 Add the brown sugar and the oats to the pan and stir everything together well. Spread the mixture out evenly over the base of the pan, then flatten down firmly with the back of a spoon.

03 Increase the temperature to 150ºC/300ºF and cook for 20 minutes. Let it sit in the warm air fryer for another 5 minutes, then let them cool completely at room temperature before transferring to the fridge to chill for an hour. Slice the flapjack into eight wedges before serving.

Dual flapjacks Follow the recipe above, but swap the round silicone pans for two smaller rectangular containers that fit the dual drawers and divide the mixture between the two. Or reduce your washing up and use foil trays/pans!

veronica's coconut oatmeal cookies

My aunt made these for us, and after just one bite, I asked for the recipe. She compiled a cookbook of her best recipes for me, including these delicious oatmeal cookies. The recipe was passed down to her from a local farmer's wife and it's now my pleasure to pass the recipe on to you, adapted for the air fryer, of course!

....

MAKES **16**
HERO **BASKET/DUAL**
PREP **10 MINUTES**
COOK TIME **12 MINUTES**
CALORIES **272**

....

175g/6oz/¾ cup unsalted butter
2 tbsp golden syrup/light corn syrup
110g/3¾oz/1¼ cups desiccated/dried shredded coconut
125g/4½oz/1¼ cups porridge/rolled oats
200g/7oz/1 cup granulated sugar
170g/6oz/1¼ cups self-raising/self-rising flour
2 tsp ground ginger

01 Put the butter into a silicone pan, cutting it into bite-sized cubes as you add it. Add the golden syrup, then transfer the pan to the air fryer basket/drawer. Set the temperature to 120ºC/250ºF and cook for 4 minutes, or until the butter has melted.

02 Transfer the butter and golden syrup to a mixing bowl and add the coconut, oats and sugar. Mix well with a wooden spoon. Gradually add the flour and the ground ginger, then use your hands to continue mixing until everything is combined and you have a cookie dough.

03 Divide the oatmeal dough into 16 portions and roll each into a ball. We found the easiest way is to use an ice cream scoop. Then you can scoop each oatmeal cookie mix into the perfect ball.

04 Because this recipe makes 16, we air fry them in batches. Place four cookies into the air fryer basket, spreading them out, or place two in each drawer if you are using a dual air fryer. Set the temperature to 180ºC/360ºF and cook for 8 minutes, or until golden. Allow to rest for 5 minutes to firm up before eating.

Make ahead If you like, you can freeze the raw dough for later, so you can have cookies in an instant! Prepare the dough as above, then spread out the cookies on a baking tray and place them flat in the freezer for an hour. Once they have firmed up, transfer to a freezer bag. This will stop them sticking together as they freeze. To cook, place as many frozen cookies as you would like to cook into the air fryer and air fry at 160ºC/320ºF for 10 minutes.

road trip raspberry & white chocolate muffins

If we are off travelling, I can guarantee these muffins will be made the day before and stored in Tupperware for those "I'm starving" moments. Whether it's on a road trip or on a plane, these travel so well.

....

MAKES **20**
HERO **BASKET/DUAL**
PREP **10 MINUTES**
COOK TIME **20 MINUTES**
CALORIES **171**

....

75g/2½oz/⅓ cup unsalted butter
1 large egg
150g/5½oz/¾ cup granulated sugar
250g/9oz/1 cup Greek yoghurt
1 tbsp vanilla extract
4 tbsp whole milk/full-fat milk
250g/9oz/2 cups self-raising/ self-rising flour
180g/6¼oz raspberries, chopped
170g/6oz/1 cup white chocolate chunks

01 Put the butter into a silicone pan, cutting it into bite-sized cubes as you add it. Transfer the pan to the air fryer basket, set the temperature to 120°C/250°F and cook for 4 minutes, or until the butter has melted.

02 Carefully transfer the melted butter to a mixing bowl and add the egg and sugar. Beat with a hand whisk until nice and creamy.

03 Add the yoghurt, vanilla and milk, and continue to mix with the whisk until you have a smooth and creamy batter. Gradually add the flour, continuing to mix as you add it. Finish by adding the chopped fruit and chocolate chunks and stirring to combine.

04 Use an ice cream scoop to add a scoop of the muffin batter into silicone muffin cups. Fill as many cups as will fit in your air fryer (I can normally fit 8 in my air fryer basket).

05 Set the temperature to 170°C/340°F and cook for 10 minutes, then cover with foil and air fry at 180°C/360°F for a further 5 minutes, or until a thermometer probe inserted into the centre of the muffins comes out clean.

06 While they are cooking, fill more cups (or you may need to wait until a batch is cooked and wash and reuse the cups, depending on how many you have). Continue to cook them in batches until all the muffins are cooked. Once cool, store in an airtight container and they will keep for up to 5 days – unless the kids raid the Tupperware without you noticing!

Dual muffins If you are making these in the dual, melt the butter in a silicone pan in a dual drawer and continue with the recipe above. Load the muffins into the drawers (we can usually fit 6 in each drawer) and set the temperature to 160°C/320°F. Cook for 10 minutes, then cover them with foil and cook at 180°C/360°F for a further 10 minutes. This is because we find they brown slightly more on top in the dual.

Mix and match This recipe works well with 180g/6¼oz of any berries – although if you are using large ones, like strawberries, chop them up first. Dom's favourite is blueberries (in photo, left), though Sofia and I love a mix of strawberries and raspberries. Or if you fancy a bit of both, separate the mixture into two bowls before adding the fruit and you can do half a batch with a mixture of strawberries and raspberries and half a batch with blueberries.

let's air fry a cheesecake

If you love cheesecake, you will love a baked cheesecake in the air fryer. The mixture is whipped up fast thanks to an electric hand mixer.
    You can also use the air fryer for melting the butter for the cheesecake crust, as well as for melting the chocolate for decorating the cheesecake.

the ultimate baked cheesecake

SERVES **8**
HERO **BASKET**
PREP **10 MINUTES**
COOK TIME **37 MINUTES**
CALORIES **718**

FOR THE COOKIE BASE
60g/2oz/¼ cup unsalted butter
200g/7oz chocolate sandwich
   cookies (we use Oreos)

FOR THE CHEESECAKE LAYER
700g/1lb 9oz full-fat cream
   cheese (we use Original
   Philadelphia)
250g/9oz/1¼ cups granulated
   sugar
3 tbsp sour cream
2 tsp vanilla extract
2 large eggs
100g/3½oz chocolate sandwich
   cookies (we use Oreos)

TO DECORATE
75g/2½oz/½ cup white
   chocolate chunks
2–3 snack bags of mini chocolate
   sandwich cookies (we use
   about 50g/1¾oz of Mini Oreos)

We flavour our easy air fryer cheesecake with Oreos. They make the delicious chocolate biscuit base and are crumbled into the batter, so you get a brilliant effect as you slice through. If you can find bags of the mini ones, they make the cutest decoration for the top, too.

01 Place a silicone pan into the air fryer basket and add the butter, cutting it into bite-sized cubes as you add it. Set the temperature to 120°C/250°F and air fry for 4 minutes, or until the butter is melted.

02 Put the cookies for the base in a mixing bowl and crush them with a rolling pin, until they are crumbs and you have no big bits left. When the air fryer beeps, transfer the melted butter to the mixing bowl with the crushed Oreos. Mix well with a fork. Tip the buttery crumbs into the bottom of a 18cm/7 inch springform pan and spread level. Press down to compact it – we always find a potato masher is useful for this – making sure it is level.

03 Put the cream cheese and sugar in a large mixing bowl and beat with an electric hand mixer on medium speed until well combined and very creamy. Add the sour cream and vanilla, and continue to mix, then add the eggs, one at a time, mixing in between each egg.

04 Finally, add the cookies, breaking them in half as you add them. Use the mixer to naturally break them down a bit more into various sizes, but don't let them get too small, as it's nice to see chunks of cookie as you slice the finished cheesecake.

05 Tip the batter over the crumb base in your pan and use the back of a spatula to level the top. Carefully place the pan into the air fryer basket. Set the temperature to 160°C/320°F and cook for 30 minutes.

CONTINUED OVERLEAF

06 When the air fryer beeps, use a thermometer probe to check that the temperature in the middle of the cheesecake is 70ºC/160ºF or above, and that the thermometer probe comes out clean. (If it isn't the correct temperature, give it another 5 minutes and then test again until it is at the required internal temperature.) Close the air fryer basket, and let it sit for another 30 minutes in the cooling air fryer, as the residual heat will continue the setting process. Once completely cool, transfer the cheesecake to the fridge and allow it to chill for 12 hours before decorating and slicing.

07 To decorate, put two-thirds of the white chocolate chunks into a silicone pan and air fry at 120ºC/250ºF for 3 minutes, or until melted. Transfer the chocolate to a piping bag and snip off the end to make a tiny hole. Drizzle the chocolate over the top of the cheesecake.

08 Use the mini cookies to decorate around the edge of the cheesecake – the melted chocolate will help secure them in place. Add some whole, but break others up to vary the look. Finish by scattering over the remaining chocolate chunks.

Dual cheesecake If using a dual air fryer, you wont be able to fit a 18cm/7 inch springform pan in. Instead, halve the quantities of the crust and cheesecake batter ingredients, and divide them between four 10cm/4 inch springform pans. Place two pans in each drawer and cook as in the main recipe, but reducing the cook time to 20 minutes. You can also save time by using the "match" feature.

Top tips

Easy crushing To crush the cookies easily, use the end of a rolling pin, standing it up and pressing down into the cookies in the bowl to make crumbs.

Use the right pan It's important that you use the right size pan, as this will determine the thickness of your cheesecake topping and make sure the cooking time is correct. If you use a smaller pan, the cheesecake layer will be deeper and it won't be set within the cooking time.

Perfect slicing To get a smooth edge to your slices, heat your knife in a jug of hot water and wipe off the water and slice whilst still hot. It will melt the cheesecake layer slightly as it goes through, creating the perfect slice.

Alarm It's easy to forget about your cheesecake when you're leaving it to cool in the air fryer before moving it to the fridge. We set an alarm on our Alexa.

Use ramekins instead This cheesecake recipe can also be made in ramekin dishes – perfect for if you want a quicker cooking method. Make the crumb crust and cheesecake batter as in the main recipe, but divide both mixtures between eight ramekins. Reduce the cook time to 15 minutes at 160ºC/320ºF, followed by a 15 minute cool down in the air fryer. An average-sized air fryer will hold four ramekins, meaning you would only need to do two batches.

Smaller air fryers If you have a small air fryer, using ramekins makes it possible for you to cook cheesecake too. You can usually fit in two ramekins at once, so this is a good solution if your air fryer is too small for a springform pan.

vanilla sprinkle cake

I loved puddings when I was little at school. Even now in my forties I want to recreate them in the air fryer. Top of the list, and also our kids' favourite, is a vanilla sprinkle cake. Made with a vanilla sponge, pink icing and, of course, plenty of sprinkles.

....

SERVES **8**
HERO **BASKET**
PREP **10 MINUTES**
COOK TIME **60 MINUTES**
CALORIES **510**

....

170g/6oz/¾ cup unsalted butter
200g/7oz/1 cup granulated sugar
4 large eggs
1 tbsp vanilla extract
6 tbsp whole milk/full-fat milk
1½ tbsp extra virgin olive oil
180g/6¼oz/1⅓ cups self-raising/self-rising flour
100g/3½oz/¾ cup icing/confectioner's sugar
⅓ tsp hot pink food colouring (or any colour you like)
2½ tbsp rainbow sprinkles

01 Put the butter and sugar in a mixing bowl and, using an electric hand mixer, beat until it becomes almost white and has a fluffy texture. Crack the eggs into the bowl, add the vanilla, milk and olive oil, and continue to whisk until smooth and creamy.

02 Sift in the flour, a bit at a time, folding it in and not over-mixing because you want a light and fluffy cake. Then pour the mixture into a 20cm/8 inch round silicone pan and place it carefully into the air fryer basket.

03 Set the temperature to 160ºC/320ºF and cook for 30 minutes. When the air fryer beeps, cover the cake in foil to prevent it over-browning on top and cook at 150ºC/300ºF for another 30 minutes, or until a thermometer probe inserted into the centre of the cake comes out clean.

04 Remove the silicone pan – it will easily peel away from the cake – and place the cake on a cooling rack to cool completely before icing.

05 Sift the icing sugar into a mixing bowl and add about 2 tablespoons water – a little at a time – mixing until you have the consistency of a thick paste. Add the food colouring a little at a time, mixing until you have the shade of pink you want. Just remember to add it slowly, because you can always add more but you can't take it away.

06 Pour the pink icing over the cooled cake, then cover it with sprinkles and leave to set. Once set, slice and serve.

Dual sprinkle cake If you have a dual air fryer, you won't be able to fit the specified cake pan in the drawer. Instead, divide the batter between four 10cm/4 inch cake tins and cook two pans in each drawer at 160ºC/320ºF for 30 minutes.

three-ingredient shortbread

I love shortbread. As a kid, every Christmas my parents' Scottish bookkeeper would gift us some shortbread. I thought it was the nicest treat ever. As a grown-up I learnt it was ridiculously easy to make and could be used in many recipes.

Let me first show you our master recipe for Scottish shortbread, and then how to transform it into chocolate orange shortbread, and strawberries and cream shortbread stacks.

....

SERVES **8**
HERO **BASKET**
PREP **5 MINUTES**
COOK TIME **35 MINUTES**
CALORIES **314**

....

240g/8¼oz/1¾ cups plain/all-purpose flour
75g/3oz/6 tbsp granulated sugar, plus extra for sprinkling
175g/6oz/¾ cup unsalted butter

01 Put the flour, sugar and butter in a mixing bowl. Use your fingertips to rub the fat into the flour, continuing until big lumps form, then bring the mixture together into a dough. The high fat content means that it forms into a dough easily; try not to over-handle the dough, because the butter will get too melty.

02 Place the dough into a 20cm/8 inch round silicone cake pan and press it down, so that it creates an even disc in the base of the silicone pan. Use a fork to crimp around the edge, like traditional shortbread and score the top to divide it into 8 wedges. Doing so now will create the lines to slice again when cooked and makes it much easier.

03 Place the silicone pan in the air fryer basket, set the temperature to 150ºC/300ºF and cook for 20 minutes. Increase the temperature to 180ºC/360ºF and cook for a further 15 minutes until light golden.

04 Remove the silicone pan from the air fryer and sprinkle the shortbread with extra sugar. Allow to rest before peeling away from the silicone. Use the original cuts as your guide to slice into eight "petticoat tails" before serving.

Smaller shortbreads As this classic shortbread won't fit the air fryer dual drawers or into a small air fryer, we recommend using a cookie cutter and making individual shortbread rounds instead. You can follow our recipe on page 217 and either enjoy as plain cookies or transform it into a strawberry and cream dessert.

Tip We find that the easiest way to press our shortbread dough down firmly into the tin is to use a potato masher.

Hot chocolate orange shortbread This is our favourite way to make shortbread and a chocolaty upgrade of traditional Scottish shortbread. Make as above, but as you add the main ingredients to the bowl, add an extra **28g/1oz/3 tablespoons plain/all-purpose flour, 60g/2oz/½ cup hot chocolate powder** and the **finely grated zest of a medium orange**, plus **2 tablespoons of the orange juice**.

strawberry shortbread stacks

Shortbread cookies are made from the shortbread dough on page 214, then loaded with fresh strawberries, and whipped cream.

SERVES **6**
HERO **BASKET/DUAL**
PREP **8 MINUTES**
COOK TIME **30 MINUTES**
CALORIES **649**

1 recipe quantity of shortbread dough (see ingredients and step 1 on page 214, but don't shape the dough)
Plain/all-purpose flour, for dusting
225g/8oz fresh strawberries
fresh mint sprigs, to decorate

CHANTILLY CREAM
240ml/8fl oz/1 cup double/ heavy cream
1 tsp vanilla extract
2 tbsp icing/confectioners' sugar, plus extra for dusting

01 Make the shortbread dough as in the recipe on page 214. Use your hands to knead everything together, then lightly flour a worktop and press the dough out to form a sheet 5mm/¼ inch thick. Using a 7cm/2¾ inch cookie cutter, stamp out 12 rounds – you will need to gather up the offcuts and reroll to make all 12 rounds. Place 4 shortbread cookies into the air fryer basket, or if using the drawers of a dual add 3 to each drawer.

02 Set the temperature to 180ºC/360ºF and cook for 10 minutes until light golden. Allow to cool on a cooling rack while you cook the remaining shortbreads. Allow all the shortbreads to cool completely before moving on to the next step.

03 Put the cream into a mixing bowl and add the vanilla extract and icing sugar. Using an electric hand mixer, whip the cream to soft peaks.

04 Slice the strawberries. Add a good spoonful of the chantilly cream to the top of six of the shortbread rounds, then top with some of the sliced strawberries. Add another shortbread on top of each stack and top it with more cream and strawberries. Add a sprig of mint to each to decorate, and dust the tops with icing sugar.

The sweetest strawberries There is nothing like strawberries in season, but at other times, they sometimes need a little help. Put your strawberries in a bowl and sprinkle over **2 tablespoons granulated sugar**. Mix well and leave to macerate for a couple of hours to soften and sweeten the fruit.

Strawberry cream You can also make the cream in these stacks strawberry flavoured, if you wish. Finely chop a couple of your sweetened strawberries and add them to the cream with the vanilla and sugar. Whisk for a few seconds until the strawberries have combined and the cream is a lovely shade of pink. If you'd like it pinker, add a few more strawberries, but be careful not to overwhip the cream or it may go grainy.

afternoon tea with classic scones

For the last recipe, we're combining some of our favourite recipes from this book to bring you an amazing air fryer afternoon tea.

lemonade scones

You can't have afternoon tea without scones! Let's first share our five-ingredient scones recipe, before running through some ideas of what to pair these scones with for your afternoon tea.

MAKES **6**
HERO **BASKET/DUAL**
PREP **8 MINUTES**
COOK TIME **14 MINUTES**
CALORIES **330**

340g/11¾oz/2½ cups self-raising/self-rising flour, plus extra for dusting
85g/3oz/7 tbsp granulated sugar
120ml/4fl oz/½ cup lemonade
120g/4¼oz/½ cup Greek yoghurt
85g/3oz raisins or sultanas
1 egg, beaten for egg wash

serving suggestions

For a traditional afternoon tea for two, we recommend you fill the top layer of a cake stand with scones; sweet treats occupy the middle layer; and the bottom layer is savoury, with sandwiches, quiche and sausage rolls.

The fun thing about afternoon tea is that wherever you have it, it will be served differently, and you can really make it your own. If you'd like to use the recipes from this book, here are our suggestions:

- Scones with clotted cream and strawberry jam
- Tuna sandwiches using Tuna Melt filling and cucumber (see page 48)
- Sandwiches with gammon from the rotisserie (see page 68)
- Impossible Quiche (see page 30)
- Sausage Rolls (see page 202)
- Raspberry and White Chocolate Muffins (see page 207)
- Sprinkle Cake (see page 212)
- Three-Ingredient Shortbread (see page 214)

01 Put the flour, sugar, lemonade and yoghurt into a mixing bowl, and mix well with a wooden spoon. Stir in the raisins, then use your hands to bring everything together into a dough. We find it easier to flour our hands when handling the dough.

02 Tip the dough onto a lightly floured worktop and knead lightly until smooth, then shape the dough with your hands, pressing it out until you have a sheet that is 2.5cm/1 inch thick. Use an 8cm/3¼ inch cookie cutter to stamp out circles of dough circles. Gather up your dough leftovers, knead back together and cut again until you have six scones.

03 Place the scones into the air fryer and brush the tops with egg wash. If you are using a basket air fryer, you will need to cook them in batches, but you should be able to fit three in each dual drawer and four in an air fryer basket.

04 Set the temperature to 180ºC/360ºF and cook for 14 minutes, or until the scones are golden outside and not doughy in the middle.

index

thank you

Wow, another air fryer book! Well, this couldn't have happened without all the amazing people who bought our first book, told their friends about it, wrote amazing reviews, bought extra copies for Christmas presents and continuously spread the word. You are our heroes and we thank you from the bottom of our hearts.

This book is a community effort and we love how your genuine feedback has shaped it. A special shout out to Sue for your support; as requested, we made you smoked haddock. To Pat, for our long-term friendship and shared love of the air fryer oven. To Allan, who asked for some chicken flavouring ideas: you were our inspiration for the seven marinades on page 37.

To our agent Clare, who continues to support us through our passion for the air fryer.

A special mention to the incredible team who produced this book: to our publisher, Denise, who always makes us think outside the box and takes our ideas to the next level; to our photographer Dan; to Becci for your beautiful food styling and awesome editing; to Nicky for your attention to detail; to Faye for your beautiful props (our favourite is the salad bowl used in the autumn salad bowl – it's so pretty); to Georgie for another beautiful design – I am amazed by how you managed to squeeze so much great content into the pages; and, finally, to Liz for her marketing know-how – we just love working with you, and we have made another great book for your mum!

To the ladies of the Inspiring Mums in Business network, who motivated me to make another book and grow our business. I love you all and the amazing businesses we are all building with each other's support. Special mention to Julie, Leanne, Kelly, Kirsty, Jayne, Alison, Tracy and Linda.

To Saskia, for your amazing Tuesday night baking classes. We look forward to them each week and love the invaluable baking skills you are teaching Sofia and Jorge. They loved recreating your flatbread for the cookbook.

To Mrs Gallagher, the best teacher I ever had. Everyone has that one amazing teacher who is remembered for years to come: that is you! I hope you like this book as much as you liked the first!

To Sarah, for your loyal friendship and your commitment to all the recipe testing. We loved your sprinkle cake adaptation the most!

To Kyle, Sofia and Jorge: you're our biggest fans and we are your biggest fans. Mum and dad are incredibly proud of the three of you and all your amazing help. Although, we are sorry to disappoint: the mac and cheese is now fully tested so no more eating mac and cheese for breakfast!

To Kath, you're doing an amazing job learning the air fryer and thank you for your years of support and friendship.

To all our suppliers: Andy and the team at Rafters of Driffield; Daniel at Elston Butchers, the butchers at Vanessa's; and the team at The Refill Jar. You have supplied us with some amazing local produce in the making of this book and it's a pleasure to shop local.

To Claire, Pete, our parents and other family and friends, for your continued support.

about the authors

Sam and Dom Milner have been air frying since 2012 and couldn't imagine day-to-day cooking without the air fryer and their other kitchen gadgets.

In late 2015, they started *Recipe This* so that they could share their love for the air fryer with others and help air-fryer beginners. They are now loved around the world for their air fryer recipes and advice.

They live in Yorkshire in the North of England with their kids Kyle, Sofia and Jorge – and three air fryer ovens, three air fryer baskets and two air fryer duals.

RecipeThis.com